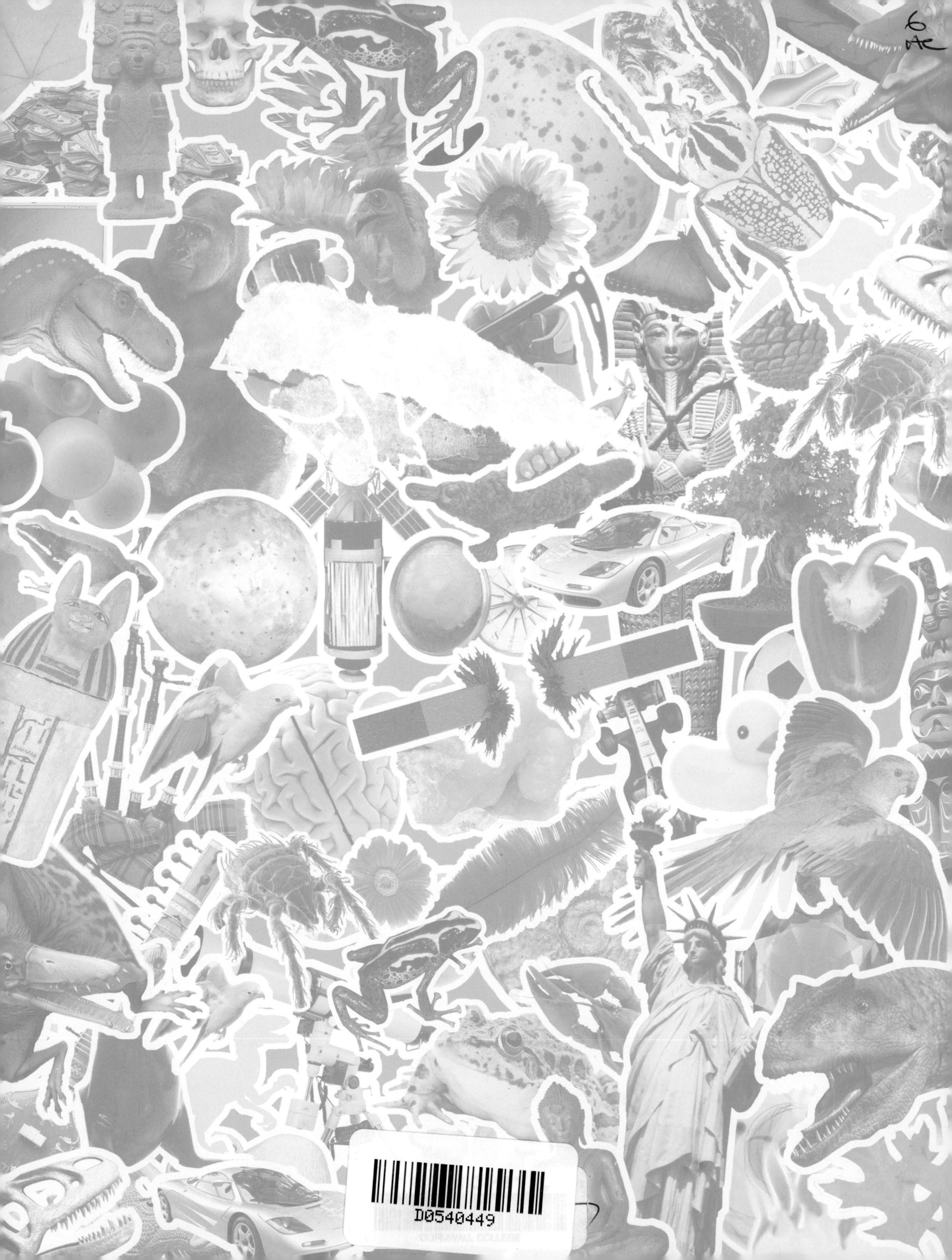

KNOW IT ALL

Facts, stats, lists, records, and more

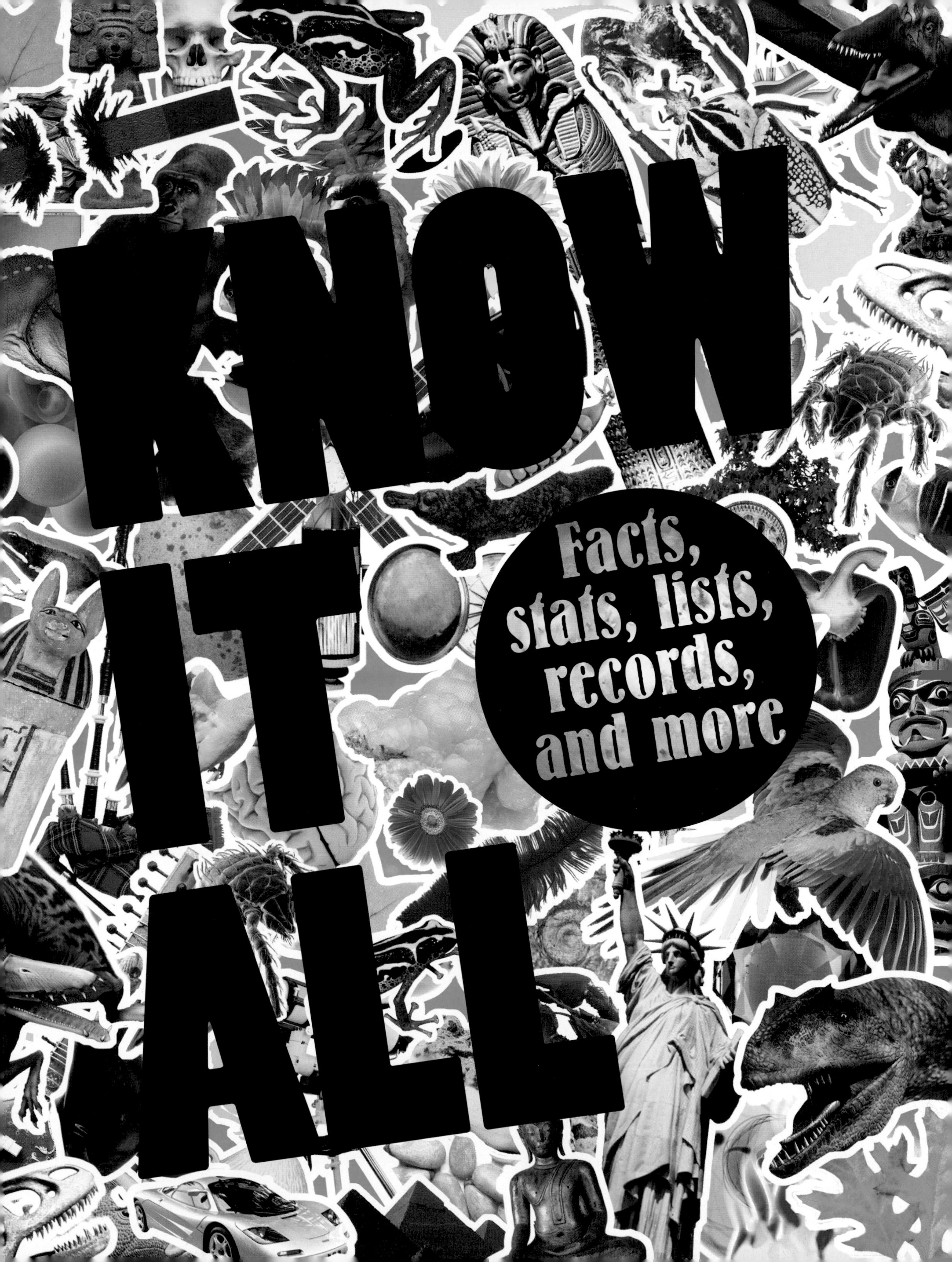

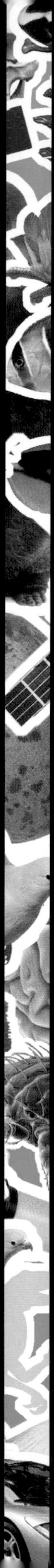

LONDON, NEW YORK,
MELBOURNE, MUNICH, AND DELHI

Senior editor Francesca Baines
Senior designer Smiljka Surla
Art editors Angela Ball, Dave Ball
Editors Hazel Beynon, Carron Brown, Jenny Finch,
Clare Hibbert, Phil Hunt, Ashwin Khurana, Fran Jones
Designers Sheila Collins, Hoa Luc,
Johnny Pau, Stefan Podhorodecki

Managing editor Linda Esposito
Managing art editors Jim Green, Diane Thistlethwaite

Consultants Philip Parker, Richard Walker
Commissioned illustrations Maltings Partnership
Picture researchers Nic Dean, Mik Gates

Publishing manager Andrew Macintyre
Category publisher Laura Buller

Production editor Andy Hilliard
Senior production controller Angela Graef
Jacket designer Hazel Martin
Jacket editor Matilda Gollon
Jacket manager Sophia M Tampakopoulos Turner

First published in Great Britain in 2010 by
Dorling Kindersley Limited,
80 Strand, London, WC2R 0RL

2 4 6 8 10 9 7 5 3 1
176246 – 08/10

A CIP catalogue record for this book
is available from the British Library

ISBN: 978-1-40535-533-9

Colour reproduction by MDP, UK
Printed and bound by Toppan, China

Discover more at
www.dk.com

DK

KNOW IT ALL

Facts, stats, lists, records, and more

Contributors
Samone Bos, Julie Ferris, Ian Graham, Susan Kennedy, Darren Naish, Jim Pipe, Carole Stott, John Woodward

Contents

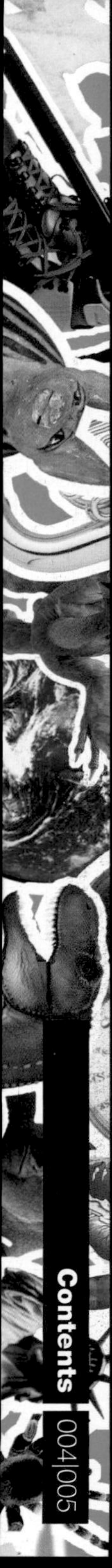

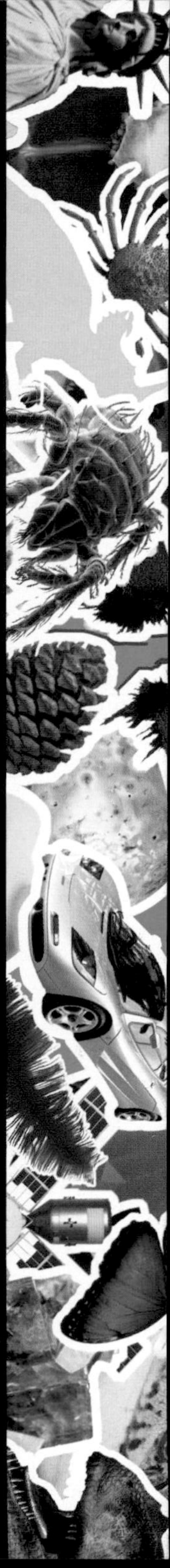

Space

How big is **the Universe?**

The Universe is very big; in fact, it is bigger than anything else we know about. We can see that it exists as far as about 13.7 billion light years (ly) from us. We also know there is more beyond the edge of the observable Universe, but we don't know how much. The Universe is expanding all the time – it is bigger now than when you started reading this sentence!

RECORD BREAKER

The largest structure in the Universe is the Sloan Great Wall. About one billion ly away from Earth, it is a **giant wall of galaxies** that stretches for 1.37 billion ly across the Universe.

Expanding Universe

01: When the Universe started in the explosive event called the Big Bang about 13.7 billion years ago, it was smaller than a full stop on this page.

02: Within a trillionth of a second it ballooned to about the size of a football pitch.

03: The young Universe was incredibly hot and made of tiny particles of matter. It has been expanding, cooling, and changing ever since.

04: In 1998, astronomers discovered that the Universe's expansion rate is not slowing down as they thought, but accelerating.

05: For the past 5–6 billion years, the Universe has been getting bigger at a faster and faster rate.

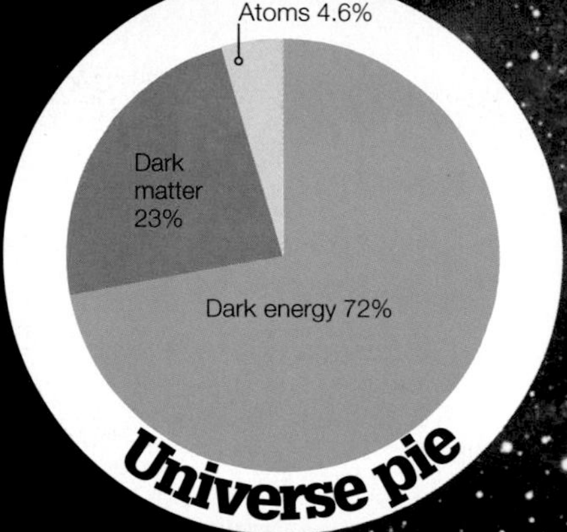

Universe pie

Calculating the scale

- We can't see the Universe's large-scale structure easily because we are inside it.
- Computers have been used to simulate a cube-shaped region (above) that is two billion ly across and populated by about 20 million galaxies.
- Superclusters are groupings of galaxy clusters, which in turn are collections of galaxies.
- The Universe is made of a huge weblike network of chains and sheets consisting of superclusters separated by huge voids.

What about me?

The most distant object that most people can see with the naked eye is the Andromeda Galaxy, 2.5 million ly away. In good conditions, some people can see the Triangulum Galaxy, 3 million ly away.

Galaxy gang

Barnard's Galaxy
10,000 ly wide

Milky Way Galaxy
100,000 ly wide

1781 William Herschel discovers Uranus, a planet twice as far from the Sun as Saturn, which until now is the most distant known planet – the known Solar System doubles in size overnight

1916 Harlow Shapley measures the size of the Milky Way and finds it is much larger than previously thought

1924 Edwin Hubble proves that small, dim patches of light are distant galaxies outside the Milky Way and so the Universe is more than just our galaxy

1989 The Great Wall, the first huge, flat sheet of superclusters, is discovered by Margaret Geller and John Huchra

2003–04 The Hubble Space Telescope looks further into ultra-deep space than ever before and sees thousands of galaxies – the most distant are 13 billion ly away

Blasts from the past

Mass interest

- Astronomers are often more interested in an object's **mass** than its size.
- Mass is the amount of **material** something is made of.
- In a star, mass determines how a star lives and for how long – the greater the mass, the shorter the **life**.
- The most **massive** stars are about 100 times the Sun's mass and the least are one-tenth of the Sun's mass.

In numbers

1.3 million
The number of Earths that could fit inside the Sun

1.4 million
The width of the Sun in kilometres (864,900 miles)

3.26 million
The Universe expands by about 72 km (45 miles) per second for every 3.26 million ly

27
The distance in light years from the Sun to the centre of the Milky Way

125 billion
The minimum number of galaxies in the Universe

I don't believe it!

Earth is in the Milky Way Galaxy, which is part of the Local Group of galaxies – one of the galaxy clusters that make up the Local Supercluster. In turn, the Local Supercluster is one of the superclusters that make the Pisces-Cetus Supercluster Complex, which is about one billion ly long and 150 million ly wide.

Astronomers have found a **huge void**: a 3.5 billion ly-wide region of space that is empty of both normal matter, such as stars and galaxies, and of dark matter (material that we know is there but scientists don't know what it is yet).

The Milky Way Galaxy belongs to a collection of more than 40 galaxies known as the Local Group. They exist in a dumbbell-shaped volume of space ten million light years across. These are some of the group's best known members.

Triangulum Galaxy
50,000 ly wide

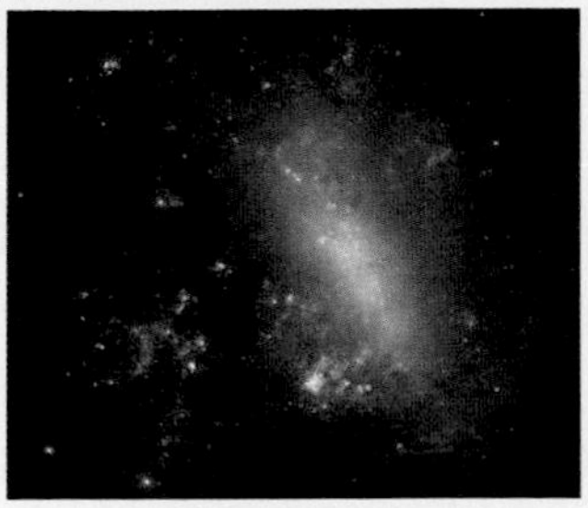

Large Magellanic Cloud
20,000 ly wide

Galaxy size

- **Galaxies are huge collections of stars, gas, dust, and dark matter all bound together by gravity.**
- The biggest galaxies are about 300,000 ly across and contain about a thousand billion stars.
- **The smallest galaxies, known as dwarf galaxies, measure a few thousand ly across and have about ten million stars.**

Galaxies have been changing in **size**, **mass**, and **shape** since they first formed billions of years ago.

Why are there **telescopes in space?**

Collecting energy
Space telescopes work in much the same way as Earth telescopes. These use a mirror to collect wavelengths of light, which are brought to a focus to form an image of the object in view.

Gamma rays

The shortest wavelengths collected from space objects are gamma rays. Space telescopes such as the Compton Gamma Ray Observatory, which recorded these rays for nine years, work in a unique way. Gamma rays cannot be brought to a focus like other wavelengths because they pass through most materials. Telescopes collecting them use detectors stacked on top of one another, which measure the way the gamma rays pass through.

Telescopes collect light and other forms of energy from stars and galaxies. The energy travels in wavelengths, but Earth's atmosphere stops some of these reaching our planet's surface. Telescopes located in space are able to collect the full range of wavelengths and give us a more complete view of the Universe. They can also be used 24 hours a day.

I don't believe it!

The Chandra X-ray Observatory orbits Earth more than a third of the way to the Moon – 200 times more distant than the Hubble Space Telescope. It needs two kilowatts of power to work – that's about the same as a hairdryer!

Tell me more: **energy from space**

The wavelengths of energy are of specific length and have their own names. Short wavelengths such as X-rays cannot travel through Earth's atmosphere. Radio wavelengths, which are longer, pass readily to Earth's surface.

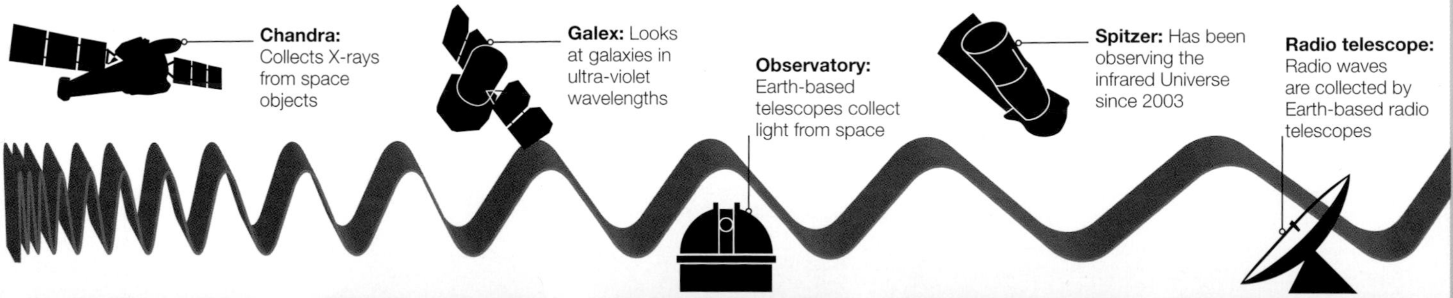
Chandra: Collects X-rays from space objects
Galex: Looks at galaxies in ultra-violet wavelengths
Observatory: Earth-based telescopes collect light from space
Spitzer: Has been observing the infrared Universe since 2003
Radio telescope: Radio waves are collected by Earth-based radio telescopes

X-rays
Spiral galaxy M81 seen at X-ray wavelengths, which are emitted by material heated around 1 million °C (1.8 million °F).

Ultra-violet rays
Bright, hot newly formed stars in M81 give off ultra-violet energy. The stars are located within the galaxy's spiral arms.

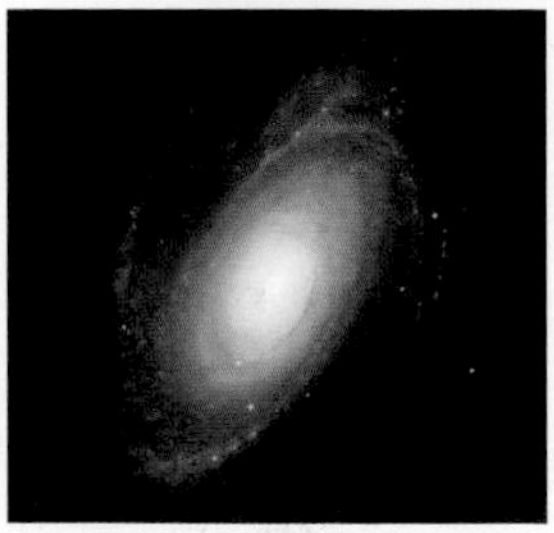

Optical wavelengths
This is how M81 looks in light wavelengths and to the human eye. It has a bright nucleus and spiral arms of stars and dust.

Infrared rays
Dust warmed by bright, young stars shines brightly at infrared wavelengths. Clumps in M81's arms are where stars are born.

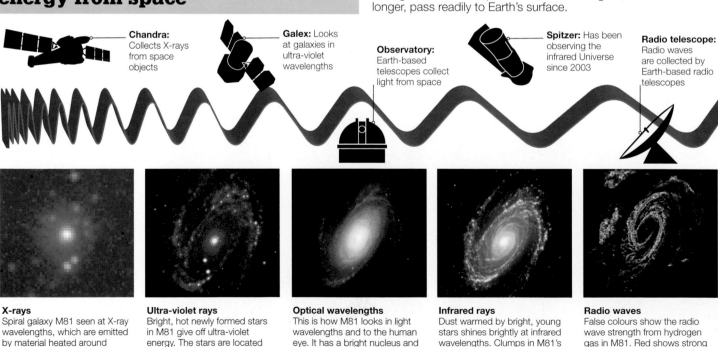

Radio waves
False colours show the radio wave strength from hydrogen gas in M81. Red shows strong emission and blue weaker.

FAST FACTS

Herschel Space Observatory

01: The Herschel Space Observatory is the most powerful infrared telescope ever to operate in space.

02: It was launched on 14 May 2009 on-board Ariane 5 from Kourou, French Guiana.

03: The telescope is orbiting the Sun 1.5 million km (932,057 miles) from Earth, facing away from the Sun.

04: Herschel is about 7.5 m (24.6 ft) high and 4 m (13.1 ft) wide. Its main mirror is 3.5 m (11.5 ft) wide.

05: It is studying dusty and cold regions of space to learn more of the origin and evolution of stars and galaxies.

06: Data from the telescope is transmitted every day to an antenna in New Norcia, Australia.

Keeping cool

Infrared telescopes like the Herschel Space Observatory are looking at some of the **coolest** objects in space. The telescope itself needs to be kept cool to make sure its own heat doesn't spoil its observations. Liquid **helium** on board keeps its temperature down to almost –273°C (–460°F).

Repair work

Once a telescope is launched in space, it is on its own. If something goes wrong, a repairman cannot be called to fix it.

The exception is the Hubble Space Telescope. It was designed so that it can be serviced and repaired in space.

Astronauts made running repairs and installed new parts on five visits to Hubble between 1993 and 2009.

Sun watcher

The Solar and Heliospheric Observatory (SOHO) is a space telescope that has been observing the Sun since 1995.

SOHO observes invisible and ultraviolet light and reveals huge prominences and outbursts of energy on the solar surface.

SOHO has 12 instruments on-board and is orbiting around the Sun at a distance of about 1.5 million km (932,000 miles) from Earth.

As SOHO images the Sun, it also records anything passing close to it, particularly **comets**. Astronomers looking through its data have discovered more than 1,600 new comets.

Space telescopes

The **Hubble** Space Telescope works about 560 km (348 miles) above Earth. It started work collecting infrared, optical, and ultraviolet energy in 1990.

The **Solar Dynamics** Observatory that launched in February 2010 will observe the Sun for five years.

The **Fermi** Gamma Ray Telescope started work above Earth in mid-2008. It is studying gamma rays from explosions in far-off galaxies.

Launched into space in 2009, **Planck** is investigating the heat that remains from the Big Bang.

WHAT'S IN A NAME?

Space telescopes are sometimes named after astronomers and scientists. The **Herschel** Space Observatory is named after brother and sister William and Caroline Herschel, while Edwin **Hubble** gave his name to the Hubble Space Telescope.

Blasts from the past

1970
Uhuru, the first X-ray space telescope is launched on 12 December and during its four-year life, it discovers 270 X-ray sources across the sky

1978
The IUE (International Ultraviolet Explorer) begins an 18-year mission, and it is the first satellite astronomers can operate in real time

1983
The first infrared space telescope is launched on 25 January – IRAS (Infrared Astronomical Satellite) is able to survey the entire sky

1990s
The microwave space telescope COBE (Cosmic Background Explorer) operates during the early part of the decade, and detects the heat left over from the Big Bang

Capturing space

Space telescopes work around the clock to collect information in a range of wavelengths. Though they image objects nearby, these telescopes usually peer into deep space to give us extraordinary views of far-off stars and galaxies.

Milky Way Galaxy This colourful view of our galaxy combines images from three telescopes (see right): Spitzer reveals dusty clouds; Chandra highlights the centre of the galaxy; and Hubble images warm gas.

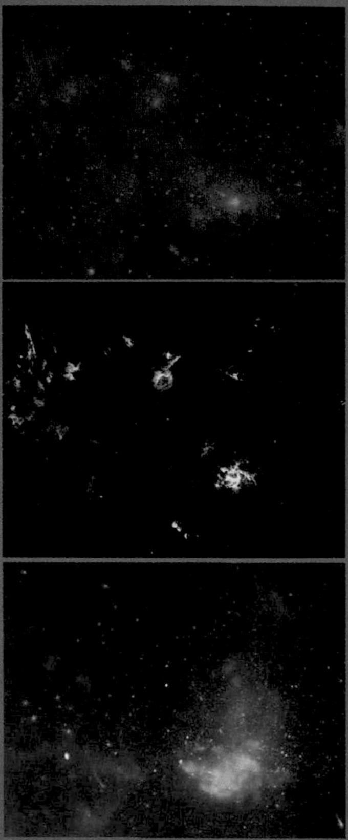

Spitzer Infrared

Hubble Near Infrared

Chandra X-ray

Pluto Two small moons, now named Nix and Hydra, were discovered when the Hubble Space Telescope took this image of Pluto (centre) in 2005. Close to Pluto is its largest moon, Charon. To the right are Nix (top) and Hydra.

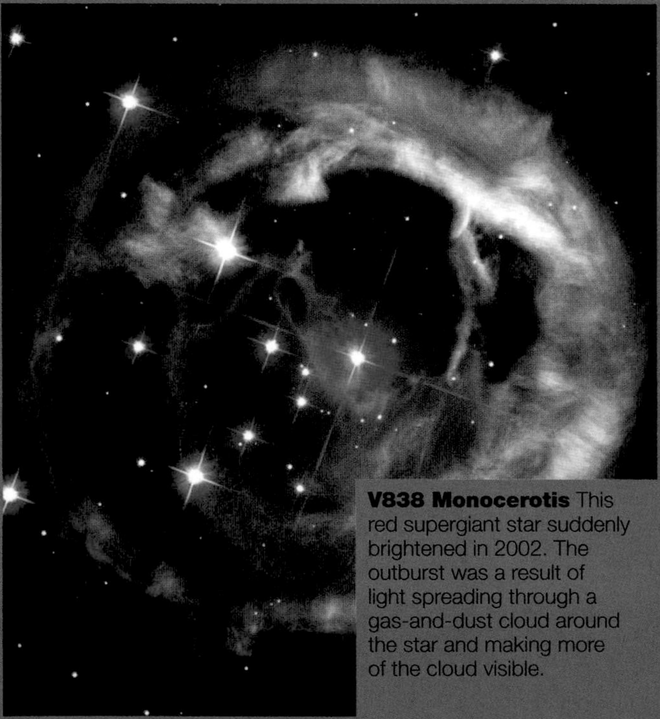

V838 Monocerotis This red supergiant star suddenly brightened in 2002. The outburst was a result of light spreading through a gas-and-dust cloud around the star and making more of the cloud visible.

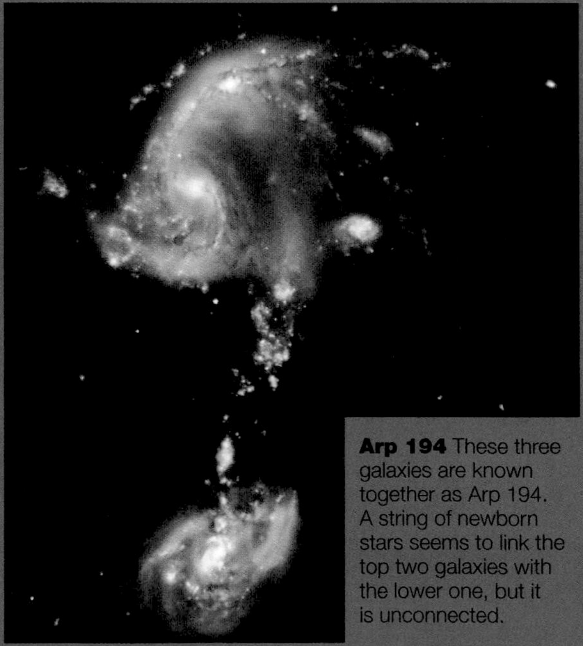

Arp 194 These three galaxies are known together as Arp 194. A string of newborn stars seems to link the top two galaxies with the lower one, but it is unconnected.

Eagle Nebula This column of gas and dust, several light years long, is just a small part of a huge star-forming region, the Eagle Nebula. Bumps in the column are dense regions where stars are taking shape.

Centre of the Milky Way The Chandra X-ray Telescope took this image of thousands of stars crowded together at the centre of the Milky Way. Within them is the massive black hole Sagittarius A*.

Helix Nebula This false-colour infrared Spitzer Telescope image shows the red remains of a star once similar to the Sun. The blue material was thrown off by the star thousands of years ago.

NGC290 The star cluster NGC290 is within the Small Magellanic Cloud, one of the closest galaxies to us. Its hundreds of young stars were created from the same cloud of gas and dust.

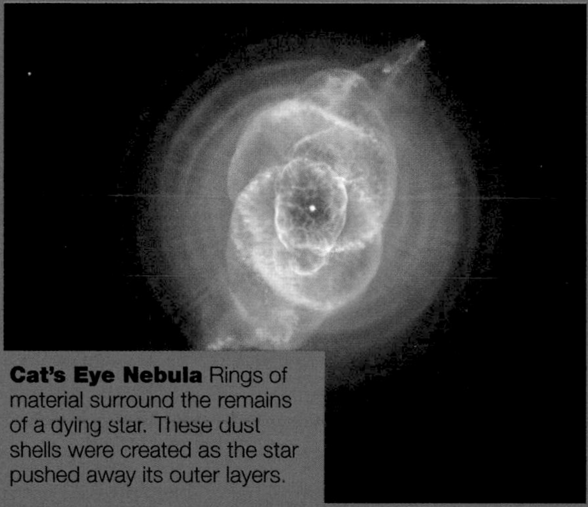

Cat's Eye Nebula Rings of material surround the remains of a dying star. These dust shells were created as the star pushed away its outer layers.

Saturn When Saturn is seen in infrared light, detail in its upper atmosphere is revealed. Blue indicates a clear view of the main cloud layer; green and yellow are thick and thin haze respectively; orange denotes high clouds.

Stephan's Quintet These five galaxies are known as Stephan's Quintet, but only four are close; the white one is unrelated.

Heat of the Big Bang The COBE (Cosmic Background Explorer) satellite was the first to make this type of image of the sky. It shows the heat remaining after the Big Bang that marked the start of the Universe.

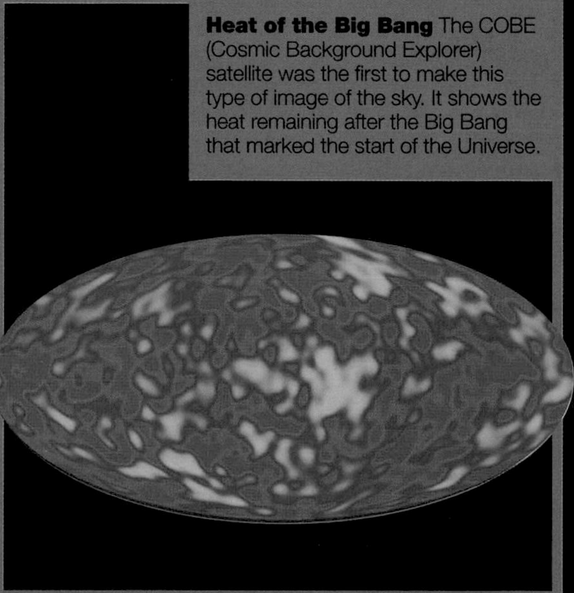

Which **star** shines the **brightest?**

The Sun is by far the brightest star in Earth's sky. The next brightest is Sirius, sometimes called the Dog Star, in the constellation of Canis Major. Sirius is 12.5 billion times fainter than the Sun, but that is because it is much further away – it is actually twice as big and 25 times brighter.

Measuring scales

- Astronomers measure the brightness of a star on two scales.
- The first, called **apparent magnitude**, gives the brightness of a star seen from Earth.
- The second, **absolute magnitude**, is a measure of the star's real brightness (its luminosity), and compares the stars as if they were the same distance from Earth.

I don't believe it!

Inside the Sun, a tug of war is going on. The Sun's gravity pulls gas in, but the pressure of the Sun's core tries to push it out. The gravity and pressure balance each other out, so the Sun keeps its spherical shape.

The Greek astronomer **Hipparchus**, who lived more than 2,000 years ago, was the first person to class stars according to their **brightness**. The brightness scales we use today are based on his work.

Ten brightest stars from Earth

1. Sun
2. Sirius
3. Canopus
4. Rigil Kentaurus
5. Arcturus
6. Vega
7. Capella
8. Rigel
9. Procyon
10. Achernar

FAST FACTS: The Sun

01: The Sun has shone for about 4.6 billion years and will continue to shine for another five billion years or so.

02: It is a huge ball of glowing gas: about 75% hydrogen, 25% helium, and tiny amounts of 90 or so other elements.

03: At the Sun's core, the temperature is 15 million °C (27 million °F), but it is a cooler 5,500°C (9,900°F) on its surface.

04: When seen in ultra-violet light (right), the Sun appears deep orange.

Living together

- Stars are born together in **clusters** from the same cloud of material and at the same time.
- Over hundreds of millions of years, the stars in a cluster **drift apart**, but many continue to live alongside another star.
- Of the 100 nearest **stellar systems** (orbiting stars), 69 are single stars, 22 are made of two stars, seven are three stars, one is a group of four, and one a group of five.

Largest constellations

The constellations come in different sizes. The five biggest are:

★ Hydra, the water snake
★ Virgo, the virgin
★ Ursa Major, the great bear
★ Cetus, the sea monster
★ Hercules

WEIRD OR WHAT?

Stars are made of gas, the density of which varies throughout the star. Much of the gas, which is mainly **hydrogen** and **helium**, is squashed in its core. At the Sun's core, the gas density is about 160 times that of water.

Star patterns

- Astronomers use a system of **constellations** to find their way amongst the night-time stars.
- A constellation is a straight-edged area of sky that includes a made-up pattern. The pattern is formed by linking the **bright stars** with imaginary lines.
- The **star patterns** are of humans, creatures, or objects. The first of these were identified about 4,000 years ago.
- There are 88 constellations – they fit together like the pieces of a **jigsaw** to make the complete sky.

In numbers

8
The average distance in light years between stars in the vicinity of the Sun

8.50
The number of minutes and seconds it takes the Sun's light to reach Earth

28
The number of objects depicted in constellations; it includes Crux (the cross), the smallest constellation of all with only four stars

109
The number of Earths that could fit across the face of the Sun

1,000
The largest stars are 1,000 times wider than the Sun; the smallest are about one-hundredth the Sun's width

14,000 km
(8,700 miles) The width of a white dwarf star, which is what the Sun will be in about five billion years

Tell me more: **Orion, the hunter**

Orion is one of 12 mythological figures in the sky and one of the easiest star patterns to see. It includes the supergiant stars Rigel and Betelgeuse, and the star-forming region of the Orion Nebula.

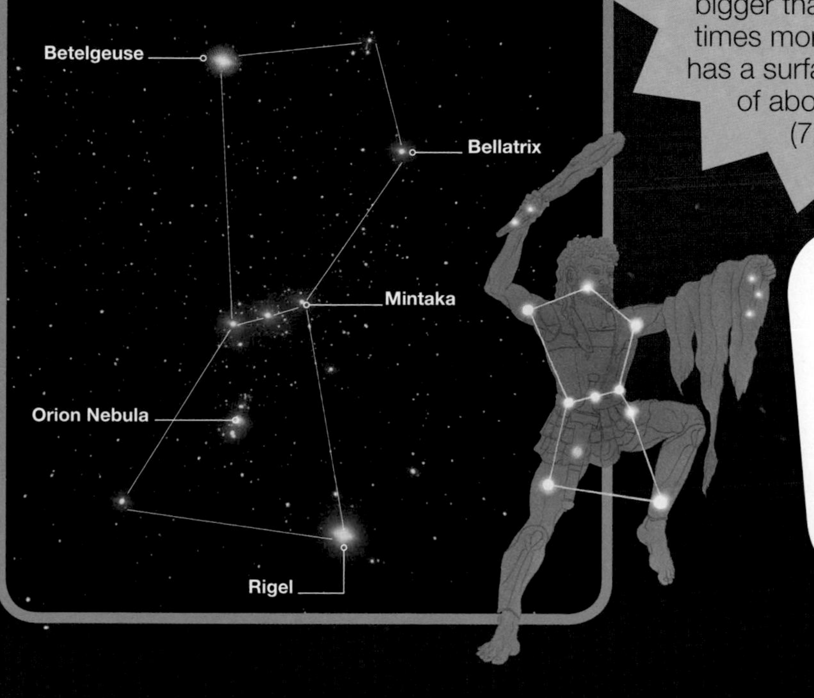

RECORD BREAKER

The hottest stars are **blue supergiants**, like Eta Carinae, which is 180 times bigger than the Sun, 100 times more massive, and has a surface temperature of about 40,000°C (72,032°F).

What about me?

On a clear night, people living in a city can see about 400 stars in their sky. In the countryside, up to about 1,200 are visible, while around 3,500 can be seen from the darkest places where there is no polluting light.

How does **space technology** affect me?

Every day we learn more about the amazing Universe we live in from the craft that explore it on our behalf. Nearer to home, hundreds of satellites orbit our planet. They transmit TV pictures around the globe, relay our phone calls, link us on the Internet, and provide data for weather forecasts, and much more. Thousands of technologies and techniques designed for space have been adapted for life on Earth.

Tell me more: **satellite orbits**

- **The path a satellite takes around Earth depends on the job it does.**
- Those in geostationary orbit are 35,786 km (22,227 miles) above the equator and stay over the same part of the surface.
- **Others in low Earth orbit are at an altitude of only a few hundred kilometres and cover the whole planet.**
- Satellites in polar orbit follow a path that takes them over Earth's poles; they observe any part of the surface twice a day.
- **Some satellites follow highly elliptical orbits that bring them close to the part of Earth they want to study and then take them farther away on the far side of the planet.**

Satellite types

Satellites orbit Earth for a number of different reasons:

- Space telescopes
- Earth observing
- Navigation
- Weather
- Spy
- Communication

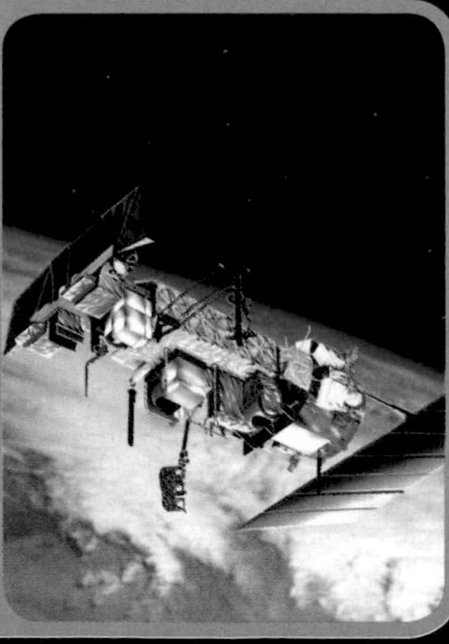

Earth watcher

Envisat, short for Environmental Satellite, is the largest satellite observing Earth's land, water, ice, and atmosphere.

Launched: 1 March 2002

Space agency: European Space Agency (ESA)

Orbit: polar

Altitude: 790 km (490 miles)

Time to orbit: 101 mins

Instruments: 9

Microgravity experiments

Astronauts working on the International Space Station (ISS) orbiting Earth perform various experiments in the weightless environment of space.

Growing plants
Astronauts travelling to Mars will need to grow their own food, so seeds and plants are being tested.

Keeping healthy
An astronaut uses equipment that tests for biological and chemical substances on the ISS.

Radiation studies
A dummy astronaut is used to check the level of radiation that astronauts experience when out in space.

Growing crystals
The ISS has three laboratories – here in the Kibo lab, a crystal-growing experiment is monitored.

Body experiments
Living in space affects the human body; astronauts routinely monitor their health and fitness.

WHAT'S IN A NAME?

More than 9,000 US students entered a competition to name a **rover** that will go to Mars in 2011. A 12-year-old girl suggested the winning name, Curiosity.

Moon explorers

Countries and regions that have sent craft to the Moon:

- USA
- RUSSIA
- EUROPE
- JAPAN
- CHINA
- INDIA

Planet explorers

Here are the most recent spacecraft to have explored each planet. Both Uranus and Neptune have been visited by only one spacecraft:

Mercury – Messenger

Venus – Magellan

Mars – Mars Express

Jupiter – Galileo

Saturn – Cassini

Uranus – Voyager 2

Neptune – Voyager 2

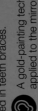

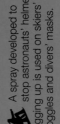

Blasts from the past

1959
Luna 1 is the first spacecraft to travel away from Earth

1962
Telstar transmits the first live TV pictures and telephone calls through space

1962
Mariner 2 flies by Venus; the first craft to fly by another planet

1970
Lunokhod 1 lands on the Moon – it is the first rover to drive across another planet

1970
Venera 7 sends the first signals from the surface of Venus

1971
Salyut 1 becomes the first space station to orbit Earth

1971
Mariner 9 orbits Mars to become the first spacecraft to orbit another planet

1995
Galileo releases a probe into Jupiter's atmosphere, the first into a giant planet's atmosphere

In numbers

4.5
The number of hours it takes for a radio message to travel from a spacecraft at Pluto to Earth

8
The number of years the Galileo craft spent exploring Jupiter and its moons

7,000+
The number of spacecraft that have been launched from Earth since 1957

65,000
The number of parts in a Voyager spacecraft

86,320
The orbits of Earth made by the Mir space station during its lifetime (1986–2001)

Space spin-offs

Materials, equipment, and techniques developed for space are also used on Earth.

- The metal nitinol was developed for space equipment that expands to full size in space. On Earth, it is used in teeth braces.
- A gold-painting technique applied to the mirror of a telescope sent to Mars is used on a thermometer for the human ear.
- A spray developed to stop astronauts' helmets fogging up is used on skiers' goggles and divers' masks.
- Breathing apparatus and clothing used by firefighters uses technology developed for spacewalking astronauts.
- At the 2008 Olympic Games, 94 per cent of the swimming gold medallists wore a seamless swimsuit that used techniques previously employed in space-shuttle design.

How do you get **into space?**

The way to get into space is on-board a rocket or a rocket-powered craft such as the space shuttle. The rocket's cargo is known as the payload and usually consists of a satellite, an interplanetary spacecraft, or a craft with astronauts. Something in the region of 250 payloads are launched into space each year.

Tell me more: **rocket stages**

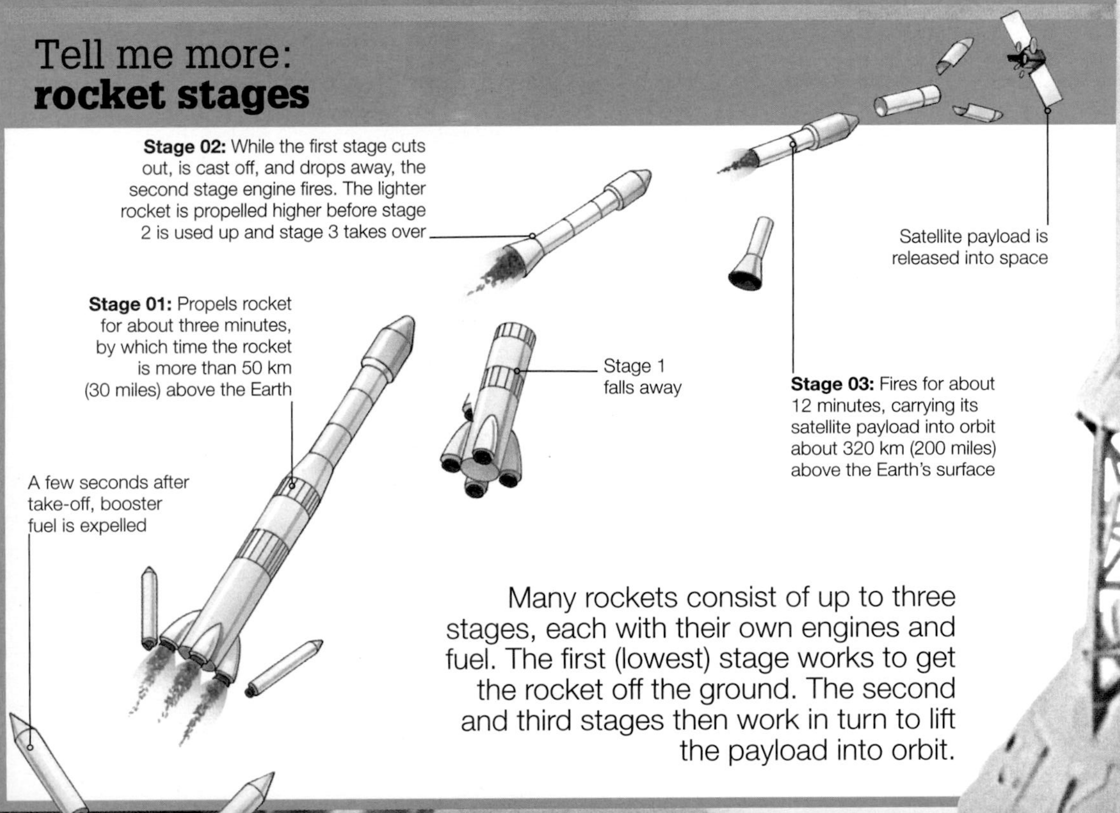

Stage 02: While the first stage cuts out, is cast off, and drops away, the second stage engine fires. The lighter rocket is propelled higher before stage 2 is used up and stage 3 takes over
Satellite payload is released into space
Stage 01: Propels rocket for about three minutes, by which time the rocket is more than 50 km (30 miles) above the Earth
Stage 1 falls away
Stage 03: Fires for about 12 minutes, carrying its satellite payload into orbit about 320 km (200 miles) above the Earth's surface
A few seconds after take-off, booster fuel is expelled

Many rockets consist of up to three stages, each with their own engines and fuel. The first (lowest) stage works to get the rocket off the ground. The second and third stages then work in turn to lift the payload into orbit.

Five shuttle orbiters

Name: Columbia
Flights: 28
First flight: April 1981
Last flight: January 2003

Name: Challenger
Flights: 10
First flight: April 1983
Last flight: January 1986

Name: Discovery
Flights: 39
First flight: August 1984
Last flight: September 2010

Name: Atlantis
Flights: 32
First flight: October 1985
Last flight: May 2010

Name: Endeavour
Flights: 25
First flight: May 1992
Last flight: July 2010

Seven launch sites

Rocket **gallery**

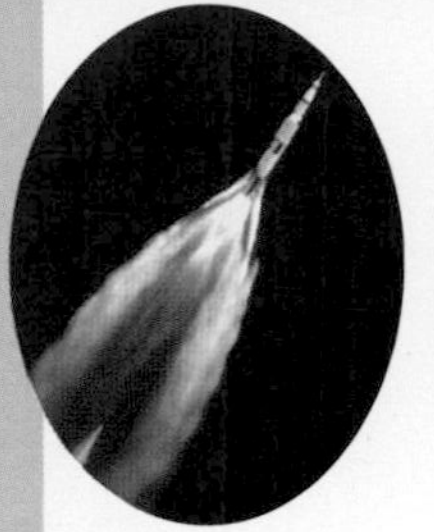

Saturn V
Thirteen US Saturn V rockets were launched between 1967 and 1973.

Ariane 5
This European rocket launches satellites and spacecraft from French Guiana.

Long March 2F
China's first astronaut was launched on-board a Long March 2F rocket in 2003.

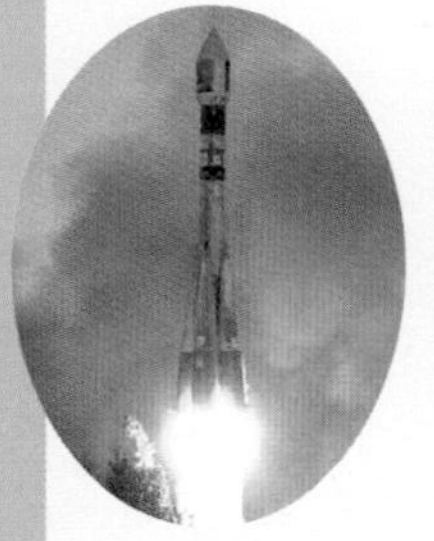

Soyuz FG
These Russian rockets take astronauts to the International Space Station.

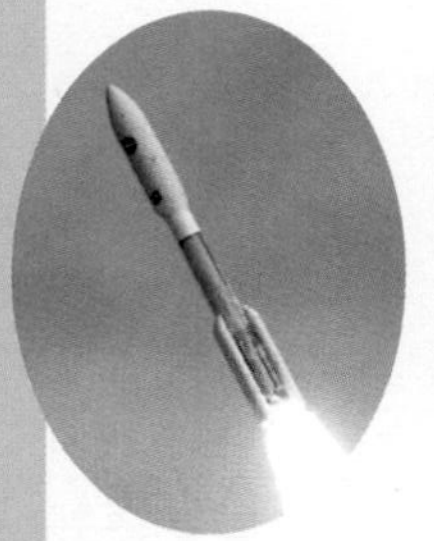

Atlas 5
Since 2002, Atlas V rockets have been taking satellites and interplanetary spacecraft from sites in the USA.

RECORD BREAKER

The biggest successful rocket was **Saturn V**, which took men to the Moon. A three-stage rocket, it was as tall as a 30-storey building (111 m/364 feet) and weighed about the same as 2,200 cars.

In numbers

11.3 km
(7 miles) The speed per second that a rocket needs to escape Earth's gravity

240 km
(150 miles) The length of wiring in a space shuttle orbiter

5,000
The approximate number of satellites launched in the past 60 years

257 billion
The amount of dollars spent by the United States on space projects each year

Blasts from the past

1926
Robert Goddard launches the first liquid-fuel rocket

1942
Under the guidance of Werner von Braun and Walter Dornberger, the first German V2 rocket is launched from Peenemunde, Germany

1944
A V2 rocket flies higher than 100 km (62 miles) and becomes the first man-made object in space

1957
The USSR launches the first satellite, Sputnik 1

1961
Russian Yuri Gagarin becomes the first human to be sent into space

1981
The launch of the space shuttle *Columbia*, the first reusable space launcher

What about me?

If you are aged 27 to 37, between 153–190 cm (5–6.2 ft) tall, and have a science-based university qualification, you could apply to be an astronaut.

SpaceShipOne

- In June 2004, SpaceShipOne became the first privately owned piloted craft to travel into space more than once.
- SpaceShipOne was carried to 15 km (9 miles) above Earth by the White Knight aircraft. Once released, it ignited its rocket engines and moved off into space.
- Its pilot, Mike Melvill, became the first commercial astronaut as he took the craft to more than 100 km (62 miles) above Earth.

Space starts about 100 km (62 miles) above Earth's surface. At this height, **99.99997 per cent** of the mass of Earth's atmosphere is below you.

What is a spacewalk?

When an astronaut goes outside a spacecraft it is described as extra-vehicular activity (EVA), or more simply, a spacewalk. The astronaut doesn't walk, but hovers and floats and pulls to move around. To make sure the astronauts don't float away, they are attached to their craft.

Blasts from the past

1965
On 18 March, Russian Alexei Leonov makes the first ever spacewalk; he spends about ten minutes outside his Voskhod 2 craft

1972
Ron Evans' 1 hour 6 minute spacewalk from Apollo 17 is one of the few occasions when an EVA has taken place outside Earth's orbit

1984
Bruce McCandless becomes the first astronaut to carry out a spacewalk when not attached to a spacecraft, in this case Challenger

2001
On 11 March, Jim Voss and Susan Helms set the record for the longest spacewalk so far; they work outside the International Space Station (ISS) for 8 hours 56 minutes.

2007
The 100th spacewalk outside the ISS is performed by Peggy Whitson and Dan Tani on 18 December; it lasts 6 hours 56 minutes

RECORD BREAKER

Anatoly Solovyev has spent more time **spacewalking** than anyone else. He has made 16 EVAs and clocked up a total of 82.22 hours. In second place is Michael Lopez-Alegria, who has spent 67.4 hours on ten EVAs.

Astronauts are **tethered** to their craft in one of a number of ways. The earliest astronauts were attached by a **cord-like restraint** that supplied oxygen. Today, they use metal and rope-like tethers, or are fixed by their feet and back to a **robotic arm**.

Creatures in space

Many living creatures other than humans have been into space. In the past 50 years these have included:

Dogs	Rabbits
Monkeys	Spiders
Rats	Jellyfish
Fish	Turtles
Bees	Newts
Mice	Crickets
Flies	Guinea pigs
Chimpanzees	Butterflies

I don't believe it!

Spacesuits used to be custom-made for particular astronauts, but now they are made so they can be quickly adjusted for different-sized wearers. Suits are kept on-board the ISS and used when needed.

WEIRD OR WHAT?

There is no washing machine in space and so astronauts wear their **clothes** for as long as they can. Shirts and trousers are changed about every ten days, and underwear and socks every other day.

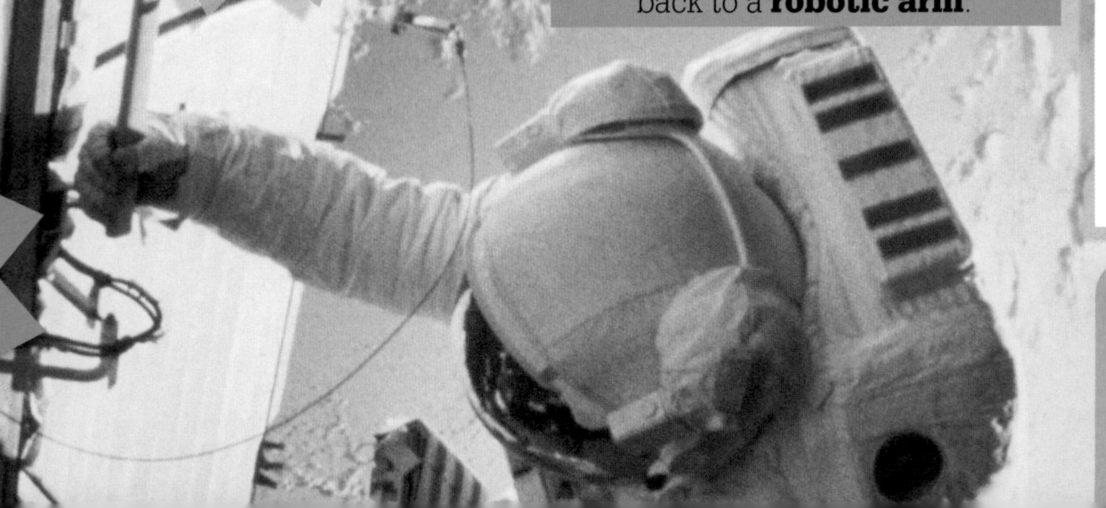

Space **wardrobe**

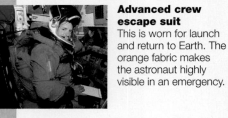

Advanced crew escape suit
This is worn for launch and return to Earth. The orange fabric makes the astronaut highly visible in an emergency.

Spacesuit
The white spacesuit protects astronauts from the space environment and supplies oxygen to breathe when they are spacewalking.

Underwear
Under the spacesuit is a one-piece stretchy suit that keeps the astronaut cool. Chilled water flows through 91.5 m (300 ft) of tubes within the suit. Under this is an adult-sized nappy!

Helmet
The main part of the helmet is a clear plastic bubble. This is covered by the extra-vehicular visor assembly. A TV camera and lights can be attached to the helmet.

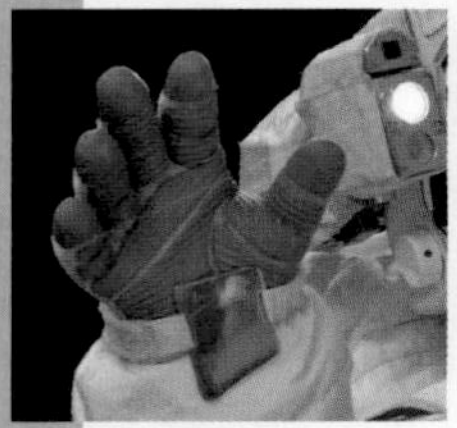

Gloves
Spacesuit gloves have a thumb and fingertips moulded from silicone rubber for sensitivity. Heaters in the fingertips prevent the astronauts' fingers getting cold.

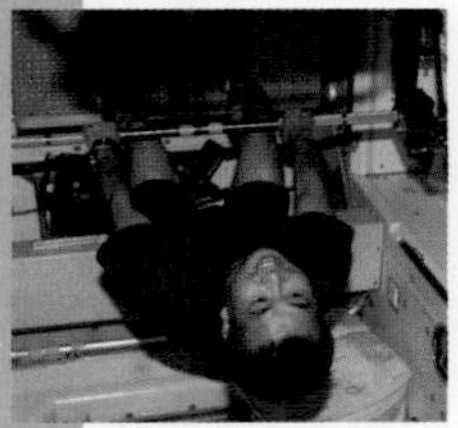

Leisurewear
An astronaut has a choice of long- and short-sleeved polo shirts, rugby shirts, jumpers, t-shirts, and shorts to wear while working, relaxing, or exercising inside their craft.

Launch essentials

Items astronauts wear or have in their pockets when they launch include:

Sunglasses	Gloves
Flares	Thermal socks
Wristwatch	ID bracelet
Sick bag	Handkerchief
Penknife	Scissors
Torch	Calculator

Spacewalkers

- **About 500 astronauts have been into space, but only about 200 have spacewalked.**
- Before leaving their craft, astronauts spend hours in an airlock to get used to the low-pressure, pure-oxygen atmosphere of their spacesuit.
- **Spacewalking astronauts wear SAFER (Simplified Aid for EVA Rescue), a backpack with rocket thrusters that propel them to their craft if their tether breaks.**
- Tasks carried out by spacewalkers include carrying out repairs, monitoring an experiment, or helping construct the ISS.
- **So far, around 800 hours have been spent on spacewalks outside the ISS.**

Moon

- So far, 12 men have walked on the Moon. They went on six different Apollo missions between 1969 and 1972.
- The first was Neil Armstrong on 21 July 1969.
- The last to step off was Eugene Cernan on 14 December 1972.
- The 12 astronauts spent 300 hours on the Moon, 80 of these outside their craft.
- The astronauts found that loping (taking long strides) or occasionally making kangaroo hops were the best ways to move across the Moon's surface.

Lost in space

Occasionally, an astronaut lets go of a tool when on a spacewalk; it drifts away and starts to make its own orbit around Earth. In November 2008, Heide Stefanyshyn-Piper was cleaning up the mess a **grease gun** had made in her tool bag when the bag and a pair of grease guns **floated away**.

Tickets to space

Astronauts from around the world are flown into space by just three countries: the USA, Russia, and China. Seven space tourists have paid about $25 million each to travel aboard a Russian Soyuz craft for a one-week stay aboard the ISS.

Dennis Tito (2001)

Mark Shuttleworth (2002)

Greg Olsen (2005)

Anousheh Ansari (2006)

Charles Simonyi (2007 and 2009)

Richard Garrott (2008)

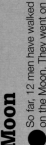

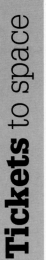

Guy Laliberté (2009)

How long does it take **to get to the Moon?**

The Moon is about 384,400 km (238,900 miles) away and it takes just over 60 hours to get there. More than 60 robotic craft and nine crewed craft have travelled to the Moon. The journey has been made by 24 men – three of them have been twice and a dozen have walked on its surface.

First to the Moon

mission	arrived	achievement
Luna 2 (USSR)	13 Sept 1959	first crash-landing
Luna 9 (USSR)	3 Feb 1966	first soft-landing
Apollo 11 (USA)	21 July 1969	first astronauts walk on Moon
Luna 16 (USSR)	20 Sept 1970	first automated sample return
Luna 17 (USSR)	17 Nov 1970	first robotic lunar rover
Apollo 15 (USA)	30 July 1971	first manned lunar rover

Moonwalkers

The 12 men that walked on the Moon spent a total of more than 300 hours on its surface, 80 of these were outside their craft. They travelled there in six separate missions. The first was Neil Armstrong on 21 July 1969. Harrison Schmitt was the last onto the Moon, but Eugene Cernan (above) was the last to step off, on 14 December 1972.

1. Neil Armstrong
2. Buzz Aldrin
3. Charles Conrad
4. Alan Bean
5. Alan Shepard
6. Edgar Mitchell
7. David Scott
8. James Irwin
9. John Young
10. Charles Duke
11. Eugene Cernan
12. Harrison Schmitt

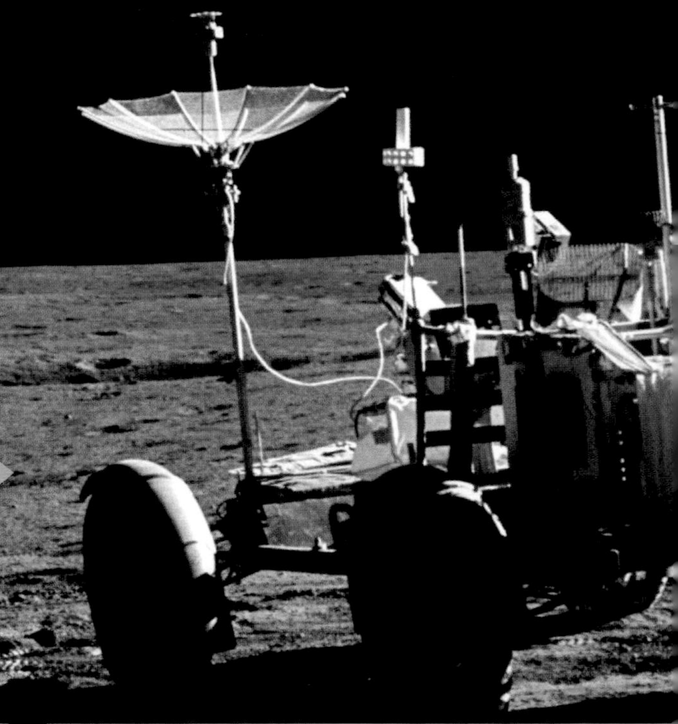

Getting around

In addition to walking, astronauts have used powered transportation to get across the Moon. **Lunar Roving Vehicles**, or rovers, were used by the six astronauts of the Apollo 15, 16, and 17 missions. These battery-driven four-wheel-drive vehicles were about the size of a small car.

Robotic rovers

- The first rover to operate on a surface other than Earth was the Soviet remote-controlled robot rover Lunokhod 1.
- It arrived on the Moon in November 1970 and spent ten months travelling across 10 km (6 miles) of the surface as it made images and tested the ground.
- Its twin, Lunokhod 2, roved over 37 km (23 miles) of a different lunar region in 1973.

Robotic missions

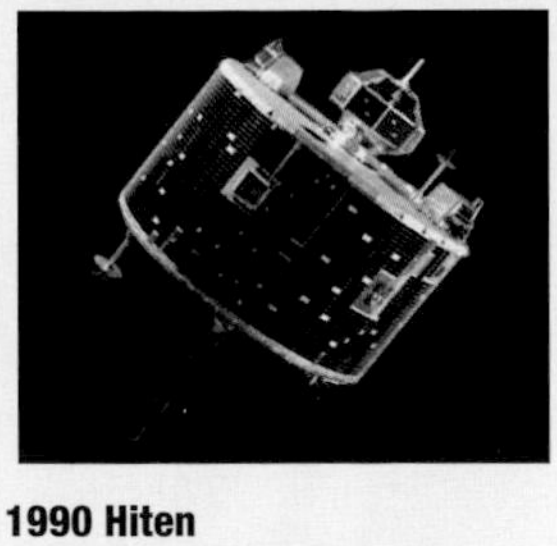

1990 Hiten
Japan became the third nation (after Russia and the USA) to put a craft into orbit around the Moon.

1994 Clementine
This US craft mapped the Moon; it took 1.8 million images of the lunar surface.

FAST FACTS

The Moon

01: Diameter 3,476 km (2,160 miles)

02: Rotation period 27.3 days

03: Orbital period 27.3 days

04: Surface temperature –150°C to 120°C (–240°F to 240°F)

05: Gravity at equator 0.165 (Earth = 1)

Take your time
It would take **160 days** to get to the Moon in a car driven at 100 kph (62 mph).

A record year

- The lunar rover speed record is 17 kph (10.56 mph). Apollo 16 astronauts John Young and Charles Duke set this in 1972 when driving to the Lunar Module (LM) from Descartes Crater.
- In 1972, Apollo 17 crew members Gene Cernan and Harrison Schmitt travelled 7.6 km (4.7 miles) from the LM, further than any others.
- Astronauts do not travel more than 9.7 km (6 miles) from the LM – at this distance, they would only just be able to walk back if their rover broke down.

Tell me more: **the far side**

- **The Moon spins once during the time it takes to orbit the Earth once, so one side of the Moon always faces Earth and the other (the far side) always faces away.**
- The first-ever pictures of the far side of the Moon were taken by the Soviet spacecraft Luna 3 in October 1959.
- **Apollo 8 crew members, James Lovell, William Anders, and Frank Borman were the first people to see the far side. They went round the back of the Moon ten times in December 1968.**
- The far side of the Moon is different from the near side. The Moon's rocky crust is 15 km (9 miles) thicker on the far side and the craters there have not been filled by volcanic lava as on the near side.

The **Moon** was originally much closer to the **Earth** than it is now. It is moving away at about 3.8 cm (1.5 in) per year.

I don't believe it!

The Moon's gravity is one-sixth of that on Earth, so heavy items, such as rocks, are much easier to pick up. Also, your Portable Life Support System – the backpack that supplied you with oxygen and kept you cool – would weigh 14 kg (31 lb) instead of the 86 kg (190 lb) it does on Earth.

About 50 robotic craft flew to the Moon between 1959 and 1976. After which no craft, either manned or robotic, journeyed there until 1990. Since then, about ten robotic craft have been there.

2003 Smart 1
The first European craft to travel to the Moon took both X-ray and infrared images.

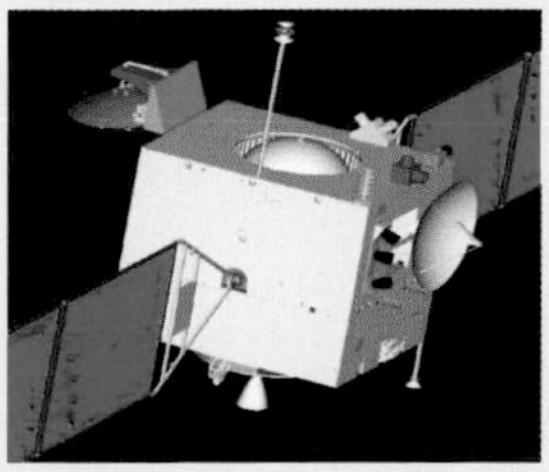

2007 Chang'e 1
The first of China's lunar missions used a craft that's named after the Chinese goddess of the Moon.

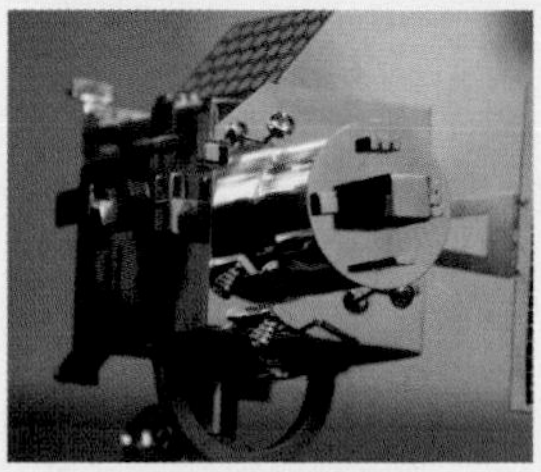

2008 Chandrayaan-1
India opened its lunar expedition with this craft that identifies water molecules in the Moon's soil.

2009 Lunar Reconnaissance Orbiter
This maps the Moon for landing sites for future manned missions.

2009 LCROSS
The Lunar Crater Observation and Sensing Satellite records water vapour on the Moon.

Who names the **stars and galaxies?**

Stars and galaxies are named according to conventions established through history. The International Astronomical Union makes sure these conventions are followed and sets up new rules when needed. Founded in 1919, the organization is based in Paris, France, and counts the majority of the world's top astronomers as its members.

WHAT'S IN A NAME?

The **Sombrero Galaxy** (below) gets its nickname from its passing resemblance to the Mexican hat. We see this spiral galaxy edge on: its core is the hat's crown, and its disc the hat's rim.

Tell me more: **naming celestial objects**

- **Objects are identified by names, letters, and numbers, or a combination of these. Some have a nickname but most are known by their official identification.**
- The brightest stars in a constellation are known by a letter of the Greek alphabet – alpha, beta, and so on – along with the constellation name. About 350 of these have a proper name too, such as Sirius.
- **Parts of Solar System objects including mountains and craters are given names. Even small rocks, such as the one on Mars named after the cartoon character Yogi bear (below), need identification.**

Asteroids

Asteroids are numbered in order of discovery and also given a name, usually suggested by the discoverer. These are all asteroids:

- **Barcelona**
- **Beethoven**
- **Chicago**
- **Elvis**
- **Eros**
- **Helsinki**
- **Hitchcock**
- **James Bond**
- **Karl Marx**
- **Kleopatra**
- **Mark Twain**
- **Michelangelo**
- **Rembrandt**
- **Sinatra**
- **Tolkien**

I can see that!

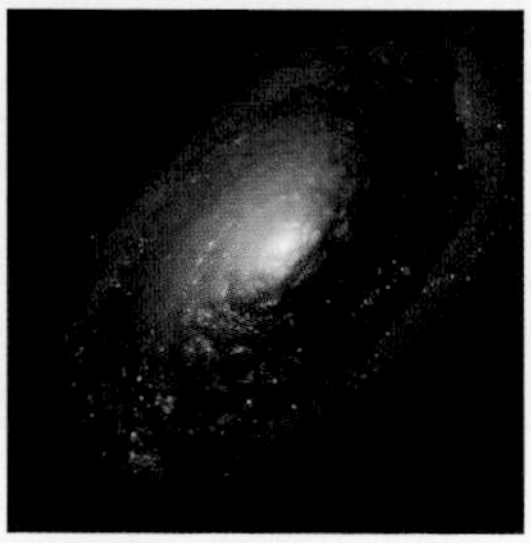

Black Eye Galaxy

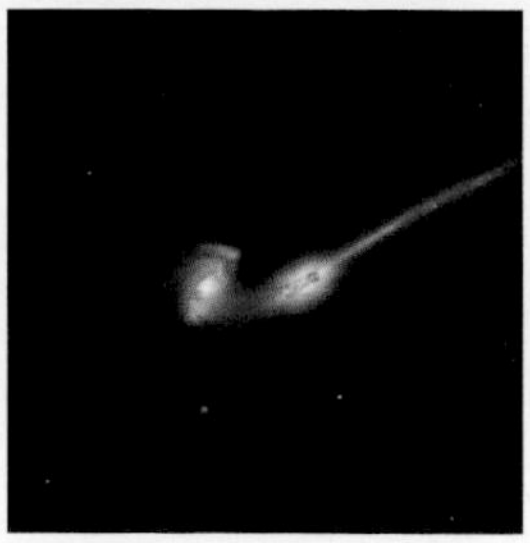

The Mice (a pair of galaxies)

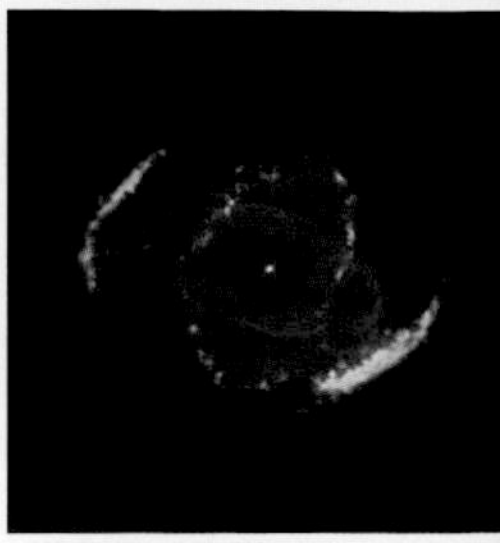

Cat's Eye Nebula

Blasts from the past

1604 German astronomer Johannes Kepler witnesses a supernova – a dying star that suddenly explodes – and the cloud of material blasted off in the explosion is named Kepler's Star

1675 French-Italian astronomer Giovanni Cassini discovers a gap in Saturn's ring, which will become known as the Cassini Division; the space orbiter sent to study Saturn in 1997 is also called Cassini

1836 English astronomer Francis Bailey describes an effect seen when sunlight shines through valleys on the edge of the Moon during a total solar eclipse – it becomes known as Bailey's Beads

1947 Bart Bok suggests that some of the Milky Way's stars are born in small, cool clouds of gas and dust; although it is many years before the Dutch-American astronomer is proved correct, the clouds are named Bok globules

In numbers

1
The number of the first asteroid to be discovered, Ceres, in 1801

8
The number of constellations named after birds; they include the peacock

110
The number of objects in Charles Messier's list and given M numbers; M1 to M110

173
The number of named volcanic sites on Jupiter's moon, Io

945,592,683
The number of stars listed in the Hubble Space Telescope's Guide Star Catalogue

What about me?

The easiest way to get a space object named after you is by discovering a comet, which will automatically take your family name.

Deep Space

Most deep space objects, such as galaxies, do not have names but are given a number according to how they appear in a catalogue. If they are in more than one catalogue, they have more than one number.

Charles Messier produced his catalogue in the late 18th century, when hunting for comets. It includes star clusters, galaxies, and nebula. Its objects are designated M with a number.

The New General Catalogue of 7,840 deep-sky objects was produced in 1888 and objects there have an NGC number. The Andromeda Galaxy is both NGC 224 and M31.

Recent catalogues include objects such as radio galaxies. Entries in the 1959 Third Cambridge Catalogue of Radio Sources have designations such as 3C 273.

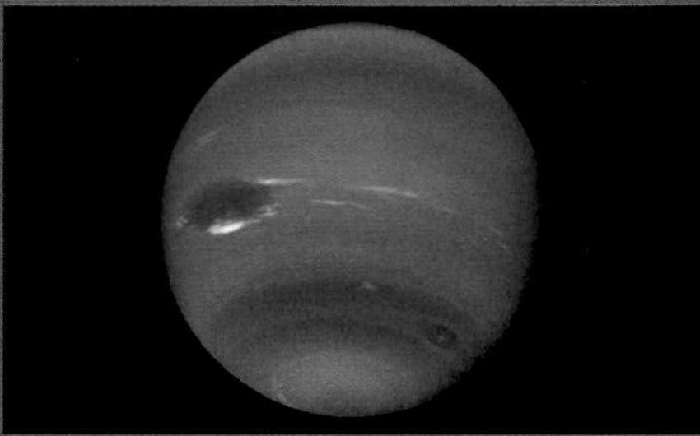

Planetary names

Mercury – messenger of the Roman gods

Venus – Roman goddess of love

Mars – Roman god of war

Jupiter – king of the Roman gods

Saturn – father of Jupiter

Uranus – god of the sky and father of Saturn

Neptune – Roman god of the sea

Woman's world

All except one of the surface features on Venus are named after women. The exception is the **Maxwell Montes** mountain range, which is named after the British physicist James Clerk Maxwell.

I don't believe it!

Some of Uranus's moons are named after characters in the plays of dramatist William Shakespeare. Two of them, Oberon and Titania, are the king and the queen of the fairies.

Many stars and galaxies are given nicknames by astronomers. It is often pretty obvious that their names come from the way they look, but it depends on what you can see.

Whirlpool Galaxy

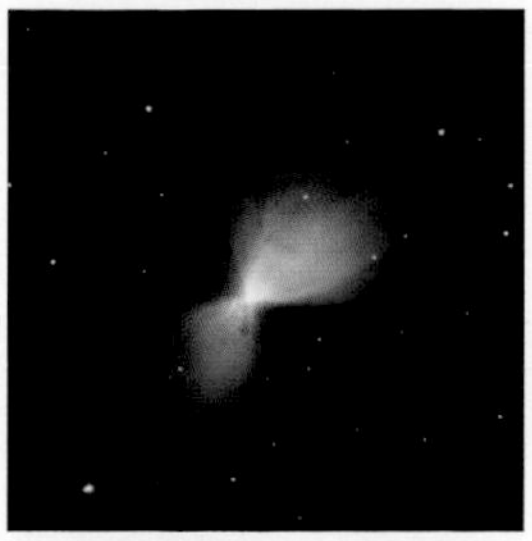

Bowtie Nebula (also known as Boomerang Nebula)

Horsehead Nebula

Jewel Box star cluster

The Mask (a pair of galaxies)

Why is **Mars red?**

Mars is known as the red planet because of the colour of its top layer of soil. This soil is rich in iron and has combined with oxygen to become a rusty red colour. From Mars's surface, you would see a rusty-red landscape and a pink sky as winds blow its fine dust into its atmosphere.

Rocky worlds

Mars is one of four rocky planets in the Solar System. Also called the terrestrial planets, they are made mainly of rock and iron.

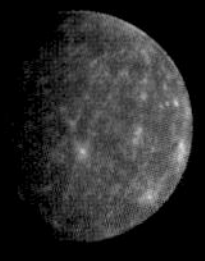

Mercury – the smallest of all the planets and the closest to the Sun. This world is grey and rocky, just like Earth's Moon.

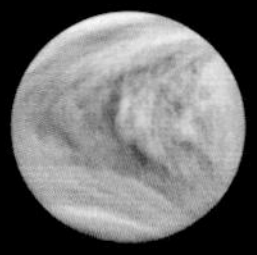

Venus – the only visible thing is Venus's thick clouds; sulphur makes them yellow in colour.

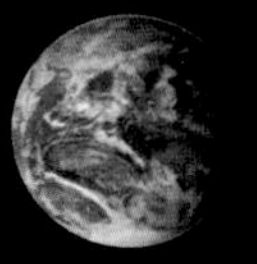

Earth – from space, Earth has three main colours: white clouds, blue oceans, and brown land.

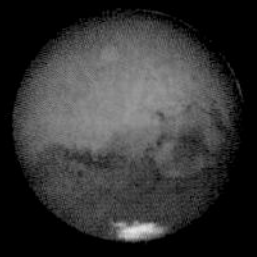

Mars – the most distant rocky planet. It is red all over except for two white caps of ice at its poles.

RECORD BREAKER

The biggest mountain in the Solar System is the Martian volcano **Olympus Mons**. It is about 24 km (15 miles) high and its base is 648 km (403 miles) across. Earth's Mount Everest is only 8.85 km (5½ miles) high.

Planet statistics

planet	average distance to Sun (km)	time to orbit the Sun	mass relative to Earth	diameter (km)	rotation period
Mercury	57.9 million (40 million miles)	88 days	0.055	4,879 (3,032 miles)	**59 days**
Venus	108.2 million (67.2 million miles)	224.7 days	0.82	12,104 (7,521 miles)	**243 days**
Earth	149.6 million (93 million miles)	365.26 days	1	12,756 (7,926 miles)	**23.9 hours**
Mars	227.9 million (141.6 million miles)	687 days	0.11	6,792 (4,220 miles)	**24.6 hours**

I don't believe it!

In the late 1800s, Italian astronomer Giovanni Schiaparelli reported seeing thin markings on Mars's surface, which he called channels. As the Italian for "channels" is *caneli*, some believed that he meant irrigation canals used by Martians to water their crops.

Blasts from the past

1965 Mariner 4 flies by Mars and takes the first close-ups of another planet

1971 Mariner 9 is the first craft to go into orbit around Mars

1976 Viking 1 and 2 land on the planet to search for life, but found none

1997 Mars Pathfinder lands and releases Sojourner, the first rover on Mars

2004 Mars Express starts mapping Mars's surface as it orbits the planet

2004 Two identical rovers, *Spirit* and *Opportunity*, land on opposite sides of the planet

2008 Mars Phoenix Lander arrives in Mars's north polar region and begins a search for water

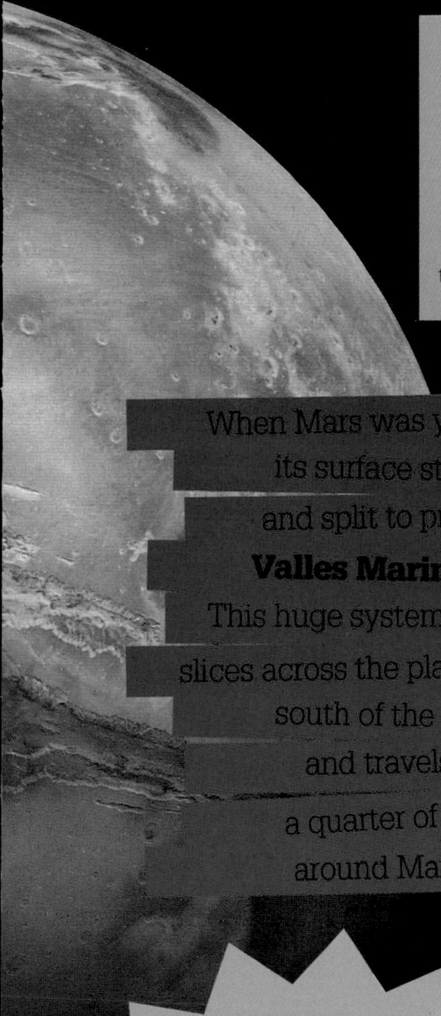

Core! That's hot!

Radioactive material inside Mars made it so hot when it was young that it melted completely. The planet's heavy iron sank to the middle and its lighter rocks floated on top. Over time, its surface cooled, but molten rock would break through the crust and flow across the planet. The giant volcanoes on Mars today grew through successive eruptions at one spot.

Martian moons

Mars has two moons, Phobos and Deimos, which were discovered in 1877. These potato-shaped lumps of rock are covered in impact craters. They were once asteroids but got captured into orbits round Mars. Both are tiny: Phobos is the largest at 27 km (17 miles) long.

When Mars was young, its surface stretched and split to produce the **Valles Marineris**. This huge system of canyons slices across the planet just south of the equator and travels about a quarter of the way around Mars.

Cratered world

There are tens of thousands of craters on Mars where asteroids crashed into the planet in the distant past. They range from simple bowl-shaped ones, less than a kilometre across, to huge basins hundreds of kilometres wide.

name	width
Hellas Planitia	2,200 km (1,367 miles)
Argyre Planitia	800 km (497 miles)
Lowell Crater	203 km (126 miles)
Columbus Crater	119 km (74 miles)
Thom Crater	24 km (15 miles)

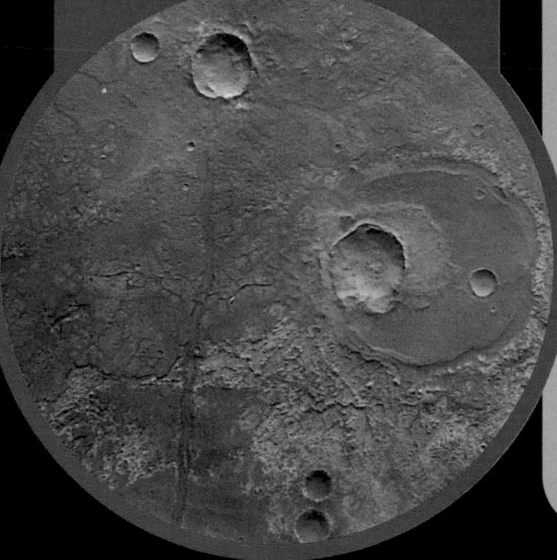

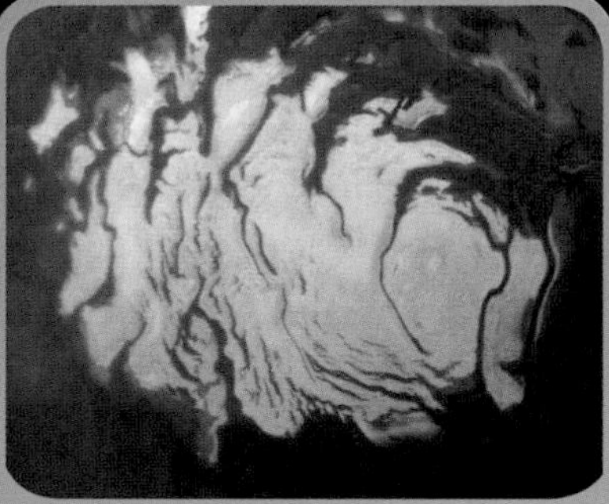

Water world

- Around 3–4 billion years ago, Mars was warmer and had liquid water. This flowed across the surface, carving out valleys and forming lakes and seas.
- There is still water on Mars today, but it is frozen. Its south polar cap (above) consists of predominantly water ice roughly centred on Mars's South Pole.
- Water exists under Mars's surface as permafrost – water ice mixed into the soil and frozen to the hardness of solid rock.
- There is also water in Mars's atmosphere. It sometimes forms clouds of water ice, and it can also settle on the ground as early morning frost.

WEIRD OR WHAT?

The **northern and southern hemispheres** of Mars are different. The north is a young low-lying plain and the south is ancient highlands. It's possible that an asteroid hit the north and blasted off some of the crust.

Five steps to landing on Mars

01: Mars could be the first planet that humans visit. We have the ability to get there; we just need to raise US$ 500 billion to build a suitable spacecraft.

02: Volunteers have already undertaken a 105-day simulated trip in an isolation unit in Moscow to test the effect of long-duration spaceflight. A 520-day trip is planned.

03: The shortest trip to Mars would last about 15 months, with only three weeks of it on the planet.

04: Living quarters for the astronauts would be sent on ahead by robotic craft.

05: The craft transporting the astronauts would be so large that it would be assembled above Earth.

WHAT'S IN A NAME?

Mars is named after the **Roman god of war**. Its moons, Phobos and Deimos, are the names of the god's horses. The mountain home of the **Greek gods** gives its name to the huge volcano on Mars, Olympus Mons.

A guide to Mars

More than 20 spacecraft have successfully explored Mars. They have flown by the planet, orbited around it, landed on it, and sent rovers across it. The first close-up images were transmitted back to Earth in 1965, and today the entire planet has been mapped.

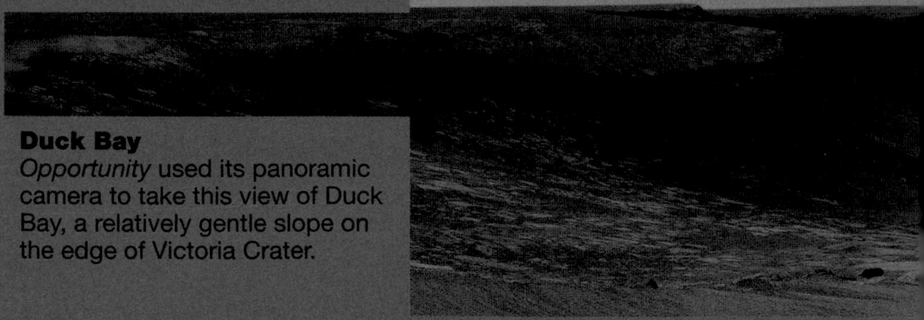

Duck Bay
Opportunity used its panoramic camera to take this view of Duck Bay, a relatively gentle slope on the edge of Victoria Crater.

Victoria Crater
The Mars rover *Opportunity* arrived at this 800-m- (0.5-mile-) wide impact crater in 2006 and spent almost two years exploring it.

Low Ridge
This image taken by *Spirit* in April 2006 shows dark volcanic rocks against the red soil on Low Ridge within Gusev Crater.

Endurance Crater
This 130-m- (427-ft-) wide impact crater was explored by *Opportunity* from May to December 2004.

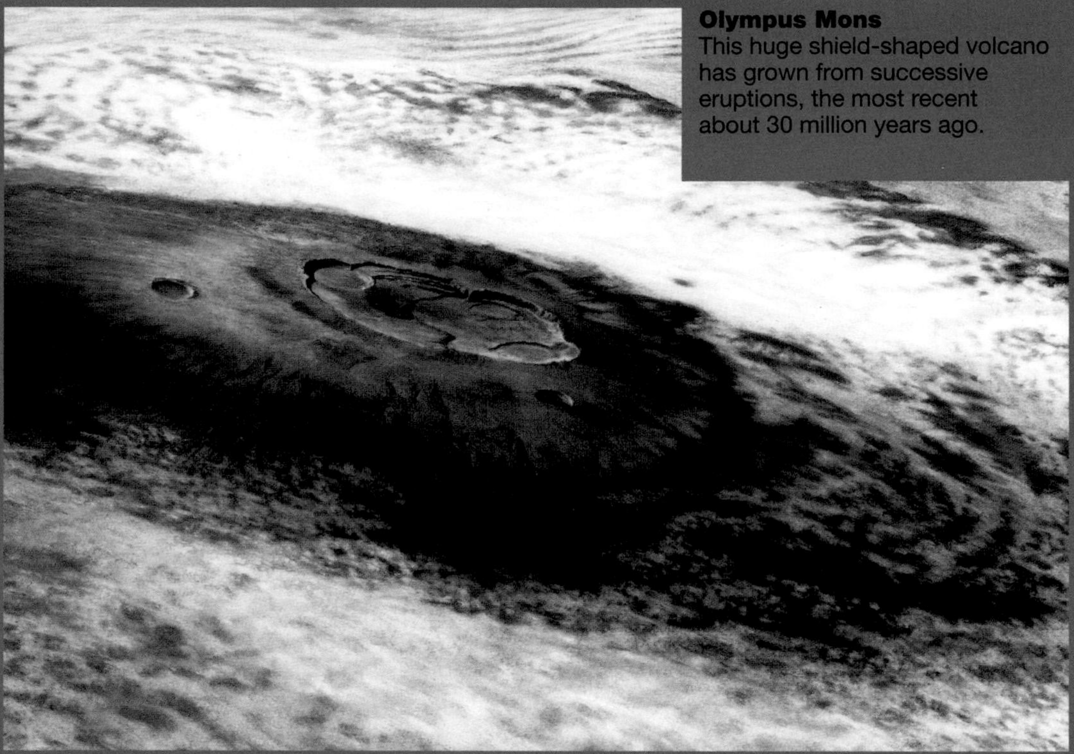

Olympus Mons
This huge shield-shaped volcano has grown from successive eruptions, the most recent about 30 million years ago.

Ares Vallis
After a seven-month journey, in 1997 the Mars Pathfinder landed in the Ares Vallis, a region that was flooded by water in the planet's early history.

Icy surface
A 10-cm- (3-in-) wide trench dug by the *Phoenix* lander craft in 2008 revealed ice under Mars's surface soil.

Echus Chasma
Formed by water cutting through young surface rock, Echus Chasma is about 100 km (62 miles) long and 10 km (6.2 miles) wide.

Why does **Saturn** have **rings?**

One theory is that the material in Saturn's rings was left over from when the giant planets formed – the material tried to join together to make a moon, but Saturn's gravity pulled it in. Another idea is that this material was from a moon that was drawn too close to the planet and broke up.

Tell me more: **ringed planets**

- **Jupiter, Saturn, Uranus, and Neptune all have rings.**
- They are the four largest Solar System planets and are known as the giant planets.
- **Saturn's rings are by far the biggest: they are the equivalent of a rocky, icy satellite about 200 km (125 miles) across.**
- There is only enough material in each of the other planets' rings to make a satellite about 10 km (6 miles) across.

Jupiter's ring system is made of three rings, the main one visible here.

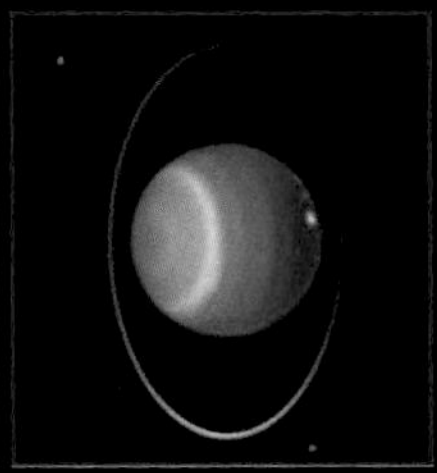

Of Uranus's 12 narrow rings, only one (the Epsilon) is easily seen.

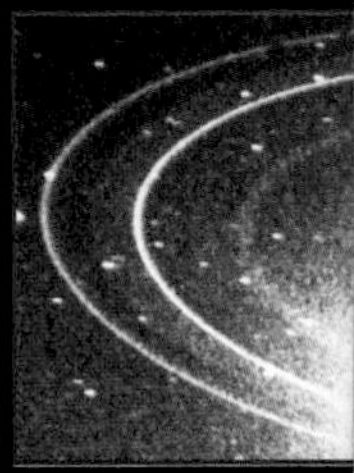

Neptune has five thin rings and a sixth partial ring.

FAST FACTS

Saturn's rings

01: Saturn has seven main rings and hundreds of smaller ringlets.

02: They are made of particles and chunks of dirty ice.

03: The pieces range from about a centimetre to 5 m (16 ft), the size of a London bus.

04: Each piece of ring material follows its own orbit around Saturn.

05: Individual rings are identified by letters in order of discovery.

06: The rings are less than 100 m (328 ft) deep, paper thin compared to the planet itself.

Mind the gap

Viewed from a distance, there are gaps between **Saturn's rings**. Even the largest of these, the 4,800-km- (2,983-mile-) wide Cassini Division, contains ring material.

Blasts from the past

1610 Saturn's rings are first seen by Galileo Galilei, who looks at them with the newly invented telescope; he thinks Saturn has two earlike handles, one on each side

1655 Christiaan Huygens realizes that what Galileo has seen is a ring of material

1977 Astronomers discover Uranus has rings when they notice a star appear to blink on and off when near the planet

1979 The rings of Jupiter are revealed when the Voyager 1 spacecraft flies by the planet

1985 Parts of Neptune's rings are detected from Earth; its complete system is revealed by the Voyager 2 spacecraft in 1989

Stormy Saturn

- Saturn looks tranquil, but its upper atmosphere is full of storms and **powerful winds** that blow up to speeds of 1,930 kph (1,200 mph).
- Its calm appearance comes from a thin layer of foggy haze that surrounds the planet.
- A region in Saturn's southern hemisphere is so stormy that it was nicknamed **Storm Alley**.
- A huge thunderstorm deep in Saturn's atmosphere has been named **Dragon Storm** because its outline resembles that of a dragon.

Cloud-top view

When we look at the gas planets such as Saturn, all we see are the high clouds in their hydrogen and helium atmospheres. Their different colours are the result of different additional elements and the temperatures of the atmospheres.

Exploration of Saturn

Four spacecraft have visited Saturn: the first three flew by; the fourth, Cassini, is in orbit around Saturn and its moons.

spacecraft	year
Pioneer 11	1979
Voyager 1	1980
Voyager 2	1981
Cassini	2004 to present

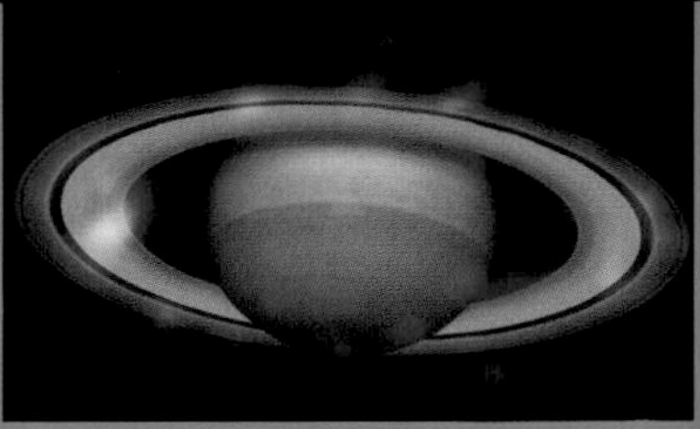

X-ray planet

- Saturn's atmosphere acts like a mirror reflecting light, and other forms of energy such as X-rays, from the Sun.
- The Chandra X-ray Observatory space telescope studied Saturn in 2004. It found that Saturn's rings sparkle in X-rays.
- The Chandra X-ray image and an optical image are combined in the image above. The blue dots are caused by X-rays from the Sun striking the oxygen atoms in the water ice of the ring particles.

Saturn's moons

Saturn has a large family of moons. At present, there are 60 known moons, with the smallest measuring just a few kilometres across.

Titan
Saturn's largest moon and the second largest moon in the Solar System.

Enceladus
Located within Saturn's rings, Enceladus's icy surface makes it shine brightly.

Mimas
Also within the rings, Mimas is an icy ball of rock that is covered with craters.

Phoebe
Phoebe is the largest of the 38 moons that orbit Saturn at great distance.

I don't believe it!

Saturn may look like a huge ball, but it is not actually spherical in shape – the planet is wider around its equator than around its poles. Saturn rotates every 10.7 hours, and as it does so material is flung outwards, resulting in its bulging equator (which is the biggest of any planet).

What about me?

Visible as a bright star for about ten months of the year, Saturn can be seen by the naked eye. Binoculars will show the rings, but a telescope is needed to see any detail.

Why do comets have tails?

For most of its life, a comet is just a lump of snow and dust orbiting through space. But if its path takes it close to the Sun, the heat turns the snow to gas and in the process releases dust. This forms two tails that make the comet easily seen from Earth.

Origins
Comets are made of pristine material that has been unchanged since the birth of the Solar System 4.6 billion years ago. They formed in the region between Jupiter and Neptune and were then dispersed by the gravitational influence of these planets. The comets that exist today are less than one-thousandth of those that existed originally.

FAST FACTS

Comets

01: Measuring a few kilometres across, the heart of a comet is an irregular-shaped spinning dirty snowball called a nucleus.

02: Trillions of comets orbit the Sun beyond Neptune, but only those that travel into the inner Solar System develop a coma – a huge spherical head of gas and dust, with gas and dust tails.

03: Gas molecules absorb sunlight, fluoresce, and produce a bluish gas tail. Dust particles just reflect light and the dust tail appears white.

04: The size of the coma and tails depend on how close the nucleus gets to the Sun. The tails can be up to 100,000,000 km (62,137,000 miles) long.

How to: **land on a comet**

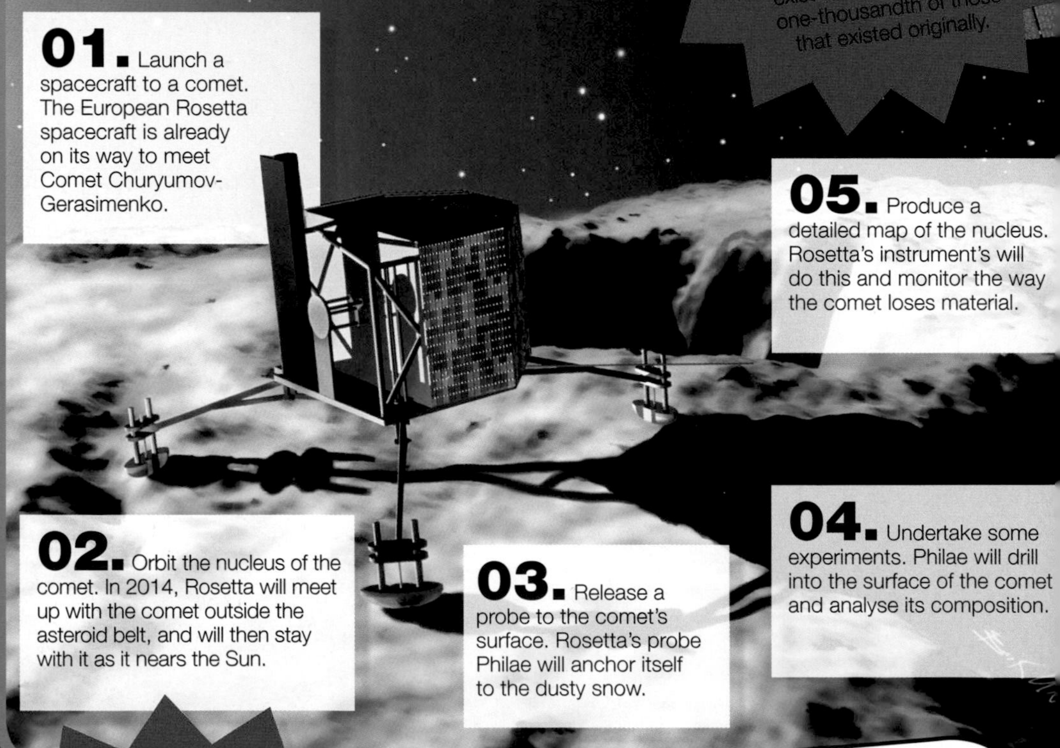

01. Launch a spacecraft to a comet. The European Rosetta spacecraft is already on its way to meet Comet Churyumov-Gerasimenko.

02. Orbit the nucleus of the comet. In 2014, Rosetta will meet up with the comet outside the asteroid belt, and will then stay with it as it nears the Sun.

03. Release a probe to the comet's surface. Rosetta's probe Philae will anchor itself to the dusty snow.

04. Undertake some experiments. Philae will drill into the surface of the comet and analyse its composition.

05. Produce a detailed map of the nucleus. Rosetta's instrument's will do this and monitor the way the comet loses material.

WHAT'S IN A NAME?
If more than one person finds a comet independently, all their names are used. **Comet Hale-Bopp**, for example, was discovered in 1995 by Alan Hale and Thomas Bopp.

What about me?

Comets visible with the naked eye appear at the rate of about four per decade. Particularly easy to see were Hale-Bopp in 1997 and McNaught in 2007.

RECORD BREAKER

Scottish-Australian astronomer Robert (Bob) McNaught, who works at the Siding Springs Observatory in New South Wales, Australia, has discovered **54 comets**, more than any other person.

Few people see **Halley's Comet** twice. American author Mark Twain didn't manage it. He wrote: "I came in with Halley's Comet in 1835. It is coming again next year, and I expect to go out with it." The comet did appear in 1910, but Twain didn't live to see it – he died one month before.

In numbers

2 m
(6.6 ft) The average depth of the layer of material lost from the nucleus of Halley's' Comet as it passes the Sun

100
The average number of hours that pass between comet discoveries by a dedicated comet-hunter

230
The number of comets that return to Earth's sky in periods of less than 200 years

3,400
The number of comets that return in periods greater than 200 years

100,000 km
(62,137 miles) The typical diameter of a comet's coma

trillion
The minimum number of comets in the Oort Cloud

Blasts from the past

Halley's comet is a rare example of a comet not being named after its discoverer. It is named after the astronomer who predicted its return – Edmond Halley. The comet appears every 76 years.

240 BCE
The earliest recognized appearance of the comet in Chinese astronomical diaries

1066
The comet hovers over the Battle of Hastings and is depicted in the Bayeux Tapestry

1301
The comet's appearance this year is used as a model for Giotto di Bondone's depiction of the Star of Bethlehem in his Nativity fresco in the Arena Chapel, Padua, Italy

1682
Viewed by English astronomer Edmond Halley when on his honeymoon in Islington, London, he predicts that the comet will return in 1758

1910
The first photograph of the comet is taken. Earth passes through the comet's tail and many people worry needlessly about being poisoned

1986
The Giotto spacecraft flies into the comet's coma and images its nucleus

On target

In July 2005, the Deep Impact spacecraft fired a missile at Comet Tempel 1. The craft photographed the collision, but the crater produced could not be seen through the huge cloud of very fine dust that formed. The Stardust craft will visit Tempel 1 in 2011 to observe changes in the comet since Deep Impact's visit.

I don't believe it!

The nucleus of a comet is so fragile that you could pull it apart with your hands. When Comet Shoemaker-Levy 9 got too close to Jupiter in 1992, the planet's gravity pulled on it and the comet broke up into 20 pieces. These all hit Jupiter in 1994.

Comets **through the ages**

Great Comet, 1577
Danish astronomer Tycho Brahe showed that this comet was much further away than the Moon, proving that comets were not part of Earth's atmosphere.

Great Comet, 1680
This comet was observed by Isaac Newton. He calculated its orbit, something never before done for a comet.

Donati, 1858
This spectacular example was the first comet to be photographed, by English photographer William Usherwood.

Tempel-Tuttle, 1866
Observations of this comet and the Leonid meteors showed how comets decay to produce meteor showers.

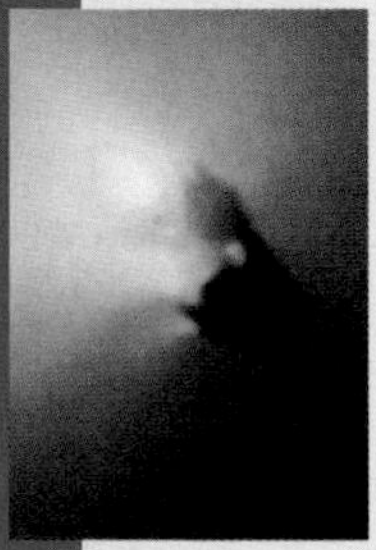

Halley, 1986
The first ever image of a cometary nucleus (Halley's) is taken by the Giotto spacecraft.

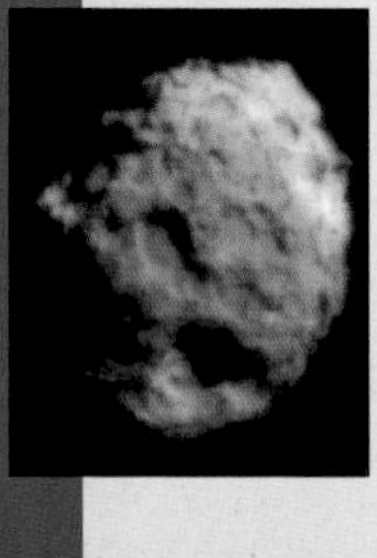

Wild 2, 2004
The Stardust spacecraft collected dust from the coma of Wild 2 – the first material returned from a comet.

What is a **meteorite?**

A meteorite is a lump of space rock that survives a fiery passage through Earth's atmosphere and hits the planet's surface. Air friction slows down the meteorite and much of the rock's surface is boiled away, leaving behind a very bright trail of gas and dust. This is seen from Earth and called a fireball.

WHAT'S IN A NAME?

Meteorites are named after the places where they are found. For example, when, on 21 September 1949, a cricket-ball sized lump of rock fell through the roof of the Prince Llewellyn hotel in Beddgelert, Wales, it was named **Beddgelert**.

Types of **meteorites**

Stony meteorites
Asteroid meteorites with compositions similar to Earth's rocky mantle are classed as stony meteorites.

Iron meteorites
Those with a composition like Earth's central iron-nickel core are classed as iron meteorites.

Stony-irons
Meteorites made from a mixture of the above are called stony-irons. They come from asteroids not big enough to melt.

Lunar meteorites
Meteorites from the Moon's surface can be recognized from their similarity to the samples brought to Earth by the Apollo astronauts.

Martian meteorites
Rock from Mars can be recognized by the small amounts of gas within it similar to that found in the Martian atmosphere.

Meteorite origins

Almost all (99.9 per cent) meteorites come from the asteroid belt – rocky material between Mars and Jupiter that was unused when the planets formed. A few (about 0.05 per cent from each) are from the surfaces of Moon and Mars, having been blasted off these planets after being hit by rocks.

Falls and finds

Meteorites are divided into falls and finds. With a fall, the fireball produced by the incoming rock is seen, the landing location is worked out, and a successful search is made. Finds are found by chance when someone picks up a strange-looking rock, or as part of an organized search.

I don't believe it!

On 10 August 1972, a space rock as bright as the full Moon moved through the sky over North America. Yet rather than hit Earth, it skipped off! It was detected at 76 km (47 miles) above Utah, then 58 km (36 miles) above Montana, but then left Earth's atmosphere and went off to orbit the Sun.

How to: **find a meteorite**

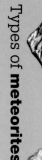

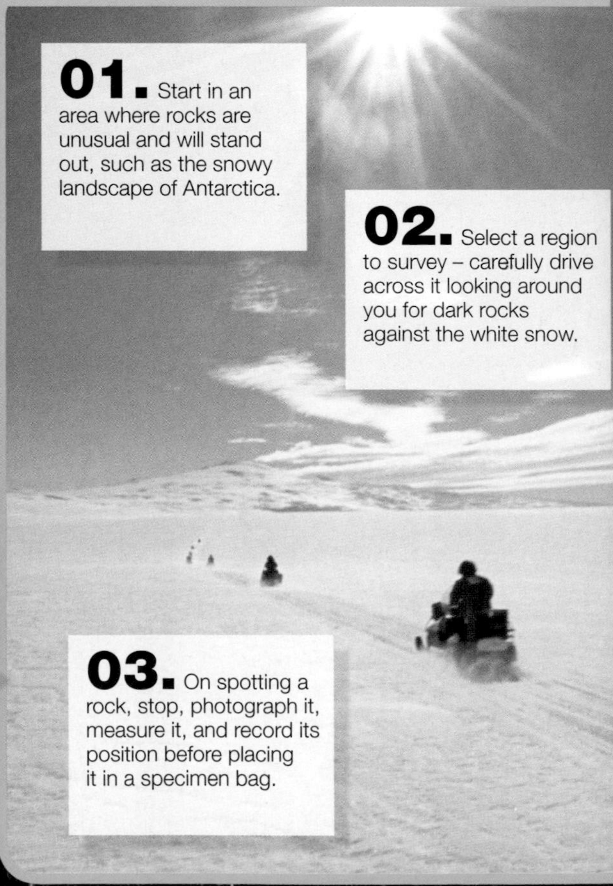

01. Start in an area where rocks are unusual and will stand out, such as the snowy landscape of Antarctica.

02. Select a region to survey – carefully drive across it looking around you for dark rocks against the white snow.

03. On spotting a rock, stop, photograph it, measure it, and record its position before placing it in a specimen bag.

Through Earth's atmosphere

- Rocky meteorites often fragment as they come through the atmosphere and form a meteorite shower.
- Space rocks weighing less than 100 kg (220 lb) before entering Earth's atmosphere have no chance of getting to the ground.
- A rock heavier than 1,000 tonnes will punch through the Earth's atmosphere like a bullet through tissue paper.

In numbers

34
The number of meteorites found that originated on Mars

1911
On 28 June of this year, a rock from Mars broke up in Earth's atmosphere and landed near Alexandria, Egypt

7,000 +
The number of meteorites have been found in searches in Antarctica

38,272
The number of named meteorites at the start of 2010

68,780
The pieces of meteorite that fell near Pultusk, Poland, in a shower in January 1868

Tell me more: Hoba West

- **The biggest meteorite found on record is the 60-tonne Hoba West.**
- This iron meteorite was discovered in Namibia, southern Africa, in 1920.
- **Hoba West weighed 66 tonnes when it was found, but since then 6 tonnes has rusted away.**
- The meteorite is still situated where it landed – the Namibian government declared it a national monument in 1955.

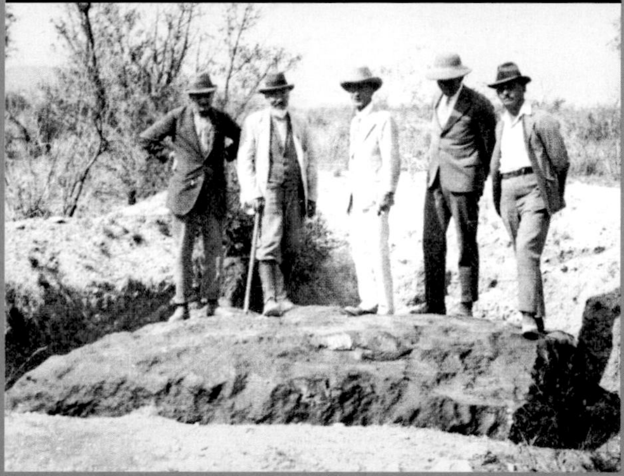

Meteor-wrongs

Harvey H. Nininger, the father of modern meteoritics (the study of meteorites) lectured about the subject all across the USA. He would ask people to bring what they thought were "rocks from space" to his meetings. Only about 1 in 100 was from space, the rest being Earth-based material.

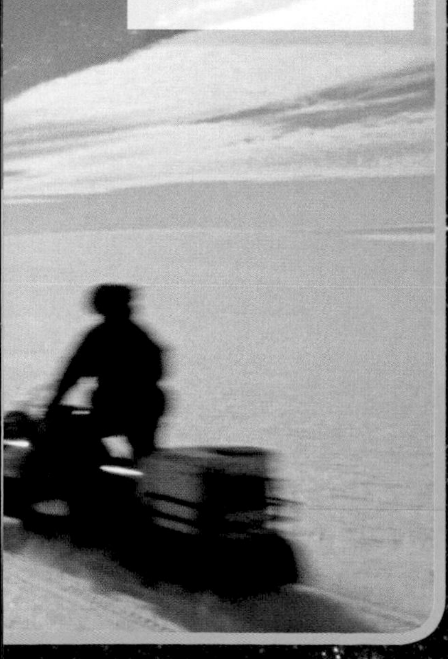

04. Return to your base where the rock's composition can be analysed and the rock verified as a meteorite.

Rock seekers

- Camera systems over the USA, Eastern Europe, and the Nullarbor Plain in Australia scan the skies for fireballs of incoming meteorites.
- Scientists search the barren, icy wastes of the Antarctic for meteorites – this is where the Martian example pictured below was found. The blue ice glacier region of Allan Hills in the eastern Antarctic has yielded thousands of meteorites.
- Searches are also carried out in desert regions such as the Sahara, North Africa. There, rocks are rare and stand out in the sandy terrain.

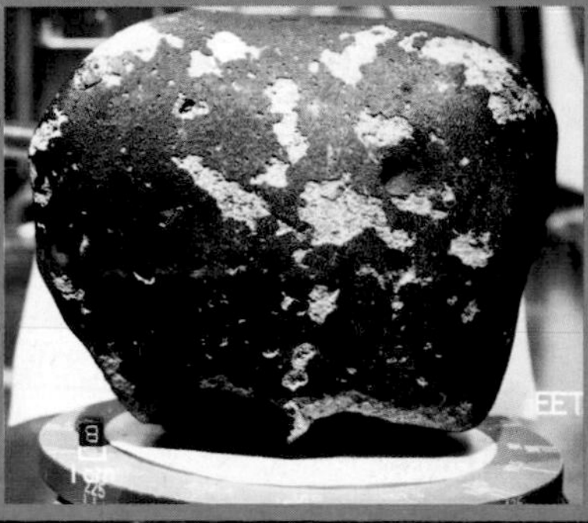

Record breakers

- The first record of a meteorite fall is in an Egyptian papyrus of 2000 BCE.
- Hoba West (see above) is the largest meteorite ever found, but the biggest now in a museum is Ahnighito (Inuit for tent). This 34-tonne iron is in the American Museum of Natural History, New York. It was found near Cape York, Greenland, in 1897 by Robert Peary.
- The largest known stony meteorite is the Jilin, which fell in Manchuria, China, on 8 March 1976. It weighs 1.77 tonnes.

Even the cheapest, most common type of meteorite costs about **US$2** a gram. Lunar and Martian meteorites cost about **US$2,000** a gram – much more than gold.

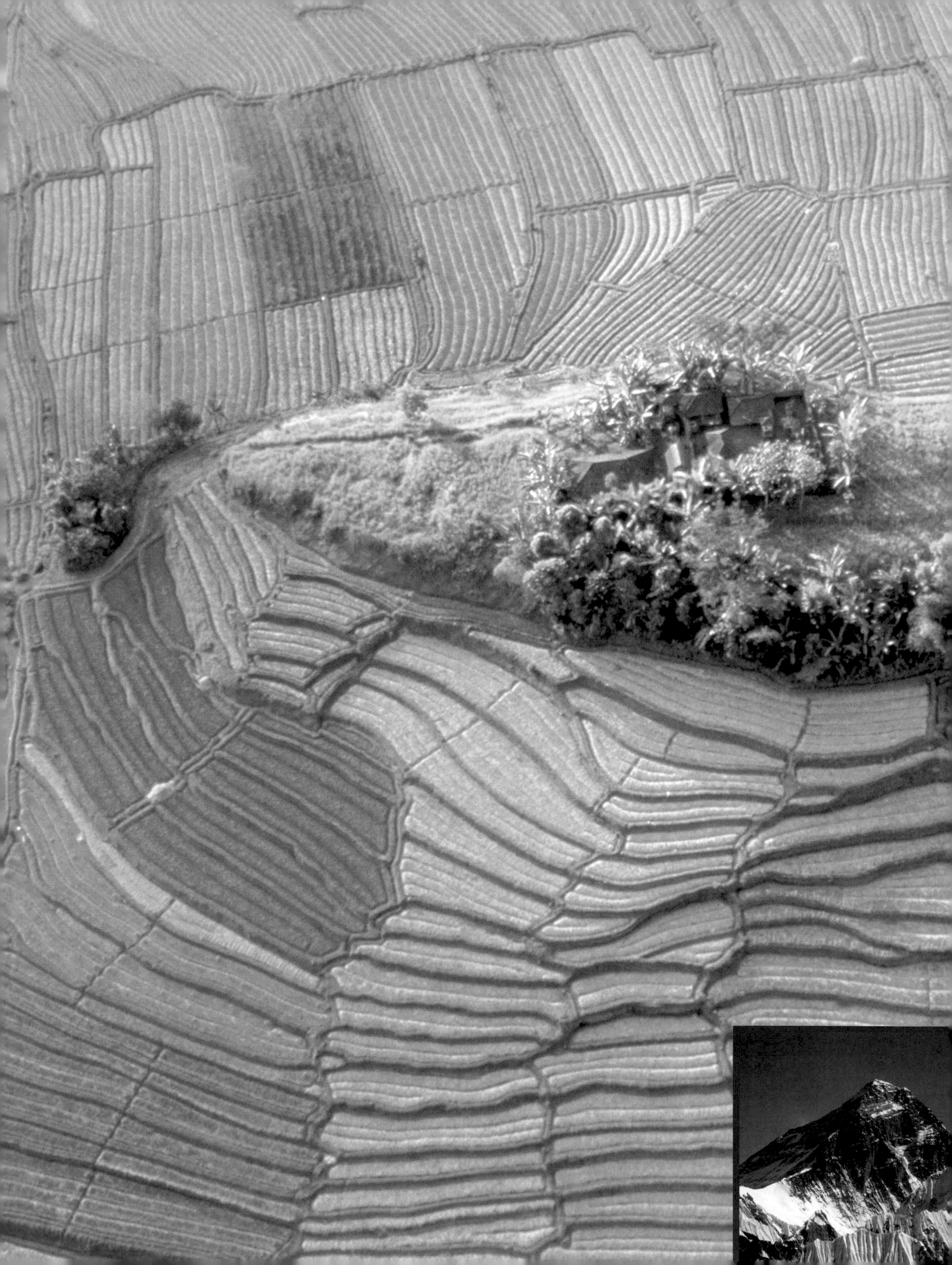

Earth

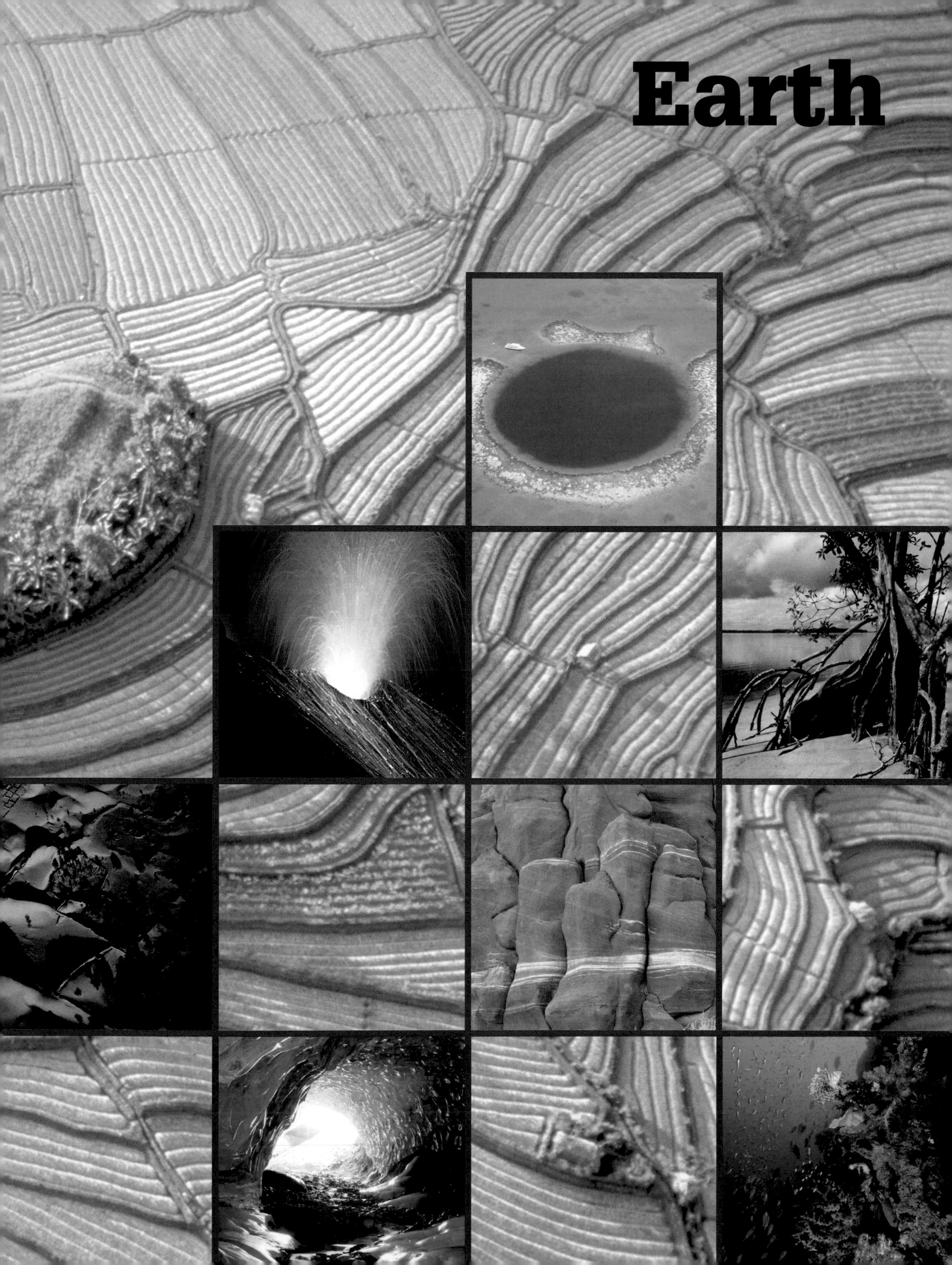

What is **geology?**

Geology is the science of rocks – how they are created and destroyed, and how they have formed our planet. This involves studying minerals, which are the natural chemical compounds that form rocks, as well as looking at the forces that drive geological processes.

In numbers

4,540 million
The number of years ago that Earth formed

4,030 million
The dating (in years) of the oldest-known rock on Earth's surface – the Acasta gneiss of northwest Canada

3,460 million
The age (in years) of the oldest fossils of living things – algal colonies called stromatolites in the rocks of Pilbara, Western Australia

230–65 million
The number of years ago that dinosaurs roamed Earth

3.6 million
The date (in years) of the first evidence of our human ancestors walking upright

FAST FACTS

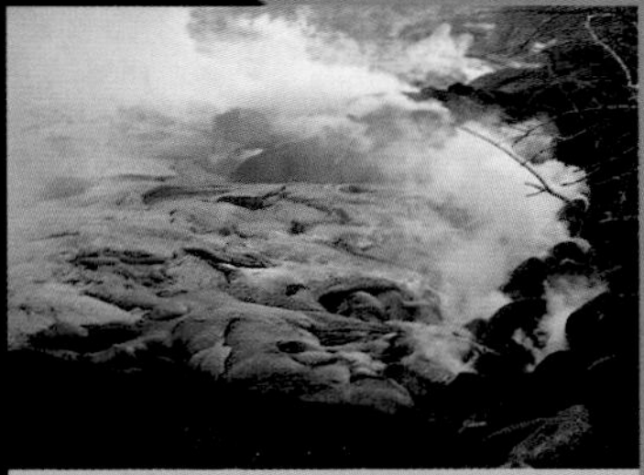

The rock cycle

01: Igneous rocks are made of minerals formed by the cooling of molten rock erupting from below Earth's crust.

02: These rocks are worn down into tiny particles (sediments), which are carried into the sea.

03: Over millions of years, the sediments are compressed to form sedimentary rocks.

04: Earth movements push these rocks up so they become land, and start wearing down.

Geological time

When geologists first began studying rocks, they had no way of knowing how old they were. They worked out which rocks were the same age by comparing the minerals and fossils they contained.

Groups of rocks are named after areas where they were studied, or an obvious feature. So Devonian rocks get their name from rock in Devon, England, while Carboniferous rocks include seams of coal, which is mostly carbon.

Older rock layers usually lie beneath younger ones, since they formed earlier. Devonian rocks are normally below carboniferous rocks, so are older. Permian rocks mainly lie above carboniferous rocks, so are younger.

These names are used to describe divisions of relative geological time. The Devonian, Carboniferous, and Permian are the three periods that led up to the age of the dinosaurs.

Geologists can now date rocks in millions of years, to give absolute geological time.

WHAT'S IN A NAME?

Geology is known as an **Earth science**. The word translates as "Earth-talk" in Greek, and since the "talk" is scientific discussion, geology does literally mean "Earth science".

I don't believe it!

Geologists can date rocks by measuring the amount of radioactive minerals (such as uranium) they contain. Over time, these turn into different minerals; by measuring this process, the rock can be dated.

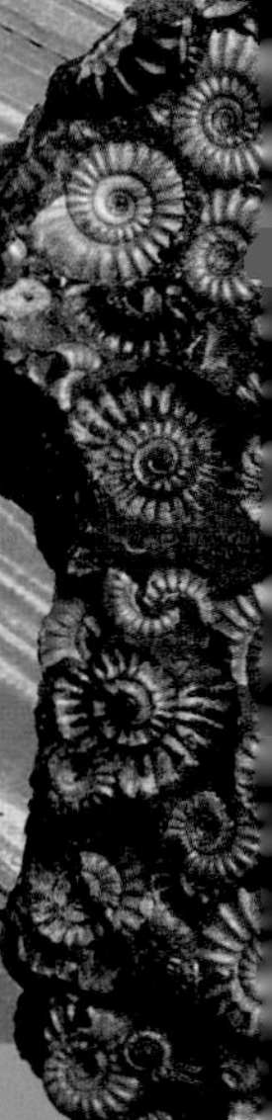

Rock types

Basalt
This dense igneous rock forms the bedrock of the ocean floors. It erupts as molten lava from oceanic volcanoes.

Granite
A very hard igneous rock, granite is mostly glassy quartz and feldspar, which often forms colourful crystals.

Sandstone
Many rocks are sedimentary – rock fragments bound together by other minerals. Sandstone is composed of sand grains.

Limestone
Another sedimentary rock, most limestones are made of the skeletons of millions of microscopic sea organisms.

Schist
Earth's oldest rocks have been squeezed and melted by massive forces to form metamorphic rocks, such as schist.

Tell me more:
fossils and geological time

Before evolution was understood, pioneer geologists realized that fossils of animals such as shellfish were clues to the age of rocks.

They guessed that all shellfish of one type lived at the same time. So all rocks containing them must be the same age.

By gathering fossils from rock layers at one site, they identified fossil groups that were typical of each layer.

If they found the same grouping in another rock outcrop far away, this showed that the rock was the same age and even part of the same layer.

This method was used to produce the first accurate geological map, published by English geologist William Smith in 1815.

Hot plates

- Earth's crust is divided into huge plates that float on the hot rock below.
- When plates push together, one slides beneath the other in a series of jerks that cause **earthquakes** and erupting **volcanoes**.
- Where plates are moving apart, **continents** split to create new oceans. Molten rock erupting from the rifts forms new ocean floors and ridges.
- Over millions of years – and at a very slow rate – this has created and destroyed **oceans**, and moved the continents into many different

WEIRD OR WHAT?

Geologists were the first to realize that Earth was **millions of years** old. Before 1800, most people would have agreed with Irish archbishop James Ussher, who calculated in 1650 that Earth was created on 23 October 4004 BCE!

Rock **strata**

Sedimentary rocks
Formed from beds of soft sediments such as sand and mud, these rocks harden into flat, solid layers called strata.

Old at heart
Different types of sediment form strata of various colours, thicknesses, and hardness. They lie in horizontal beds, with the youngest on top.

Buckle up
If strata are squeezed by earth movements, they buckle and fold. Often, only one side of the fold is seen as sloping or even vertical strata.

Fault line
Extreme pressure or tension can snap the strata, so they slip out of alignment. This is called a fault.

Blasts from the past

1075
Chinese scholar Shen Kuo describes the rock cycle, realizing that ancient seashells found in rocks on land show that the rocks originally formed on the sea bed, from sediments eroded from mountains

1830
Scottish geologist Charles Lyell suggests that gradual processes occurring all around us could cause massive geological upheavals over millions of years

1915
German meteorologist Alfred Wegener publishes his theory of continental drift, suggesting that the continents move around the globe and were once joined together

1960
US geologist Harry Hess shows how ocean-floor spreading could cause continental drift; this is the basis of plate tectonic theory, which explains earthquakes and revolutionizes geology

Where do **metals come from?**

Metals are part of the rocks that form our planet – they are all around us in the solid bedrock, scattered stones, and soft soil. Yet most of these metals don't look like the tough, shiny materials we are used to because they have been transformed by chemical reactions with other elements.

Mercury is a very strange metal because it is a liquid at room temperature. It has to be cooled to –39°C (–38°F) before it becomes solid

FAST FACTS

Metals and minerals

01: All pure metals are elements, which means that they contain just one kind of atom. Three-quarters of the 94 elements that occur naturally on Earth are metals.

02: Most pure metals naturally react with other elements to form the chemical compounds we call minerals.

03: The most familiar of these is iron oxide, a compound of iron and oxygen that we know as rust.

04: Iron oxide doesn't look like metallic iron. Yet if it is heated with something called a reducing agent, this soaks up the oxygen and turns the oxide into pure metal.

05: Most of the commonest metals are produced in a similar way, from oxides and other compounds known as metal ores.

I don't believe it!

Some metals are so reactive that they cannot exist in pure form on Earth. When iron reacts with oxygen it turns to rust, but when potassium meets oxygen, it bursts into flames.

What is so special **about metals?**

■ Nearly all pure, refined metals are dense, opaque, shiny solids. Most are quite hard, but some are surprisingly soft.

◆ Many metals are extremely strong for their weight and can carry heavy loads and resist impacts.

⬟ Metals can be easily worked or formed into shapes without cracking or crumbling, especially when hot.

⬢ Most metals are good conductors of electricity. This makes them essential to modern technology.

Tell me more: **precious metals**

■ Precious metals such as silver and gold boil up from Earth's interior wherever there are volcanoes and hot springs. The hot water deposits the metals in cracks in the rock called hydrothermal veins.

■ **The most precious metals such as gold and platinum do not react easily with other elements to form compound minerals. This means that they are found as veins and nuggets of pure metal.**

■ Non-reactive precious metals do not oxidize (react with oxygen) in air, which is why gold always stays shiny.

Metal ores

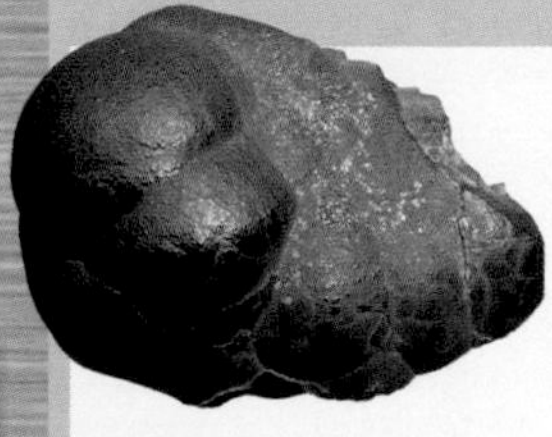

Iron
The most important iron ore is haematite, or iron oxide (rust). It often occurs in rounded, rusty-looking nodules that feel very heavy when you pick them up.

Aluminium
This extremely common metal is found in more than 270 different minerals. It is most easily extracted from a sedimentary rock called bauxite.

Copper
Some copper is found in pure form, but most is obtained from a brassy and metallic compound of iron, sulphur, and copper called chalcopyrite.

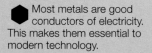

Tin
The primary ore of tin is cassiterite. This oxide, a compound of tin and oxygen, is usually found in regions where local rock has been heated by molten magma.

9000 BCE
Pure copper discovered in mineral veins in the Middle East is worked into some of the oldest-known metal tools, marking the beginning of the Copper Age

4000 BCE
Some of the earliest gold ornaments are made from pure gold nuggets and, because of its beauty and rarity, it immediately becomes a symbol of wealth

3000 BCE
The Bronze Age begins when Middle Eastern metalworkers discover that an alloy of tin and copper is both easier to cast than copper and much stronger

1800 BCE
Metalworkers find ways of generating enough heat to turn iron oxide into tough metallic iron – this marks the start of the Iron Age

1942
The nuclear age begins when the radioactive metallic element uranium is used to generate energy for the first time, in Chicago, USA

lasts from the past

How to: **pan for gold**

01. Find an upland stream with a bed of sand and fine gravel and scoop some of the material into a broad, shallow pan.

02. Submerge your pan in about 15 cm (6 in) of running water, then stir the contents with your fingers to wash out any mud.

03. Shake the pan underwater to help the heaviest minerals (which might include gold) sink to the bottom of the pan.

04. Tilt the pan and swirl it beneath the surface so the water washes away the lighter particles. Swirl and shake the pan again.

05. Eventually, you will get down to the heaviest minerals – most will be dark, but you may find some shiny gold!

RECORD BREAKER

Gold is the most workable of all metals. A single gram (0.03 oz) can be beaten into 1 sq m (10 sq ft), and 28 g (1 oz) into 28 sq m (300 sq ft). The resulting "gold leaf" is almost transparent!

Lead
Most lead is extracted from the heavy metallic crystals of a compound of lead and sulphur known as galena. Lead is a poisonous metal used to make batteries.

Zinc
This whitish metal occurs in sphalerite, which is a compound of zinc, iron, and sulphur. Zinc is combined with copper to make shiny, yellow brass.

Both **copper** and **tin** are quite soft metals, but if they are mixed together, the resulting **alloy** – bronze – is much harder than either!

Metal **world**

Our modern world relies on metal products. Here are eight metals and a few examples of their uses:

Aluminium
Used to make drinks cans, foil, pipes for the building industry, car parts, aircraft, and computers.

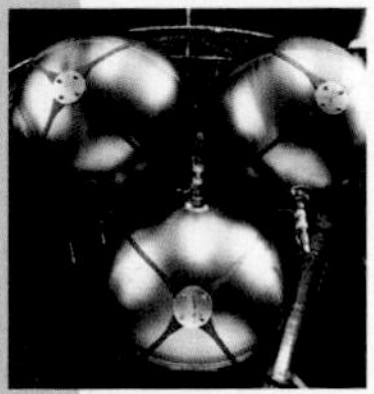

Titanium
Car parts, tennis racquets, wristwatches, aircraft and spacecraft parts, and pressure-proof deep-sea capsules all contain titanium.

Copper
Used for piping, computer components, electrical wire. Alloyed with tin to make bronze and with zinc to make brass.

Iron
Refined into steel, it is used to make cars, tools, fencing wire, ships, bicycles, and steel-framed skyscrapers.

Nickel
Mainly alloyed with iron to make stainless steel for cutlery and similar items, but also made into coins, magnets, and nickel-plated guitar

Zinc
Often added to steel to stop it rusting, so features in chains, cables, and corrugated sheets. Alloyed with copper to make brass. Also used in batteries.

Lead
Alloyed with tin to make the solder used to build electronic circuits. Also features in car batteries, bullets, and radiation shielding.

Tin
Principally alloyed with lead to make solder, but also used to make tin-plated steel cans. Alloyed with copper to make bronze.

Why are there so many **volcanic islands?**

Most of the islands found in the oceans are, or were, volcanoes that have erupted from the ocean floor. Many of these volcanoes are part of long chains, while others form the bedrock of coral islands. A large number are long extinct – and actually subsiding beneath the waves – but some are still spectacularly active!

RECORD BREAKER

In 1815, the biggest explosion in recorded history occurred during an eruption on **Sumbawa** island, Indonesia. It blasted 151 km^3 (36 $miles^3$) of rock dust into the atmosphere.

FAST FACTS

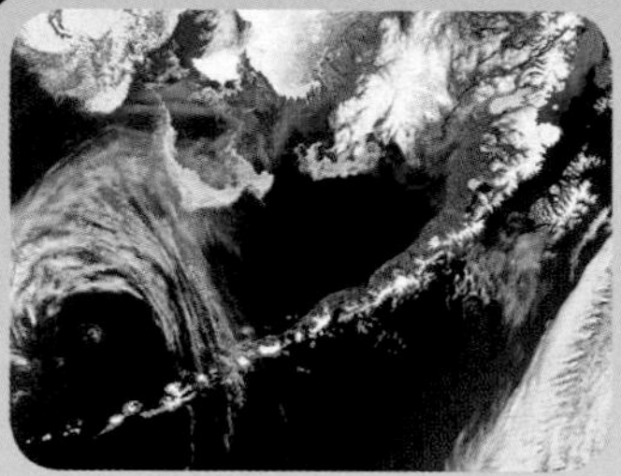

The Pacific Ring of Fire

01: All around the Pacific, ocean floor is sinking into the hot interior of Earth at destructive plate boundaries.

02: As one plate is dragged beneath another, the sinking rock melts and chains of volcanoes erupt from the edge of the overlying plate.

03: Where it plunges beneath other plates of oceanic crust, it creates island arcs such the Aleutian Islands (above) that curve across 2,500 km (1,550 miles) of ocean from Alaska to Siberia.

04: Other Pacific island arcs include the Kuril Islands and Japan, the Mariana Islands, the Philippines, Tonga, and Bougainville.

Three types of volcanic island

▲ **Rift volcanoes** Ocean floors are made of basalt rock that erupts from spreading rifts in Earth's crust called mid-ocean ridges. Some very active sections of these rifts have formed volcanic islands.

▲ **Island arcs** Earth's crust is always moving, and where two plates of oceanic crust are pushing together, one is steadily destroyed. This creates a long line of volcanic islands along the plate boundary.

▲ **Hotspot chains** Many volcanic islands form over hotspots in the deep mantle beneath Earth's crust. As the moving crust creeps over the hotspot, the heat forms a chain of volcanic islands.

How to: **know when to leave a volcanic island**

01. Be aware of ground tremors and minor earthquakes. If you suddenly start noticing these on a volcanic island, then an eruption is likely.

02. Listen for ominous rumbling, humming, or buzzing – and keep an eye on animals that might have better hearing than you do. If they start behaving oddly, it might mean something!

I don't believe it!

Mont Pelée on the island of Martinique is one of many volcanoes that form an island arc in the Caribbean. In May 1902, it exploded and swamped the nearby city of St Pierre with red-hot rock and gas, killing more than 30,000 people within two minutes. There were just two survivors – and one was a prisoner in the city jail!

Island arcs

- The volcanoes that form island arcs erupt sticky lava that often plugs their craters and solidifies, trapping volcanic gas.
- Over many decades or centuries, the pressure builds up until the rocks plugging the volcanic vent give way and cause an explosive eruption.
- This blasts huge amounts of molten lava and rock debris high into the sky, such as in the 1991 eruption on Mount Pinatubo in the Philippines (pictured).
- Sometimes, the top is blown off a whole island. A famous example of this was the explosion of Krakatau, Indonesia, in 1883.

The long, narrow island of Java is a string of **volcanic islands** that have become joined together. It has at least 20 active volcanoes – one for every 50 km (31 miles) of its length.

WEIRD OR WHAT?

When volcanoes erupt beneath the ocean, the lava turns to rock where it meets cold water, but it stays liquid inside. Volcanic pressure makes it burst out from **ruptures** in the rock's surface. This creates tumbled heaps of cushion-shaped rocks known as **pillow lava**.

05. Ignore anyone who says that the volcano is extinct – any volcano that has erupted in the last 10,000 years could do so again!

04. Sniff the air. If you smell anything sulphurous, it could be volcanic gases escaping from molten rock rising within the volcano and about to erupt from its crater.

03. Watch for any steam or smoke coming from the crater, or any change in the shape of the volcano. Internal pressure can make the whole mountain bulge outwards!

In numbers

76
The number of active volcanoes in Indonesia

260
The number of coral atolls in the tropical oceans, each crowning an extinct volcano

800
The number of volcanic hot springs on Iceland

10,205 m
(33,480 ft) The total height of the highest volcano on Hawaii, from its base on the Pacific Ocean floor – this makes it the highest mountain on Earth

90,000
The number of people killed by the 1815 explosion of Mount Tambora on Sumbawa, Indonesia

FAST FACTS

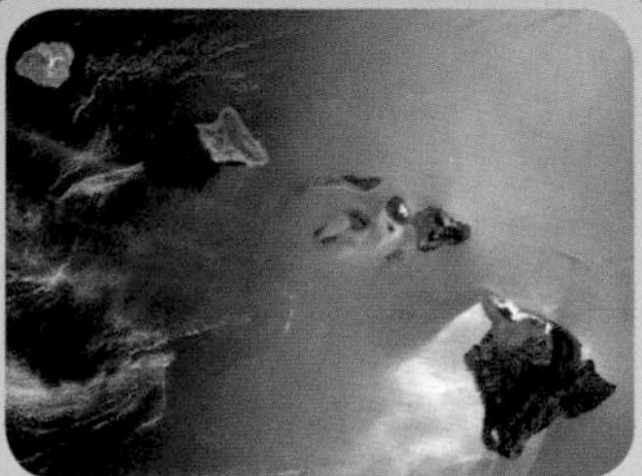

Hotspot chains

01: Some volcanic islands have no connection with plate boundaries, but are formed by isolated heat plumes below Earth's crust.

02: Even though the plates are constantly moving, these hotspots stay in the same place. So the islands eventually move off the hotspots that created them.

03: When this happens , the island's volcano becomes extinct. Meanwhile, a new volcano erupts from the part of the ocean floor now over the hotspot.

04: Over millions of years, this process builds a chain of islands such as those that make up Hawaii (above), but only the most recent one, nearest the hotspot, has an active volcano.

Volcanic islands from space

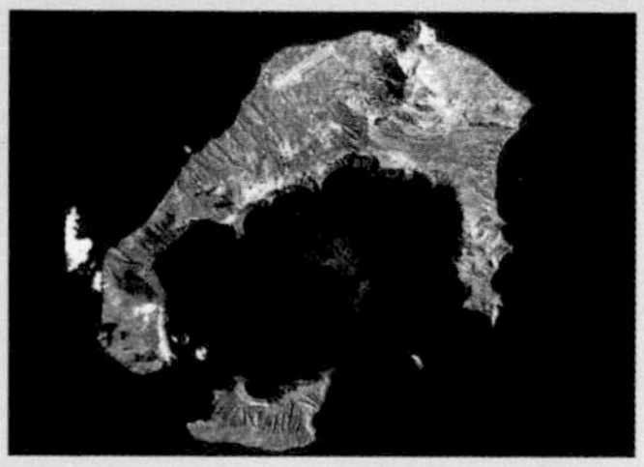

Santorini
This Greek island exploded about 1630 BCE, causing devastating tsunamis. A new volcano is growing in the middle of the vast crater left by the explosion.

Mount Cleveland
This is one of many active volcanoes in the Aleutian island arc. Its eruption in 2006 was photographed by an astronaut on the International Space Station.

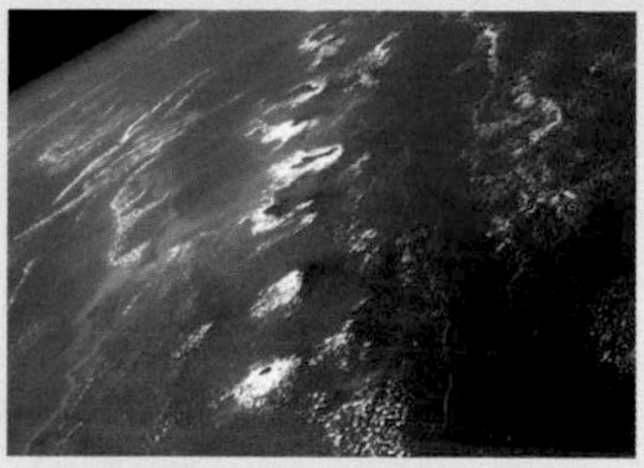

Java
The Indonesian island of Java has many volcanoes. A few are seen here, including Merapi (lower left), Indonesia's most active volcano.

Anak Krakatau
The "Child of Krakatau" is a volcano that, in 1927, emerged from the explosion crater of Krakatau. Solid black lava is spilling into the sea and new plants are growing in the east.

What's so wonderful about **the Galápagos Islands?**

The Galápagos are a group of volcanic islands lying on the equator in the eastern Pacific, close to South America. The oldest volcanoes boiled up from the ocean floor less than ten million years ago, creating islands of bare rock. These were gradually colonized by plants and animals, some of which – such as the land iguanas pictured here – have evolved into weird forms that are found nowhere else on Earth.

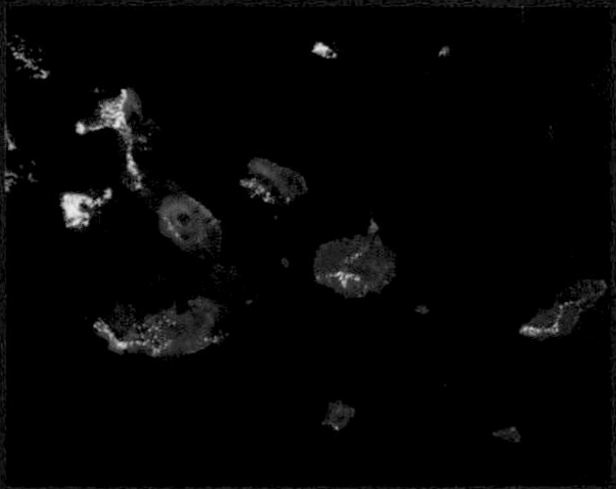

01: Hotspot chains
The Galápagos have erupted over a hotspot that now lies beneath the most western island of Fernandina. All the islands are being carried east by the gradual movement of the ocean floor, at the rate of 3.7 cm (1.5 in) a year. This means that in about 26 million years they will crash into South America!

02: Active volcanoes
The active volcanoes on Fernandina and nearby Isabela erupt liquid lava that burns everything in its path. It spreads out and cools to form broad sheets of basalt rock that, over time, turn a rusty brown colour. These barren wastes of bare rock are only slowly colonized by plant life, though many seabirds nest on the lava fields.

03: Green islands
While the young islands of the Western Galápagos are still volcanically active, the volcanoes on older eastern islands such as San Cristóbal and Española are extinct. There, volcanic rock has formed fertile soils that support lush vegetation, which in turn provides food for rare creatures such as giant tortoises.

04: Breeding seabirds
The Galápagos make ideal nesting sites for ocean birds. They include the waved albatros the cormorant, the frigatebird (above), and the blue-footed booby. All these birds feed at se either by catching fish or – in the case of the frigatebird – stealing them from other seabirds!

05: Weird wildlife

The animals of the Galápagos have been isolated for so long that they have evolved quite differently from their mainland relatives. They include giant tortoises weighing up to 250 kg (550 lb) and the marine iguana, a lizard that dives into the cold ocean to graze on seaweed.

06: Cradle of evolution

In 1835, the Galápagos were visited by Charles Darwin. Intrigued by the strange animals, he noticed that the giant tortoises and some birds varied from island to island. Later, he realized that they had changed over time to suit the conditions on each island – an insight that was key to his world-changing theory of evolution.

07: Marine riches

Although they lie on the equator, the islands are washed by cold ocean currents flowing north from the icy Southern Ocean. The water is rich in nutrients that support plankton. This then feeds vast shoals of fish, which attract predators such as sharks and seabirds. The Galápagos have been declared a marine wildlife reserve.

08: Magical land

The volcanic landscapes, exciting wildlife, and scientific importance of the Galápagos have made them a major tourist destination. Each year, thousands of people travel to the islands yet, despite this, most of the islands retain the magical quality of a place almost untouched by the modern world.

What created **the Himalayas?**

Most mountains are created by forces pushing the great plates of Earth's crust together. Where ocean floor is being driven beneath a continent, the fringes of the continent are crumpled and folded into mountain ranges. The Himalayas, though, are unique because they are being forced up by a head-on collision between two continents.

Tell me more: **crumple zone**

▲During the age of the dinosaurs, India was an island continent, moving north towards Asia at the rate of up to 15 cm (6 in) a year.

▲**Roughly 50 million years ago, India crashed into Asia. The collision slowed it down, but it kept on moving north at more than 5 cm (2 in) per year.**

▲India is now ploughing beneath Asia, rucking up its edge to form the mountain ridges of the Himalayas, the Karakoram, and the Hindu Kush.

▲**This mountain system is the highest on Earth, containing all of the world's "eight-thousanders" – peaks that rise above 8,000 m (26,250 ft).**

Although India is still pushing north into Asia, there have been no major **earthquakes** in the region since the 1950s. Scientists fear that the strain is building up and could be released as a massive earthquake in the near future.

I don't believe it!

Sedimentary rocks that had formed on the ocean floor between India and Asia were squeezed between the two continents and pushed up into mountains. This means that you can find fossils of shellfish at least 5 km (3 miles) above sea level.

In numbers

2.5 million sq km
(965,000 sq miles) The area covered by the Tibetan plateau – the biggest and highest in the world

2,400 km
(1,490 miles) The length of the Himalayan mountain range from Afghanistan in the northwest to China in the east

2,000 km
(1,240 miles) The total distance that India has pushed north into Asia since the two continents collided

14
The number of Himalayan peaks that are more than 8,000 m (26,250 ft) high

5 cm
(2 in) The rate at which the Himalayas are still rising each decade

Ice mass

There are about 15,000 **glaciers** in the Himalayas, which, together with expanses of frozen ground, form the largest area of ice outside the polar regions.

WEIRD OR WHAT?

When high mountains are created, a chemical process called **weathering**, which absorbs carbon dioxide (CO_2), wears them away. The Himalayas may have absorbed enough CO_2 to cool the planet and trigger the ice ages!

Top ten Himalayan peaks

Mount Everest
8,848 m (29,029 ft)

K2
8,611 m (28,251 ft)

Kangchenjunga
8,586 m (28,169 ft)

Lhotse
8,516 m (27,940 ft)

Monsoon maker

In summer, the Tibetan plateau warms up, heating the air above. The air rises, drawing in the warm, moist air from the Indian Ocean that causes the torrential rain of the summer monsoon in India.

As the moist air is drawn north over India, it meets the rock wall of the Himalayas. It spills the rest of its rain on the south side of the mountains, creating lush forests and great rivers such as the Indus, Ganges, and Brahmaputra.

The air that reaches the north side of the mountains in summer has lost all its moisture, so the Tibetan plateau gets little rain. It is just as dry in winter, when sinking cold air stops clouds forming; it means the region is a near-desert.

High tea

The air is thin at high altitude because there is less weight of air above to squeeze it together. This **reduced atmospheric pressure** also allows water to boil at a lower temperature, so Tibetans routinely drink their tea while it is still boiling. Don't try this at home!

RECORD BREAKER

In 1978, Italian Reinhold Messner and Austrian Peter Habeler were the **first mountaineers** to climb Mount Everest without using bottled oxygen – a feat thought impossible.

On the move

The Himalayas owe their amazing **height** to the fact that India is still pushing north into Asia. If it stopped moving, the Himalayas and the Tibetan plateau would gradually settle lower and lower, like a heap of wet cement.

FAST FACTS

Thin air

01: As you climb higher, the air gets thinner, so every lungful of air that you breathe contains fewer molecules of vital oxygen.

02: On Himalayan peaks above 7,000 m (23,000 ft), there is less than half the usual amount of oxygen measured at sea level.

03: Even on the Tibetan plateau there is only 60 per cent of the oxygen at sea level.

04: Despite this, almost three million people live on its dry grasslands. Their bodies have adapted to the thin air. In particular, their blood has more red cells to absorb oxygen.

05: Others gasp for breath and suffer altitude sickness, which forces most climbers to use breathing equipment.

The highest mountains in the Himalayas are also the highest in the world. They include famed peaks such as Mount Everest and K2 as well as others like Dhaulagiri, which, for the first decades of the 19th century, was believed to be the world's tallest mountain.

Makalu
8,485 m (27,838 ft)

Cho Oyu
8,188 m (26,864 ft)

Dhaulagiri
8,167 m (26,795 ft)

Manaslu
8,163 m (26,781 ft)

Nanga Parbat
8,126 m (26,660 ft)

Annapurna
8,091 m (26,545 ft)

How deep is the **Grand Canyon?**

The canyon is a gigantic gash in the Arizona Desert that is more than 1,800 m (5,905 ft) deep. It was carved out by the Colorado River over the past 20 million years, as it flowed over rock layers that were slowly being forced upwards by massive earth movements. As fast as the rocks rose, the river cut down through them to create the most spectacular river gorge on Earth.

Tell me more: **rock layers**

The walls of the Grand Canyon are made up of layers of rocks, with the oldest at the bottom and the youngest at the top. Most of these rocks are hardened beds of sand and mud that formed on the floor of an ancient ocean.

250 million years old: Creamy white Kaibab Limestone forms the rim of the canyon. Younger rocks above it have eroded away.
260 million years old: The Coconino Sandstone is a layer of solidified desert sand dunes.
330 million years old: The Redwall Limestone is a hard rock that forms a sheer cliff up to 150 m (492 ft) high.
530 million years old: The soft mudstone of the Bright Angel Shale wears away easily, allowing the upper layers to collapse.
540 million years old: Dark brown Tapeats Sandstone forms vertical walls in the lower region.
1,700 million years old: At the bottom of the canyon is the very hard Vishnu Schist.

WEIRD OR WHAT?

When the first **Spanish explorers** saw the Grand Canyon in 1540, they thought the river was just 2 m (6 ft) wide because it was so far down. It is actually about 100 times wider!

Climate change and water abstraction for cities and farming have led to the **Colorado River** drying up. In some years, so little water flows down the lower course of the river that it doesn't even reach the sea.

Formation facts

01: The Grand Canyon slices through the Colorado Plateau, which was pushed up by the same forces that created the Rocky Mountains.

02: The whole process started about 70 million years ago, when huge dinosaurs such as *T rex* were prowling the land.

03: The Grand Canyon is in a desert so how did the river have the power to gouge it out of the rock? The fact is that the desert does get rare – yet massive – rainstorms.

04: These flash floods cascade into the river, carving deep side-canyons and, over millions of years, the Grand Canyon itself was formed.

FAST FACTS

Grand Canyon

01: In summer, the temperature in the inner canyon can soar above 38°C (100°F).

02: In winter, the temperature on the North Rim of the canyon (the highest part) can plunge below −18°C (0°F), and access is impossible because of heavy snow.

03: The temperature range in the canyon means that anyone climbing from the bottom to the top passes through the same range of environments as a traveller journeying from hot, dry Mexico to mild, wet Canada.

04: These environments have created five "life zones" that range from hot desert to icy mountain grassland.

In numbers

349 km
(217 miles) The total length of the Grand Canyon

6 km
(4 miles) The narrowest distance between the upper cliffs

30 km
(19 miles) The widest part of the canyon

1.83 km
(1.14 miles) The maximum depth of the canyon

56°C
(133°F) The range of temperatures experienced in the canyon, from the highest in the summer to the lowest in the winter

22
The number of major rock layers in the canyon walls

10 years
The average time it has taken the river to deepen the canyon by just 1 mm (0.04 in)

Six ways to see **the Grand Canyon**

Look down
Observe from the amazing Skywalk platform or one of the viewpoints on the rim.

Walk
Only fit people should hike trails that lead from the canyon rim to the river below.

Ride
Hire a mule and ride down a trail. A great option if you're not up to walking.

Fly
Climb into a plane or helicopter for a canyon flyover. Spectacular!

Raft
Take an exhilarating trip down the river in a white-water raft. Only for the brave!

Take the train
See the canyon from a vintage Pullman car on the Coconino Canyon Train.

WHAT'S IN A NAME?

The river that formed the Grand Canyon was named the **Rio Colorado**, or "Red River" because the water was full of reddish rock debris. The water is now less red in colour than it was because much of the red sediment is trapped by a dam upriver from the canyon.

Some reasons NOT to hike to the bottom of the Grand Canyon

01 It's a long way, and you've got to get all the way back up to the top again. In fact, hiking down to the river and back up to the rim in one day is almost impossible.

02 High temperatures near the bottom can cause heatstroke, and if that doesn't get you, there is a serious risk of dehydration as you climb back up.

03 Every year the Grand Canyon Park Service has to rescue hundreds of hikers who think they are fit enough to tackle the climb, but find out that they are not.

04 Since the 1970s, more than 280 people have died in the canyon by falling, drowning, being hit by rockfalls, or suffering fatal health problems such as hypothermia or heart attacks.

I don't believe it!

Although the rocks on the rim of the Grand Canyon now lie up to 2,450 m (8,038 ft) above sea level, they contain the fossils of fish, corals, and clams that once lived in the ocean.

What's so strange about the **Namib Desert?**

The spectacular Namib Desert on the Atlantic fringe of southwest Africa is a land of vast sand dunes, gravel plains, and bare rock. Despite the desert having little rainfall, thick sea fogs blow in from the ocean to blanket the dunes and supply life-giving moisture to the amazing plants and animals that make the desert their home.

WEIRD OR WHAT?

Although the Namib Desert is one of the most barren places on Earth, the sea nearby teems with life, including clouds of **plankton** that support vast shoals of fish, which feed masses of seabirds and **Cape fur seals**.

Beetle juice

The long-legged beetle gathers vital water by climbing to the crest of a desert dune at dawn on a foggy morning, facing the wind, and raising its tail. The **fog condenses** on its body to **form water** drops that trickle down into its mouth. It may gather almost half its own body weight of water like this in a single morning.

The weird **welwitschia** of the Namib Desert is one of the rarest and longest-surviving plants on Earth, capable of living for up to 2,500 years! The largest welwitschias can grow up to 1.4 m (4.6 ft) high.

Tell me more: **fog desert**

The desert climate of the Namib is created mainly by dry air sinking over the tropics, generating high atmospheric pressure. This stops warm air rising from near ground level to form clouds and rain.

Offshore in the Atlantic, the cold Benguela Current flows north from Antarctica. As moist air moving in from the ocean blows over the cold water flow, its moisture turns to rain and dense sea fog.

All the rain falls on the sea, so by the time the air reaches the land there is no rain left. The thick fog rolls in over the desert but is soon dispersed by the tropical sun, and any moisture on the ground surface evaporates.

Namib **life**

Scorpion
Armoured scorpions emerge from their burrows at night and use the powerful stings on their tails to kill insects, spiders, lizards, and mice.

FAST FACTS

01: On average, the Namib gets less than 12 mm (0.5 in) of rain a year.

02: Despite this, the air near the coast is sometimes saturated with moisture.

03: Compared to most deserts, the Namib is quite cool – average annual temperature on the coast is below 16°C (61°F).

04: Maximum daytime air temperatures rarely exceed 40°C (104°F).

05: At night in winter, air temperatures can fall close to freezing point.

In numbers

80,900 sq km
(31,200 sq miles) The area of the Namib Desert

1,600 km
(1,000 miles) The length of the desert from north to south

140 km
(87 miles) The width of the desert at its widest point

160
The number of days each year that the coast is shrouded in fog

5–15
The number of days of annual rainfall

I don't believe it!

The shores of the Namib Desert contain the richest diamond deposits in the world. Originally formed in volcanic rocks far inland, the diamonds were carried to the ocean by the Orange River and spread along the coast by ocean currents.

Creepy coast!

The Atlantic fringe of the northern Namib is known as the Skeleton Coast because it is littered with the remains of ships wrecked by high winds or lost in dense fog. Many of these wrecks now lie up to 50 m (160 ft) from the shore, overwhelmed by desert sand that is gradually creeping towards the sea.

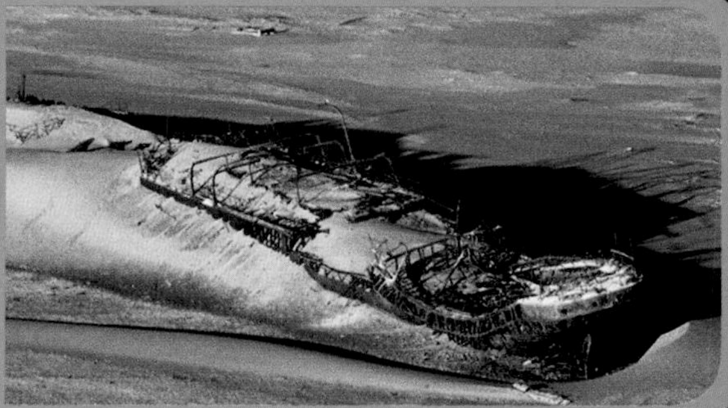

Desert dunes

Much of the southern Namib Desert is a "sand sea" of enormous sharp-crested dunes, covering some 34,000 sq km (13,120 sq miles) and extending right down to the seashore.

Most of the dunes form long parallel ridges aligned northwest to southeast. They are up to 50 km (31 miles) long and 1.5–2.5 km (1–1.5 miles) apart. They average more than 150 m (492 ft) high.

The coastal dunes are pale yellow-brown, but moving inland they become darker brown to brick red. This is because the sand of the older inland dunes has become coated with rusty iron oxide.

More mobile crescent-shaped dunes also creep over the land surface as sand blows up the windward side, drops over the crest, and settles on the leeward side. They can move at rates of up to 15 m (49 ft) per year.

FAST FACTS

Plant survivors

01: Only the toughest plants can survive in the Namib Desert. Some of the most abundant are not really plants at all, but lichens – fungus-like organisms that grow on west-facing slopes where they are able to absorb moisture from sea fogs.

02: Unique to the Namib, the welwitschia plant grows just one pair of long leaves that split into tattered, Sun-blackened ribbons that curl over the ground and soak up the dew.

03: The peculiar half-mens tree is a cactus-like plant with a single, tall trunk crowned by a small tuft of crinkled, leathery leaves. It soaks up water from the ground after rare rainstorms, and stores it in its thick, spiny trunk.

04: The window plant grows mostly underground, but produces thick, juicy leaves at the surface that look like flattened pebbles. Each has a glassy "window" in the top that lets in the light the plant needs to grow!

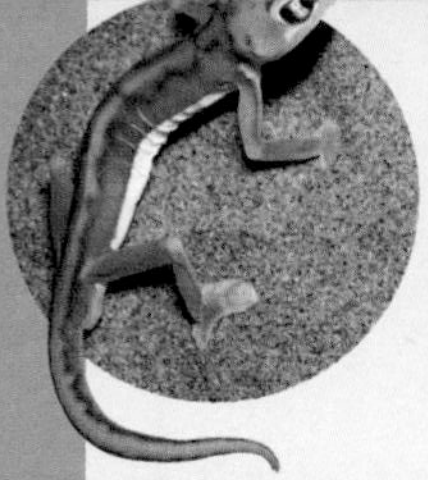

Web-footed gecko
This little lizard has webbed toes to stop it sinking into the desert sand when hunting for insects at night. The toes also make useful burrowing tools.

Sidewinder viper
Sand can be difficult for a snake to negotiate, but the venomous sidewinder does so by coiling its body into loops that pull it sideways over the sand.

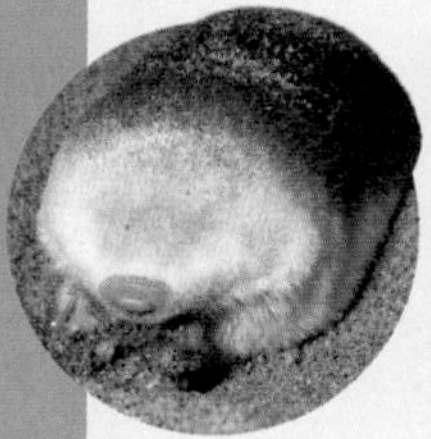

Golden mole
Named for the metallic sheen on its fur, the golden mole burrows through the sand hunting for termites. It rarely surfaces, and is quite blind!

Gemsbok
This antelope can allow its body temperature to rise well above normal before it starts to sweat and lose vital moisture. This enables it to go for days without water.

Brown hyena
The shaggy-coated brown hyena prowls the Skeleton Coast looking for dead animals swept in by the tide. It also preys on fur seal pups.

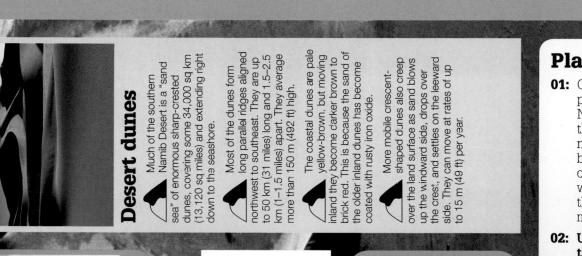

Sandgrouse
A male sandgrouse flies a long way to collect water. At a waterhole, he soaks up water in his breast feathers, then flies to his nest to give his chicks a drink.

How do **caves** form?

Caves are large, natural holes in rock or ice. They can be created in various ways, but most caves are hollowed out of rock by water – or by water that is loaded with stones that grind away the rock like sandpaper. Some caves are just single chambers, while others are part of a network where many caves are linked by narrow passages.

WHAT'S IN A NAME?

The Yucatan in Mexico has a network of underground caves. Some cave ceilings have collapsed to form sinkholes called cenotes, which means "**well**" in the ancient Mayan language of Mexico.

01. Don't even think of doing it alone. You need experienced back up, so join a caving club.

02. Check the weather. Many caves may flood to the ceiling if there is a sudden rainstorm, leaving you with no air to breathe.

FAST FACTS

Limestone caves

01: The most spectacular caves form in a rock called limestone. Over hundreds of years, the rock is dissolved by rainwater.

02: As the water seeps down through cracks and joints in the rock, it enlarges them into vertical holes.

03: The water flows through narrow winding tunnels or potholes that lead to underground rivers.

04: Sometimes, the cave roof collapses to create huge underground caverns with strange rock formations shaped by dripping water.

Blasts from the past

32,000 YEARS OLD
The approximate age of the earliest known cave paintings, in the Chauvet Cave in southern France that show animals, including lions, bears, rhinos, and hyenas

25,000 YEARS OLD
Spectacularly lifelike images of woolly mammoths, horses, cattle, reindeer, and some humans are made on the walls of Pech Merle Cave in southern France

15,000 YEARS OLD
The date of paintings in the Altamira Cave in northern Spain, which include a herd of bison that are painted so beautifully that they were an inspiration for the great Spanish artist Pablo Picasso

12,000 YEARS OLD
The radio-carbon date of the paintings in Las Monedas Cave in northern Spain, borne out by images of reindeer, which died out in Spain when the ice age ended

Strange cave formations

The water that flows through limestone caves contains a mineral called calcite. As it is deposited, the mineral gradually builds up to create strange and beautiful shapes.

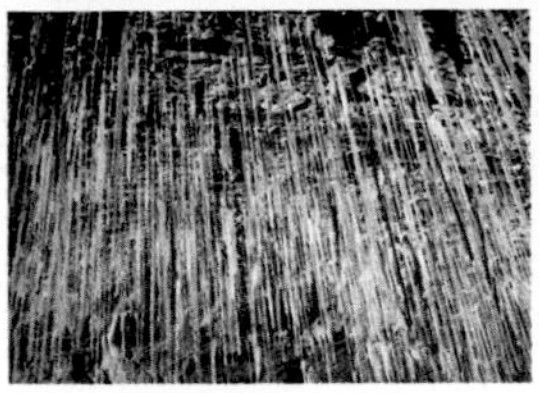

Straw stalactites
Water seeping through a cave roof interacts with air, which crystallizes the dissolved calcite and forms delicate "straws".

Stalactites
Larger flows of water from the cave roof build up bigger hanging structures shaped like inverted cones.

Stalagmites
Where the dripping water lands on the cave floor, more calcite is deposited. Over time, this builds up into conical structures.

Flowstones
If mineral-loaded water flows over a boulder, the minerals stick to the rock in fluted layers that hang like curtains.

Cave pearls
Water dripping into a cave pool deposits calcite on sand grains. As the layers of calcite build up, they form pearl-like spheres.

What about me?

Some people still live in houses based on natural caves carved out of solid rock. In Spain, whole villages of cave houses have been dug out of the hard ground.

In numbers

2,191 m
(7,188 ft) The depth of the deepest-known cave system, Voronya Cave in Georgia, southwest Asia

4.6 km
(2.9 miles) The length of the largest single cave passage ever discovered, in the Son Doong Cave in Vietnam

700 m
(2,296 ft) The length of the world's largest cavern, the Sarawak chamber in the Gunung Mulu caves of Borneo, which is more than 300 m (984 ft) wide and 100 m (328 ft) high

67 m
(220 ft) The height of the world's tallest stalagmite, in the Cueva San Martin Infierno, Cuba

12 m
(39 ft) The length of the biggest known free-hanging stalactite, in the Sistema Chac Mol, Mexico

How to: explore a limestone cave

05. Remember the way out! This might involve leaving markers made of coloured tape.

04. Find a way in. You may have to climb down a rope or squeeze through a tiny gap.

03. Get kitted out with a helmet, boots, protective overalls, and at least two powerful torches. Add plenty of rope, a first-aid kit, and some emergency food.

WEIRD OR WHAT?

A few caves, such as Grotte Casteret in Spain, are just cold enough for water to freeze. This creates glittering, glassy **ice falls** cascading to the cave floor.

I don't believe it!

Caves make ideal refuges for bats. Bracken Cave in Texas is the summer home of an amazing 20 million Mexican free-tailed bats, which pour out of the cave entrance every night to feast on flying insects. The floor of the cave is covered with piles of bat poo!

Coastal caves

The power of the sea enables caves to be created in very hard rock on the coast. These caves are much easier and safer to explore than limestone caves.

Painted Cave
This is the world's longest sea cave, on Santa Cruz Island, California. It is 370 m (1,214 ft) long and is home to sea lions.

The Blue Grotto
This cave on the island of Capri, Italy, owes its name to the way the sunlight glows through an underwater entrance.

Fingal's Cave
Beside Fingal's Cave on Staffa, Scotland, are hexagonal columns formed as volcanic rock cooled, shrank, and split.

The **coldest caves** in the world are formed by meltwater from glaciers pouring into crevasses and flowing through icy tunnels. The cave walls glow blue as sunlight filters through the ice.

How does water **shape the Earth?**

Water is the defining feature of our planet. There may be ice and water vapour on other planets in the Solar System, but only Earth definitely has oceans, rivers, and lakes of liquid water, covering two-thirds of the planet. The other third – the land – owes most of its character to water erosion and the spread of plants, which could not exist without water. Indeed, without water, there would be no life.

FAST FACTS

H_2O

01: Water is a chemical compound of two gases, hydrogen and oxygen. Two atoms of hydrogen are bonded to one atom of oxygen to make each molecule of water: H_2O.

02: The three atoms in each water molecule are held together by electrostatic charges that make them form a flattened triangle.

03: Each molecule has a negative charge on the oxygen atom and a positive charge on each hydrogen atom, so it behaves like a tiny triangular magnet.

04: This makes the molecules stick together loosely as a liquid. If they are heated, the added energy makes them burst apart to form a gas – water vapour.

05: On the other hand, if water is cooled to below 0°C (32°F) the molecules lock together in the regular, rigid crystal structure of solid ice.

Some underground water reservoirs were formed long ago in regions that are now deserts. Sealed in by more rock, the water may be 20,000 years old. One of these **desert reservoirs** lies beneath the eastern Sahara, and contains around 150,000 km^3 (36,000 $miles^3$) of water!

Tell me more: **water cycle**

All life on land relies on the water cycle, which delivers water from the oceans to the continents and back again.

02: Here, it cools and condenses into the tiny water droplets that form clouds.
01: The heat of the Sun turns salty ocean water to pure water vapour, which rises into the air.

Weird properties of water

Water is strange stuff. For one thing, it is very heavy, which is odd considering that it is made of two gases – and that one of these gases, hydrogen, is the lightest substance in the Universe!

Uniquely, water expands as it freezes. So ice is less dense than water, and this is why it floats. Just think – if water behaved like any other substance, lakes would not freeze over in winter. They would freeze under!

Water molecules stick together so strongly at the water surface that they form an elastic film called surface tension. This is strong enough for small animals to walk on.

The forces that make water molecules cling together also make them cling to atoms of other substances such as salt, pulling them apart and dissolving them. In fact, water can dissolve more substances than any other liquid.

WEIRD OR WHAT?

Water can turn to **vapour** at quite low temperatures. It doesn't need to be boiling. It can even do it at near **freezing point** – which means that floating ice, water, and water vapour can all exist in the same place at the same time!

I don't believe it!

Most of the water on Earth probably erupted from massive volcanoes some four billion years ago, collecting as water vapour in the atmosphere. As the planet cooled, the vapour turned to rain that poured down for millions of years to create the oceans!

Rivers, lakes, and wetlands

The pure, fresh water that falls as rain forms flowing streams and rivers, broad lakes and ponds, and various types of watery wetlands.

Rivers
Rain drains off the land in streams that join together to form rivers of fresh water. Most of these flow into the sea.

Lakes
In some places, streams and rivers flow into hollows in the ground, filling them up to create ponds and large lakes.

Swamps
The edges of lakes and rivers can become choked with reeds and other vegetation, creating swamps and marshes.

Bogs
Heavy rain encourages the growth of bog mosses, which form thick, spongy masses of acid peat dotted with bog pools.

03: Winds blow the clouds over the land.
04: There, they tend to spill their moisture as rain.
05: In cold regions, rain falls as snow. This can build up to form thick ice sheets that lock up the water for thousands of years.
06: The rain drains off the land in rivers that flow back to the sea, carrying minerals with them.

Some areas of the land get hardly any rain or snow. Parts of the **Atacama Desert** in South America have had no rain at all since records began… and possibly no rain for centuries!

Hidden water

- **Rain falls to the ground, where it usually soaked up by porous rocks to form reservoirs of ground water.**
- Water keeps draining down until it reaches a waterproof layer of rock that stops it sinking any further.
- **The layers above fill up with water – the top of the water-saturated layer is called the water table.**
- If you dig a hole down to this point, the bottom of the hole will fill with water.

Ice ages

- Earth has passed through many cold phases in its history, mainly because of regular changes in its orbit around the Sun.
- During these cold phases, temperatures in many areas are too low for snow to melt, so it gets thicker each year and is compressed into ice.
- The colder it is, the bigger the area that is covered with ice. Such periods of Earth history are known as ice ages.
- The most recent ice age began about two million years ago. It hasn't finished yet – we are just living in a relatively warm spell!
- At the peak of the recent ice age, some 20,000 years ago, so much water was locked up as ice that sea levels fell by 100 m (330 ft).

In numbers

97% The percentage of Earth's water contained in the oceans

3% The percentage of Earth's water that is "fresh" and not salty

69% The percentage of fresh water that is frozen into ice sheets and glaciers

30% The percentage of fresh water that is hidden underground

1% The percentage of fresh water that forms rivers, lakes, wetlands, and living things

Why do **storms** happen?

Storms are caused by the Sun heating the Earth's surface and generating powerful air currents in the lower atmosphere. These create swirling weather systems known as cyclones, which store up vast amounts of water and energy in towering storm clouds. Eventually, all this water and energy is released as rain, hail, lightning, and wind.

FAST FACTS

Cyclones

01: Land and water heated by the Sun warms the air above it. This expands and becomes less dense than the surrounding air, so it travels upwards.

02: The upward movement of this warm air creates a zone of low atmospheric pressure.

03: The surrounding air is under higher pressure, so swirls into the low-pressure zone to replace the rising air. This is a cyclone.

04: The bigger the pressure difference, the faster the airflow. So very low pressure at the cyclone's centre generates high winds.

05: The rising air contains invisible water vapour that has evaporated from Sun-warmed oceans, lakes, and vegetation.

06: As the water vapour is carried higher, it cools and turns into the tiny water droplets that form clouds.

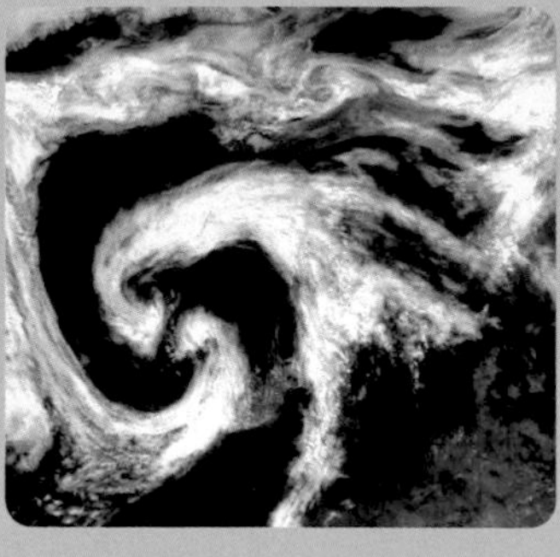

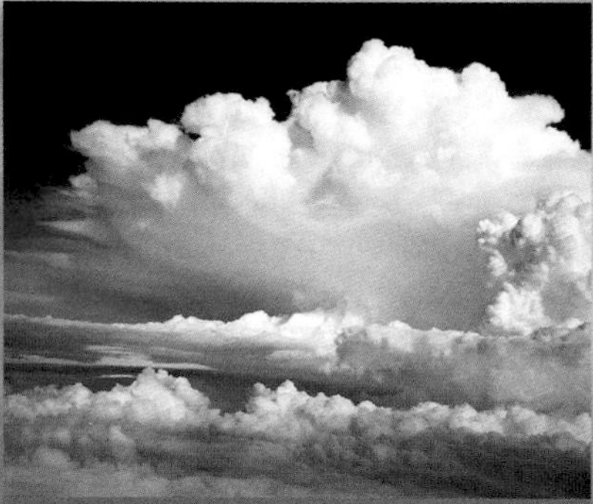

Building storm clouds

Water vapour evaporating from an ocean absorbs energy from the water and carries it up into the sky. So water vapour contains more energy than water.

When the vapour turns into cloud droplets, the energy is released, warming the air. The warmth makes the air expand and rise, carrying the water with it.

If all water vapour turns to cloud droplets, the process stops, forming the relatively small clouds we see in fair weather.

But if massive evaporation generates enough water vapour, the process can carry on, building colossal storm clouds containing vast amounts of water.

The cloud droplets gradually fuse together until they form much bigger drops that fall as torrential rain.

Tell me more: **hailstones and tornadoes**

■ **As water vapour turns to cloud droplets inside a storm cloud, it releases energy as heat. This generates powerful updraughts in the core of the cloud that can reach speeds of 160 kph (100 mph) or more!**

■ The tops of storm clouds are made of tiny ice crystals. These grow heavier until they fall through the cloud, but are then hurled up again by the updraughts. As they are tossed around, they gather layers of ice and turn into hailstones.

■ **The updraughts created by massive storm clouds may suck in so much air from below that they turn into spinning tornadoes, powerful enough to toss cars into the air and rip the roofs off houses.**

I don't believe it!

A typical cloud may be hundreds of metres high, but a storm cloud may have a total height of 10 km (6 miles) or more!

RECORD BREAKER

The biggest **hailstone** on record fell in Nebraska, USA, on 22 June 2003. It measured 17.8 cm (7 in) across – almost as big as a soccer ball!

Supercharged clouds

Ice crystals and water droplets are tossed around in storm clouds, building up static electricity.

This charges up the whole cloud like a giant battery, with the positive charge at the top and the negative charge at the bottom. It also creates a positive charge on the ground below the cloud.

In a 10-km (6-mile high cloud, the difference between the positive and negative charges can build up to 100 million volts!

Eventually, the huge voltage overcomes the electrical resistance of the air, and the electricity in the cloud flashes to the ground as lightning.

WEIRD OR WHAT?

Electrical storms can create bizarre effects, including **ball lightning** – fireballs up to 2 m (6½ ft) across that last longer than the split-second flashes of normal lightning, move at random making hissing noises, then vanish or explode!

A really big **storm cloud** can contain an amazing 250,000 tonnes of water – that's the weight of 1,000 jumbo jets!

How to: tell how close a storm is

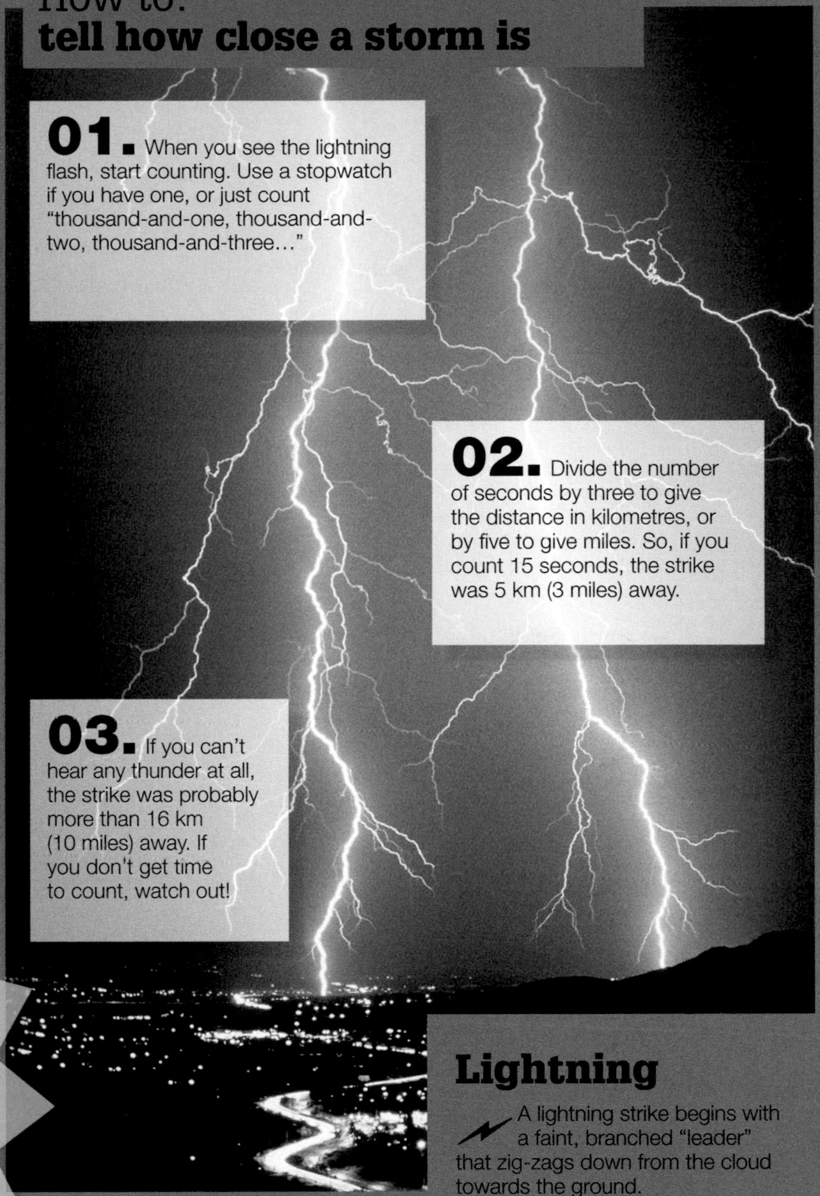

01. When you see the lightning flash, start counting. Use a stopwatch if you have one, or just count "thousand-and-one, thousand-and-two, thousand-and-three…"

02. Divide the number of seconds by three to give the distance in kilometres, or by five to give miles. So, if you count 15 seconds, the strike was 5 km (3 miles) away.

03. If you can't hear any thunder at all, the strike was probably more than 16 km (10 miles) away. If you don't get time to count, watch out!

Lightning

A lightning strike begins with a faint, branched "leader" that zig-zags down from the cloud towards the ground.

When this makes contact – usually with a high point such as a tree – the main discharge shoots back up the leader with a much brighter flash.

Within a fraction of a second, the massive voltage heats the air along the path of the lightning strike to an incredibly high temperature.

The intense heat makes air in the strike path expand explosively, causing the crackling shockwave that we call thunder.

In numbers

16 million
The number of thunderstorms that break out worldwide every year

100
The number of lightning strikes, worldwide, every second

3,000 to 1
The odds against being struck by lightning in your lifetime

1,200
The number of tornadoes reported in the United States each year

695
The number of people killed by the most deadly tornado in history – the Tri-state Twister that hit Missouri, Illinois, and Indiana on 18 March 1925

Red-hot lightning

The temperature of the air in a lightning strike is approximately **30,000°C** (54,000°F) – six times hotter than the surface of the Sun!

Tell me more: **hurricanes**

The biggest, most powerful storms on Earth are the massive cyclones that build up over tropical oceans. Up to 800 km (500 miles) across, they are known as hurricanes, tropical cyclones, or typhoons. Intense evaporation of the warm surface water creates immense storm clouds that form a revolving spiral around a central "eye", causing high winds, torrential rain, and huge ocean waves. If these storms strike land, they destroy virtually everything in their path.

Screaming wind
The eye of a hurricane is strangely calm, but it is surrounded by a wall of very high storm clouds that generate powerful updraughts, sucking in air like a massive vacuum cleaner. This produces winds of up to 300 kph (186 mph) – enough to create huge ocean waves and flatten many buildings that lie in the path of the storm.

Torrential rain
The battering winds are accompanied by epic rainfall, so heavy that it almost defies belief. When Hurricane Mitch struck Central America in 1998, it dumped 127 cm (50 in) of rain in a few hours – equivalent to half the typical annual rainfall! The enormous volume of water pours off the landscape in flash floods and mudslides.

Storm surge
The atmospheric pressure at the eye of the storm is very low, so winds and surrounding air pressure push up a moving body of water – a storm surge. As the surge nears the coast, it generates huge waves more than 10 m (33 ft) high. A storm surge flooded New Orleans when the city was struck by Hurricane Katrina in 2005.

Hurricane Katrina
A satellite image of Hurricane Katrina taken on the morning of 28 August 2005, when the Category Five storm was located in the Gulf of Mexico and generating winds of almost 280 kph (175 mph). The following day, the storm hit the Gulf Coast of the United States with devastating consequences.

Destructive power
The combined effects of the high winds, flash floods, mudslides, and storm surges can cause major destruction: large ships are lifted on to land, houses swept away, and whole towns buried beneath deep mud. A major hurricane can even set off an earthquake because the air pressure is so low that it can allow Earth's crust to rise!

Shattered lives
Hurricanes kill more people than tornadoes, volcanoes, and earthquakes combined. This is partly because they are so frequent – in 2005, there were 13 hurricanes in the north Atlantic alone. Most victims are killed by mudslides and storm surges, the latter accounting for more than 200,000 deaths when Cyclone Nargis hit Myanmar in 2008.

Tracking the storm
Satellite technology allows us to track hurricanes as they build up and move across the oceans. Specially equipped aircraft even fly into the storms to collect data! Nothing can stop a hurricane – all that can be done is to prepare for the worst and, if necessary, evacuate areas at risk. Such measures cause chaos, but they also save lives.

FAST FACTS

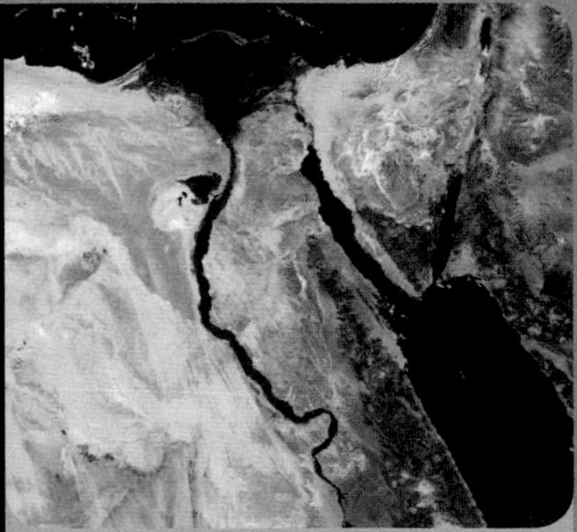

River Nile

01: The Nile has two sources, forming two great rivers that come together at the Sudanese city of Khartoum.

02: The White Nile flows steadily from Lake Victoria, fed by the daily rain that falls on the tropical forests of equatorial Africa.

03: The Blue Nile flows from Lake Tana in the Ethiopian Highlands. During the summer rainy season, it swells to a torrent, but in the winter dry season, it often shrinks to a trickle.

04: North of Khartoum, there is just one major tributary, the River Atbarah, which flows only in the summer rainy season.

Blasts from the past

48 BCE
After arriving in Egypt, Julius Caesar declares that the source of the Nile is the world's greatest unsolved mystery

66
Roman Emperor Nero despatches two military officers to find the source of the Nile, but they find their route upriver blocked by the immense swamp of the Sudd

1618
Spanish Jesuit missionary Pedro Páez becomes the first European to lay eyes on the source of the Blue Nile

1858
British explorer John Hanning Speke reaches the south shore of Lake Victoria and guesses it is the source of the White Nile; his guess is confirmed in 1860.

2004
An expedition led by South African Hendri Coetzee is the first to navigate the entire length of the river from the source of the White Nile to the Mediterranean – the journey takes four months and two weeks.

What's special about the **River Nile?**

Flowing north from the equator to the Mediterranean, the Nile is the longest river in the world. For most of its course, it flows through some of the most barren terrain on Earth – including the hot Sahara Desert – where its waters create a green ribbon of fertile land.

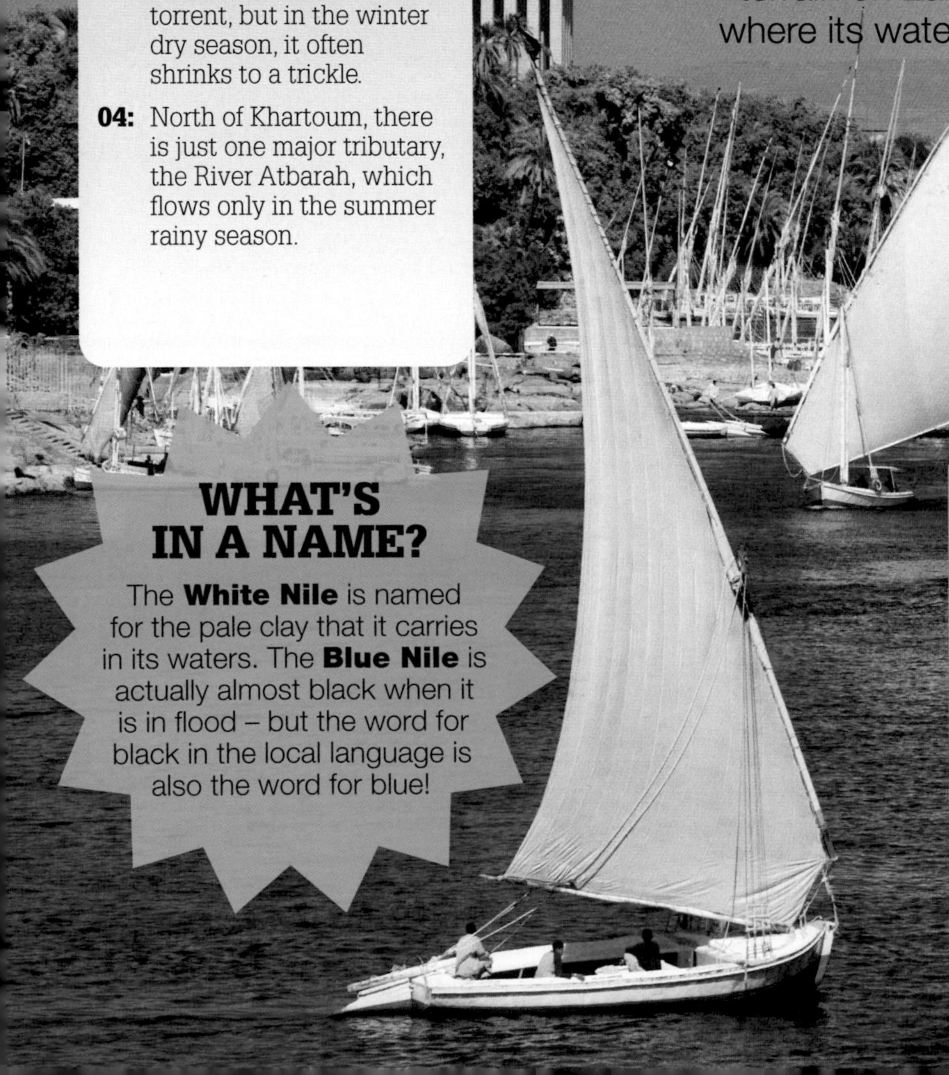

WHAT'S IN A NAME?

The **White Nile** is named for the pale clay that it carries in its waters. The **Blue Nile** is actually almost black when it is in flood – but the word for black in the local language is also the word for blue!

Nile landscapes

Tis Issat Falls
Near its source at Lake Tana, the Blue Nile plunges some 45 m (148 ft) over this spectacular waterfall.

The Sudd
In southern Sudan, the White Nile flows into this vast, reed-choked marshland that covers some 30,000 sq km (11,580 sq miles).

Tell me more: **Nile floods**

■ During the summer rainy season, so much water flows down the Blue Nile that it once flooded the banks of the Nile in Egypt.

■ **As it receded, the floodwater left behind a layer of fertile black silt that enriched the soil, enabling the local farmers to grow crops.**

■ Despite the agricultural value of the floods, they could be destructive, so in the 20th century two dams were built at Aswan in southern Egypt to control the water flow.

■ **Today, the River Nile no longer floods every summer, and the supply of fertile soil has dried up.**

Cotton is grown along the banks of the Nile.

I don't believe it!

At least half of the water that flows into the reed swamp known as the Sudd never flows out – it just evaporates. This means the river flowing out of the Sudd is only half the size of the one that flows into it.

Egyptian desert
In northern Sudan and Egypt, the river flows almost entirely through desert. The river bank is green, but the hills are made of rock and sand.

Nile Delta
North of Cairo, the River Nile flows over the fertile, low-lying Nile Delta and into the Mediterranean Sea.

In numbers

6,650 km (4,132 miles) The length of the Nile from Lake Victoria to the Mediterranean

3,000 years The amazingly long lifespan of the ancient Egyptian civilization, made possible by the river

80 km^3 (19 miles^3) The amount of water that flows down the Nile each year

10% The percentage of the land area of Africa that is drained by the river and its tributaries

6 The number of countries that the Nile flows through

3 The percentage of land area in Egypt that is fertile enough for farming – entirely thanks to the River Nile

RECORD BREAKER

Lake Victoria, the source of the White Nile, is the **largest tropical lake**, with an area of 68,800 sq km (26,564 sq miles). It is also the third largest of all lakes – the Caspian Sea and Lake Superior are larger.

Aswan High Dam

01: The flow of the Nile through Egypt is controlled by the Aswan High Dam, which uses the energy of the river to generate electricity.

02: Completed in 1970 after ten years of work, the dam is 111 m (364 ft) high and replaces an earlier, much lower dam from 1902.

03: The valley above the dam is now a vast reservoir called Lake Nasser. It is 550 km (342 miles) long and holds more than 100 km^3 (24 miles^3) of water.

04: The water in Lake Nasser helped protect Egypt from the drought and terrible famines that hit Sudan and Ethiopia in the 1980s.

Nile **monuments**

Pyramids
The ancient Egyptians built more than 100 pyramids (tombs for royalty) along the west bank of the Nile.

Temples
The cities of the Nile featured magnificent temples such as those at Karnak (above) and the Temple of Edfu.

Statues
The temples and palaces of ancient Egypt were adorned with statues of gods and royal figures.

Tombs
Underground tombs preserve vivid images of daily life on the Nile, such as this hunting and fishing scene.

Why is the **Indian Ocean so beautiful?**

Of all the world's oceans, the Indian Ocean is the only one that is mainly tropical, with glorious clear water, fabulous coral reefs, and magical islands inhabited by strange creatures. However, the ocean is also a place of drama and danger, for it is regularly pounded by intense storms, swept by tsunamis, and rocked by catastrophic volcanic eruptions.

Crystal seas

- In the tropical Indian Ocean, the heat of the Sun creates a layer of warm surface water that floats on the colder water below.
- As the layers generally do not mix, nutrients in the cooler, deeper water do not reach the surface where they would fuel plankton growth.
- It means that few plankton live in the surface water, so it is crystal clear. It also means there is little food for marine life.
- Most of the fish and animals live in local upwelling zones where nutrient-rich water is dragged up from the depths by ocean currents.
- The other hotspots of marine life are coral reefs. These are built by corals living in partnership with plantlike algae that, acting together, make their own food.

FAST FACTS

Grinding plates

01: The Indian Ocean formed over the last 120 million years as the continents of India and Australia moved away from Africa.

02: It is expanding from a spreading rift in the ocean floor called the Mid-Indian Ridge. The rift extends into the Red Sea, which is also getting wider.

03: The movement is dragging the eastern Indian Ocean floor northeast beneath Indonesia, creating a long chain of volcanic islands.

04: The same movement is driving India into Asia, piling up the massive crumple zone of the Himalayas and the Tibet plateau.

05: Past volcanic activity has created many other submerged ocean ridges, some now capped by islands such as the Maldives.

Tell me more: **mangroves**

- Tidal mudflats on tropical Indian Ocean shores are colonized by evergreen trees called mangroves, forming dense, impenetrable swamps.
- **Most trees could not grow in the salty mud, but mangroves have roots that can absorb air and draw in water while excluding salt.**
- Mangrove swamps teem with wildlife, including fiddler crabs and strange fish called mudskippers that can live out of water and even climb trees!
- **At high tide, the tangled tree roots provide safety for young fish – many of the big oceanic fish start life among the mangroves.**

In the 16th and 17th centuries, the Moluccas and Banda Islands in the eastern Indian Ocean were known as the **Spice Islands**, because they were the only known sources of **cloves**, **mace**, and **nutmeg**. The spices were so rare that they were worth more than their weight in gold!

Ocean giants

The warm waters of the Indian Ocean are home to some of the largest, most spectacular fish, mammals, and other sea creatures to be found anywhere on Earth.

Great white shark
The most feared fish in the ocean, this powerful killer shark is common off southern Africa, where it preys on Cape fur seals.

Giant tortoise
The largest population of giant tortoises (152,000) live on Aldabra, north of Madagascar. The biggest weighs 360 kg (793 lb)!

Manta ray
The manta ray is a plankton-eating giant that "flies" through the ocean open-mouthed, filtering the tiny animals from water.

Komodo dragon
Measuring up to 3 m (10 ft) long, the world's largest lizard lives only on the island of Komodo, where it is the top predator.

Whale shark
Biggest of all fish, the whale shark feeds on plankton. Despite growing to a huge 14 m (46 ft) long, this fish is quite harmless.

Saltwater crocodile
This hunter lives mainly in mangroves, but often swims out to sea. It is very dangerous, and kills about 1,000 people each year!

Volcanic Indonesia

The Indian Ocean floor grinds beneath another plate of Earth's crust that lies under Indonesia. The long, curved boundary is marked by an underwater chasm called the Java Trench.

Molten rock erupting from the edge of the overlying plate has created a chain of volcanoes that formed Sumatra, Java, and other islands.

The volcanoes include the island of Krakatau between Sumatra and Java. When it erupted in 1883, the explosion caused waves up to 42 m (138 ft) high that killed at least 36,000 people!

The region is also an earthquake zone – it was a powerful earthquake in the Java Trench that caused the Asian Tsunami of 2004.

I don't believe it!

Ocean currents flowing west around southern Africa clash with storm waves moving east, building up colossal "rogue waves" up to 20 m (66 ft) high! Such waves can endanger large ships, and several have disappeared from these waters without a trace.

RECORD BREAKER

Weighing up to 17 kg (37 lb), the **coco-de-mer** is the world's biggest seed. It floats in the sea to other islands, but despite this, the parent tree grows in just one valley in the **Seychelles**.

In numbers

73.6 million sq km
(28.4 million sq miles) The area of the Indian Ocean

3,890 m
(12,760 ft) The average depth of the ocean

7,258 m
(23,812 ft) The maximum depth of the ocean, in the Java Trench

22°C
(72°F) The minimum surface temperature in the tropical Indian Ocean

9
The average annual number of tropical cyclones in the tropical Indian Ocean since 2000

Islands in the Sun

Maldives
The Maldives are low-lying coral islands surrounded by coral reefs, but the islands are endangered by rising sea levels.

Seychelles
These islands were separated from the Indian continent about 65 million years ago by the spreading rift of the Mid-Indian Ridge.

Aldabra
Just north of Madagascar, Aldabra is a huge coral atoll – a reef crowning an old, extinct volcano that has sunk under the waves.

Réunion
Lying over a hotspot below Earth's crust, this island has a volcano that erupts every few years, spilling molten rock into its tropical forests.

Dinosaurs

When did **dinosaurs rule the Earth?**

Dinosaurs dominated our planet during the Mesozoic, 251 to 65 million years ago (mya), a time that we split into the Triassic, Jurassic, and Cretaceous periods. Great changes took place in the Mesozoic. Many new plant and animal groups appeared, but there were also mass extinctions.

How to: **be *Eoraptor*, one of the first-ever dinos**

01. Have long legs for running away from giant reptile predators. Be small (turkey-sized) for extra speediness.

02. Don't have specialized teeth. Be versatile so you can catch and eat just about anything.

03. Walk upright rather than on all-fours. You need your clawed hands free to grab at animal prey.

04. Be warm-blooded. You need to be able to cope with both hot and cold climates.

Naming history

Mesozoic means "time of middle animals". The creatures of this era came between those of the Palaeozoic (545–251 mya) and the Cenozoic (65 mya to the present).

The **Triassic Period** was named in 1834 for its three-fold rock sequence: black shales, chalk, and red sandstone.

The **Jurassic Period** is named after the Jura Mountains in Switzerland, the place where the first Jurassic rocks were identified in 1795.

Creta is Latin for "chalk", and the **Cretaceous Period** was when huge chalk cliffs were laid down (made up of the fossilized remains of billions of tiny plankton).

12 animal groups that appeared in the **Mesozoic**

Stony corals
The corals that form coral reefs evolved in the Triassic from ancestors that resembled modern sea anemones.

Crabs
The first crabs appeared in the Jurassic. Crabs are crustaceans, closely related to lobsters but with a short, tucked-in tail.

Social insects
Wasps, bees, and ants appeared in the Jurassic or Cretaceous. The earliest were solitary, but group living evolved by 100 mya.

Teleost fishes
Most familiar bony fish are teleosts, which evolved in the Triassic. Examples include eels, herring, cod, carp, and salmon.

Frogs
The earliest true frogs are from the Jurassic. Frogs are tail-less amphibians with short bodies and hind legs built for jumping.

Mammals
Warm-blooded, hairy mammals evolved during the Triassic. Mammals were successful in the Mesozoic, but mostly tiny.

Blasts from the past

251 million years ago The Triassic Period begins
199 mya End of the Triassic Period and start of the Jurassic Period
145 mya The Jurassic Period ends and the Cretaceous Period begins
100 mya The Early Cretaceous ends and the Late Cretaceous begins
65 mya A global mass extinction event brings the Cretaceous Period to an end
1840 The English geologist John Phillips coins the name "Mesozoic"

Plants of the Mesozoic

New greenery appeared on land and in the sea, joining more ancient plants:

Pre-Mesozoic	Mesozoic
Ferns	Bennettitaleans (now extinct)
Horsetails	Flowering plants
Cycads	Palms
Conifers	Modern seaweeds
Ginkgos	Grasses

With just one supercontinent in the Triassic, there was less cooling by sea winds. Inland **temperatures soared** to 50°C (122°F).

FAST FACTS

The Mesozoic world

01: The Mesozoic atmosphere was different from today's: there was less oxygen and more carbon dioxide (CO_2).

02: Mesozoic Earth was a hothouse, with warm climates and little or no ice at the poles.

03: Sea levels were high due to the lack of ice. Low-lying regions were often covered by shallow, tropical seas.

04: At the start of the Triassic, conditions were dry and deserts were widespread.

05: The world became wetter during the Jurassic. Tropical forests and other moist habitats appeared.

Tell me more: **Earth's moving continents**

Landmasses are always moving. Oceans slowly open as continents pull apart, or close as continents push together.

At the beginning of the Triassic, there was one single supercontinent, Pangaea, and a single enormous ocean, Panthalassa.

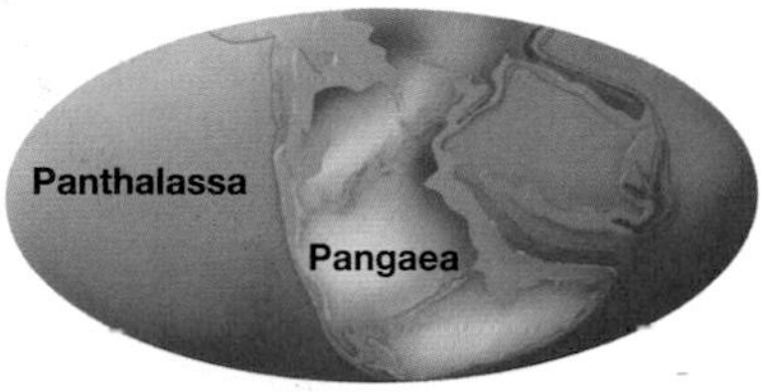

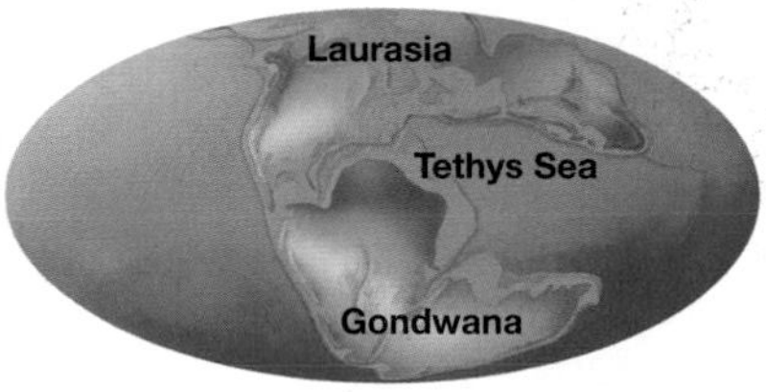

Early in the Jurassic, Pangaea split into Laurasia and Gondwana, separated by the Tethys Sea.

During the Cretaceous, the continents split apart and moved nearer to their current positions.

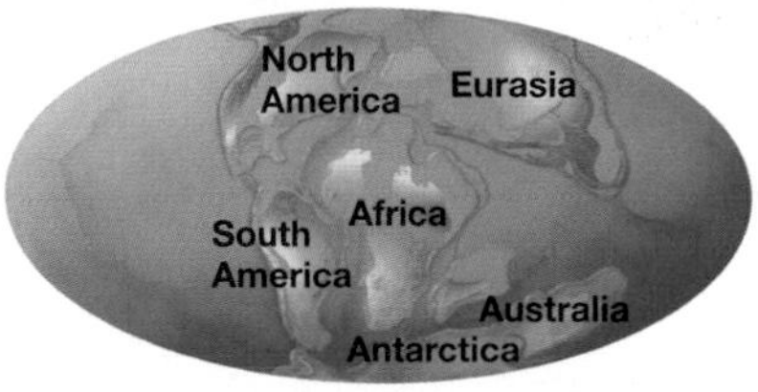

Which of these appeared in the Mesozoic?

(answers at bottom of page)

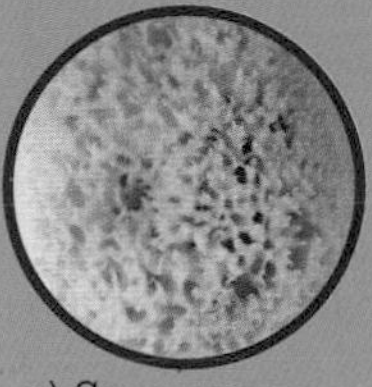
a) Sponges

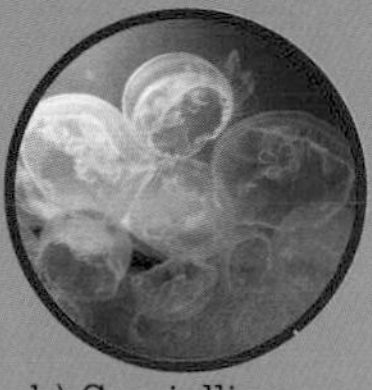
b) Sea jellies

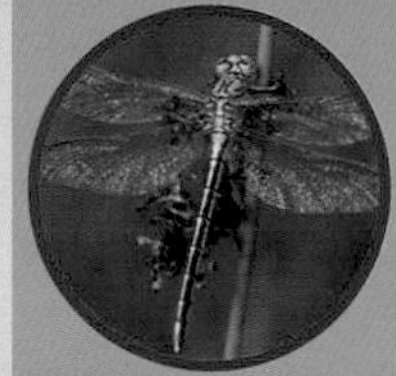
c) Dragonflies

d) Sharks

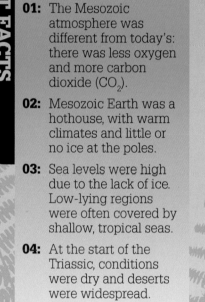

Turtles
The earliest fossil turtles are from the Triassic. Turtles are unique reptiles where the ribcage has become a shell.

Pterosaurs
Small, primitive pterosaurs (flying reptiles) appeared in the Triassic. The group survived to the end of the Cretaceous.

Dinosaurs
Like pterosaurs, dinosaurs are reptiles. The first dinosaurs evolved from small, slender-legged reptiles during the Triassic.

Birds
The earliest birds evolved in the Jurassic from small, long-armed dinosaurs. Birds are feathered dinosaurs.

Plesiosaurs
The first plesiosaurs appeared in the Triassic. These sea-going reptiles had long necks and two pairs of paddlelike limbs.

Snakes
The oldest known fossil snakes date to the Cretaceous. Snakes evolved from burrowing or swimming lizards.

ANSWERS: None of them! These are all ancient groups that evolved *before* the start of the Mesozoic. Sponges and sea jellies evolved more than 500 mya. The earliest sharks are about 400 million years old, while dragonflies appeared more than 300 mya.

Tell me more:
ancient four-legged creatures

Hundreds of different groups of animals came and went before the first dinosaur appeared about 230 million years ago. Backboned animals with arms, legs, fingers, and toes are called tetrapods, and the first tetrapod evolved from fish about 375 million years ago (mya). Over the next few hundred million years, an amazing variety of tetrapods evolved, from giant amphibians to odd mammal ancestors.

01. *Proterogyrinus*
(Early Carboniferous)
Many predatory, amphibious tetrapods evolved in the Carboniferous (350–300 mya). *Proterogyrinus* had a 2-m (6.5-ft) body and fanglike teeth.

02. *Phlegethontia*
(Late Carboniferous)
You can usually tell tetrapods from their fish ancestors because they have legs. However, limbs were lost several times during tetrapod evolution. Snakelike *Phlegethontia* slithered along looking for prey.

03. *Amphibamus*
(Late Carboniferous)
Amphibamus looked like a salamander and was around 20 cm (8 in) long. It probably lived on land and hunted insects and other small prey. It may have had a "tadpole" stage, when it lived in water and had gills.

04. *Spinoaequalis*
(Late Carboniferous)
Most early reptiles lived on land, but some took to life in water. *Spinoaequalis* was a small early reptile that lived about 300 mya. Tall, bony rods on its tail skeleton show that it had a deep, paddlelike tail. It almost certainly used this for swimming.

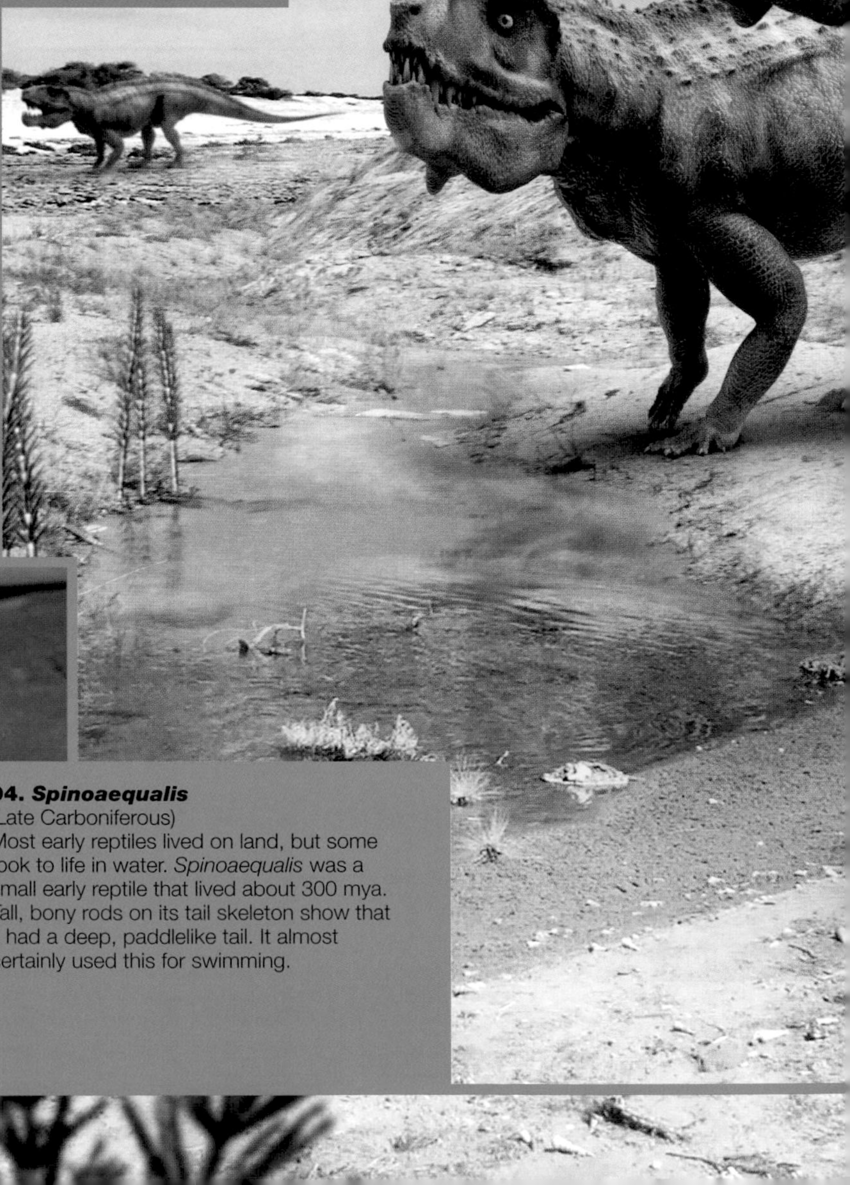

05. *Moschops*
(Late Permian)
Mammals are the only survivors of a group called the synapsids. During the Permian (299–251 mya), synapsids were the most important land animals. *Moschops* was a giant, plant-eating synapsid with a thick skull. *Moschops* males probably headbutted each other to fight for females.

06. *Varanops*
(Early Permian)
Synapsids gave rise to mammals during the Triassic (251–199 mya), but the earliest synapsids looked more like lizards. *Varanops* was a 1-m- (3.3-ft-) long predator that hunted insects and other small animals. It had numerous sharply pointed teeth. Later synapsid groups had teeth that were specialized for particular foods.

07. *Metoposaurus*
(Late Triassic)
Metoposaurus was related to *Amphibamus*, but about ten times the size. Special grooves on the bones of its skull suggest that it had a lateral line system, like sharks do. Lateral lines allow aquatic animals to sense vibrations in the water. *Metoposaurus* almost certainly skulked in the water, preying on fish and other animals.

08. *Postosuchus*
(Late Triassic)
The crurotarsans were predatory reptile cousins of dinosaurs and pterosaurs. Most walked on four legs, but some walked on two, just like meat-eating dinosaurs. *Postosuchus* was a giant crurotarsan with a huge head and short arms. It died out at the end of the Triassic.

Neck posture

After plugging together sauropod neck bones, some scientists have argued that sauropod necks must have been straight, horizontal, and incapable of much up-and-down movement.

However, living animals all hold their necks up, even if their bones suggest a horizontal neck pose. It's most likely that sauropods had raised necks and a strongly bent head-neck junction.

Modern animals show that keeping the neck in a raised posture is not difficult. Special muscles hold up the neck with minimal effort – keeping the neck upright uses less energy than holding it out straight.

Computer modelling indicates that bony struts on the vertebrae helped conduct stress and support the weight of the neck. Hollow air sacs – like honeycomb – also made the neck lighter than it looked.

In numbers

19
The number of vertebrae in the neck of the Chinese sauropod *Mamenchisaurus*

26
The average number of eggs in a sauropod nest

30
The age (in years) at which a sauropod reached its adult size

60 m
(200 ft) The likely length of *Amphicoelias*, the largest known sauropod

500–600
The number of peglike teeth in the jaws of *Nigersaurus*

Air sac facts

Sauropod bones, especially the vertebrae and ribs, have distinctive openings called pneumatic foramina.

These openings show that the bones contained air-filled sacs, just like the bones of modern birds.

As in birds, the sacs were connected to the lungs by tubes. Sacs were located throughout the body.

The air-sac system meant that sauropods were surprisingly light for their size – perhaps 10 per cent lighter than they would have been without the sacs.

Light as air

In sauropods such as ***Giraffatitan***, nearly 90 per cent of the bone was taken up by air. The neck of ***Giraffatitan*** was 8.5 m (28 ft) long, but weighed only around 600 kg (1,320 lb).

Tell me more: **sauropod necks**

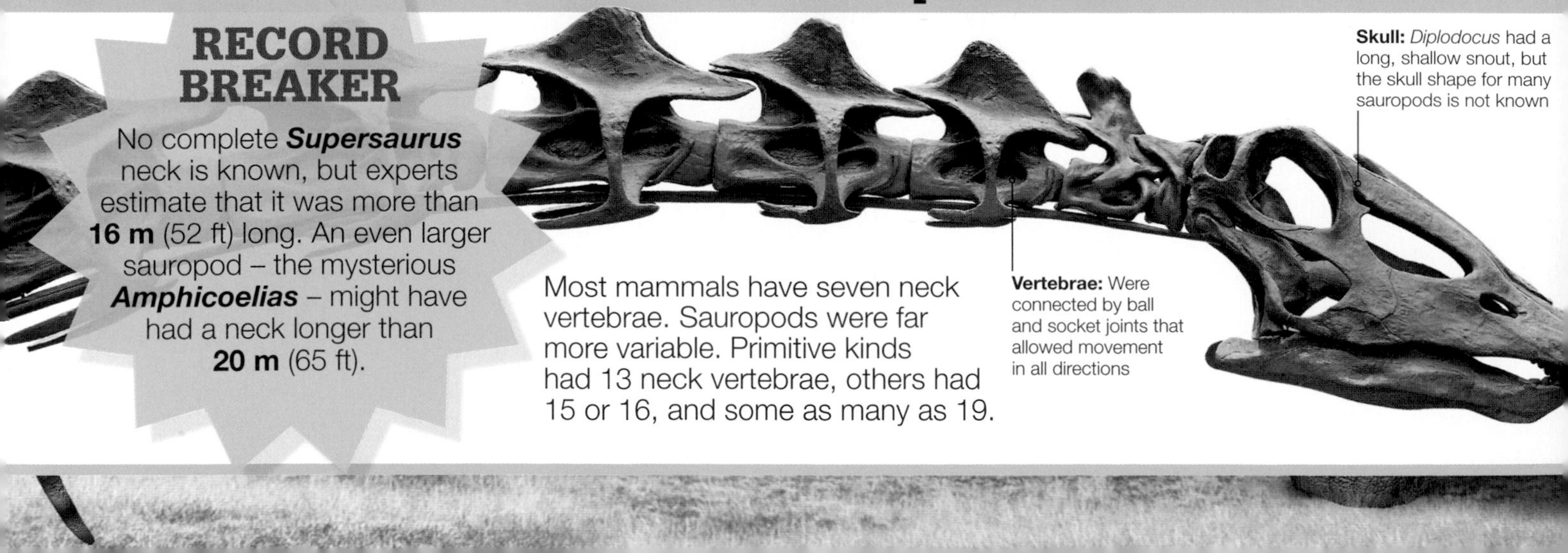

Skull: *Diplodocus* had a long, shallow snout, but the skull shape for many sauropods is not known
Vertebrae: Were connected by ball and socket joints that allowed movement in all directions

RECORD BREAKER

No complete ***Supersaurus*** neck is known, but experts estimate that it was more than **16 m** (52 ft) long. An even larger sauropod – the mysterious ***Amphicoelias*** – might have had a neck longer than **20 m** (65 ft).

Most mammals have seven neck vertebrae. Sauropods were far more variable. Primitive kinds had 13 neck vertebrae, others had 15 or 16, and some as many as 19.

How did dino **giants** hold up their **necks?**

The giant plant-eating sauropods are famous for their incredibly long necks. Experts have argued for decades about how these dinosaurs held up their necks, and what they used them for. We now know that sauropod necks were remarkably light for their size, and were probably held in raised postures.

FAST FACTS

Sauropods

01: Sauropods lived in the Triassic, Jurassic, and Cretaceous periods.

02: Sauropod fossils have been found worldwide.

03: More than 100 different sauropods have been named.

04: *Diplodocus* and its relatives had longer tails and short arms.

05: *Brachiosaurus* and its relatives had shorter tails and long arms.

Some sauropod necks were more than **15 m (50 ft)** long. Even the long neck of the modern giraffe is short (at 2.4 m, or 8 ft) compared to the longest sauropod neck.

Super giants
Sauropods thrived for more than **100 million years**. Almost all sauropods had long necks and big bodies. However, at least one kind evolved a short neck, and a few sauropods were only as big as horses.

Advantages of a long neck

01 It allows you to reach higher up into the trees than other herbivores, and so avoid competition for food.

02 You can reach a large area without moving much, so you can save energy.

03 The size of your neck can show how strong and healthy you are, and make you more attractive to mates.

04 You can use your neck as a weapon for fighting enemies or competitors.

05 With your head high, you can see, smell, or hear danger from far off.

06 A long windpipe can make super-loud noises that travel vast distances.

Disadvantages of a long neck

01 Long necks lose a lot of heat, so you can only live in warm climates.

02 You need special tricks to move air in and out of a long windpipe. Sauropods had a special air-sac system.

03 Pumping blood up a long neck to the head requires strong blood vessels, a big heart, and high blood pressure.

04 Long windpipes are more prone to fungal diseases and other infections.

05 Growing all that extra bone, muscle, and skin uses up a lot of energy.

Tell me more: **rearing up**

Diplodocus and its relatives could probably rear up on their back legs. This allowed them to reach even higher into the trees, perhaps to heights of 12 m (40 ft) or more.

Vertebrae: Were tall and able to support the massive muscles and ligaments needed to haul the body upright
Body: Was short for a sauropod, so it was easier for the animal to raise itself into a bipedal position
Tail: Had a heavy, muscled base that counterbalanced the body and neck
Forelimbs: Were short and light, so they helped minimize the weight at the front of the body
Thighbones: Were sturdy enough to take the animal's total body weight

Which dinos were **super predators?**

Giant megalosauroids and allosauroids were some of most successful predators of the Jurassic and Cretaceous periods. Some were even larger than *T rex*! They ambushed prey with killer bites. One group of megalosauroids, the spinosaurids, were long-snouted fish-eaters.

Tyrannosaurus belonged to a different group of **theropods** (two-legged predatory dinosaurs) called the coelurosaurs.

Tell me more: ***Allosaurus* features**

S-shaped neck: Meant *Allosaurus* could pull back when biting, for extra wrenching power
Large size: Of 8 m (26.2 ft) nose to tail meant *Allosaurus* could overpower large prey
Skull: Carried shocks and stresses away from the teeth and back along the jaws
Powerful arms: Allowed *Allosaurus* to restrain prey
Huge muscles: On thighs and calfs would have given the animal a powerful kick
Flexible fingers: Ended with curved claws for latching on to prey

In numbers

7
The number of tiny serrations per 1 mm (0.04 in) on the teeth of *Baryonyx*; (two serrations per mm is more typical)

1.8 m
(6 ft) Possible skull length of *Giganotosaurus*

64
The number of teeth present in the lower jaws of *Baryonyx*; (most big, predatory dinosaurs had half as many)

37 cm
(14.5 in) Length along the curve of *Megaraptor*'s largest hand claw

50
The number of vertebrae that make up the tail bone of the theropod *Allosaurus*

Big beasts!

***Spinosaurus* probably weighed more than 10 tonnes and was 18 m (59 ft) long.**

The large megalosauroid *Torvosaurus* weighed in at just 2 tonnes.

***Saurophaganax* was one of the biggest allosauroids, also weighing around 2 tonnes.**

The monster allosauroid *Giganotosaurus* was similar in size to *T rex* – about 13 m (42.5 ft) long and weighing less than 10 tonnes.

Rough lives

Fossil evidence of injuries:

- **One *Allosaurus* has a hole in a tail bone that was clearly made by a stegosaur's tail spike**
- **A Chinese *Sinraptor* bears facial injuries that seem to have been inflicted by a fellow *Sinraptor***
- **Healed ribs in *Neovenator* suggest that it either had a nasty fall or was badly hurt in battle**

Stiffened tail: Helped the animal keep its balance when running
Hind legs: Enabled the dinosaur to run fast and ambush prey

WHAT'S IN A NAME?

The name ***Torvosaurus*** has its roots in two ancient languages. *Torvo* comes from the Latin word for "savage" and *saurus* comes from the Greek word for "lizard".

Crests, horns, and ridges

Many super predators had odd skull structures. Most were for display but some were used as weapons.

- *Spinosaurus* had a ridged crest in front of its eyes
- Both *Baryonyx* and *Suchomimus* had long ridges up the middle of the snout
- *Acrocanthosaurus* had bony lumps above and behind each eye socket
- *Monolophosaurus* (below) had a knobbly ridge running along its snout and over its eyes
- *Allosaurus* had triangular horns in front of its eyes and paired ridges along its snout

FAST FACTS

Super predators

01: Most big theropods had a deep, narrow snout, with air-filled sacs along each side.

02: *Carcharodontosaurus* and *Allosaurus* had some binocular ("two-eyed") vision even though their eyes faced sideways. Seeing with both eyes at once allowed them to judge distance.

03: Theropods had an excellent sense of smell.

04: All theropods had a V-shaped wishbone, perhaps to provide strength to the chest.

05: The arms were stout with large muscles.

06: Most theropods had three large, clawed fingers. Some had a fourth, clawless finger.

07: Most theropods had four toes. The first toe was small, however, and didn't reach the ground.

08: The tail was strong, muscular, and used for balance.

Lost to science

The original *Spinosaurus* specimen, discovered by Ernst Stromer in 1912, was **destroyed during World War II**, when Munich's natural history museum was bombed. Other *Spinosaurus* specimens have been discovered since, but none are as complete as the original find.

Five spinosaurid skull facts

- Most megalosauroids had short skulls, but spinosaurids had long snouts, like a crocodile's.
- The gumlines were not straight, but followed an S-shaped curve.
- The teeth were arranged along the S-shaped curve, so they pointed forwards and downwards as well as backwards.
- Spinosaurid teeth were relatively conical and rounded in cross-section (rather than flattened from side to side).
- The nostril openings were located far back, away from the tip of the snout.

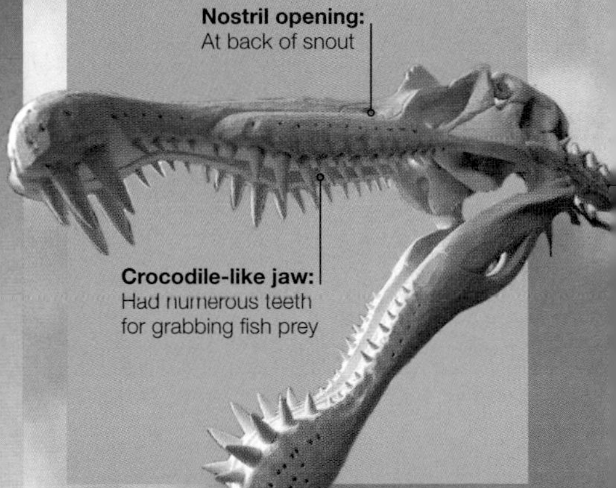

Nostril opening: At back of snout
Crocodile-like jaw: Had numerous teeth for grabbing fish prey

Super predator discovery sites

- **Agadez, Niger:** *Suchomimus*
- **Bahariya, Egypt:** *Spinosaurus, Carcharodontosaurus*
- **Calvados, France:** *Poekilopleuron, Dubreuillosaurus*
- **Ceará, Brazil:** *Irritator*
- **Colorado, USA:** *Allosaurus, Torvosaurus*
- **Fukui Prefecture, Japan:** *Fukuiraptor*
- **Isle of Wight, UK:** *Neovenator*
- **Mendoza Province, Argentina:** *Aerosteon*
- **Oklahoma, USA:** *Acrocanthosaurus*
- **Patagonia, Argentina:** *Mapusaurus, Giganotosaurus, Megaraptor*
- **Queensland, Australia:** *Australovenator*
- **Sichuan, China:** *Sinraptor, Yangchuanosaurus*
- **Surrey, UK:** *Baryonyx*

Why did some **dinos have armour?**

During the Jurassic and Cretaceous, a group of dinosaurs called thyreophorans evolved. Virtually all thyreophorans were four-legged plant-eaters that ate low-growing plants. What made thyreophorans unusual was that they possessed rows of armoured plates (scutes) that ran along their necks, backs, and tails.

Four kinds of **thyreophoran**

Scutellosaurus
One of the earliest thyreophorans, *Scutellosaurus* could walk on two legs and had a long tail. It had parallel rows of small scutes along its body and tail.

Scelidosaurus
Larger and heavier than *Scutellosaurus*, *Scelidosaurus* walked on all fours all of the time. Its rows of plates covered more of its body.

Stegosaurs
Famous for their arching backs and cluster of deadly tail spikes, stegosaurs such as *Kentrosaurus* had two rows of plates or spikes.

Ankylosaurs
Edmontonia was one of the ankylosaurs – the tanks of the dinosaur world. It had a broad body dotted with scutes, stout limbs, and a distinctive, bony skull.

FAST FACTS

Thyreophoran skulls

01: All thyreophorans, including this *Huayangosaurus*, had beaklike mouths.

02: Unlike most reptiles, thyreophorans had cheeks.

03: Stegosaur skulls were long and narrow. The animals were picky feeders, choosing the best leaves and fruit.

04: Ankylosaurs had wide muzzles and probably took broad mouthfuls of vegetation.

05: Some ankylosaurs had bony loops in their snouts. Perhaps these made their calls louder.

06: Thyreophoran teeth were small, with large serrated edges.

In numbers

1.1 m
(3.6 ft) Length of the longest spike on the stegosaur *Loricatosaurus*

60 cm
(2 ft) Width of the biggest ankylosaur tail club

17
The number of plates on the neck, back, and tail of *Stegosaurus*

900
The number of *Kentrosaurus* bones discovered at Tendaguru, Tanzania

718 megapascals
The estimated force of a blow from a big ankylosaur tail club – enough to break bone!

One ***Tyrannosaurus*** fossil had ankylosaur plates in its stomach – with bite marks on them. Not even armour plating was protection from a determined *T rex*!

I don't believe it!

Until the discovery of *Miragaia* in 2009, stegosaurs were seen as short-necked grazers. *Miragaia* had 17 neck vertebrae – more than most sauropods. With this long neck, it could have reached up into foliage 3 m (10 ft) off the ground.

Tell me more: *Stegosaurus*

Stegosaurus's small, narrow skull could only house a small brain.

Its plates were probably brightly coloured and used for display, to intimidate rivals, and to attract mates.

Its plates were too fragile to be armour and lacked enough blood vessels to be able to control body temperature.

Its throat was covered with buttonlike scutes called ossicles.

Huge shoulder muscles allowed *Stegosaurus* to quickly turn, when whipping its tail.

***Stegosaurus* had two pairs of long tail spikes for self-defence.**

Growing-up

Like all dinosaurs, thyreophorans hatched from eggs. A few fossil eggs might be from thyreophorans, but no one has found a nest of thyreophoran eggs yet.

Some baby ankylosaurs have been discovered curled up together. This suggests they lived together as youngsters.

Fossils show that thyreophoran babies had limited armour. The scutes grew as the animals matured.

Baby *Stegosaurus* tracks were found in 2007. There were no adult tracks nearby, so maybe stegosaur babies looked after themselves.

WHAT'S IN A NAME?

The armoured dinosaur *Minmi* is named after the place in Australia where it was found in the 1970s. For more than a decade, *Minmi* had the **shortest dinosaur name** – now *Mei* is the shortest.

Ankylosaur armour

Short horns stuck outwards and backwards from the back of the skull in some ankylosaurs, such as this *Gargoyleosaurus*.

***Ankylosaurus* and *Euoplocephalus* had armour plates on their eyelids.**

Some ankylosaurs had an armour plate over the cheek.

There was a mosaic of armour on top of the skull.

Collarlike rings of plates covered the top of the neck.

In some ankylosaurs, long spikes stuck out from the neck and shoulders.

Some ankylosaurs had scutes on their arms and legs as well as on their bodies.

The ankylosaur *Edmontonia* had forked spikes. No one knows why.

The small Chinese ankylosaur *Liaoningosaurus* had a large armour plate over its belly.

A protective shield grew over the hips of *Polacanthus* and some other ankylosaurs.

Some ankylosaurs had big, triangular scutes sticking out of the sides of their tails.

Key thyreophoran fossil sites
Colorado, USA
Alberta, Canada
Sichuan, China
Gobi Desert, Mongolia
Lourinhã, Portugal
Dorset, UK

Which **dinosaurs** became **birds?**

Birds evolved during the Jurassic from small, feathered dinosaurs called maniraptorans. Many maniraptorans were so birdlike that it would have been hard to tell these animals apart when they were alive. They had downy feathers for warmth, and showy plumage for display.

How to: be feathery like *Caudipteryx*

01. You'll need a fan of colourful feathers at the end of your tail. Use this fan to impress likely mates.

02. You also need a crest of longer feathers sticking up on the top of your head. This is for display, as well.

03. Your hands, especially your second finger, have extra-long feathers. Are these the beginning of wings?

04. Grow soft, downy fuzz on your body to keep you nice and warm, whatever the weather.

05. Make sure your feet and lower legs are free of feathers (unlike those of some of your maniraptoran cousins).

The story of feathered dinosaurs

- Maniraptorans evolved during the Middle Jurassic (about 170 million years ago).
- **Early birds, troodontids, and dromaeosaurids were all small, feathered predators with long feathers on the arms and legs. Their shared ancestor must have looked like this, too.**
- Troodontids and dromaeosaurids are grouped together as the deinonychosaurs.
- **Oviraptors, troodontids, and dromaeosaurids started out small, but all evolved much larger sizes later on in their history.**
- The tiniest feathered dinosaurs were the scansoriopterygids. One species, *Epidendrosaurus*, was the same size as a sparrow!
- **Were scansoriopterygids early birds or closer to oviraptors? No one is sure.**

RECORD BREAKER

More than **1,000 specimens** have been found of the Cretaceous bird *Confuciusornis*. Most maniraptorans are known from a single fossil.

FAST FACTS

Maniraptorans

01: Maniraptorans had relatively large brains for dinosaurs. They used the brain for processing sensory information, not for thinking!

02: The eyes were large, and maniraptorans had excellent eyesight.

03: Maniraptorans had three-fingered hands. The thumb was the shortest finger.

04: Maniraptorans typically had deep, narrow bodies.

05: Oviraptors and birds evolved shortened tails.

06: Of the four toes, the first was short and did not reach the ground.

07: In birds, the first toe was longer – useful for perching and grabbing prey.

Catching and killing

All maniraptoran hands had three sharp claws, and were held with the palms facing in. Small animals could be grabbed by "clapping" the hands together.

Dromaeosaurids and troodontids had sickle-shaped claws to pin down and kill lizards and small mammals.

Caudipteryx and other oviraptors probably used their beak and buck teeth to snatch leaves, fruit, or small animals.

Dromaeosaurids and troodontids had serrated teeth that were good at slicing through flesh.

Small maniraptorans preyed on insects, lizards, and other small animals. Those longer than 2 m (6.6 ft) hunted plant-eating dinosaurs and other larger animals.

Early bird

Discovered in Germany in 1861, *Archaeopteryx* is still the **oldest known fossil bird**. It lived 150 million years ago in the Jurassic Period. With its large hand claws and toothed jaw, it was extremely similar to small dromaeosaurids.

Seven exciting feathered finds

01: ***Caudipteryx*** *(China, 1998)* – an early oviraptor

02: ***Bambiraptor*** *(USA, 2000)* – a long-legged dromaeosaurid

03: ***Mei*** *(China, 2004)* – a troodontid found curled up in a sleeping position

04: ***Buitreraptor*** *(Argentina, 2005)* – a long-snouted dromaeosaurid

05: ***Mahakala*** *(Mongolia, 2007)* – a primitive dromaeosaurid from the Gobi Desert

06: ***Shanag*** *(Mongolia, 2007)* – a crow-sized dromaeosaurid known from part of a skull

07: ***Hesperonychus*** *(Canada, 2009)* – a tiny dromaeosaurid, related to *Microraptor*

Tell me more: **anatomy of *Epidexipteryx***

Discovered in China, *Epidexipteryx* was one of the tiny scansoriopterygids. These long-fingered maniraptorans were tree-climbers that ate insects.

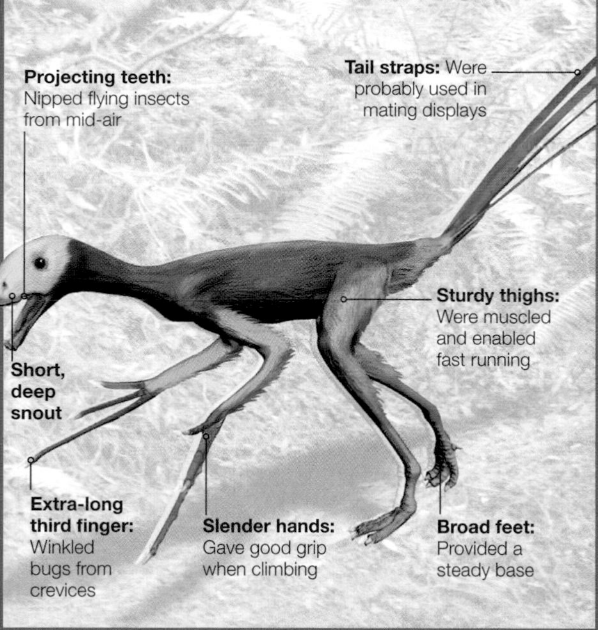

Projecting teeth: Nipped flying insects from mid-air
Tail straps: Were probably used in mating displays
Sturdy thighs: Were muscled and enabled fast running
Short, deep snout
Extra-long third finger: Winkled bugs from crevices
Slender hands: Gave good grip when climbing
Broad feet: Provided a steady base

Five theories for how flight evolved

01: Maybe small maniraptorans were tree-climbers that began to glide from tree to tree, and later took to flapping.

02: Perhaps maniraptorans used their feathered arms to "boost" their speed as they ran on the ground.

03: An old idea is that the wings were stretched out to grab insects, and that the flight stroke evolved from this.

04: Another idea is that bird ancestors "flew" underwater, and later took to the air. Since maniraptorans were not aquatic, this is not likely.

05: Some modern bird chicks flutter their arms when running up slopes or tree trunks. Maybe maniraptorans did this too, and the flight stroke soon followed.

Spectacular feathered **fossils from China** show that some birdlike maniraptorans were very peculiar, with buck teeth, or winglike legs.

Main maniraptoran groups

Dromaeosaurids
Predators with long arms and raised, sickle-shaped claws on their second toes.

Oviraptors
Short-snouted maniraptorans, equipped with a few projecting teeth or a toothless beak.

Troodontids
Predators or omnivores with closely packed, serrated teeth, and long legs.

Birds
The first birds were small, long-armed, toothed predators of insects and lizards.

FAST FACTS

Pterosaur wings

01: A unique bone (the pteroid) helped control the front segment of the wing.

03: Large blood vessels in the wing could absorb or release heat.

04: The wings folded away when not in use.

05: Rodlike fibres gave the wings their shape.

06: Muscles controlled the wing surfaces and helped the animal fly.

07: The front edge of the wing had a air-filled layer of cushioning.

08: The back legs were connected to the main wing membrane, and helped to control it.

Which reptiles ruled the skies?

Pterosaurs were not dinosaurs, but close relatives. They ruled the air while dinosaurs dominated life on land. Recent discoveries have shed new light on these remarkable reptiles – including how they flew and what foods they ate.

How to: **be the biggest pterosaur ever**

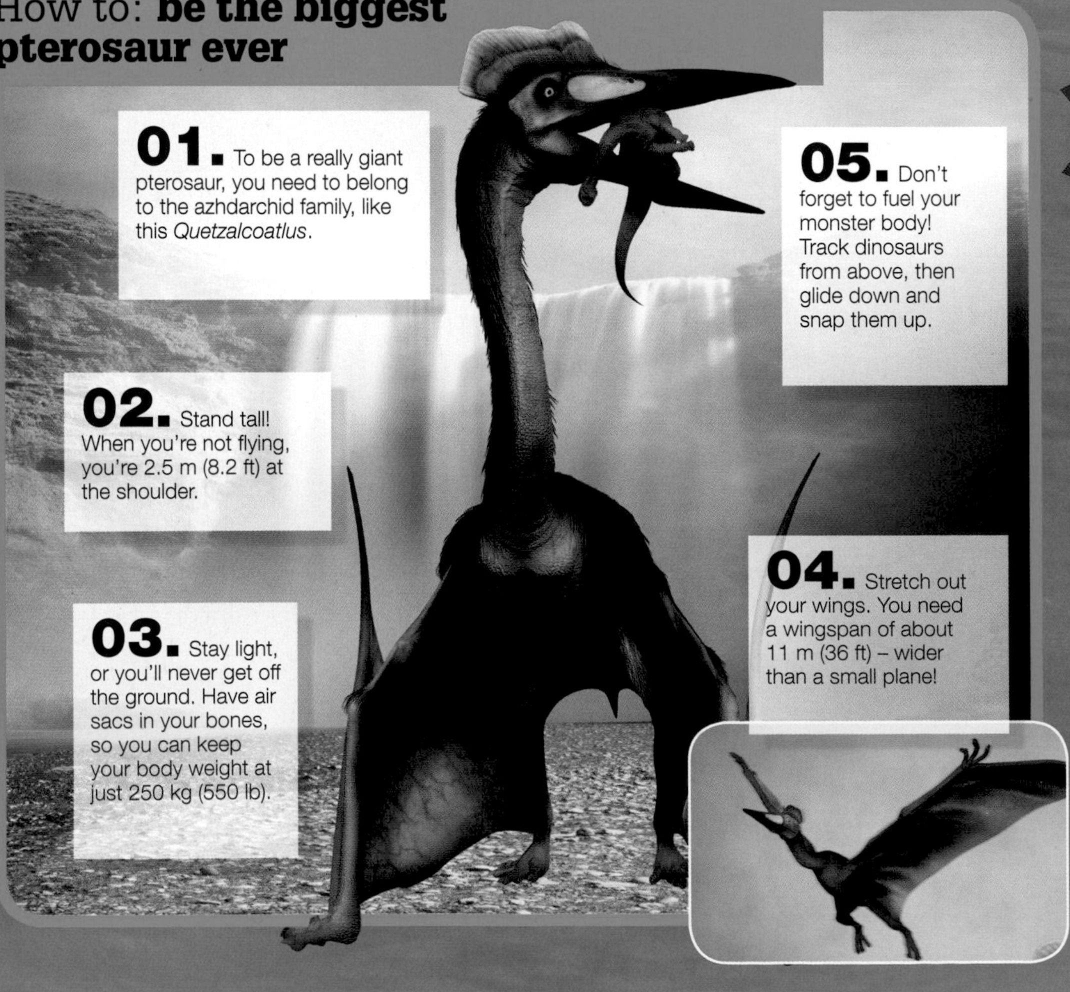

01. To be a really giant pterosaur, you need to belong to the azhdarchid family, like this *Quetzalcoatlus*.

02. Stand tall! When you're not flying, you're 2.5 m (8.2 ft) at the shoulder.

03. Stay light, or you'll never get off the ground. Have air sacs in your bones, so you can keep your body weight at just 250 kg (550 lb).

04. Stretch out your wings. You need a wingspan of about 11 m (36 ft) – wider than a small plane!

05. Don't forget to fuel your monster body! Track dinosaurs from above, then glide down and snap them up.

In birds, part of the brain called the **flocculus** helps control eye, head, and neck movement. The pterosaur's flocculus was even bigger than that of birds. So pterosaurs were probably very good at controlling their heads and keeping a fixed gaze.

Top pterosaur localities

- At Solnhofen, Germany, limestone layers hold Jurassic pterosaurs such as *Rhamphorhynchus*.
- Karatau, Kazahkstan, has specimens of the small pterosaurs *Sordes* and *Batrachognathus*.
- In Brazil, fossil-hunters have found fine Cretaceous pterosaurs, some with wing membranes.
- Liaoning Province in China has revealed exceptional pterosaur fossils.

Tell me more: **pterosaur breathing apparatus**

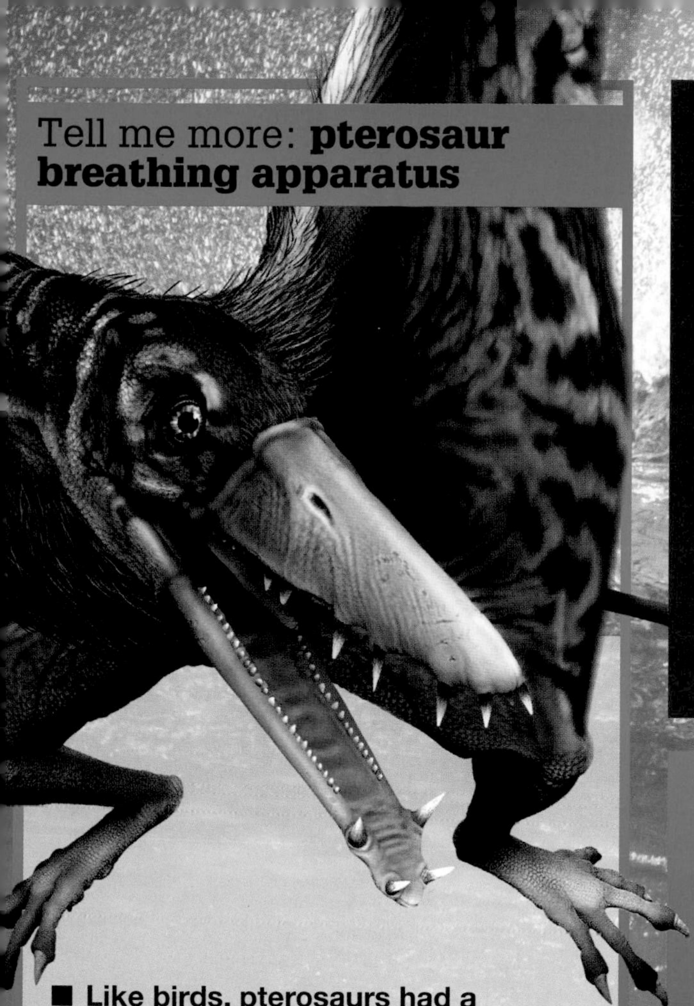

■ Like birds, pterosaurs had a large breastbone that extended from the front of the ribcage to the belly.

■ Small, serrated bones called sternal ribs connected the breastbone with the ribs.

■ When the pterosaur breathed in, muscles pulled the sternal ribs (and therefore the breastbone) down.

■ As the breastbone moved down, all the air sacs inside the body filled with air.

■ When the rib muscles relaxed, the breastbone moved back up.

■ As the breastbone moved up, air was pushed out of all the air sacs, and out of the animal's throat.

Pterosaur teeth

Dimorphodon had a deep snout and conical teeth for grabbing and subduing small prey.

Dsungaripterus had big, blunt teeth for crushing shellfish.

Pteranodon had a long, gently upcurved, toothless beak.

Ctenochasma had hundreds of long, fine teeth for filtering tiny prey from the water.

Quetzalcoatlus had a toothless, storklike beak, useful for seizing small animals and fruit.

Ornithocheirus had clusters of fangs for snatching fish and squid from the waves.

Open ocean
For a long time experts thought all pterosaurs lived by the sea. *Pteranodon* probably fed out at sea like a modern albatross.

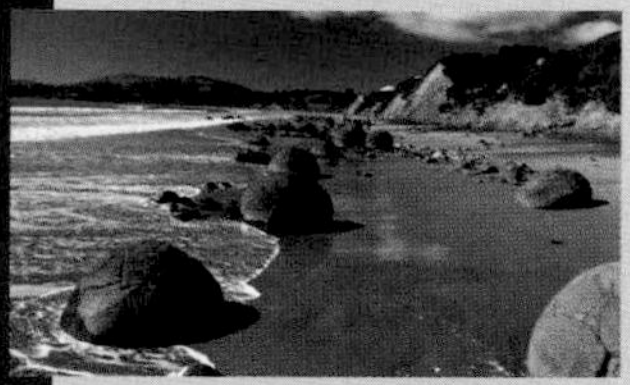

Seashores
Many pterodactyls nested along coastlines, just like modern seabirds. Here, they had easy access to fish and shellfish.

Woodlands
Anurognathus and some of its relatives lived in woodland where they hunted insects. They may have been nocturnal like bats.

Fern meadows
Azhdarchids, such as *Quetzalcoatlus*, pursued prey far inland. Their many habitats included fern meadows and woodlands.

Freshwater lakes
Many Cretaceous pterosaurs fished in freshwater lakes. They include *Dsungaripterus* and *Ctenochasma*.

How to: **fly like a pterosaur**

01. ■ Thrust your wings down and back, in order to power yourself forwards. This is your downstroke.

02. ■ Now contract your muscles to raise your wings, which are slightly folded. This is your midway position.

03. ■ Once your wings are at their highest point (the upstroke), get ready for the next downstroke!

ANSWER: All of these ideas have been put forward by experts at some time or another, but h) is the only likely purpose of the crest; b), f), and g) may also have been true; a), c) d), and e) are just plain silly!

Which ancient lizard **looks like a fish?**

Ichthyosaurs were marine reptiles with streamlined bodies, paddlelike limbs, pointed snouts, and a tail fin. Some looked like swordfish, some were deep-diving squid-eaters with huge eyes, and some were giant, sharp-toothed predators. Despite their success, they died out before the end of the Cretaceous, perhaps because of competition from new sharks.

WHAT'S IN A NAME?

Ichthyosaur means "fish lizard". Ichthyosaurs evolved **fishy features** to adapt to life in the sea, but their lizardlike ancestors lived on land.

FAST FACTS

Ichthyosaurs

01: Ichthyosaurs evolved during the Triassic.

02: The first ichthyosaurs were small – less than 1 m (3.3 ft) long.

03: Ichthyosaurs lived in oceans worldwide.

04: Ichthyosaurs lacked scales and had smooth, tight skin.

05: Ichthyosaurs did not come ashore to lay eggs. They had live young out at sea.

06: Ichthyosaurs did not rely on sonar like dolphins. They relied on sight and smell.

07: Later ichthyosaurs were probably warm-blooded.

Tell me more: **ichthyosaur anatomy**

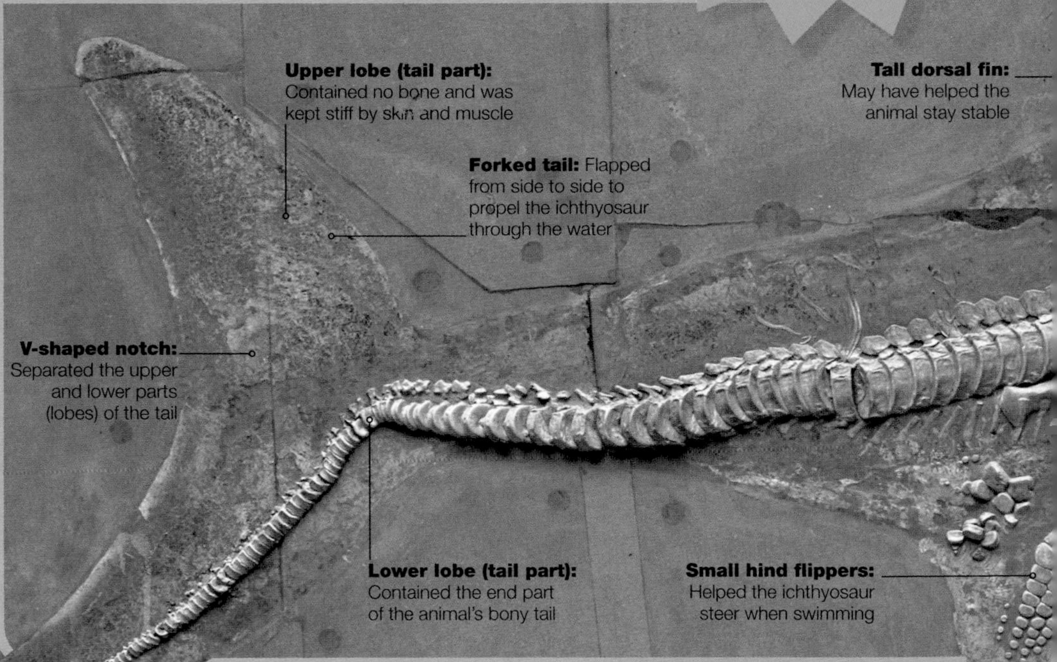

Upper lobe (tail part): Contained no bone and was kept stiff by skin and muscle
Tall dorsal fin: May have helped the animal stay stable
Forked tail: Flapped from side to side to propel the ichthyosaur through the water
V-shaped notch: Separated the upper and lower parts (lobes) of the tail
Lower lobe (tail part): Contained the end part of the animal's bony tail
Small hind flippers: Helped the ichthyosaur steer when swimming

I don't believe it!

Some ichthyosaurs grew new fingers to broaden their paddles, and new phalanges (finger bones) to lengthen them. *Platypterygius* had ten fingers per paddle, and some fingers were made up of more than 30 phalanges!

In numbers

1 or 2 The usual number of babies found inside fossilized pregnant female ichthyosaurs

11 The exceptionally high number of babies preserved within one pregnant ichthyosaur

6.8 kph (4.2 mph) The average swimming speed of the tuna-shaped *Stenopterygius*

26 cm (10.2 in) The minimum eyeball size in the large ichthyosaur *Temnodontosaurus*

600 m (2,000 ft) The likely depth to which *Ophthalmosaurus* could dive

120 The number of vertebrae present in some long-bodied ichthyosaurs

RECORD BREAKER

The 23-cm (9-in) eyes of ***Ophthalmosaurus*** were, for its body size, the largest of any vertebrate. Scientists have worked out that this ichthyosaur's sight was as keen as that of cats and other animals with excellent night vision.

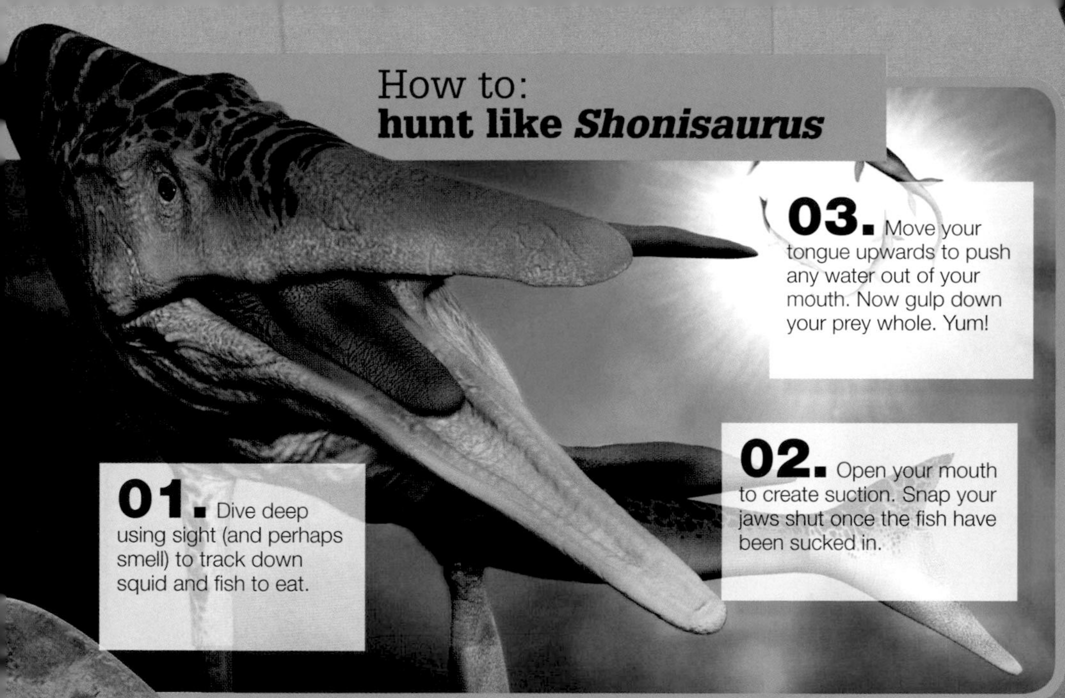

How to: **hunt like *Shonisaurus***

01. Dive deep using sight (and perhaps smell) to track down squid and fish to eat.

02. Open your mouth to create suction. Snap your jaws shut once the fish have been sucked in.

03. Move your tongue upwards to push any water out of your mouth. Now gulp down your prey whole. Yum!

Changing appearances

At first, ichthyosaurs were thought to be straight-tailed, like crocodiles. Palaeontologists thought the bent tail had been accidentally broken.

Later finds showed that advanced ichthyosaurs were shark-shaped animals with dorsal fins and forked tails.

A couple of experts have suggested that ichthyosaurs used their front fins to "fly" underwater, like penguins. However, this idea is not widely accepted.

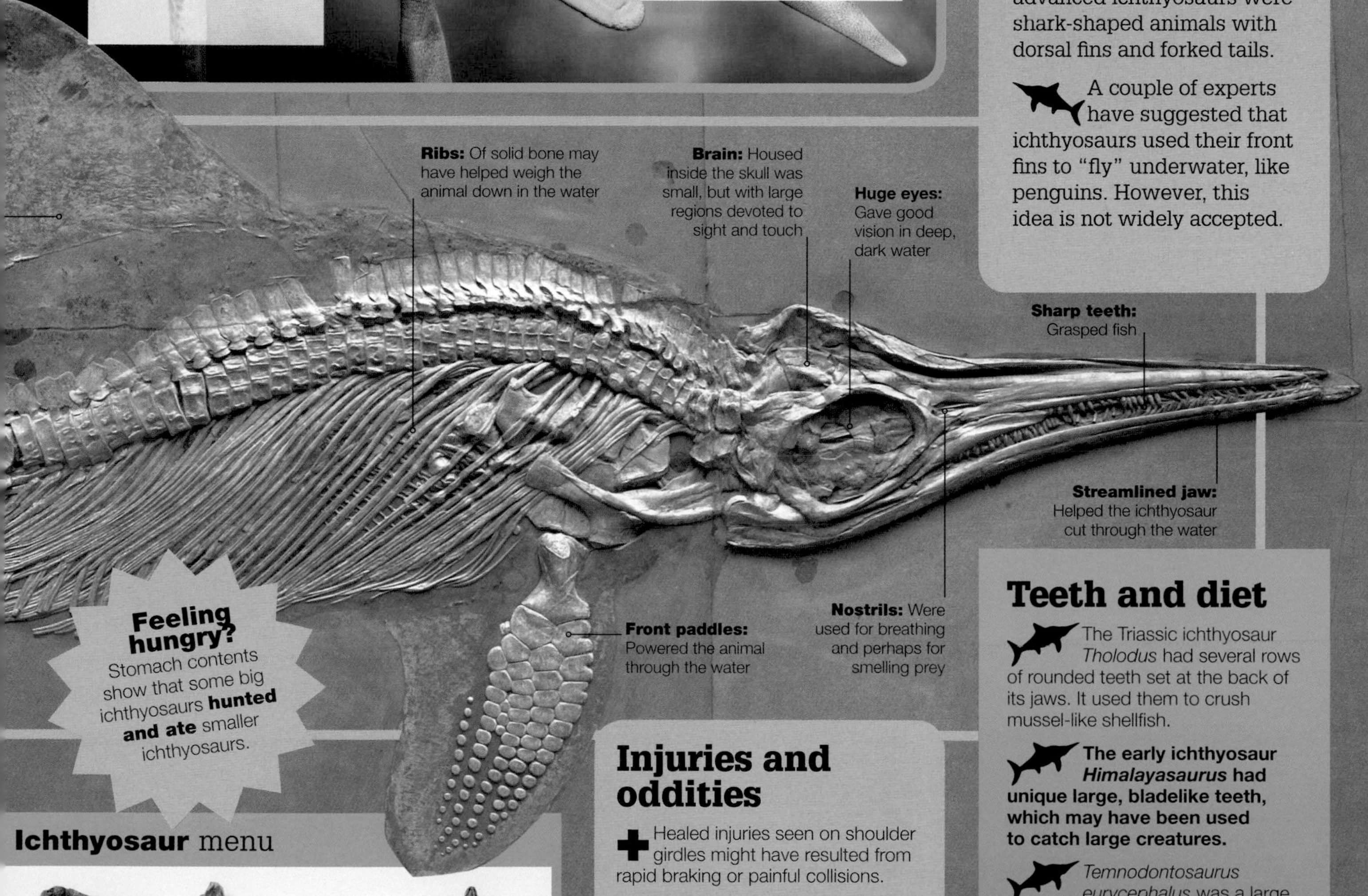
Ribs: Of solid bone may have helped weigh the animal down in the water
Brain: Housed inside the skull was small, but with large regions devoted to sight and touch
Huge eyes: Gave good vision in deep, dark water
Sharp teeth: Grasped fish
Streamlined jaw: Helped the ichthyosaur cut through the water
Nostrils: Were used for breathing and perhaps for smelling prey
Front paddles: Powered the animal through the water

Feeling hungry? Stomach contents show that some big ichthyosaurs **hunted and ate** smaller ichthyosaurs.

Ichthyosaur menu

Shellfish
Fish
Turtles
Belemnites (extinct squidlike creatures)
Seabirds

Injuries and oddities

- Healed injuries seen on shoulder girdles might have resulted from rapid braking or painful collisions.
- In some ichthyosaur specimens, one front paddle is longer than the other. No one knows why.
- Sometimes ichthyosaur nostrils are asymmetrical – different to each other in shape and size.
- Bite marks on some ichthyosaur bones show that they were preyed on by other marine reptiles.
- Fractured ribs seen in some ichthyosaurs suggest that some species fought by ramming each other's bodies.

Teeth and diet

The Triassic ichthyosaur *Tholodus* had several rows of rounded teeth set at the back of its jaws. It used them to crush mussel-like shellfish.

The early ichthyosaur *Himalayasaurus* had unique large, bladelike teeth, which may have been used to catch large creatures.

Temnodontosaurus eurycephalus was a large ichthyosaur very like a killer whale. It had deep jaws and massive teeth.

Leptonectoids were ichthyosaurs that looked like swordfish. They had slender paddles and very long upper jaws. They probably chased belemnites, squid, and small fish.

Platypterygius from the Cretaceous ate whatever it could catch. Fossiliized stomach contents have included turtles, seabirds, and fish.

Which animals lived in the Ice Age?

The Pleistocene – the time from 2.5 million to 10,000 years ago – had several ice ages, when polar ice covered northern parts of Europe, Asia, and North America. Many land mammals had thick coats to cope with cold climates. Others lived in warmer parts of the world.

The Pleistocene world

- With so much sea water locked up in polar ice, Pleistocene sea levels were as much as 120 m (400 ft) lower than present ones.
- **The Bering land bridge connected North America to Asia. Mammoths, jaguars, and lions crossed between the two.**
- The Central American land bridge formed before the Pleistocene. It allowed sloths, armadillos, and capybaras to move north, and big cats, horses, and camels to move south.
- **Australia and New Guinea were linked during the Pleistocene. Both had marsupial wolves and kangaroos.**
- Africa and Arabia were connected to Asia long before the Pleistocene started. African animals migrated to Asia and Europe, and vice versa.

RECORD BREAKER

The steppe mammoth was one of the **biggest mammoths** – it stood 4.5 m (14.8 ft) tall!

There were about **a dozen** mammoth species, found across Africa, Asia, Europe, and North America.

How to: be a woolly mammoth

01. Survive when food is scarce by drawing on stored energy in your large, fatty hump (like a modern camel's).

02. Have large, broad teeth so that you can browse on grass, leaves, and other plant foods.

03. Stay cosy in the bitter cold. You'll need a layer of fat beneath the skin, a thick, hairy undercoat, and coarse, 1-m- (3.3-ft-) long top hairs.

04. Use your long, curved tusks to battle rivals, dig up plants, and scrape bark off trees.

Back to life

Scientists have taken DNA from a brilliantly preserved frozen baby mammoth carcass, known as the Yamal mammoth. They may be able to use it to create a clone – and bring mammoths back from extinction!

Cave art

Works of art by early people tell us a lot about extinct and modern animals.

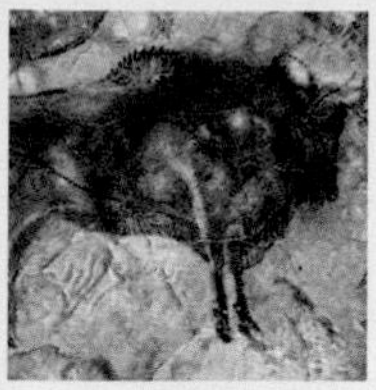

Pleistocene bison looked like modern kinds, but with thick manes and beards.

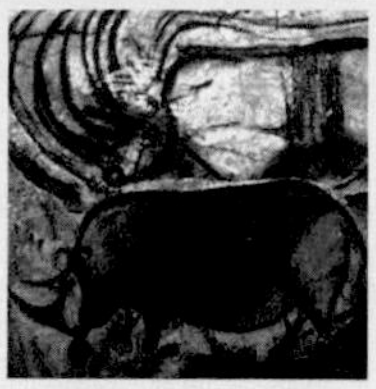

Cave art shows that the woolly rhinoceros had a band of darker hair around its middle.

The antlers on these red deer stags were probably exaggerated to look impressive.

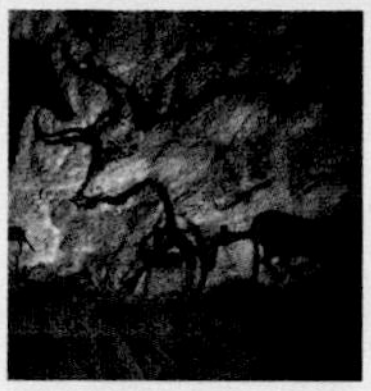

The aurochs was a huge wild cow that stood 2 m (6.6 ft) at the shoulder.

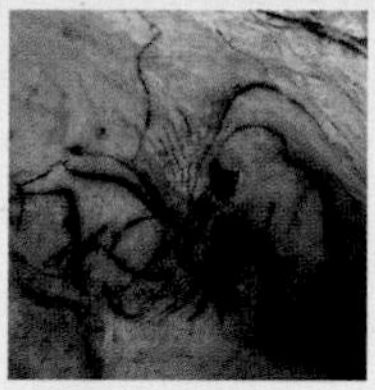

Here, a mammoth overlaps an aurochs. The two wouldn't have been so close in life!

Top spots for Pleistocene mammal fossils

- Inside ancient limestone caves
- Frozen in the Siberian or Alaskan tundra
- In the peat bogs of Ireland, Denmark, and Germany
- At the bottom of the North Sea (it was dry land for part of the Pleistocene)
- Submerged in the swamps of Kentucky, Florida
- In ancient riverbank deposits worldwide
- In sediments from ancient lakes, such as Lake Turkana in Kenya
- In the tar pits of California and Peru

Pleistocene predators

- Australia was home to the gigantic lizard *Varanus priscus*, which was up to 7 m (23 ft) long.
- There were giant cheetahs – 50 per cent bigger than modern ones – in Europe and Asia.
- Lions inhabited Europe, Asia, Africa, and North and South America.
- *Smilodon* from the Americas is the best known sabre-toothed cat.
- Other sabre-toothed cats lived in Africa, Europe, and Asia.
- Large, wolflike dogs lived in the Americas and Europe.

Mega deer
The giant deer *Megaloceros* was 2 m (6.6 ft) tall at the shoulder. Its **huge antlers** spanned 3.6 m (11.8 ft).

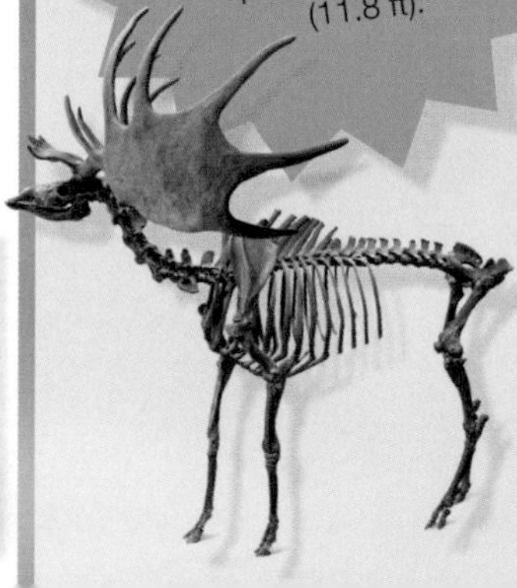

05. Pick grasses, buds, and flowers with your long, flexible trunk, which has two bendy "fingers" at the tip.

Six Pleistocene plant-eaters

The giant beaver *Castoroides* was 2.5 m (8.2 ft) long and weighed 100 kg (220 lb). It lived in North America.

Weighing 4 tonnes, *Megatherium* was a giant ground sloth with deadly claws to use in self defence.

Glyptodon lived in the Americas and looked like a giant armadillo. It was the same size as a VW Beetle car.

Coelodonta was a woolly rhino found across Europe and Asia. It was the same size as a modern white rhino.

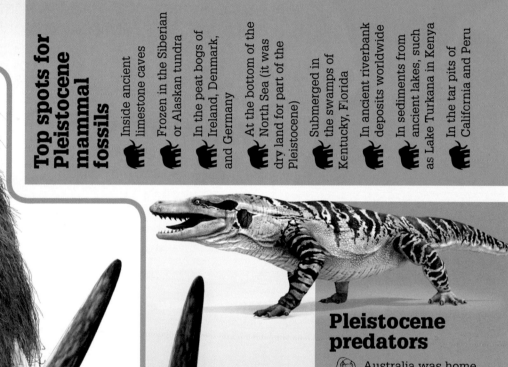

Macrauchenia looked a bit like a llama, but with a tapir's trunk. It was about the same size as a camel.

Where did the earliest humans come from?

Humans are part of a bigger family, called the hominids, that evolved in Africa. Chimps, gorillas, and other great apes are hominids, too. Around seven million years ago, humans split from the apes. Our species – *Homo sapiens* – is about 200,000 years old.

Five facts about Neanderthals

01: Neanderthals evolved in Europe about 350,000 years ago and died out around 30,000 years ago.

02: Archaeologists have found fossils of more than 275 Neanderthals at 70 different sites in Europe and Asia.

03: Neanderthals had bigger brains – and bigger noses! – than us.

04: Neanderthal bodies were short and stocky – ideal for ice age conditions.

05: Could Neanderthals talk? Scientists are still arguing about that!

Using tools

Tool use is not unique to modern humans. Other living hominids – gorillas and chimps – use and make tools too. This chimpanzee is using a stick to dig out termites.

What about me?

Today, *Homo sapiens* is the only hominin (human) species. But more than 20 hominin species have been named from fossils. Some were similar to us, but others were quite different.

Tell me more: **hominin family tree**

Fossils show that humans evolved about seven million years ago (mya). Our fossil history was complicated and many hominin species came and went over the years.

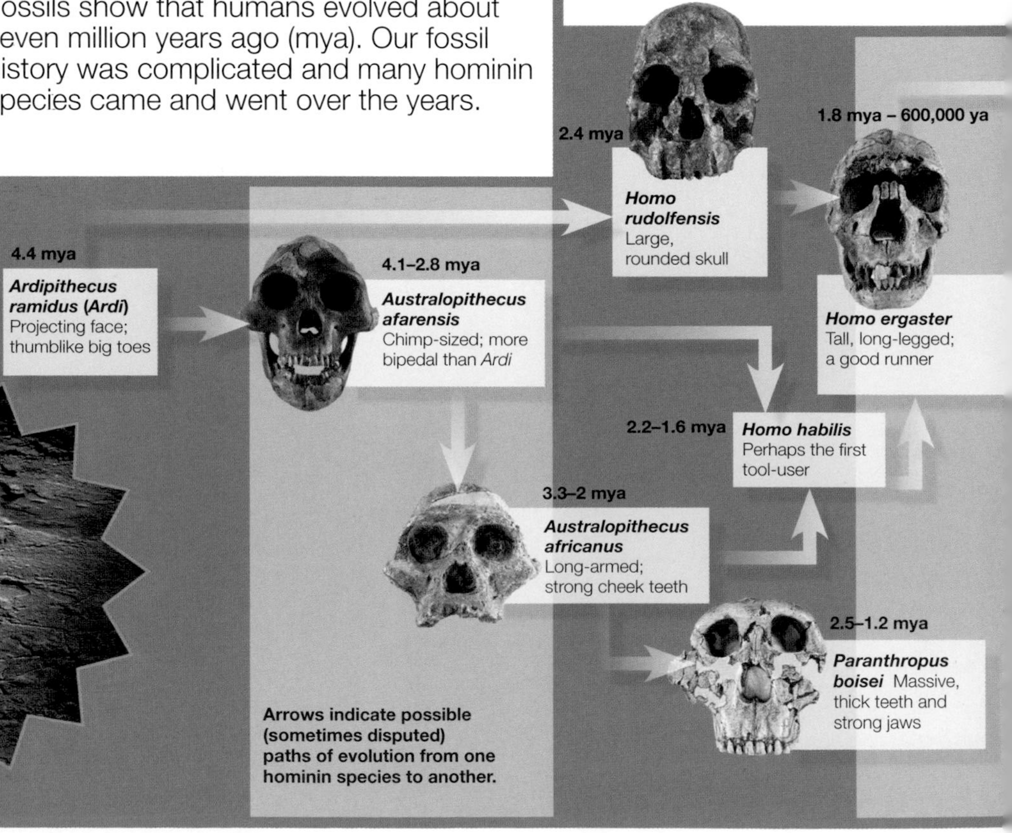

4.4 mya
Ardipithecus ramidus (Ardi) Projecting face; thumblike big toes
4.1–2.8 mya
Australopithecus afarensis Chimp-sized; more bipedal than *Ardi*
3.3–2 mya
Australopithecus africanus Long-armed; strong cheek teeth
2.4 mya
Homo rudolfensis Large, rounded skull
2.2–1.6 mya
Homo habilis Perhaps the first tool-user
1.8 mya – 600,000 ya
Homo ergaster Tall, long-legged; a good runner
2.5–1.2 mya
Paranthropus boisei Massive, thick teeth and strong jaws
Arrows indicate possible (sometimes disputed) paths of evolution from one hominin species to another.

Walking styles

Fossil tracks in Tanzania show that australopithecines (extinct hominids from the *Australopithecus* species) could **walk upright**. Their feet and toes were more flexible than ours, but they already had an arch in the foot.

What's the difference?

apes
- forward-projecting face
- long upper canine teeth
- small brain at 300–350 cm^3 (18–21 in^3)
- long arms
- able to knuckle-walk
- thumblike big toe

early humans
- forward-projecting face
- long upper canine teeth
- small brain at 380–430 cm^3 (23–26 in^3)
- shorter arms
- unable to knuckle-walk
- thumblike big toe

modern humans
- flattened face
- shorter upper canine teeth
- large brain at 1,400 cm^3 (85 in^3)
- shorter arms
- unable to knuckle-walk
- forward-pointing big toe

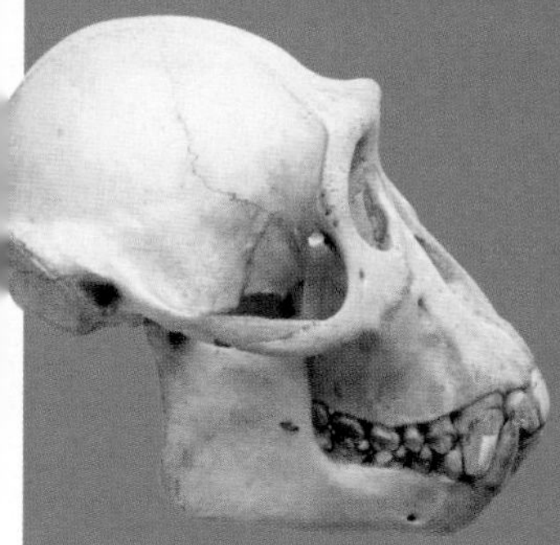
Chimpanzee skull

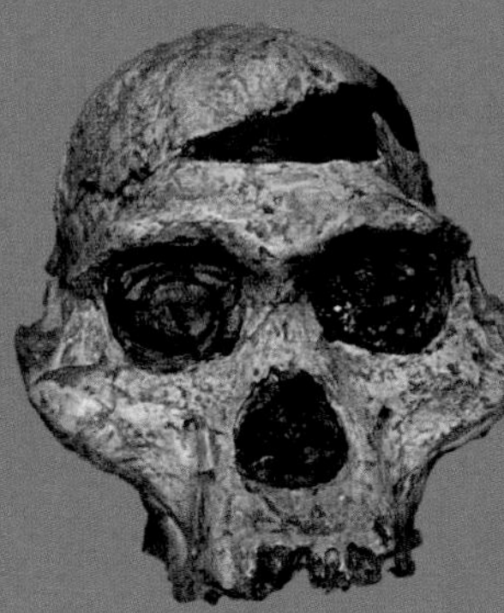
Australopithecine skull

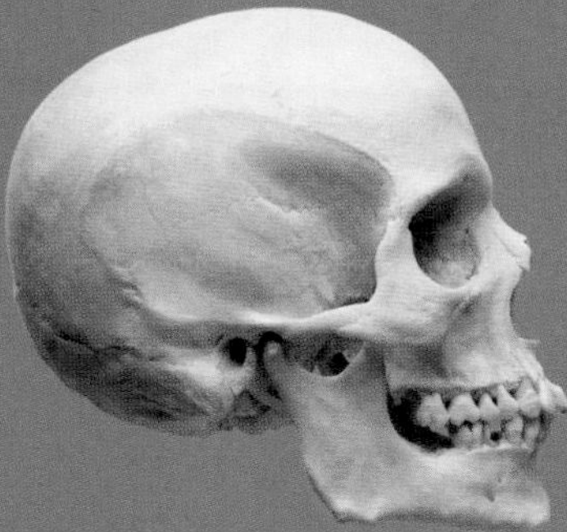
Modern human skull

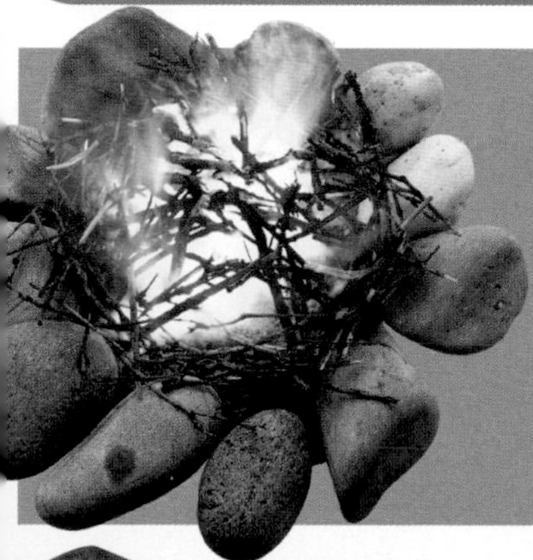

Five fire facts

- Experts disagree over which hominin species was the first to use fire.
- *Homo ergaster* and *Hcmo erectus* may have used fire for cooking 1.6 million years ago.
- Humans used fire long before they knew how to light one. If they found a natural fire – after a lightning strike, for example – they kept it going.
- Knowing how to use fire meant humans could settle in colder climates. Humans colonized cold northern Europe more than 600,000 years ago.
- By about 50,000 years ago, Neanderthals and *Homo sapiens* were using fire to stay warm and cook meat. They struck flints to produce sparks that lit dry wood.

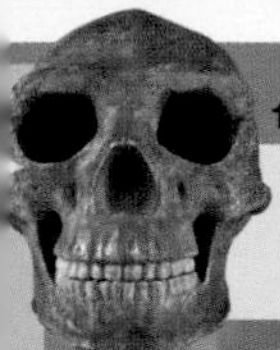
1.8 mya – 27,000 ya
Homo erectus Long-lived; thick jaw bones; brow ridges

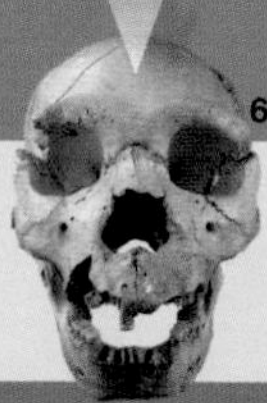
600,000–250,000 ya
Homo heidelbergensis Neanderthal-like; robust limbs; large brain; thick skull

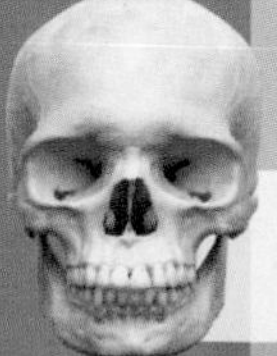
200,000 ya – present
Homo sapiens Flat face; projecting chin; small brow ridges

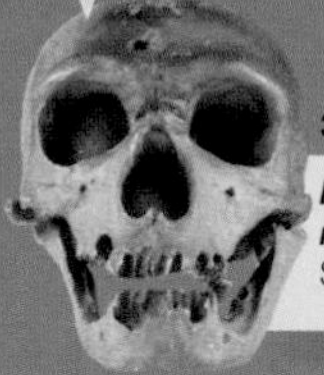
350,000–30,000 ya
Homo neanderthalensis Stocky; large brain

I don't believe it!

In 2004, a new hominin was found on the island of Flores in Indonesia. *Homo floresiensis* has been nicknamed "the Hobbit" after the little characters in JRR Tolkien's books. The hominin stood just 1 m (3.3 ft) tall.

Chimplike climber

Australopithecus afarensis is one of the **earliest hominins**. Its long arms and curved finger bones suggest that it was very good at climbing trees.

Five special fossil finds

01 *Australopithecus bahrelghazali* (named 1997) Discovered in Chad, further north in Africa than most australopithecines, this find proves that the group was more widespread than experts first thought.

02 *Homo antecessor* (named 1997) A Spanish species that seems to show that *Homo ergaster*-like hominins staged an early colonization of Europe.

03 *Kenyanthropus platyops* (named 2001) A weird hominin that has a flattened face and very narrow nose.

04 *Orrorin tugenensis* (named 2001) A controversial hominin whose leg bones suggest that it was one of the first bipedal walkers.

05 *Sahelanthropus tchadensis* (named 2002) A hominid that might be close to the ancestor of the chimp and hominin lineages.

FAST FACTS

Human migration

01: Hominids and hominins evolved in Africa.

02: By about 1.8 mya, *Homo erectus* occurred in Asia.

03: *Homo erectus* spread across Asia and parts of Europe, and survived until 27,000 years ago.

04: The earliest members of a group of species that later included Neanderthals may have moved out of Africa about 1 mya.

05: Several other species left Africa independently. The ancestors of *Homo floresiensis* left Africa more than 100,000 years ago.

06: *Homo sapiens* evolved in Africa about 200,000 years ago, and migrated to Europe and Asia about 45,000 years ago.

Who brings fossil animals back to life?

How to: **reconstruct an *Edmontosaurus***

Scientists work together with specialist artists (palaeo-artists) to create lifelike paintings and models of fossil animals. It is one of the main ways they show off their finds. The process is not easy. Often, scientists cannot agree on basic details. Artists need a thorough knowledge of modern animal anatomy.

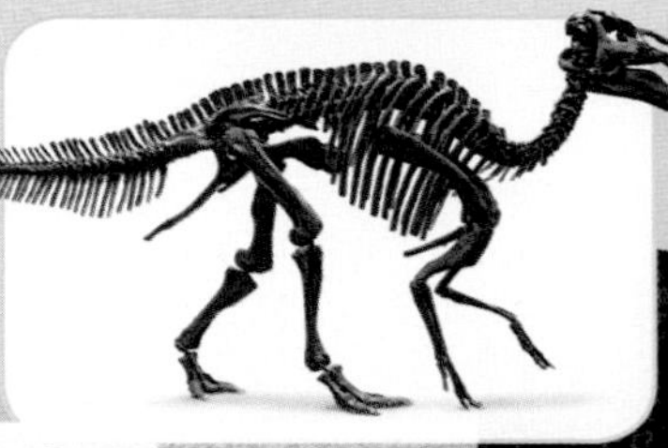

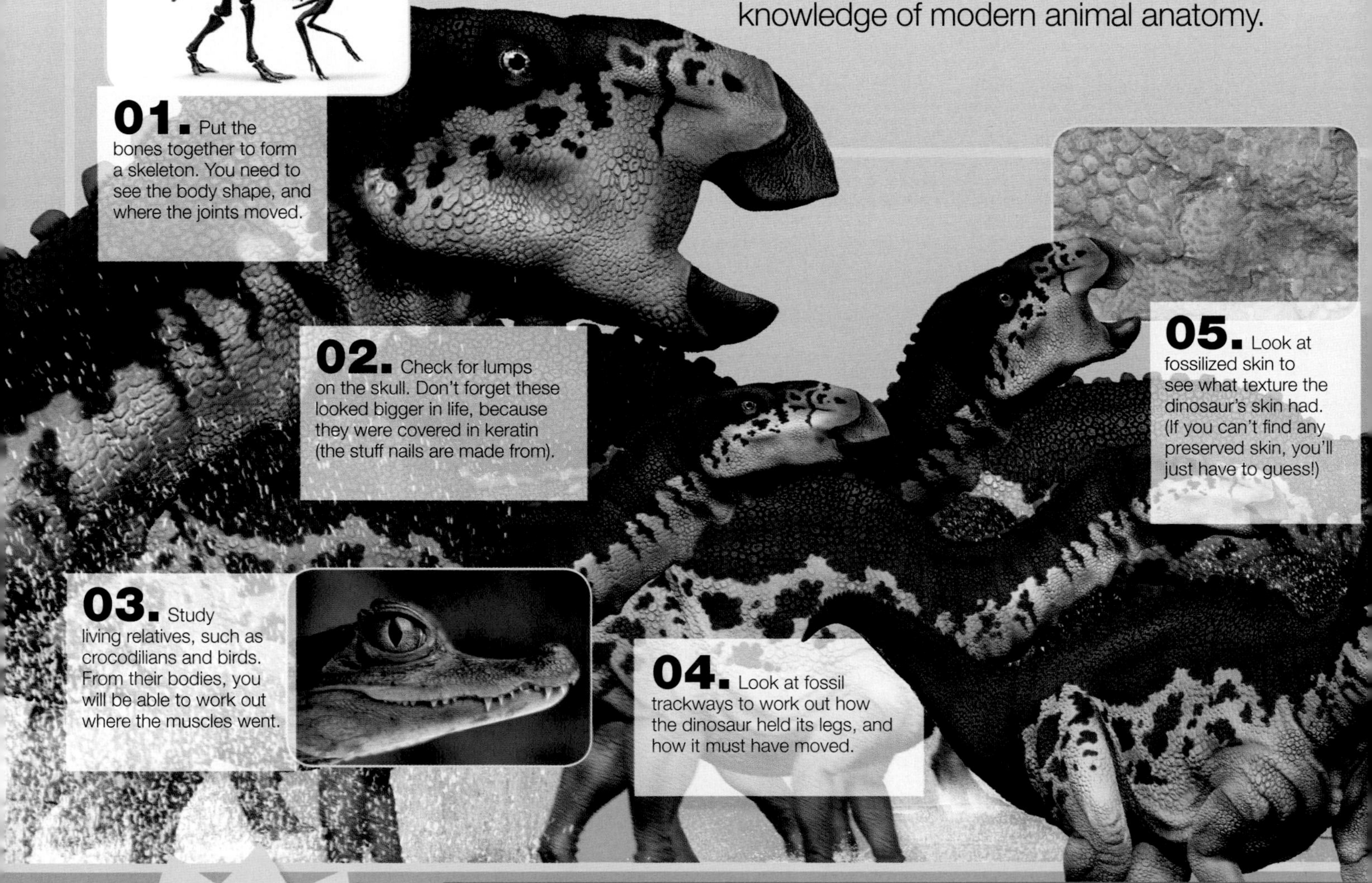

01. Put the bones together to form a skeleton. You need to see the body shape, and where the joints moved.

02. Check for lumps on the skull. Don't forget these looked bigger in life, because they were covered in keratin (the stuff nails are made from).

03. Study living relatives, such as crocodilians and birds. From their bodies, you will be able to work out where the muscles went.

04. Look at fossil trackways to work out how the dinosaur held its legs, and how it must have moved.

05. Look at fossilized skin to see what texture the dinosaur's skin had. (If you can't find any preserved skin, you'll just have to guess!)

WHAT'S IN A NAME?

Palaeo-art is the name for reconstructing fossil animals. But the same word means prehistoric cave art. So some experts prefer the term **palaeontography** for fossil reconstruction.

Top tools for cleaning a fossil

Hammer and chisel: Used for removing large chunks of rock

Saw: Used closer to the fossilized bone, to clean away smaller areas of rock

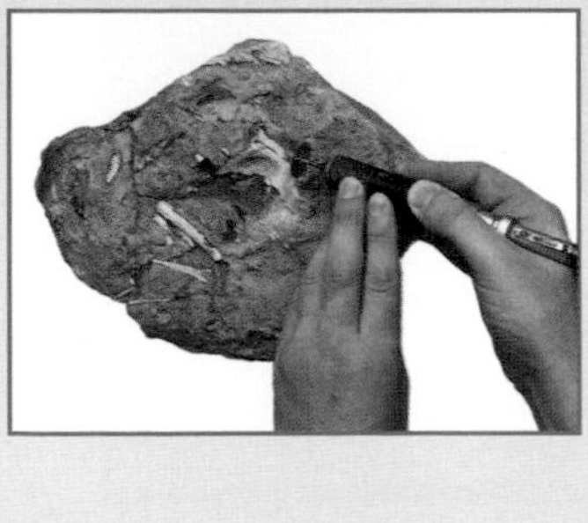

Dental drill: Used for the delicate cleaning that reveals the fine details

Different techniques

01: Artists sketch their reconstructions before producing paintings. They base their work on fossils.

02: Artists often study mounted skeletons – but sometimes these have been put together incorrectly.

03: Some artists make a model of the skeleton, then work with clay to add an accurate body shape.

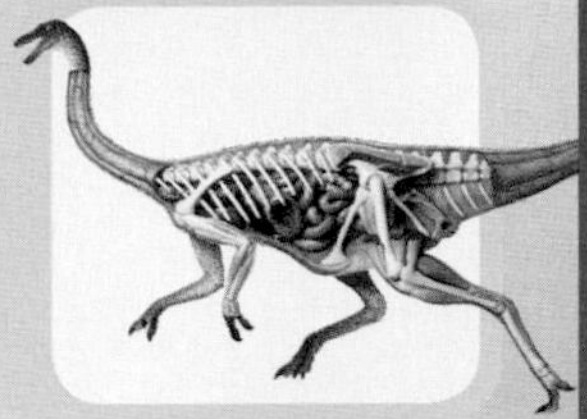

04: Many people create CG (computer generated) models. The results can be spectacular!

Special insights

The better preserved a fossil is, the more it can tell us:

Fossils from fine limestones and other rocks sometimes show the outline of the body.

Some fossils even reveal details such as skin colour and patterns.

Volcanic ash can rapidly bury a dead animal and preserve parts that normally rot. Some still have fur or feathers.

Bodies preserved in permafrost (ground that is always frozen) may still have skin and muscle.

Mammoths and other Pleistocene animals were painted by prehistoric people. Cave art helps us to reconstruct them with confidence.

Colour **rules**

Studying living animals allows scientists to make educated guesses about the colours and patterns of extinct creatures:

Elephant
Large animals have plain colours. They rely on size and loud noises to attract mates.

Arabian oryx
Large desert animals are often pale. Dark colours would absorb more of the Sun's heat.

Cape buffalo
Being dark makes herd animals appear as one large mass and puts off predators.

Okapi
Forest animals sometimes have stripes that look like lines of light and shadow.

Tragopan
Animals that live in shady habitats may have bright or iridescent (metallic) display patches for attracting females.

Peacock
Crests and other display structures are usually brightly coloured to catch a mate's attention.

06. Feed all the data you've gathered into your computer. Use special software to build a 3D model of *Edmontosaurus*.

Onscreen reconstructions

The Lost World (1925) was one of the first films to feature stop-motion dinosaurs and other prehistoric animals. The effects look poor to modern eyes, but were revolutionary for the time and amazed audiences. ***Jurassic Park*** (1993) aimed to bring accurate CG dinosaurs to the big screen. The tyrannosaur looked excellent but the "raptors" (based on *Deinonychus*) were wrongly given scaly bodies instead of feathers. ***Walking with Dinosaurs*** (1999) showed that low-budget CG could be produced for TV. Some of the animals, such as the *Tyrannosaurus*, were highly inaccurate, but others, including *Iguanodon* and some of the marine reptiles, were portrayed very well.

Three positive results of palaeo-art

01 Reconstructions help people to picture an animal – and be amazed by it.

02 Many scientists were inspired at an early age by murals, paintings, or sculptures.

03 Some details about body size and shape aren't obvious until a reconstruction is made.

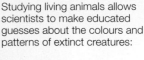

Five famous palaeo-artists

Charles Knight: A hugely influential American artist, who produced work from the 1890s to the 1950s. During this time, the public's understanding of the prehistoric world was based almost entirely on his art.

Zdeněk Burian: A Czech artist whose best known work was produced in the 1960s and 1970s. He painted detailed, vibrant landscapes.

Greg Paul: An American artist who has pioneered the scientifically accurate reconstruction of dinosaurs.

Tell me more: **reading fossils**

Fossils can tell palaeontologists about when a creature lived, and give clues to its features and characteristics. The story changes as new fossil discoveries provide new details. Oviraptorids were originally believed to be egg-stealing predators (oviraptorid means "egg thief"). One skeleton was discovered close to an egg-filled nest thought to belong to the horned dinosaur *Protoceratops*. Experts assumed that the oviraptorid had been caught stealing and was killed. Recently, the oviraptorid *Citipati* has been discovered sitting on top of the same kind of nest. This shows that oviraptorids were not stealing other dinosaurs' eggs, but looking after their own.

Citipati

Fossils give experts the details they need to paint an accurate picture of dinosaur lives. *Citipati* was one of many birdlike dinosaurs of the late Cretaceous era. It would have had feathers on its arms, tail, and body. More complete fossils of smaller relatives show that there was a fanlike arrangement of tail feathers and long feathers on the arms and hands. Like many oviraptorids, *Citipati* had a large, hollow, bony crest on its head. This might have been used in mating displays.

Flexible neck: Arrangement and number of vertebrae show that *Citipati* had a long and flexible neck
Large eye socket: Indicates that *Citipati* had large eyes and good eyesight
Upper skeleton: Had mostly been worn away by wind (the arms and legs were not yet exposed when the fossil was discovered)
Long arm: Gave the dinosaur good reach for pulling at branches on trees and shrubs or for grabbing animal prey
Nostrils: Were either side of the bony crest that projected upwards from the beak
Protective position: Arm sheltering eggs mirrors a protective posture used by today's nesting birds
Strong beak: Parrotlike beak around powerful, toothless jaws could have cracked nuts, seeds, and other hard objects
Long feathers: Would have covered the arms of a live *Citipati*, and helped keep its eggs warm while it was sitting on its nest

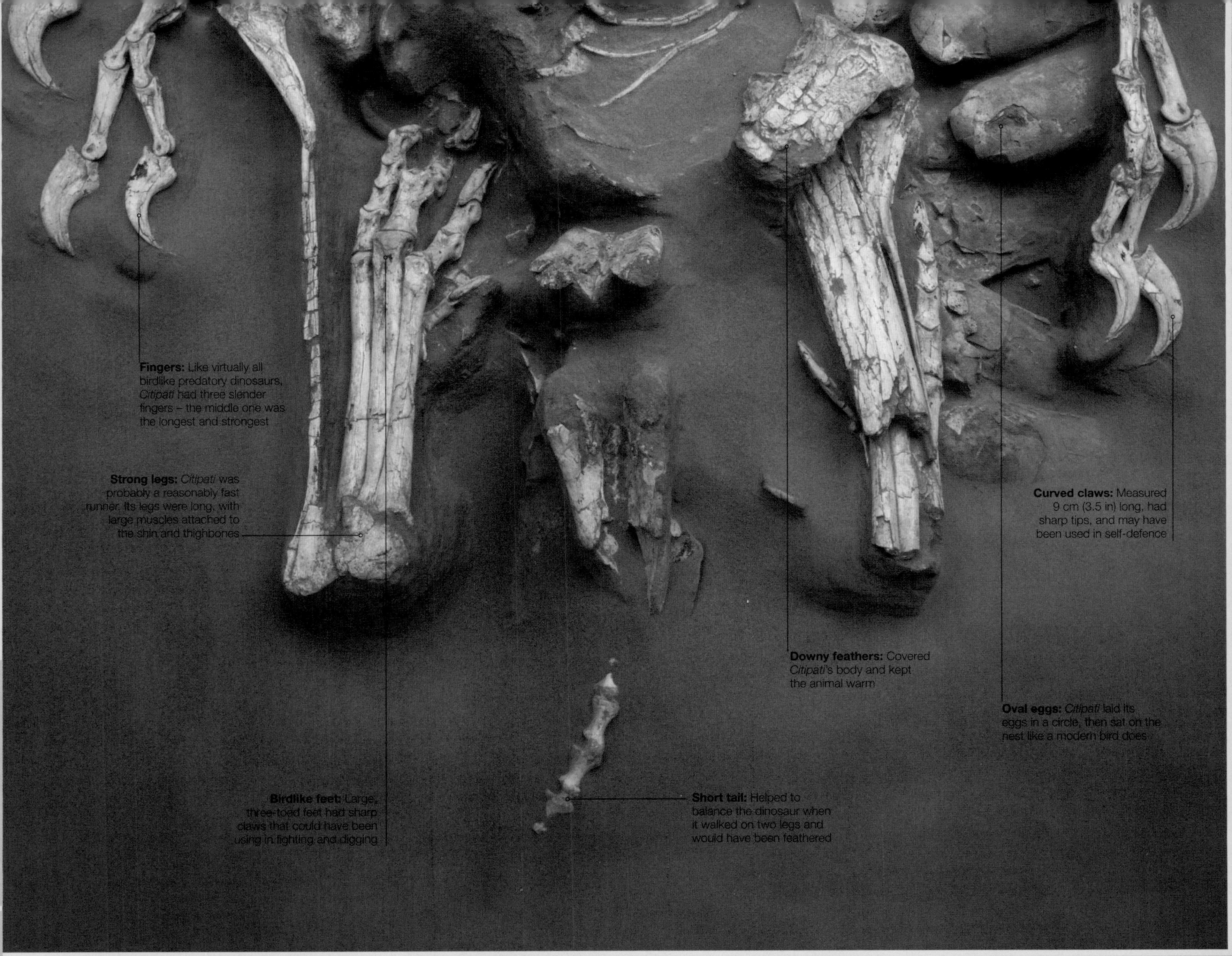
Fingers: Like virtually all birdlike predatory dinosaurs, *Citipati* had three slender fingers – the middle one was the longest and strongest
Strong legs: *Citipati* was probably a reasonably fast runner. Its legs were long, with large muscles attached to the shin and thighbones
Birdlike feet: Large, three-toed feet had sharp claws that could have been using in fighting and digging
Short tail: Helped to balance the dinosaur when it walked on two legs and would have been feathered
Downy feathers: Covered *Citipati*'s body and kept the animal warm
Curved claws: Measured 9 cm (3.5 in) long, had sharp tips, and may have been used in self-defence
Oval eggs: *Citipati* laid its eggs in a circle, then sat on the nest like a modern bird does

Nature

What is evolution?

Evolution is the gradual change over time that produces new species. Life on Earth began billions of years ago. Some organisms, because of their genetic make-up, have always been more likely to survive and breed than others. This natural selection is the driving force of evolution – and it has led to today's amazing diversity of species.

Blasts from the past

3.5 billion years ago (bya)
Earliest life-forms – bacteria

3.4 bya
First stromatolites

565 million years ago (mya)
Ediacarans – first complex animals

545 mya
Molluscs evolve protective shells

520 mya
Explosion of ocean life, including sponges, worms, and arthropods

480 mya
First vertebrate – a jawless fish

460 mya
First land plants

428 mya
First land animals – arthropods

420 mya
First fish with jaws

400 mya
First insects

375 mya
Tiktaalik marks transition between fish and tetrapods (four-legged creatures)

360 mya
First land vertebrates

315 mya
First reptiles, such as *Hylonomus*

295 mya
Sail-backed reptiles, such as *Dimetrodon*

245 mya
Marine reptiles, such as nothosaurs and ichthyosaurs

228 mya
First dinosaurs, such as *Eoraptor*

200 mya
First, shrewlike mammals

151 mya
First known birds

130 mya
First flowering plants

122 mya
First feathered dinosaurs, such as *Microraptor*

65 mya
Mass extinction of many animal groups, including the dinosaurs

62 mya
Explosion of new mammal species

60 mya
First grasses

7 mya
Earliest hominins (humans), such as *Sahelanthropus*

1.8 mya
Homo habilis, a possible ancestor of modern humans

Fantastic fossil evidence

- The coiled shells of sea creatures called ammonites evolved from ancestors with straight and curved shells.
- Cynodonts were the first reptiles to have mammal features, such as hair and warm-blooded bodies, but they still laid eggs.
- Charles Darwin found the remains of an extinct mammal, *Glyptodon*, and realized it was a relative of modern armadillos living in South America.
- A *Sahelanthropus* skull known as "Toumai" belongs to an apelike human who lived around seven million years ago – about the time that chimps and humans parted company from a common ancestor.
- Stromatolites – structures made up of bacteria and sediment – are the oldest-known fossils. Living stromatolites can be seen in the warm, shallow waters off the coast of Western Australia.

How to: evolve (over many generations

01. Get better at escaping predators. You need to be able to outrun animals that prey on primitive rabbits like yourself.

02. Grow slightly longer legs – that'll make you faster. Certain genes in your body will make this possible.

Growing apart

Asiatic and American **black bears** shared a common ancestor about four million years ago. They still look alike because of their similar habitat and diet.

In North America, **polar bears** evolved from **brown bears** around 100,000 years ago. Brown bears eat plants as well as meat; polar bears are meat-eaters.

What about me?

Human evolution continues. In the past 10,000 years, for example, Europeans have evolved a tolerance for milk and cheese into adulthood, whereas people from China and most of Africa have not.

05. Evolve – slowly – over time. Over many generations, more and more of your species will have longer legs. One day, you'll all have become modern, long-legged rabbits.

04. Pass on your advantage! Your longer-legged offspring will have a greater chance of survival.

03. Breed and produce lots of young. Being more likely to survive and breed is called natural selection.

When they become separated, animal populations may evolve into new species. This happens as each group adapts to its different environment.

The **Galápagos Islands** in the Pacific Ocean are home to many creatures that are found nowhere else on Earth. These include the marine iguana.

Madagascar separated from mainland Africa about 160 million years ago. Of its land mammals, 98 per cent are unique, including 50 types of lemur.

FAST FACTS

Evolutionary experts

Jean-Baptiste Lamarck (1744–1829) argued wrongly that organisms could pass on features they acquired in their lifetime.

Charles Darwin (1809–1882) came up with the theory of evolution by natural selection.

Gregor Mendel (1822–1884) guessed that tiny particles (genes) pass on characteristics.

James Watson (b. 1928), **Francis Crick** (1916–2004), and **Rosalind Franklin** (1920–1958) discovered the structure of DNA, which contains the instructions for life.

Richard Dawkins (b. 1941) put forward the "selfish gene" idea that organisms exist only to pass on their DNA.

RECORD BREAKER

In 2001, a **bacterium** was killing 99 per cent of male blue moon butterflies. The immune ones bred – and the population evolved and recovered in just a year.

I don't believe it!

Humans and our closest relatives, chimps, have about three billion DNA bases or "letters". The recipe for building a chimp is 96 per cent identical to that for a human.

Hey, good-looking...

Peacocks
Male peacocks evolved brightly coloured tail feathers. The glossy feathers show females that the male is in good health.

Elephant seals
Male elephant seals are more than twice the size of females. Being big and strong means they can overcome male rivals.

Red deer
Male red deer compete for females by roaring and fighting. They have evolved impressive antlers and a fearsome bellow.

Alien life?

In the late 1970s scientists were astonished to find fish, mussels, and crabs living in the dark ocean depths around bubbling springs called "**black smokers**". If life could survive there, where else might it be?

Nine incredible examples of animals that evolved... and one that didn't!

01. In just three million years, 14 finch species have evolved in the Galápagos Islands.

Large ground finch: Lives on the ground and has a big beak for crushing large, hard seeds.

Vegetarian finch: Lives in trees and has a parrotlike beak for eating fruit and seeds.

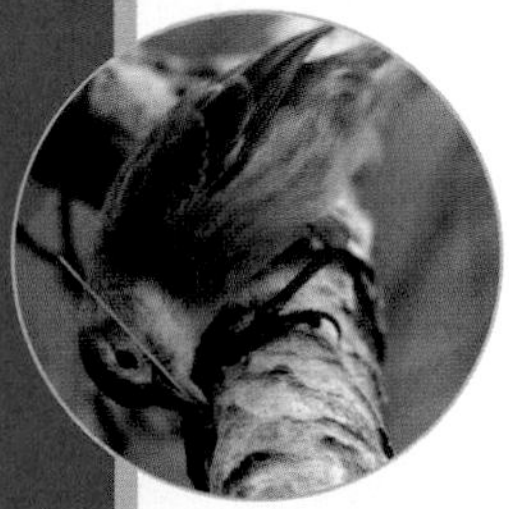

Woodpecker finch: Lives in trees and has a probing beak for finding and eating grubs and insects.

Medium tree finch: Lives in trees and has a bill adapted for grasping insects, buds, and leaves.

Medium ground finch: Lives on the ground. Its beak size shows natural selection in action (birds with larger beaks are more successful during periods of drought).

Cactus finch: Lives on cacti and has a beak suitable for eating cactus nectar, fruit, and seeds.

02. Over about 3.6 million years, Australian lizards called skinks lost their limbs. They spend most of their time "swimming" through sand or soil, so arms and legs just get in the way.

03. Cane toads were introduced into Australia in 1935. Today's toads have legs 10 per cent longer than their ancestors', so they are able to move faster and further.

04. Whales may have evolved from a deerlike land mammal. *Indohyus* lived 47 million years ago and had an ear bone like a whale's.

06. *Tiktaalik* lived 375 million years ago. This fish could prop itself up on its front fins, so it is a key link to the first land animals.

07. Bighorn sheep have become about 20 per cent smaller in the past 30 years. This is because human hunters shoot the biggest animals.

05. The moray eel cannot create enough suction to draw in prey as other fish do. The eel has evolved a second set of hidden jaws. They pop out and drag food into the mouth.

09. Darwin predicted that only a moth with a 28-cm (11-in) mouthpart could feed from this star orchid. The moth was discovered 40 years later.

08. Sticklebacks lose their spiny back fins if they live in predator-free lakes. These fish will become a new species.

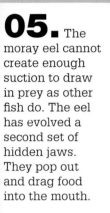

Still going strong...
The coelacanth was thought to have died out with the dinosaurs, until fishermen caught one in 1938. Its perfect body design has not changed for 400 million years.

Why do flowers look and smell so good?

FAST FACTS

Flowering plants

01: Flowering plants occur in almost every land habitat on Earth.

02: Sea grasses are the only flowering plants in the sea.

03: There are two main groups of flowering plants: monocots and dicots.

04: Monocots have leaves with parallel veins, and flower parts arranged in threes.

05: Dicots have net-veined leaves, and flower parts in fours or fives.

06: Some flowers open during the day and close when it is dark.

07: Flowering plants provide food for our livestock and also for us.

08: Flowering plants produce vegetables and fruit, as well as grains, nuts, oils, sugars, and spices.

Plants use bright flowers and strong scents to attract insects, bats, and birds, which feed on nectar inside the flower. The animals enable flowering plants to reproduce by carrying their pollen – which brushes on to them as they feed – from flower to flower.

The *Puya raimondi* is a very rare plant that grows in the Andes Mountains of South America. It may wait an incredible **140 years** before blooming and then dying! Its stunning flower head can be 10 m (33 ft) tall.

How to: **attract a hummingbird**

01. Choose your flower shape carefully. A long tube is a good match for a hummingbird's beak.

02. Don't bother too much about scent. Hummingbirds have a poor sense of smell, so they rely on sight.

03. Use bold, bright colours to draw attention to yourself. Hummingbirds are especially attracted to the colour red.

04. Make your visitor reach deep for the nectar. That way, its body will be dusted with lots of pollen.

Some families of **flowering plants**

Water lilies
These freshwater plants have their roots in the soil, while their leaves and flowers float on the surface.

Grasses
Rice, wheat, maize, and bamboo are all types of grasses. They have small flowers without petals.

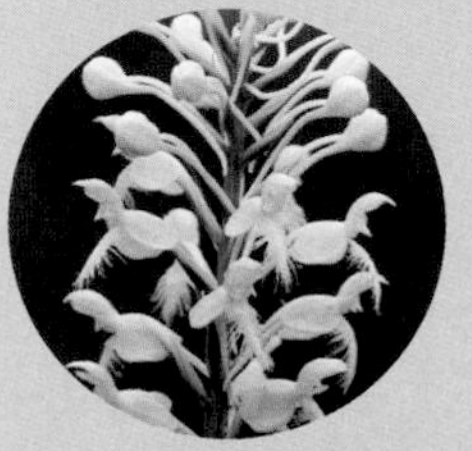

Orchids
There are 25,000 species of orchid, making it the largest plant family. Many have delicate clusters of flowers.

Palms
Tropical flowering plants, palms have evergreen leaves and a straight stem with no branches.

Lilies
This family of plants with strongly scented flowers includes daffodils, tulips, onions, and garlic.

Laurels
The laurel family includes evergreen shrubs and trees, such as avocados and cinnamon.

Which of these is the odd one out?

(answer at bottom of page)

a) Tomato

b) Aubergine

c) Raspberry

d) Apple

e) Squash

f) Turnip

Never eat flowers unless you know they're edible. Some can make you ill and **some can kill**.

Five flowers you can eat

Flower cookery has been traced back to Roman times:

- In the past, carnation petals were soaked in wine or used to decorate cakes.
- Nasturtium and cornflower petals have a sweet, spicy flavour a bit like watercress.
- Marigold petals can taste spicy, bitter, tangy, or peppery.
- Young dandelions taste sweet, but mature ones are bitter.
- In China, peony petals are boiled and sweetened for a tea-time treat.

In numbers

90 cm
(3 ft) The width of the world's largest flower, *Rafflesia*

6
The number of weeks it takes a mouse-ear cress to complete its life cycle

12
The number of watermeal flowers, the world's smallest, that could fit on a pinhead

100 m
(328 ft) The height of the Tasmanian swamp gum, the world's tallest flowering plant

258,000
The known number of species of flowering plant

Blasts from the past

130 mya
Flowering plants appear

90 mya
Flowering plants are widespread, replacing tree ferns, cycads, and conifers

70 mya
Woodlands of flowering trees replace conifer forests

55 mya
Grasses are widespread

10,000 years ago
Humans first grow crops such as wheat and barley

1500s
Tomatoes, maize, potatoes, and pineapples are brought from the New World to Europe and Asia

1983
Scientists create the first genetically modified (GM) flowering plant, a tobacco plant

Magnolias
Among the first flowering plants to evolve, these are woody shrubs and trees, often with large flowers.

Carrots
The plants in this family have hollow stems and small, aromatic flowers on umbrella-like flower stalks.

Peas
Many plants from this group are grown as crops, including clover, beans, lentils, peas, and peanuts.

Sunflowers
This is the second-largest plant family, with 23,000 species, from daisies to dandelions and lettuce.

Eight deadly flowering plants

Don't be fooled by the pretty flowers and juicy-looking berries. These plants are poisonous, so **don't touch** and **never taste**.

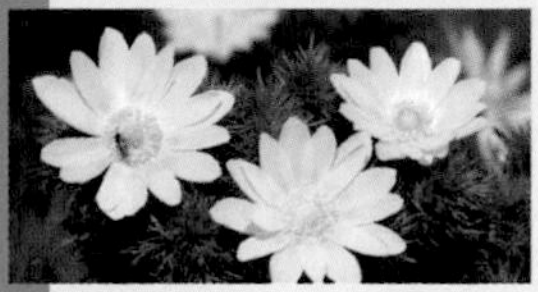

Adonis

Daphne

Lily of the valley
Convallaria majalis

Deadly nightshade
Atropa belladonna

Hemlock
Conium maculatum

Angel's trumpet
Datura innoxia

Oleander
Nerium oleander

Autumn crocus
Colchicum

Answer: The turnip is the odd one out, because it is a vegetable, while the others are all fruit. Fruit come from flowers.

How can a cactus **survive in the desert?**

Cacti are nature's water bottles, with tough, waxy skin to seal in moisture. Their thin, sharp spines lose less water than ordinary leaves – and also put off plant-eating animals. When the rains come, a cactus's shallow roots take up enough water to last all year.

WHAT'S IN A NAME?

The name **cactus** comes from the Greek word *kaktos*, which means "prickly plant". *Opuntia* cacti are known as "**prickly pears**" because they bear red and green fruit.

Tell me more: **cacti**

- Cacti are flowering plants shaped like barrels, pillars, cushions, or candelabra.
- **There are two main groups of cacti: those that grow in the desert (usually spine-covered), and those that grow in the rainforest (often without spines).**
- Cacti belong to a group of water-storing plants known as succulents.
- **Most cacti are native to the Americas, though the mistletoe cactus is from Africa, Sri Lanka, and India.**
- Too much water or too much cold can kill a cactus.
- **Cacti grow slowly, but they can live for more than 200 years.**
- Most cacti are small but some can grow to 3 m (9.8 ft) or more.

How to: **look after a cactus**

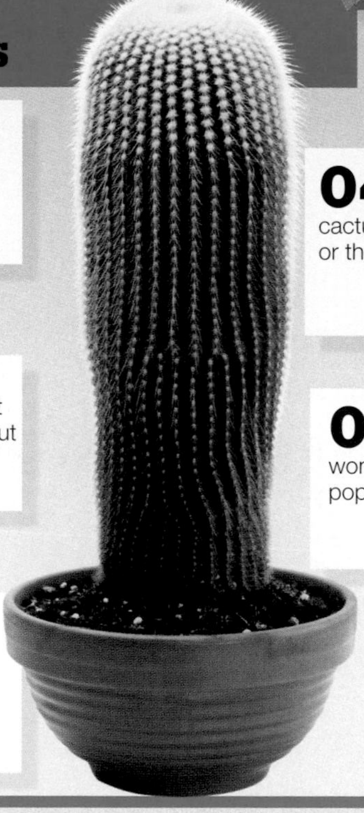

01. Plant your cactus in a pot that's slighter bigger than it.

02. Place the pot near a bright window, but not in direct sunlight.

03. Water the cactus once a month, and not at all in winter.

04. Give your cactus plant food two or three times a year.

05. That's it! No wonder cacti are such popular house plants!

Some cacti are extremely small and look just **like pebbles**. It's almost impossible to spot them except when they are in flower.

Name that **cactus**

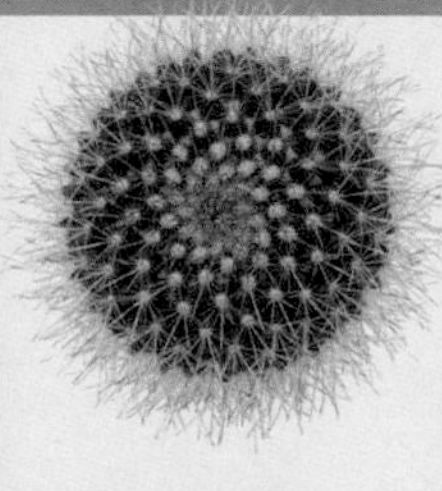

Fishhook cactus
This genus of small cacti gets its name from the plants' hooked spines.

Hedgehog cactus
This cactus's fleshy fruit has prickly spines, like the animal. It's also delicious!

Melon cactus
It's not difficult to see how this plump, round cactus got its name.

Old man cactus
The long, white hairs that cover this tall cactus look like a fluffy white "beard".

Bishop's cap cactus
This cactus has four or five ribs that make it look like a bishop's mitre or headdress.

Four curious **cacti**

Pincushion cactus
Found in southern Canada, this cactus can survive being covered by snow for months at a time.

Rose cactus
A close relative of the very first cacti, this has leaves and looks more like an orange bush than its desert cousins.

Christmas cactus
In the wild, this cactus grows in the rainforests of Brazil. It's a favourite house plant around Christmas time.

Queen of the night
This cactus is known for its sweet-smelling flowers, which only fully open for two hours at night.

I don't believe it!

The rangers of Saguaro National Park, Arizona, USA, are putting microchips into large roadside cacti. They are trying to deter **cactus rustlers**, who sell stolen saguaros to plant nurseries and homeowners.

Ten uses for a saguaro

For centuries, the people who live in and around the Sonoran Desert have found uses for saguaro cacti:

- The strong woody ribs have built shelters, fences, lances, arrows, drills, and toys.
- Parts of the cactus give up chemicals that can tan leather or waterproof clothing and tents.
- The figlike fruit can be eaten raw or cooked, or turned into jam or syrup.
- The fruit are also fermented to make saguaro wine.
- The Hohokam people decorated sea shells with saguaro juice vinegar around 1200 CE.
- Saguaro fruit juice is an ingredient sometimes used in traditional medicines.
- Saguaro seeds are pressed for cooking oils, milled for flour, or fed to chickens.
- The spines are used as needles for tattooing and sewing.
- The bloom of the saguaro is the state flower of Arizona.
- The saguaro has also starred in countless Westerns.

In numbers

12 m
(39.4 ft) The height of a fully grown giant saguaro cactus – about the same as a three-storey house

750 litres
(165 gallons) How much water the roots of a saguaro cactus can soak up during a single rainfall

40 million
The number of seeds a saguaro cactus produces during its lifetime

2,000
The number of known cactus species

Six threats to saguaro cacti

- Animals eat the cactus seeds and seedlings.
- **Seedlings may be trampled by cattle and other livestock.**
- Big freezes wipe out thousands of plants.
- **If a lightning bolt cracks a saguaro, the plant may rot inside.**
- Severe droughts weaken and kill cacti.
- **Wildfires can wipe out large forests of saguaro cacti.**

Four other **dryland plants**

Hen and chicks are so-called because new plantlets develop in a cluster around the parent plant, like chicks around a hen. They grow low to the ground.

Yuccas belong to a family of desert plants known as agaves. They store water in their tall, swordlike leaves.

Stone plants grow partly buried in the ground, which helps to prevent water loss. Some only need water two or three times per year, but they do grow extremely slowly.

The welwitschia of the Namib Desert can live for 2,000 years. Dew runs off its two leaves and is taken up by the 3-m- (10-ft-) long roots.

WEIRD OR WHAT?

The jumping cholla is a cactus with stems that fall off so easily they seem to **jump out** and bite you when you pass by!

What on **Earth** are **algae?**

They're not animals or plants… but they're definitely alive! Algae are a large group of living things that include seaweeds and plankton. Though they don't have leaves or roots, many algae are plantlike. They use sunlight to combine carbon dioxide and water to produce food. In the process, they release more oxygen than all of the world's plants combined!

In numbers

60 m
(197 ft) The length of mature giant kelp – that's one-and-a-half times the height of an oak tree

360 m
(1,180 ft) How deep in the ocean living algae have been found

7,000+
The number of species of green algae

1,800,000,000
The age in years of the oldest algae fossil

Meet the curious **algae cousins**

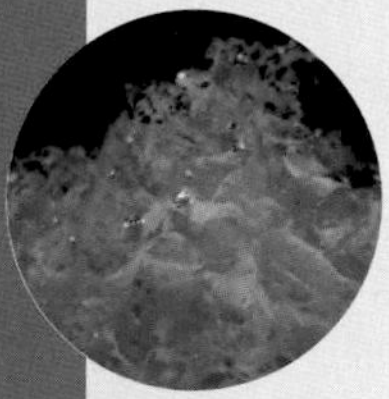

Green algae
Range from green seaweeds, such as this sea lettuce, to freshwater pondweeds, such as blanketweed.

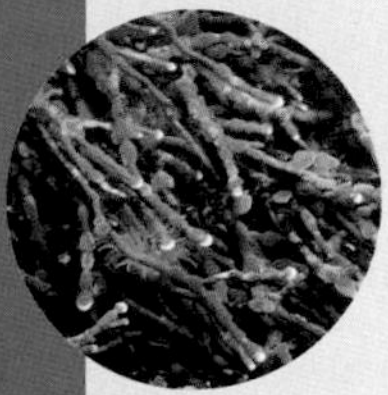

Red algae
Include purple, brown, and black seaweeds, as well as red, such as this coralline red algae.

Brown algae
Coloured greenish-brown, these are mostly large seaweeds and include giant kelp.

Golden algae
Tiny freshwater organisms that make energy from sunshine, but sometimes feed on bacteria.

Diatoms
Have super-thin shells. Some form part of plankton, the mass of tiny organisms that float in the oceans.

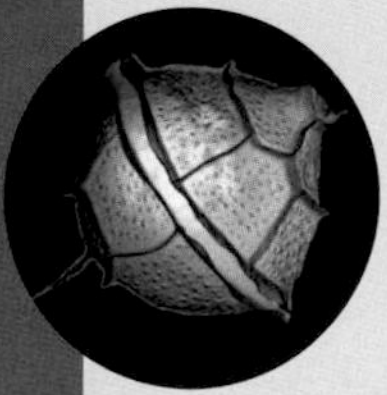

Dinoflagellates
Float freely as plankton. They're easiest to spot at night because some of them glow in the dark.

Three best buddies

01: The lichens that grow on rocks and walls are algae and fungi living together. The algae give the fungi food in return for a cosy living environment.

02: The tiny animals that build coral reefs depend on live-in algae called zooxanthellae for food. The algae give coral reefs their colour.

03: Some green algae live inside simple animals called sponges, safe from predators. In return, they provide the sponges with oxygen and sugars.

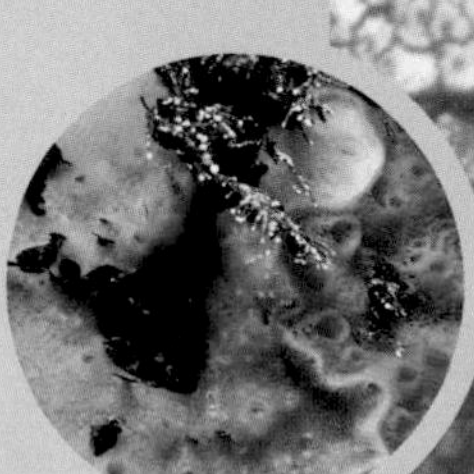

How to: **turn algae into biofuel**

01. Cultivate special oily algae in ponds – just add sunlight and waste carbon dioxide.

02. Check on the algae regularly. Add extra nutrients to help them grow.

03. Now extract the oil. Crush the algae in a press, or add chemicals that will separate out the oil.

Super-tough slime

- Some diatoms thrive in the Arctic ice, surviving temperatures below freezing.
- **Snow algae live up to their name. These tough organisms are found in the Himalayas, the Alps, and other snow-capped mountains.**
- Scientists think they may find algae in the underground ice on two of Jupiter's moons: Europa and Ganymede.
- **Some algae live in hot springs. They can cope with the high temperatures and poisonous sulphur.**
- In 2005, European scientists exposed a container of lichens to the cold vacuum of space for 15 days. Incredibly, they survived!

Nine amazing algae uses

- Seaweeds have been used as fertilizer for centuries.
- Seaweed contains growth hormones. It helps the grass on damaged football pitches grow back quickly.
- Seaweeds are healthy foods. They are high in protein, low in fat, and contain iron, calcium, potassium, and other minerals.
- The carrageenan in red algae makes things smooth and creamy – it's used in toothpaste, chocolate milk, and ice cream.
- Red algae also contain agar, a substance that is used to thicken cosmetics and shoe polish, among other things.
- Scientists grow bacteria in the laboratory in agar gel.
- A red seaweed called nori is used in sushi wraps and other Japanese dishes.
- Scientists are making a safe hair dye from seaweed.
- Scientists are investigating whether a seaweed diet could help cows' digestion. They hope to reduce the methane (a greenhouse gas) cows give off when they break wind.

I don't believe it!

The microscopic algae that live in the oceans are so small that 1,000 individuals could fit on a pinhead. But hot, calm weather can lead to huge **"blooms" of algae**. Big enough to be seen from space, these turn the sea pale turquoise.

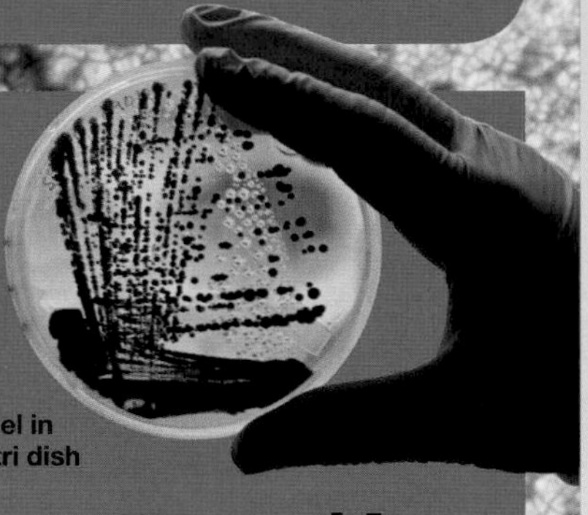

biofuel in a Petri dish

Power your ride with pond scum

01 In the next few years, scientists hope to use oily algae to develop new biofuels, nicknamed "oilgae".

02 Don't be surprised – some oil and gas fields are partly the fossilized remains of algae.

03 Growing 1 kg (2.2 lb) of algae takes in 2.2 kg (4.8 lb) of carbon dioxide, so the process will combat global warming at the same time.

04 Algae can produce more oil in an area the size of a two-car garage than a football field of soya beans.

04. Next, turn your algae oil into biodiesel – a renewable "green" fuel.

05. Fill up your car's tank, and off you go!

Four reasons to love algae

01: Algae are at the bottom of food chains or food webs in rivers, lakes, and seas.

02: Algae suck in carbon dioxide – the gas that is created by traffic and other forms of human pollution.

03: Three billion years ago, ancestors of algae called cyanobacteria started using sunlight to make food and release oxygen.

04: Breathe in… and thank the algae that produce more than 50 per cent of our planet's oxygen.

WEIRD OR WHAT?

American scientists hope that pond scum will provide **a cure for Parkinson's**, a disease that badly affects speech and movement. They will inject the algae into the diseased brain, then fit a light into the skull. It sounds crazy, but it's already worked in mice!

Designer algae

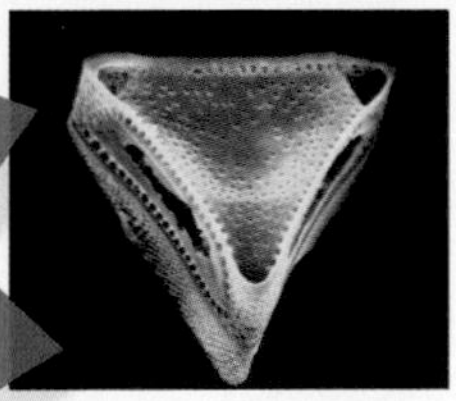

Diatom
Seen under a microscope, diatoms look more like art than living organisms. They make beautiful fossils.

Dulse
This red alga is as rubbery and springy as an elastic band. It's also delicious fried and served with butter.

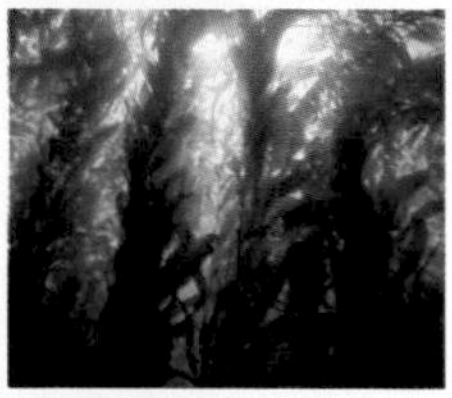

Giant kelp
This seaweed forms underwater "forests" in shallow seas. Gas-filled floats keep it upright.

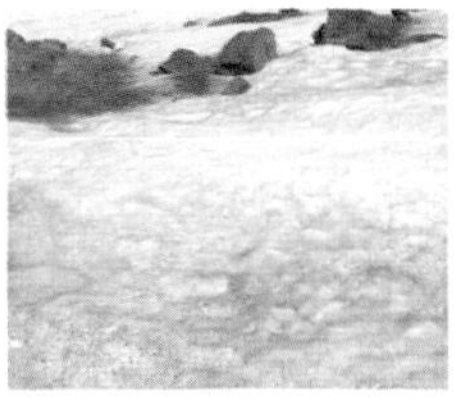

Snow algae
Nicknamed "watermelon snow", this algae forms pink or red blooms on the surface of Arctic ice.

How **big** is **a swarm?**

A giant creature is heading your way. As it closes in, you're shocked to see that it's actually thousands of smaller creatures. It's a swarm! The biggest swarms can be seen from space. Pacific waters turn red when krill congregate. A swarm of locusts can blot out the Sun, and millions of cicadas turn a forest floor into a heaving carpet.

Five reasons to **gang up**

Finding a mate
As dusk falls in the mangrove swamps of Thailand, thousands of fireflies gang up to find a mate. They flash in unison, forming a large, flickering cloud.

Keeping snug
In Canada, hundreds of garter snakes snuggle up all winter in underground dens. Coiling their bodies together helps them keep warm.

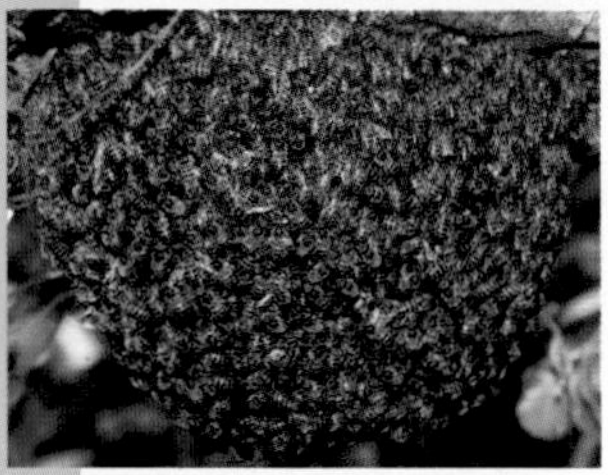

House hunting
Bees swarm when their colony gets too crowded. While scouts look for a new nest, the other bees hang out and crawl over one another in a bee ball.

Saving energy
Birds such as geese flock together to go on long migrations. Flying in a "V" cuts down on air resistance and allows the birds to glide and save energy.

Safety
Loners are often the first animals to be gobbled up by predators. Many fish swim together in groups known as schools or shoals.

How to:
avoid being chomped by a piranha

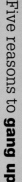

01. Piranhas are only found in certain Amazonian rivers. If you're worried, don't swim in South America!

02. If you must take the plunge, try to keep quiet. Noise and splashing attract hungry piranha packs.

03. Like sharks, piranhas get very excited when they smell blood. If you cut yourself, get out of the water – quick!

04. Don't swim in the dry season. Water levels are low and there are thousands of young piranhas looking for foo

In numbers

300 million
The number of monarch butterflies that migrate each year from Canada to Mexico – a distance of more than 3,000 km (1,865 miles)

50 billion
The total number of locusts in the 50 swarms that invaded Kenya in 1954; together, the swarms covered an area of more than 1,000 sq km (386 sq miles)

30,000
The number of pieces of slain prey carried back to the nest each day by a swarm of army ants

1 trillion
The number of American periodical cicadas in a swarm – luckily, they only swarm once every 17 years

Avoiding the traffic

In the rainforests of South America, columns of army ants swarm over the forest floor. Like rush-hour commuters, they want to avoid traffic jams, so they follow a three-lane highway laid down by ant scouts. Returning ants in the middle lane use their antennae to avoid bumping into ants heading off for work in the two outer lanes.

Swarming tips
(for Christmas Island red crabs)

01 Gang up with 100 million other red crabs and form large columns. Leave the forest and head for the coast.

02 Who needs a map? Just follow the same route as last year. Show no fear as you cross railway lines, climb down cliffs, and clamber over any obstacles in your way.

03 After a quick dip in the Indian Ocean to top up on mineral salts and water, it's time to breed. If you're a male, dig a nice burrow along the shore to attract a mate.

04 Take one last dip before heading back inshore. It's a good idea to travel in the early morning or late afternoon, to avoid shrivelling up in the baking-hot midday Sun.

Outswarmed!
Columns of Christmas Island red crabs have to watch out for **supercolonies** of yellow crazy ants. The insects are just 4 mm (0.2 in) long, but they form colonies more than 3,000-strong. They kill and eat millions of red crabs.

Biblical plagues
The Bible mentions a swarm of gnats attacking the Ancient Egyptians. This was followed by a **swarm of locusts** that blocked out the Sun for three days. Historians think this plague probably really happened, in around 1470 BCE.

Four scary swarms

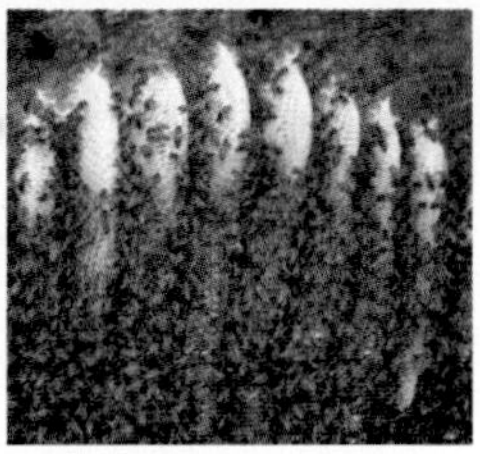

Killer bees
Never get too close to a hive of African "killer" bees. To protect their queen, the bees will swarm and chase you for more than 1 km (0.6 miles).

Birds
Flocks of ravens have been known to peck lambs to death. No wonder a group of these birds is known as "an unkindness of ravens"!

Jellyfish
The polluted waters off Tokyo and Sydney attract trillions of jellyfish. It's easier for them to prey on fish in shallow waters. Bathers beware!

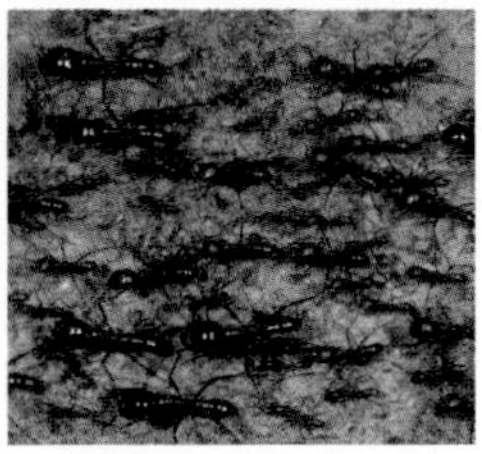

Army ants
These tiny terrors tear apart anything they meet with their small but powerful jaws. Army ants on the march can eat a cow in just a few hours.

Top ten swarm movies

- ***Arachnophobia*** (1990) – spiders
- ***The Birds*** (1963) – seagulls and other birds
- ***Frogs*** (1972) – snakes, birds, and frogs
- ***Indiana Jones and the Kingdom of the Crystal Skull*** (2008) – army ants
- ***The Mummy*** (1999) – flesh-eating scarab beetles
- ***Piranha*** (1978) – piranhas
- ***Squirm*** (1976) – killer worms
- ***Starship Troopers*** (1997) – giant alien spiders
- ***The Swarm*** (1974) – killer bees
- ***Them!*** (1954) – giant ants

WEIRD OR WHAT?
The **Atlantic palolo** is a little, red worm that lives on coral reefs. On one night of the year, all the palolos break in half and send their rear ends up to the surface to breed. The seas look like spaghetti soup!

In 1869, countless millions of **ladybirds** invaded southern England. In one seaside town, Ramsgate, a new job was created to rid the streets of all the beetle bodies: "ladybird shoveller".

I don't believe it!
When Mormon crickets get hungry, they go on the march, crossing western North America in columns up to 8 km (5 miles) long. They'll eat anything in their path, including any slowcoach Mormon crickets.

Luckless lemmings

- Lemmings are small rodents that live in the Arctic.
- Every three or four years, Norwegian lemmings breed so fast that they swarm off in all directions to search for food.
- Despite the stories, lemming hordes don't really commit suicide. Some lemmings fall off cliffs, probably by mistake, while others drown if they have to swim too far before reaching new land.
- The suicide myth is partly due to a faked 1958 documentary in which a turntable was used to hurl lemmings off a cliff!

Why is an **octopus so spineless?**

Octopuses belong to a group of animals called molluscs that have no backbone. Although they are spineless, octopuses are well able to look after themselves – they don't need shells to protect them like some other molluscs. They've got big brains, lightning reflexes, and all sorts of special tricks.

WHAT'S IN A NAME?

Octopuses, squid, cuttlefish, and nautiluses make up a group known as the **cephalopods**, which means "head-foot". They have a distinct head circled by limbs – tentacles or arms.

Tell me more: **super senses**

Chromatophores: Are tiny cells filled with chemicals that allow the octopus to change its skin colour
Reflecting cells: Pick up on nearby light, helping the octopus to match its surroundings
Suckers: Work independently, so each can send messages to the brain
Sensors: On the suckers can touch, taste, and smell

FAST FACTS

Home, sweet home

01: Octopuses live on their own, and spend a lot of time in their dens.

02: Octopus dens are often in underwater caves or in crevices in coral reefs.

03: Octopuses have also made dens in sunken ships, empty seashells, and even old cans and bottles.

04: Some mother octopuses do not eat, so they don't have to leave their dens.

05: Octopuses are very house proud – they move around rocks and shells to make a better shelter.

06: Some octopuses have two dens – one near to good hunting and another for eating in.

Super-smart

Otopuses in captivity have proved time and again how brainy they are:

- They can reach out of their tank to help themselves to food bins.
- They can find their way through complicated underwater mazes.
- They can use their arms to unscrew the lid of a jar and take out a treat to eat.
- They "play" at tossing small toys up and catching them again.
- They have personalities. Some like to be stroked, while others prefer to be left alone.

Cephalopod family

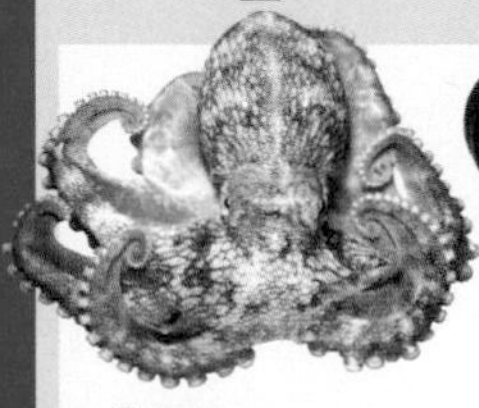

Octopus
300 species
Very intelligent, eight-armed cephalopods that are mostly found in shallower waters, especially coral reefs. The largest species weigh more than 70 kg (165 lb).

Squid
300 species
Cephalopods with eight arms and two tentacles or, in some species, ten long arms. The body is supported by a feathery structure, the pen.

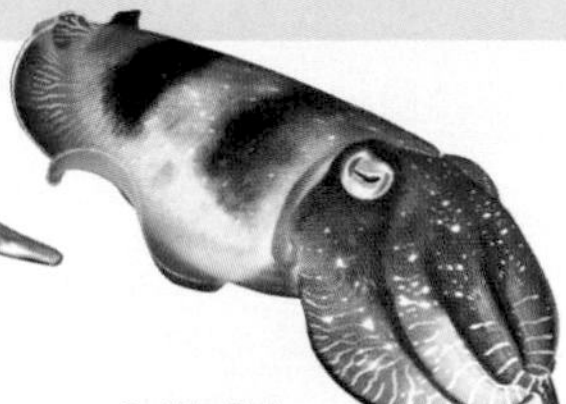

Cuttlefish
120 species
Cephalopods with eight arms and two tentacles, known for changing colour. They have an internal shell, the cuttlebone, and are up to 25 cm (9.8 in) long.

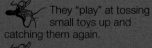

Nautilus
6 species
Cephalopods with an external shell and up to 90 suckerless tentacles. They have relatively poor eyesight but live long lives (up to 20 years).

I don't believe it!

Ancient sailors told tales of giant squid sinking ships. Though **jumbo squid** are only 2 m (6.6 ft) long, they can still wreak havoc. They ram divers, bite rowing boat oars in half, and squirt fishermen with ink and jets of water.

How to: **swim like a squid**

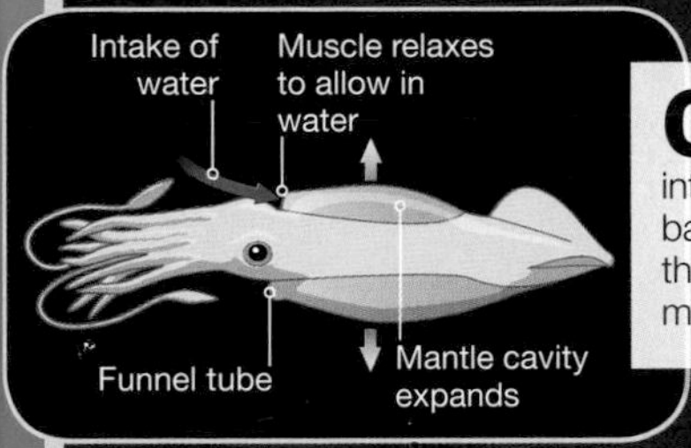

01. Suck water into your mantle – the bag of skin and muscle that contains your major organs.

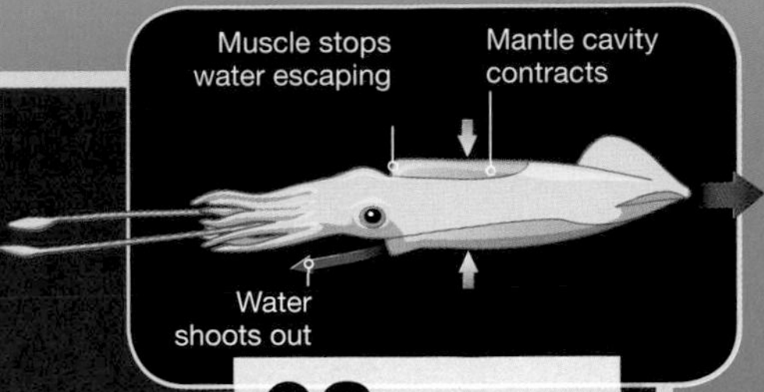

02. Blow the water out through your funnel tube. This creates a fast, strong jet that propels you forwards.

03. To change direction, point your funnel tube a different way. Let your tentacles trail and just go with the flow.

Large eyes: Let in plenty of light, giving the octopus excellent eyesight and even night vision

Eye pupil: Always stays horizontal, so the octopus is able to identify shapes whatever position it is in

Thin muscle layer: Allows the octopus to alter its skin texture

Arms: Help the octopus to "crawl" along the seabed

Most cephalopods **live fast and die young**. Their average lifespan is between one and two years. The exception is the nautilus, which lives for up to 20 years.

Scary squid

Up to 15 m (49 ft) long, the colossal squid is something of a monster. Its **dinner-plate-sized eyes** are the largest of any known animal and it has powerful, beaklike jaws. A speedy swimmer, it uses its long tentacles to grab prey.

Six odd deep-sea **cephalopods**

The dumbo octopus has two fins that look like the big ears of Walt Disney's flying elephant. Waving these fins helps the octopus to move about.

The curious-looking piglet squid is about the same size as an avocado. It gets its name from its piglike snout.

The cockatoo squid holds its tentacles in a sort of crest over its head.

The vampire squid has webbed skin between its arms, which looks like a bat's wing. It hangs in the water by drooping its arms to form an umbrella shape.

The flapjack octopus looks a bit like a pancake, thanks to the webs of skin linking its arms.

The glass squid has an almost transparent body, so predators look right through it!

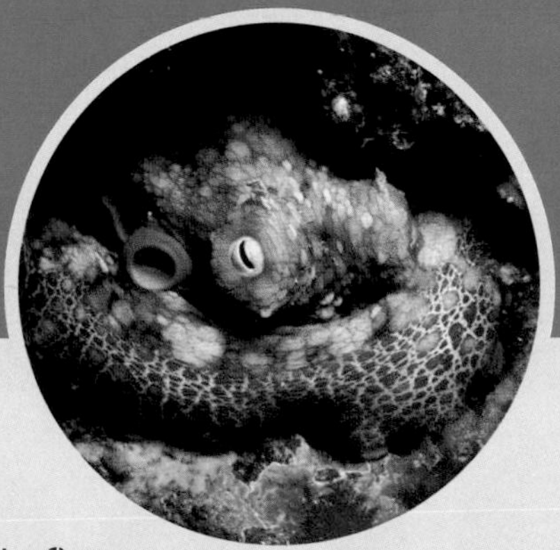

Eight top tactics

01 Flying squid: Smaller squid species jump out of the water to escape predators.

02 Bright spark: One deep-sea octopus has body parts that glow bright green, perhaps to attract prey.

03 Poison dwarf: The blue-ringed octopus is the size of a golf ball, but it's packed with enough poison to kill 26 people in minutes.

04 Disappearing act: An octopus's skin has cells and muscles that can change its colour and even its texture. It can turn its skin red and bumpy to hide in a coral reef.

05 Faking it: The mimic octopus can change its colour and shape to look like a sea snake or a giant crab.

06 Snap decision: Some octopuses can detach an arm if a predator grabs it, and then grow a replacement.

07 Escape artist: Most octopuses can shoot a dark cloud of ink into the water to confuse an attacker. Some can even squirt the ink to form an octopus shape!

08 Using weapons: The blanket octopus rips the poisonous tentacles off a Portuguese man-of-war jellyfish, then uses them to fight off predators.

Why are **sharks so scary?**

There's one word you never want to hear at the beach: "Shark!" Actually, shark attacks are very rare. You're far more likely to be killed by a charging hippo. Sharks are incredible killing machines, though, and they've been terrorizing the oceans for around 400 million years.

Seven secrets of shark success

01: Variety: There are more than 400 shark species.

02: Movement: The shark's tail and fins propel it through the water at 35 kph (22 mph) or more.

03: Size: A large body can power through the water quicker than a small one.

04: Drag reduction: The skin has toothlike scales (denticles) that channel water over the body.

05: Senses: As well as smell, sight, hearing, and taste, sharks can detect movement, and electric signals given off by prey.

06: Teeth: Razor-sharp, they include thin ones for slicing fish and jagged ones for tearing off chunks of seal flesh.

07: Jaws: These are loose and can push out to take a bigger bite.

How to attack like a great white shark

01. Circle your prey – then come at it from beneath. The sheer force will thrust you both out of the water.

02. With the seal (or fish) safely trapped in your jaws, you can deliver your killer bite in mid-air.

RECORD BREAKER

The shortfin mako is the cheetah among sharks. It "sprints" at speeds of up to 50 kph (31 mph). This **burst of speed** enables it to catch fast prey such as tuna.

Four oddballs

The **megamouth** is a 5.5-m- (18-ft-) long monster. Like whale and basking sharks, it filter-feeds, sieving prey from the water.

It's not just its strange head that makes a **hammerhead** so unusual. Females can reproduce without mating!

The long, eel-like **frilled shark** closely resembles early sharks. The first sharks appeared about 400 million years ago – before the dinosaurs!

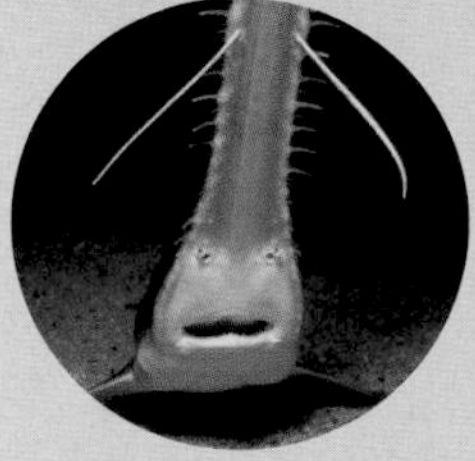

The **longnose sawshark** lives up to its name! It uses its "saw" to slash at schools of fish, or to rummage in the sandy seabed for shellfish.

Pearly whites

A **shark's teeth** are constantly being lost. They're replaced by new ones growing in a row behind them, which are always brand new and at the ready!

Five hunting **tactics**

Thresher sharks
Work in pairs. They thrash their long tails to herd fish into shallower waters. Then the sharks take turns to grab a bite.

Mako sharks
Have a very cunning trick. They sometimes bite off their victim's tail – that slows it down!

Basking sharks
Feed on tiny shellfish called copepods. They swim along, open-mouthed, fluttering their gills to swallow any trapped food.

Tiger sharks
Will eat almost anything – turtles, seabirds, and even small whales. Their super senses allow them to hunt in murky waters.

Tasselled wobbegongs
Are so well camouflaged they blend in with the seabed. They lie in wait till a fish gets close enough, then ambush it.

03. Release your prey. Wait for it to die of blood loss from your initial killer bite.

04. Your prey's well and truly dead. Snatch it up again, dive down deep, and set about devouring it!

Ten objects from sharks' stomachs

Sharks have a habit of taking a bite out of just about any floating object they find:

Car license plates

Tennis balls

Tyres

Pieces of armour

An entire reindeer (without the antlers!)

A cannon ball

A live turtle (it survived!)

***The Times* newspaper**

A barrel of nails

A tattooed arm (part of a murder victim)

Tips on avoiding a shark attack

01 Never ever go swimming alone.

02 Never enter shark-infested waters – especially if you're bleeding.

03 Avoid midnight dips, because many shark species hunt at night.

04 If you do spot a shark, swim quickly back to shore with a minimum of splashing.

05 Leave shiny jewellery back on the beach (it glints like fish scales).

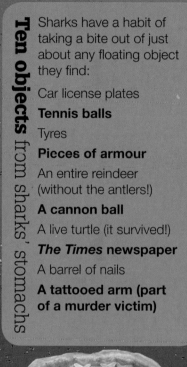

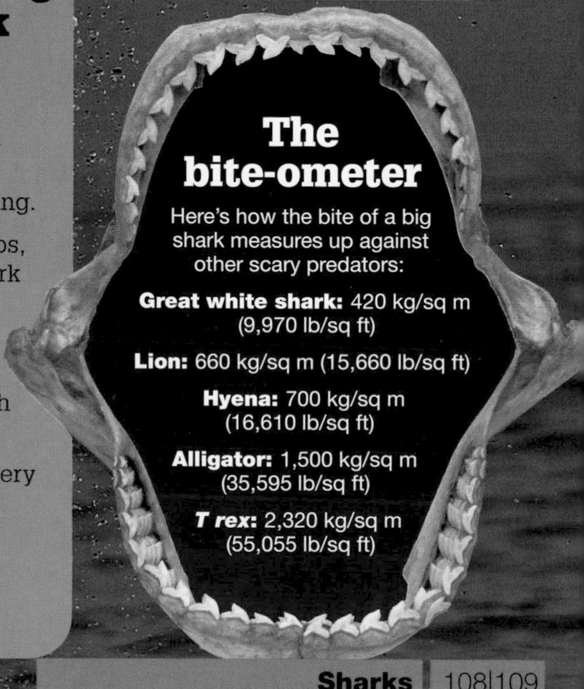

The bite-ometer

Here's how the bite of a big shark measures up against other scary predators:

Great white shark: 420 kg/sq m (9,970 lb/sq ft)

Lion: 660 kg/sq m (15,660 lb/sq ft)

Hyena: 700 kg/sq m (16,610 lb/sq ft)

Alligator: 1,500 kg/sq m (35,595 lb/sq ft)

***T rex*:** 2,320 kg/sq m (55,055 lb/sq ft)

In numbers

100 The number of years a whale shark may live

9 tonnes The quantity of meat that a great white eats in a year

1/4 How much of a full shark's body weight is made up by its stomach

12 m (40 ft) The length of a whale shark (the biggest shark)

20 tonnes The weight of a whale shark

15 cm (6 in) The length of the smallest shark, the dwarf lanternshark

Where can you **find a parasite?**

Parasites live off another living thing, feeding from their host without helping it in return. They can be hard to spot, as most are a lot smaller than their host. Some, such as ticks, fleas, and lice, live on the skin. Others, such as roundworms, live and feed inside the host's body.

Six steps to lingering death (if you're a cloverworm)

01: Some clover plants attract a female wasp to attack the cloverworms that eat them.

02: If they detect the wasp, the cloverworms fling themselves off the edge of the leaf. They stay attached by spinning a single thread of silk.

03: This tactic puts off most wasps, but not all. One species slides down the thread, then paralyses its caterpillar prey with a sting.

04: Next, the wasp lays its eggs inside the caterpillar's body.

05: The caterpillar recovers from the sting and climbs back up the thread, unaware of its deadly cargo.

06: As the wasp young grow inside the caterpillar's body, they slowly eat it from the inside out.

Four parasite facts

Every living thing has at least one parasite that lives inside or on it. Many, including humans, have far more.

Parasites may make up the majority of species on Earth. They may even outnumber "free-living" species by four to one.

Some parasites have parasites, and some of *those* parasites even have their own parasites!

Parasites are often insects, but can also include flatworms, fish, crustaceans, and birds.

How to: **suck blood like a chigger**

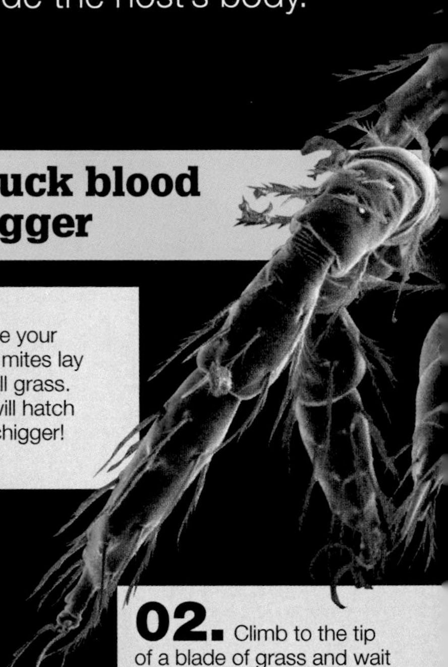

01. Have your parent harvest mites lay their eggs in tall grass. One of these will hatch into you, little chigger!

02. Climb to the tip of a blade of grass and wait for a host to pass by. Any warm-blooded mammal will do.

Tell me more: **mosquito senses**

Mosquitoes have been buzzing around for more than 100 million years, and in that time they've become expert trackers:

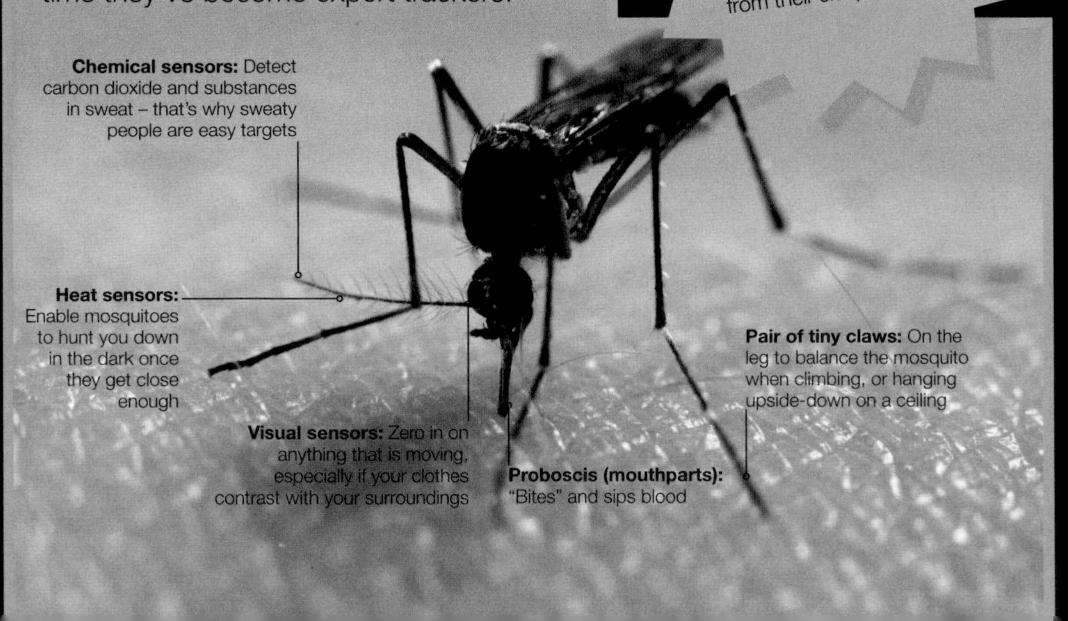
Chemical sensors: Detect carbon dioxide and substances in sweat – that's why sweaty people are easy targets
Heat sensors: Enable mosquitoes to hunt you down in the dark once they get close enough
Visual sensors: Zero in on anything that is moving, especially if your clothes contrast with your surroundings
Proboscis (mouthparts): "Bites" and sips blood
Pair of tiny claws: On the leg to balance the mosquito when climbing, or hanging upside-down on a ceiling

Night feeders

Bedbugs can flatten their oval bodies to squeeze into tight spots between the bed sheets. At night they crawl from their hiding places, following the trail of warmth and carbon dioxide coming from their sleeping host.

03. Landed yourself a human? After brushing on to some clothing, crawl to a safe, cosy place – just under the underwear elastic is perfect!

04. Now chew a hole in your victim's skin. Chemicals in your spit turn the wound into a slurpable soup. Yum! Don't worry about the chemicals giving your host a rash.

05. Finished feeding? Drop to the ground. Here you can develop into an adult harvest mite.

The candirú is just 4 cm (1.5 in) long but it's **an alarming fish**. It's said to track down urine in river water and force its way into people's body passageways.

Record-breaking scroungers

01 The giant Amazon leech, which is up to 46 cm (18 in) long, can suck in four times its body weight in blood!

02 The record jump for a flea (usually 2–8 mm (0.1–0.3 in) long) is 33 cm (13 in). You'd need to jump over a 50-storey building to match that.

03 Ticks are champion fasters – some can last for more than a year without a meal.

Mass killers

Female mosquitoes feed on human blood to provide protein for their eggs. Some species infect humans with the disease malaria. This kills up to 1.5 million people per year and affects another 300 million.

When an infected tsetse fly bites its victim, it injects a tiny parasite into the bloodstream. This eventually invades the brain, causing drowsiness and fever known as "sleeping sickness", which kills 40,000 people per year.

Fleas on rats carried the potentially fatal disease known as bubonic plague. The Black Death was an epidemic of this plague that wiped out some 75 million people worldwide between 1347 and 1351.

Top five **uninvited guests (for humans)**

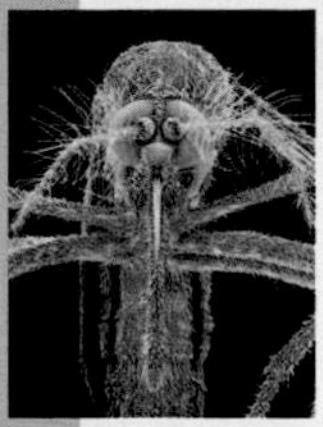

Midges
Biting flies come in all shapes and sizes. Some are so small that they are nicknamed "no-see-'ums"!

Fleas
These agile critters have super-long legs. They leap great distances at lightning speed.

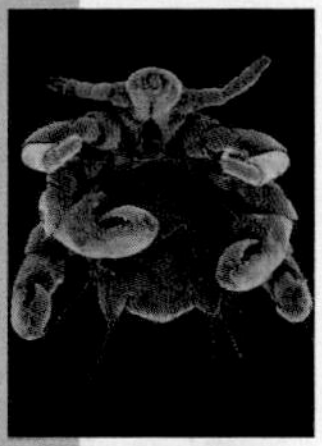

Lice
They can't hop, skip, or jump, but lice make skin (and hair) crawl! They cling on by the claws.

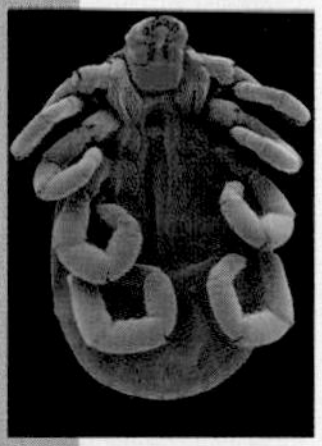

Ticks
Less mobile than lice, ticks nestle in warm, moist places, such as the crotch or armpit.

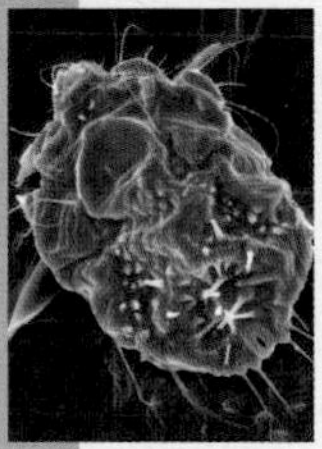

Scabies mites
The females burrow under our skin to lay eggs, causing an itchy rash.

Name that sucker

Tapeworm
Gets its name from its long, segmented body, which resembles a measuring tape!

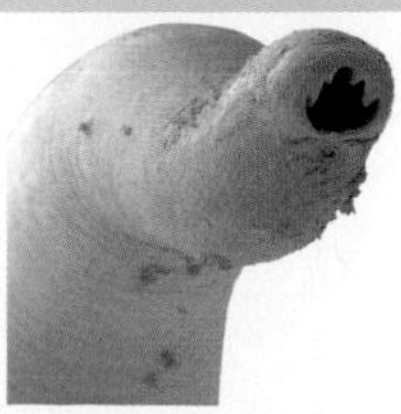

Hookworm
Has distinctive curved hooks that it uses to cling onto the inside of its host's intestine.

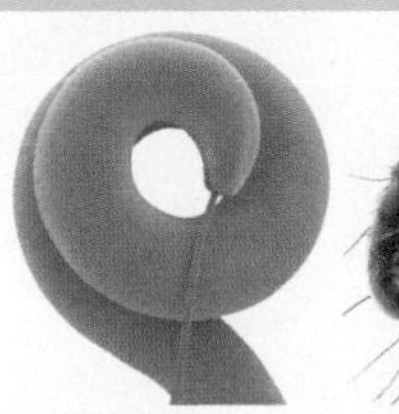

Whipworm
Looks a bit like a curled-up whip, with wider "handles" at the rear end.

Crab louse
Is named for the outsize claws with which it clings to its host's pubic hair.

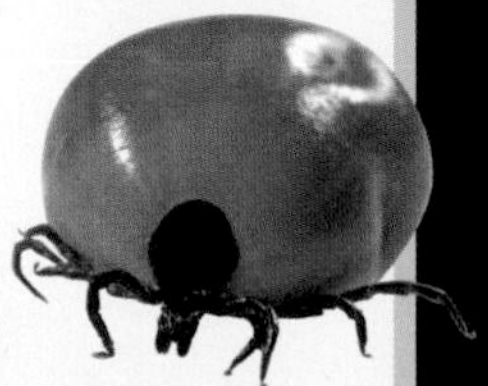

Castor bean tick
Is so-called because of its round, beanlike shape. Sometimes it has mottled patterning.

In numbers

1,000
The number of segments that make up the body of a tapeworm

8 m
(26 ft) The length a tapeworm can grow

200
The number of times its original size a castor bean tick can swell when full of blood

200,000
How many eggs a female ringworm produces in a day

30
The number of different mite species that one Mexican parrot carries just on its feathers – the bird is a walking zoo!

Why are beetles built **like tanks?**

Beetles, like other insects, have a hard outer skeleton made of overlapping plates. These plates form a flexible suit of armour. Beetles also have hardened front wings. Thanks to their tough body design, beetles survive in just about every habitat on Earth, apart from the poles and oceans.

Beetle defences

Camouflage: One African beetle resembles dead, velvety moss and has antennae (feelers) that look like dried twigs.

Scary features: Longhorn beetles can put up a fight with their strong mandibles (jaws) and "horns" (antennae).

Mimics: Some beetles look just like wasps and bees. They're harmless – but would-be predators won't risk being stung.

Bad smell: A stink beetle stands on its head and sprays foul-smelling liquid at its enemies.

Poison: Blister beetles are often colourful – a warning that they are poisonous.

Playing dead: Many weevils fall to the ground and play dead. They fold their legs around their body so they look like seeds or bits of soil.

Run away!: Darkling beetles make a dash for it, tiger beetles take to the air, and flea beetles leap for safety.

How to: see off a rival, stag-beetle style

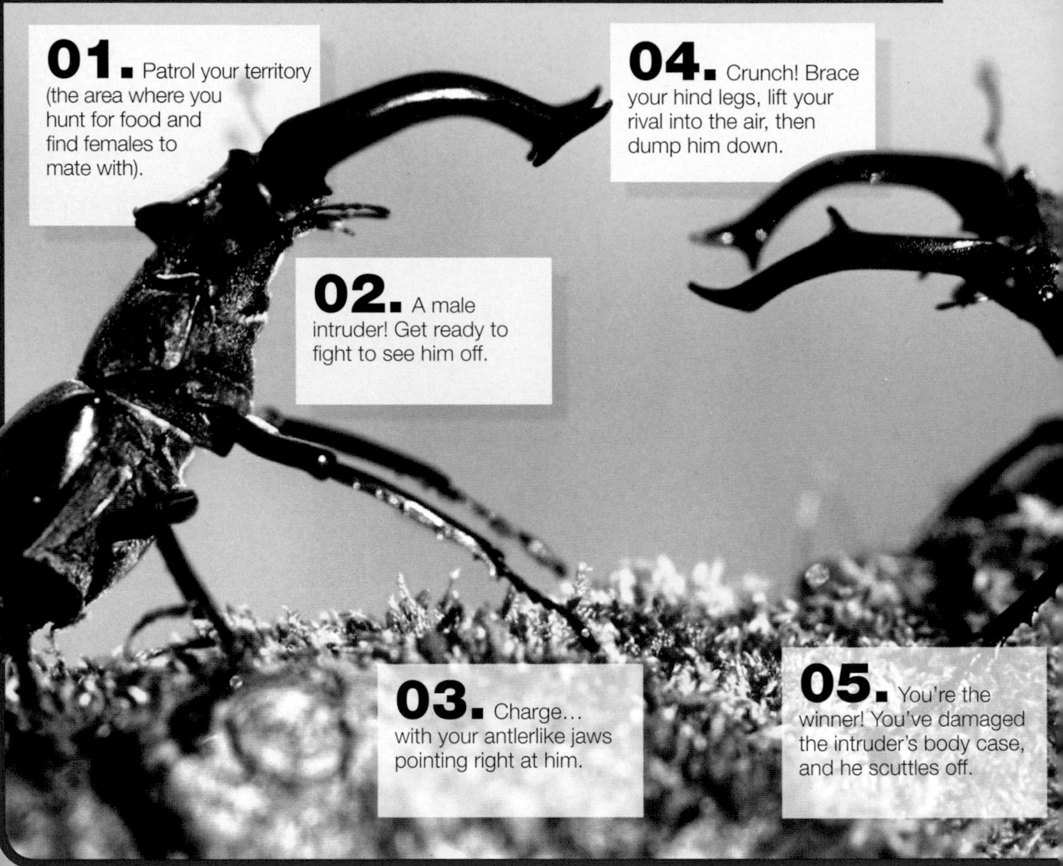

01. Patrol your territory (the area where you hunt for food and find females to mate with).

02. A male intruder! Get ready to fight to see him off.

03. Charge… with your antlerlike jaws pointing right at him.

04. Crunch! Brace your hind legs, lift your rival into the air, then dump him down.

05. You're the winner! You've damaged the intruder's body case, and he scuttles off.

What's for dinner?

Some beetles are meat-eating predators, while others feast on plants. Whatever their diet, each type of beetle has a specific design of mouthparts to make the most of each meal.

A **tiger beetle**'s strong, large jaws are perfect for slicing up insect prey.

Weevils have long snouts tipped with biting jaws for nibbling plant parts.

Blister beetles have tubelike mouthparts and sometimes suck nectar from flowers.

Large-headed beetles can crush snail shells with their powerful jaws.

Cigarette beetles munch on tobacco leaves and other dried plant products.

The gardener's friend, **ladybirds** gobble up aphids and other plant-eating pests.

Bess beetles, shown here with a beetle grub, chew up wood from old, rotting logs.

Which of these is *not* a beetle? (answer at bottom of page)

a) Damsel bug

b) Cockroach

c) Stink bug

d) Froghopper

I don't believe it!

When a bombardier beetle is attacked, it mixes two chemicals stored in its abdomen to create a jet of hot poison. This sprays out of the beetle's body with an explosive "POP!" With its abdomen tucked between its legs, a bombardier can blast at enemies coming from any direction.

Sacred scarab

The dung, or scarab, beetle was sacred to the **Ancient Egyptians**. The way scarabs roll balls of dung reminded them of their creator god rolling the Sun across the sky each day.

In numbers

16 cm
(6.3 in) The lengths of the three largest beetles – Titan, Goliath, and Hercules beetles

480 kph
(300 mph) The estimated speed of a tiger beetle if it were the same size as a human – it is the fastest land animal for its size

370,000
The number of known beetle species, though more are found each year

Six helpful beetles

The Romans believed cutting a scarab beetle in half and tying both bits to your arm cured fever.

Tiger beetles are used as pest control against the mole crickets that infest rice paddies (fields).

The irritating liquid from blister beetles can burn off warts.

Skin beetles feed on dead flesh, skin, and hair. Taxidermists (people who preserve dead animals) and museums use them to clean skeletons.

Carrion and rove beetles help to solve crimes. Forensic scientists can tell a corpse's time of death by the insects found in and around the body.

The ancient Chinese sometimes caught fireflies in see-through jars and used them as lanterns.

FAST FACTS

Fireflies

01: Fireflies are not flies but beetles. Males can fly but females don't have wings, so they let the males know where they are by glowing.

02: A firefly's glow is made by a chemical reaction that gives off energy in the form of light.

03: At sunset, a firefly on a branch turns on its lantern to let other fireflies know it's there. More females join in, lighting up the whole tree!

04: Firefly larvae, called glow-worms, give off light to warn predators not to eat them.

05: Most fireflies give off a blue or green light from their abdomen, but the young of some beetles, known as "railroad worms", also make a red light on their head.

Legs **fit for...**

Grabbing: Many beetles have claws at the end of each leg segment.

Scuttling: Ground beetles have long, slender legs for scampering and running.

Digging: Most kinds of dung beetle have broad legs covered in spines.

Swimming: Diving beetles have curved, paddlelike legs covered in bristles.

Hopping: Flea beetles have extra-large hind legs built for leaping.

Mating: The claws of male flower beetles are adapted for clinging on to the female.

ANSWER: None of them are beetles. a), c), and d) are bugs (unlike beetles, they have sucking mouthparts); b) is a roach (unlike beetles, they have no larval stage – froghoppers hatch from their eggs looking very like adults).

Tell me more: **beetles**

Over millions of years, beetle bodies have adapted to an amazing variety of lifestyles. The long legs of the tiger beetle help it run down prey over the sand dunes, while the giant horns of the rhinoceros beetle are used in fierce clashes with other males.

Whirligig beetles
These water beetles spend much of their time swimming on the surface of ponds. To help them look out for prey, they have divided eyes – one half to watch under the water, and the other to see above the surface. When they dive, they carry an air bubble down with them.

Jewel beetles
These come in brilliant metallic colours and their shiny wing cases are used to make jewellery and ornaments in parts of Asia. The striped love beetle's "shell" works like prism, giving a rainbow tint to its green colouring.

Colorado potato beetles
Native to the southwestern United States, these beetles are one of the most destructive insect pests. They attack crops of potatoes, tomatoes, and aubergines. They are resistant to insecticides, but farmers can spray crops with a fungus that kills the beetles.

Rhinoceros beetles
When female rhinoceros beetles are ready to mate, they give off a smell th brings males flying in. Rivals bob thei heads in threat, then the headbutting levering, and tossing starts. The lose is the one that's knocked off its perch

Tiger beetles
Night hunters with big, bulging eyes, tiger beetles pursue their prey at speeds of up to 8 kph (5 mph). They are also fast flyers. The beetles' long legs hold their bodies high above the hot sand of their desert habitat.

Flour beetles
These insect pests feed on wheat and other cereals and cause costly damage if they infest a farmer's grain silo. Flour beetle young, known as mealworms, are raised commercially to feed pet reptiles and birds, or to be used as fishing bait.

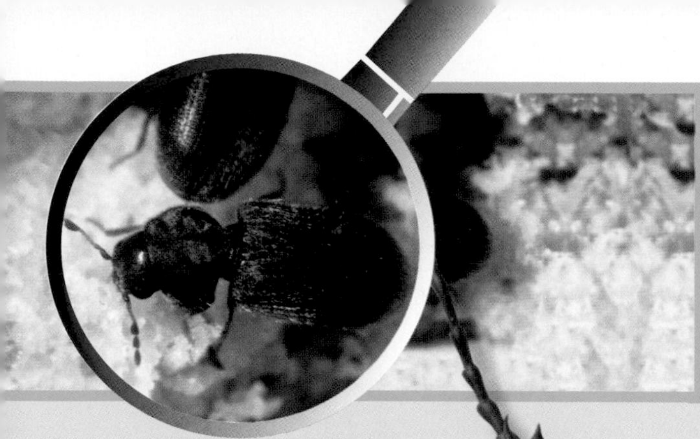

Bread beetles
Also known as biscuit beetles or drugstore beetles, these insect pests feed on a variety of foods. They have been known to eat bread, biscuits, spices, books, leather, and even medicines and drugs. Female bread beetles may lay as many as 75 eggs at a time.

Christmas beetles
These scarab beetles appear in large numbers around December, when it is summer in their native Australia. Having two front legs of different lengths gives them a better grip on their preferred food, eucalyptus leaves.

Goliath beetles
Found in African tropical forests, Goliath beetles are 16 cm (6.3 in) long and are among the world's largest insects. When fully grown, their larvae weigh as much as 100 g (3.5 oz). Goliath beetles feed on plant sap and fruit.

Blister beetles
All beetles are poisonous, but blister beetles are especially dangerous to horses and livestock. During summer, striped blister beetles swarm together to feed on alfalfa hay. A few of them gobbled down in a single clump of hay can be enough to kill a horse.

Deathwatch beetles
Deep inside the timbers where they developed as larvae, adult deathwatch beetles call to each other at mating time by tapping their heads. The eerie ticking sound gave the beetles their name.

Dung beetles
These scarab beetles roll lumps of dung along the ground to form a ball. The beetles bury the dung ball in their burrow and lay their eggs inside. Why? Because dung is their young's favourite food!

Sexton beetles
These scavengers feed on rotting animal flesh. They have special sensors that can sniff out the body of a dead mouse from more than 1 km (0.6 miles) away.

Bark beetles
When these pests bore into the wood of elm trees, they spread a fungus known as Dutch elm disease. The fungus has wiped out huge numbers of elms in Europe and North America.

How can a **frog leap so far?**

Most frogs have long, muscular hind legs and long feet. These allow frogs to push hard against the ground when they jump. Frogs also store jumping energy by stretching their tendons like springs. This extra power helps many frogs to leap 10 to 20 times their body length.

All together, now!

- Male frogs croak in a midnight chorus to attract females and frighten away rivals.
- Most male frogs have an inflatable, balloonlike vocal sac in the floor of their mouths to make their croak louder.
- The croak of an American bullfrog is said to sound like the words "jug o' rum"!
- The tiny painted reed frog has the loudest frog call for its size. Males can be heard almost 2 km (1.2 miles) away from their pond.
- Male white-lipped frogs make extra noise by pounding their vocal sac on the ground as they call.

How to: **jump like a frog**

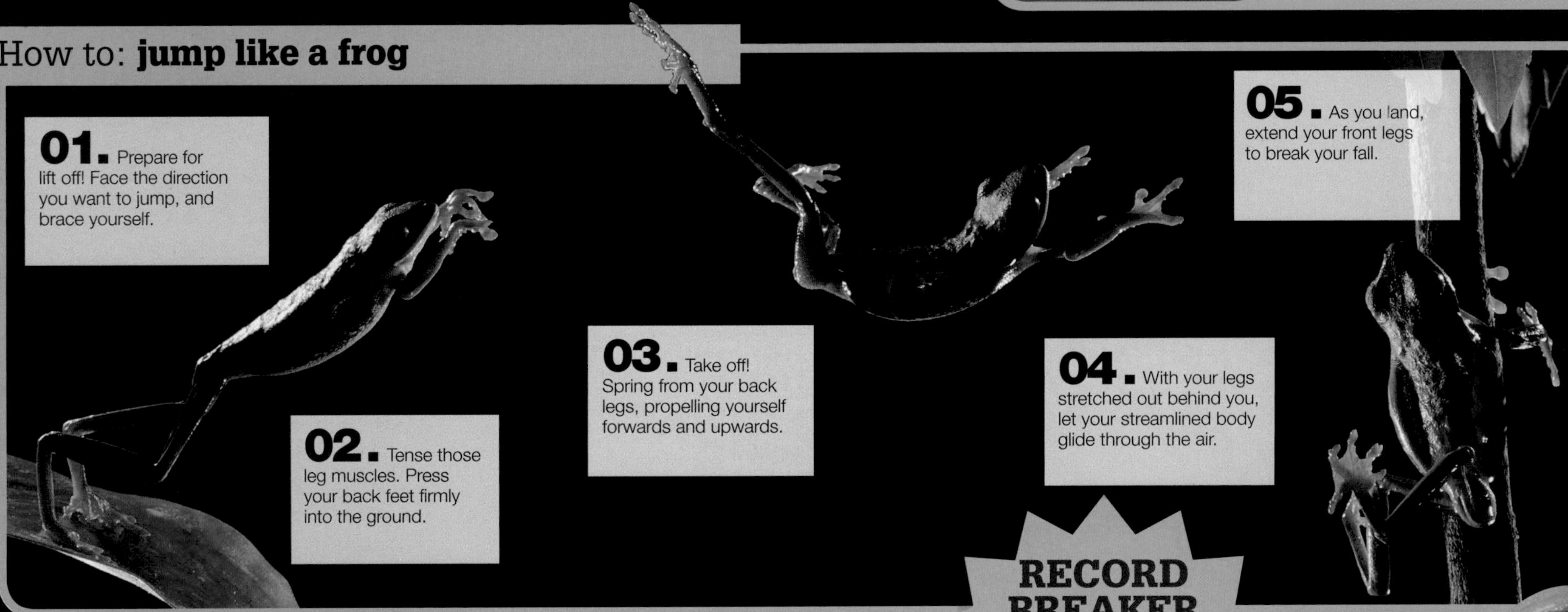

01. Prepare for lift off! Face the direction you want to jump, and brace yourself.

02. Tense those leg muscles. Press your back feet firmly into the ground.

03. Take off! Spring from your back legs, propelling yourself forwards and upwards.

04. With your legs stretched out behind you, let your streamlined body glide through the air.

05. As you land, extend your front legs to break your fall.

I don't believe it!

A frog shuts its eyes when it catches prey, so it must take careful aim. It also seems to blink when it swallows: its eyes sink into its skull to help force food down its throat.

RECORD BREAKER

The well-named **rocket frog** can jump an amazing 50 times the length of its body in one leap, more than 2 m (6.6 ft).

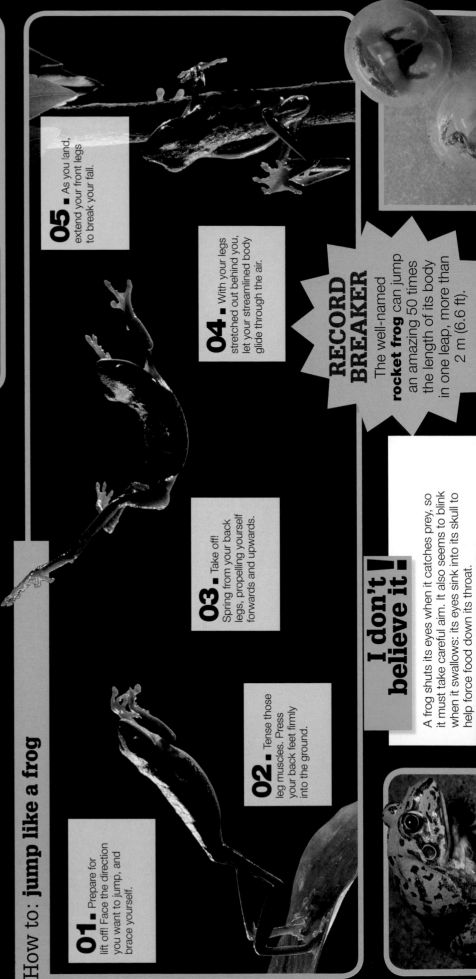

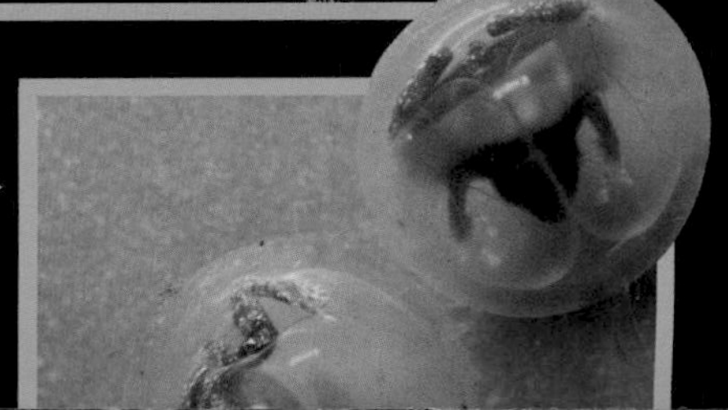

Survivors of hot and cold

The water-holding frog survives the heat of the Australian desert in a burrow. Its "cocoon" of skin traps enough water to last the frog until the next rains – nine months later!

The wood frog lives in the far north of North America. It survives winter lows of –6°C (21°F) by turning into a "frog-sicle"! Up to 65 per cent of its body's fluids turn to ice and even its organs stop working.

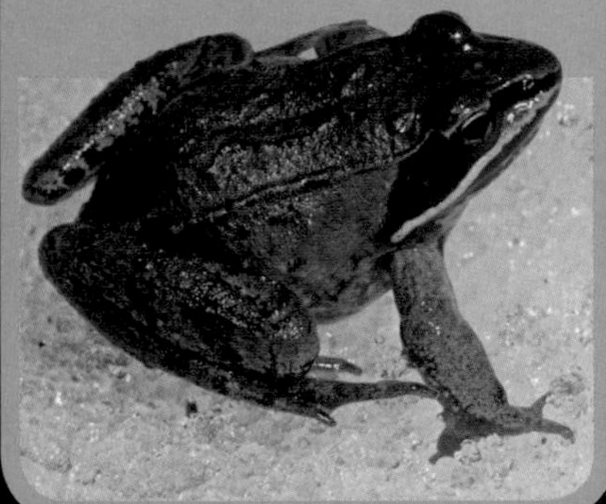

FAST FACTS

Tadpole food

01: Frogs may look cute, but, like most amphibians, they're cannibals. Adult frogs will often eat tadpoles.

02: Tadpoles will eat other tadpoles – though they try to avoid gobbling up their siblings.

03: Tadpoles may nibble off the legs of early developers, so it pays to be a late bloomer!

04: Some tree frogs lay an extra egg for the tadpoles to feed on!

Some frogs, such as the Mexican tree frog, lie on their back and play dead when threatened.

What about me?

If you pick up a frog, don't be offended if it pees. It might empty its bladder to lose weight, so it can jump further to safety. (Never hold a frog for too long – salts in your sweat can be dangerous to it.)

In numbers

3/20
The fraction of a second it takes a frog to shoot out its tongue and catch its prey

5
The number of frogs that grow up to breed, from the 2,000 or so eggs in a blob of frogspawn

30 cm
(12 in) The body length of the record-breaking Goliath frog

37
The age of the oldest known frog, first tagged in the 1970s

60 million
The number of frogs whose legs are eaten in France each year

Eggs, tadpoles, and froglets

Fiji tree frogs hatch as fully formed froglets!

Now extinct, the **gastric brooding frog** "ate" its eggs so the tadpoles could develop in its stomach.

Some **poison dart frog** mums give their tadpoles a piggyback to the nearest pool after they hatch.

The **Surinam toad**'s eggs develop on the female's back. The offspring hop off when they're froglets!

The **male pouched frog** of Australia has pouches on either side of its body where its young develop.

Paradox frog tadpoles are 22 cm (8.7 in) long. They "grow" into frogs that are just 6.5 cm (2.6 in).

Six freaky frogs

Giant Titicaca frog
Living in Lake Titicaca, high in the Andes of South America, this is one of the few amphibians that never needs to surface for air. Instead, it takes in oxygen from the water through its wrinkled skin.

Ornate horned frog
With its mottled green and brown skin, this frog is perfectly camouflaged hiding under leaves. When a worm, mouse, or other frog passes by, it lunges at its victim and gobbles it up.

Mossy frog
Native to Vietnam, this tree frog has bumpy, speckled skin that looks just like moss or lichen. When alarmed, the frog rolls into a ball and plays dead till the danger has passed.

Glass frog
There are more than 100 species of glass frogs. They live in trees in Central and South American rainforests. They have hardly any pigment in their transparent skin, so their organs show through.

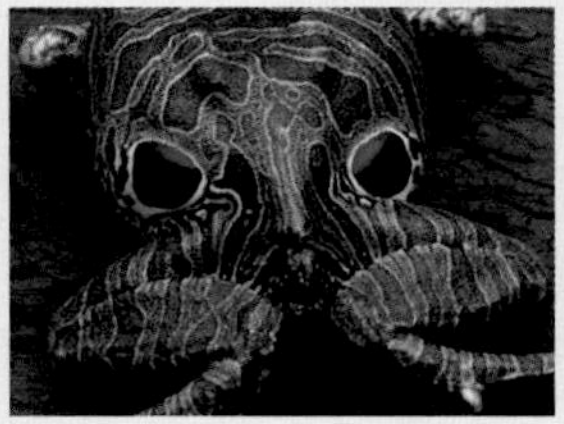

False-eyed frog
This frog has two large spots on its bottom that look like the eyes of a much larger animal and scare off most predators. If that doesn't do the trick, the frog produces sticky, foul-smelling "tears". Yuck!

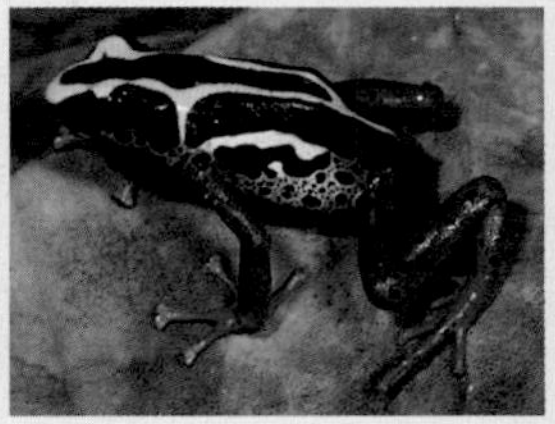

Dyeing dart frog
Like all poison dart frogs, this frog is brilliantly coloured – a warning that its skin contains deadly toxins. Tribal peoples collect this poison to use on their arrows, which is how poison dart frogs get their name.

How fast can **a crocodile swim?**

A crocodile can swim at speeds of up to 30 kph (18 mph) – and even faster if it's chasing prey or escaping danger. Crocodiles are superb swimmers. They hold their front legs flat against their sides and use their powerful tails to propel themselves through the water. They use the back feet as rudders to steer left and right.

Meet the **crocodilians**

Crocodilians are reptiles – scaly-skinned animals with backbones. They hunt in water but lay their eggs on land.

Crocodile
Living in both salt- and freshwater in Asia, Australia, and Africa, crocodiles eat mammals, birds, and fish.

Alligator
The only crocodilian to hibernate during the coldest months of the year, the alligator lives mainly in North America.

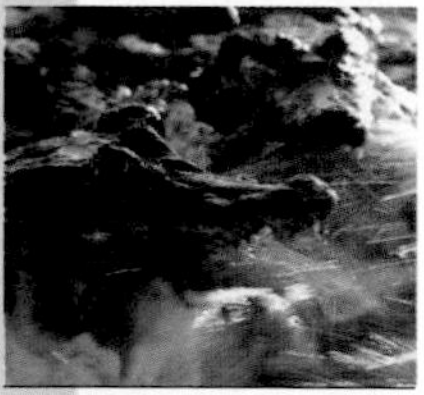

Caiman
The most common of the crocodilians, caimans live in Central and South America.

Gharial
With a narrow snout, this large, slender crocodilian from the Indian subcontinent eats mainly fish.

See and feel

Crocodiles can see underwater, thanks to a **transparent lid** that protects the eye. They also have excellent **night vision**. Sensory buds around the jaws allow crocodiles to detect vibrations – crucial when hunting in murky water.

I don't believe it!

If you shed "crocodile tears" people think you are faking it. That's because crocodiles "cry" while they are eating their victims. But it's not because they are feeling remorse: as they swallow down great lumps of meat, their jaw muscles expand and contract. The pressure created by the moving muscles squeezes tears out of the crocodile's tear glands.

Jaw-dropping

01 Crocodiles have **34 teeth** on each jaw, which are continuously replaced as they fall out.

02 Their **teeth can't cut meat or chew**, so a crocodile swallows its prey whole, or takes a bite, holds tight, and spins round furiously until the piece of meat breaks off.

03 The Greek writer Herodotus reported that crocodiles have rotten food **picked out of their teeth by birds**.

04 A crocodile can **go without food** for many months and then eat half its body weight in a single meal.

05 Despite having powerful jaws, a crocodile **cannot open its mouth if it is held shut**, with an elastic band, for example. Any volunteers to test this theory?

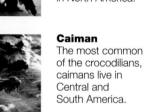

In numbers

23
The number of crocodilian species

230 million
How many years ago the first crocodilians appeared (about the same time as the dinosaurs)

134
The estimated age in years of the oldest captive crocodile

68
The number of teeth a crocodile has (they are constantly falling out and being replaced)

10–15
The average number of minutes a crocodile can hold its breath underwater

The **largest crocodile** on record is a giant saltwater crocodile that measured 8.6 m (28 ft) and weighed 352 kg (2,980 lb). It was shot in Queensland, Australia, in 1957.

[redacted]

Crocodile or alligator?

If you ever find yourself up close and personal with a large reptile and cannot decide if it is a crocodile or an alligator, here are two key things to look out for:

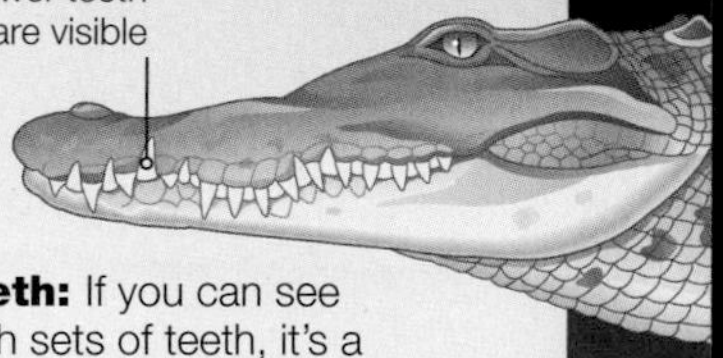

Teeth: If you can see both sets of teeth, it's a crocodile. An alligator's lower jaw is slightly smaller than its upper jaw, so the bottom row of teeth is hidden when the mouth is closed.

Alligator: Wide, U-shaped snout

Snout: What's the overall jaw shape? Crocodiles have long, pointed snouts, shaped like a "V". Alligators have more rounded snouts, like the letter "U".

WEIRD OR WHAT?

When a crocodile lays an egg, it's neither **male nor female**. Temperature determines the sex. If the nest is around 31.6°C (88.8°F), males are produced. Females develop at slightly lower and higher temperatures.

How to: raise a family like a Nile crocodile

01. Lay 20 to 80 eggs in a hollow of soil or plant material. Cover them so they keep warm.

02. Guard the eggs from predators for three months – sleep nearby and check on them regularly.

03. At hatching time, help your young break out by cracking the shells carefully with your teeth.

04. Transport your babies safely to the river in your mouth. Watch over them for about two years.

How **big** is a bird of prey?

Birds of prey, or raptors, are birds that hunt other animals for food. They include huge eagles and condors with a wingspan of up to 3 m (9.8 ft), as well as pigeon-sized kestrels and merlins. Most birds of prey have sharp sight, a hooked bill, and large, curved claws called talons.

Guide to behaving like a vulture

- Use uplifting currents of air to get high in the sky and soar in circles.
- Why waste time and effort hunting live prey? The dead don't fight back!
- Pee on your legs to chill out – the evaporating liquid cools your body.
- Throw up on enemies – the stomach acids in your vomit will burn their flesh.
- Show good parenting by half-digesting food before you feed chunks to your chicks (Most birds of prey feed their offspring pieces of raw flesh.

How to: **catch a fish supper if you're an osprey**

01. Fly over the lake or sea, about 30 m (100 ft) above the surface. Once you spot a fish, hover for an instant.

02. Plummet towards your prey, plunging feet-first into the water.

03. Snatch a fish in your talons. Fly up, out of the water, turning the fish head-forwards to reduce drag.

04. Fly back to your nest and feed your hungry chicks – or find a quiet perch and devour the fish yourself!

I don't believe it!

For thousands of years, nomadic peoples in Central Asia have trained golden eagles to hunt for them. Training can take four years, and the eagle will obey only its trainer. The bird is used to hunt young deer, foxes, and even young wolves.

Types of bird of prey

Eagles
65 species
Large, powerful birds with broad wings, a heavy head and beak, and huge, taloned feet.

Falcons
66 species
Medium-sized raptors with narrow, pointed wings that are built for speed.

Kestrels
15 species
The most common European raptors, these falcons hover while hunting.

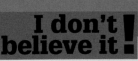

Hawks
56 species
Agile woodland raptors with shorter wings and longer tails, built for flying among trees.

Tell me more: **golden eagle**

Strong body: Weighs as much as 7 kg (15.5 lb)
Keen eyes: Can spot a rabbit more than 1 km (0.6 miles) away
Hooked beak: Rips off chunks of flesh
Powerful wings: Span more than 2 m (7 ft)
Sharp claws: Grasp prey

In numbers

4
The number of months a year that a Swainson's hawk spends travelling between its breeding and winter habitats

6 m
(20 ft) The depth of the largest nest ever recorded; built by bald eagles, it was also 3 m (9.5 ft) across

4,000–10,000 km
(2,500–6,250 miles) How far south an osprey flies to reach its winter feeding grounds

7,200
The approximate number of feathers on a bald eagle

RECORD BREAKER

The fastest animal in the world is the **peregrine falcon**, which has been filmed diving down on prey at speeds of more than 320 kph (200 mph).

What's for dinner?

- Harpy eagles grab sloths and monkeys in their sharp claws.
- The crested serpent eagle has scaly legs to protect against bites from its preferred prey – snakes.
- Kites eat creepy-crawlies, small mammals, and carrion. They also raid rubbish bins.
- Kestrels eat all sorts, including grasshoppers, frogs, small snakes, lizards, bats, and mice.
- The northern caracara (a falcon) gobbles down worms, baby birds, crabs, and turtles.
- Bald eagles often steal or "pirate" fish from other birds.

Eight flying machines inspired by birds

- BAE Hawk – a jet made famous by the Red Arrows team.
- F-15 Eagle – a fighter plane that can outclimb a *Saturn V* rocket.
- Fw 200 Condor – a German aircraft used in World War II.
- Harrier Jump Jet – a military jet that takes off vertically.
- *Millennium Falcon* – Han Solo's spaceship in *Star Wars*.
- SH-60 Seahawk – a US Navy search-and-rescue helicopter.
- V-22 Osprey – an aircraft with rotor blades that can fly like a plane or take off like a helicopter.
- The Vulture – a futuristic robot spy plane under development.

Buzzards
25 species
Medium to large hawks with strong bodies and broad wings. They prey on rabbits and rodents.

Harriers
18 species
Slender-bodied raptors, with long wings, tails, and legs. They fly close to the ground.

Kites
25 species
Lightweight, soaring birds with long wings and weak legs. They nest in large groups.

Old World vultures
16 species
Large birds that feed on dead animals (carrion). They are close cousins of eagles and hawks.

New World vultures and condors
7 species
Giant, soaring birds, usually found in mountain regions.

Secretary bird
1 species
A long-legged hunter of the African savannah that stamps its prey to death.

Osprey
1 species
Also known as a sea eagle, a large, fish-eating bird of prey with a 2-m (6.6-ft) wingspan.

What goes bump **in the night?**

At sunset, most animals head for the safety of their den, burrow, or nest, but some are just getting going. Many of these "nocturnal" (night-time) creatures are mammals. Their warm-blooded bodies and furry coats allow them to keep warm and active at night when temperatures fall.

Seven noises in the night

- Tarsiers are tiny primates, about the size of a human fist. Rival males trill like birds, while tarsier groups chirp together like crickets.
- Baby opossums travel with their mother at night. If they get lost, they let out a sneezing sound to tell her where they are.
- Hedgehogs communicate at night with grunts and snuffles. They may scream if they are threatened.
- The spotted hyena's whoops, giggles, and cackles have earned it the nickname "laughing" hyena.
- Many owls hoot to keep in touch or to tell other owls to keep away, but some, such as screech and barn owls, screech or even scream.
- Foxes call out with a hoarse-sounding bark as they go about their territory. They also cry, squeal, squeak, and purr.
- Male crickets chirp at night to attract female mates – and to tell other males to stay out of their territory.

Seven night senses

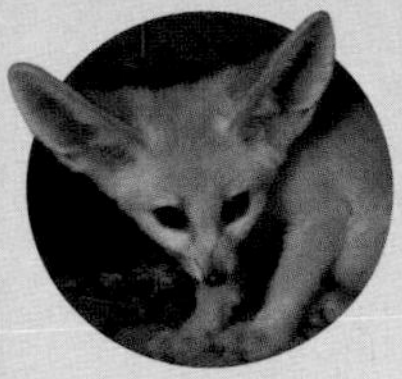

Big ears
The fennec fox's outsize ears funnel sound from prey right into the eardrum.

Aye-sight
The aye-aye sees well in the dark – its huge eyes let in what little light there is.

Super sniffer
Pen-tailed tree shrews have an amazing sense of smell.

Good vibrations
The bird-eating spider's leg hairs pick up vibrations in the air from other animals.

Whiskers
Like all cats, a tiger uses its whiskers to sense air currents and work out what's near.

How to: **howl like a wolf**

01. Find a wide open space to howl in. A good howl can be heard more than 10 km (6 miles) away.

02. Say it like it is. A deep, loud howl accompanied by a few barks will rally the pack. Longer howls warn other wolf packs to stay away.

03. Face upwards to carry your cries further. Forget the myths – wolves don't really howl *at* the Moon (though moonlit nights are good for hunting).

04. Pick a different note to your pack mates. Singing in harmony makes it sound like there are more of you. Altogether now: **OWWWOOOHHH!**

In numbers

1.5 m
(5 ft) The wingspan of the largest bat, the giant golden-crowned flying fox

20 g
(0.7 oz) The weight of a teeny-tiny marsupial called the pilbara ningaui (a bit heavier than a CD)

45 cm
(18 in) The length of an aardvark's tongue – perfect for slurping up termites and ants!

10,000 tonnes
The weight of insects eaten each year by a single roost of free-tailed bats

Although some nocturnal animals have excellent night vision, most rely on other senses to find their way – and their prey.

Heat sensors
Pits beween a snake's eyes and nostrils can detect heat from its warm-blooded prey.

Echolocation
A bat's squeaks echo as they bounce off objects, telling the bat where the objects are.

Pouched night prowlers

Marsupials are mammals that give birth to tiny young that develop in a pouch on the mother's body. Many are up and about at night.

Though it hunts in the dark for insects and other small prey, the grey four-eyed opossum doesn't really live up to its name. Its two extra "eyes" are just white spots.

In the hot season, kangaroos rest in the day and feed at night. They have enough spring in their legs to leap over your head.

Koalas spend most of their time lounging in the fork of a tree. Their diet of eucalyptus leaves doesn't provide much energy, so they snooze up to 20 hours per day.

Wombats leave their burrows at night to avoid losing water from their bodies in the hot daytime Sun.

The size of a small dog, a Tasmanian devil scavenges dead prey at night, but will also hunt wombats and small kangaroos. It gobbles down the fur and bones as well as the flesh.

Tell me more: owl features

Head: Swivels almost all the way round, to pick up noises from any direction
Large eyes: Make the most of any moonlight
Soft feathers: Muffle the sound of beating wings
Hooked beak: Tears apart voles, mice, and rats
Talons: Grip prey securely

I don't believe it!

A duck-billed platypus hunts underwater in the dark, but closes its eyes, ears, and nose each time it dives. So how does it find its prey? Sensors in its bill detect tiny electric currents generated by shrimps, insects, and worms hiding in the mud.

WEIRD OR WHAT?

When attacked, a **Virginia opossum** falls into a coma that can last up to four hours. It lies on its side, mouth and eyes open, tongue lolling, and with a nasty green fluid trickling out of its bum. What self-respecting predator would want to eat that?

Seven night stalkers

01: Leopards will patiently stalk prey for hours. They've even dragged sleeping humans from their beds without waking anyone else!

02: Tigers are soft-footed night hunters. They edge slowly towards deer or other prey… and then pounce!

03: Foxes are cunning midnight raiders. Poultry farmers hate these notorious chicken-snatchers.

04: White-tailed mongooses make their attack in lightning-quick time. They have to, before their snake prey can inflict a venomous bite.

05: Coyotes often hunt and scavenge alone, but sometimes work as a pack. They can bring down prey as large as adult elk, but usually target newborns.

06: Black caimans hunt at night. These fearsome reptiles are 5 m (16.5 ft) long and, like other crocodilians, kill their prey by drowning it.

07: Whitetip reef sharks hunt in the moonlight, then spend the day resting on the ocean floor or in caves.

Life in dark, spooky caves

A fish called the cave angel lives only in waterfalls inside caves in Thailand. Pink and eyeless, it clings to the slimy rocks and feeds on bacteria in the water.

In Bracken Cave, Texas, USA, skunks and raccoons grope their way around the floor looking for fallen baby bats to munch on.

It's hard to hunt in a pitch-black cave. The Texas blind salamander can go without food for up to six years.

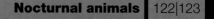

Ten amazing bats

Most bats prefer to avoid daytime predators and competition with birds. These night flyers navigate by listening to the echoes of their own high-pitched squeaks. Wrinkly skin around their ears helps to channel the returning sounds.

03: The **Australian ghost bat** (below) swoops down on frogs, lizards, birds, and small mammals. It wraps its wings around the prey as it delivers a killer bite, then flies back to its roost to eat. It usually roosts in colonies in caves, old mine tunnels, or in deep cracks in rocks.

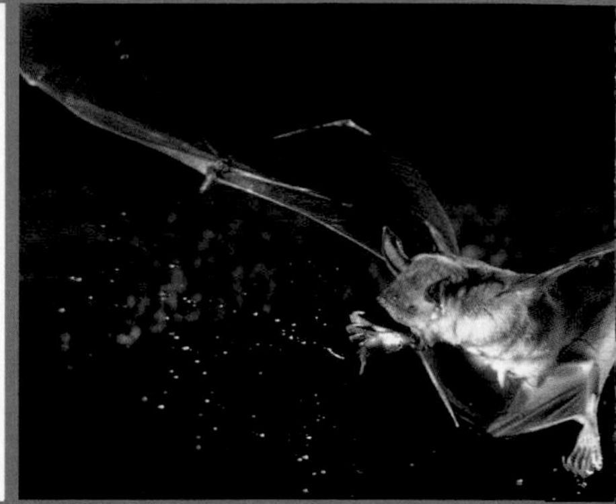

04: The **fisherman bat** (above) of Central and South America uses its squeaky sonar (sound navigation) to scan the surfaces of rivers, lakes, and seas for ripples made by fish. Then it swoops down and snatches its prey (up to 7 cm/2.8 in long) in its impressive, hooked claws.

01: A **long-eared bat** relies on its huge, concertina ears to hear the gentle beating of a moth's wings. The bat flies face down, so the tips of the ears point forwards. When resting, the bat allows its ears to curl down.

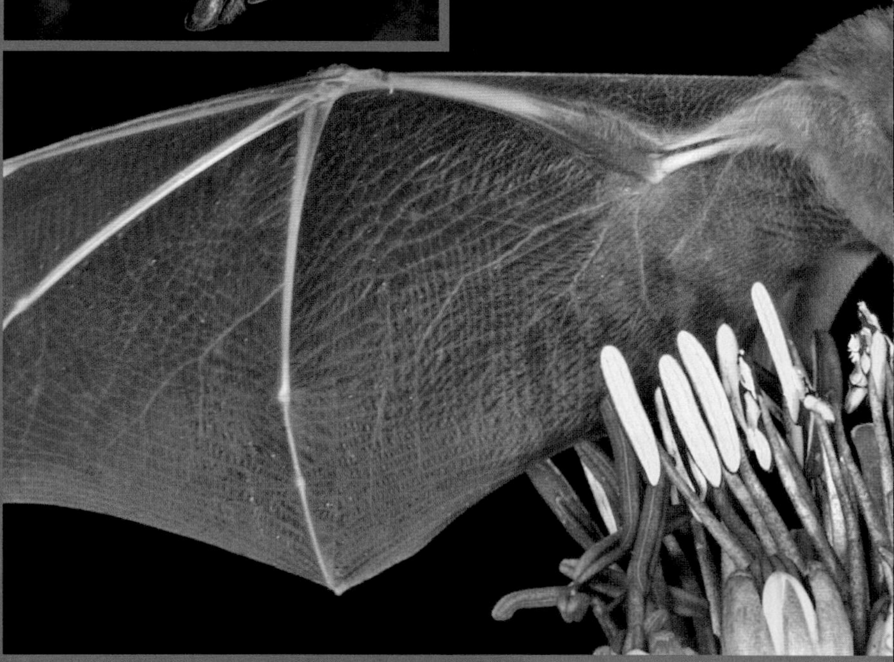

02: **Fringe-lipped bats** circle ponds, listening for telltale croaks. Once they locate a frog, they zoom down, grab it, then return to their perch to feed. The bats can tell poisonous frogs from non-poisonous ones by their calls.

05: In New Zealand, the **lesser short-tailed bat** feeds on the forest floor. While it is clambering about looking for insects or fallen fruit, it folds each wing inside a leathery "pocket" where it won't get damaged. This frees up its arms for walking on like front legs.

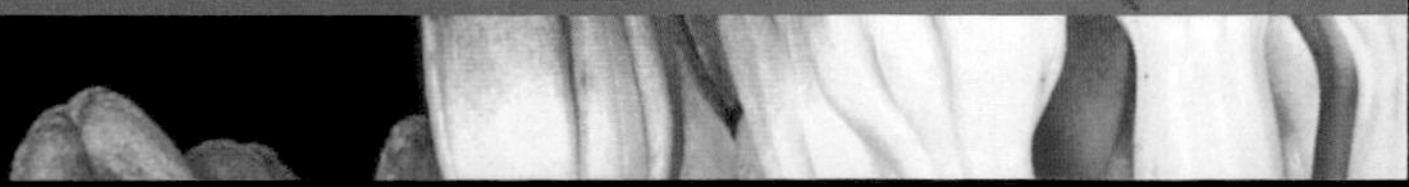

06: Vampire bats land a distance away from sleeping prey, then scuttle up close. After biting into a soft part of the skin, such as an ear, they lap up the blood like a cat drinking milk.

07: Many bats prefer to roost in caves and old buildings. However flying foxes and fruit bats often roost out in the open. They may hang from tree branches in "camps" up to 200,000 strong. **Egyptian fruit bats** have even been known to roost in ancient pyramids!

08: The **blossom bat** measures just 7.5 cm (3 in). It has a super-long tongue for drinking nectar from flowers. Snakes and other sneaky predators hide in fruit trees and wait for the bats to come to them.

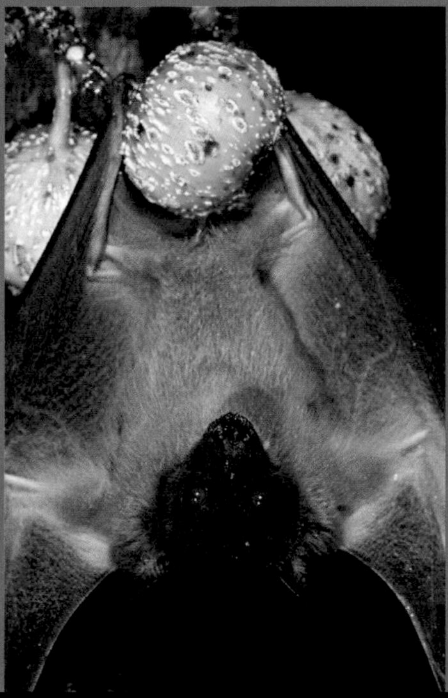

09: Named for their doglike muzzles, there are many species of flying fox, including this **greater musky fruit bat**. It locates figs and other fruits by sight and smell, then harvests them with its feet.

10: As their front limbs are wings, bats have no fingers to grip with. That's why they tend to rest by hanging upside down, like this **flying fox**, holding on with the long, curved claws of their feet.

Why are **whales so big?**

A blue whale is the biggest animal ever. It can grow up to 33 m (108 ft) long and weighs the same as 30 elephants. On land, such a large animal would collapse under its own weight, but the water supports its bulky body. A whale's size puts off predators, and its blubber helps it to stay warm in polar waters.

FAST FACTS

Cetaceans

01: Whales, dolphins, and porpoises are all cetaceans, a group of marine mammals.

02: Like all mammals, they are warm-blooded, give birth to live young, breathe air, and have some hair (whiskers).

03: Toothed whales include porpoises, dolphins, beaked whales, and orcas (killer whales).

04: Porpoises are smaller than dolphins and have rounded, beakless heads.

05: Baleen whales feed by filtering small sea creatures through bristly plates in their mouths. They include right, blue, and humpback whales.

06: Cetaceans have a layer of blubber (fatty tissue) that keeps them warm and stores energy.

How to: **dive like a sperm whale**

01. Raise your huge tail flukes (lobes) in the air – this is called "fluking up".

02. Dive, dive, dive in a vertical descent. It will take you about 15 minutes to reach a depth of 1,000 m (3,280 ft). Cut your heart rate by half to save oxygen.

04. Time's up! Take another quarter of an hour or so to get back to the surface.

05. Clear the water you took in during the dive. Each time you breathe out, a jet of water is forced through your blowhole.

Spectacular leaps

Many **dolphins** leap into the air as they swim. This "porpoising" technique may help to reduce drag.

When the **spinner dolphin** leaps, it twirls its body around and around in mid-air.

Right whales and other large whales breach (rise out of the water) to show off to mates and rivals.

The **humpback whale** is named for its habit of arching its back out of the water before a dive.

I don't believe it!

Each autumn, humpback whales migrate an incredible 5,000 km (3,100 miles) from their feeding grounds around the poles. In winter they breed and give birth in warmer, sheltered waters.

Funny features

The extremely rare **Ganges river dolphin** has a super-long beak packed with sharp teeth.

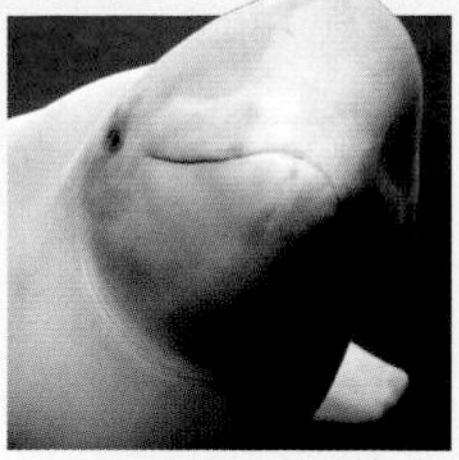

The **beluga whale** lives in Arctic waters. Its white skin is good camouflage at the ocean's silvery surface.

Resembling a unicorn's horn, the spiral "tusk" on the male **narwhal**'s head is actually a very long tooth.

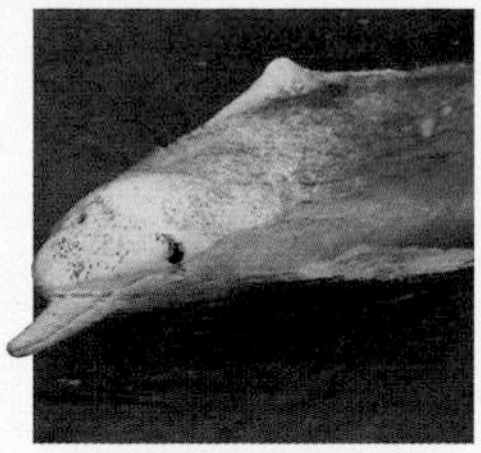

Some **Indo-Pacific humpbacked dolphins** look pink but most are grey or white. All are born black!

Two large teeth jut from the jaw of **Blainville's beaked whale**. They are often encrusted with barnacles.

Most **Risso's dolphins** are covered in scars. Why? Because other Risso's dolphins have bitten them!

03. Forage for food. Remember you only have about half an hour before you start running out of oxygen.

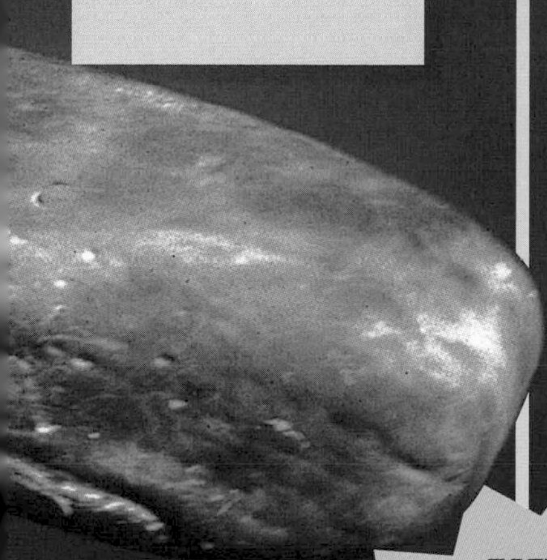

Tell me more: dolphin design

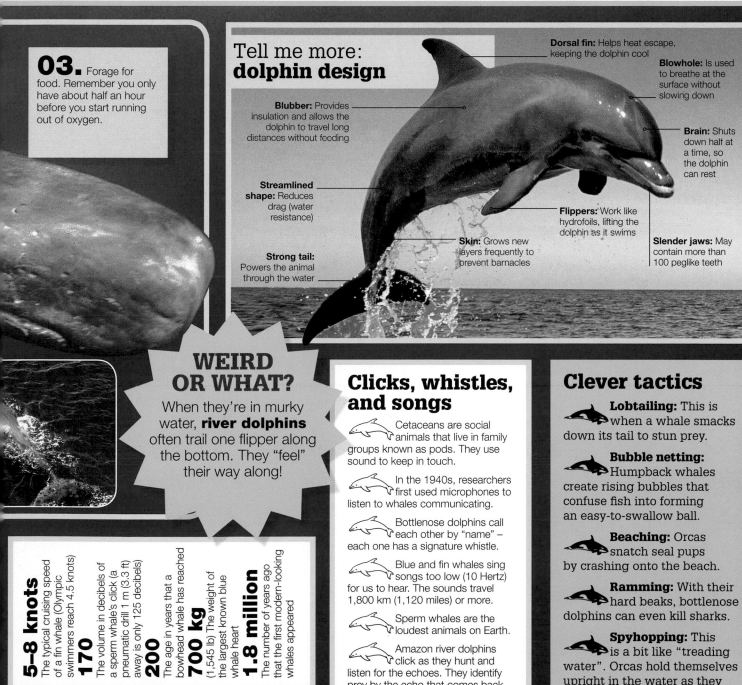

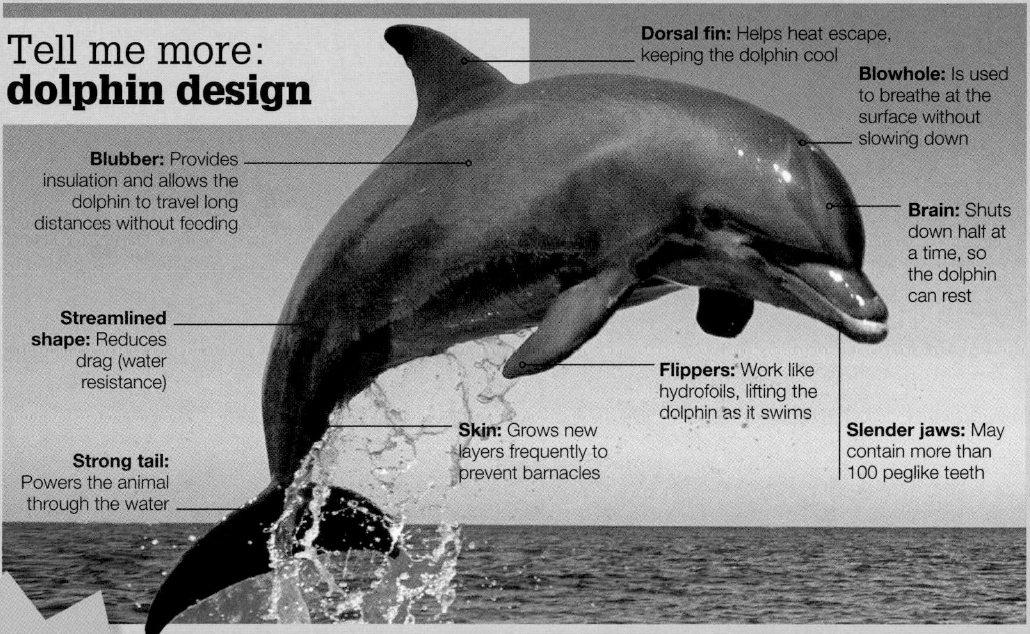

Dorsal fin: Helps heat escape, keeping the dolphin cool
Blowhole: Is used to breathe at the surface without slowing down
Blubber: Provides insulation and allows the dolphin to travel long distances without feeding
Brain: Shuts down half at a time, so the dolphin can rest
Streamlined shape: Reduces drag (water resistance)
Flippers: Work like hydrofoils, lifting the dolphin as it swims
Skin: Grows new layers frequently to prevent barnacles
Slender jaws: May contain more than 100 peglike teeth
Strong tail: Powers the animal through the water

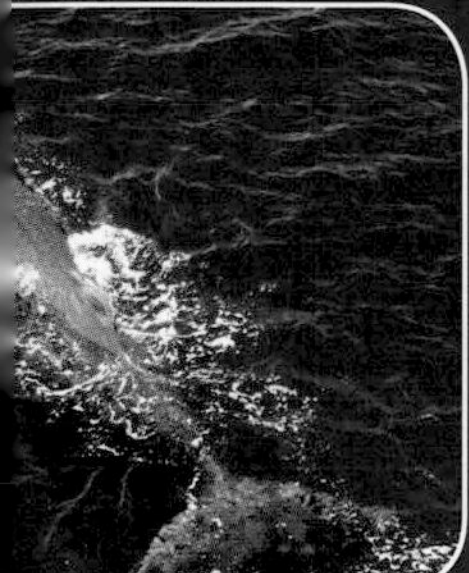

WEIRD OR WHAT?

When they're in murky water, **river dolphins** often trail one flipper along the bottom. They "feel" their way along!

Clicks, whistles, and songs

- Cetaceans are social animals that live in family groups known as pods. They use sound to keep in touch.
- In the 1940s, researchers first used microphones to listen to whales communicating.
- Bottlenose dolphins call each other by "name" – each one has a signature whistle.
- Blue and fin whales sing songs too low (10 Hertz) for us to hear. The sounds travel 1,800 km (1,120 miles) or more.
- Sperm whales are the loudest animals on Earth.
- Amazon river dolphins click as they hunt and listen for the echoes. They identify prey by the echo that comes back.

Clever tactics

- **Lobtailing:** This is when a whale smacks down its tail to stun prey.
- **Bubble netting:** Humpback whales create rising bubbles that confuse fish into forming an easy-to-swallow ball.
- **Beaching:** Orcas snatch seal pups by crashing onto the beach.
- **Ramming:** With their hard beaks, bottlenose dolphins can even kill sharks.
- **Spyhopping:** This is a bit like "treading water". Orcas hold themselves upright in the water as they peer about for prey.

In numbers

5–8 knots The typical cruising speed of a fin whale (Olympic swimmers reach 4.5 knots)

170 The volume in decibels of a sperm whale's click (a pneumatic drill 1 m (3.3 ft) away is only 125 decibels)

200 The age in years that a bowhead whale has reached

700 kg (1,545 lb) The weight of the largest known blue whale heart

1.8 million The number of years ago that the first modern-looking whales appeared

Can all **big cats roar?**

There are at least 38 species of wild cat. With their agile bodies, super-fast reflexes, and camouflaged fur, cats are born predators. There are seven species of big cat: the tiger, lion, leopard, jaguar, cheetah, snow leopard, and clouded leopard. Only the first four of these can roar.

WHAT'S IN A NAME?
The distinctive spots on a jaguar or leopard's coat are known as **rosettes** because they resemble rose flowers.

Tell me more: **tiger physique**

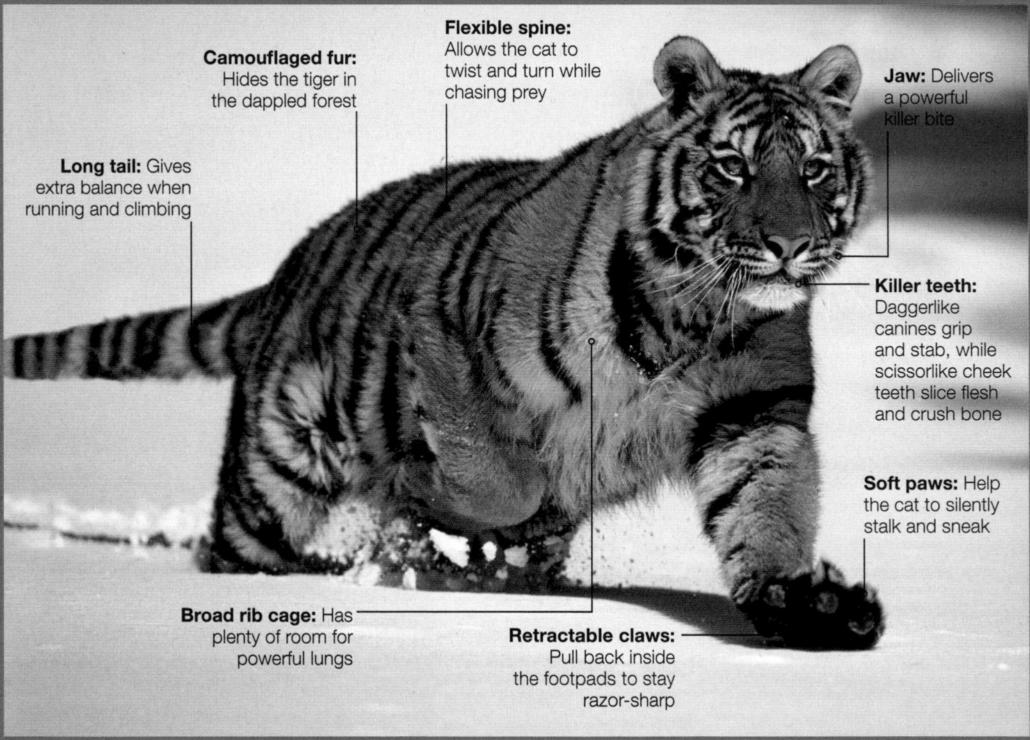

Camouflaged fur: Hides the tiger in the dappled forest
Flexible spine: Allows the cat to twist and turn while chasing prey
Jaw: Delivers a powerful killer bite
Long tail: Gives extra balance when running and climbing
Killer teeth: Daggerlike canines grip and stab, while scissorlike cheek teeth slice flesh and crush bone
Soft paws: Help the cat to silently stalk and sneak
Broad rib cage: Has plenty of room for powerful lungs
Retractable claws: Pull back inside the footpads to stay razor-sharp

FAST FACTS

Cat senses

01: Large, forward-facing eyes judge distances well. Cats also have excellent night vision.

02: Large, movable ear flaps direct sound into a cat's inner ear.

03: The Jacobson's organ is a special sensor in the roof of a cat's mouth that detects smelly messages from other felines.

04: A cat's highly sensitive whiskers help it to judge gaps and find its way in the dark, just by touching objects or sensing air currents.

05: Cats right themselves as they fall, always landing on their feet.

Cat cousins

Tiger
The largest big cats, tigers are usually orange and black. Of the five types, the Bengal is most common and the Siberian is biggest.

Lion
The "king of the jungle" actually lives on the grassy plains of Africa. It has the loudest roar and is the only cat to live in groups.

Leopard
This cat is famous for its spots, but some leopards, known as panthers, have plain black fur. Leopards are smaller than jaguars.

Jaguar
The jaguar lives in the rainforests of Central and South America. It has a squat body and a bite that can crush a turtle's shell.

Cheetah
Equipped with long legs, the cheetah is the fastest land animal. It can sprint at more than 110 kph (68 mph) in short bursts.

Snow leopard
Adapted to life in the mountains of Central Asia, this cat has a thick, warm coat, strong lungs, and stocky legs for climbing.

Six hunting **techniques**

Speed: Unlike most cats, cheetahs are active in the day. They rely on raw speed to catch prey.

Stealth: Most big cats are stalk-and-pounce hunters. Tigers creep up on prey such as sambar deer.

Swimming: Jaguars are strong swimmers. They scoop fish from the water in their heavy paws.

Climbing: Leopards are especially at home in the trees. They hoard prey in a "larder" in the branches.

Leaping: Snow leopards ambush prey in their mountain habitat. They can leap as far as 14 m (45 ft).

Working together: Lions hunt in groups to take down buffaloes, hippos, and other large prey.

How *not* to: **be eaten by a lion**

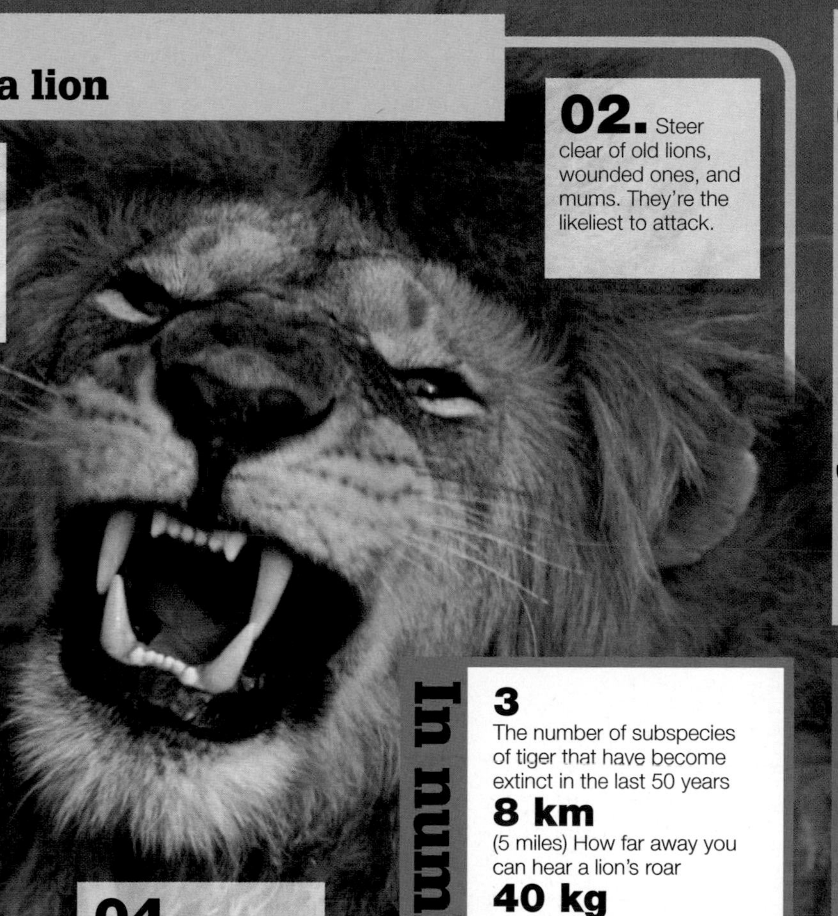

01. Avoid tall grass, as lions love to hide in it. They hunt at night, so light a fire if you're out.

02. Steer clear of old lions, wounded ones, and mums. They're the likeliest to attack.

03. If a lion's ears are flattened and its tail is swinging, it's angry! Don't run away, though, or it will charge.

04. Back away slowly. If the lion runs towards you, try to stare it down. (This takes a lot of guts!)

Big cat's diary

Day 1:
Lion cubs are born blind and helpless

3 weeks:
First, wobbly steps

7–8 months:
Cubs are weaned off their mother's milk

11 months:
Cubs take part in kills

2 years:
80 per cent of cubs don't reach this age, due to lack of food or being eaten by predators

3 years:
Male cubs leave the pride – they will live alone until they're strong enough to take over a pride of their own

8–10 years:
The average age that a lion dies

In numbers

3
The number of subspecies of tiger that have become extinct in the last 50 years

8 km
(5 miles) How far away you can hear a lion's roar

40 kg
(88 lb) The amount of meat a tiger can eat in one go

150
The number of breaths a cheetah takes in a minute when running at full speed

What's on the menu?

Big cats will eat most animals when they're hungry, including monkeys, birds, and mice.

Lions living near the Namib coast have been observed eating seals, cormorants, and even a beached whale.

Tigers have a special liking for porcupines, despite the danger from the poisonous quills. To get more fibre, they will eat fruit.

Leopards tuck into wild dogs and baboons.

Jaguars will attack young black caimans (crocodilians) in the water.

Clouded leopard
Smallest of the seven big cats, the clouded leopard lives in Asia. It is an expert tree-climber, preying on gibbons and macaques.

Pulling faces
Male lions sometimes **grimace** to expose the Jacobson's organ in their mouth. The organ picks up smells given off by females ready to mate.

I don't believe it!

When a young male takes over a pride, it kills and may even eat any cubs. It does this so it can mate with the females and produce offspring of its own.

How **small** is a **mouse?**

Mice include some of the smallest mammals. Their minute bodies have tiny skeletons, so they can squeeze through teeny-tiny holes – some as small as 1 cm (0.3 in). If the head can fit through, then the body can. Mice, rats, and their relatives are all rodents, part of a group that also includes squirrels and beavers. They live all over the world except for the polar regions.

Do mice like cheese?

Scientists have discovered that mice wrinkle up their noses at the strong smell and rich taste of cheese. Their main diet is grains and fruit. Mice prefer sugary foods, especially muesli, and do not like cheese.

Tell me more: **house mouse**

The house mouse is the most common species of mouse. Less than 10 cm (4 in) long, it scampers about on all fours, but stands on its hind legs to fight or eat.

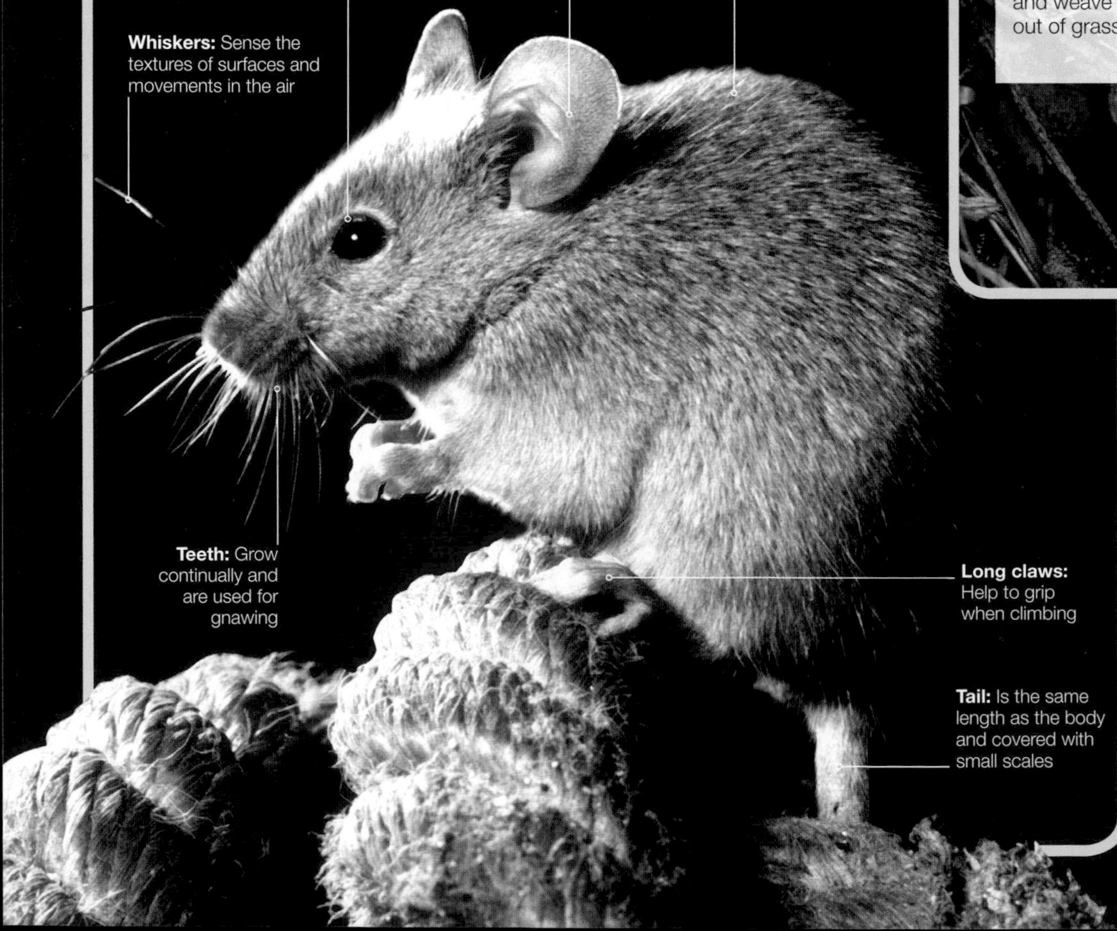
Eyesight: Is poor, with no colour vision
Ears: Are hairless and extremely sensitive to sounds
Short fur: Is grey or brown
Whiskers: Sense the textures of surfaces and movements in the air
Teeth: Grow continually and are used for gnawing
Long claws: Help to grip when climbing
Tail: Is the same length as the body and covered with small scales

How to: **hibernate if you're a do**

01. Start eating a lot. You need to be double your usual weight before you hibernate.

02. Find a pile of leaves on the ground and weave a cosy nest out of grasses.

03. When the weather gets colder, curl into a tight ball in your nest and fall asleep.

Types of nest

- Most mice can adapt to nest just about **anywhere**, but some are more fussy.
- Mice may live together in large colonies, digging out a **burrow system** of interconnecting tunnels.
- Some mice move into the **abandoned nests** of other animals, such as birds or rats.
- Harvest mice weave intricate **ball-shaped nests** from grass.
- House mice move in with people, living behind **skirting boards**, under floors, and inside sofas.

DO NOT DISTURB!

Found across Europe, Africa, and Asia, **common dormice** hibernate when food is scarce to save energy. They go for weeks at a time without moving, and spend up to three-quarters of their life asleep!

FAST FACTS

Families

01: House mice can have up to 10 litters a year.

02: Pregnancy lasts for about 20 days.

03: There are about four to nine babies in each litter.

04: Baby mice are called kittens. They are born hairless.

05: A female mouse can become pregnant again 48 hours after giving birth.

06: Female mice can breed at 42 days old.

se

04. Lower your body temperature and slow your heartbeat. Stay like this for six months.

05. Wake up! You are ravenous. Go and find something to eat!

Tooth facts

An adult mouse has 16 teeth, which it uses for gnawing and chewing its food.

Mice have one upper pair and one lower pair of long, chisel-like incisor teeth at the front of the mouth.

Mice have 12 broader cheek teeth called molars that they use for chewing food into small particles.

During gnawing, lips are sucked into the gap between the incisors and molars. This stops inedible stuff bitten off by incisors entering the mouth.

The incisor teeth grow continuously. Each pair is kept sharp and at the right length by scraping against the other pair.

WEIRD OR WHAT?

Some rodents, including mice, hamsters, and guinea pigs, **eat their own droppings**. They do it to take in nutrients released by bacteria in their intestines.

I don't believe it!

Hopping mice do not drink. They get all the water they need from their diet of seeds, berries, leaves, green plants, and insects.

WHAT'S IN A NAME?

The word "mouse" comes from the word for "thief" in Sanskrit, an ancient Indian language.

Five rodent relatives

As well as mice, the rodent family includes rats, gerbils, hamsters, lemmings, voles, and muskrats. They all have incisors that never stop growing.

Harvest mouse
This small European and Asian mouse has a prehensile tail, which it uses like a fifth limb. Found in cereal fields and hedgerows, it feeds on seeds and insects.

Bank vole
About 10 cm (4 in) long, this vole lives in hedgerows and woodland across Europe and Asia. It eats insects as well as leaves, fruits, and nuts.

Norway lemming
Lemmings are solitary rodents with thick, long fur that live in the tundra near the Arctic. They do not hibernate in winter, but instead live in burrows under the snow.

Golden hamster
Native to Syria, the golden hamster is a popular pet. In captivity it is nocturnal, but in the wild it is active by day. Its cheek pouches hoard and transport food.

Dune hairy-footed gerbil
Gerbils live in dry places with harsh climates. This one is found in the Namib Desert of southern Africa. Hair protects the feet from the heat of the desert sand.

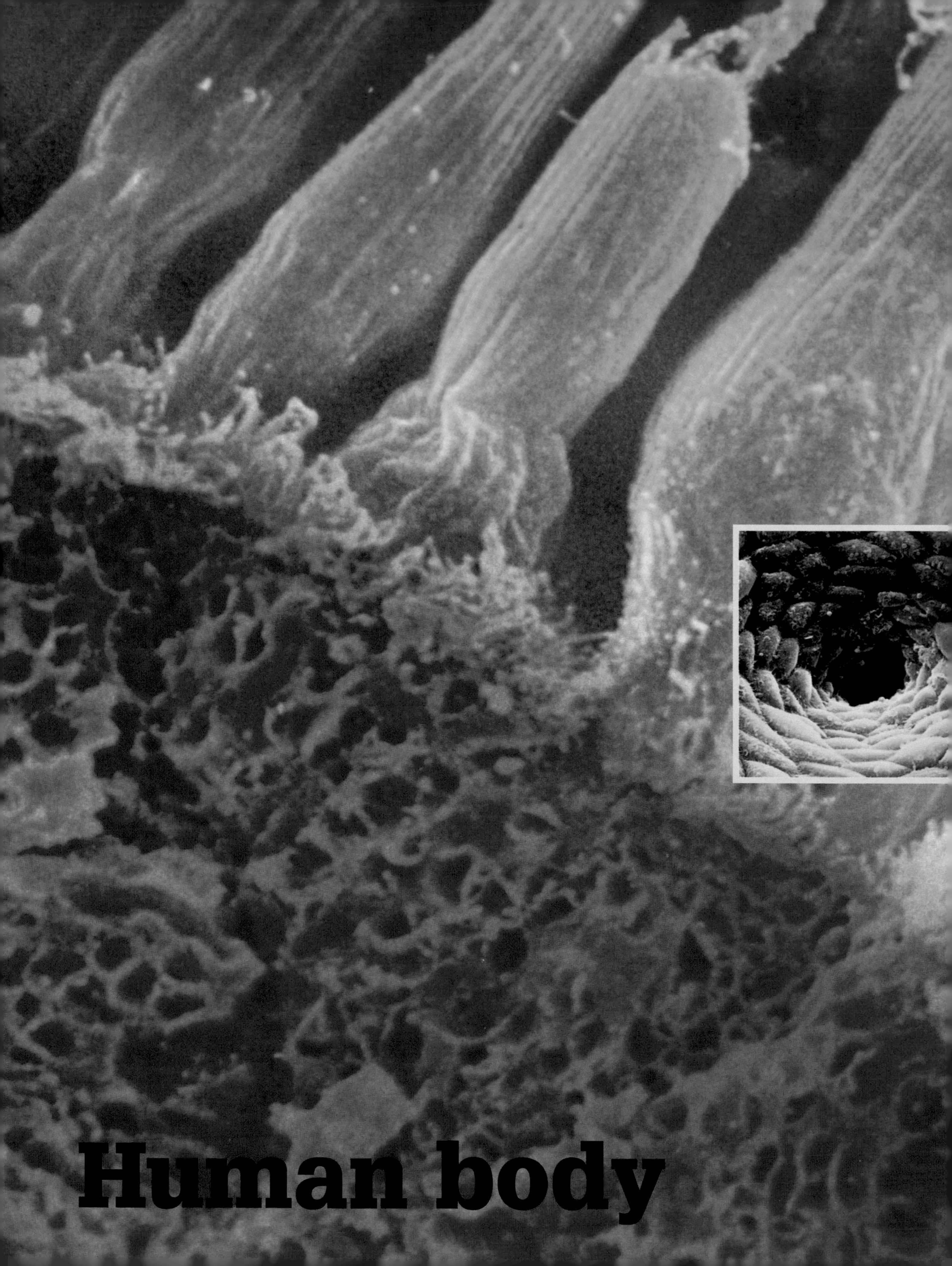

Human body

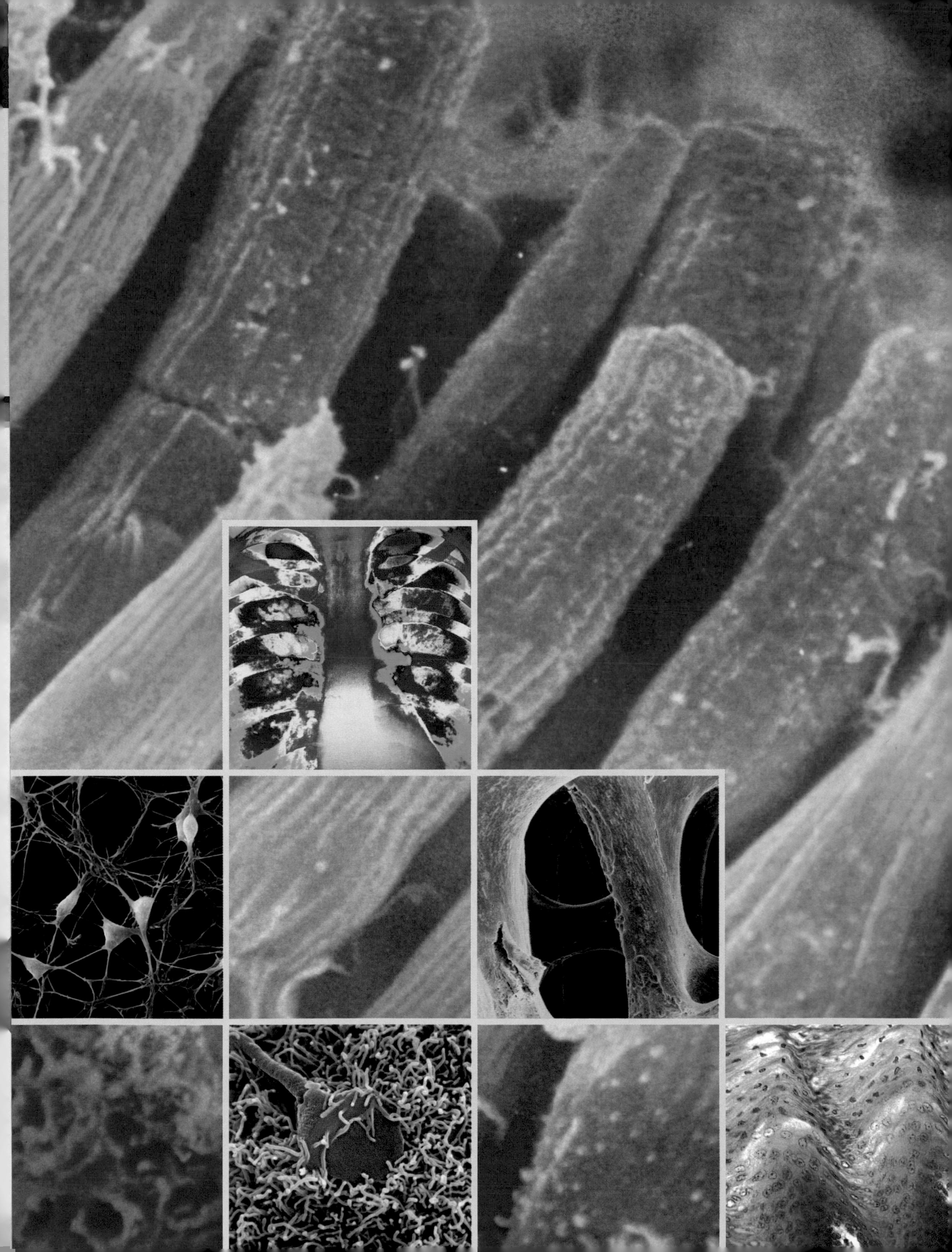

Vital organs

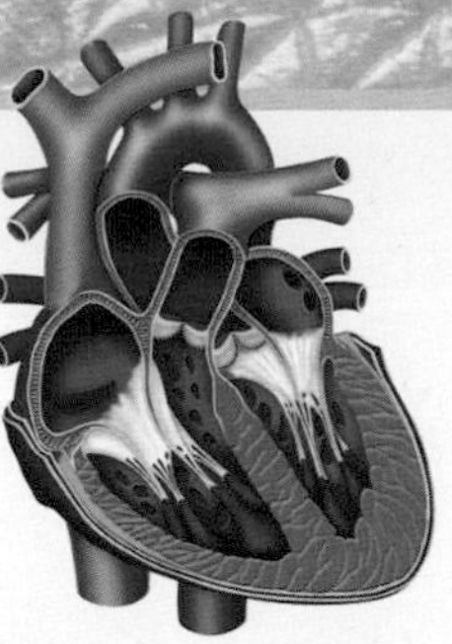

Heart
A muscular pump, the heart powers oxygen-rich blood around the body to "feed" your body cells. Throughout your life, the heart keeps pumping without ever tiring.

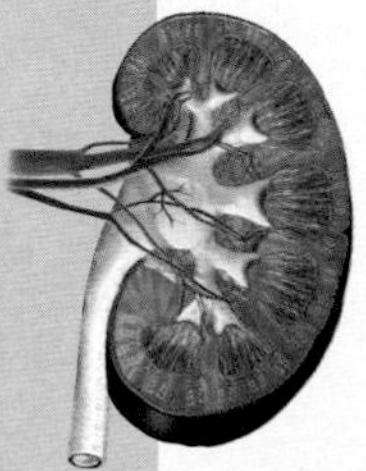

Kidneys
Remove waste products produced by cells along with excess water from the blood. These are then released from your body when you pee.

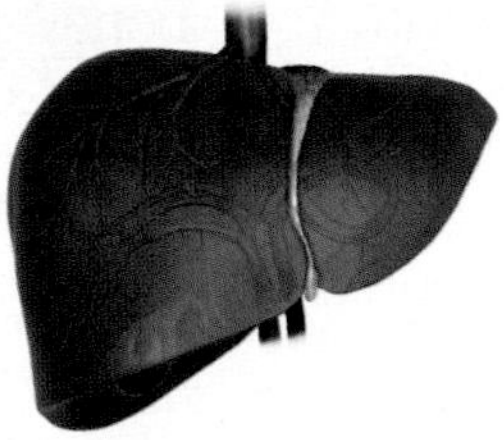

Liver
Processes some nutrients and stores others, and removes harmful substances from the blood. It also recycles worn-out red blood cells.

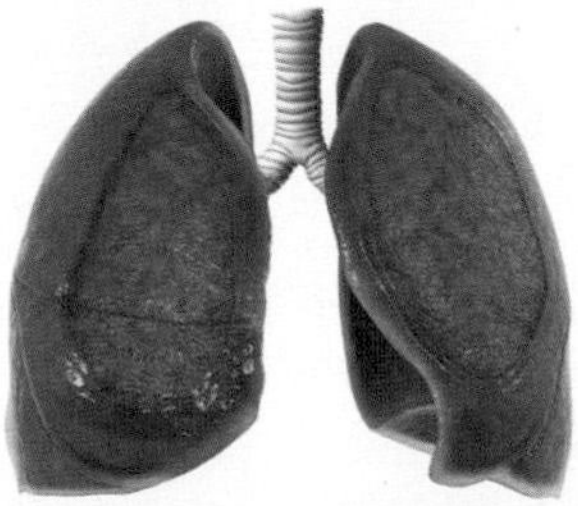

Lungs
Deliver oxygen from the air to your bloodstream when you breathe in. They also release waste carbon dioxide from the blood when you breathe out.

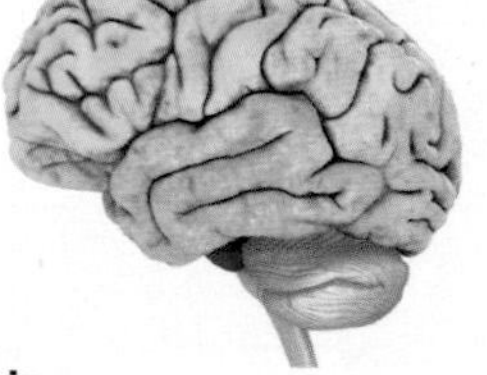

Brain
Collects, interprets, and sends out information through the nervous system enabling you to move, feel, think, and remember.

What is your **largest body organ?**

Parts of the body that perform a specific function, such as the heart and lungs, are called organs. The largest organ in the human body is the skin, which can cover an area of more than 2 sq m (20 sq ft). Some body organs are vital to sustain life but, when damaged, many can now be replaced by a healthy organ from a donor.

RECORD BREAKER

Due to a rare medical condition, known as Ehlers-Danlos syndrome, Englishman Gary Turner has the world's **stretchiest skin**.

Skin functions

- ✔ **Keeps germs and water out**
- ✔ **Keeps body fluids in**
- ✔ **Detects touch, pressure, pain, heat, and cold**
- ✔ **Filters out harmful UV rays in sunlight**
- ✔ **Helps the body maintain a constant internal temperature**
- ✔ **Makes vitamin D**

How to: **transplant a heart**

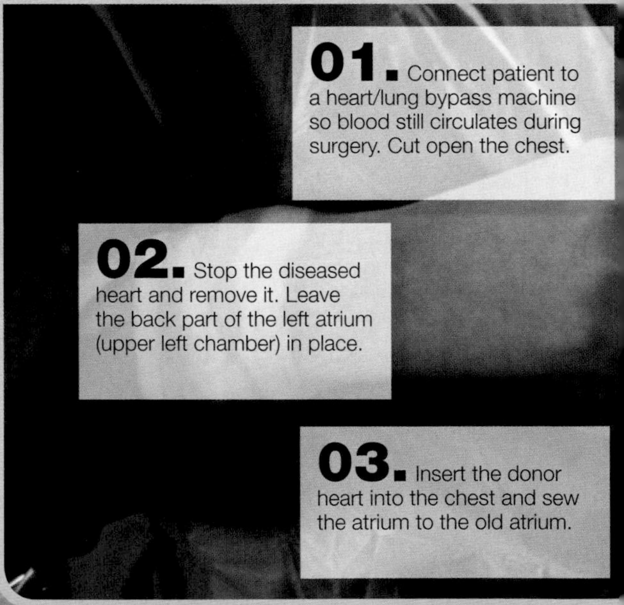

01. Connect patient to a heart/lung bypass machine so blood still circulates during surgery. Cut open the chest.

02. Stop the diseased heart and remove it. Leave the back part of the left atrium (upper left chamber) in place.

03. Insert the donor heart into the chest and sew the atrium to the old atrium.

What's it for?

No one knows for sure what an appendix does. Scientists once thought that this finger-sized tube attached to the large intestine was used by our ancestors to digest tough plant food. Experts now think the appendix might play a role in the immune system by storing helpful bacteria.

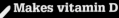

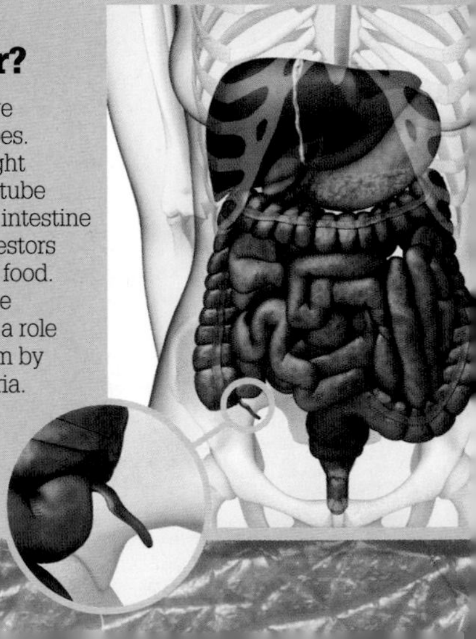

Bladder basics

- The bladder is a hollow, muscular organ that can store about 0.6 litres (1 pint) of urine.
- Urine is made in the kidneys and transported to the bladder via two narrow tubes called ureters.
- As the bladder fills with urine, it expands and its wall stretches. When the bladder is fully expanded, stretch receptors in the wall send messages to your brain telling you it's time to find a loo.
- A sphincter muscle keeps the exit from the bladder to a tube called the urethra closed until your brain instructs it to relax. Then, the bladder wall contracts and forces the urine down and out. Remember to flush!

Wee recipe

95 per cent water

urea and uric acid

bicarbonate ions

creatinine

calcium

magnesium

salts (phosphate, potassium, sodium, and sulphate ions)

Your stomach secretes **hydrochloric acid** to help with digestion. The acid is so corrosive, it could eat through metal, but the walls of the stomach are protected from the acid by a layer of mucus.

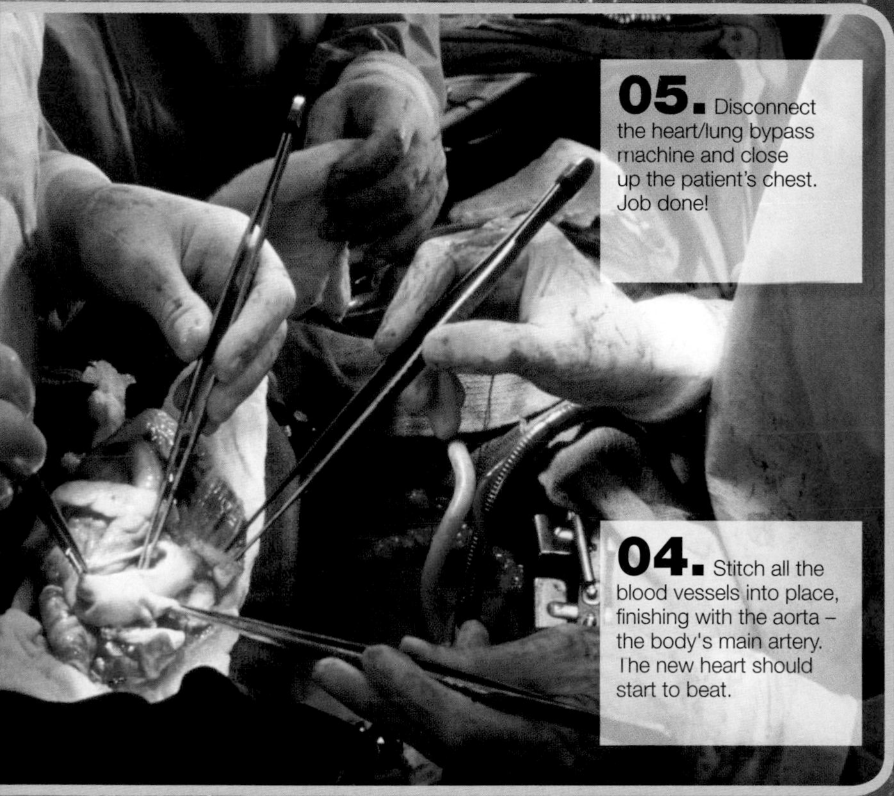

05. Disconnect the heart/lung bypass machine and close up the patient's chest. Job done!

04. Stitch all the blood vessels into place, finishing with the aorta – the body's main artery. The new heart should start to beat.

Transplant organs

These organs can be transplanted from a donor to replace a diseased organ in a recipient's body:

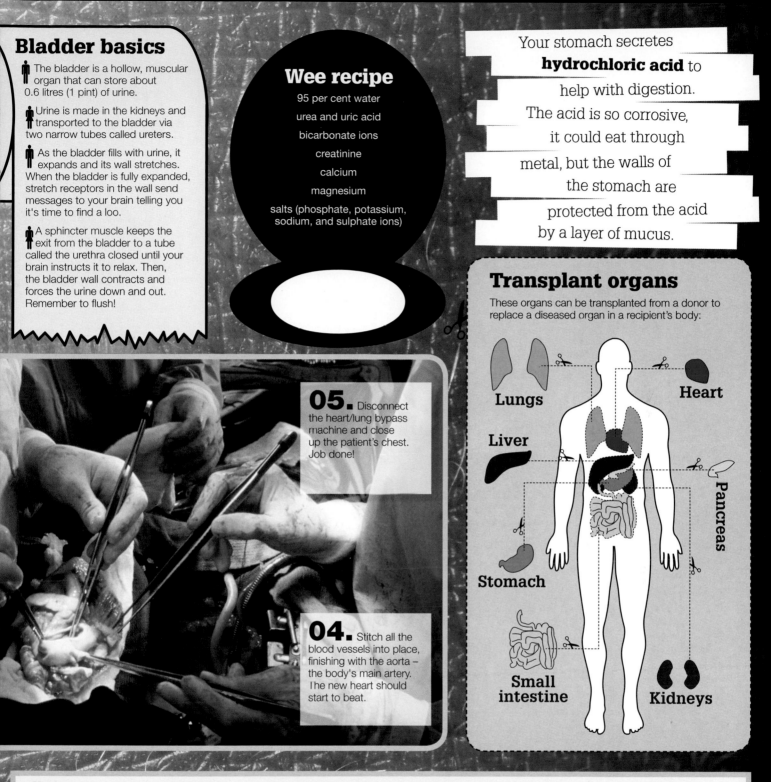

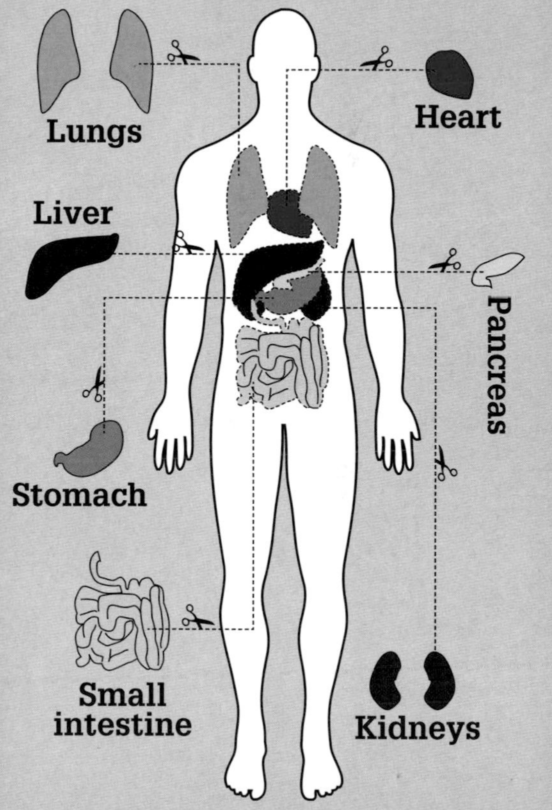

Some more organs

organ	system	location	function
gallbladder	digestive	underside of liver	squeezes a green fluid called bile into your small intestine to help break down fat in food
large intestine	digestive	abdomen – final part of digestive tract	converts food waste into poo
spleen	lymphatic	between stomach and diaphragm on left side of body	removes viruses and bacteria from the blood, helping to protect you from infection
larynx	respiratory	top of windpipe in the throat	contains vocal cords and creates sounds for speech
tongue	digestive	mouth	flexible muscle used to move and taste food

What is a body system?

Organs and tissues that work together in the body are described as systems. For example, all the parts of the digestive system – from the mouth to the stomach, liver, and intestines – play a role in processing food. Body systems are interdependent, relying on one another to function properly.

Tell me more: **breathing in... and out**

Breathing brings fresh air containing oxygen into the lungs and removes stale air containing carbon dioxide. Lungs do not have muscles, so the diaphragm (a dome-shaped muscle under the lungs) and rib muscles must do the work.

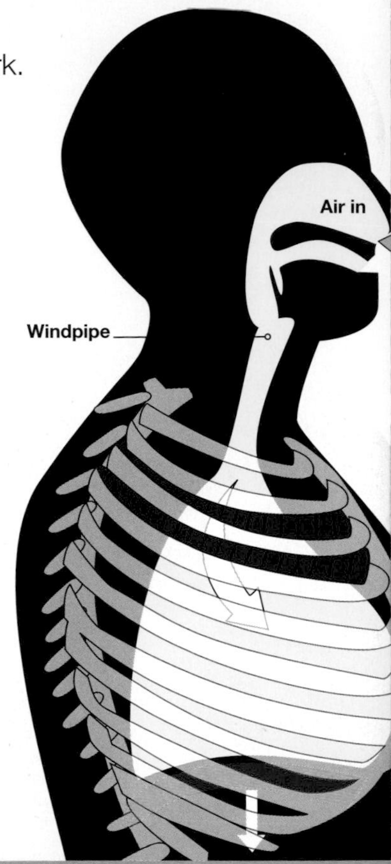

01: Contract and flatten your diaphragm, and contract the muscles between your ribs. This will increase the space in the chest cavity.

02: Your lungs will expand to fill the space, sucking in oxygen-rich air through your nose and down your throat and windpipe.

03: In your lungs,the oxygen passes into your bloodstream, so it can travel to your heart to be pumped around the body with a supply of oxygen for cells.

The head houses and protects key parts of the nervous system including its control centre, the brain, and those vital sense organs, the eyes, ears, tongue, and nose.

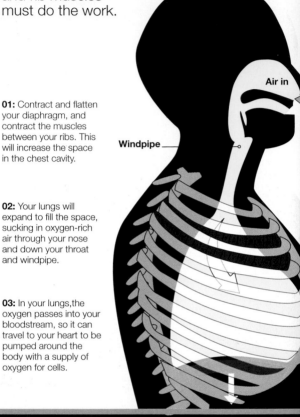

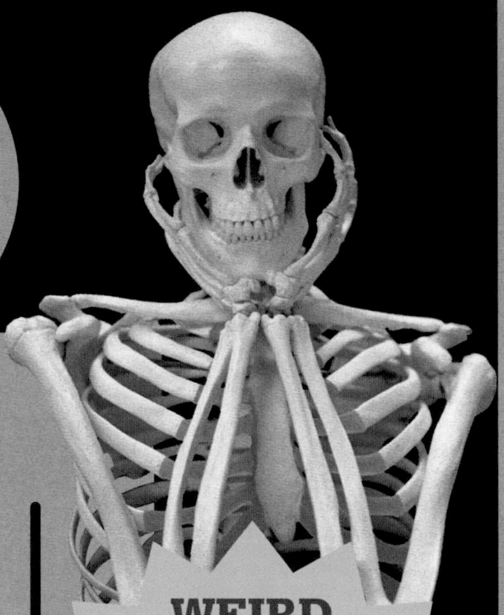

Body systems

- **01: Integumentary:** skin, hair, and nails
- **02: Muscular:** muscles
- **03: Skeletal:** bones
- **04: Cardiovascular:** heart and blood vessels
- **05: Respiratory:** breathing organs
- **06: Digestive:** food-processing organs
- **07: Reproductive:** sex organs
- **08: Lymphatic and immune:** fluid draining and disease defence
- **09: Nervous:** brain and body control
- **10: Urinary:** waste removal
- **11: Endocrine:** hormone production

WEIRD OR WHAT?

You had more bones when you were born than you do now. **Babies** have about **300 bones**, but as you grow some, such as those in your skull, fuse together.

In numbers

650
The number of skeletal muscles in the body

9 m
(30 ft) The combined length of organs in the digestive system

206
The number of bones in an adult's body

320
The number of movable and semi-movable joints in the body

Every minute, when not exercising, you breathe in and out about **6 litres** (3,370 in^3) of air. Exhaled air contains about 100 times the concentration of carbon dioxide than air that is breathed in.

What about me?

If your blood vessels were laid end to end, they would stretch around Earth two and a half times.

Handy guide

Although testosterone is the male sex hormone, it is present in females too. If you had a high level of testosterone before you were born, your ring finger is usually longer than your index finger.

Index finger

Ring finger

Hormones

01: Made up of a number of different glands, the endocrine system releases chemical messengers called hormones into your bloodstream.

02: Release of a hormone called melatonin peaks at night to make you drowsy; during the day less is needed.

03: The endocrine system controls more than 30 hormones. Some of the activities they help to control include:

- How and when you grow
- When you feel hungry
- Glucose (sugar) levels in your bloodstream
- Sleep
- Dealing with stress

Temperature control

Humans are warm-blooded mammals and several body systems are involved in maintaining a constant internal temperature of 37°C (98.6°F).

Nervous system
Nerves relay information about body temperature to the brain, which instructs the other systems to take action.

Integumentary system
Receptors in the skin detect changes in external temperature. If too hot, sweat glands release sweat, which evaporates on the skin's surface to cool the body.

Cardiovascular system
Blood vessels near the surface of the skin widen to radiate heat from the body when hot, or narrow to reduce heat lost through the skin when cold.

Endocrine system
If too cold, adrenal glands produce more adrenaline and noradrenaline to speed up the rate of chemical reactions in cells to increase body heat.

Muscular system
If too cold, involuntary shivering makes muscles contract and release heat to warm the body.

04: Now relax your diaphragm so it pushes up and the muscles between your ribs decrease the space in your chest cavity.

05: This forces your lungs to shrink and squeeze out stale air containing the waste carbon dioxide.

Air out

Ribs

Intercostal muscles

Lungs

Diaphragm

WHAT'S IN A NAME?

The word **"hormone"** comes from a Greek word meaning to excite or set in motion.

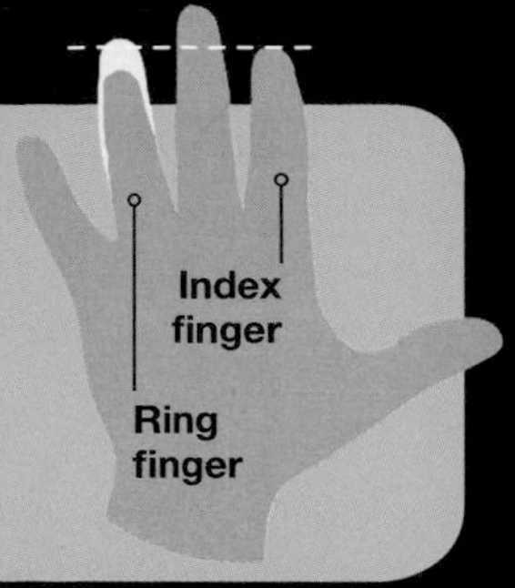

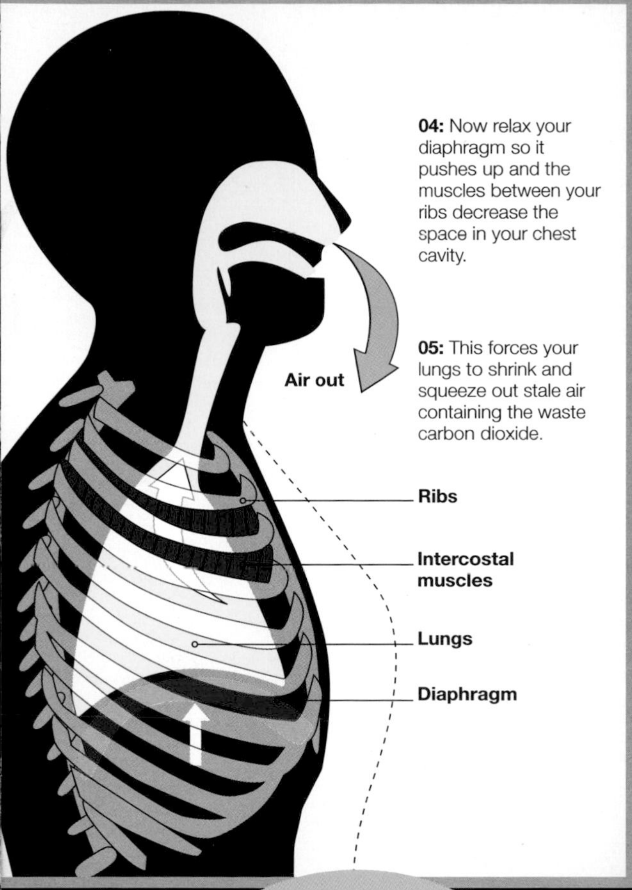

WEIRD OR WHAT?

Muscles make up almost **half your body weight**. When you do a lot of exercise, your muscles develop, which means you can sometimes gain weight.

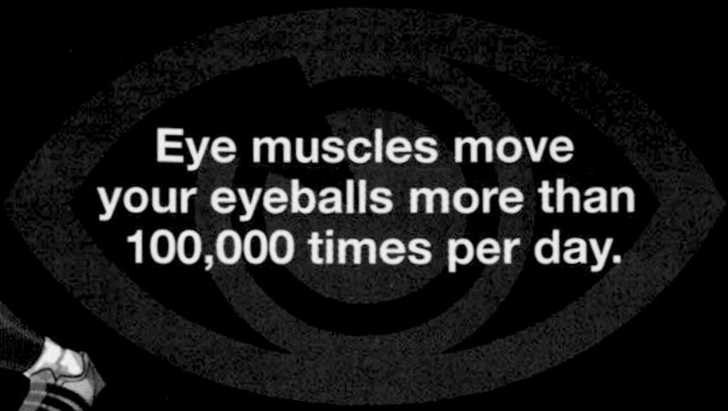

Eye muscles move your eyeballs more than 100,000 times per day.

Ten things you can't do without a nervous system

Smell

Taste

See

Hear

Think

Remember

Dream

Touch

Move

Breathe

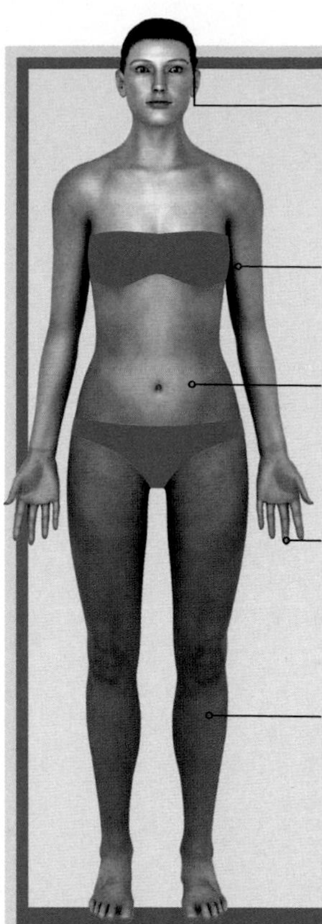
Hair: Grows from scalp and protects top of head
Skin: Forms a protective barrier
Fat layer: Insulates the body
Fingernails: Protect ends of the fingers and thumbs
Brown melanin: Pigment in skin that filters out harmful rays of the Sun

Integumentary system

Together, skin, hair, and nails make up the body's protective outer covering. They form a waterproof and germ-proof barrier between the delicate internal organs and the outside world.

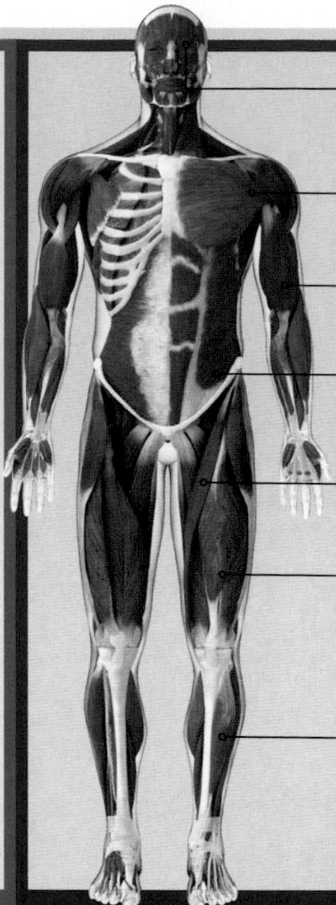
Orbicularis oculi: Closes the eyes
Pectoralis major: Pulls the arm forwards and towards the body
Biceps brachii: Bends the arm at the elbow
External oblique: Twists the trunk and bends it sideways
Sartorius: Bends the thigh at the hip and rotates it outwards
Quadriceps femoris: Straightens the leg at the knee and bends the thigh at the hip
Tibialis anterior: Lifts the foot upwards and inwards

Muscular system

Muscles attached to the skeleton pull the bones to move the body. Smooth muscle produces movement in walls of hollow organs, such as the intestines. Cardiac muscle makes the heart beat.

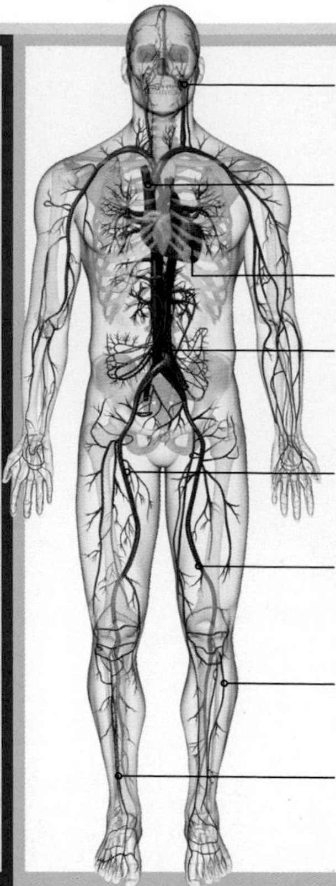
Internal jugular vein: Collects blood from the brain
Superior vena cava: Drains blood from the upper body
Heart: Pumps blood along blood vessels
Descending aorta: Supplies blood to abdomen and legs
Femoral artery: Supplies the thigh and knee
Femoral vein: Carries blood from the thigh
Small saphenous vein: Drains the foot and lower leg
Anterior tibial artery: Supplies the lower leg and foot

Cardiovascular system

The heart pumps oxygen-rich blood along arteries (red) to the body's tissues via tiny blood vessels called capillaries. Veins (blue) return oxygen-poor blood to the heart.

Tell me more: **body systems**

Each body system carries out an important function, such as processing food, transporting blood around the body, or providing the body with oxygen. For a healthy body to function efficiently, the systems work together in a synchronized way, controlled mainly by the brain and nervous system.

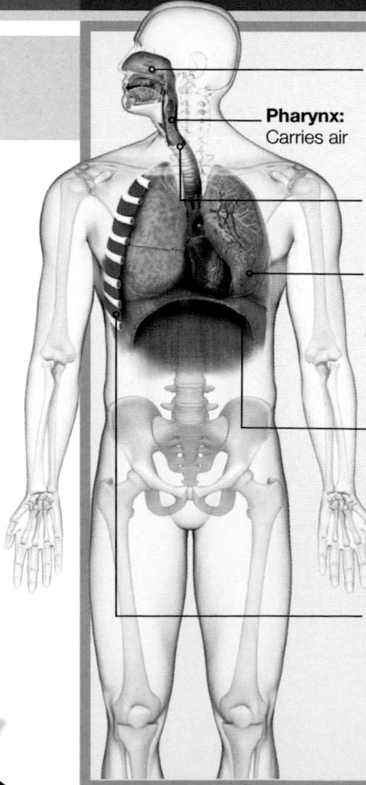
Nasal cavity: Cleans, warms, and moistens inhaled air
Pharynx: Carries air
Larynx (or voicebox): produces sounds
Lungs: Supply the body with oxygen and remove waste carbon dioxide
Diaphragm: Domed muscle that helps breathing movements of the lungs
Intercostal muscle: Moves ribs to aid breathing

Respiratory system

Air enters the lungs via the nasal cavity and pharynx (throat). In the lungs, oxygen is absorbed into the blood and waste carbon dioxide is removed from the blood.

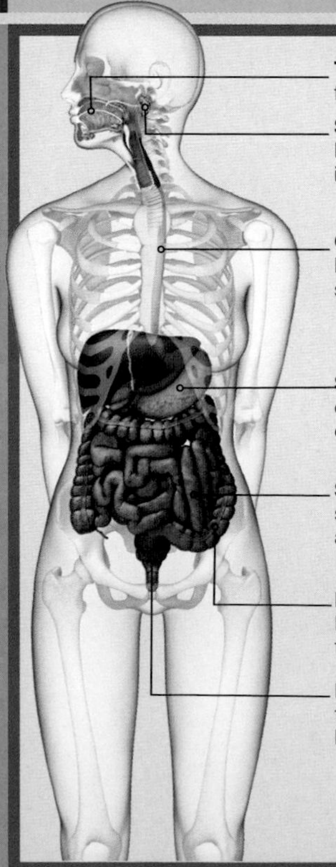
Teeth: Chop and crush food into small pieces
Salivary gland: Releases watery saliva into the mouth
Oesophagus: Pushes food to the stomach
Stomach: Stores, churns, and partially digests food
Small intestine: Main site of digestion and absorption of food
Large intestine: Forms and transports faeces
Rectum: Stores faeces until it can be released

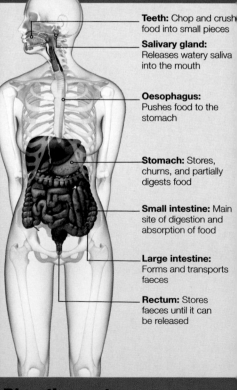

Digestive system

Food is swallowed down the oesophagus to the stomach. As the food passes through the stomach and intestines, it is digested and nutrients are absorbed into the bloodstream.

Male and female

The reproductive system is unique. It is the only system that differs dramatically between males and females and also functions for only part of a lifetime.

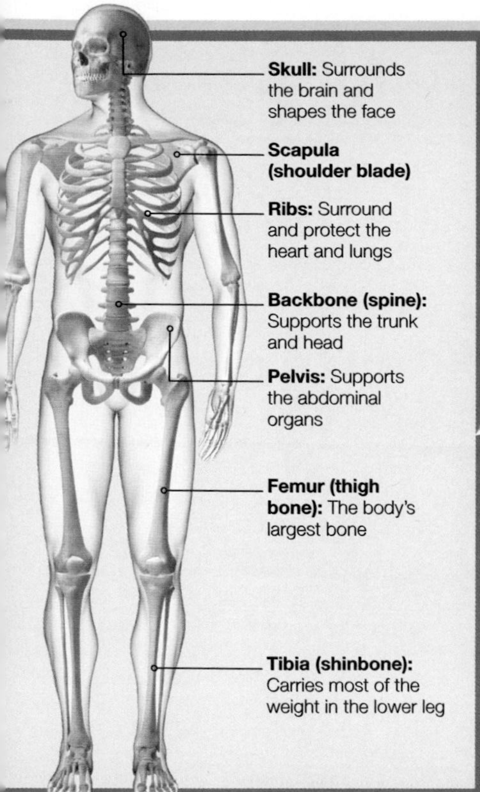
Skull: Surrounds the brain and shapes the face
Scapula (shoulder blade)
Ribs: Surround and protect the heart and lungs
Backbone (spine): Supports the trunk and head
Pelvis: Supports the abdominal organs
Femur (thigh bone): The body's largest bone
Tibia (shinbone): Carries most of the weight in the lower leg

Skeletal system

This jointed framework of bones supports the body and allows it to move. Some bones protect delicate body organs. For example, skull bones protect the brain.

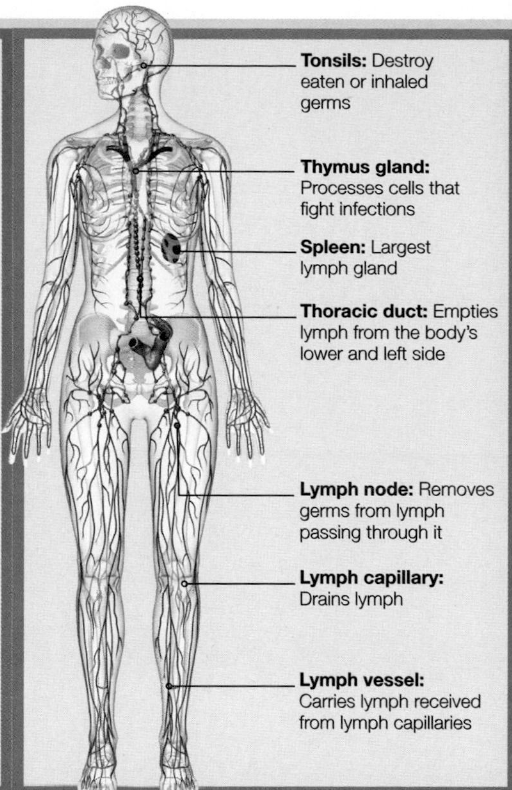
Tonsils: Destroy eaten or inhaled germs
Thymus gland: Processes cells that fight infections
Spleen: Largest lymph gland
Thoracic duct: Empties lymph from the body's lower and left side
Lymph node: Removes germs from lymph passing through it
Lymph capillary: Drains lymph
Lymph vessel: Carries lymph received from lymph capillaries

Lymphatic and Immune system

The lymphatic system drains excess fluid (lymph) from the tissues and filters out germs. The immune system prevents infectious diseases by detecting and destroying invading germs.

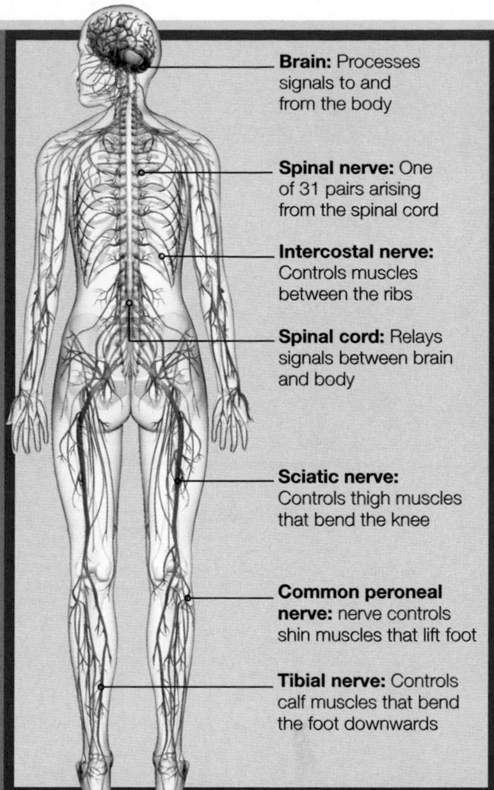
Brain: Processes signals to and from the body
Spinal nerve: One of 31 pairs arising from the spinal cord
Intercostal nerve: Controls muscles between the ribs
Spinal cord: Relays signals between brain and body
Sciatic nerve: Controls thigh muscles that bend the knee
Common peroneal nerve: nerve controls shin muscles that lift foot
Tibial nerve: Controls calf muscles that bend the foot downwards

Nervous system

Sensory information is relayed by nerves to the spinal cord and brain, which receive and process the information then send out instructions to parts of the body via the nerves.

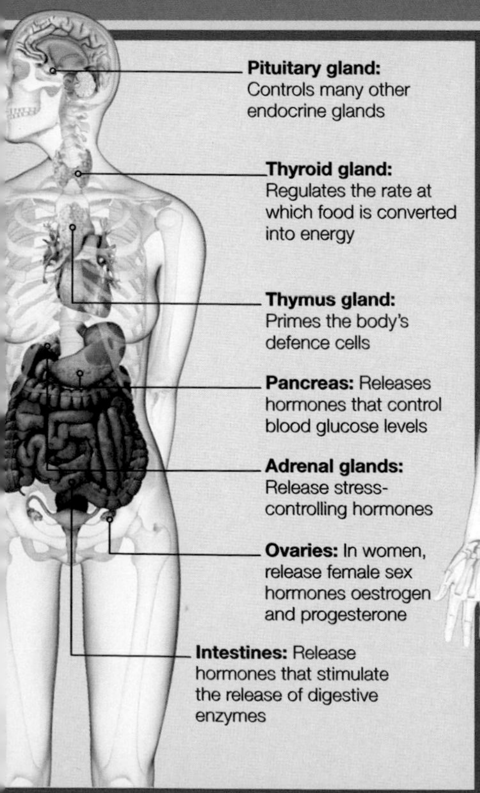
Pituitary gland: Controls many other endocrine glands
Thyroid gland: Regulates the rate at which food is converted into energy
Thymus gland: Primes the body's defence cells
Pancreas: Releases hormones that control blood glucose levels
Adrenal glands: Release stress-controlling hormones
Ovaries: In women, release female sex hormones oestrogen and progesterone
Intestines: Release hormones that stimulate the release of digestive enzymes

Endocrine system

he organs in this system produce messenger hemicals called hormones that trigger growth nd maintain body functions. Male bodies roduce the sex hormone testosterone.

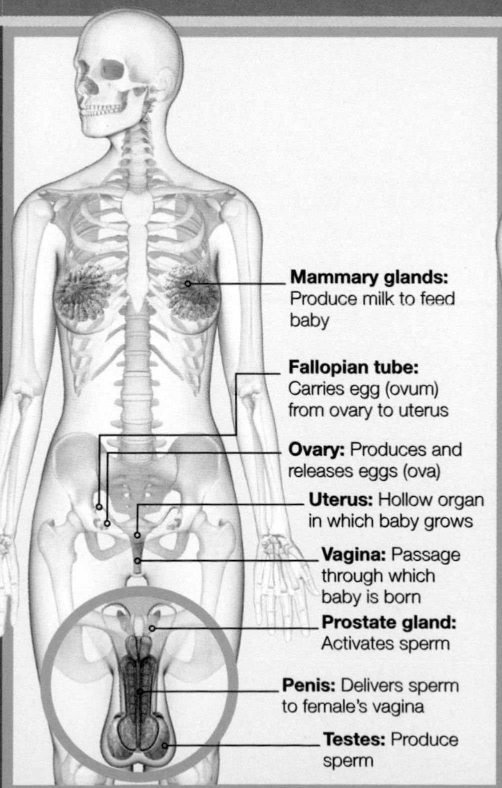
Mammary glands: Produce milk to feed baby
Fallopian tube: Carries egg (ovum) from ovary to uterus
Ovary: Produces and releases eggs (ova)
Uterus: Hollow organ in which baby grows
Vagina: Passage through which baby is born
Prostate gland: Activates sperm
Penis: Delivers sperm to female's vagina
Testes: Produce sperm

Reproductive system

Men and women have very different reproductive systems. A female (main image) produces eggs, while the male (circle) produces sperm. When an egg is fertilized by a sperm, it develops into a baby.

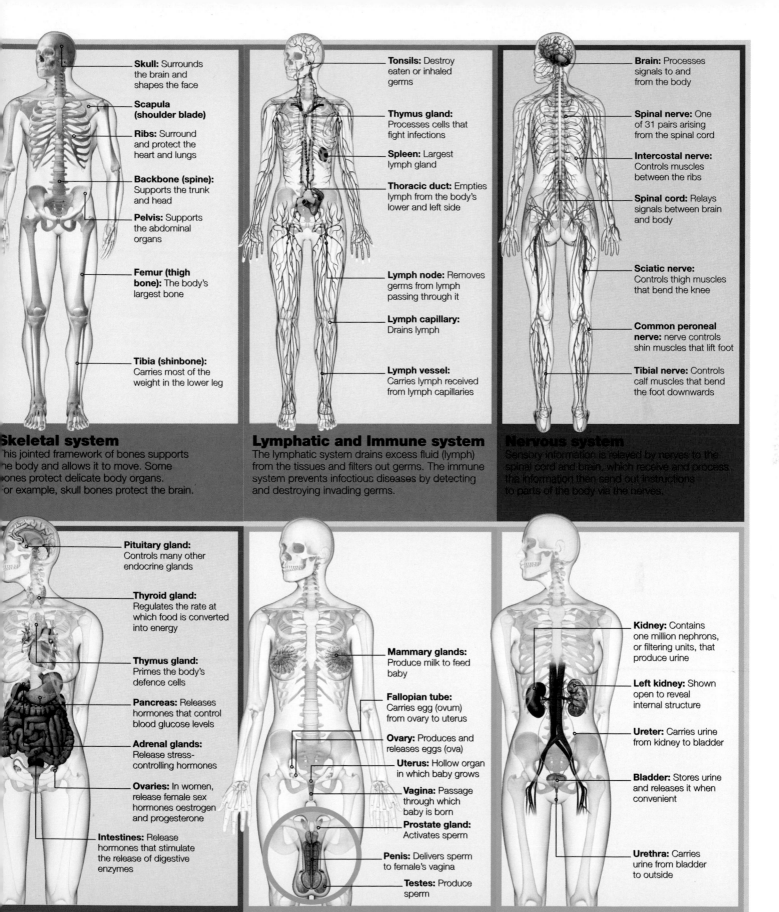

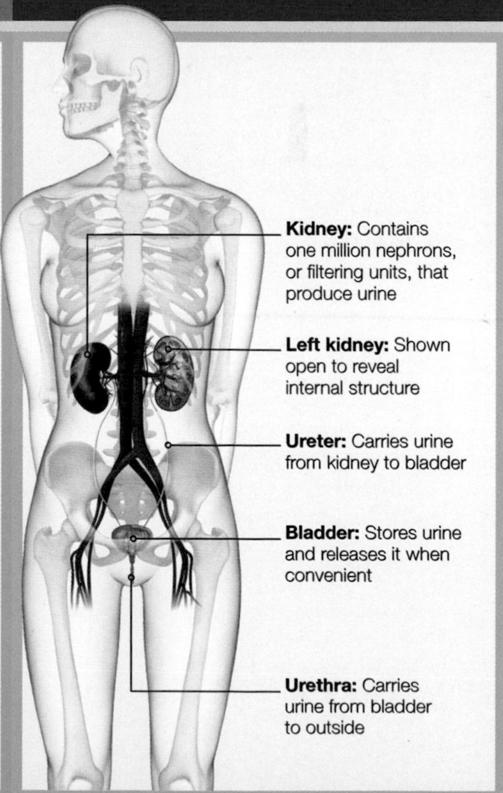
Kidney: Contains one million nephrons, or filtering units, that produce urine
Left kidney: Shown open to reveal internal structure
Ureter: Carries urine from kidney to bladder
Bladder: Stores urine and releases it when convenient
Urethra: Carries urine from bladder to outside

Urinary system

Kidneys form urine from waste substances and excess water and salts in the blood, which is stored in the bladder. When the bladder is full, urine is expelled from the body via the urethra.

Blasts from the past

1866
German priest and scientist Gregor Mendel publishes his results of experiments on the laws of inheritance, confirming that genes come in pairs, with one inherited from each parent

1869
Swiss biologist Johannes Friedrich Miescher identifies a substance in the nucleus of white blood cells, which is later called deoxyribonucleic acid (DNA)

1910
US scientist Thomas Hunt Morgan studies genetic variations in fruit flies and confirms that genes are carried on chromosomes

1944
Canadian and American scientists Oswald Avery, Colin MacLeod, and Maclyn McCarty prove that genes are made of DNA

1952
British physicist Rosalind Franklin produces an image of a DNA molecule using X-ray diffraction

1953
Briton Francis Crick and American James Watson use Franklin's DNA image and earlier research to work out the double helix structure of DNA

1972
US scientist Paul Berg successfully cuts and splices DNA to create the first genetically engineered strand of DNA

1984
Danish scientist Steen Willadsen sucessfully clones a sheep from embryo cells

2003
The international Human Genome Project team announce the completion of the human genome sequence

2009
A German Shepherd search and rescue police dog, who rescued the last person alive following the attacks in New York on 9/11, is cloned to create five puppies

What is **DNA?**

The nucleus of a body cell contains the instructions to make the proteins that determine how that cell functions and what your body looks like. These instructions, or genes, are carried on structures called chromosomes, which are made from deoxyribonucleic acid, or DNA.

Counting chromosomes

Each body cell has 46 chromosomes in 23 pairs. One chromosome from each pair is inherited from your mother and one from your father. One pair of chromosomes determines your gender. Two "X"s makes a girl and "XY" makes a boy.

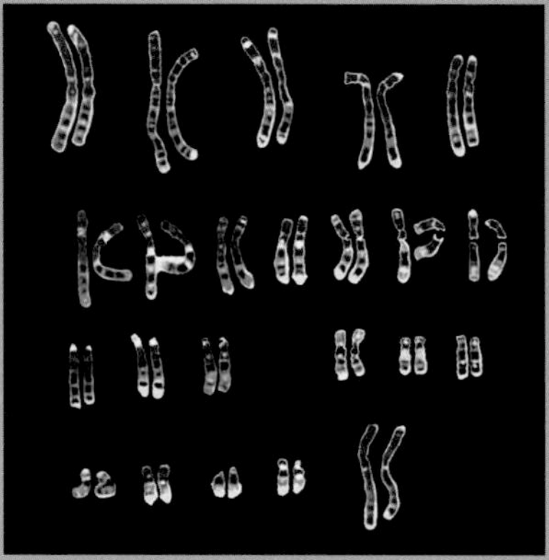

If the DNA from just **one cell** were stretched out, it would be about 2 m (6 ft) long.

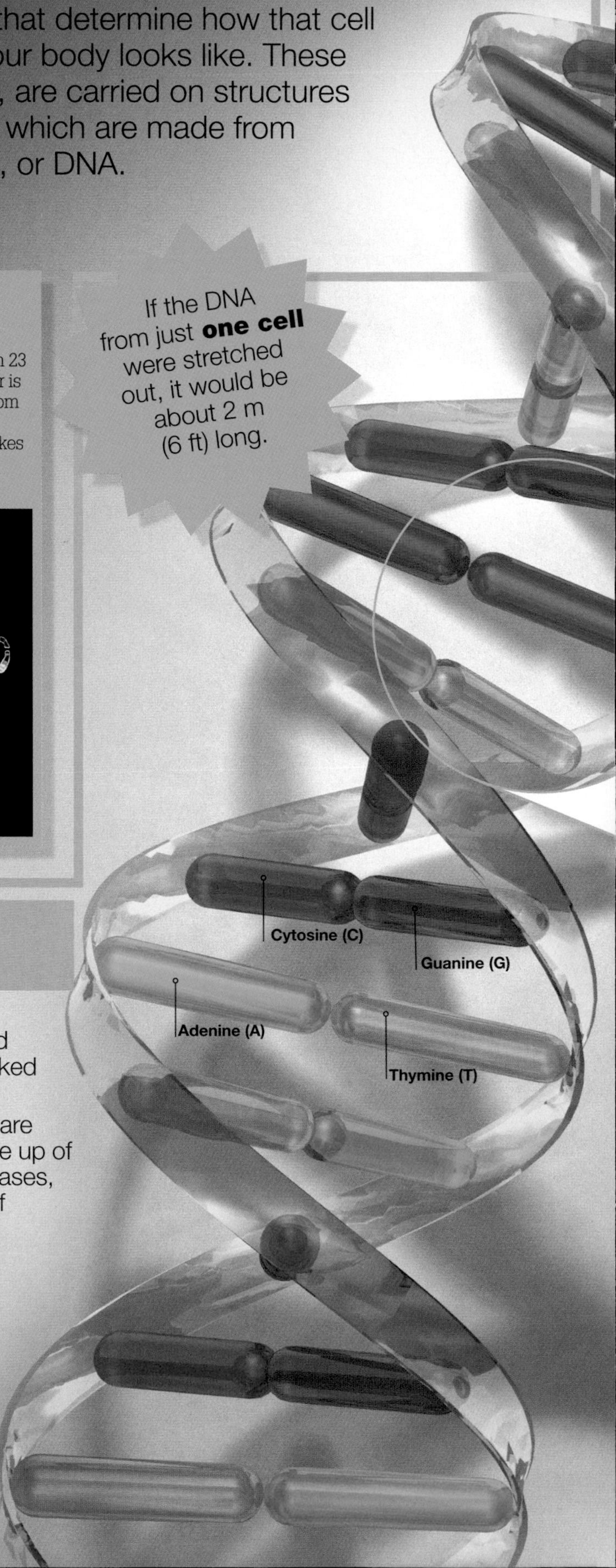

Tell me more: **DNA structure**

- DNA is shaped like a double helix, or twisted ladder, made up of two linked strands.
- The two DNA strands are joined by "rungs" made up of paired chemicals, called bases, that provide the "letters" of the instructions in genes.
- There are four bases: adenine (A), thymine (T), guanine (G), and cytosine (C).
- A is always paired with a T and every C with a G.

Spot the difference!

Identical twins may share the same genes, but they do not have matching fingerprints. The pattern of whorls and ridges will be similar, but fingerprints are also influenced by environmental factors in the womb before birth, so twins will have slightly different print patterns.

FAST FACTS: Human genome

01: The complete DNA sequence of our chromosomes is called a genome.

02: The Human Genome Project united scientists around the world in the challenge to identify the entire sequence of DNA bases in a human cell.

03: They discovered that the human genome is made up of 3.2 billion pairs of bases.

04: Just 3 per cent of the DNA bases make the 20,000–25,000 genes of the genome.

05: The average gene is about 10,000 bases long.

06: The rest of the genome is known as "junk DNA". Scientists don't yet know what its function is

DNA identity

01 Although 99.9 per cent of DNA is the same in every person (99.95 per cent in siblings), there are sections that are highly variable and unique to each individual (apart from identical twins).

02 Forensic scientists can analyse a DNA sample to create a unique DNA profile of an individual. This can be used to identify victims or criminals. It's called a genetic fingerprint.

03 DNA can be extracted from samples of body fluids found at a crime scene, or from cheek cells collected by rubbing a cotton swab inside the mouth.

How to: **catch a criminal**

Victim

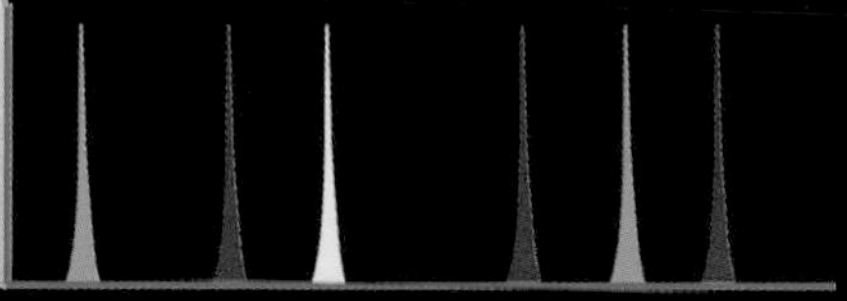

01. Search the crime scene for any physical evidence such as body fluids or strands of hair and take them back to the forensic lab for analysis. Extract key sections of DNA from the evidence collected to create a DNA fingerprint.

Crime scene sample

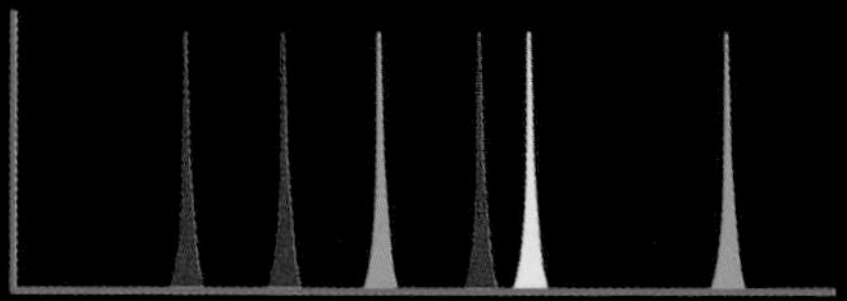

02. Create a fingerprint of the victim's DNA to check whether the physical evidence collected at the scene belongs to them. If it doesn't, the crime scene evidence could help identify the criminal culprit.

Suspect 1

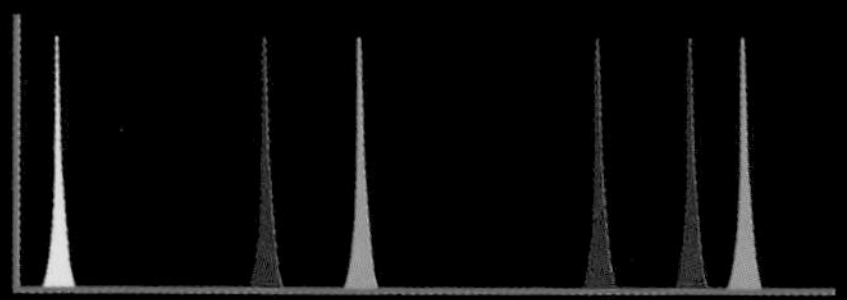

03. Once police have identified a suspect, scrape cells from inside the suspect's cheek and use them to build a DNA fingerprint. Look for a match with the crime scene DNA. This suspect is clearly innocent.

Suspect 2

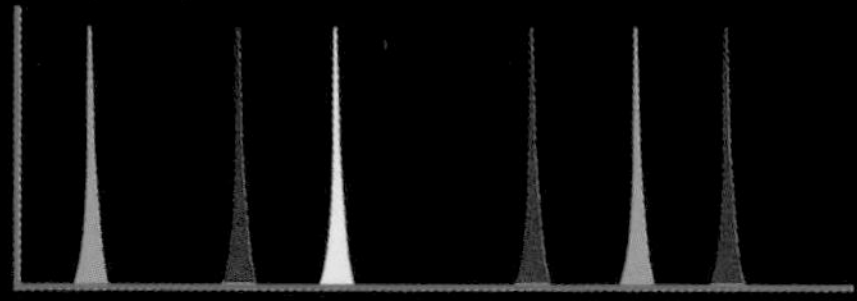

04. Collect DNA from a second suspect and compare to the crime scene sample. This suspect was at the scene!

We humans share 96 per cent of our DNA with **chimpanzees** and a surprising 80 per cent of human genes are the same as those found in mice. So squeak up if you have a fondness for bananas!

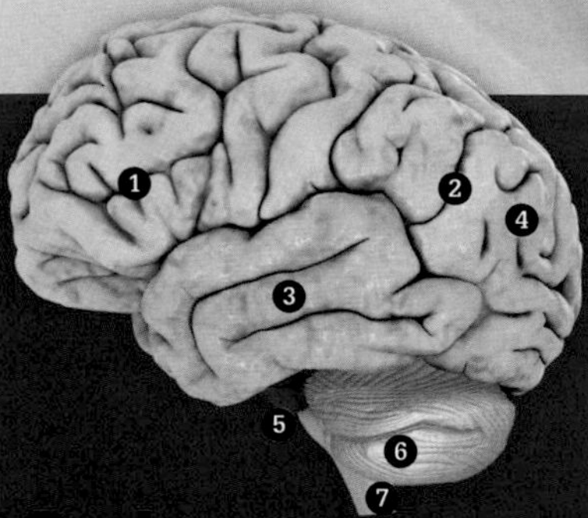

Brain map

01 Frontal lobe controls personality, speech, and emotion

02 Parietal lobe processes sensory data

03 Temporal lobe identifies and processes sound

04 Occipital lobe processes visual information

05 Pituitary gland releases many hormones

06 Cerebellum helps control movement and balance

07 Brain stem links brain to body and controls heartbeat and breathing

Long-term memory types

Procedural: Learned skills such as riding a bicycle or playing guitar

Semantic: Words, languages, and facts

Episodic: Significant events in your life

How do you **think?**

The brain is the control centre of your nervous system and is more complex than any computer. It is packed with 100 billion nerve cells (neurons) that process and pass on information in the form of electric signals from your sense organs and other receptors. These are then stored in your memory.

WEIRD OR WHAT?

The brain cannot feel pain. This means that **brain surgeons** can probe areas of the brain while the patient is awake.

Neurons in the brain are tiny – 30,000 could fit on the head of a pin. The longest neuron extends about 1 m (3 ft) from the base of the spine to the big toe.

Tell me more: **neuron anatomy**

Neurons are nerve cells that transmit information as electric signals.

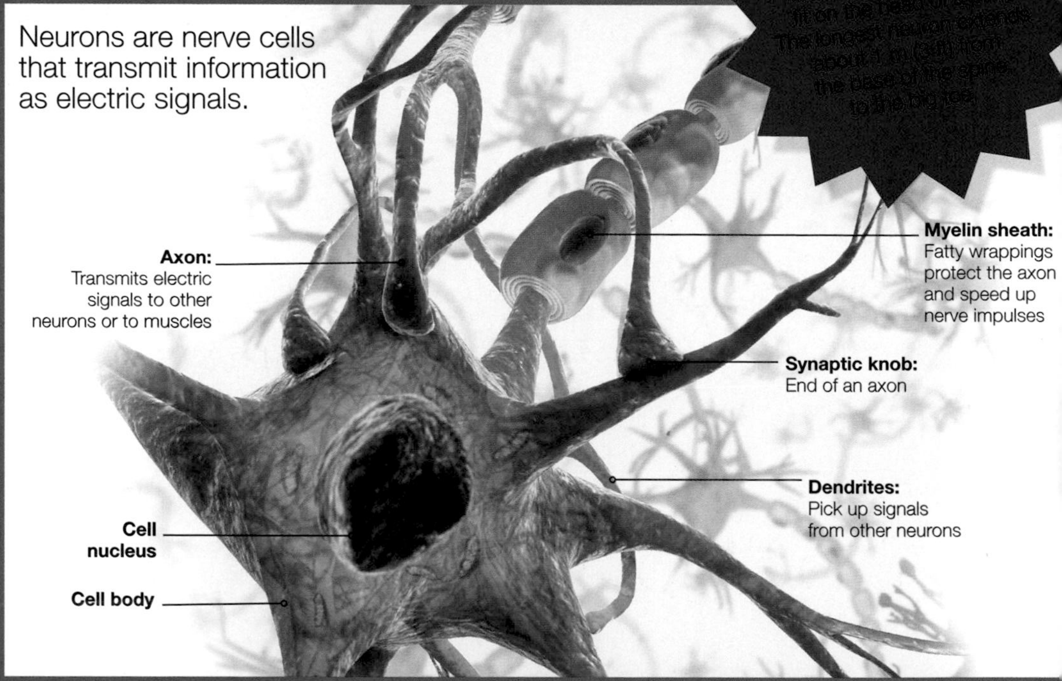

Range of emotions

Emotions are triggered in our brains and are beyond our conscious control. Here are four main types:

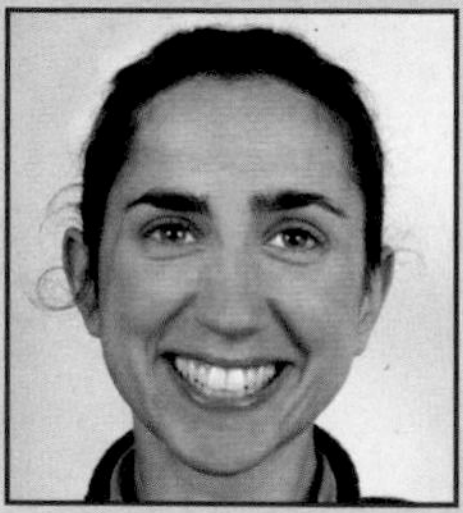

Happy
Feelings of contentment, love, pleasure, and joy

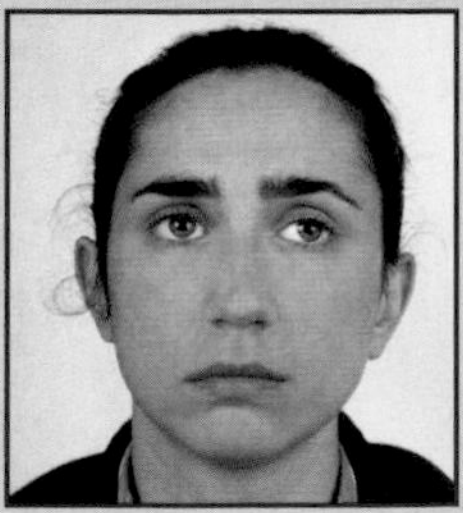

Sad
Feelings of loss, grief, and helplessness

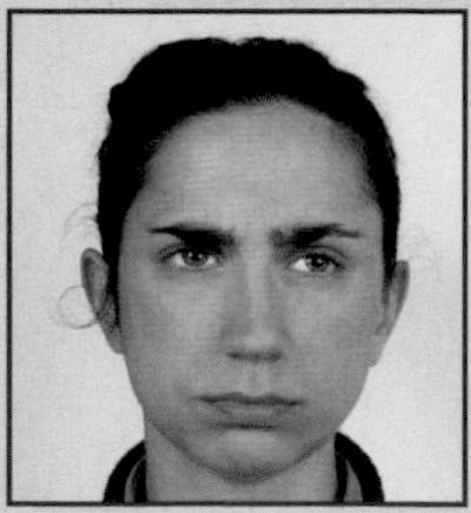

Anger
Feelings of aggression and outrage

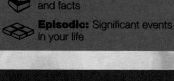

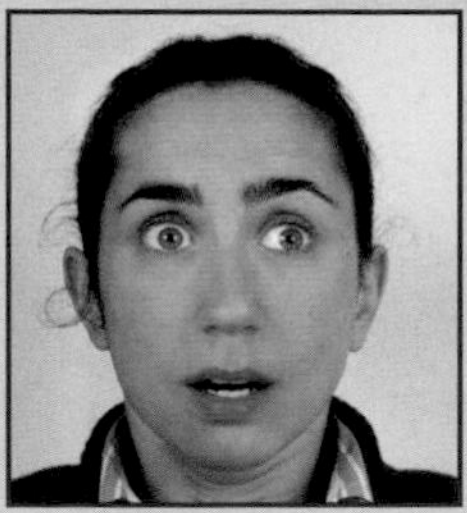

Fear
Feelings of apprehension about what might happen

Brain tasks

- ✔ Controls breathing, heart rate, and body temperature
- ✔ Instructs muscles to contract and pull on the skeleton so your body can move
- ✔ Processes information from sense organs and skin receptors, so you can feel and experience your surroundings
- ✔ Stores and retrieves memories
- ✔ Thinks, reasons, and imagines
- ✔ Produces and controls emotions

Visual tricks

Your brain uses clues in your surroundings to make sense of what you see, but sometimes the images are confusing and the brain is tricked.

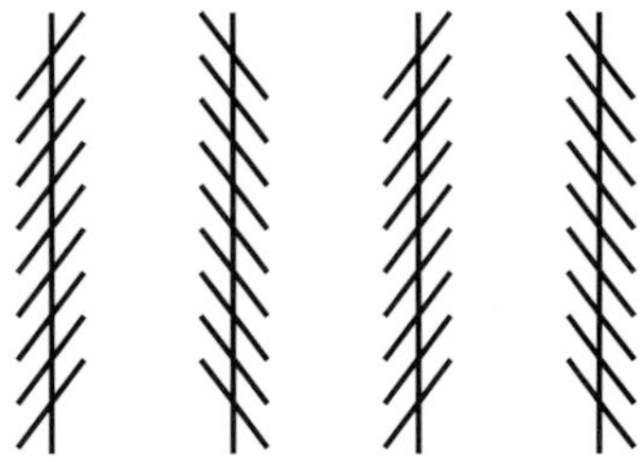

These four parallel lines may appear to lean slightly to the left or right, but they are actually perfectly straight.

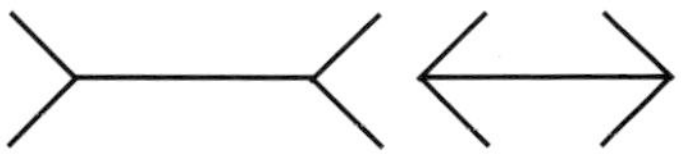

The line on the left may look as if it's longer than the one on the right, but they are exactly the same length.

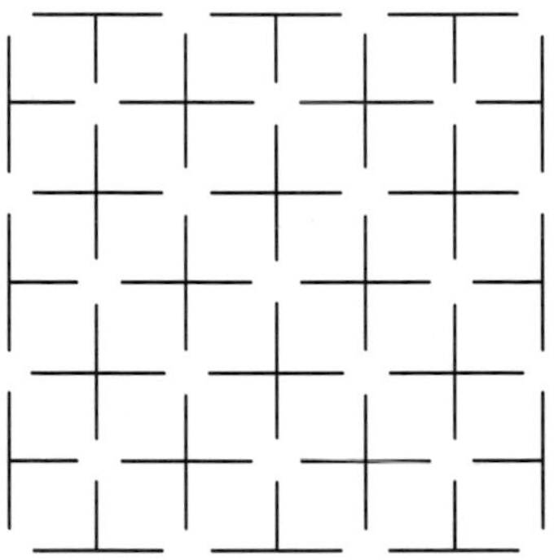

The grid lines seem to be joined by a pattern of white circles, but these are just gaps between the lines.

Blood to the head

- The brain is covered in a 645-km (400-mile) network of arteries, veins, and capillaries.
- About 20 per cent of the body's oxygen intake is reserved for the brain even though it makes up a mere 2 per cent of the body's mass.

■ If the brain's blood supply is cut off, unconsciousness can occur in 10 seconds.

- [illegible]
- [illegible]

Five ways to improve your memory

01: Link new ideas to things you already know so they connect to information already stored in your long-term memory.

02: Divide long number sequences, such as phone numbers, into smaller chunks that are easier to remember.

03: Invent a mnemonic by using the first letter of each item to make up a sentence. For example, "Richard of York gave battle in vain" can help you remember the colours of the rainbow: red, orange, yellow, green, blue, indigo, violet.

04: Read written information out loud and then rewrite it to reinforce your memory of it.

05: Get a good night's sleep – it is hard to concentrate and remember things if you are tired.

How to: remember

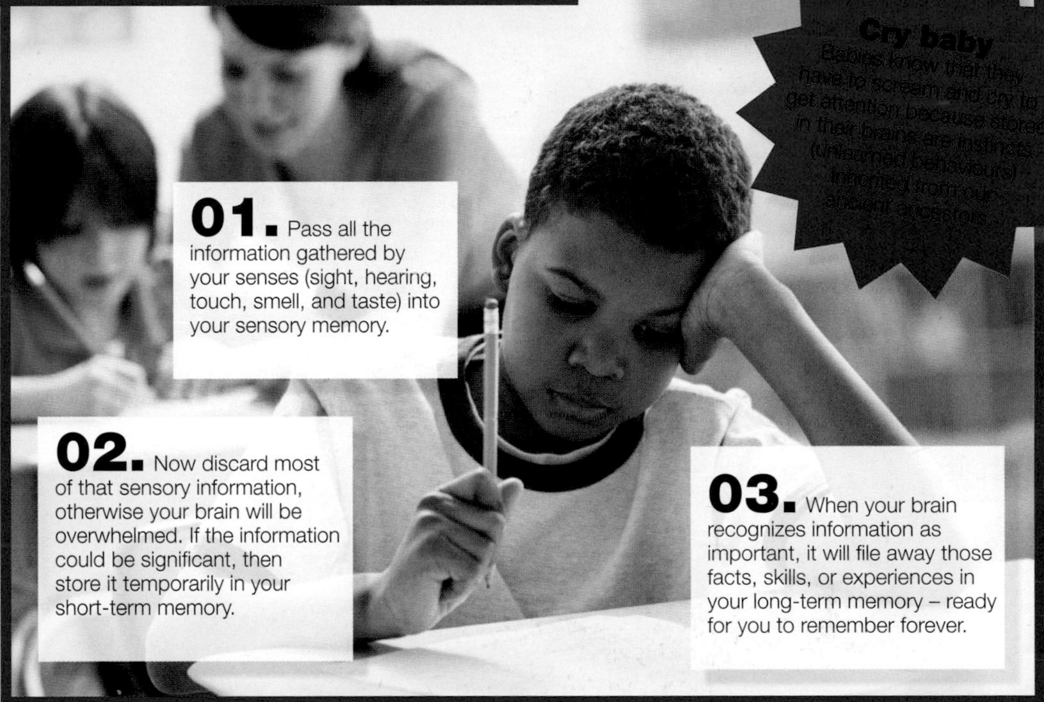

01. Pass all the information gathered by your senses (sight, hearing, touch, smell, and taste) into your sensory memory.

02. Now discard most of that sensory information, otherwise your brain will be overwhelmed. If the information could be significant, then store it temporarily in your short-term memory.

03. When your brain recognizes information as important, it will file away those facts, skills, or experiences in your long-term memory – ready for you to remember forever.

Cry baby

Babies know that they have to scream and cry to get attention because stored in their brains are instincts (unlearned behaviours) inherited from our ancient ancestors.

Left or right?

The left half of the brain controls the right side of the body, and the right half of the brain controls the left side.

For most people, the left half of the brain dominates and they are right-handed.

In 10 per cent of the population, the right half of the brain dominates and these people are left-handed.

Famous left-handers include Italian artist Leonardo da Vinci, English scientist Isaac Newton, and US President Barack Obama (pictured).

Ambidextrous people can use both hands equally well.

You can also have a dominant eye and a dominant foot.

Butter brain

Brain tissue is so soft that it could be easily sliced through with a butter knife. Luckily, the **brain** is protected by the tough bones of the **skull**.

FAST FACTS

Consciousness

01: Consciousness is awareness of your own existence and of your surroundings.

02: Consciousness is not controlled by one particular part of the brain, but depends on activity throughout the outer layer of the cerebrum – the part of the brain that is responsible for memory, thinking, personality, and so on.

03: Humans don't develop a sense of self until they are about 18 months old.

Why do you **need to sleep?**

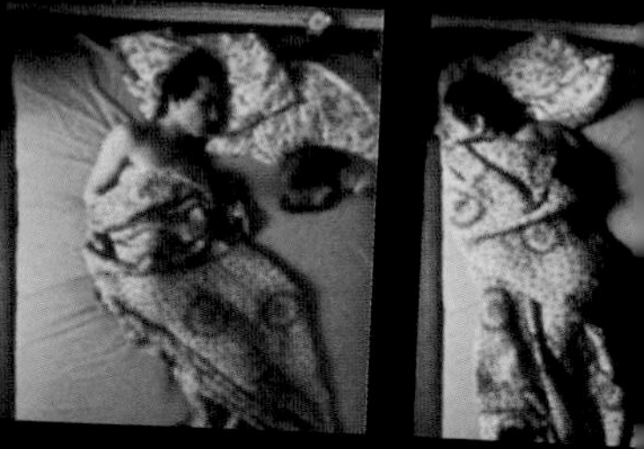

No one knows for sure, but most scientists believe that during sleep the brain organizes, processes and stores information, and produces memories. It also gives your body time to rest. If you don't get enough sleep, you can become irritable and find it hard to concentrate.

WEIRD OR WHAT?

Diaries from the days before the electric light bulb was invented reveal that our **ancestors slept longer** hours than we do. Maybe the light bulb wasn't such a bright idea!

How to: **sleep**

01. Lie down, shut your eyes, and relax your muscles. Don't worry if your muscles occasionally twitch or jerk. This is perfectly normal.

02. Slow down your brainwaves from active beta waves to the more relaxed alpha waves.

03. Slow down your breathing and reduce your body temperature. You will only roll over occasionally, so slow down your heart rate.

04. Enter non-rapid eye movement (NREM) sleep by slowing your brainwaves from alpha to delta. It should be really hard to wake you now.

05. At several points in the night, raise brainwave level back up to alpha to enter rapid eye movement (REM) sleep. This is the time to dream.

How much sleep?

age	hours a day
newborns	10.5–18
3–11 months	9–12 (plus several naps)
1–3 years	12–14
3–5 years	11–13
5–12 years	10–11
11–17 years	8.5–9.25
adults	7–9

The electrical activity of brain cells can be measured using special equipment. The main waves are known as **beta** (consciously alert), **alpha** (physically and mentally relaxed), **theta** (sleeping with reduced consciousness), and **delta** (deep sleep).

Sleep pattern

Each night you repeat the NREM and REM stages about every 90 minutes until you wake up. The REM periods become a little longer as the night passes, which is why your longest dreams happen in the morning. During REM sleep, muscles are paralysed so you can't act out your dreams.

Sleep checklist

Lying down
Eyes closed
Unconscious to the surrounding environment
Can only hear loud noises
✓ Occasionally moves body
Slow heart rate
Slow, rhythmic breathing

Sleep disorders

Sleep walking
Some people can get out of bed when they are fast asleep and walk around. Sleepwalkers have been known to drive cars and even commit murder while unconscious.

Snoring
This noise is caused when soft tissue at the back of the throat relaxes and vibrates during breathing.

Teeth grinding
Clenching or grinding teeth during sleep is called "bruxism". It can damage teeth, so sufferers often wear mouth guards.

Sleep talking
Some sleep talkers make just random noises, but others hold long one-sided conversations.

Sleep eating
Sleep eaters raid the fridge while fast asleep. The only clue to their nocturnal activities the next morning is crumbs in the bed.

In numbers

1/3
The proportion of an average lifetime spent asleep

6 years
The amount of time spent dreaming in an average lifetime

11 days
How long American Randy Gardner went without sleep in 1964 – a very dangerous world record, so don't try to beat it

20%
The estimated percentage of people that snore

100,000
The number of car crashes every year in the US caused by drivers falling asleep

Sleep deprivation may have contributed to disasters such as the Chernobyl nuclear accident in 1986 and the Exxon Valdex oil tanker spill in 1989.

WHAT'S IN A NAME?

Taking naps in the day rather than a long sleep at night is called "**Da Vinci sleep**" after the Italian artist and serial napper Leonardo da Vinci. Yachtswoman Ellen McArthur used this power-napping technique in her record-breaking solo circumnavigation of the globe, taking frequent ten-minute naps.

Tall stories

Kids' bodies release more growth hormone during sleep, so too many late nights can leave you short-tempered… and short!

When you wake up after a good night's sleep, you will be about 3 cm (1 in) taller than when you went to bed. During the day, gravity compresses the discs in your spine making you shorter, but as you sleep the discs expand again.

Dream theories

The ancient Sumerians of Mesopotamia (modern-day Iraq) recorded dreams on stone tablets 5,000 years ago. The dreams were believed to be predictions about what the future held.

The Ancient Egyptians believed they could communicate with the gods through their dreams.

Swiss psychiatrist Carl Jung thought dreams helped us to resolve emotional issues.

In the 1970s, US scientists Allan Hobson and Robert McCarley argued that dreams were caused by electrical brain impulses pulling imagery from random memories.

Dreams

01: You dream several times a night, but only remember dreams if you are woken during them.

02: You forget most of your dreams within ten minutes of waking.

03: People who have been blind since birth have dreams with sounds but no pictures.

04: Some people dream only in black and white, not colour.

05: You incorporate physical sensations and environmental factors into your dreams, such as feeling thirsty, needing the toilet, or hearing car sirens.

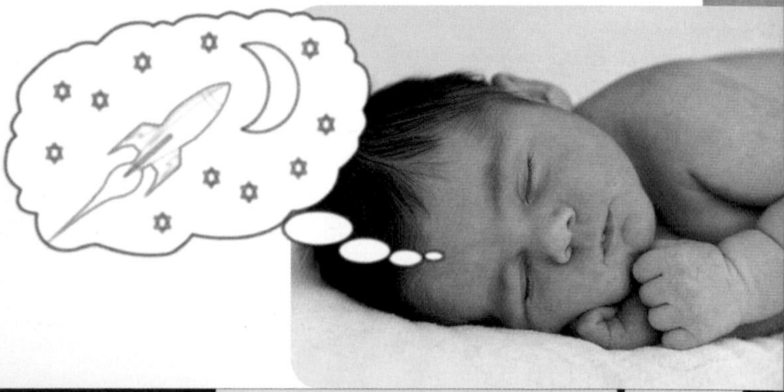

Why do **some smells trigger memories?**

Senses

Senses help us to perceive our environment.

- **Sight**
- **Hearing**
- **Taste**
- **Smell**
- **Touch**

The scent of freshly cut grass can remind you of summer or the smell of a logfire can trigger memories of a winter's day. This is because the olfactory bulb – which transmits information about smells detected in your nostrils – is connected to the parts of the brain that process emotion and memories.

Telltale smell
The **durian fruit** of southeast Asia has a pungent aroma that people either love or hate. Some describe it as smelling like stale sick or dirty toilets! The smell is so strong that in Singapore people are banned from carrying the fruit on public transport.

Baby smell
The average person can detect more than **10,000 different smells**. Research has also shown that mothers can smell the difference between a vest worn by their baby and one worn by another baby only days after their child's birth.

FAST FACTS

Odours

01: Chemicals that are volatile (can easily turn into a gas) give off molecules, or odours, that are released into the air.

02: Substances such as salt and sugar have strong tastes but are odourless because they are not volatile and do not evaporate into a gas.

03: Perfumes contain a variety of chemical compounds that evaporate easily.

04: The gas used to cook and heat some homes is odourless, so gas companies add a smelly chemical to it so people can detect gas leaks.

WHAT'S IN A NAME?
People who cannot smell have a condition called "**anosmia**". Some people are born with anosmia, while others develop it later in life.

How to: **smell**

01. Breathe in air and collect the odours arriving in your nostrils on your olfactory epithelium – a patch of tissue on the roof of your nasal cavity packed with receptor cells.

02. Secrete watery mucus from the glands beneath the epithelium to help dissolve the odours.

03. Make sure your different receptor cells respond to the correct odour molecules and send information to your olfactory bulb. Transmit this odour information to your brain.

04. Get your brain to interpret the smell by analysing the different elements and comparing them to smells stored in your memory database.

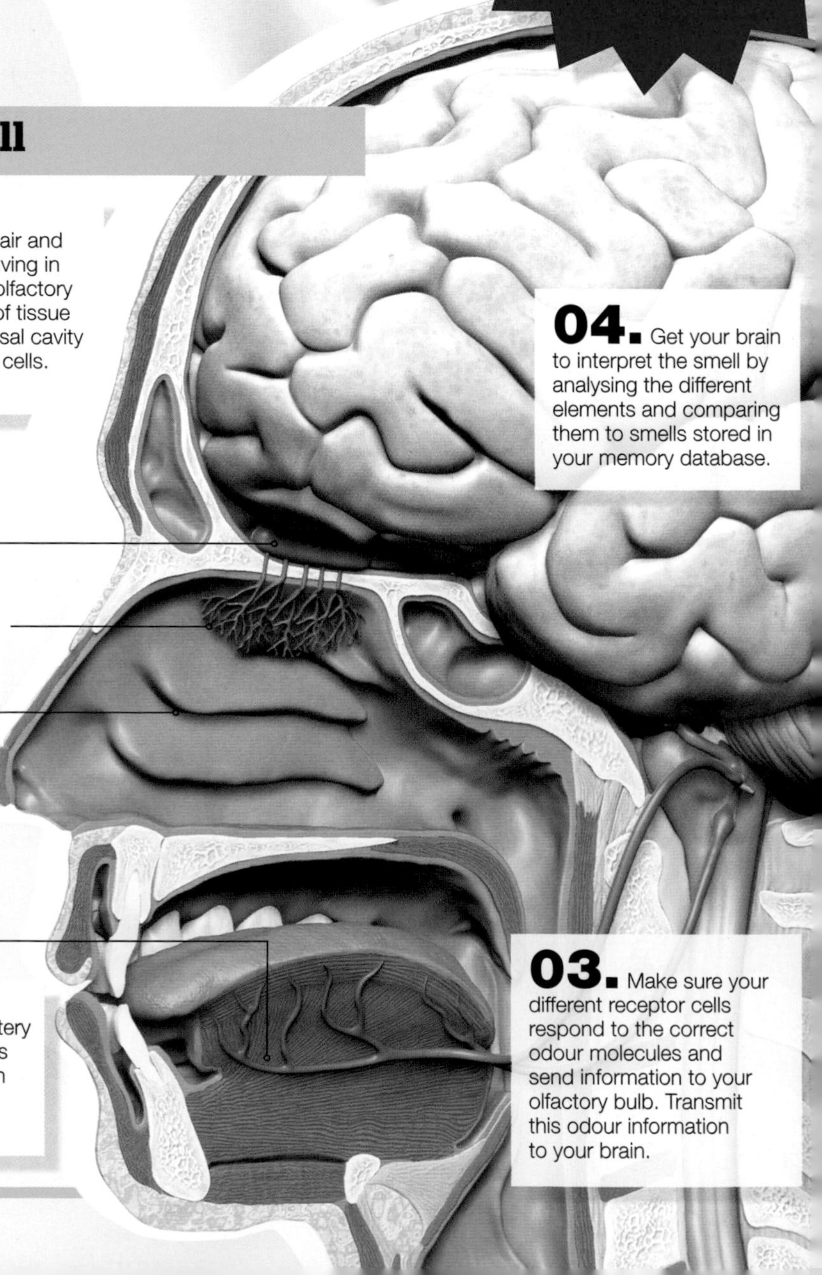

Olfactory bulb: Carries nerve impulses to the brain
Olfactory epithelium: Collects smells arriving in nasal cavity
Nasal cavity: Chamber where incoming air is warmed or cooled to body temperature
Nerve fibres: gather data from taste buds, which may help to identify a smell

Unusual favourite smells

Not everyone loves the smell of flowers or cut grass – especially if you suffer from hay fever. Here are some unusual favourite alternatives:

- **Damp dog**
- **Sun cream**
- **Old book**
- **Coal cellar**
- **Wet earth**

I don't believe it!

Researchers at the University of California tested volunteers to see if they could track scents by smell alone. The volunteers were blindfolded and wore gloves and earplugs to block out their other senses. Although a lot slower than sniffer dogs, two-thirds of the group were able to track the scent.

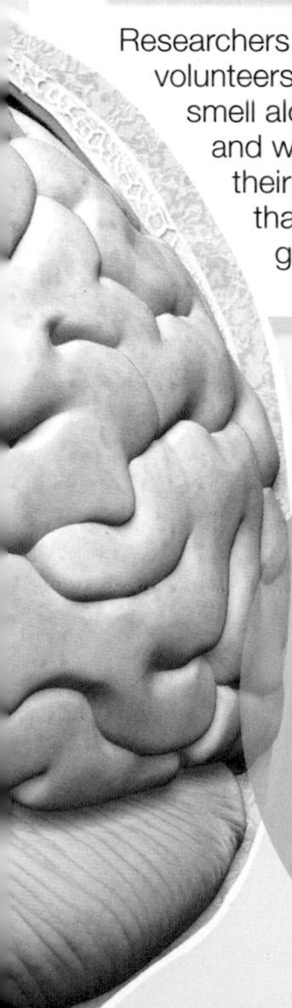

WEIRD OR WHAT?

The Israeli army has invented a "skunk" bomb to disperse rioting crowds. A synthetic version of the **foul-smelling liquid** squirted by skunks is sprayed over a crowd, forcing them to leave the scene in a hurry!

The power of smell

For the Dogon people of Mali in West Africa (pictured), smell and sound are closely linked because both travel through the air. The Dogon also believe that speech – with the correct grammar and pronunciation – smells pleasant. So, watch your language!

How smell can save your life

Your nose can be a real life saver, sniffing out potential dangers that you might otherwise miss.

Smelling smoke alerts you to fire before you see it.

The smell of rotten food makes you recoil before you eat it.

The smell of success

In numbers

100
How many times more powerful a dog's sense of smell is than a human's

10,000
The number of different odours the average human can recognize

2 million
The approximate number of adults in the USA who have no sense of smell

40 million
The number of odour receptor cells found in your nasal cavity

Nobel smell

US scientists Richard Axel and Linda Buck won the **Nobel Prize for Medicine** in 2004 for their research into how the brain recognizes smells. They discovered that more than 1,000 different genes encode olfactory receptors in the nose – the largest gene family in the human genome.

What about me?

When you have a blocked nose, food can taste bland. This is because our sense of smell is responsible for about 80 per cent of what we taste.

Why brush your **teeth?**

Dentists recommend you clean your teeth for three minutes twice a day to prevent tooth decay and gum disease. Brushing with toothpaste removes plaque – a sticky layer of bacteria and food that coats the teeth. If the plaque is not removed, it can lead to tooth decay.

700 BCE
Wealthy Etruscans use human teeth bought and pulled from poor people to fill gummy gaps; they wire the teeth to neighbouring healthy gnashers

1533–1603 CE
The art of making dentures dies out with the Etruscan civilization and Queen Elizabeth I of England plugs the gaps in her rotten teeth with pieces of cloth to improve her appearance in public

1700s
The teeth of executed criminals and teeth unscrupulously acquired by grave robbers are used to make dentures – these often carry disease and

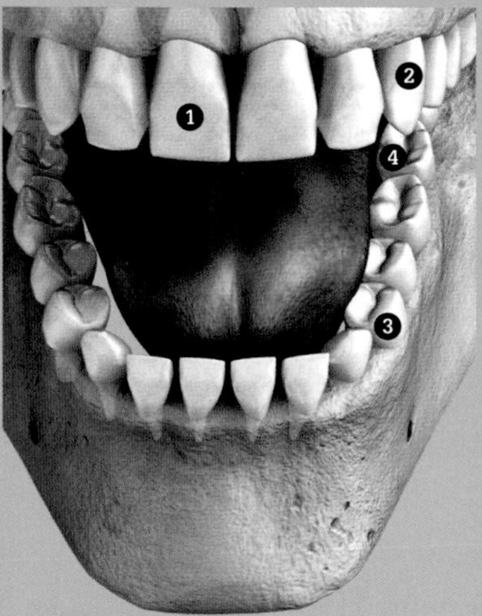

Tooth types

01 **Incisors**
Function: Chisel-like teeth used for cutting food
Number in mouth: 8

02 **Canines**
Function: Sharp, pointed teeth used for tearing and gripping food
Number in mouth: 4

03 **Premolars**
Function: Ridged teeth used for crushing and grinding food
Number in mouth: 8

04 **Molars**
Function: Teeth with a broad surface used to grind food before swallowing
Number in mouth: 12

Milk teeth

Teeth start forming while a baby is still in the mother's womb.

Babies start teething when they are about six months old, and the first teeth begin to emerge.

By the age of two, a child will usually have a full set of 20 milk teeth.

When the child reaches five or six, their milk teeth start to fall out, making way for adult teeth.

In many English-speaking countries, children believe that if they place a milk tooth under their pillow at night the tooth fairy will swap it for money. In Spanish-speaking countries, a mouse collects the teeth.

I don't believe it!

George Washington, the first president of the USA, wore false teeth made from hippopotamus ivory fitted with human teeth and parts of horse and donkey teeth.

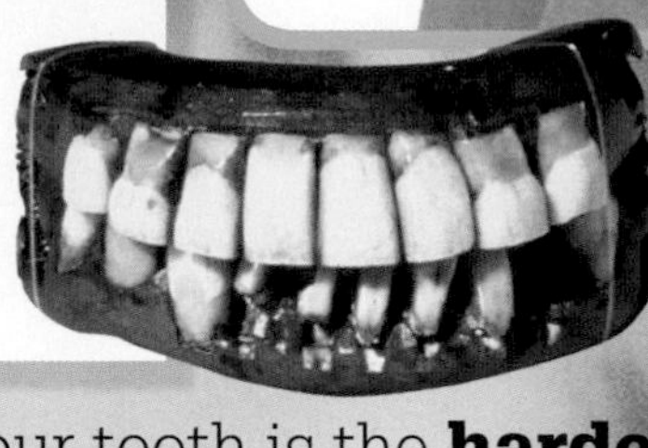

The enamel on your teeth is the **hardest substance** in your body.

How to: **chew your food**

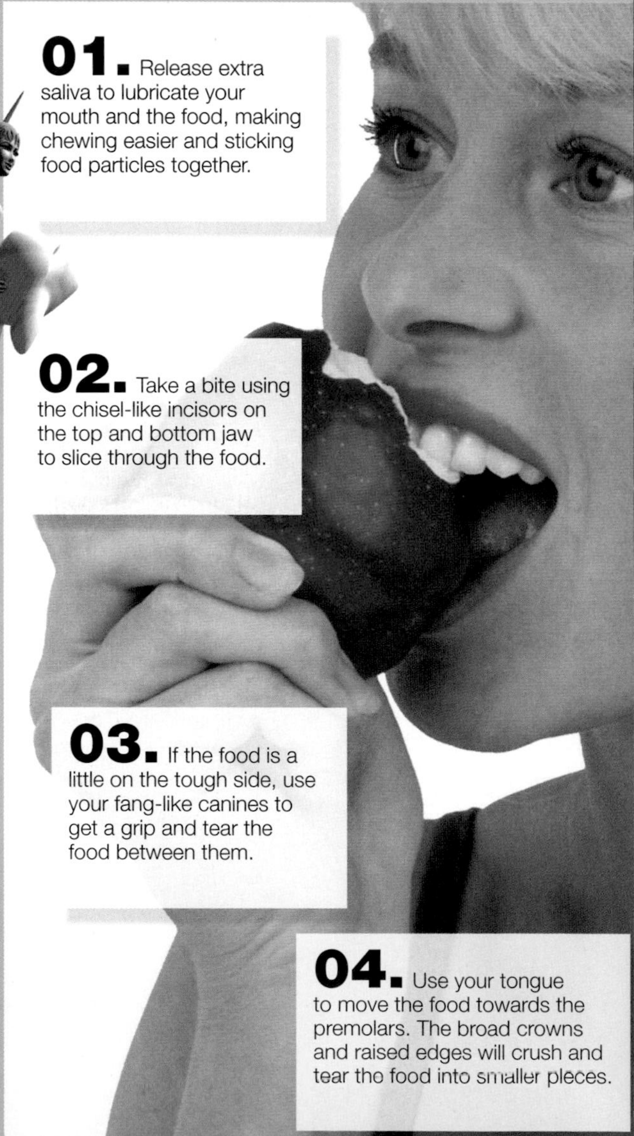

01. Release extra saliva to lubricate your mouth and the food, making chewing easier and sticking food particles together.

02. Take a bite using the chisel-like incisors on the top and bottom jaw to slice through the food.

03. If the food is a little on the tough side, use your fang-like canines to get a grip and tear the food between them.

04. Use your tongue to move the food towards the premolars. The broad crowns and raised edges will crush and tear the food into smaller pieces.

Researchers studying teeth from a **Stone Age graveyard** in Pakistan found evidence that drill tools made from flint were used to remove decay 9,000 years ago.

Blasts from the past

1774 The first porcelain teeth are created, but they chip and break very easily and look unnaturally white

1815 The loss of 50,000 healthy young men at the Battle of Waterloo between Britain and France is good news for tooth scavengers and denture makers; "Waterloo teeth" become the height of fashion and are worn with honour

1850s Developments in rubber moulding lead to the invention of properly fitted dentures

2000s Modern dentures are made-to-measure for every patient out of acrylic resin and other plastics

(caption, left column top) are only worn for the sake of appearance – they are removed in order to eat

Ouch!
Until the 19th century, **tooth extractions** were often carried out by barbers in between haircuts.

Teeth cleaning

01 Chewing on a twig or root with antiseptic properties was a common practice in many ancient civilizations.

02 Ancient Egyptians rubbed their teeth with a powder made from egg shells, myrrh, pumice stone, and ox hooves.

03 The ancient Chinese invented the first toothbrush. They attached pig bristles to a bamboo stick.

04 In 18th-century Europe people used their fingers to rub their teeth with bicarbonate of soda.

05 Teeth cleaning become a daily practice in American homes only after World War II, when returning soldiers brought the habit home with them.

06 The first electric toothbrush was made in 1939 in Switzerland, but they didn't go on sale until the 1960s.

06. Use the tongue to move the pulped food to the rear of the mouth ready for swallowing

WEIRD OR WHAT?
The bristles of **toothbrushes** were originally made from the hair of hogs and cows.

05. Give the food a final hammering between the large molars at the back of the jaw. They will grind the food into a moist, soft pulp.

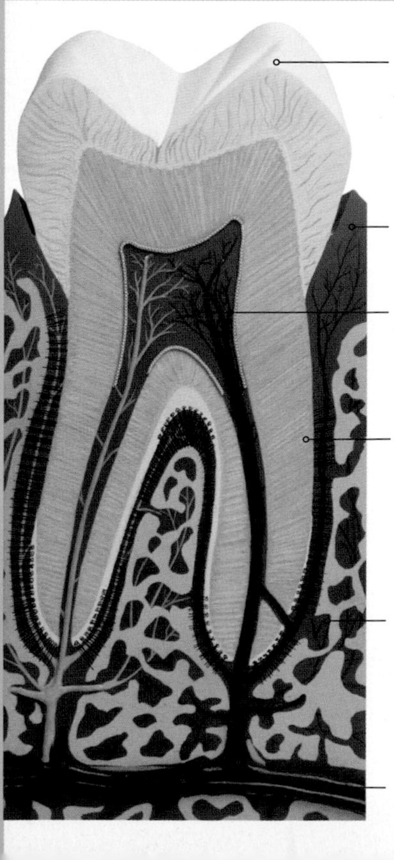

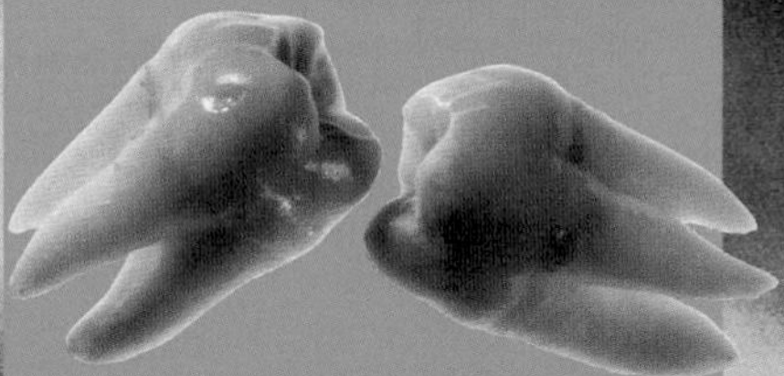

Wisdom teeth

Wisdom teeth (rear molars) usually emerge when you are older and wiser, between the ages of 17 and 25.

Most people have four wisdom teeth.

If they don't come through properly or fail to emerge at all, it may become necessary to have them removed.

In Turkey, the name of the wisdom tooth refers directly to the age at which they appear and is called *20 yas disi* (20th year tooth).

Scientists in Japan have tried extracting stem cells from wisdom tooth pulp. This could help future medical research.

Tell me more:
anatomy of a tooth

Enamel: Hard white substance covering the crown of the tooth

Gum: Tissue surrounding the base of the tooth

Pulp: Soft tissue in the centre of the tooth

Dentine: Hard, bone-like substance that makes up the bulk of the tooth

Jaw bone: Part of the skull that holds the teeth

Blood vessels and nerves

The **Temple of the Tooth** in Sri Lanka is believed to house the left upper canine tooth of Buddha. This precious relic attracts pilgrims bearing lotus blossoms every day.

Telling the tooth!

Forensic dentists study teeth to identify victims. They compare the teeth to dental records or photos of missing people. The teeth can also indicate how old the victim was.

The first recorded case of bite mark evidence securing a conviction was in a trial in Texas, US, in 1954. A piece of cheese with a bite mark taken out of it was left at the crime scene. The accused was told to bite into another piece of cheese in the courtroom and the bite marks were compared for a match.

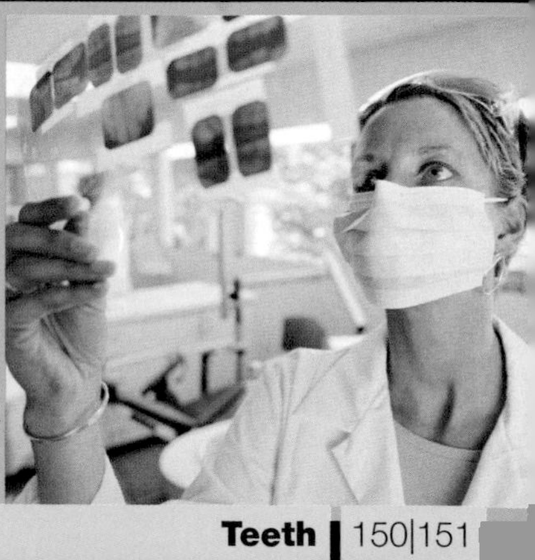

How do we **communicate?**

Just like our close ape relatives, we communicate with each other through facial expressions, gestures, and touch. But one way of communicating – spoken language – is unique to humans. Our vocal cords create sounds that are shaped into words by the tongue and lips. These words are picked up by the ears and sent to the brain, where they are interpreted into the language that we understand.

Tell me more: **language**

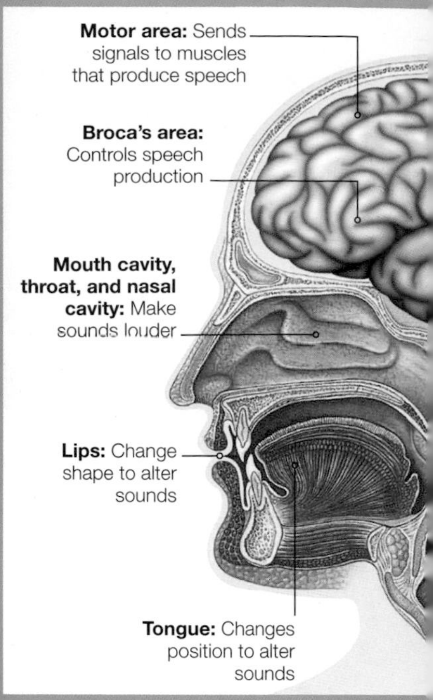

Motor area: Sends signals to muscles that produce speech
Broca's area: Controls speech production
Mouth cavity, throat, and nasal cavity: Make sounds louder
Lips: Change shape to alter sounds
Tongue: Changes position to alter sounds

Holding a conversation

01: When sound waves arrive in your pinna (ear flap) they are directed into your inner ear via the ear canal.

02: The sound waves are converted into electrical nerve impulses by the cochlea and sent to the auditory area of your brain.

03: The auditory area, analyses speech sounds and voice tones and sends the information on to Wernicke's area to make sense of what was said.

04:. This information then goes to Broca's area of your brain, which will work out a suitable response. It instructs your brain's motor area to tell the muscles in your larynx to activate your vocal cords.

05: Broca's area also tells breathing muscles to force air past the vocal cords to make them vibrate and produce sounds, and instructs the muscles in your tongue, lower jaw, and lips to move so you can respond.

Making waves

Sound waves are created by vibrations coming from an object, such as someone talking, a dog barking, or a musical instrument. This **vibration** moves through the air in the form of pressure waves, disturbing particles of air as it moves.

FAST FACTS

Sign language

01: Many deaf people communicate by using sign language.

02: Sign languages vary around the world, but in all of them words and phrases are formed by making signs with the hands and through facial expressions.

03: Sign language can be used to tell jokes and sing songs... in fact, anything spoken languages can do.

04: People who are deaf and blind can communicate through tactile signing, by touching the hands of the signer or through finger spelling. They can also use a method called tadoma in which they hold the speaker's face and feel for lip movements and vocal cord vibrations.

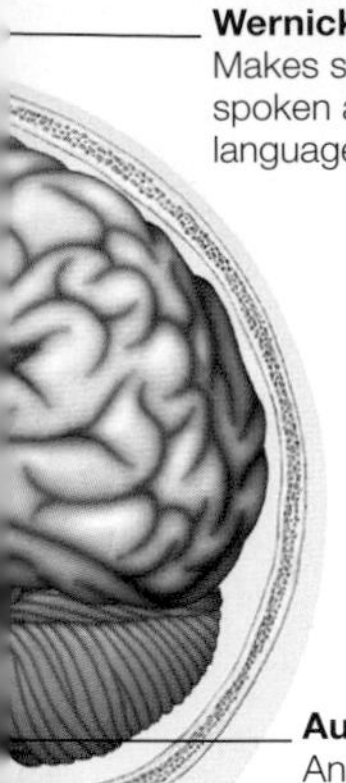

Wernicke's area: Makes sense of spoken and written language

Auditory area: Analyses speech sounds and tone of voice

Larynx: Contains vocal cords

Vocal cords: Vibrate when air passes over them, creating sounds

Breaking voices

When a boy reaches puberty, his **larynx** gets bigger and his vocal cords lengthen and thicken, which causes the voice to sound deeper. As his body adjusts to this change, his voice may occasionally "break".

Body language

More than half of human communication is non-verbal through expressions and gestures:

- **Happy** (smiling)
- **Sad** (crying)
- **Angry** (narrowed eyes and clenched fists)
- **Nervous** (biting nails)
- **Defensive** (crossed arms)
- **Confident** (locked hands behind head)
- **Bored** (inspecting fingernails or looking at watch)

Learning languages

The younger you are the easier it is to learn another language, but scientists cannot agree why this is. Maybe it's because the young brain is more "plastic" and has a greater capacity for learning.

More people in the world are multilingual (able to speak more than one language) than single-language speakers.

People who can speak lots of different languages are known as polyglots. *The Lord of the Rings* author JRR Tolkien was fluent in 13 languages, could get by in 12 others, and even invented his own languages.

When hands are better than words

Directing traffic in a busy city

Doing a deal on a stock exchange

Demonstrating safety procedures

Refereeing at a football match

Asking people to keep quiet – ssshh...

Calling a taxi to stop for you

Clapping to show appreciation

Ten most widely spoken languages

language	approx no. of speakers
Chinese Mandarin	1,213,000,000
Spanish	329,000,000
English	328,000,000
Arabic	221,000,000
Hindi	182,000,000
Bengali	181,000,000
Portuguese	178,000,000
Russian	144,000,000
Japanese	122,000,000
German	90,000,000

Tell me more: **the ear**

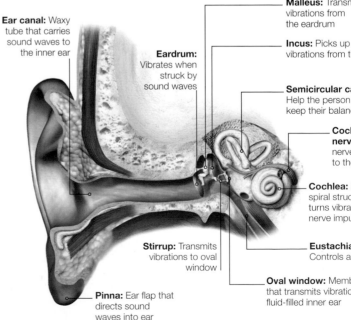

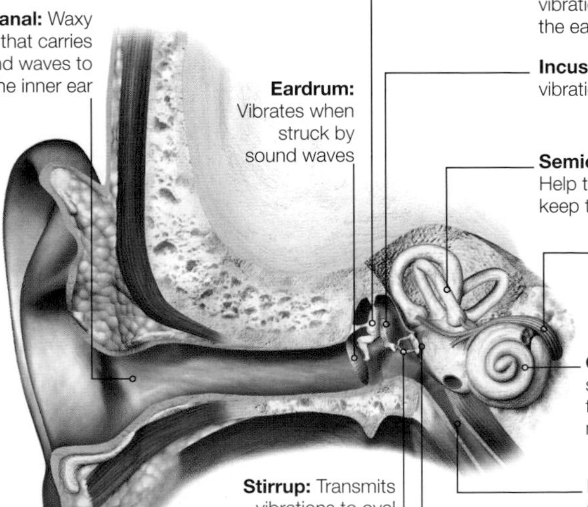

Ear canal: Waxy tube that carries sound waves to the inner ear

Eardrum: Vibrates when struck by sound waves

Malleus: Transmits vibrations from the eardrum

Incus: Picks up vibrations from the malleus

Semicircular canals: Help the person to keep their balance

Cochlear nerve: Carries nerve impulses to the brain

Cochlea: Fluid-filled spiral structure that turns vibrations into nerve impulses

Eustachian tube: Controls air pressure

Oval window: Membrane that transmits vibrations to fluid-filled inner ear

Stirrup: Transmits vibrations to oval window

Pinna: Ear flap that directs sound waves into ear

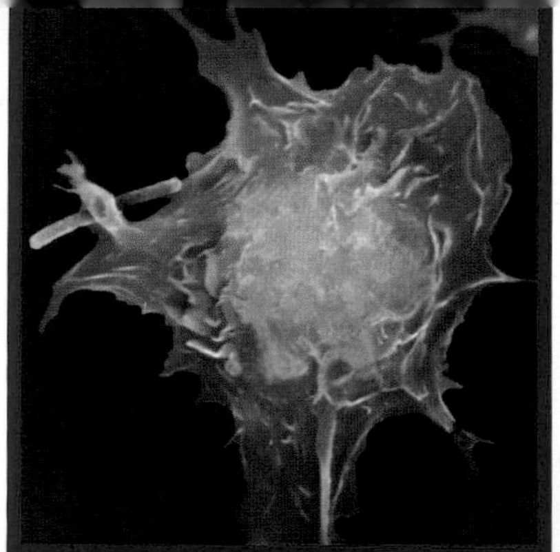

How does your body **fight illness?**

Your body has several lines of defence against pathogens, or germs. The skin forms a barrier to stop invading pathogens, while chemicals in tears and acidic stomach juices also deter bacteria. Pathogens that do breach these defences are targeted by white blood cells and other weapons of the immune (defence) system.

White cell warriors

White blood cells target pathogens in a number of ways. Macrophages, for example, are white blood cells that have left the blood vessel in search of bacterial infections. They engulf bacteria and kill the ingested pathogen.

Types of pathogen

Virus
Infectious agent that invades and reproduces inside cells, causing diseases such as colds, chickenpox, and flu.

Bacteria
Single-celled microscopic organisms that release toxins and cause diseases such as food poisoning and sore throats.

Parasites
Organisms such as tapeworms that make the body their food source.

Fungi
Moulds that infect the skin causing irritation, such as athlete's foot.

In numbers

Average life expectancy

35
Ancient Greece (c. 300 BCE)

40
Industrial Revolution (1800s)

47.3
USA (1900)

31.8
Swaziland (2009)

64.7
India (2009)

82.6
Japan (2009)

How to: **heal a cut**

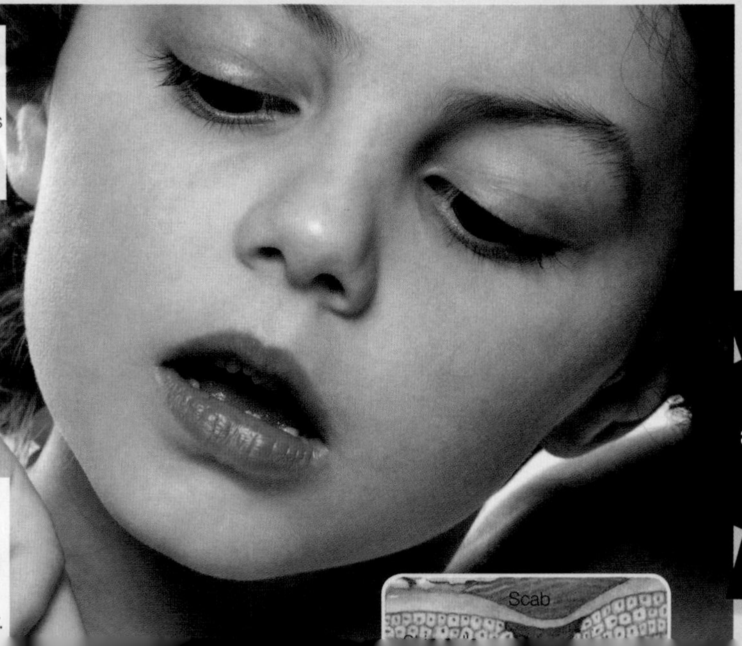

01. Release histamine to widen blood vessels and provide access to white blood cells.

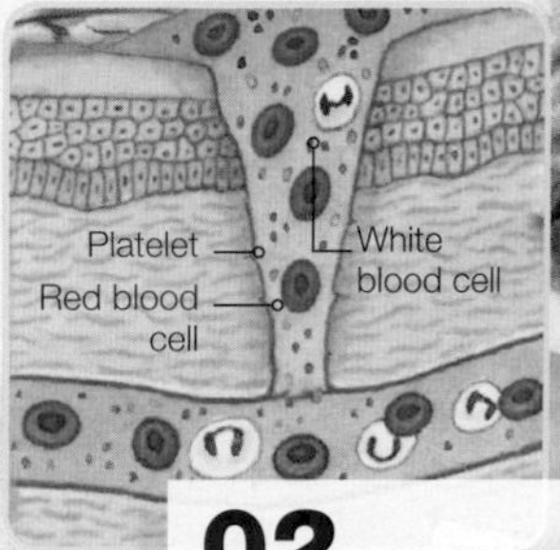

02. Send white blood cells to destroy pathogens in the cut, and make platelets become sticky and group together.

WEIRD OR WHAT?

In the 1600s, Italian doctor Santorio Santorio conducted an experiment. He suspended a "**weighing chair**" from the ceiling so he could compare the weight of what he had eaten with the weight of his poo and urine.

How doctors make a diagnosis

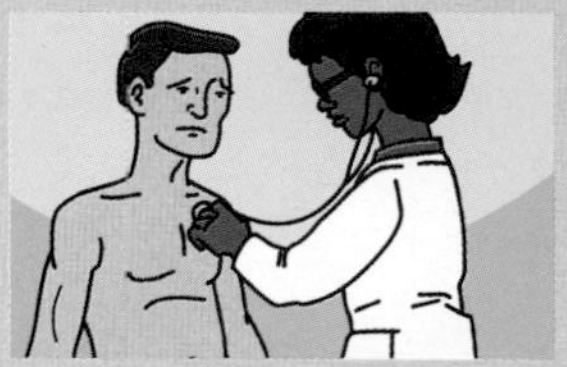

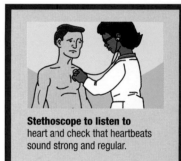

Stethoscope to listen to heart and check that heartbeats sound strong and regular.

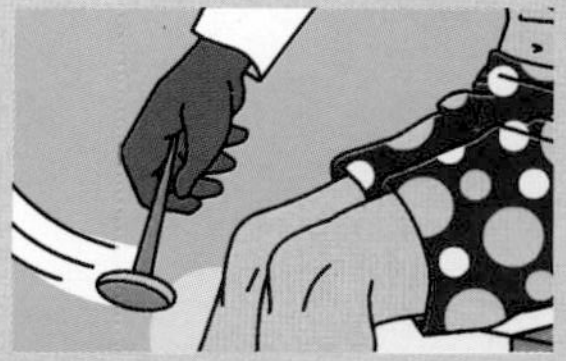

Reflex hammer to test reflexes in your nervous system and your spinal cord.

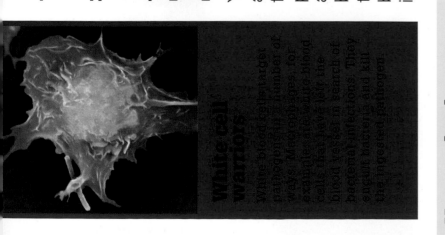

Tongue depressor to examine the mouth and throat for signs

To identify a disease, doctors consider symptoms and signs. Symptoms are things experienced by the patient, such as pain or swelling. Signs are what the doctor observes during a physical examination and the results of medical tests. Tests can include:

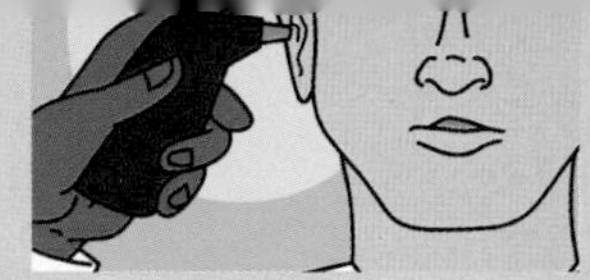

Thermometer to measure body temperature, which can be an indicator of underlying infection.

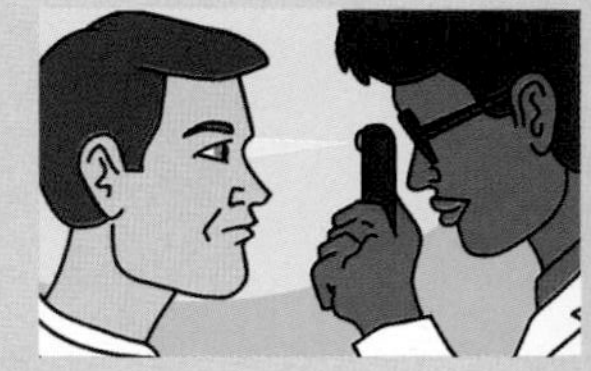

Ophthalmoscope to examine inside the eye to check the health of the retina.

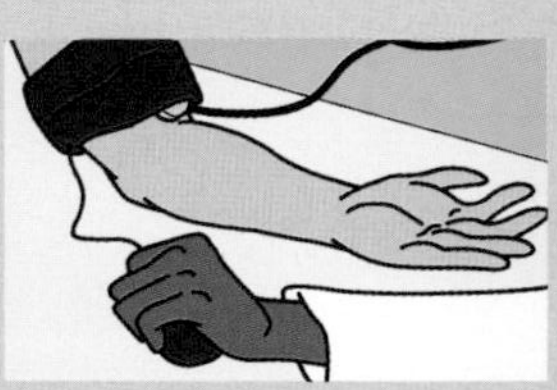

Sphygmomanometer to measure blood pressure, which may seem too high or low for the patient's age and weight.

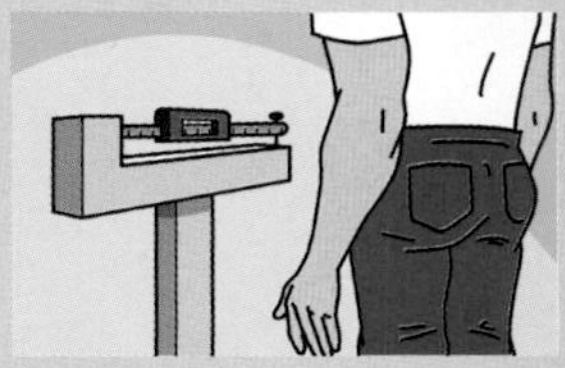

Scales to check body weight to make sure that patient is not gaining or losing too much weight.

I don't believe it!

The punishment for a doctor found guilty of medical incompetence in ancient Babylon was to have his hands cut off.

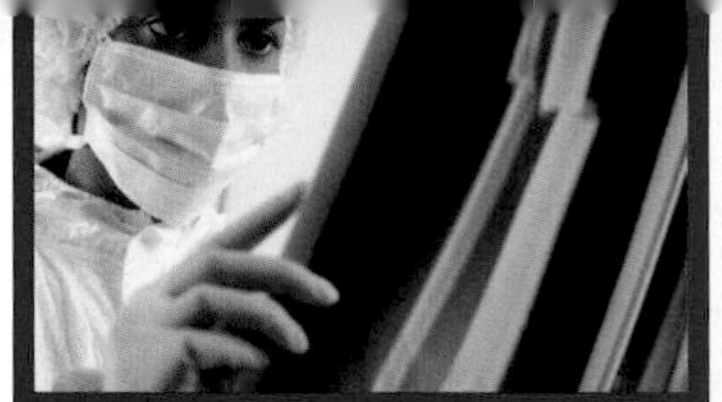

Medical specialisms

Anaesthesia – controlling pain

Cardiology – heart and blood vessels

Dermatology – skin

Endocrinology – endocrine system

Gastroenterology – digestive system

Geriatrics – elderly patients

Gynaecology – female reproductive organs

Haematology – blood

Hepatology – liver

Nephrology – kidneys

Neurology – brain and nervous system

Oncology – cancer

Ophthalmology – eyes

Orthopaedics – muscular and skeletal systems

Otolaryngology – ear, nose, and throat

Paediatrics – children

Pathology – examining body samples to diagnose disease

Plastic surgery – appearance and reconstruction

Psychiatry – emotional and behavioural disorders

Pulmonology – lungs and respiratory system

Radiology – X-rays and medical imaging

Rheumatology – inflammatory diseases such as arthritis

Urology – urinary tract

03. Release chemicals from platelets and tissue around the cut to create strands of a protein called fibrin.

04. Use platelets to form a plug to stop bleeding and a net of fibrin threads to trap red blood cells and form a clot to reinforce the platelet plug.

05. Form a scab around the cut's surface to protect the area and produce new skin cells from wounded tissue to repair the damage.

The **stethoscope** was invented by French doctor René Laënnec in 1816. Doctors normally listened to a patient's heart by pressing their ear against the chest. Laënnec couldn't hear the heart of an overweight female patient due to the "great degree of fatness", so he used paper rolled into a tube to amplify the sound.

FAST FACTS

Vaccinations

01: Vaccinations can provide the body with immunity to certain diseases.

02: When you are given a vaccination, your body is injected with a substance that triggers the body's immune system's cells to produce antibodies.

03: The first vaccination was given by British doctor Edward Jenner in 1796.

04: The word vaccine comes from *vacca*, the Latin word for cow.

05: Following a vaccination campaign in the 1970s, smallpox became the only infectious disease to have been eradicated.

06: Vaccines are used to protect against many diseases today, including flu, measles, and cholera.

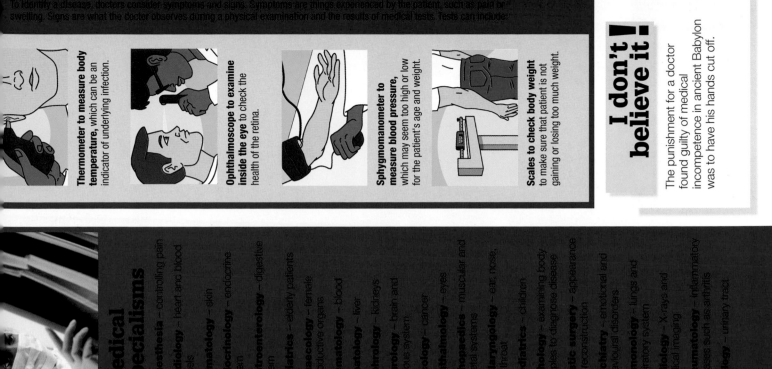

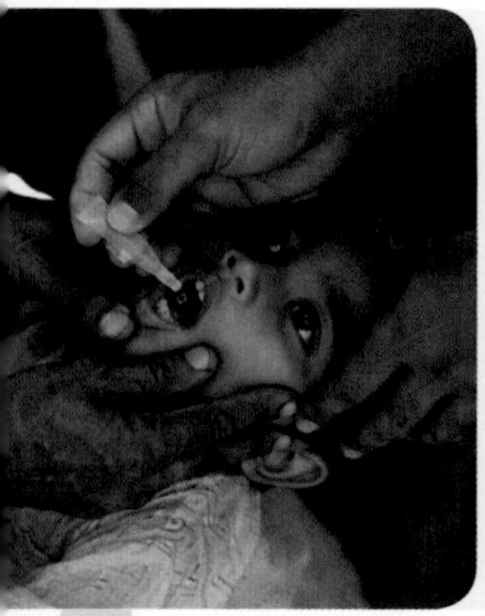

After completing their training, many doctors swear an oath to practise medicine ethically. It is based on the **Hippocratic oath**, named after Hippocrates, an Ancient Greek physician in the 4th century BCE – although no one knows if he really wrote it!

Five ways to keep healthy

- Do at least one hour of exercise per day
- **Walk to school**
- Eat five portions of fruit and vegetables every day
- **Drink plenty of water**
- Never smoke cigarettes

Gallery of pathogens (germs)

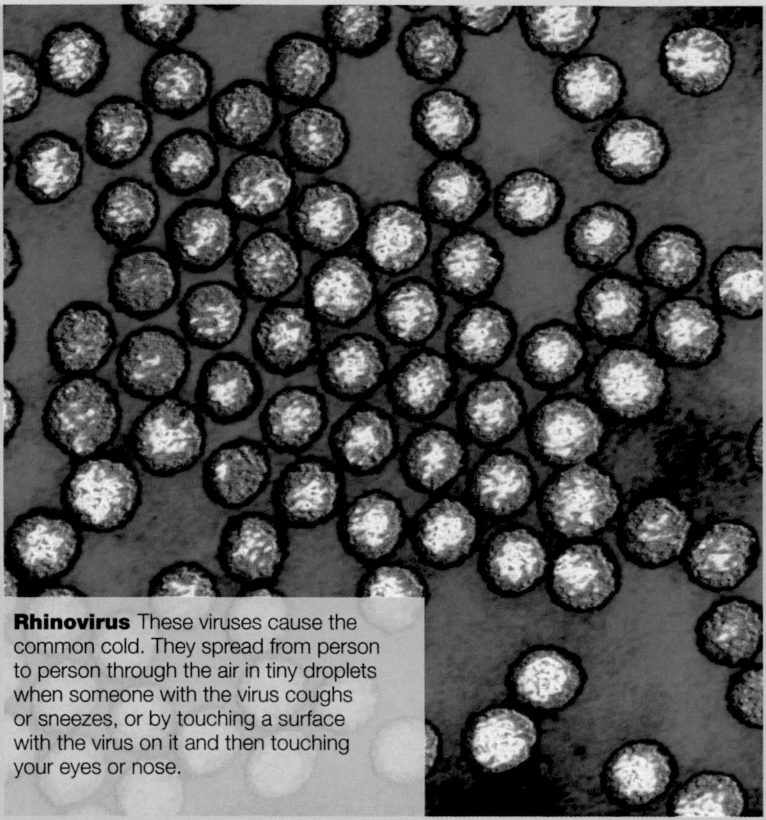

Rhinovirus These viruses cause the common cold. They spread from person to person through the air in tiny droplets when someone with the virus coughs or sneezes, or by touching a surface with the virus on it and then touching your eyes or nose.

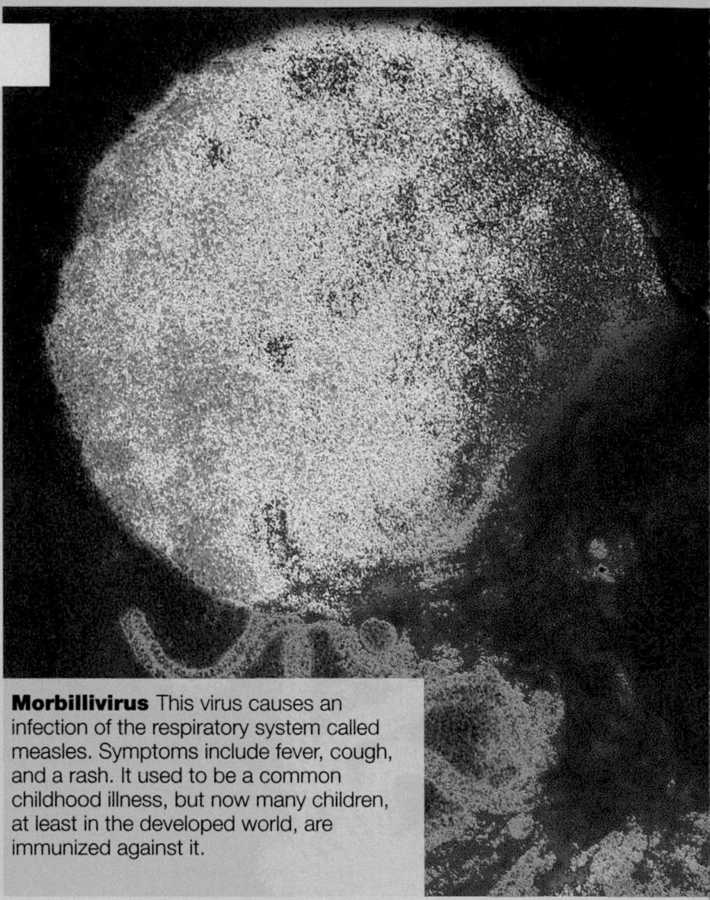

Morbillivirus This virus causes an infection of the respiratory system called measles. Symptoms include fever, cough, and a rash. It used to be a common childhood illness, but now many children, at least in the developed world, are immunized against it.

Viruses

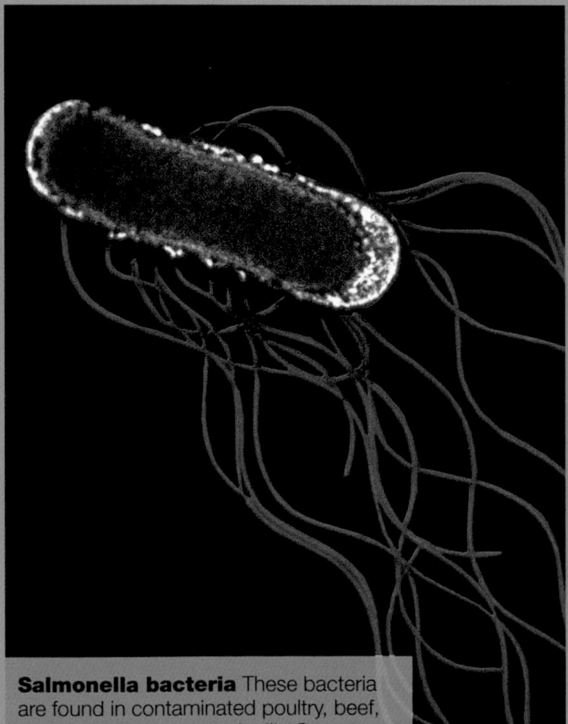

Salmonella bacteria These bacteria are found in contaminated poultry, beef, and eggs, and untreated milk. Symptoms of salmonella food poisoning are diarrhoea, vomiting, stomach cramps, and fever. It is important to cook food properly to kill off the bacteria.

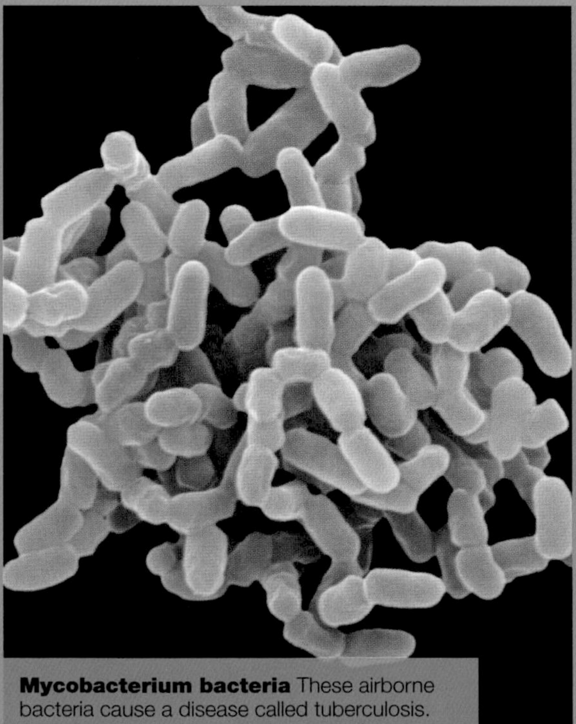

Mycobacterium bacteria These airborne bacteria cause a disease called tuberculosis. Symptoms include a chronic cough, fever, and weight loss. If left untreated, tuberculosis can kill more than half of its victims. Despite vaccination programmes, many people worldwide still get infected with this disease.

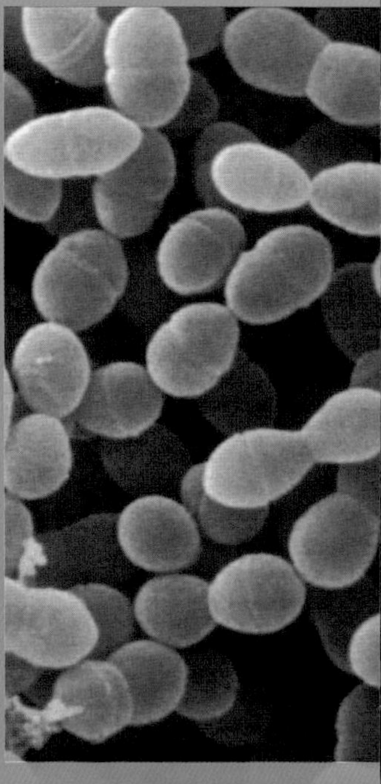

Streptococcus bacteria These bacteria can infect different parts of the body, but one common illness they cause is strep throat – an infection of the throat, larynx, and tonsils. It can be treated with antibiotics.

Bacteria

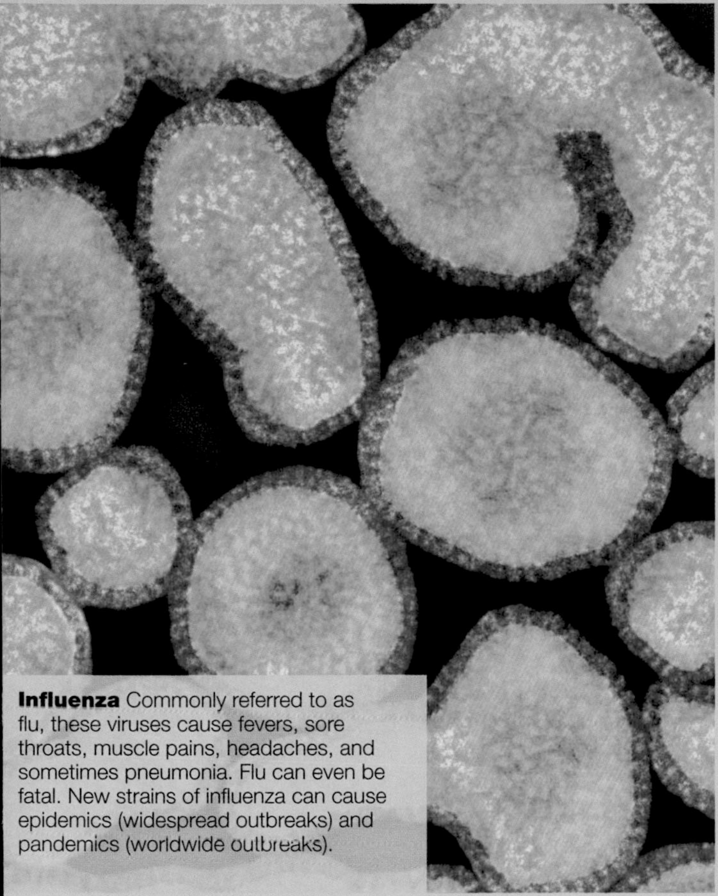

Influenza Commonly referred to as flu, these viruses cause fevers, sore throats, muscle pains, headaches, and sometimes pneumonia. Flu can even be fatal. New strains of influenza can cause epidemics (widespread outbreaks) and pandemics (worldwide outbreaks).

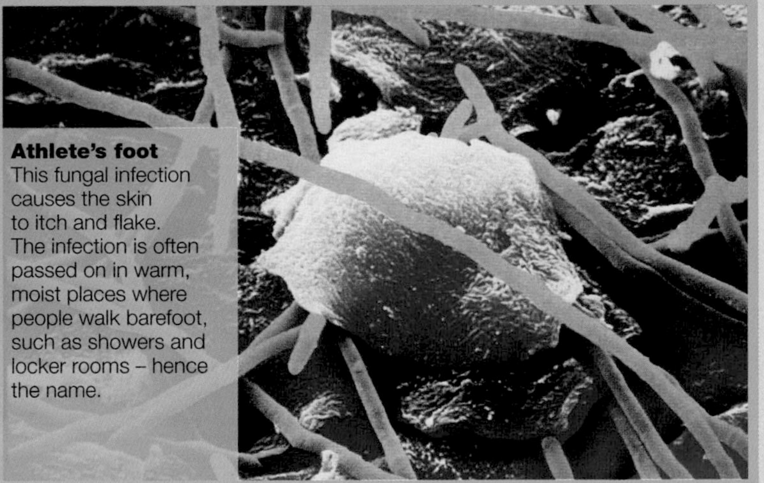

Athlete's foot This fungal infection causes the skin to itch and flake. The infection is often passed on in warm, moist places where people walk barefoot, such as showers and locker rooms – hence the name.

Ringworm Like athlete's foot, this is a fungal infection of the skin. There are no worms, just a ring-like red rash on the skin. Fungal infections are very contagious, but good hygiene, such as not sharing towels, can reduce the risk of infection.

Fungi

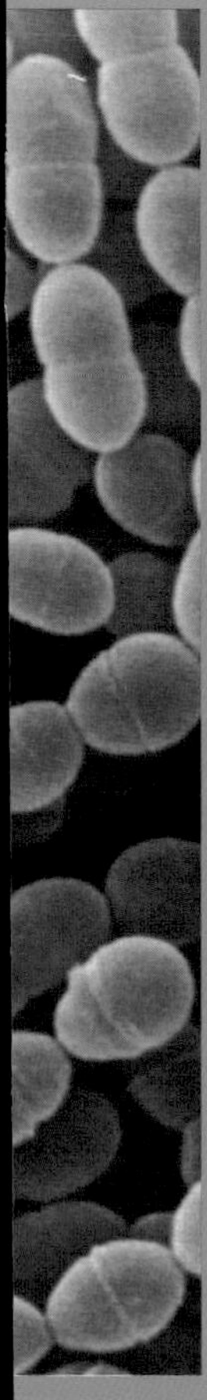

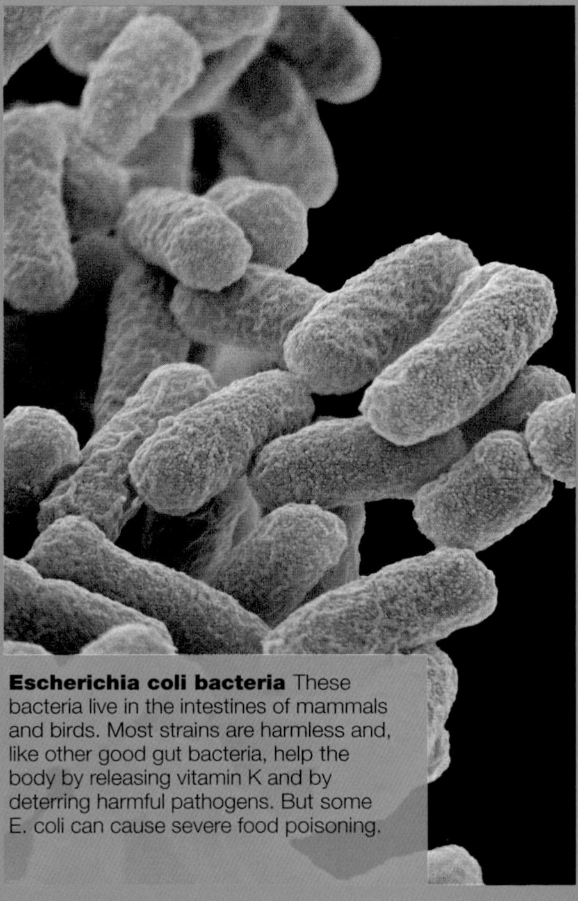

Escherichia coli bacteria These bacteria live in the intestines of mammals and birds. Most strains are harmless and, like other good gut bacteria, help the body by releasing vitamin K and by deterring harmful pathogens. But some E. coli can cause severe food poisoning.

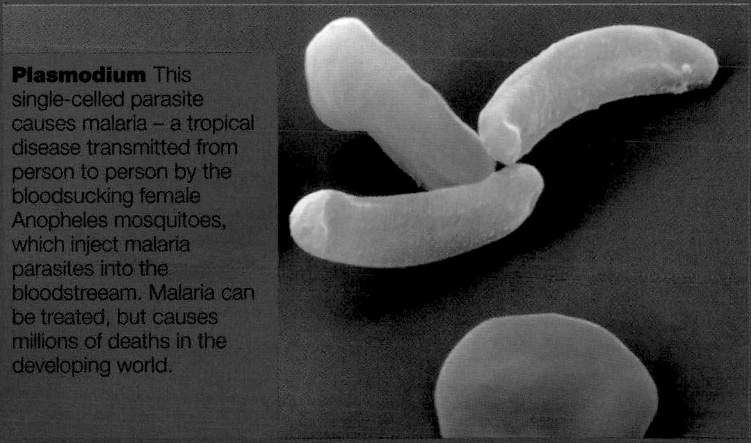

Plasmodium This single-celled parasite causes malaria – a tropical disease transmitted from person to person by the bloodsucking female Anopheles mosquitoes, which inject malaria parasites into the bloodstreeam. Malaria can be treated, but causes millions of deaths in the developing world.

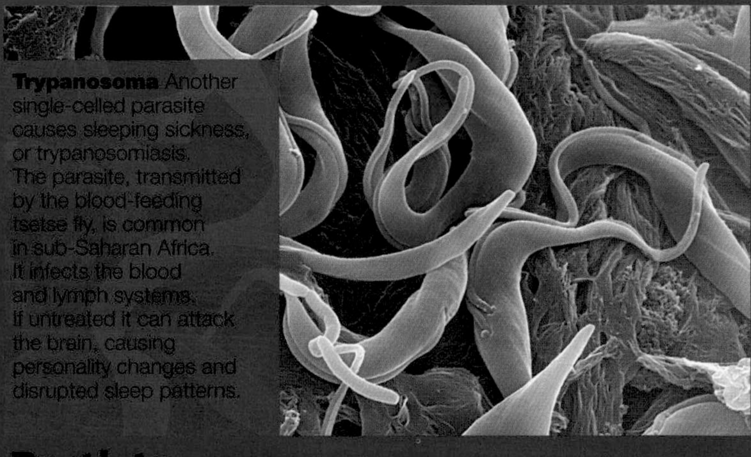

Trypanosoma Another single-celled parasite causes sleeping sickness, or trypanosomiasis. The parasite, transmitted by the blood-feeding tsetse fly, is common in sub-Saharan Africa. It infects the blood and lymph systems. If untreated it can attack the brain, causing personality changes and disrupted sleep patterns.

Protists

Science and technology

E Plan
WD 0.65
10x

Why are numbers so useful?

Without numbers, we wouldn't know how big something is, the temperature, or the date or time. There would be no speed limits on roads, but there would be no cars or roads either, because numbers are essential to make them.

In numbers

12
The number of people who have walked on the Moon

50,000
The average number of bees in a hive

1 million+
The number of insect species

620 million
The number of cars in the world

6.8 billion
The number of people in the world

What is a googol?
A googol is a huge number. It is 1 followed by 100 zeros (see below). When **mathematician** Edward Kasner was trying to think of a name for this number, his nine-year-old nephew, Milton, suggested "googol".

How to: count to 27 in Papua New Guinea

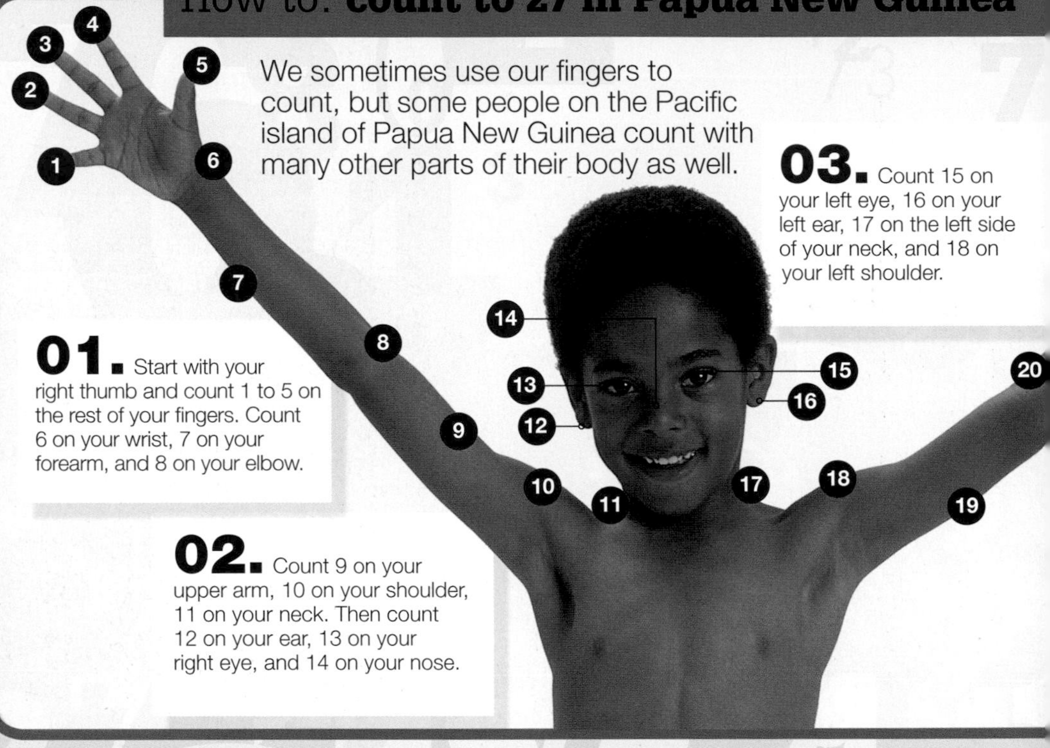

We sometimes use our fingers to count, but some people on the Pacific island of Papua New Guinea count with many other parts of their body as well.

01. Start with your right thumb and count 1 to 5 on the rest of your fingers. Count 6 on your wrist, 7 on your forearm, and 8 on your elbow.

02. Count 9 on your upper arm, 10 on your shoulder, 11 on your neck. Then count 12 on your ear, 13 on your right eye, and 14 on your nose.

03. Count 15 on your left eye, 16 on your left ear, 17 on the left side of your neck, and 18 on your left shoulder.

10,00

Why is zero so important?

○ Zero is important in two ways. First, zero is a number. Second, it lets us tell the difference between numbers like 11, 101, and 1001.

○ In our counting system, the position of a number matters. From right to left, the positions are ones, tens, hundreds, thousands, and so on.

○ The zeros in 1,001 show that there are no tens and no hundreds, so the number is one thousand and one.

Seven mathematicians

Pythagoras (c.570–495 BCE)

Archimedes (c.287–212 BCE)

Johannes Kepler (1571–1630)

Developed Pythagoras' Theorem and advocated the notion that Earth was spherical rather than flat.

Discovered Archimedes' Principle – an object in water experiences an upwards force equal to the weight of water it displaces.

Discovered the laws of planetary motion.

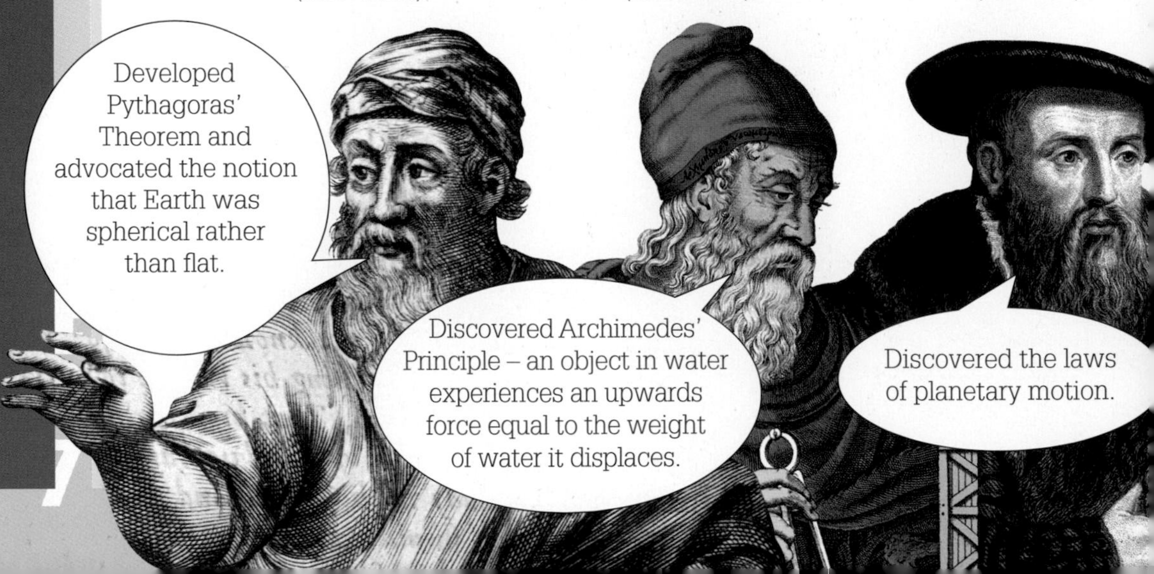

How do you make pi?

Divide the circumference of any circle by the same circle's diameter and you'll always get the same number – 3.14159. In mathematics, a number that never changes is called a constant. This constant is also called pi (pronounced pie). It's written as the Greek letter π.

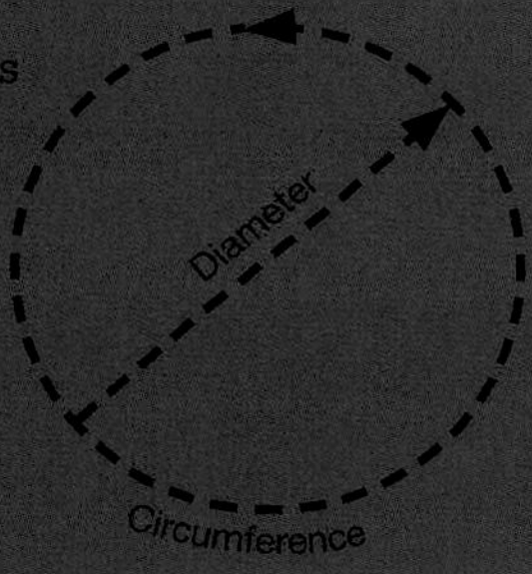

Why do we count in tens?

We count in tens because we have ten fingers. Computers count in twos – they don't have ten fingers, but they can turn electric currents off and on, which represent the numbers zero and one. Numbers based on ten are **decimal** numbers. Numbers based on two are called **binary** numbers.

Numbers in nature

- Nature seems to be random, but numbers can be found everywhere in the natural world.
- One set of numbers present in nature is known as the Fibonacci series.
- Each number in the Fibonacci series is found by adding the two previous numbers – 0, 1, 1, 2, 3, 5, 8, 13, 21, 34, and so on.
- The spiral patterns of sunflower seeds and pine cones (above), the shape of snail shells, and the arrangement of leaves on plant stems all follow the Fibonacci series.

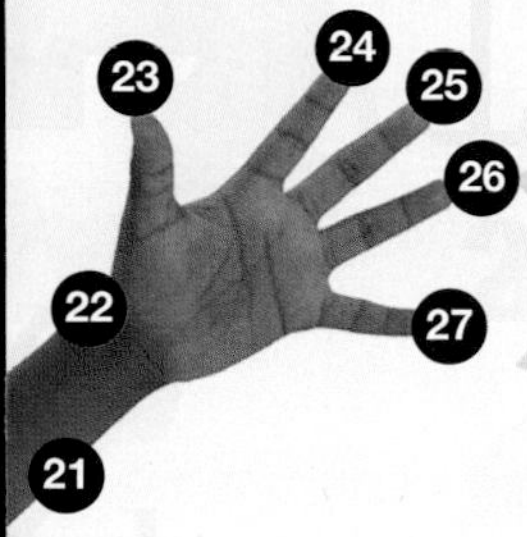

Why is a "baker's dozen" not 12?

A dozen is 12, but the English term "baker's dozen" is actually 13. In 13th-century England, a baker could have a hand cut off for selling loaves that were below the required weight. So, when they sold loaves, they added a free loaf to every 12 loaves to make sure that the bread was never under-weight.

04. Then count in the same way down your left arm and hand, reaching "27" on the little finger of your left hand.

Five types of numbers

01: Natural numbers
The counting numbers – 1, 2, 3, and so on

02: Integers
Counting numbers (1, 2, 3, and so on) and their negatives (–1, –2, –3, and so on)

03: Rational numbers
Counting numbers (1, 2, 3, and so on) and fractions (¼, ½, ¾, and so on)

04: Prime numbers
Numbers that can be divided only by themselves and one

05: Perfect numbers
Numbers that are the sum of all their factors, such as 6. It can be divided by 1, 2, and 3, and it is also the sum of 1, 2, and 3

How big is infinity?

Infinity is bigger than any other number. In fact, it's so big that it can't be counted. It's written as a symbol called a **lemniscate** that looks like a number 8 lying on its side.

0,000,000,000,000,000,000,000,000,000,000

Some of the most important discoveries in history have been made by mathematicians, who are able to make sense of the numbers in our world.

Rene Descartes (1596–1650) | **Pierre de Fermat** (1601–1665) | **Sir Isaac Newton** (1643–1727) | **Gottfried Leibniz** (1646–1716)

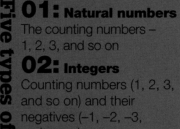

Created analytical geometry, the study of geometry using algebra.
Invented the theory of probability.
Discovered the laws of motion and gravitation, and invented calculus.
Invented calculus independently of Newton.

What's so great about **wheels?**

Wheels are really simple objects – just discs or hoops with a hole in the middle for an axle – but we'd find it hard to live without them. They are not just used on cars, bikes, and other vehicles – many machines have wheels inside.

Variations **on wheels**

Pulley
A pulley is a wheel with a groove around the edge into which a rope or cable fits.

Gears
A gear is a wheel with teeth around its edge. The teeth of two gears turn each other around.

Flywheel
A flywheel is a heavy wheel that stores energy when it spins.

The world's fastest car wheels help jet-powered cars to set speed records. These wheels are made of **solid metal**, because they spin so fast that rubber tyres would fly apart.

Who invented the wheel?

- Noone knows who invented the wheel.
- Cartwheels were used in an ancient land called Mesopotamia (modern-day Iraq) about 5,500 years ago.
- The idea for the first cartwheel might have come from the potter's wheel. This was a spinning wooden table used for making clay pots. It was in use for perhaps one thousand years before someone thought of turning it into a cartwheel.

Spokes

Spokes are rods or wires that connect a wheel's hub, in the middle, to its rim.

Most bicycles have wheels with wire spokes.

Some racing bicycles have solid wheels with no spokes.

Traditional horse-drawn carriages have wheels with wooden spokes.

FAST FACTS

Tyres through the ages

01: The first tyres were made of iron about 2,800 years ago. They were fitted around wooden wheels to stop them wearing down so fast.

02: The first cars and bicycles had solid rubber tyres.

03: Pneumatic (air-filled) tyres began replacing solid tyres on cars and bicycles in the 1890s.

Wacky wheels

Unicycle: One wheel with a seat on top. It's more difficult to balance on one wheel than two.

Uno motorbike: Looks like half a bike, as if it has only one wheel. It actually has two, but they are side by side instead of one in front of the other!

Segway: A two-wheeled electric vehicle that balances by itself. The rider stands on a platform between the wheels. Leaning forward speeds it up, leaning back slows it down. Leaning to one side makes it turn.

Gyroscope
A gyroscope is a wheel that resists being tipped over when it is spinning very fast.

Water wheel
A water wheel is a wheel turned by running water in a river to operate a machine.

WEIRD OR WHAT?

Scientists have made working wheels so small that more than **100,000** of them would fit across the width of a human hair. Making things this small is called nanotechnology.

Airliner wheels

Aircraft wheels and tyres have to be very strong to land a plane safely.

01: When a large plane touches down, its main wheels spin from 0 to 250 kph (155 mph) in a fraction of a second.

02: A puff of smoke from the tyres shows the moment the wheels touch the ground.

03: The nose wheel of a Boeing 737 is about the same size as a car wheel. It's designed to go faster than a racing car while holding up the weight of three family cars.

Space wheels

The US space agency NASA needed wheels for the rover vehicles it sent to the Moon and Mars. They had to be light and reliable.

01 Three of the Apollo Moon-landing missions took lunar rovers with them. The wheels were made of springy wire mesh.

02 The *Spirit* and *Opportunity* rovers sent to Mars had aluminium wheels with spiral spokes. The spaces between the spokes were filled with foam to stop stones getting stuck in them.

Some wheels are great fun

01 Ferris wheels like the London Eye and the Singapore Flyer take you high up into the sky and back to Earth.

02 Playground roundabouts whirl you round and round as fast as you like.

03 Bikes are a fun way to get around, if you can keep your balance.

04 Skateboards are great for stunts and jumps.

05 Roller skates put wheels on your feet. Quads have two wheels in front and two at the back, while rollerblades have up to five wheels in a line.

06 A Catherine wheel is a wheel-shaped firework that spins when it is lit.

Tell me more: **changing a racing-car wheel**

It takes less than ten seconds to change the wheels of a racing car.

0.0 seconds The moment the car stops in the pits, about 20 mechanics swarm around it. One mechanic, called the lollipop man, holds a "Brakes on" sign in front of the car to remind the driver to keep a foot on the brakes.

0.2 seconds A mechanic at each wheel uses an air-powered wrench to remove the single nut that holds on each wheel.

1.0 seconds The car is jacked up off the ground by mechanics at the front and back.

1.5 seconds The old wheels are pulled off, and new ones are pushed on.

2.5 seconds While the wheels are being changed, a fuel hose is connected to the car to fill up its fuel tank.

3.5 seconds Mechanics tighten the wheel nuts, and the jacks are lowered.

3.8 seconds The lollipop man shows the driver a sign to put the car in first gear. A mechanic cleans his or her helmet visor.

7.0 seconds The fuel hose is pulled away from the car.

7.3 seconds The lollipop man lifts his or her sign and the driver sets off.

Why are there **so many materials?**

Thousands of different materials are used to make millions of things. This is because all materials have strengths and weaknesses. Wood is good for building a fence, but not for making clothes; rubber is perfect for making a car's tyres, but not its wheels. Each material is chosen because it has the right properties for the job it has to do.

What is an alloy?
An alloy is a mixture of one metal with other metals or non-metals. Alloys usually have different properties from the materials they contain. For example, **steel** is an alloy that is stronger than either of the materials it contains – iron and carbon.

01. Load iron ore, coke (from coal), limestone, and dolomite into a blast furnace. Heat them to make molten iron.

02. Pour the molten iron into a Basic Oxygen Furnace and add scrap steel, to produce molten steel.

Five types of **glass**

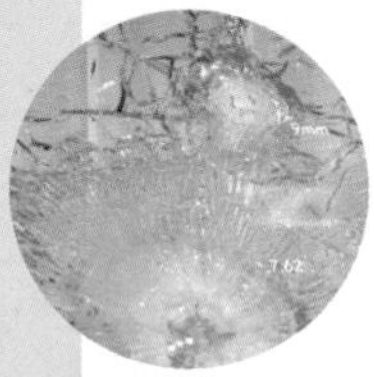

Bullet-proof
Glass that is able to stop a bullet, made from layers of compressed laminated glass.

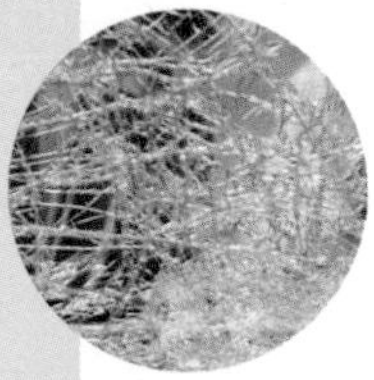

Laminated
Glass made from a sheet of clear plastic glued between two sheets of glass.

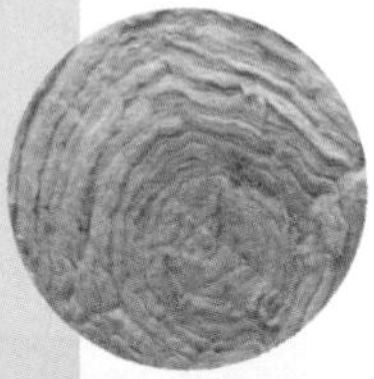

Glass wool
An insulating material with a fluffy, woolly texture made from glass fibres.

Lead crystal
Glass that contains lead, giving it a sparkling appearance for glassware.

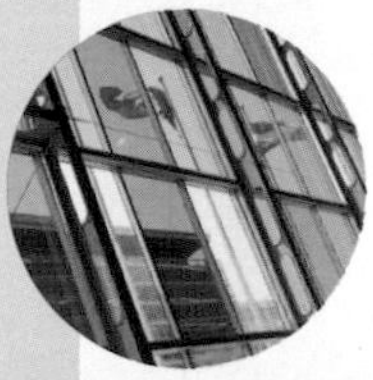

Stained
Coloured glass made into pictures and patterns for windows and ornaments.

Alloys list

There are many varieties of alloys, which are made from mixtures of materials.

alloy	contains
brass	copper and zinc
bronze	copper and tin
cupronickel	copper and nickel
conel	iron, nickel, and chromium
stainless steel	iron, carbon, and chromium
steel	iron and carbon
sterling silver	silver and copper
pewter	tin, lead, and copper

RECORD BREAKER

The strongest known material is called **graphene**. It is 200 times stronger than steel and is made of carbon.

WHAT'S IN A NAME?

Raw materials are the basic substances we make things from. They come from nature and include wood, bamboo, stone, wool, crude oil, and plant fibres such as cotton, sisal, and hemp.

Metals are extracted from rocks called ores that are dug out of the Earth. An ore called **bauxite** contains aluminium, while **chalcocite** is an ore that contains copper. An ore has to be processed – often by using heat and chemicals – to get the metal out.

How to: **make steel**

05. Roll the slabs between heavy rollers to produce sheet steel for industry.

04. Cast the molten steel into slabs.

03. Refine the molten steel with agents to remove oxygen, hydrogen, and nitrogen and produce low-carbon steel.

Five extreme materials

Titanium is a metal used in military jet-planes. It is as strong as steel but half the weight, and it can withstand high temperatures.

Kevlar is a very strong fibre, used to make bullet-proof vests and ultra-strong ropes.

Carbon-carbon is a material used in rockets and spacecraft because it can withstand very high temperatures.

Aerogel is a clear, jelly-like material so light that it is almost not there! It has been used in a spacecraft to trap particles from a comet without damaging them.

Aluminium honeycomb is used to make helicopter rotor blades and parts for aircraft and racing cars because of its lightness combined with its strength.

Six types of plastic

- **Polycarbonate** – a hard plastic used for making CDs, DVDs, and spectacles.
- **Polyethylene** – also known as polythene, the most wicely used plastic (80 million tonnes a year) is used mainly for packaging, bags, and bottles.
- **Polypropylene** – the second most commonly used plastic, used for packaging, textiles, ropes, food containers, and some barknotes.
- **Polystyrene** – used to make plastic cutlery, CD cases, plastic models, and packaging foam.
- **PTFE** – also called Teflon, used as a non-stick coating for cooking pots and pans.
- **PVC** – polyvinyl chloride, the third most widely used plastic, features in plumbing pipes, window frames, upholstery, flooring, and inflatables.

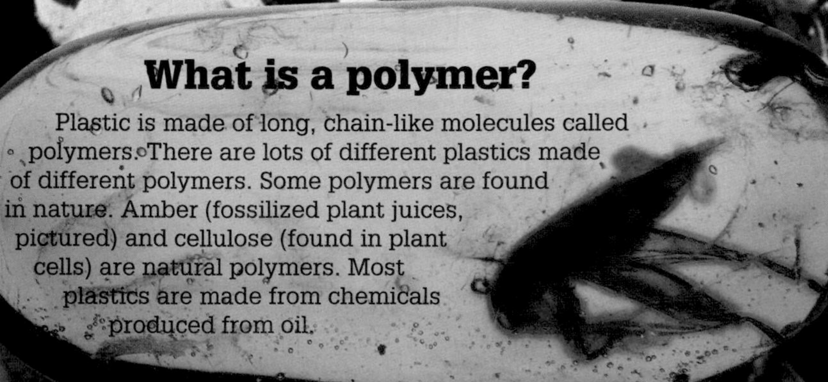

What is a polymer?

Plastic is made of long, chain-like molecules called polymers. There are lots of different plastics made of different polymers. Some polymers are found in nature. Amber (fossilized plant juices, pictured) and cellulose (found in plant cells) are natural polymers. Most plastics are made from chemicals produced from oil.

Why does my bike rust?

Some materials, such as iron, react with oxygen in the air. When iron, water and air meet, the iron combines with oxygen and changes into **iron oxide**, which is also known as rust. Bicycles are made of steel, which contains iron.

Why do magnets **stick to fridges?**

What is a magnet?
A magnet is a substance or an object that attracts iron. The region around a magnet, where magnetic forces act, is called a magnetic field.

Fridge magnets stick to fridges because magnets stick to steel… and fridges are made of steel. Magnets can do a lot more than stick cartoon characters on a fridge door, though. Many of the things we use every day would not work without magnets – and if Earth itself were not magnetic, we'd be in real trouble!

How to: **see a magnetic field**

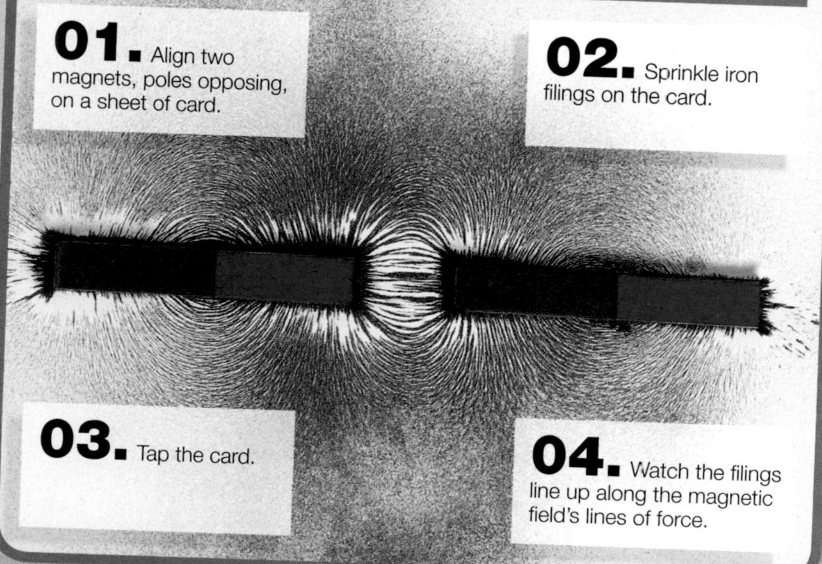

01. Align two magnets, poles opposing, on a sheet of card.

02. Sprinkle iron filings on the card.

03. Tap the card.

04. Watch the filings line up along the magnetic field's lines of force.

Ten things that use magnetism

Magnets are found in lots of everyday things. Each time you use a computer or its printer, listen to music, charge your mobile phone battery, or travel in a car, plane or train, you're using magnets.

- ✔ Microphones
- ✔ Loudspeakers
- ✔ Electric motors
- ✔ Electromagnets
- ✔ Transformers
- ✔ Generators
- ✔ Computer disc drives
- ✔ Compasses
- ✔ Power supplies
- ✔ Battery chargers

Tell me more: **inside a magnet**

If you could look inside a magnet, you would see tiny regions called domains. Inside each domain, all the magnetic particles of matter are lined up in the same direction.

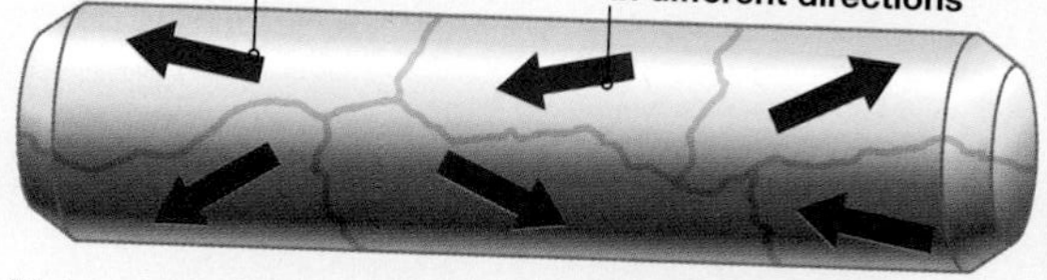

01: In an unmagnetized piece of iron, the domains point in different directions. Their magnetic forces cancel each other out.

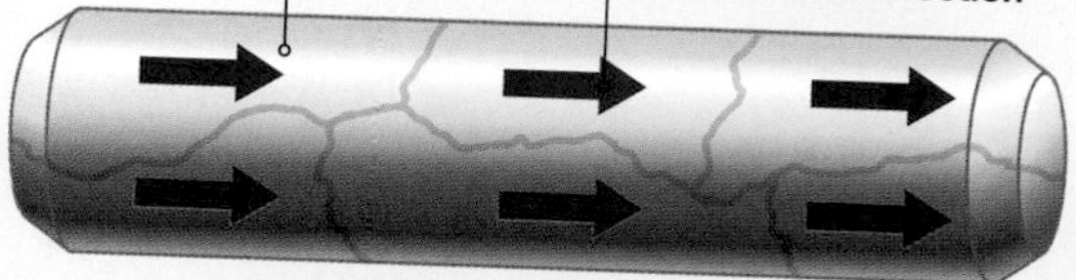

02: When the iron is magnetized, the domains point in the same direction and their magnetic forces add together.

Natural magnets

Some rocks in nature contain iron and are magnetic. People in the ancient world discovered magnetism when they noticed the magnetic effects of some of these rocks:

- Magnetite (also called lodestone) is the most magnetic natural rock. It was used to make the first magnetic compasses.
- Pyrrhotite is a bronze-coloured, weakly magnetic rock.
- Tantalite is a rust-coloured magnetic rock.
- Franklinite is a weakly magnetic black rock found in Franklin, New Jersey, USA.

What is an electromagnet?

Unlike fridge and bar magnets, which are magnetic all the time, electromagnets can be **switched off**. An electromagnet has a coil of wire that becomes magnetic when an electric current flows through it. A piece of iron inside the coil concentrates the magnetic field and makes an electromagnet more powerful.

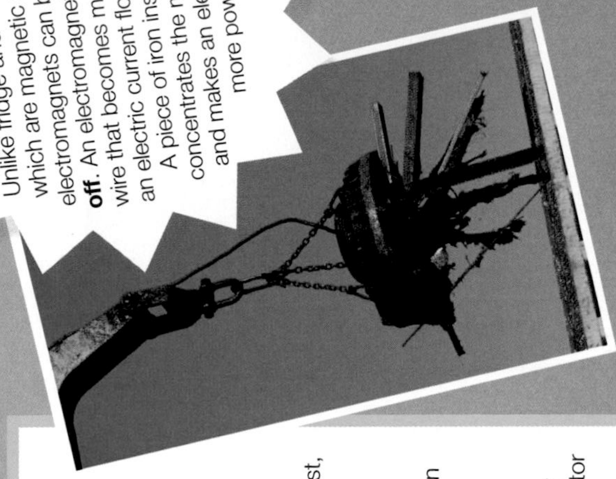

The magnet found inside an MRI scanner is **extremely powerful** – as well as being able to move objects such as scissors, chairs, and oxygen tanks, it can even move a **forklift truck** across a room.

Blasts from the past

580 BCE
Greek philosopher Thales of Miletus writes about the magnetic effects of lodestone

1086
Chinese scientist Shen Kua describes a magnetic compass

1600
William Gilbert, an English scientist, describes Earth's magnetism

1819
Danish scientist Hans Oersted discovers electromagnetism when he notices that electric currents produce magnetic fields

1821
English scientist Michael Faraday builds the first simple electric motor

1831
Michael Faraday discovers electromagnetic induction – the ability of a changing magnetic field to make an electric current flow in a wire

1906
Pierre Weiss, a French physicist, describes the domain theory of magnetism

1939
German-born scientist Walter Elsasser suggests that Earth's magnetism is caused by swirling motions in the liquid part of Earth's metal core

How does magnetism light up the sky?

Planet Earth is magnetic. It is surrounded by a magnetic field that protects us from particles speeding through space from the Sun. When these particles plunge into the atmosphere at Earth's magnetic poles, they make the air glow. A shimmering glow in the sky near the poles is called an aurora.

FAST FACTS

Magnets

01: Opposite magnetic poles attract – and the same poles repel each other.

02: Halving the distance between two magnets quadruples the magnetic force between them.

03: A magnet can be made of iron, steel, nickel, or cobalt.

04: If you break a magnet in two, you don't get a north pole and a south pole – you get two new magnets, each with a north pole and south pole.

05: If a magnet is heated to a certain temperature, called the Curie Point, it loses its magnetism. The Curie Point for iron is 770°C (1,418°F).

Magnetic fields

- **The strength of a magnetic field is measured in tesla.**
- The strength of Earth's magnetic field is about 50 millionths of a tesla.
- **A fridge magnet is about 100 times more powerful than Earth's magnetic field.**
- Most MRI (Magnetic Resonance Imaging) body scanners in hospitals use a 1.5 tesla magnet.
- **The most powerful MRI scanner used on humans has a 9.4 tesla magnet weighing more than 40 tonnes!**
- The strongest magnets built by scientists so far have a field strength of about 100 tesla.

I don't believe it!

In 2009, scientists at the Jet Propulsion Laboratory in California were able to make a live mouse float in mid-air by placing it in a magnetic field 300,000 times stronger than Earth's!

What's so special about lasers?

A laser is a device that produces an intense beam of pure light. When the laser was first developed, it was called "an invention looking for a use", because no-one knew what to do with it. Today, the special qualities of their light mean that lasers have many applications – you probably use a laser every day without even knowing it.

Why is laser light different?

Light is made of **electromagnetic waves**. Normally, the waves are different lengths, randomly mixed up together, and going in different directions. Light from a laser is made of waves that are all the same length, all in step with each other, and all going in the same direction.

Did you use a laser today?

You can find lasers in all sorts of places:

- ✔ **CD players**
- ✔ **DVD players**
- ✔ **Telephone lines**
- ✔ **Cable television**
- ✔ **Laser printers**
- ✔ **Games consoles**
- ✔ **Barcode readers in shops**
- ✔ **Visual effects in stage shows**
- ✔ **Scientific research**
- ✔ **Hospitals**
- ✔ **Industry**

Tell me more: **how does a laser work?**

A laser can be made from a solid material, a liquid, or a gas – this is called the lasing medium. Energy, usually electricity or bright light, is pumped into the lasing medium, where atoms soak up this energy and release it again as light. The light bounces between two mirrors, gaining in strength as it does so. One of the mirrors lets some light through – this is the laser beam.

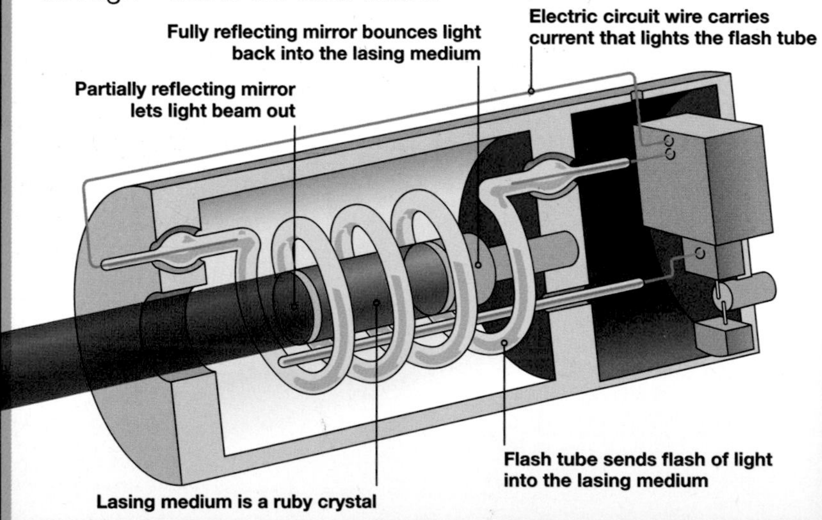
Fully reflecting mirror bounces light back into the lasing medium
Electric circuit wire carries current that lights the flash tube
Partially reflecting mirror lets light beam out
Flash tube sends flash of light into the lasing medium
Lasing medium is a ruby crystal

WHAT'S IN A NAME?

The word laser is made up from the first letters of **L**ight **A**mplification by **S**timulated **E**mission of **R**adiation, which is a scientist's way of describing how a laser works.

Can you tie a laser beam in a knot?

Light usually travels in straight lines, but a laser beam can be bent by shining it through a very thin strand of glass called an optical fibre. The light stays inside the glass fibre, even if the fibre is bent or tied in a knot. So the answer is yes!

In numbers

Less than 0.001 watts
The power of a laser pointer (a pen-like device that uses a laser to shine a spot of light on something)

Up to 0.01 watts
The power of the laser in a DVD player

0.25 watts
The power of lasers in DVD burners

30–100 watts
The power of a surgical laser

100–3000 watts
The power of an industrial laser

Tell me more: **laser reflectors on the Moon**

- The Apollo 11 astronauts took a laser reflector to the Moon in 1969 – it is the only Apollo 11 experiment still working.
- Two more laser reflectors were placed on the Moon by Apollos 14 and 15.
- The Apollo 15 laser reflector is three times the size of the other two.
- The Russian Lunokhod 1 and 2 lunar landers also carried laser reflectors.
- Lunar laser reflectors are used to measure the distance from Earth to the Moon and show that the Moon is moving away from Earth at the rate of 3.8 cm (1.5 in) per year.

How to: **use a laser to measure the distance to the Moon**

01. Ask an astronaut to take a reflector to the Moon for you.

02. Fire a laser at the reflector – measure how long it takes for the light to bounce back from the reflector.

03. Using the formula speed x time = distance, calculate how far the light has travelled.

04. Divide the distance by two, because the light travelled to the Moon and back again.

How are lasers used in medicine?

- Lasers are used in surgery to cut through flesh.
- The heat produced by a laser can vaporize living cells and seal leaking blood vessels.
- A laser can also change the shape of a cornea in the eye to correct long or short sight.
- Medical lasers are sometimes used to remove warts.

The world's **smallest laser** is only 44 billionths of a metre across. A line of more than 2,000 of them would fit across the **width** of a **human hair.**

Have you seen a hologram today?

- Imagine a photograph that lets you see behind a subject in it.
- It's not magic – it's a 3D picture called a hologram.
- A hologram is a special image created by a laser.
- A hologram is neither a picture nor photograph.
- It is a complex pattern that interferes with light to produce an image.
- Holograms are used on credit cards, DVD cases, and computer software packages.
- Holograms can also be found on some banknotes to show that the note is genuine because they are difficult to fake.

FAST FACTS

01: The scientific principle of the laser was predicted by Albert Einstein in 1916.

02: The first working laser was built by Theodore Maiman in 1960.

03: The first item bought after being scanned by a laser barcode scanner was a pack of chewing gum from a US supermarket in June 1974.

04: The most powerful laser beams can cut through the toughest materials, even diamond.

05: At the National Ignition Facility (NIF) in California, USA, 192 laser beams are produced at the same time.

06: The NIF lasers are designed to be fired at a tiny pellet of fuel in a quest to produce energy by a process called nuclear fusion, the same process that powers the Sun.

WEIRD OR WHAT?

The musician Jean-Michel Jarre is famous for playing a **laser harp** in his concerts. Blocking each of the instrument's laser beams with his hand produces a different musical note.

How does **science catch criminals?**

Criminals always take something away from a crime scene with them and leave something of their own behind. For example, they might unknowingly carry away fibres from a carpet and leave fingerprints behind. Crime Scene Investigators (CSIs) look for these tell-tale pieces of evidence and scientists use them to link criminals with their crimes.

In numbers

100
The number of hairs that fall out of a healthy scalp every day, so there's a good chance that a criminal will drop a hair or two at a crime scene

240+
The number of prisoners freed in the USA as a result of DNA tests on evidence from past crimes

5 million
The number of people whose DNA is stored in the UK national DNA database

55 million
The number of people whose fingerprints are kept on file by the FBI in the USA

How do crime scientists match bullets with guns?

[illegible]

WHAT'S IN A NAME?

Crime scientists are also called **forensic scientists**. "Forensic" means to do with a court of law.

Ten things CSIs search for at a crime scene

- ✔ Fingerprints
- ✔ Shoe prints
- ✔ Tyre prints
- ✔ Hair
- ✔ Fibres
- ✔ Documents
- ✔ Blood and other body fluids
- ✔ Illegal drugs
- ✔ Weapons
- ✔ Bullets

I don't believe it!

Crime scientists can tell how long a body has been lying undiscovered by studying the creepy-crawlies living on it!

Reading the code

- DNA (deoxyribonucleic acid) is a biological code found inside the body's cells.
- Apart from identical twins, everybody has different DNA.
- If DNA found at a crime scene is the same as DNA taken from a suspect, this proves the suspect was at the crime scene.
- Matching various samples of DNA like this is known as DNA profiling.
- The chance of a wrong identification being made from a good DNA profile is one in several billion.

Crime scientists list

Ten kinds of crime scientists and what they specialize in:

01 Forensic anthropologist (skeletons)
02 Forensic DNA analyst (DNA)
03 Forensic ballistics analyst (firearms)
04 Forensic entomologist (insects)
05 Forensic odontologist (teeth)
06 Forensic psychologist (psychology)
07 Forensic digital analyst (computers, mobile phones, digital cameras)
08 Forensic geologist (soil and rock)
09 Forensic engineer (structures)
10 Forensic document analyst (documents)

1247 The first book on forensic science is written in China by Sung Tzuh
1642 The University of Leipzig starts teaching forensic medicine
1889 Alexandre Lacassagne shows that a bullet can be matched to the gun that fired it
1892 Fingerprints are used to convict a murderer for the first time
1901 Karl Landsteiner creates the ABO system of blood types
1910 The world's first crime laboratory opens in Marseilles, France
1921 The first lie detector machine is built
1936 Maggots are first used to estimate the time of a person's death
1975 The FBI creates the first computerized fingerprint identification system
1984 Alec Jeffreys invents genetic profiling
1986 Genetic profiling is used to solve a murder for the first time

Blasts from the past

How to lift fingerprints

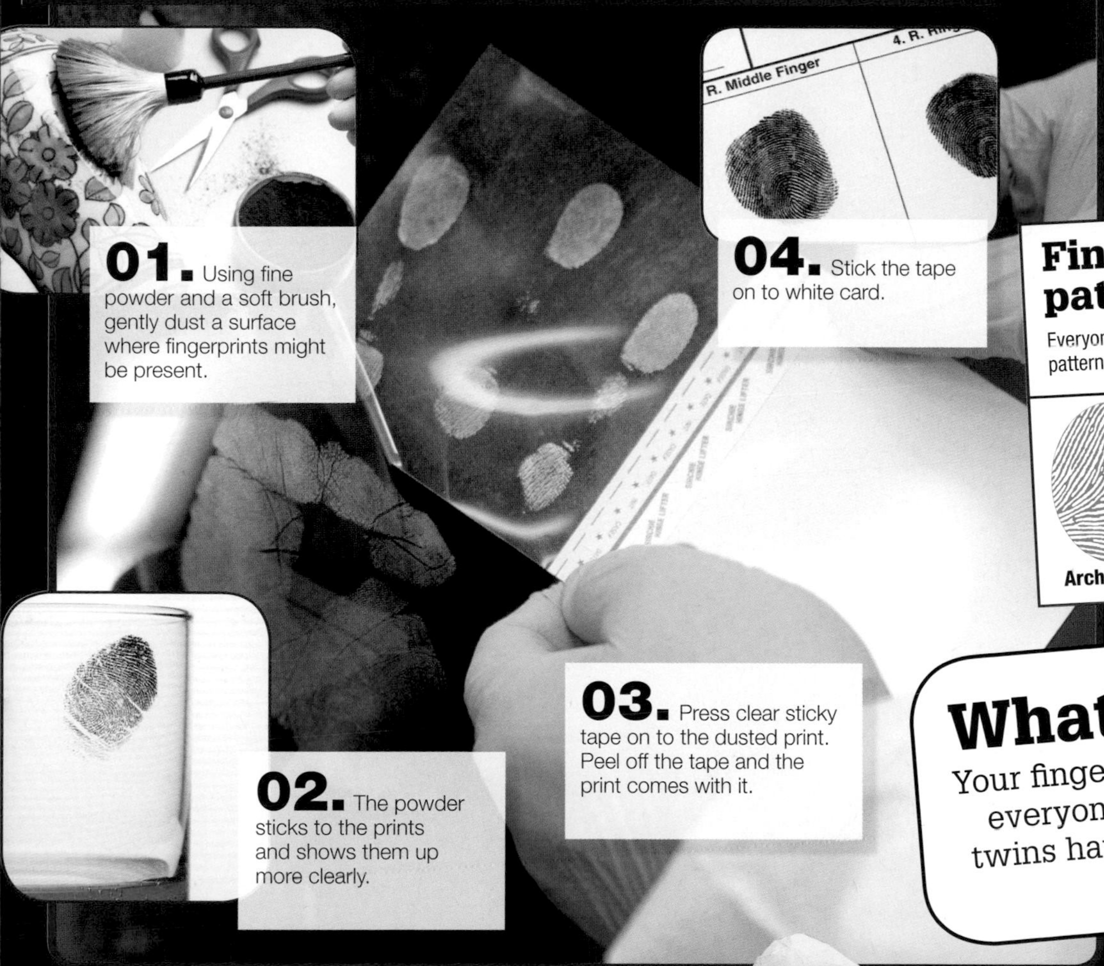

01. Using fine powder and a soft brush, gently dust a surface where fingerprints might be present.

02. The powder sticks to the prints and shows them up more clearly.

03. Press clear sticky tape on to the dusted print. Peel off the tape and the print comes with it.

04. Stick the tape on to white card.

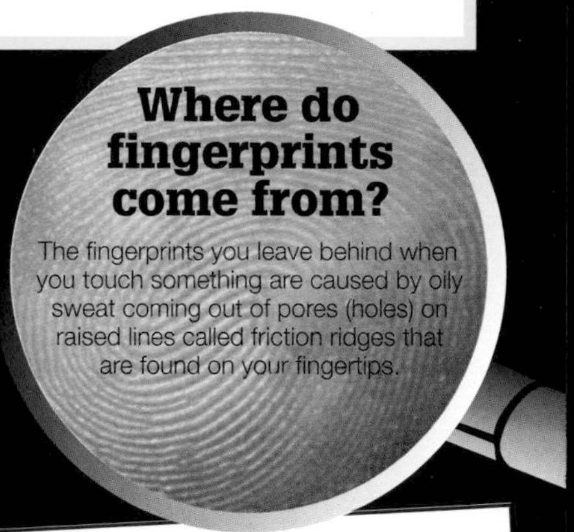

Where do fingerprints come from?

The fingerprints you leave behind when you touch something are caused by oily sweat coming out of pores (holes) on raised lines called friction ridges that are found on your fingertips.

Fingerprint patterns

Everyone's fingerprints belong to one of three basic patterns:

What about me?

Your fingerprints are different from everyone else's. Even identical twins have different fingerprints.

Whose prints are these?

[illegible]

Things crime scene investigators wear

CSIs have to take care not to contaminate a crime scene with their own hair, fibres, sweat, or fingerprints. They wear:

- Latex gloves on their hands
- A papery-plastic suit that covers their whole body
- A hood that covers their hair
- Over-shoes that cover their feet
- A face mask

How do microscopes **magnify things?**

FAST FACTS

Magnifying facts

01: More than 2,000 years ago, glass balls filled with water were used in Ancient Greece and Rome to magnify things.

02: Glass lenses called reading stones were used from around 1,000 years ago.

03: A single lens used to magnify something is called a simple microscope.

04: Microscopes with two or more lenses are known as compound microscopes.

05: The magnifying power of a microscope is found by multiplying the power of the eyepiece (usually about ten) by the power of the lens focusing in on the object.

06: Compound microscopes usually have at least three objective lenses with different magnifying powers.

Most microscopes work by using lenses to bend light rays. The human eye can see things as small as the width of a human hair, but microscopes let us see things that are far smaller than this. The most powerful microscopes make images of individual atoms.

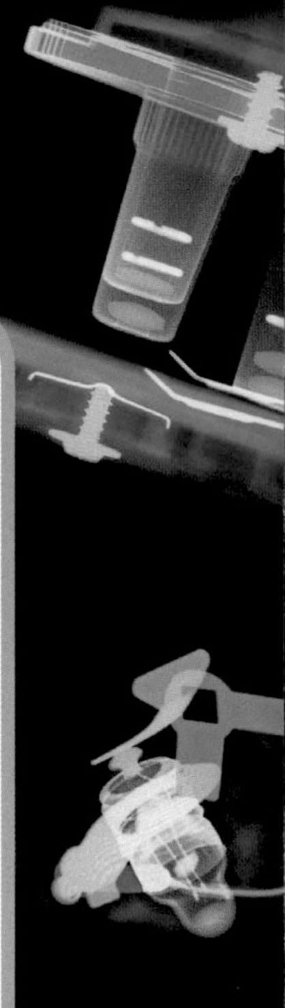

How to: **use an optical microscope**

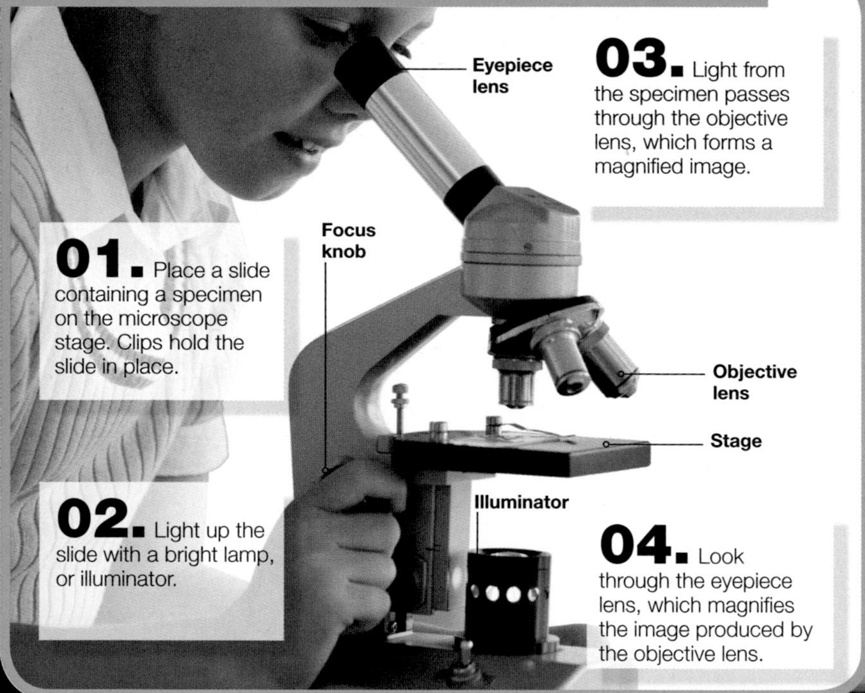

01. Place a slide containing a specimen on the microscope stage. Clips hold the slide in place.

02. Light up the slide with a bright lamp, or illuminator.

03. Light from the specimen passes through the objective lens, which forms a magnified image.

04. Look through the eyepiece lens, which magnifies the image produced by the objective lens.

Who invented the microscope?
No one knows who invented the simple microscope, because it happened so long ago! The **compound microscope** was probably invented by a Dutch lens maker called Zacharias Janssen in the 1590s.

Looking closer… and closer

Surface of tongue
magnified 1,000 times

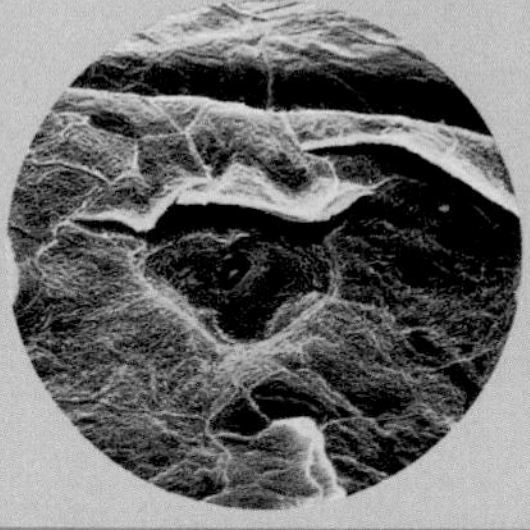

Snail's teeth
magnified 4,000 times

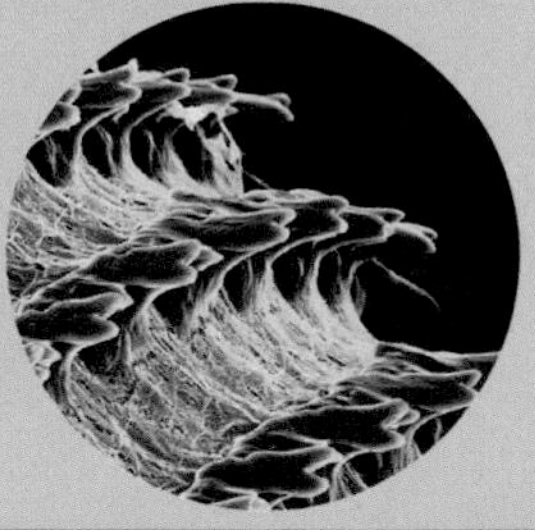

Snowflake
magnified 6,500 times

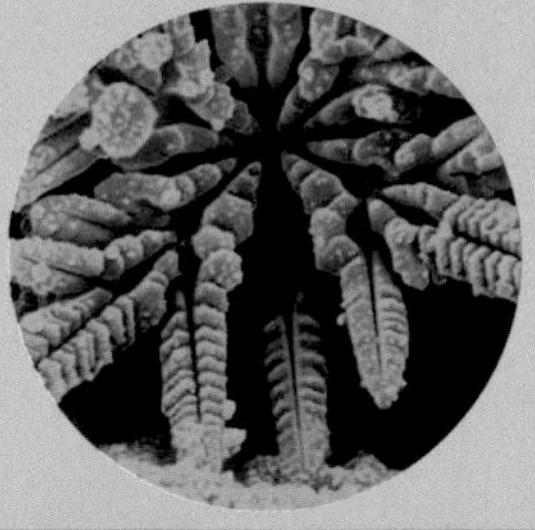

Virus
magnified about 100,000 tim

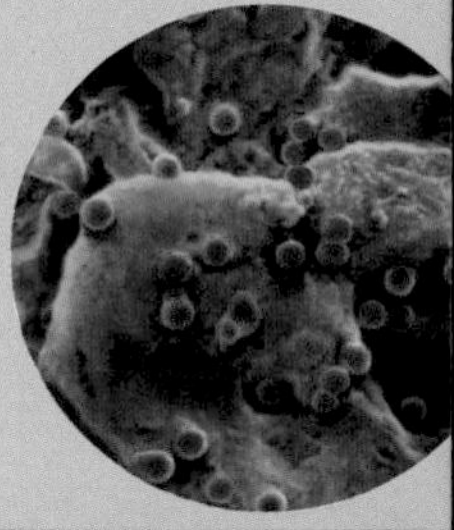

Blasts from the past

9th century
Abbas Ibn Firnas invents lens-shaped glass pebbles called reading stones

13th century
The Arab scientist Alhazen writes about using lenses for magnification

1595
Dutch lens-maker Zacharias Janssen makes the first compound microscope by placing two lenses inside a tube

1625
John Faber invents the name "microscope" for an instrument that uses lenses for magnification

1667
Robert Hooke publishes his book, called *Micrographia*, about his observations using a microscope

1675
Anton van Leeuwenhoek uses a simple microscope with one lens to study insects, cells, and bacteria

1931
Ernst Ruska invents the electron microscope

1981
Gerd Binnig and Heinrich Rohrer invent the scanning tunnelling microscope, a type of scanning probe microscope

1986
Gerd Binnig, Calvin Quate, and Christoph Gerber develop the atomic force microscope, another type of scanning probe microscope

WEIRD OR WHAT?

On 28 September 1989, Don Eigler became the first person to move and control an **individual atom**. He used a scanning tunnelling microscope to move 35 xenon atoms to spell the name of the company he worked for – IBM.

Types of **microscopes**

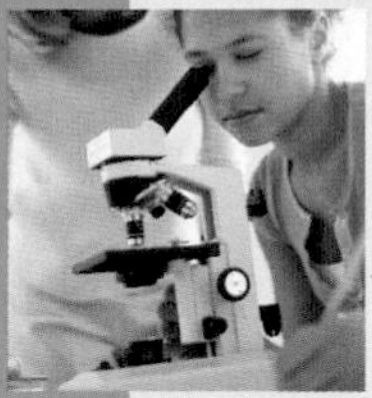

Optical microscope
The most widely used type of microscope. It uses light to magnify an object up to about 1,500 times.

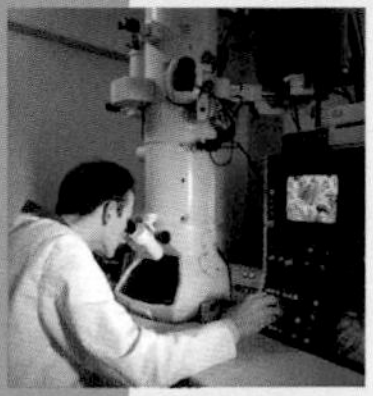

Electron microscope
This microscope uses an electron beam instead of light to form images. Magnifies up to two million times.

Scanning probe microscope
Capable of producing images of individual atoms, this microscope can magnify up to 100 million times.

Binocular microscope
This features two eyepieces instead of just one, so the user doesn't have to close one eye to view.

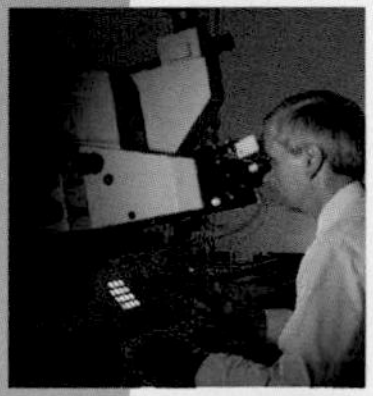

Stereo microscope
A binocular microscope with two objective lenses as well as two eyepieces to generate a 3D view.

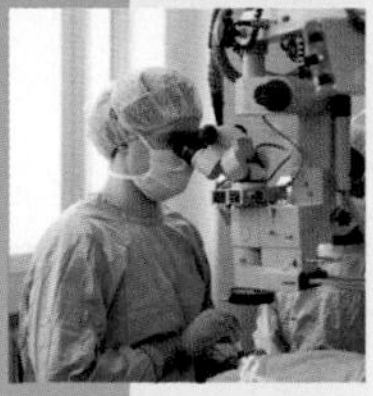

Operating microscope
Another binocular microscope used by surgeons to carry out intricate operations on tiny areas of the body.

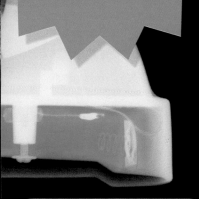

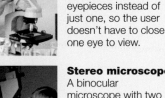

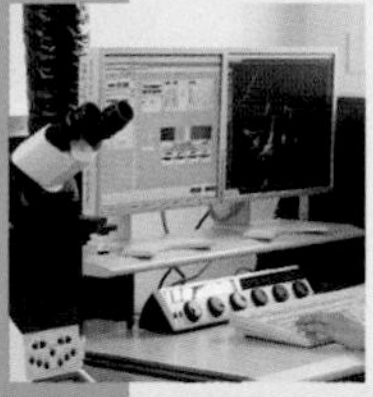

Digital microscope
This high-tech microscope is capable of sending digital images to a computer.

Tell me more: **electron microscope**

- Electron microscopes use a beam of electrons to create images.
- Electrons can't go through glass lenses, so electron microscopes use magnetic lenses.
- Air is sucked out of the microscope to stop it getting in the way of the electrons.
- Electrons bounce off the specimen or go through it and then make an image on a screen.
- An electron microscope can make images of objects 500,000 times smaller than the human eye can see.
- Electron microscopes made it possible to see viruses for the first time.

New microscopes

New types of microscopes are still being invented. At the California Institute of Technology in 2008, Changhuei Yang invented a **new optical microscope that doesn't need lenses**. The pocket-sized instrument uses the same type of light-sensitive chip that is found in digital cameras.

RECORD BREAKER

The world's **most powerful microscope** is called TEAM 0.5. TEAM stands for Transmission Electron Aberration-corrected Microscope. Located at the Lawrence Berkeley National Laboratory, California, it can see objects as small as half the width of a hydrogen atom.

Under the microscope

The invention of the microscope revealed a world teeming with tiny creatures, as well as the amazing structure of the human body. For scientists, it was like a new toy – they looked at water, blood, plants, and even scrapings from their own teeth!

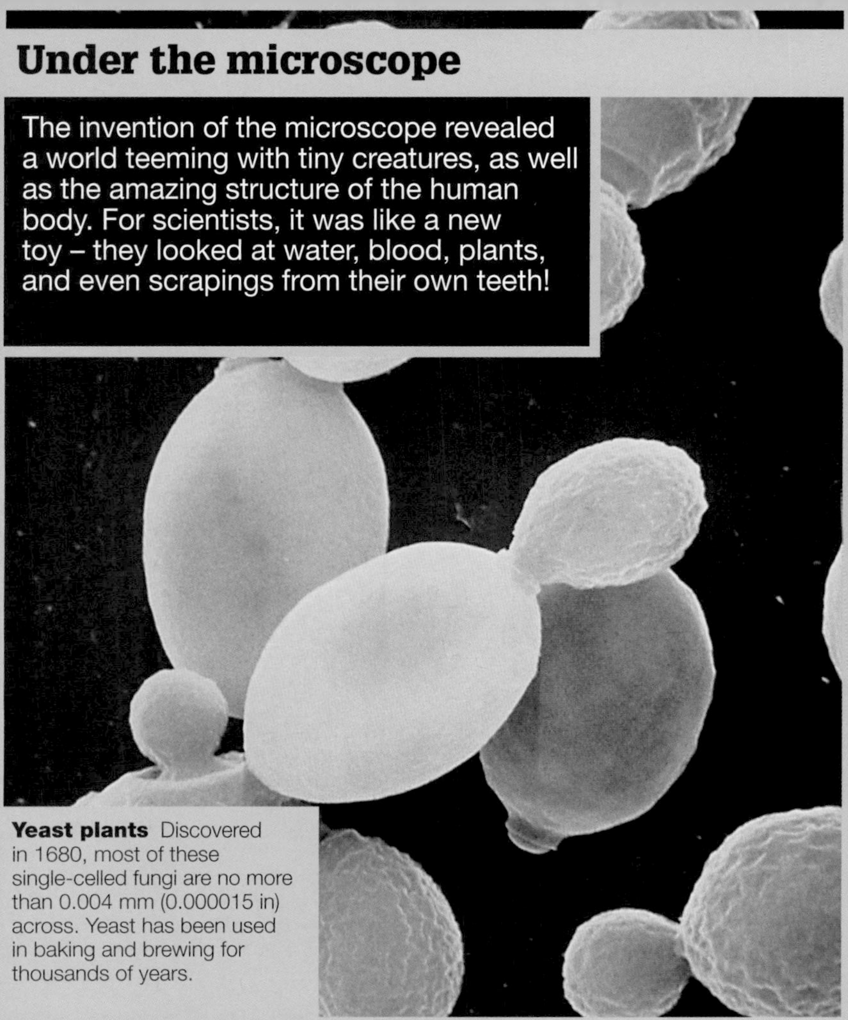

Yeast plants Discovered in 1680, most of these single-celled fungi are no more than 0.004 mm (0.000015 in) across. Yeast has been used in baking and brewing for thousands of years.

Rotifers These tiny creatures, mostly less than 0.5 mm (0.02 in) long, are made up of about 1,000 cells and live in water and wet soil. Rotifers were first spotted in 1696.

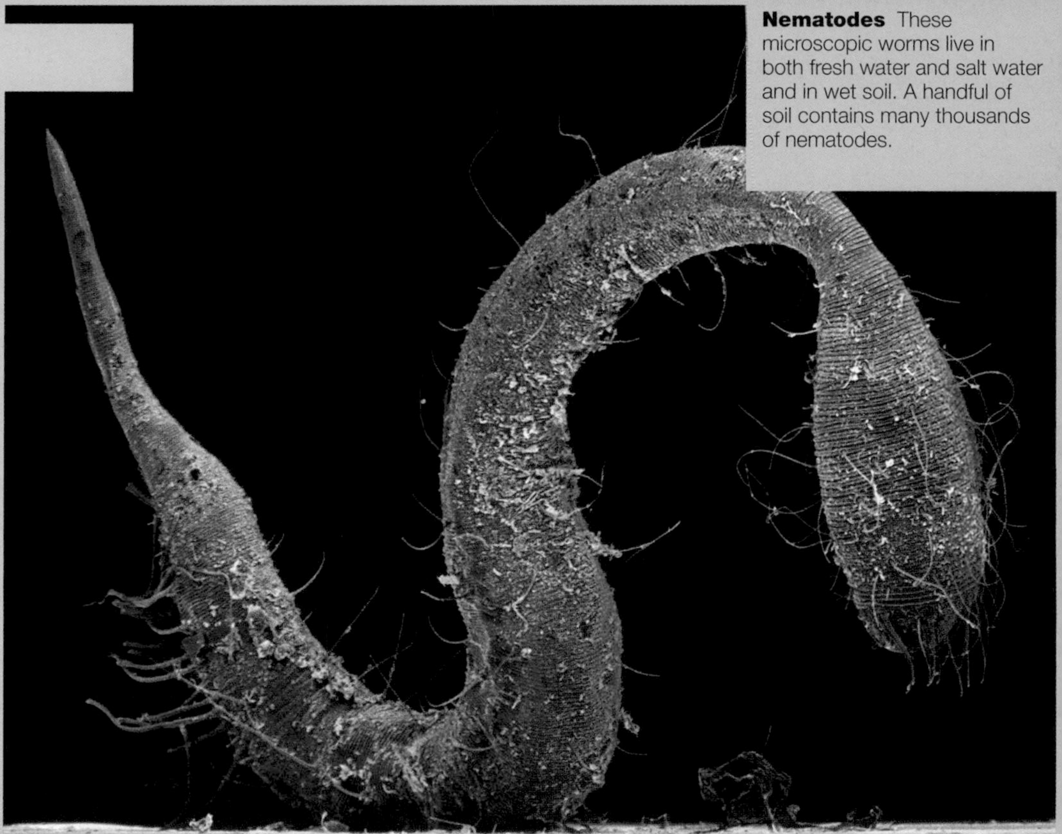

Nematodes These microscopic worms live in both fresh water and salt water and in wet soil. A handful of soil contains many thousands of nematodes.

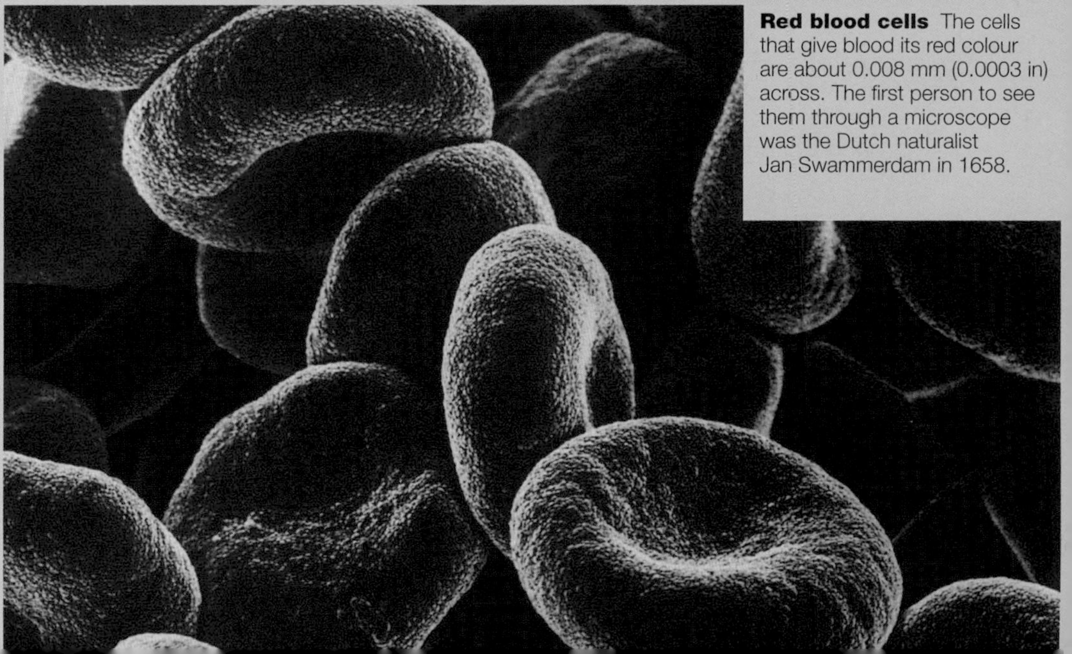

Red blood cells The cells that give blood its red colour are about 0.008 mm (0.0003 in) across. The first person to see them through a microscope was the Dutch naturalist Jan Swammerdam in 1658.

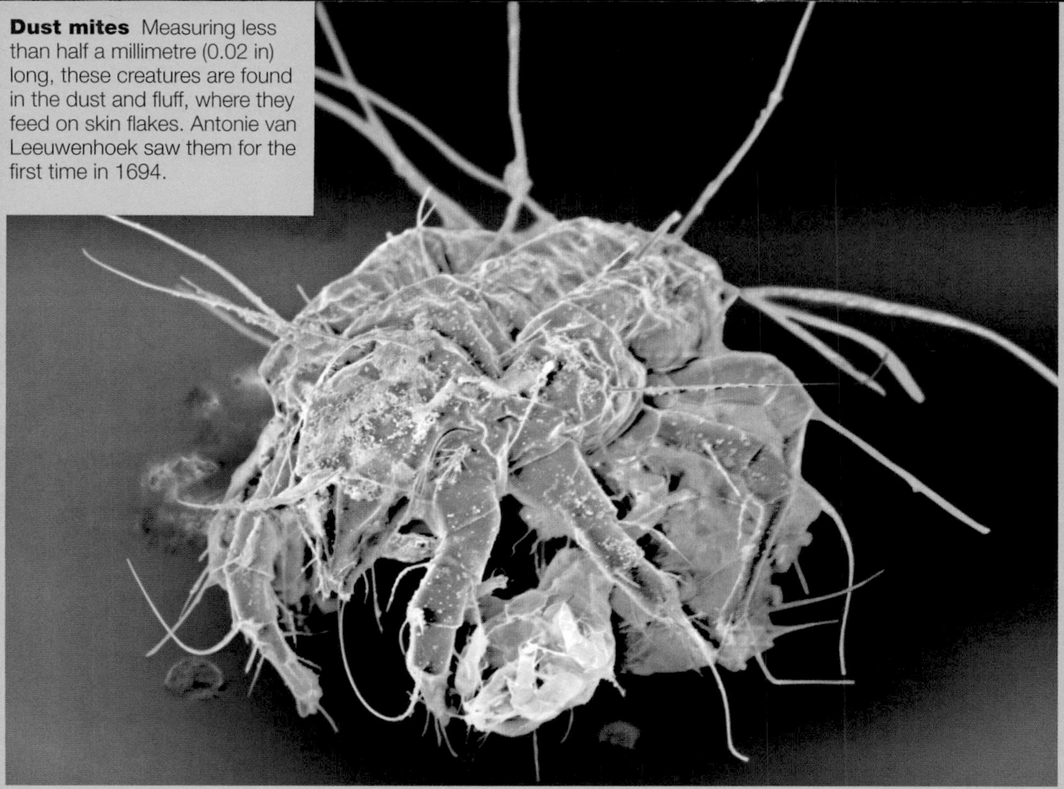

Dust mites Measuring less than half a millimetre (0.02 in) long, these creatures are found in the dust and fluff, where they feed on skin flakes. Antonie van Leeuwenhoek saw them for the first time in 1694.

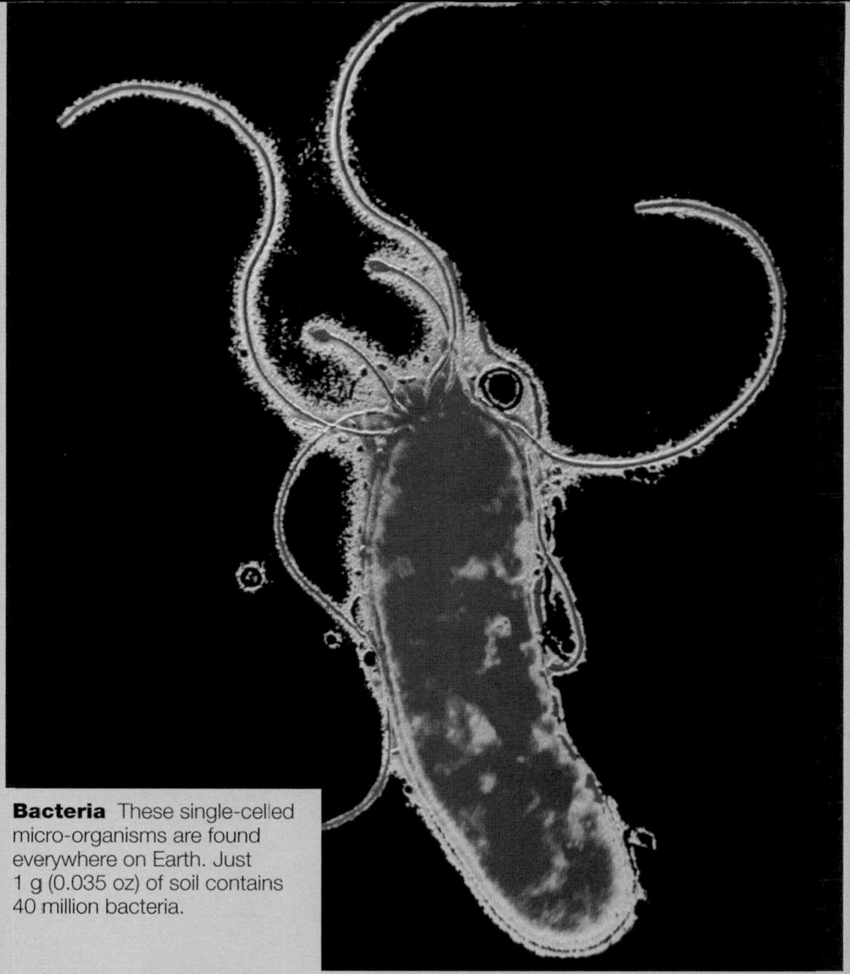

Bacteria These single-celled micro-organisms are found everywhere on Earth. Just 1 g (0.035 oz) of soil contains 40 million bacteria.

The cell nucleus This is the part of a living cell that contains most of the cell's genetic material and controls its activities. It may have been seen by several pioneers in microscopy, but was described in detail for the first time in 1804 by Franz Bauer and named in 1831 by Robert Brown.

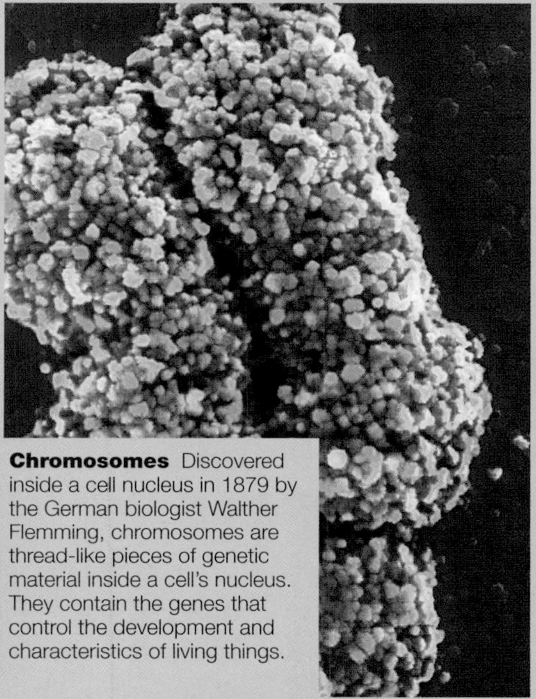

Chromosomes Discovered inside a cell nucleus in 1879 by the German biologist Walther Flemming, chromosomes are thread-like pieces of genetic material inside a cell's nucleus. They contain the genes that control the development and characteristics of living things.

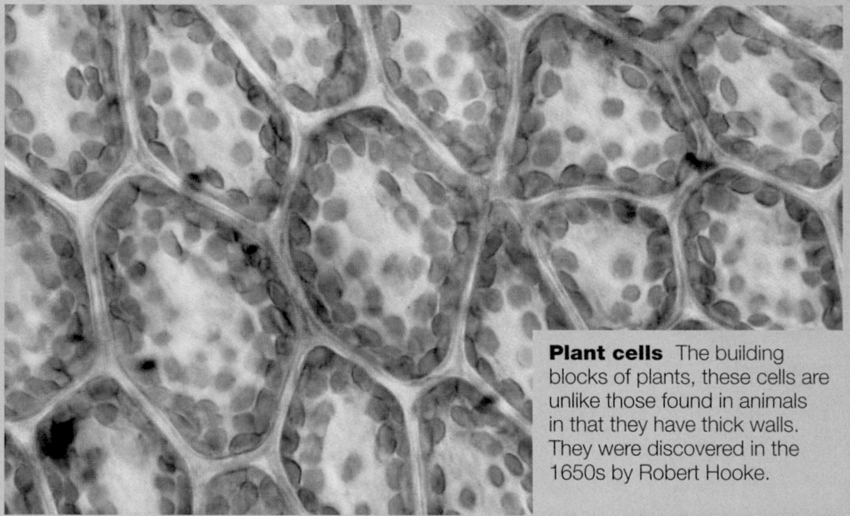

Plant cells The building blocks of plants, these cells are unlike those found in animals in that they have thick walls. They were discovered in the 1650s by Robert Hooke.

Why is **uranium dangerous?**

Uranium is radioactive. And there's the problem – because radioactivity is dangerous, uranium is dangerous. Radioactive substances can cause sickness, burns, cancer, and even death. Even though it's dangerous, radioactivity can be useful too. For example, without it, you might not be able to turn your lights on.

Cockroaches can survive up to 16 times more radiation than humans. **Fruit flies** are even tougher – they are able to survive up to 160 times more radiation than us!

Where do radioactive substances come from?

01 Primordial – these are radioisotopes that have existed since before Earth was formed.

02 Cosmogenic – these are created when a cosmic ray (a particle from space) hits the nucleus of an atom and changes it.

03 Produced by humans – many of the radioisotopes used in industry and medicine are made in nuclear reactors. Some of the radioactive particles found in nature today were produced by nuclear weapons tests in the past.

What is radioactivity?

Radioactivity is a property of some **atoms** that are so unstable that they break up all by themselves. They fire out particles or rays. When they do this, it's called radioactive decay.

Using radioactivity

Radioactive materials are used in a number of ways:

- Nuclear power stations use radioactivity to generate electricity for millions of people.
- Gamma rays kill bugs, so they are used to sterilize medical equipment.
- In industry, gamma rays are used like high-powered X-rays to look for cracks in metal parts.
- In medicine, radiotherapy uses radiation to kill cancer cells.
- Smoke detectors contain a radioactive element called americum.
- Radioactive tracing uses radioactive substances to find out where something goes or how fast it moves.
- Carbon dating is used to find out how old a once-living object (such as wood or bone) is by measuring the amount of carbon-14 (a radioisotope) it contains.
- In paper-making, radioactivity is used to make sure that the paper is the right thickness.

Nuclear spacecraft

The **space probes** that explore the furthest planets go so far from the Sun that they cannot use solar energy to make the electricity they need. Instead, they have nuclear-powered generators for making electricity.

Half-lives

Some radioisotopes decay faster than others. The time it takes for half of the atoms in a piece of a radioactive element to decay is called the element's half-life. Half-lives can range from a fraction of a second to billions of years.

radioisotope	half-life
polonium-214	160 microseconds
radium-221	30 seconds
strontium-90	9 minutes
carbon-14	5,730 years
uranium-238	4,500 million years

I don't believe it!

When radioactivity was discovered, some people thought that it was good for them. They drank glowing radioactive drinks, not knowing how seriously dangerous they were.

Tell me more: types of radiation

Radioactive substances give out three types of radiation: alpha, beta, and gamma radiation.

α Alpha radiation: Alpha radiation is made of particles. These alpha particles can be stopped easily by a sheet of paper or your hand.

β Beta radiation: Beta radiation is also made of particles. Beta particles pass through paper, but they can be stopped by a sheet of aluminium foil.

γ Gamma radiation: Gamma radiation is made of waves. Gamma rays pass through most materials and can only be stopped by a sheet of lead or a concrete wall.

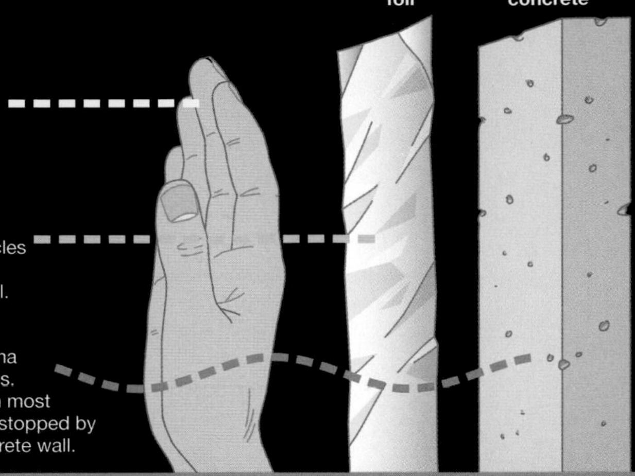

Nuclear accidents

1957: The core of the Windscale nuclear reactor in England caught fire. Radioactive material was released.

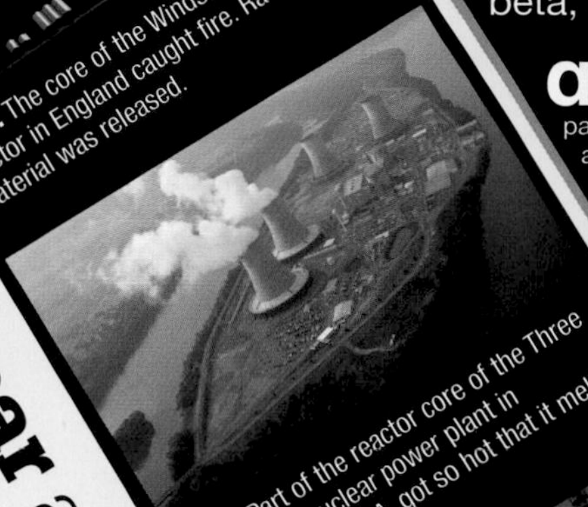

1979: Part of the reactor core of the Three Mile Island nuclear power plant in Pennsylvania, USA, got so hot that it melted.

1986: A reactor at the Chernobyl nuclear power plant in the Ukraine exploded and burned. It is the world's worst nuclear accident.

Radioactivity

- There are about 1,800 radioisotopes.
- About 200 radioisotopes are used in industry and medicine.
- More than 10,000 hospitals worldwide use radioisotopes in medicine.
- The radioisotope most commonly used in hospitals is technetium-99.
- The average nuclear reactor needs about 25 tonnes of new uranium fuel a year.
- 50,000 tonnes of uranium ore has to be mined to produce 25 tonnes of reactor fuel.

Blasts from the past

1896 Henri Becquerel discovers that uranium gives out unknown rays; one year later, Ernest Rutherford uncovers alpha and beta radiation, while in 1898 Marie Curie and her husband Pierre discover the radioactive elements radium and polonium

1942 Enrico Fermi produces the first self-sustaining nuclear chain reaction at the University of Chicago

1951 Electricity is produced from nuclear energy for the first time, using the Experimental Breeder Reactor 1 (EBR-1) in Idaho, USA

1954 The USS *Nautilus*, the world's first nuclear-powered submarine, is launched

1972 Pioneer 10, the first nuclear-powered interplanetary space probe, is launched

What are isotopes?

An atom can have two types of particles in its nucleus – **protons** and **neutrons**. Atoms of the same element have the same number of protons, but can have different numbers of neutrons. Atoms of the same element with different neutrons are called isotopes. Radioactive isotopes are called **radioisotopes**.

Ten radioisotopes

The number after an isotope's name shows how many particles (protons and neutrons) there are in its nucleus. Uranium-235 has 92 protons and 143 neutrons in its nucleus. Uranium-238 has three more neutrons.

Actinium-225
Americum-241
Carbon-14
Cobalt-60
Plutonium-239
Polonium-210
Radium-226
Strontium-90
Thallium-204
Uranium-235

Uranium-235

Where do most **people** live in **Canada?**

Most people live in the south of the country, within 160 km (100 miles) of the US border, where the climate is warmer and the winters are less severe than in the vast area of lakes, forests, and swamps further north. More than 75 per cent of Canadian people live in cities.

WHAT'S IN A NAME?

When French explorer Jacques Cartier (1491–1557) was exploring the St Lawrence River in the 1530s, he asked the local inhabitants where they lived. They replied "**kanata**", which means "village" in the Iroquois language – and that's how Canada got its name.

Five facts about the CN Tower, Toronto

01 The CN Tower is 553.33 m (1,815 ft) tall.

02 It took 40 months to build and was opened to the public in June 1976.

03 The elevators travel at a speed of 6 m (20 ft) per second (except in high winds).

04 Two-thirds of the way up, visitors can walk on a glass floor 372 m (1,222 ft) above the ground.

05 Lightning strikes the tower an average of 75 times per year.

In numbers

42
The number of Canadian national parks

5,959 m
(19,583 ft) The height of Mount Logan, Canada's highest mountain

7,604 km
(4,724 miles) The length of the Trans–Canada Highway, which links the west and east coasts

8,893 km
(5,526 miles) The total length of the border with the US

243,000 km
(151,100 miles) The total length of Canada's coastline

812,129
The population of Ottawa, Canada's capital city

33.4 million
The population of Canada

The red maple leaf, recognized everywhere in the world as the national emblem of Canada, was adopted as the national flag in 1965.

Ten ways to enjoy the **Canadian wilderness**

Heli-skiing

Snowboarding

Hiking in the Rocky Mountains

Ocean kayaking

Polar bear watching

Dog sledding

Mountain biking

Inventive minds

Canadians claim **Alexander Graham Bell**, inventor of the telephone, as their own. Born in Scotland, he later moved to Canada where he made his all-important experiments with sound. Here are some other Canadian bright sparks:

- **James Naismith** Came up with the idea of nailing a peach basket to the wall and aiming a soccer ball through it. Basketball was born!
- **Frederick Banting** Won a Nobel Prize for isolating the hormone insulin and discovering a successful treatment for diabetes.
- **Thomas Ahearn** Invented many electrical products, including the first electric oven.
- **Reginald Fessenden** Credited with making the first broadcast of the human voice in 1905.
- **Arthur Sicard** Marketed a canny device for clearing snow – the snowblower.

Fast-food favourite

Ask for **poutine** in any fast-food outlet or diner in Canada and you will get a plate of French fries covered with fresh curd cheese and brown gravy. This dish, invented in Québec in the 1950s, has become a national favourite.

I don't believe it!

Canada isn't all forests, frozen lakes, and rocky shores – Okanagan desert in southern British Columbia is Canada's only true desert, a vast, arid landscape that is home to many rare birds of prey.

The world's longest public ice rink is a 7.8-km (4.8-mile) section of the Rideau Canal in the heart of Ottawa, which freezes over from December to February.

Sports medley

- Ice hockey (known as "hockey") is the national winter sport. It is played by 25 per cent of the male population of Canada.
- The national summer sport is lacrosse, a field game that originated among the Iroquois nation, who are said to have played it with teams of 1,000 people.
- *Hockey Night in Canada* is the world's longest running TV sports show – it has been on the air since 1952.
- Canada has hosted the Summer Olympics once (Montreal 1976) and the Winter Olympics twice (Calgary 1988 and Vancouver 2010).
- The official mascots for the Vancouver Olympics, **Miga**, **Quatchi**, and **Sumi**, were based on Native American mythical animals.

Canada's oldest national park is **Banff National Park**, which was created in 1885 in Alberta's Rocky Mountains.

French or English?

- Canada has two official languages, English and French (except in Québec, where French is the only official language).
- 20.6 million Canadians (58 per cent) speak English at home, and 6.6 million (22 per cent) speak French.
- Montreal, the capital of Québec, is the second largest French-speaking city in the world, after Paris, France.
- Chinese is the most widely spoken language in Canada after English and French, and is spoken by 2.6 per cent of the population.

Salmon fishing

Going to the rodeo at Calgary

River rafting

RECORD BREAKER

The world's **biggest tides** are found in the Bay of Fundy in Nova Scotia, where the tidal range (the difference in height between low and high tides) can be as much as 17 m (55 ft).

Which is the **highest** capital in the world?

The Andes were once part of the **Spanish Empire**. The seven countries of the Andes region were founded after South America was freed from Spanish rule in 1823.

Say it in Quechua? After Spanish, the most widely spoken **language** in the Andes is Quechua, the language of the Incas.

La Paz, the capital of Bolivia, is 3,631 m (11,912 ft) above sea level. Bolivia is the highest country in the Andes, the mountain chain that extends north–south all the way down the western coast of South America. It is the longest mountain chain in the world.

Tell me more: **the Andes**

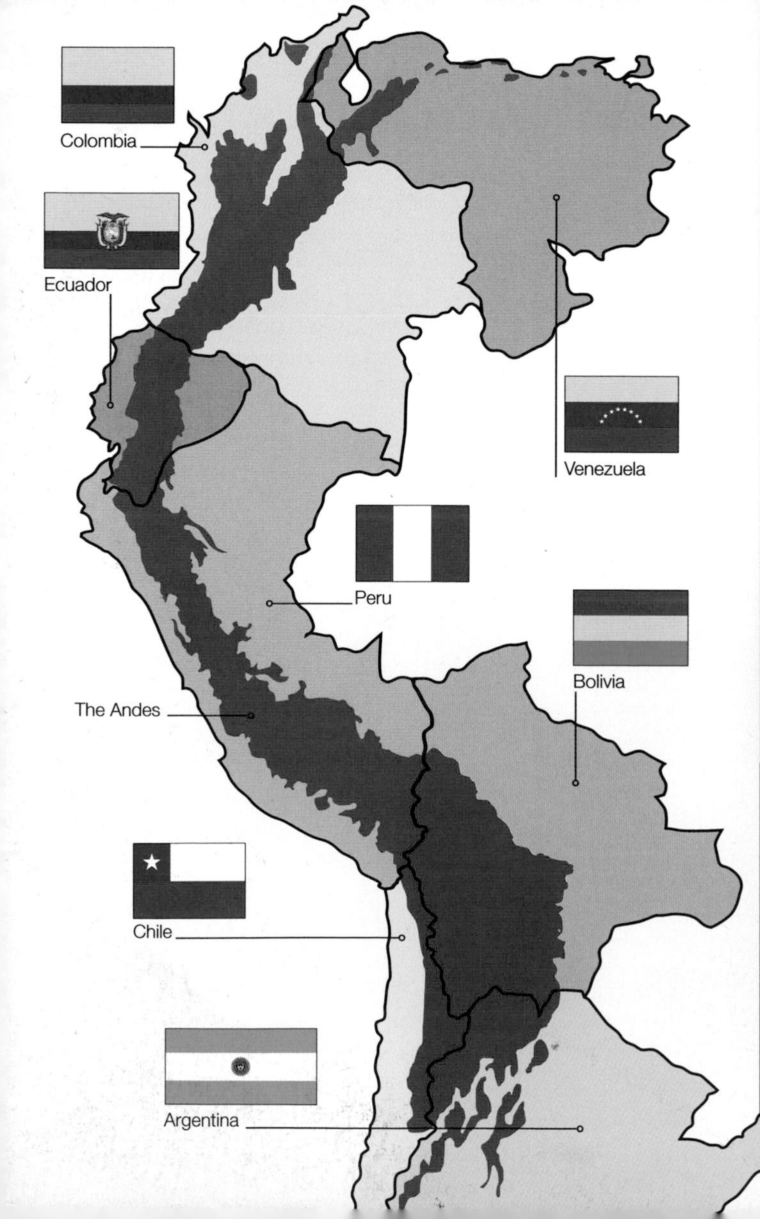

The Andes

01: Length
8,900 km (5,500 miles)

02: Maximum width
640 km (398 miles)

03: Highest mountain
Aconcagua (Argentina) 6,962 m (22,841 ft)

04: Highest active volcano
Ojos del Salado (Argentina/Chile) 6,891 m (22,608 ft)

05: Highest navigable lake (in the world)
Lake Titicaca (Bolivia/Peru) 3,812 m (12,507 ft)

06: Largest salt flat (in the world)
Salar de Uyuni (Bolivia) 10,582 sq km (4,085 sq miles)

Living at altitude

- Many people in the Central Andes (Bolivia and Peru) live above 3,000 m (10,000 ft).
- At high altitudes, the oxygen in the atmosphere thins, making it difficult to breathe.
- The body adjusts by increasing the lung size to absorb more oxygen.
- More oxygen-carrying red blood cells are produced.
- Shepherds in Peru sometimes live at more than 5,000 m (17,000 ft). Phew!

WHAT'S IN A NAME?

Argentina: Means "land of silver".

Bolivia: Named after Simón Bolívar, liberator of South America

Chile and **Peru** are both local Quechuan names.

Colombia: Named after Christopher Columbus – although he never went there.

Ecuador: Gets its name from its location – it straddles the equator.

Venezuela: So called because it reminded early European explorers of Venice.

Five facts about the Andes

01 About 95 per cent of the world's emeralds come from Colombia.

02 Two Chilean writers have won the Nobel Prize for Literature: Gabriela Mistral (1889–1957) and Pablo Neruda (1904–1973).

03 Argentina is the fifth largest wine-producing country in the world.

04 Guinea pigs are eaten throughout the Andes and provide an important source of protein.

05 The Inca city of Machu Picchu attracts more than 400,000 visitors a year.

I don't believe it!

Panama hats actually come from Ecuador. The straw hats got their name because they were shipped through the Panama Canal on their way to the USA.

..ake Titicaca

The Incas believed that the god Viracocha rose from the deep ..aters of Lake Titicaca to create the ..orld, Sun, and stars.

Lake Titicaca is always cold because it is fed by water ..om glaciers high in the Andes.

The Isla del Sol, the largest of the lake's islands, has many Inca ruins.

A small group of people known as the Uros live on ..oating islands, made from totora ..eds that grow in the lake.

The interwoven reeds form long roots that mat together and are ..chored with sticks to the bottom .. the lake. As the reeds begin to ..t, new layers are laid on top.

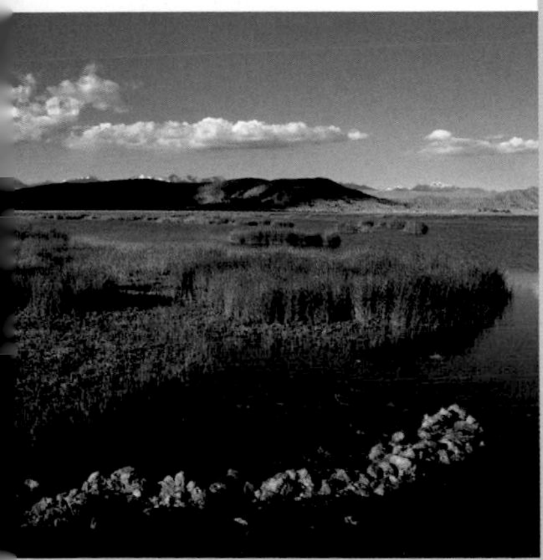

Three facts about the Uros

01: The Uro people use bundles of dried totora reeds to make their houses, furniture, and boats. The white pithy part of the reeds is used to relieve pain.

02: The islanders support themselves by fishing and selling brightly coloured textiles and woven goods to tourists.

03: Their boats, which are shaped like canoes and often have animal heads at the prow, are used for fishing and transporting visitors to the islands.

Incredible Incas

The Incas built more than 40,000 km (24,855 miles) of **roads**. They had no wheeled transport, so travelled everywhere on foot using **llamas** as pack animals.

Early Andean civilizations

Humans have lived in the Andes region for at least 13,000 years – perhaps far longer. The first civilizations emerged in the region nearly 3,000 years ago.

- The **Nazca** people of Peru (100 BCE to 500 CE) drew lines in the desert to make vast, geometric patterns.
- The **Moche** rulers of north Peru (c. 1 CE to c. 800 CE) were buried in garments decorated with gold and silver.
- **Tiwanaku** was a large city on Lake Titicaca that flourished from 500–950 CE.
- The **Chimú** of Chan Chan, Peru, (c. 900–1470 CE) were highly skilled gold-workers.
- The **Inca** Empire (c. 1200–1533 CE) was the largest in ancient America, extending over most of the Andes until the Spanish conquest in 1533.

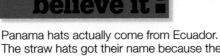

Chimú gold burial mask

Does anything **grow** in the Sahara?

Although much of the Sahara is too hot and dry for most plants to survive, trees such as palms grow around oases – fertile spots in the desert fed with water from underground springs. Farmers living beside the oases grow crops in small tree-shaded gardens.

Tell me more: **deserts**

- A desert is an area with low precipitation (rain, snow, or mist).
- **One-fifth of the Earth's land mass is covered by desert.**
- The driest desert in the world is the Atacama in Chile, where it hasn't rained since records began.
- **The Arctic and Antarctica are both technically deserts because of the low precipitation.**

FAST FACTS: The Sahara

01: The Sahara is the largest desert in the world, covering most of north and west Africa.

02: Its highest peak is Emi Koussi at a height of 3,415 m (11,204 ft).

03: The highest temperature ever recorded was 57°C (136°F) in 1922.

04: The average rainfall in the Sahara is 76 mm (3 in) per year.

05: Only about one-fifth of the Sahara is sand. The rest is made up of mountains, rocks, and gravel.

Three Saharan winds

01 Haboob Sudden, violent wind that causes dust storms (below).

02 Harmattan Blows in winter, carrying dust and sand all the way to the Caribbean.

03 Khamsin Hot, dusty wind that blows for 50 days a year.

Rock art
Cave paintings in the mountains of Tassili-n'Ajjer, Algeria, record a time when the Sahara **teemed with wildlife**. Some of the paintings show humans hunting with bows and herding cattle.

Ten deserts around the world

Sahara Desert (North Africa) 9,100,000 sq km (3,500,000 sq miles)

Arabian Desert (Arabian Peninsula) 2,330,000 sq km (900,000 sq miles)

Gobi Desert (Mongolia and China) 1,300,000 sq km (500,000 sq miles)

Patagonia Desert (South America) 673,000 sq km (260,000 sq miles)

Chihuahuan Desert (Mexico) 450,000 sq km (175,000 sq miles)

How to: **get on a camel**

01. Make sure the camel is sitting down and approach it from the left.

02. Put your left foot in the stirrup, and throw your right leg over the saddle.

03. Sit firmly and stay calm – the camel will know if you are nervous.

04. Hold the reins and lean back as the camel lurches to its feet.

05. Keep a tight hold of the reins and prepare for a bumpy ride!

The growing desert

- **The Sahara is advancing south at an estimated rate of 5 to 10 km (3 to 6 miles) a year, through a process known as desertification.**
- Causes of desertification include over-grazing, poor soil management, and global climate change.
- **Desertification swallows up farmland, threatening millions with starvation.**
- One plan is to grow a 7,000 km (4,340-mile) wall of acacia trees to hold back the desert.

Desert nomads

- **The Tuareg are a nomadic people who controlled trade routes across the Sahara for more than 2,000 years.**
- They moved their herds from place to place in the desert, living in temporary tented settlements.
- **Tuareg men wear veils to protect their faces from dust and sand.**
- Many Tuareg have now abandoned the nomadic way of life to settle as farmers in towns and villages.

Five camel facts

01: Camels were introduced to the Sahara from Asia about 2,000 years ago.

02: They can last up to seven days without food or water by storing fat in their humps.

03: Their large, flat, round feet keep them from sinking into soft sand.

04: A large camel can drink 80 litres (21 gallons) of water in ten minutes.

05: Camels can carry up 450 kg (990 lb) in weight.

I don't believe it!

The Tree of Ténéré, once a well-known landmark in the Sahara, was an acacia tree that grew entirely on its own in a corner of northwest Niger. In 1973, a truck driver demolished the solitary tree. It has now been replaced by a metal sculpture.

WHAT'S IN A NAME?

The collective name for the countries of northwest Africa (Morocco, Tunisia, Algeria, Mauritania, and Libya) is the **Maghreb**, which comes from an Arabic word, *al-maghrib*, meaning "the land where the Sun sets".

Great Basin Desert (USA) 492,000 sq km (190,000 sq miles)

Great Sandy Desert (Australia): 450,000 sq km (175,000 sq miles)

Great Victoria Desert (Australia) 338,500 sq km (150,000 sq miles)

Kalahari Desert (Southern Africa) 260,000 sq km (100,000 sq miles)

Syrian Desert (Middle East) 260,000 sq km (100,000 sq miles)

Where can you **find ostrich farms?**

Ostriches have been farmed for 150 years in the Karoo region of South Africa. Native to Africa, ostriches are bred for their skins, feathers, and meat, which is high in protein and low in fat.

FAST FACTS

Southern Africa

Population: 121 million

Highest mountain: Mount Ntlenyana (Lesotho) 3,482 m (11,424 ft)

Deserts: Namib Desert; Kalahari Desert

Longest river: Zambezi 3,540 km (2,200 miles)

Most populated city: Johannesburg (South Africa) 3.3 million

In numbers

4 The number of official languages in Botswana

5 The number of World Heritage sites in Zimbabwe

108 m (360 ft) The height of the Victoria Falls

80,900 sq km (31,200 sq miles) The area of the Namib Desert in Namibia

1,337,186 The population of Swaziland, the smallest country in southern Africa

470,000,000 The population of South Africa

WHAT'S IN A NAME?

Scottish explorer David Livingstone named the **Victoria Falls**, on the Zambezi River, after Queen Victoria, the reigning British monarch, in 1855. The local name is *Mosi-oa-Tunya* ("the smoke that thunders").

Tell me more: **countries of Southern Africa**

Southern Africa is made up of nine countries. Much of the landscape is dry grassland (savannah).

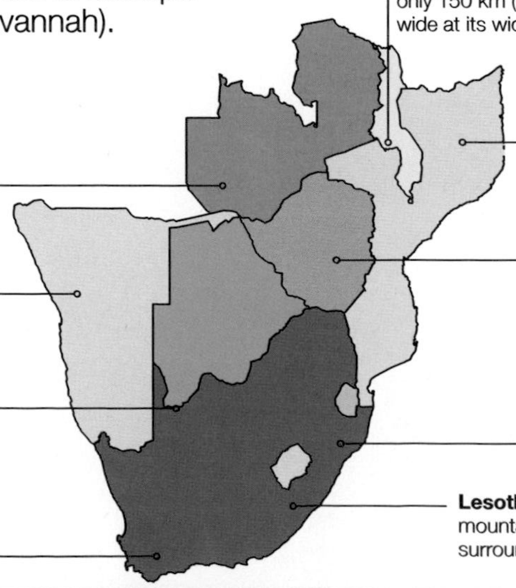
Malawi: A densely populated country that is only 150 km (93 miles) wide at its widest part
Zambia: Contains the largest copper reserves in the world
Mozambique: Has suffered years of civil war, floods, and drought
Namibia: The last African colony to win independence, in 1990
Zimbabwe: One of the world's poorest countries with high unemployment
Botswana: Nearly 17 per cent of the country is a protected wildlife area
Swaziland: A tiny kingdom that sits on a series of plateaus
South Africa: Has vast mineral resources such as diamonds, gold, and coal
Lesotho: A small mountainous country, surrounded by South Africa

If a South African policeman asks you to stop at the next **"robot"**, don't go looking for a remote-controlled humanoid. He simply wants you to pull up at the next set of **traffic lights**.

Five ways to spend time in **southern Africa**

01: Enjoy the unique wildlife in Botswana's Okavango Delta.

02: See the elephants in Etosha National Park, Namibia.

03: Abseil down the gorges of the Victoria Falls.

04: Swim with manta rays off the coast of Mozambique.

05: Watch migrating whales off the southern tip of Africa.

The Cradle of Humankind

The Cradle of Humankind site in Gauteng, South Africa, is a complex of limestone caves that contains the richest collection of hominin (human ancestor) fossils anywhere in the world.

Soccer City

The Soccer City stadium in Johannesburg, South Africa, holds 94,700 spectators. Its design was inspired by the **calabash** – a traditional round African cooking pot.

African anthem

01 The South African national anthem has lines in five languages: Xhosa, Zulu, Afrikaans, Sesotho, and English.

02 The opening verse *Nkosi Sikelel' iAfrika* (God Bless Africa) was the anthem of the African freedom movement, who campaigned for equal rights for black people.

03 It was written by schoolteacher Enoch Sontonga for his school choir in 1897.

Peoples of southern Africa

The four major ethnic groups of southern Africa are the **Ndebele, Zulu**, **Shona**, and **Xhosa.**

Ndebele women traditionally adorned themselves with copper and brass rings around their arms, legs, and neck. They also wore elaborate beaded headdresses and neck hoops.

Once scattered throughout southern Africa, the **San** people are traditional hunter-gatherers. Today they live mostly in the Kalahari Desert of Botswana.

Apartheid

From 1948–1994, the white South African vernment enforced a system known as apartheid. Black eople were not allowed to **vote**, were forced to carry dentity cards, and had to live in separate "homelands".

I don't believe it!

Vilakazi Street is the most famous street in Soweto, South Africa. It was once home to two Nobel Peace prize winners – Nelson Mandela and Archbishop Desmond Tutu (below), who both won the prize for their opposition to apartheid.

Flagging it up

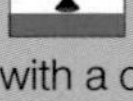

The flag of **Lesotho** features a black, conical straw hat with a complicated topknot, which is the traditional headwear of the local Basotho people.

The flag of **Mozambique** has a crossed rifle and hoe on top of an open book to symbolize the struggle for freedom, agriculture, and education.

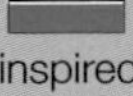

The black and white stripes on the **Botswana** flag are inspired by the zebra, the national animal. The blue colour is for water.

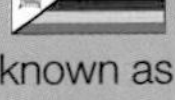

The flag of **Zimbabwe** features a stone bird, known as the bird of Zimbabwe.

The flag of **South Africa** has six colours: black, green, and red (the colours of the African freedom movement), and blue, yellow, and white.

Where is **hot water** always on tap?

In Iceland, underground geothermic (naturally hot) water is piped directly into most homes. The country lies on the Mid-Atlantic Ridge, a fault in the Earth's crust that is constantly bubbling up hot magma and lava. The underground heat produced by volcanoes is used to produce most of Iceland's electricity.

FAST FACTS

Iceland

01: The first settlers were Vikings, who arrived from Norway in the 9th century.

02: Iceland is in the North Atlantic and is the most westerly country in Europe.

03: It lies close to the Arctic Circle but has a mild climate thanks to the warm waters of the Gulf Stream.

04: The country's nearest neighbour is Greenland, 287 km (178 miles) away.

05: Most Icelandic people live in coastal areas. The uninhabited centre consists mainly of rocky mountains and plateaus.

In 985, Erik the Red left Iceland to start a colony in Greenland. In 1002, his son **Leif Erikson** (below) landed in North America at a place he called Vinland – some 500 years before Christopher Columbus got there.

Five facts about geysers

01 Geysers are small vents that spout fountains of boiling hot water into the sky.

02 Iceland has around 200 geysers.

03 **Strokkur**, Iceland's most famous geyser, spouts water every five minutes.

04 There are about 1,000 active geysers in the world.

05 More than half of them are in the Yellowstone National Park, USA.

Tell me more: **land of fire and ice**

- Glaciers in Iceland cover more than 11 per cent of the total land area.
- **The largest glacier, Vatnajökull, covers an area of 8,100 sq km (3,127 sq miles).**
- There are more than 100 volcanoes in Iceland, at least 30 of which are active.
- **On average, a volcano erupts every five years on Iceland.**
- Iceland's most famous volcano, Mount Hekla, has erupted 18 times in the past 1,000 years.

Tell me more: **the Blue Lagoon**

- People bathe all year round in the Blue Lagoon, even when it's snowing.
- **The temperature of the water is about 38°C (100°F).**
- The mix of salt, minerals, and algae in the water give it a rich blue colour.
- **The white mud that lines the lagoon is said to be good for certain skin conditions, such as eczema.**
- The geothermal water comes from boreholes deep underground. Used to generate electricity in a nearby power plant, the water is then cooled before it enters the lagoon.

WHAT'S IN A NAME?

In Iceland, your first name is followed by your **father's name**. If you are a girl called Gudrun and your father's name is Magnus, your full name is **Gudrun Magnusdottir** (Gudrun, daughter of Magnus). Your brother Olaf would be **Olaf Magnusson** (Olaf, son of Magnus).

In numbers

2
The number of hours of sunlight a day in December

90
The percentage of homes in Iceland with geothermal heating

1,339 km
(832 miles) The length of Route 1, Iceland's ring road

80,000
The estimated number of ponies in Iceland

306,000
The population of Iceland

Five things you may not know about Iceland

- The national sport is **glima**, a form of Viking wrestling that has been around since the 12th century.
- The Icelandic language is descended from the language of the **sagas** – stories that told the family histories of the first Icelandic settlers.
- More books and magazines are published per head of the population of Iceland than in any other country in the world.
- Icelandic phone directories list people by their first names.
- Founded in 930, Iceland's parliament, the **Althing** (below), is the oldest parliament in the world.

At midwinter feasts, Icelanders tuck into **thorramatur** – snacks of smoked and salted lamb, singed sheep's head, blood sausage, pickled salmon, and rotten shark.

I don't believe it!

Iceland has thirteen Santa Clauses – troll brothers who make mischief on the 13 nights before Christmas. They leave presents for children who have been good all year, and potatoes for those who have misbehaved!

An island is born

In 1963, a violent eruption off the coast of Iceland was the first sign that a new volcanic island was emerging from the sea. Given the name of **Surtsey** after Surtur, the Norse god of fire, it now stands 150 m (492 ft) high.

Five Icelandic animals

Arctic fox
The only mammal native to Iceland.

Icelandic pony
The Vikings brought these sturdy animals to Iceland.

Icelandic sheepdog
A Viking introduction and still used for herding sheep.

White-tailed sea eagle
Iceland's largest bird of prey.

Puffin
Millions of puffins breed on Iceland.

Which is the **largest** country in the world?

Russia is so large that you could fit Canada (the second-largest country) into it twice. Siberia – the part of Russia that is in Asia, stretching from the Ural Mountains to the Pacific Ocean – accounts for more than 75 per cent of the country's total land area.

FAST FACTS: Siberia

01: Siberia consists of tundra (treeless plain with permanently frozen undersoil), taiga (swampy coniferous forest), and steppes (grasslands).

02: Lake Baikal in Siberia is the deepest lake in the world.

03: Siberia is rich in natural resources, especially coal, gold, iron ore, oil, and natural gas.

04: The original inhabitants of Siberia were nomadic herders. Today, they make up less than ten per cent of the population.

05: Under the Soviets, millions of Russians were deported to forced labour camps in Siberia.

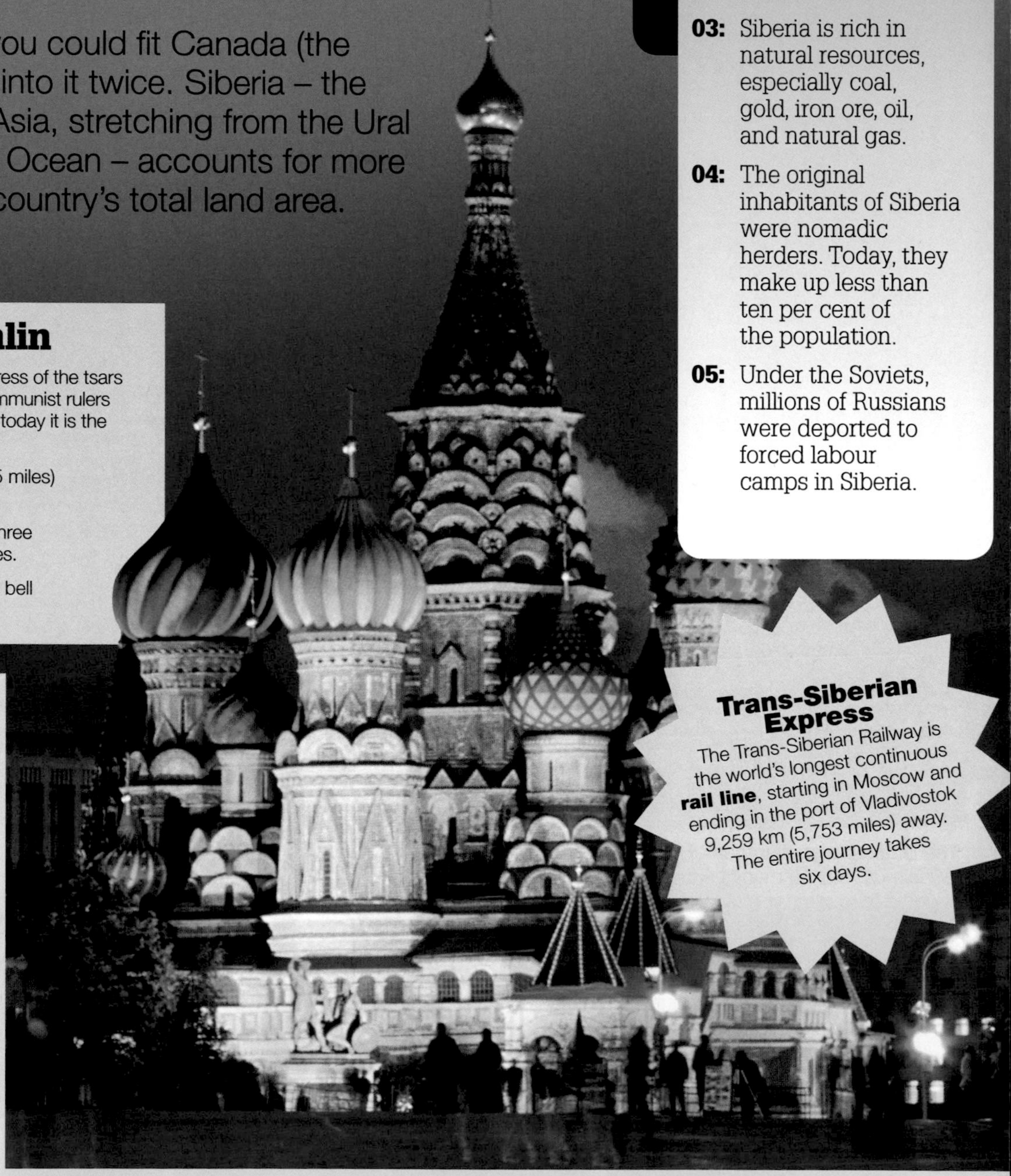

Check out the Kremlin

The Moscow Kremlin was the medieval fortress of the tsars (rulers of Russia). In 1918, Russia's new communist rulers set up their government in the Kremlin, and today it is the official residence of the president of Russia.

- The walls of the fortress are 2 km (1.25 miles) long and date from the 15th century.
- The buildings inside the walls include three cathedrals, one church, and four palaces.
- The Kremlin houses the world's largest bell and the world's largest cannon.

What was the Soviet Union?

- A federation of 15 republics ruled by the Communist Party. The Soviet Union of Socialist Republics (USSR) existed from 1921 to 1991.
- The first leader of the Soviet Union was Vladimir Ilyich Lenin (1870–1924). He was succeeded by Joseph Stalin (1897–1953), a ruthless dictator responsible for the deaths of millions of people.
- Following the collapse of communism, the 15 republics of the Soviet Union split up to form independent countries.

Trans-Siberian Express

The Trans-Siberian Railway is the world's longest continuous **rail line**, starting in Moscow and ending in the port of Vladivostok 9,259 km (5,753 miles) away. The entire journey takes six days.

Countries that were former **Soviet republics**

Armenia, Azerbaijan, Belarus, Estonia, Georgia, Kazakhstan, Kyrgyzstan, Latvia, Lithuania

Russian dishes

blini small thin pancakes
borsch beetroot soup
pelmeni minced meat wrapped in thin dough
pirozhki small buns stuffed with meat or other filling
okroshka spicy vegetable soup
shashlik meat skewers cooked over a charcoal grill
schi cabbage soup

In numbers

40
The number of national parks

49
The percentage of Russian households that own pets

160
The number of ethnic groups in Russia

322
The total number of Olympic medals won by Russians

5,642 m
(18,510 ft) The height of Mount Elbrus, Russia's highest mountain

37,000 km
(23,000 miles) The total length of Russia's coastline

9.2 million
The population of Moscow, Russia's largest city

40 million
The number of Internet users in Russia

Six famous Russians

Peter the Great
Tsar from 1682–1725, he transformed Russia into a major power and founded the city of St Petersburg.

Pyotr Ilyich Tchaikovsky
Composer of the music to the ballets *The Nutcracker*, *Swan Lake*, and *Sleeping Beauty*.

Dmitri Mendeleev
His Periodic Table of the elements was a breakthrough discovery in science.

Leo Tolstoy
Wrote many great novels, the most famous of which is *War and Peace.*

Grigorii Rasputin
The "mad monk" who claimed he could cure the last tsar's son of the blood condition haemophilia.

Vladimir Ilyich Lenin
Revolutionary leader and creator of the Soviet Union.

Credit crunch

In 2008, Russia had 74 billionaires, more than any other country in the world. By 2009, the number had fallen by nearly two-thirds, to 27.

The 25 richest people in Russia lost more than US$ 230 billion between them in less than six months.

Known as "oligarchs", many Russian billionaires had made their fortunes by taking over state-owned energy and mining industries in the 1990s.

In 2009, 17 per cent of Russians (24 million people) were living below the poverty line.

WHAT'S IN A NAME?

Russia gets its name from Norse (Scandinavian) adventurers who traded along Russian rivers and were known as the **Rus**. A Rus ruler, **Rurik**, founded a state at Kiev in 862 and his descendants became the first tsars of Russia.

The **State Hermitage Museum** in St Petersburg contains 2.7 million items. It would take 11 years to view every exhibit on display, assuming you spent one minute in front of each one.

Tea note

Russians like their tea very strong and black. They often swallow a spoonful of jam between sips to help the powerful brew go down.

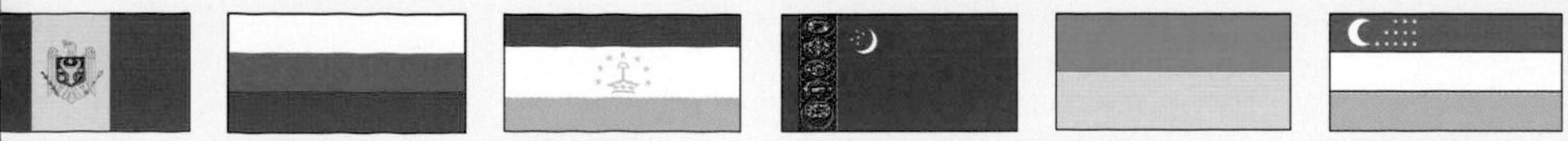

Moldova | Russian Federation | Tajikistan | Turkmenistan | Ukraine | Uzbekistan

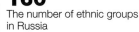

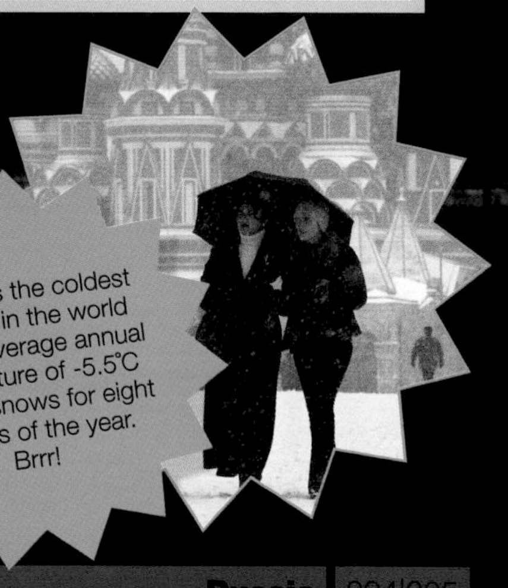

Russia is the coldest country in the world with an average annual temperature of -5.5°C (22°F). It snows for eight months of the year. Brrr!

What is the **smallest** country in the world?

Although it is part of the city of Rome, the Vatican City is an independent country with its own head of state, the Pope, the leader of the Roman Catholic Church. Most people who live in the Vatican City work for the Holy See, the body that governs the Roman Catholic Church.

Easter blessing
Each year, tens of thousands of people crowd into St Peter's Square on **Easter Sunday** to hear the Pope delive his Easter message. On average, 11,000 people visit the Vatican City every day!

Tell me more: **The Vatican City**

- The Vatican City State was founded on 11 February 1929.
- **It has its own radio and television stations, and a weekly newspaper.**
- It issues its own passports, stamps, and coins.
- **The Vatican Gardens occupy more than half of the city's land area.**
- The Pope lives in the Papal Palace, next to St Peter's Square.
- **A painted white line on the pavement shows where Rome ends and the Vatican City begins.**

Five facts about St Peter's Basilica

- This enormous church took 122 years to build (1504–1626).
- It can hold up to 60,000 worshippers at a time.
- The length of the nave is 218 m (715 ft).
- Its magnificent dome has a height of 138 m (452 ft) and a diameter of 42 m (137 ft).
- There are 491 steps to the top of the dome (there is also a lift!).

Three tourist attractions

The Sistine Chapel
The ceiling, painted by Michelangelo, took four years to complete.

The Vatican Museum
This vast building contains more than 14.5 km (9 miles) of galleries.

The Raphael Rooms
The private apartments of Pope Julius II were painted by Raphael.

St Peter's Square

- Although it is called a square, it is actually an oval.
- Renaissance architect Gian Lorenzo Bernini designed the colonnades (lines of columns).
- The square contains 140 statues of saints.
- The Egyptian obelisk in the centre of square was brought to Rome in 37 CE.

In 2007, the Vatican City became the first **carbon-neutral state** in the world. It planted a forest on land it owns in Hungary to offset its carbon usage.

I don't believe it!

The ATM (cashpoint) in the Vatican Bank has instructions in Latin (among other languages). Latin is the universal language of the Roman Catholic Church.

Monaco is the most crowded country in the world, where 33,000 people live in an area of 1.95 sq km (0.75 sq miles). Compared with that, the 826 residents of the Vatican City have plenty of elbow room!

Swiss Guard
The Pope's private bodyguard, known as the Swiss Guard, was founded in 1505 during the reign of Pope Julius II. Recruits must be male, Swiss, Roman Catholic, unmarried, and at least 1.74 m (5 ft 7 in) tall.

Top ten smallest countries

01: Vatican City
0.44 sq km (0.17 sq miles)

02: Monaco
1.9 sq km (0.75 sq miles)

03: Nauru
21 sq km (8 sq miles)

04: Tuvalu
26 sq km (10 sq miles)

05: San Marino
61 sq km (24 sq miles)

06: Liechtenstein
160 sq km (62 sq miles)

07: Marshall Islands
180 sq km (70 sq miles)

08: St Kitts and Nevis
269 sq km (101 sq miles)

09: Maldives
300 sq km (120 sq miles)

10: Seychelles
434 sq km (107 sq miles)

How to: **elect a new pope**

01. Immediately after the death of a pope, the 120 most senior cardinals in the Catholic Church come to the Vatican to elect a successor.

02. If no candidate receives a two-thirds majority, the ballot papers are burned in a special stove (above) with a handful of straw.

03. The straw creates black smoke, which means that voting continues. When at last a pope is elected, a chemical is burned to give white smoke.

04. The new pope is led on to the balcony overlooking St Peter's Square. The senior cardinal announces "*Habemus Papam*" ("We have a pope").

Can you really **ski in Dubai?**

In the tiny state of Dubai on the Arabian Peninsula, there is a massive indoor ski resort, where visitors can ski on real snow even when the temperature is 40ºC (104ºF) outside. Dubai is one of the United Arab Emirates – a federation of seven states, each ruled by its own independent emir, or prince.

RECORD BREAKER

Qatar sits on the single largest reservoir of **natural gas** in the world. The gas field is half the size of the entire country.

FAST FACTS

Gulf States

01: Countries: Bahrain, Kuwait, Oman, Qatar, Saudi Arabia, United Arab Emirates

02: Largest country: Saudi Arabia 2,331,000 sq km (899,766 sq miles)

03: Smallest country: Bahrain 678 sq km (262 sq miles)

04: Biggest city: Riyadh (Saudi Arabia) – population 5.1 million

05: Language: Arabic

Every year, two million people visit the holy city of **Mecca** in Saudi Arabia to make the Muslim pilgrimage known as the **hajj**.

United Arab Emirates

- The United Arab Emirates (UAE) was created in 1971.
- It is a federation of seven small emirates (kingdoms): Abu Dhabi, Dubai, Sharjah, Ajman, Umm al-Qaiwain, Ras al-Khaimah, and Fujairah.
- Abu Dhabi, the capital of the UAE has a population of 930,000.
- Locals account for only 18 per cent of the population. The largest group are temporary migrant workers from south Asia.

The Arabian Peninsula is home to the camel-herding **Bedu** (Bedouin). About 500,000 Bedu still follow the traditional nomadic way of life.

Tell me more: Saudi Arabia

- It is the birthplace of Islam and contains the holy cities of Mecca and Medina.
- **The king's official title is the "Custodian of the Two Holy Mosques".**
- Saudi Arabia is an absolute monarchy – a state that is ruled by a hereditary leader.
- **It owns 25 per cent of the world's total oil reserves.**
- It is the only country in the world where women are banned from driving on public roads.
- **More than 95 per cent of the land is desert.**

RECORD BREAKER

The **Burj Khalifa**, in Dubai, is the world's tallest tower. Opened in 2010, the 828-m- (2,717-ft-) high skyscraper was named after the president of the UAE.

Empty Quarter

- The Empty Quarter (Rub 'al Khali) at the south end of the Arabian Peninsula is the largest sand desert in the world at about 650,000 sq km (250,000 sq miles).
- Summer temperatures can reach 55°C (131°F) during the day and fall below freezing at night.
- The desert is entirely uninhabited, and much of it has never been explored.

Holy smoke!

- **Frankincense is the aromatic resin of a desert shrub that grows only in the desert of southern Oman.**
- Arab traders carried it across the desert along the Incense Trail – a journey of 3,200 km (2,000 miles).
- **It was used in religious ceremonies – and to mask unpleasant smells.**
- According to the Bible, frankincense was one of the gifts the three wise men brought to the baby Jesus.

Tell me more: **Arab dress**

Igal: Double black cord that holds the *gutra* in place
Gutra: Head covering that is usually white in summer, and red and white checked in winter
Bisht: Outer cloak of soft wool, usually black, brown, or grey
Dishdasha: Long-sleeved (usually white) garment that covers the whole body

Desert Storm

In August 1990, Iraqi forces invaded the tiny oil-rich state of Kuwait. In February 1991, the Iraqi leader, Saddam Hussein, was forced to withdraw his troops when a US-led force of 34 nations launched the military offensive called Operation Desert Storm.

Whacky buildings

As Dubai became one of the world's most luxurious holiday resorts in the mid 2000s, its buildings got taller and more extraordinary.

- The spire of Burj Khalifa tower can be seen from 95 km (60 miles) away.
- Developments include man-made islands built to look like a palm tree and a world map when seen from the air.
- At one time, 25 per cent of all the world's cranes were said to be working in Dubai.
- The world's economic crisis called a halt to the Dubai building boom in 2009, leaving manyprojects unfinished.

Traditional Arab sports

Camel racing

Horse racing

Falconry

Dhow (sailboat) racing

The island state of **Bahrain** is made up of one large island and 32 smaller ones. The **King Fahd Causeway**, which is 28 km (17 miles) long, links it to Saudi Arabia.

How many people live in India?

India is the second most populated country in the world after China, with a population of 1.7 billion. Although India is just over one-third the size of the USA, more than five times as many people live there.

Land of contrasts

Mountains
To the north of the country lie the snow-capped peaks of the Himalayas, the highest mountain range on Earth.

Plains
The plains that stretch across northern India consist of fertile farmland, where rice, wheat, and other crops are cultivated.

Desert
To the west lies the vast Thar Desert, where temperatures can reach 50°C (122°F). People living here rely on camels for food and transport.

Forest
India's hills are covered in lush forests, where valuable timber and orchids grow. Forests of tropical palms cover lowland areas in the west.

Beaches
With 7,000 km (4,350 miles) of coastline, India has many beautiful beaches and has become a popular tourist destination.

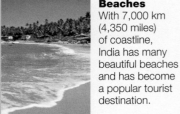

Top five big cities

01 Mumbai
With a population of almost 14 million, Mumbai is the largest city in India.

02 New Delhi
The capital of the country and the seat of Indian government.

03 Bangalore
The country's fastest-growing city and centre of research and new industry, especially Information Technology.

04 Kolkata
Once the capital of India, Kolkata is a bustling city in the east of the country.

05 Chennai
The biggest city in the south of India, Chennai began as an important trading post and port.

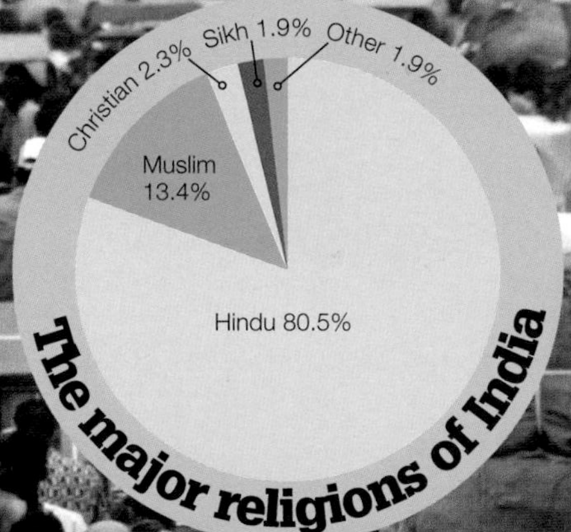

India has **18 official languages**. The most widely spoken is Hindi, the first language of 41 per cent of people. English is not an official language, but is the most important one for Indian business and government.

India's longest rivers

- **Indus**
  3,000 km (2,000 miles)
- **Brahmaputra**
  2,900 km (1,800 miles)
- **Ganges**
  2,510 km (1,560 miles)

Five facts about India

- India is the world's largest democracy. In the 2009 elections, 714,000,000 people were eligible to vote.
- **More than two-thirds of the population live in rural areas, in farming communities.**
- Indian Railways is the largest employer in the world with an estimated 1.6 million employees. Each day, it transports more than 13 million passengers, and 1.3 million tonnes of freight.
- **India has the most extensive postal system in the world, with 155,333 post offices.**
- The Indians are frequent cinema-goers. In 2003, 2,860,000,000 people went to the cinema in India, compared with 1,421,000,000 in the USA.

How to: **make a cup of tea**

01. Visit a tea plantation to pick some fresh leaves. You only want the top two leaves and bud from each branch.

02. Lay the leaves out to lose a little moisture, then crush them and leave for about two hours to develop the flavour. Next, heat the leaves to dry them out.

03. Check the quality and flavour of the leaves – you can blend different types to get the right taste.

04. Put several spoonfuls of tea leaves in a warmed pot, and add boiling water. Leave for a few minutes, then pour into a cup. Add milk and sugar to taste and enjoy!

India and China are the largest producers of tea in the world, but Indians drink the most tea.

Amazing architecture

Temples
India has beautiful and important buildings from all the major religions. The Hindu **Brihadishvara Temple** is in Tamil Nadu in southern India.

Forts
Warring rulers built defensive forts throughout India to protect their kingdoms. **Mehrangarh Fort**, in Rajasthan, rises out of a rocky outcrop.

Palaces
During the 20th century, many Indian princes built magnificent and luxurious palaces, such as the **City Palace** in Udaipur.

Tombs
The **Taj Mahal** is in fact a tomb, built by emperor Shah Jahan in the 17th century in memory of his wife. The two of them lie buried here, side by side.

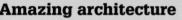

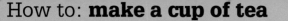

The national sport of India is hockey, but the most popular sport is **cricket**. Indians are crazy about cricket and will play it anywhere they can swing a bat.

Four **Hindu festivals**

Holi
A festival marking the end of winter. On the second day, people throw coloured powder and water over each other.

Janmashtami
The birth of the Hindu god Lord Krishna is marked by fasting until midnight, then feasting. Children often dress up as Krishna.

Diwali
Hindus light oil lamps to mark the triumph of good over evil, and remember the return of the god Rama from exile.

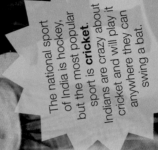

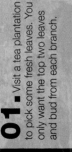

Dussehra
People celebrate the defeat of the demon-king, Ravana, by the god Rama by burning effigies of Ravana, his brother, and his son.

River Ganges

The River Ganges is a holy river, sacred to the Hindu religion. As it flows east, from the mountains of the Himalayas to the Bay of Bengal, cities, farms, and temples line its banks.

01: The source of the River Ganges is the **Gangotri Glacier** at Gaumukh, 3,892 m (12,770 ft) high in the Himalayas. At its source, the river is called the Bhagirathi. It becomes the Ganges when it joins the Alaknandra River.

02: As the river's torrents rush down the mountains, they cut through rocky gorges. The Ganges leaves the Himalayas at the holy city of Rishikesh, where **white-water rafting** through the rapids is a popular sport.

03: At the city of **Haridwar**, the river meets the plains. Haridwar is an important place of Hindu pilgrimage. Many pilgrims take jars of water from the Ganges away with them to use in religious rituals at home.

05: The holiest place on this sacred river is the city of **Varanasi**, said to have been founded by the Hindu god Shiva. There pilgrims flock down flights of steps, known as *ghats,* to be purified by the holy water.

06: As the river flows across the plains of **central India**, it deposits fertile mud, making the land rich for farming. Rice and wheat are the most important crops, but maize, sugarcane, and cotton are also grown here.

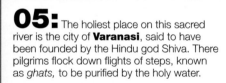

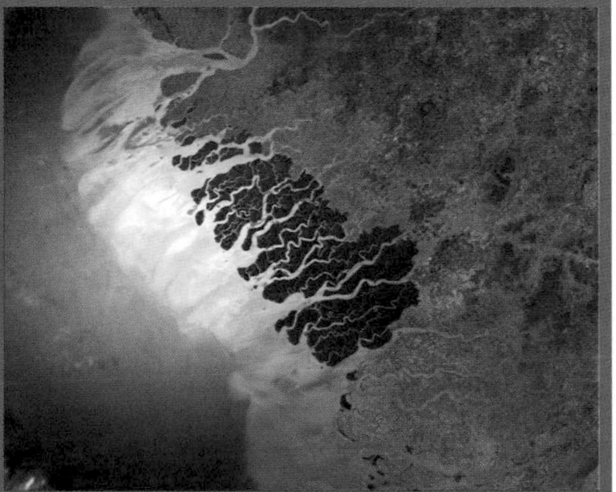

04: In 2001, an important Hindu festival, the **Maha Kumbh Mela**, took place in the city of Allahabad. More than 70 million pilgrims took part in the festival, which is held only once every 144 years.

07: At the edge of the delta is a vast area of mangrove forest, called the **Sunderbans** (in green above) which stretches from the state of West Bengal, in India, to Bangladesh. The area is a protected national park and is rich in wildlife.

08: The Ganges meets the Indian Ocean at the **Bay of Bengal**, where it forms the largest delta in the world, some 350 km (220 miles) across. This is one of the most fertile farming areas in the world.

Where is the rice bowl of Asia?

Thailand is the largest exporter of rice in the world. Rice farming probably originated in Thailand's fertile river valleys about 6,000 years ago. Today, more than 3,000 different varieties are grown in flooded rice fields called paddies.

Ten facts about Thailand

01: The emblem of Thailand is the garuda, a mythical birdlike creature (above).

02: Until 1939, the country was known as Siam.

03: It has a population of 65 million.

04: It is the only country in Southeast Asia never to have been colonized.

05: Most people in Thailand are Buddhists.

06: Up to 14 million tourists visit Thailand each year.

07: Thai boxing is the national sport.

08: The currency is the baht.

09: Thais consider it rude to touch someone's head.

10: Thailand is shaped like an elephant's head with a long trunk.

I don't believe it!

Thailand's ninth king, Bhumibol Adulyadej, succeeded his brother to the throne in 1946 at the age of 19. He is currently the world's longest-serving head of state.

FAST FACTS

Bangkok

01: It was founded as the royal capital in 1782.

02: It lies on the Chao Phraya River.

03: It has a population of 6 million.

04: Bangkok is the world's third most visited city, after Paris and London.

05: Its sprawling business districts contain more than 800 skyscrapers.

06: One unusual high-rise building is the Elephant Tower (above) built in the shape of

Floating markets

Thailand's floating markets draw thousands of tourists every year. **Boats** are piled high with tropical fruit, vegetables, and local dishes prepared on floating kitchens.

How to: grow rice

01. Sow the seeds in a flooded field. When the stalks are about 15 cm (6 in) tall, replant them in bundles (to deter weeds).

Thais traditionally celebrate **Songkran**, the spring New Year festival, by cleaning their houses from top to bottom, putting on new clothes, and having water fights in the street.

Five popular **Thai dishes**

- **Tom yam kung** (hot and sour shrimp soup)
- **Kaeng khiao wan kai** (green chicken curry)
- **Pad thai** (fried noodles)
- **Phat kraphao** (meat fried with sweet basil)
- **Kaeng phet ped yang** (roast duck in red curry)

02. Drain the field before harvesting. Cut the stems and tie into sheaves for threshing (separating the grains from the plant).

03. Hold the rice sheaf above your head, then strike it against a hard surface until all the grains fall out.

04. Put the grains in a milling machine to remove the outer brown husk, leaving smooth white grains of rice.

In numbers

102
The number of national parks in Thailand

106
The number of Thai airports

304 m
(997 ft) The height of Baiyoke II Tower, Thailand's tallest building

3,219 km
(2,000 miles) The total length of Thailand's coastline

513,120 sq km
(198,116 sq miles) The area of Thailand

Asian tsunami

The Indian Ocean tsunami that struck Thailand on the morning of 26 December 2004 was the worst natural disaster in the country's history. More than 5,400 people were killed and tens of thousands were left homeless.

Tell me more: **elephants**

- Elephants have special importance for the people of Thailand.
- **13 March is celebrated as National Elephant Day.**
- It is considered lucky to walk three times under an elephant.
- **Rare white elephants are a symbol of royal power.**
- Elephants used to be taken from the wild to work in the logging industry until Thailand banned commercial logging in 1989.
- **Thailand has about 3,000 domesticated elephants.**
- There are now only about 1,500 elephants left in the wild in Thailand.

Five things to see in **Thailand**

Wat Benchamabophit
Also known as the Marble Temple, Wat Benchamabophit in Bangkok was built as a royal monastery in 1900.

Elephants
Thailand is home to many elephant camps where tourists can learn to ride an elephant or trek through the jungle.

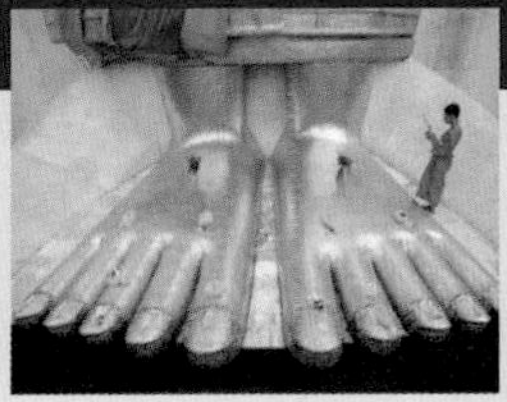

Giant Buddha
The giant standing Buddha at Wat Intharawihan in Bangkok stands 32 m (109 ft) high and took 60 years to complete.

Grand Palace
Built in 1782, the Grand Palace in Bangkok was the official residence of the kings of Siam for 150 years.

Khao Yai National Park
Thailand's oldest national park is home to more than 150 different species of animals, including tigers and macaques.

How many people **live in Tokyo?**

More than 35 million people live in the Greater Tokyo Area, making it the largest capital city in the world. Greater Tokyo includes the old city of Tokyo and four other cities around Tokyo Bay.

The Japanese have the **highest life expectancy** in the world. More than 40,000 people are more than 100 years old, a number that is expected to rise to 1 million by 2050.

Island nation

- Japan is made up of four main islands and more than 3,000 smaller islands.
- The four largest islands are **Hokkaido, Honshu, Shikoku** and **Kyushu**, which make up 97 per cent of the total land area.
- The islands of Japan extend 2,400 km (1,500 miles) from north to south.
- More than four-fifths of Japan is mountainous. Most of the population live in the crowded areas along the coast.

In numbers

28
The number of national parks in Japan

36
The number of professional football teams in Japan

47
The number of prefectures (administrative areas)

123
The number of gold medals won by Japanese athletes in the Olympic Games

8.5 million
The number of foreign tourists to Japan each year

WHAT'S IN A NAME?

Tsunami is a Japanese word that literally means "harbour wave".

FAST FACTS

Earthquakes

01: Japan lies in an earthquake zone on the junction of four of Earth's tectonic plates.

02: Up to 1,500 earthquakes are recorded in Japan each year.

03: One in five of all major earthquakes occurs in Japan.

04: More than 100,000 people died in the Tokyo earthquake of 1923, the worst in Japan's history.

05: The Japanese use the "shindo" scale to measure the intensity of their earthquakes.

06: Tsunamis (huge sea waves caused by underwater earthquakes) frequently strike the Japanese coast.

Tell me more: Tokyo

- Tokyo is on Honshu, the largest of Japan's four main islands.
- **It was called Edo until 1868, when it became the imperial capital.**
- It is a major world financial centre, together with London and New York.
- **Up to 4 million commuters per day pass through Tokyo's Shinjuku Station.**
- Tokyo's official emblem is a green gingko leaf – a symbol of prosperity and tranquillity.

Four largest islands

Hokkaido
A rural, forested island, with long, cold winters. This northerly island is covered in snow for four months of the year.

Honshu
Has hot, humid summers and cold, snowy winters. Its many volcanoes include Mount Fuji, Japan's highest mountain.

Five Japanese **martial arts**

Aikido
Opponents try to defend themselves while protecting their attacker from injury.

Ju-jitsu
Contestants try to disable their opponents by putting them off-balance.

Karate
Combatants attack their opponents with strikes from the legs, hands, elbows, and head.

Kendo
Opponents deliver blows to targeted areas using bamboo sticks as swords.

Sumo wrestling
Contestants try to throw their opponents to the ground, or push them out of the ring.

How to: **wear a kimono**

The kimono, a floor-length robe with square-cut sleeves, is the traditional dress of Japanese men and women.

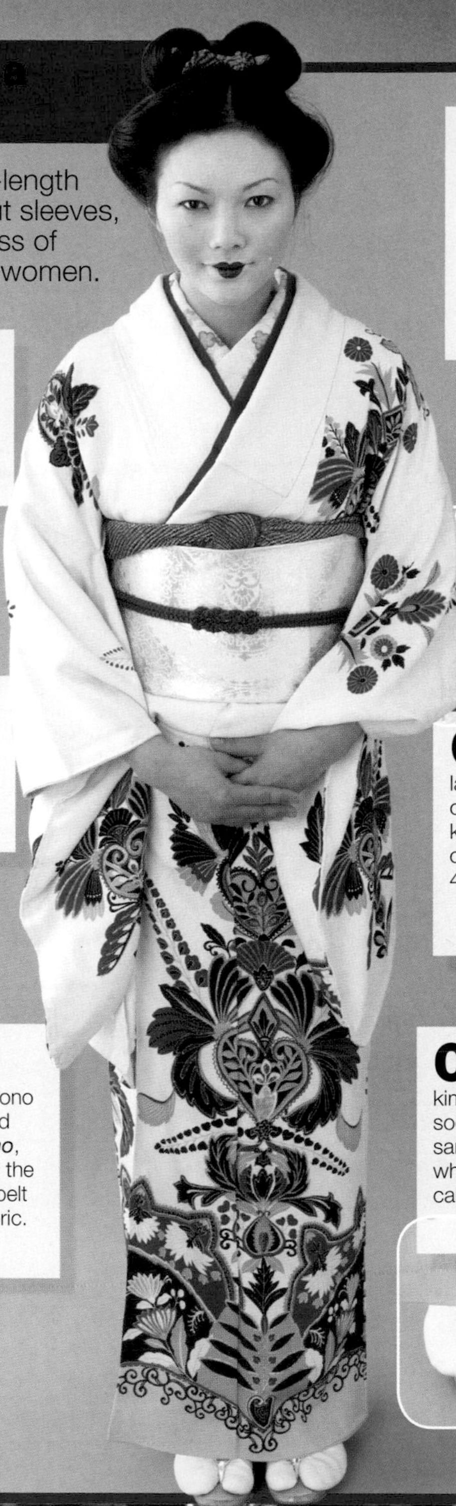

01. Put on the kimono, making sure the seam runs down the centre of your back.

02. Wrap the right side of the kimono over your body, then drape the left side across it.

03. Pull up the material so that the kimono ends at your ankles, and tie a belt, the *koshi-himo*, around your waist. Fold the extra material over the belt and smooth out the fabric.

04. Place a second belt, the *date-jime*, over the *koshi-himo* belt and tie at the back. Bring the ends to the front and tie again.

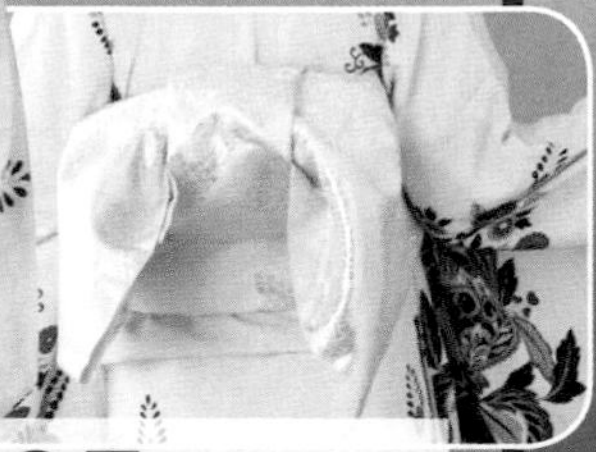

05. Tie the last belt, the obi, in a complicated butterfly knot at the back. The obi is usually about 4 m (13 ft) long.

06. Wear your kimono with white socks and wooden sandals over a simple white undergarment, called a *juban*.

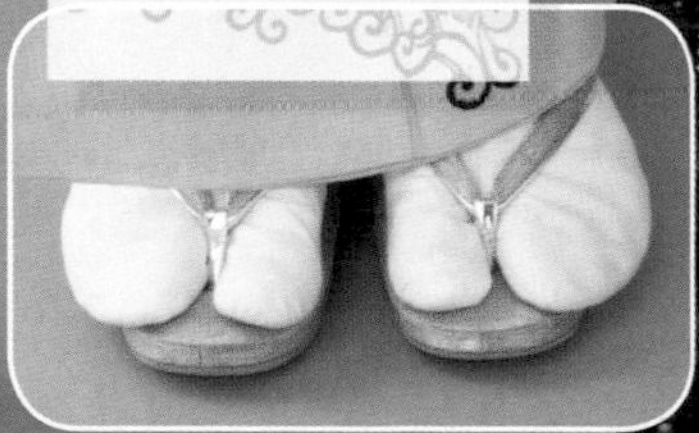

Shikoku
The smallest of Japan's main islands. Shikoku's largest city, Matsuyama, is famous for its 400-year-old castle.

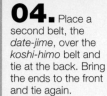

Kyushu
The island is noted for its natural hot springs, the most famous of which are at Beppu on the east coast.

Fishy stories

- One-third of all tuna caught in the world is eaten in Japan.
- Seafood is often served raw, either plain (*sashimi*) or rolled with rice (*sushi*).
- Many Japanese consider whale meat a delicacy.
- It takes Japanese chefs up to ten years of training to learn how to remove the lethal parts from *fugu*, a Japanese dish made from pufferfish meat. Mistakes can prove fatal!
- The Tsukiji fish market in Tokyo is the largest fish market in the world.

What is the **Outback?**

Australia has dazzling beaches, lush vineyards, and steamy swamps, but three-quarters of the country is desert or semi-desert. These hot, dry areas are known as the Outback, and people, plants, and animals have to be tough to survive there.

Helicopter herders

The Outback is home to some of the largest **cattle ranches** in the world. Several ranches cover such vast areas that ranchers have to use helicopters to move their herds about.

FAST FACTS

Aborigines

01: The Aboriginal people have lived in Australia for more than 40,000 years.

02: They believe the world was created by supernatural ancestors in a time before humans existed, called the Dreamtime.

03: It is estimated that 90 per cent of the Aboriginal population was wiped out by diseases, such as smallpox, after the British arrived in Australia in 1788.

04: In 2006, the estimated Aboriginal population was 517,200, about 2.5 per cent of the total population of Australia.

In numbers

3
The number of time zones across the country

6
Australia is the world's sixth-largest country, just a bit smaller than the USA

86 per cent
The percentage of the population that lives in coastal areas

4,000 km
(2,500 miles) The width of the country from east to west

25,760 km
(16,000 miles) The length of the Australian coastline

21 million
The population of Australia

How to: **make a digeridoo**

01. Take time to find the right piece of wood, such as eucalyptus. You need a tree that has been hollowed out by termites.

02. Cut the wood to the right length and strip off the bark. Smoot down the outside, then paint your instrument.

Outback animals

All these creatures have special techniques for dealing with desert life.

Thorny devil
The ridges over this lizard's back allow it to collect water on its body and then pour it into its mouth.

Emu
This is the second-largest bird in the world. It keeps cool by panting, which helps to take heat from its body.

Dingo
This desert dog preserves its energy by hunting at dawn or dusk, and sleeping in the hottest parts of day.

Kangaroo
The kangaroo's powerful hopping helps it to cover a large area in search of something to eat.

School of the Air

Children growing up on farms in the Outback may be hundreds of miles from the nearest school, so instead they have their lessons at the School of the Air, so-called because, in the past, teachers and pupils used **two-way radios**. Today, teaching is all done by webcam. The school has an average of 120 pupils each year.

04. Now practice blowing until you get a rich, droning sound. Then try holding the note. Remember to breathe!

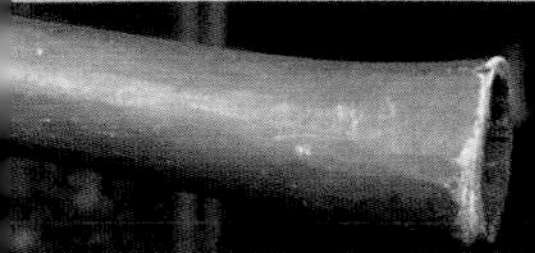

03. Take some beeswax and place it around the top edge of the digeridoo to make a mouthpiece.

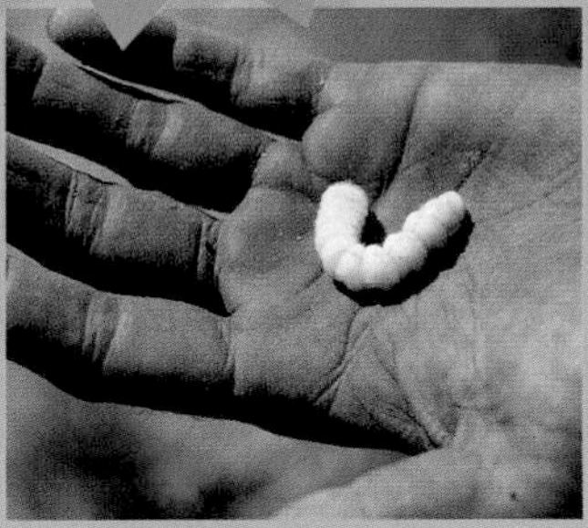

Good grub

The Outback is full of foods that grow in the wild, known as bush tucker. Aborigines have been eating these foods for thousands of years.

On the menu is a wide range of plants and nuts, as well as emu, kangaroo, crocodile, and insects such as witchetty grubs (large moth larvae).

The grubs are very nutritious and can be eaten raw (when they taste like almonds or peanut butter) or cooked (when they taste like roast chicken). Sounds delicious!

Eucalyptus

The eucalyptus, or gum tree, is Australia's most famous plant.

There are 700 species of eucalyptus and all but 15 of them are found in Australia.

They are some of the tallest trees in the world, with one famous specimen measuring 99.6 m (327 ft).

The plant is evergreen, with tough waxy leaves that are poisonous to most animals, but koalas and possums don't seem to mind.

The flowers of the trees provide nectar for birds, bats, insects, and possums.

Eucalyptus leaves are rich in oil that is valuable as a natural disinfectant.

Getting about

Flying doctors
If someone needs emergency medical help in the Outback, a doctor from the Flying Doctor service will fly out to treat them.

Air Mail
Farmers living in remote areas of the Outback have all their mail delivered by plane.

Road trains
Commercial trucks, known as road trains, are used for transporting heavy loads over long distances in the Outback. Road trains can pull several trailers behind them at once.

Tell me more: **shearing a sheep**

- Take your sheep and make sure its fleece is clean.
- **Sit the animal with its back towards you, and try to make it relaxed.**
- Carefully cut off the wool close to the body to remove the fleece in one piece.
- **It should take about 15 to 20 minutes to shear one sheep.**

Five things you might not expect to find **in the Outback**

Going underground
In the opal-mining town of Coober Pedy it gets seriously hot, so homes, shops, and even churches are underground.

Uluru
Out of a flat plain in Central Australia looms the massive red rock of Uluru, a sacred site of the Aboriginal people.

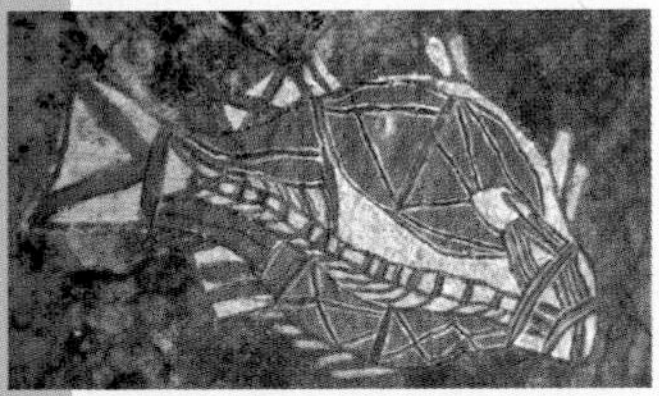

Rock art
For thousands of years, Aborigines have painted animals and people on the walls of caves and rocks.

Is that a camel?
Camels were brought to the Outback in the 19th century to transport goods. Many still live there, some in the wild.

Bottomless boats
Every year, a unusual race takes place near Alice Springs. Contestants run down a dry river bed, while holding on to bottomless boats.

How many islands are there in the **South Pacific?**

In the 18th century, trade attracted European sailors to the South Pacific, and many islands became **colonies**. But between 1962–1980, most islands gained **independence** (or partial independence) from their colonial rulers.

The Pacific Ocean is so vast that nobody knows how many islands there are. It is thought that there are between 20,000–30,000, most of which lie in the South Pacific. Some are high volcanic islands, while others are low-lying atolls – coral reefs that lie on underwater volcanoes – and are mostly uninhabited.

WHAT'S IN A NAME?

The islands of the South Pacific are divided into three groups.

Polynesia
Means "many islands". Includes the Cook Islands, Tonga, Tahiti, and Tuvalu.

Micronesia
Means "small islands". Includes the Marshall Islands, Soloman Islands, and Guam.

Melanesia
Means "black islands". Includes the islands of New Caledonia, Vanuatu, and Fiji.

OUTRIGGER CANOES

For thousands of years, **Pacific islanders** have made canoes of all shapes and sizes. Typically, the canoes have floats called outriggers attached, to make them stable.

Coconut crab

The world's largest crab is the coconut crab, which can measure 1 m (3.3 ft) across, from claw to claw. It's also the heaviest land crab, weighing up to 4 kg (8.25 lb).

This giant crustacean is found on the islands of the Pacific and Indian oceans. It lives in a burrow during the day and comes out at night to feed.

Its main food is coconuts. The crab climbs up the palm trees to get them and snips their stems with its powerful pincers.

On the ground, the crab tears off the outer layers of the coconut and pounds it open, breaking into the tasty flesh inside.

Sadly, because the coconut crab is slow on land and is easily caught by predators, the species is becoming rare.

Dangers of island life

Rising sea levels
Some low-lying islands in the South Pacific are already experiencing serious problems with rising sea levels, caused by global warming and the melting of the polar icecaps.

Tropical cyclones
Parts of the South Pacific lie in the path of hurricanes, called tropical cyclones. Torrential rain and powerful winds at speeds of up to 200 kph (125 mph) can cause terrible destruction.

Volcanoes and earthquakes
The South Pacific is an area of volcanic activity, earthquakes, and tsunamis. These huge, powerful waves are particularly destructive to low-lying islands.

FAST FACTS

Coconuts

01: Coconut palms are usually found in the tropics, and grow best in warm, wet, and sunny conditions.

02: A coconut is not a nut but a big seed.

03: The seed is covered in a thick coat of fibres, called a husk, which protects the seed when it's ripe and drops from the tree.

04: The seeds float and often wash up on distant beaches and take root.

05: Coconut palms can survive in salty water or sandy soil, and their roots help to hold the soil together, making it possible for other plants to survive around them.

06: The fibres from the husk, called coir, can be used to make rope, matting, and bedding, and the shells make good fuel.

I don't believe it!

Tattoos became fashionable among the European aristocracy after the Prince of Wales, the future King Edward VII of England, got a tattoo on his arm in 1862.

War in the Pacific

During World War II (1939–1945), much of the conflict between the USA and Japan took part in the South Pacific, as both sides fought to control the different islands. The seas here are littered with the **wrecks** of warships and planes.

In 1777, the British explorer, Captain James Cook saw islanders **surfing** on long wooden surfboards **in Tahiti**. He noted in his diary how much fun they seemed to be having!

Body beautiful?

The word "tattoo" comes from the Polynesian word "tatau" and was probably picked up by European sailors visiting the South Pacific in the 18th century.

It soon became the fashion for sailors to have tattoos.

In the South Pacific, having a tattoo marks a boy's passage to manhood.

On some Pacific Islands, full-body tattoos used to be common. Today, some men have complex tattoos around their buttocks and thighs, which look like britches.

Having a tattoo done is a long and painful process, as indelible (permanent) ink is inserted under the skin with needles.

Complex tattoo patterns are designed to inspire fear in enemies, and are believed to act like armour, giving the bearer the powers of his ancestors.

It is also traditional for women in the South Pacific to have tattoos, but the designs are usually much smaller.

Three island sports

Rugby
The islands of Samoa and Tonga may be small nations, but they have world-class rugby teams.

Surfing
Big beaches mean giant waves and some of the best surfing in the world.

Kirititi
A Samoan version of cricket – *kirititi* – is played with colourful clubs and involves dancing.

WEIRD OR WHAT?

On many Pacific Islands, special occasions are marked by drinking **kava**. Traditionally, kava is made by chewing the root of a particular plant, spitting it out onto leaves, adding water, and then straining the mixture through coconut fibres. The kava is served in half coconut shells and offered to guests, who should drain the cup!

Tell me more: **ten South Pacific islands**

Vanuatu

Number of islands:
4 main islands and
80 smaller ones
Area: 12,189 sq km (4,706 sq miles)
Population: 219,000

Vanuatu is a chain of mountainous, volcanic islands, covered with lush rainforests. There are nine active volcanoes on Vanuatu, including Mount Yasur (left), on the island of Tanna. Vanuatu's sub-tropical climate is ideal for growing cocoa, coffee, bananas, and coconuts.

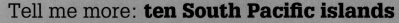

Samoa

Number of islands:
2 main islands and
several uninhabited ones
Area: 2,831 sq km (1,093 sq miles)
Population: 220,000

The International Date Line, the imaginary line that marks where one day ends and the next begins, lies just west of Samoa, which means it is the last place on Earth to see the Sun set each day. Islands just a short distance to the east are one day ahead of Samoa.

Fiji

Number of islands:
About 330 islands,
110 inhabited
Area: 18,274 sq km (7,055 sq miles)
Population: 945,000

Fiji is the perfect desert island with tropical rainforests and white sandy beaches, fringed with coral reefs. 87 per cent of the population live on Fiji's two major islands, Viti Levu and Vanua Levu.

Easter Island

Number of islands: 1
Area: 164 sq km (63 sq miles)
Population: 4,780

This isolated island is famous for its 887 giant *moai* – stone statues that represent ancient ancestors. Nearly all the island's trees were cut down to make the statues.

Area: 1,045 sq km (403 sq miles)
Population: 180,000
Tahiti is the main island of French Polynesia, although it measures only 45 km (28 miles) across at its widest point. Its many lagoons are home to a variety of sea creatures such as manta rays, barracuda, sea cucumbers, sharks, and dolphins.

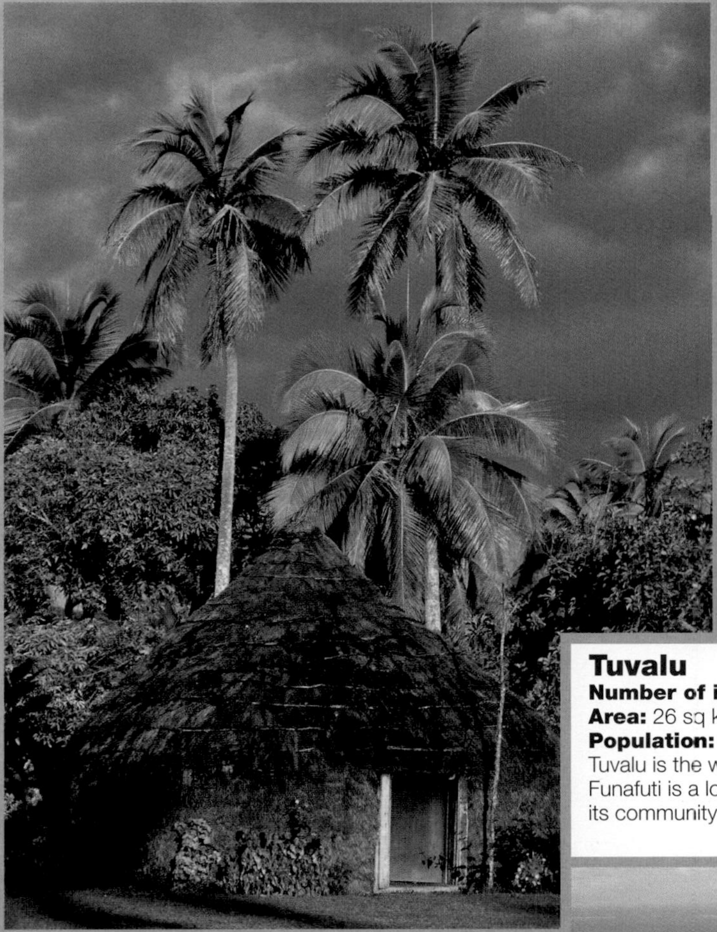

New Caledonia
Number of islands: 1 main island and several small atolls
Area: 18,575 sq km (7,175 sq miles)
Population: 227,400
Almost half the population of New Caledonia is made up of a people known as the Kanaks. The Kanaks have a strong identity and culture, based around clans. Each clan has its own "big hut" where members gather for important meetings.

Solomon Islands
Number of islands: 992 islands, 347 inhabited
Area: 28,896 sq km (11,156 sq miles)
Population: 596,000
The Solomon Islands are wonderful for diving and snorkelling. The coral reefs and sunken wrecks from World War II teem with tropical fish.

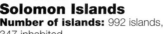

Tonga
Number of islands: 169 islands, 36 inhabited
Area: 747 sq km (288 sq miles)
Population: 121,000
When British explorer Captain Cook landed on Tonga in 1773, he declared that the country should be called the "Friendly Islands" because the people were so warm.

Tuvalu
Number of islands: 9
Area: 26 sq km (10 sq miles)
Population: 12,370
Tuvalu is the world's fourth-smallest country. The island of Funafuti is a long, low-lying strip of land, and the future of its community is seriously threatened by rising sea levels.

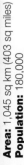

Cook Islands
Number of islands: 15
Area: 236 sq km (91 sq miles)
Population: 11,870
These islands are spread out over a large area, extending 1,433 km (890 miles) from north to south. Most of the islanders are of Maori descent and live on Rarotonga, the largest island.

Does anyone live **in the Arctic?**

About four million people live in the Arctic Circle, with the largest communities in Russia, Norway, and Finland. Traditionally, native Arctic peoples have survived by hunting reindeer and fishing in the Arctic seas. But today, many Arctic communities lead more modern lifestyles.

Tell me more: the Arctic Circle

The Arctic Circle is the area within the imaginary line at the parallel of latitude 66.5 degrees north of the equator. Eight countries have territories here.

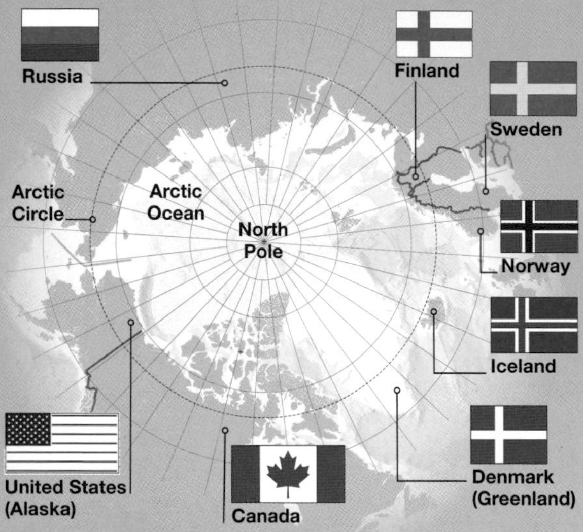

Alaska is the largest US State in size, but the **least densely populated**. It was bought from Russia in 1867 for US$ 7.2 million.

Northern Lights

On cold, clear nights, great sheets of bright colours sometimes appear to ripple across the skies in the far north. This is the **Aurora Borealis**, or Northern Lights – an effect caused by particles from the Sun releasing energy in Earth's atmosphere.

Native people

- There are more than 30 different groups of Arctic peoples.
- **The Inuit of Canada, USA (Alaska), and Greenland live the farthest north and hunt seals, walruses, and narwhals.**
- The Sami people are found in Norway, Sweden, Finland, and Russia. Traditionally, they are reindeer-herders, but today only 10 per cent follow the nomadic way of life.
- **Many different Arctic peoples live across Northern Russia. Several, such as the Chukchi, Dolgan, Evenk, Khanty, Nenet (below), and Yakut, herd reindeer.**

Frozen food

Traditionally, Arctic people have eaten the animals and fish in their local environment. Their diet is high on meat, because it is too cold to grow fruit or vegetables. A typical Arctic diet includes:

- **Fish**
- **Narwhal**
- **Polar bear**
- **Reindeer**
- **Seabirds**
- **Seal**
- **Walrus**
- **Whale**

Life on the move

Many native peoples are nomadic reindeer-hunters who build temporary shelters from the materials that are available to them.

Nenet winter camp
The winter tents of the Nenet reindeer-herders are made from reindeer skin.

Cree winter tent
Cree hunters leave their villages in northern Canada for many months to find the best hunting grounds.

Khanty summer camp
The summer tents of the nomadic Khanty reindeer-herders of Siberia are made of canvas.

FAST FACTS

Arctic sports

Blanket tossing	Reindeer racing
High kicking	**Seal skinning**
Husky racing	Tug-of-war
Piggy-back	**Wrestling**

Reindeer or caribou?

If you come across this large deer in North America, it's called a **caribou**, but if you're in Europe or Asia, it's known as a **reindeer**. The Arctic caribou live in herds and migrate in search of food – northwards in the summer, and then south to winter pastures.

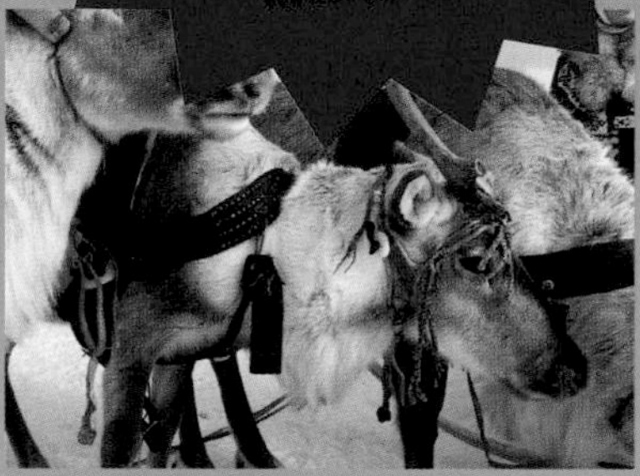

Summer fruit

In summer, wild berries such as cranberries and cloudberries grow in the warmer areas. They can be eaten fresh or made into **jam** for the winter months.

Dolgan huts
The huts of the Siberian Dolgan people are built on sleds so reindeer can pull them from place to place.

Inuit igloo
When the Inuit go on long hunting trips, they build shelters from blocks of ice, called igloos.

Six reasons to keep reindeer

01: Getting about
Reindeer can be trained to pull sleds and even be ridden like horses.

02: Milk
Their milk can be drunk or made into cheese, butter, or yoghurt.

03: Blood
The blood of freshly killed reindeer is often used to make sausages.

04: Meat
Reindeer meat can be eaten raw, frozen, or cooked.

05: Antlers
These can be carved into tools, harpoon needles, snow goggles, and decorative objects.

06: Skins
Reindeer hides are used to make clothes, bedding, and tents.

The North Pole

- **The Geographic North Pole is the point exactly 90 degrees north, in the centre of the Arctic Circle.**
- It lies on the constantly shifting ice of the Arctic Ocean.
- **The nearest land is Greenland, 650 km (400 miles) away.**
- The first explorer to reach the North Pole was American Robert Peary in 1909, with the help of a team of Inuit.
- **In the summer months at the North Pole, the Sun never sinks below the horizon. In the winter months, it never rises above it.**
- The North Pole is warmer than the South Pole because the Arctic Ocean is not as cold as the frozen land at the South Pole.
- **The North Magnetic Pole is where the needle of a compass points and is always moving.**

Dressed for the cold

Sami
Many Sami still wear traditional clothes with bands of bright yellow and red. In winter, they wear thick fur coats (parkas).

Nganasan
The Nganasan traditionally wear reindeer skins with the fur turned inside. The skins are often decorated with bright fabrics.

Nenet
Although they wear modern clothes in the towns, the Nenet often wear long reindeer-skin coats on hunting trips.

Inuit
Traditionally, Inuit clothes are made from seal skins, although sometimes Arctic fox or polar bear fur is used.

Society and culture

Hankook
Herald Sun
NEC
nab
FLYING START

How do people **worship?**

People choose to worship in different ways. Following a faith or religion can be deeply personal, or something that is shared and celebrated within communities. Some worshippers observe the traditional customs of a particular religion. They may attend a mosque, church, or temple at regular times. Other people worship in private, or not at all.

Prayer

The nature of prayer is different across faiths and is sometimes unique to the person praying. Some worshippers pray in large groups by singing or chanting, while others pray privately or in silence. Prayers are generally a way to **communicate** with a higher power or consciousness.

Counting prayers

Many worshippers use beads to track the number of prayers, chants, or devotions they utter. In some religions, these beads guard against bad spirits.

Tasbih beads
Muslim
(33 or 99 beads)

Rosary beads
Roman Catholic
(more than 50 beads)

Japa mala beads
Hindu
(usually 108 beads)

Komboskini
Greek Orthodox
(100 knots)

Mala beads
Buddhist
(usually 108 beads)

Anglican Rosary
Anglican Christian
(33 beads)

Who's who of religion

Siddharta Gautama
Born in 563 BCE
Indian prince and founder of Buddhism

Jesus Christ
Born 4 BCE
Jewish carpenter and founder of Christianity

Moses
Born c.1400 BCE
Wrote the Torah, religious book of Judaism

Guru Nanak Dev Ji
Born 1469 CE
Grainary manager, and founder of Sikhism

Muhammad
Born 570 CE
Shepherd merchant, Prophet, and founder of Islam

Zoroaster
Born 628 BCE
Prophet, philosopher, and poet, and founder of Zoroastrianism

Lao Tse
Born c. 600 BCE
Philosopher and founder of Taoism

Mahavira
Born 599 BCE
Indian prince and founder of Jainism

Baha'u'llah
Born 1817 CE
Author and messenger, founder of Bahá'í faith

MAJOR FAITHS

Listed are the proportion of the world's population that follow the six major religions. The remaining population follow other faiths, or are non-religious.

Christianity 33.3%
Islam 21%
Hinduism 13.2%
Buddhism 5.8%
Sikhism 0.4%
Judaism 0.23%

Six pilgrim hotspots

01: Mecca, Saudi Arabia (Islam)
Islam's holiest site

02: Jerusalem, Israel (Judaism)
Religious Jews pray at the Wailing Wall

03: Rome, Italy (Christianity)
A holy place for Catholics

04: Amritsar, India (Sikhism)
Home of the spectacular Golden Temple

05: Badrinath, India (Hinduism)
A Hindu holy town

06: Lumbini, Nepal (Buddhism)
The bithplace of Buddha

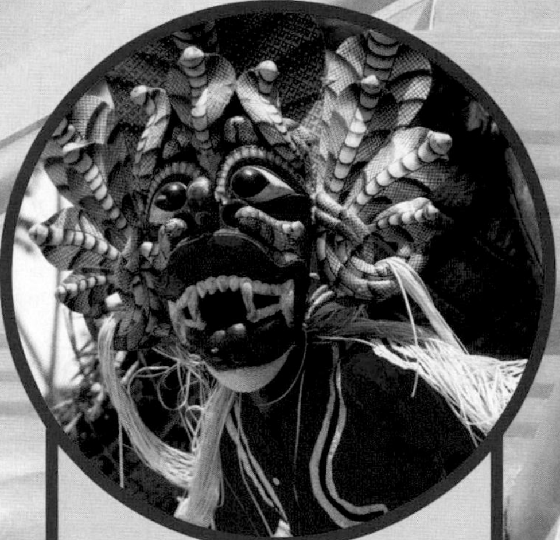

Mount Fuji in Japan is sacred to the **Shinto** faith, and has many **shrines** where pilgrims honour Sengren-Sama, the goddess of the rising Sun.

Spirit religions

Throughout the world, small groups of indigenous people worship the spirits they believe dwell in people, animals, places, and their dead ancestors.

These "spirit" religions existed long before the creation of the world's main religions.

Special religious figures, called shamans, contact the spirits, usually through rituals, such as dancing or drumming, and with the help of masks, which help them reach a state where they can travel to the spirit world.

The spirits may guide the shamans to heal people, predict the future, resolve disputes, or ward off evil spirits.

Holy smoke
Incense is used in most major religions. In some religions, these natural, **aromatic substances** are burned as part of an offering to a deity, and in other religions it assists prayer.

Big Buddha statues

01: Ushiku Amida Buddha, Japan (above)
120 m (394 ft)

02: Great Buddha Lingshan, China
100 m (328 ft)

03: Buddha of Monywa, Myanmar
90 m (300 ft)

04: Leshan Buddha, China
71 m (233 ft)

05: Nihonji Daibutsu, Japan
31 m (101 ft)

Holy hat **parade**

Religious headgear can be ceremonial or for daily wear.

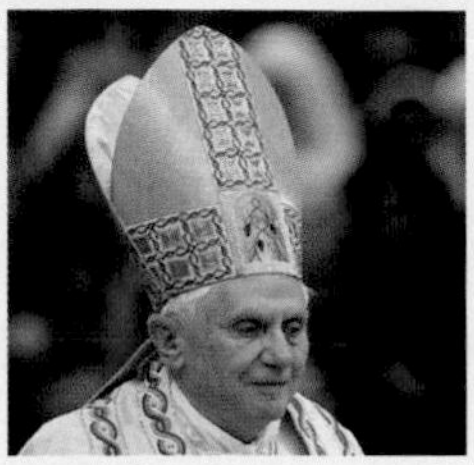

Mitre
Ceremonial headdress of Christian clergy, including the Catholic church.

Songkok
Also known as a kopiah, this hat is worn by some Muslim men in southeast Asia.

Wimple
This head-covering is worn by some Christian nuns; it accompanies the habit (tunic).

Hijab
Traditionally, a headscarf is worn by Muslim women; the style differs between cultures.

Kamilavkion
They are worn by Orthodox Christian and Eastern Catholic monks.

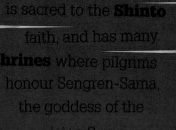

Kippah
Some Jewish men choose to wear this rounded skullcap, also known as a yarmulke.

What are **symbols?**

Symbols tell us important information without using words. Some symbols are used to represent a country, group, culture, or set of beliefs. The most effective symbols are simple and immediately understood.

Religious symbols

Religions use many symbols to express their morals, beliefs, teachings, and experiences. Here are just a few religious symbols used:

Islam
Star and crescent

Judaism
Star of David

Jainism
Ahisma hand

Buddhism
Wheel of Dharma

Christianity
Crucifix

Sikhism
Khanda

Hinduism
Lotus flower

Taoism
Yin and Yang

Zoroastrianism
Faravahar

Shinto
Torii

Braille alphabet

At the age of four Louis Braille lost his sight. He invented the Braille alphabet in 1829 to help other blind or vision-impaired people to read and write. It uses combinations of **six raised dots** to represent letters and numbers.

King of the symbols

Lions are a symbol of strength and power in many cultures. They were often used to represent families on **coats of arms** in medieval times. In **Buddhism**, the lion can symbolize the Buddha, who was a royal prince.

Capricorn
Dec 23 – Jan 20
Symbol: Goat
Ambitious, will climb every mountain

Aquarius
Jan 21 – Feb 19
Symbol: Waterbearer
Kind to others, cool, makes own path

Pisces
Feb 20 – Mar 20
Symbol: Fish
Dreamy, artistic, bit wet behind the ears

Aries
Mar 21 – Apr 20
Symbol: Ram
Courageous, direct, not too sheepish

Taurus
Apr 21 – May 21
Symbol: Bull
Tender, stubborn, can be hot-tempered

Gemini
May 22 – Jun 21
Symbol: Twins
Chatty, restless, double the fun

Cancer
Jun 22 – Jul 22
Symbol: Crab
Gentle, sensitive, can get crabby

Leo
Jul 23 – Aug 22
Symbol: Lion
Courageous, noble, fine head of hair

Virgo
Aug 23 – Sep 23
Symbol: Maiden
Clever, helpful, bit of a neat freak

Libra
Sep 24 – Oct 23
Symbol: Scales
Likeable, fair, keeps things in balance

Scorpio
Oct 24 – Nov 22
Symbol: Scorpion
Secretive, loyal, can have sting in tail

Sagittarius
Nov 23 – Dec 22
Symbol: Archer
Optimistic, brave, right on target

Wheel of fortune

In astronomy, the zodiac is a ring of 12 constellations that the Sun passes through in each year. Animals and mythological beings symbolize these constellations. Astrologers attempt to predict the future by reading the zodiac's movements. They believe the star sign we are born under shapes our personality.

Gemstones

Rare and beautiful gemstones have traditionally held special meaning across many different cultures. "Birth stones" are used to symbolize the time (usually month) of birth. Some stones are believed to have magical or healing energies.

Ruby
The king of stones – in ancient Burma nobles would lodge rubies in their teeth to signify power. In India, they are a symbol of royalty.

Emerald
This stone is a symbol of spring, rain, and fertile soil. In some cultures, emeralds are an antidote for poison and a cure for leprosy.

Blue sapphire
The sapphire's deep blue colour is believed to symbolize the heavens. The stone represents faith, hope, and destiny.

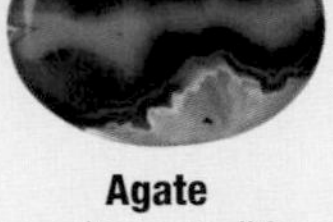

Agate
Some cultures traditionally carve eyes into this white stone in an attempt to diminish bad luck.

Turquoise
This stone is used to represent the gods in ancient Mesoamerican cultures. It also protected the dead from evil spirits in Ancient Egypt.

Tell me more: **Chess**

Chess was first played in India in the 6th century. Modern versions of the game symbolize a battle for power between kings, queens, and armies.

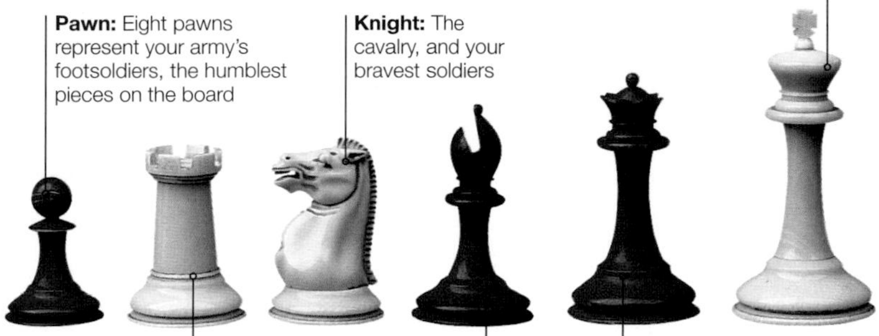

King: The most important piece on the board that your rival must capture. Known as the Shah in Persia

Pawn: Eight pawns represent your army's footsoldiers, the humblest pieces on the board

Knight: The cavalry, and your bravest soldiers

ok: This was originally a chariot, or "rokh" in Persian. This piece came a "rocca", which eans fortress in Italian

Bishop: This piece started out as an elephant, the groove marking a tusk. In Europe it was thought to look more like a bishop's mitre

Queen: This piece was first a councilor or vizier. In the East, viziers held all the real power at court

Peace symbols

Militaries around the world are identified by uniforms, emblems, and symbols. Peace also has its own symbols.

CND sign
Created in 1958 and later adopted by the Campaign for Nuclear Disarmament group.

Olive branch
A symbol from ancient Greece, extending an olive branch means to settle an argument.

V-sign
Used as a symbol of peace in the anti-war protests of the 1960s.

Dove
Traditionally Jewish and Christian symbols of peace. The dove sometimes carries an olive branch.

White poppy
This flower honours the victims of all wars around the world.

How to: **read tea leaves**

01. Prepare a cup of tea using loose tea leaves. While convenient, a tea bag will not work here.

02. Think of a question as you drink the tea, such as, "Is tomorrow a good day to go to the beach?"

03. When you have drunk most of the tea, swirl the tea leaves in the bottom of the cup.

04. Gently turn the cup upside-down onto its saucer, and wait a few minutes for the leaves to show.

05. Look into the cup and search for shapes. If you see the sun, your question is answered.

All-seeing symbol

The Eye of Providence is a symbol that dates back to Ancient Egypt. In some cultures, it represents an **all-seeing god**. It is often shown in a triangle, surrounded by Sun-like rays. Today, it can be seen on the reverse side of the US one-dollar note.

What goes around...

The most effective symbols are instant and universal. This means they can be immediately understood anywhere in the world. Recyclable items are often labelled with continuous arrows, like this symbol from Japan.

In numbers

0 The continuous circle represents both non-being and eternity

1 Stands for oneness with the Universe, God, and the individual

2 Represents opposites, such as life and death, and light and dark, but also represents pairs

3 A sacred number in most religions, representing birth, life, and death; mind, body, and soul; and past, present, and future

4 The number of the square, four represents Earth and completeness; the elements of earth, air, fire, and water; and the points of a compass

Pirate symbols

In the 17th century, pirates flew Jolly Roger flags to strike fear into other ships. These flags identified the ships crew as lawless. Some flags were plain black, while others showed symbols of death.

Cutlass: Belonged to brightly dressed pirate Jack Rackham, known as "Calico Jack".

Skull and crossbones: Flown by pirate Edward England, who was known for not killing his captives unless it was absolutely necessary.

Hourglass: Emanuel Wynne first flew a Jolly Roger flag. The hourglass meant there was little time left to surrender.

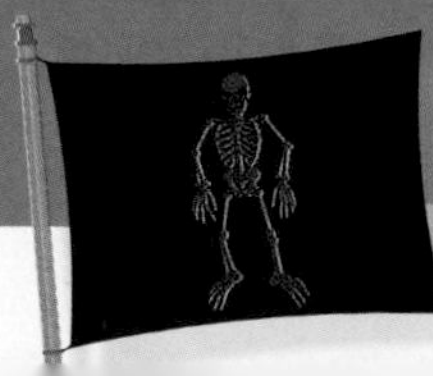

Death: The flag of Edward Low whose crew set him adrift in a dinghy.

Why do we have **myths?**

In ancient times, myths helped people to understand the world. Before scientific discoveries, things like the sky, the Moon, and natural disasters were believed to be supernatural. People told stories to help explain these things as well as historic events. Over time, these myths came to be believed as fact.

Sun stories

- Ra, the Ancient Egyptian Sun god, spent all his time in a boat. He could be seen sailing across the sky during the day, but disappeared into the dark underworld at night.
- Viracocha, the Inca god of creation, ordered the Sun, Moon, and stars to rise from Lake Titicaca and light up the world. Inti, the Sun god, was father of all the emperors.
- When the Japanese Sun goddess Amaterasu hid in a cave to avoid her brother's practical jokes, the world was plunged into darkness.
- A Sun goddess to the Native American Cherokees wept and hid when her daughter died from a rattlesnake bite. The world grew dark and her tears caused a flood.
- In Chinese myth, ten Suns took turns in lighting up the sky. One day, they played together and scorched Earth. The Emperor punished them by asking the Heavenly Archer to shoot them from the sky. Nine Suns fell and turned into crows.

How to: **stop a vampire**

01. Bury the dead upside-down with extra nails to close the coffin. This will prevent them from being possessed by vampires in the first place.

02. Hand a mirror to a suspected vampire, and say his hair is messy. If there is no reflection, you are dealing with a vampire.

03. Lure your suspected vampire to a day at the beach. The sunshine will reduce him to a pile of ashes.

04. Keep garlic, holy water, and a crucifix handy at all times. You never know when a vampire might strike.

05. Ask a vampire-hunter to drive a wooden stake through the vampire's heart if you are attacked.

A Chinese airline paid 2.33 million yuan (more than $280,000) for the phone number **8888 8888** in 2003.

WEIRD OR WHAT?

In 1987, a flotilla of 24 boats used £1 million worth of **sonar technology** to search for the **Loch Ness Monster**. Three crescent-shaped marks did appear in the sonar reports, but these were explained as being fish or possibly seals.

Four mythical **beasts**

Bunyip
(lake monster)
Aboriginal Australian

Totem pole

These carved cedar sculptures are symbols of the indigenous people of the **Pacific Northwest**, USA. Some of the images carved tell myths and legends, and others explain important cultural beliefs.

Werewolves

- Werewolves (or lycanthropes) are mythological creatures said to shapeshift from human to wolf-like form, especially when there is a Full Moon.
- It was believed an ordinary person could become a werewolf after being bitten or scratched by a werewolf, or placed under a curse.
- In Estonia in the 17th century, a youngman was brought to trial accused of being a werewolf and he confessed that he was!

Kraken
(squid-like sea monster)
Scandinavian

Chupacabra
(vampire-like creature that kills farm and forest animals)
Latin America

Unicorn
(magical, horned horse)
Medieval Europe

Fairy fakes

In 1917, two cousins, Elsie Wright and Frances Griffith, claimed to have photographed fairies in Cottingley, UK. Many people, including Sir Arthur Conan Doyle (the author of *Sherlock Holmes*), believed the girls, although in the 1970s the photos were revealed to be a hoax.

Five famous mythological places

- **Atlantis** was the Ancient Greek city that sunk into the ocean after an earthquake, according to Plato.
- **El Dorado** was the Lost City of Gold that lured Spanish conquistadors for centuries in search of its riches.
- **Great South Land** (*Terra Australis Incognita*) was suggested by Aristotle, who believed that a southern continent existed to balance the Northern Hemisphere.
- **Valhalla** was an enormous hallwhere the most courageous Vikings killed in battle were thought to hang out with the Norse god Odin.
- **Camelot**. This was the castle that was home to the legendary King Arthur and his court.

Afterlife

Mexican people honour the **Day of the Dead** on 1 November each year. Families pray to the souls of relatives who have passed away, hoping they will return to Earth for one night. Candles are lit so the souls can find their way back.

What is an urban myth?

These are modern myths that start out as a joke, or a horror story. The most hair-raising tales soon spread through the community.

- Wild alligators roam the sewers of New York City, USA, after they were flushed down toilets as babies.
- If you swallow chewing gum, it will stay undigested in your gut for seven years.
- A woman undid her fancy hairstyle after many years and unleashed a nest of killer spiders.

Dragons

Chinese dragons
This legendary creature symbolizes success and power. It has control over weather, such as rainfall.

George and the dragon
Saint George slayed a dragon and rescued a princess. George protected himself with the sign of a cross.

Viking dragon
Viking sailors carved dragons on the prow of their ships to scare away sea monsters and spirits.

Ljubljana dragon
The city of Ljubljana, capital of Slovenia, is protected by a friendly dragon, which is also a symbol of the city.

What is philosophy?

Philosophers raise many questions about existence, knowledge, and reason. The main role of the philosopher is to challenge commonplace ideas, and suggest new ways of thinking about life. Philosophy means "love of wisdom" in Greek.

Pythagoras
Born 495 BCE
This mathematician is widely known as the father of numbers. The Pythagorean theorem explains how to calculate the longest side of a right-angled triangle.

Socrates
Born 469 BCE
Popular and with many followers, he asked questions like "What is beauty?" His disrespect for the gods, though, made Athenians angry, and he was sentenced to death.

Plato
Born 429 BCE
Wrote down and shared many of Socrates' conversations. His most famous philosophical work was perhaps *The Republic*, which suggested a new type of government.

Aristotle
Born 384 BCE
A student at Plato's academy, Aristotle had a strong interest in science, and named many plants on his travels. He taught Alexander the Great.

Seven branches of philosophy
(and the basic questions they ask)

Aesthetics
What is beautiful or ugly?
Epistemology
What is knowledge?
Ethics
What is moral (right and wrong)?
Logic
What is logic?
Metaphysics
What is real?
Political philosophy
What form should government take?
Social philosophy
What is society?

Six teachings of Confucius
(Chinese philosopher, 551–479 BCE)

A man who has committed a mistake and does not correct it is committing another mistake.

Everything has its beauty, but not everyone sees it.

Real knowledge is to know the extent of one's ignorance.

Look for an occupation that you like, and you will not need to labour for a single day in your life.

Our greatest glory is not in never failing, but in rising every time we fail.

Ten schools of thought-isms

Existentialism: Finding the human self using free will. Set own values.

Nihilism: Morality does not truly exist. Life is without purpose.

Secular humanism: Humans can lead ethical, just, and happy lives without religious laws.

Objectivism: Happiness is the moral purpose of life. Respect individual rights.

Absurdism: Humans will never know if the Universe has meaning; to search is absurd.

Positivism: True knowledge is only based on real experiences.

Eight famous

Renee Descartes
1596–1650
The "father of modern philosophy"

Immanuel Kant
1724–1804
Questioned pure reason

> I think, therefore I am.

> If man makes himself a worm, he must not complain when he is trodden on.

[redacted]

- Anarchism rose as a philosophical movement in the mid 19th century.
- Anarchists do not believe in government. They argue that common sense would allow people to form a functional society. Without laws, citizens would be free to develop their own sense of morals and ethics.
- The only common "rule" anarchists agree on is that there should be no government.

Blasts from the past

650 BCE The Ancient Greeks get philosophical; Thales of Miletus rejects mythology and believes that life started from water

480 BCE Chinese philosopher Confucius spends final years of life recording his wisdom in texts called *The Five Classics*

470 BCE Chinese philosopher Lao Tzu dies, aged 130; he is considered the "wise man" in Taoist philosophy

399 BCE Socrates condemned to death for corrupting the minds of Athens' youth

161 CE Roman emperor Marcus Aurelius considers himself philosopher-king, follows Stoic philosophy of virtue, and sells own possessions to help in time of famine

427 St Augustine, Bishop of Hippo (now in Algeria), uses Plato's ancient philosophies in an attempt to prove the existence of a Christian God

1170 Ibn Rushid, Muslim philosopher, believes government and religion should separate

[redacted]

Food for thought

Make like a philosopher, and figure out these eternal philosophical questions.

- What is "good"?
- What is "evil"?
- What is the meaning of life?
- What is?
- What is truth?
- What is time?
- Do we have free will?

- **Epicureanism:** Happiness comes from living moderately. Excess ends in unhappiness.
- **Utilitarianism:** Actions should result in the greatest good for the greatest number of people.
- **Determinism:** Everything in life is determined by an existing chain of events.
- **Solipsism:** All that truly exists is one's mind.

I don't believe it!

The third Thursday of every November is World Philosophy Day. For Existentialists, this is the day to think about the world as we know it… or don't.

Penny for your thoughts

In 18th-century London, **coffee shops** were popular hangouts for students and intellectuals to meet and discuss ideas. Bottomless cups of coffee were offered for a penny, so they became known as Penny Universities.

modern philosophers

Karl Marx
1818–1883
Founder of Communism

Friedrich Nietzsche
1844–1990
Campaigned against morality

Bertrand Russell
1872–1970
Favoured logic and common sense

Jean-Paul Sartre
1905–1980
Existentialist

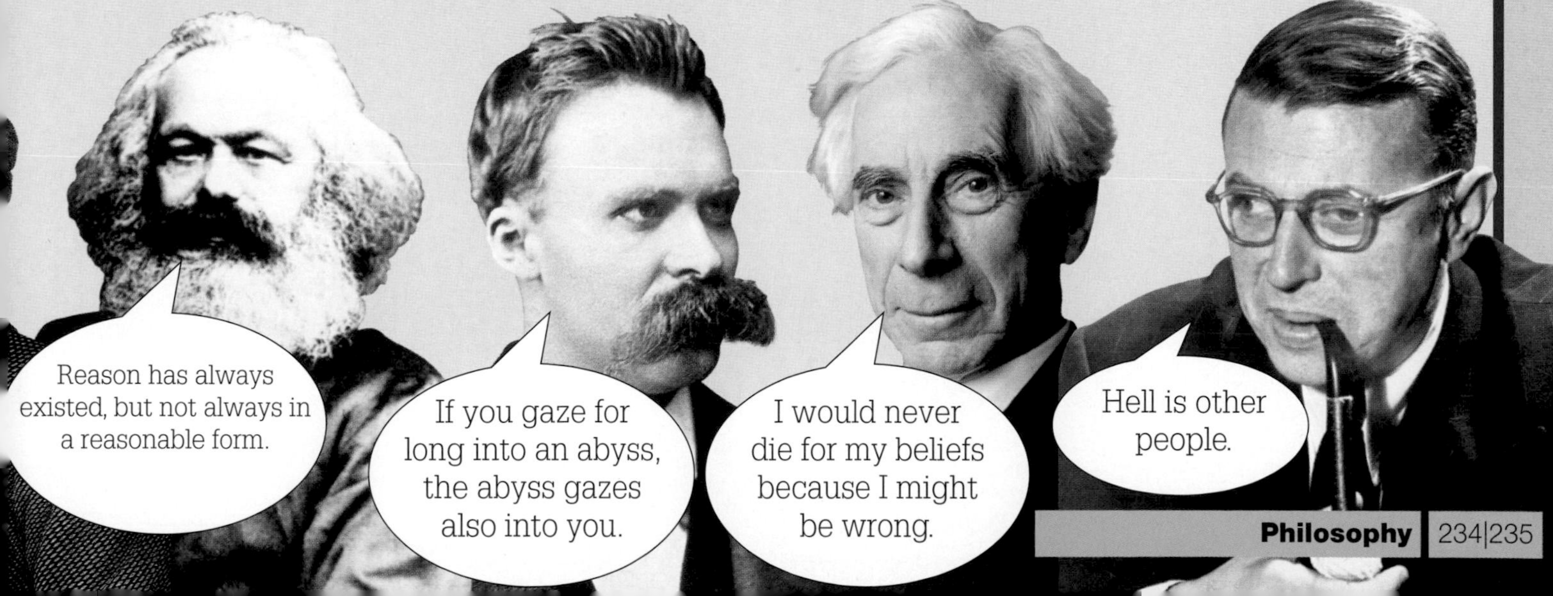

Reason has always existed, but not always in a reasonable form.
If you gaze for long into an abyss, the abyss gazes also into you.
I would never die for my beliefs because I might be wrong.
Hell is other people.

Blasts from the past

59 BCE
Julius Caesar starts the first newspaper, *Acta Diurna* (Daily Acts)

1048 CE
Bi Sheng creates moveable type on porcelain tablets in China

1450
German Johannes Gutenburg invents the printing press

1586
First magazine published by Swiss painter Josse Amman, showing women's fashions

1899
About 5,000 New York newspaper boys strike against poor pay; they are led by 13-year-old, Kid Blink (nicknamed because he was blind in one eye)

1926
During Britain's General Strike, BBC radio broadcasts five news bulletins a day as there are no newspapers published

1960
Theorist Marshall McLuhan uses the word "global village" to describe the worldwide effect of television news reporting

1976
One of the first live worldwide satellite TV broadcasts was on 1 October 1976; it was a boxing match called the "Thrilla in Manila" between Muhammad Ali and Smokin' Joe Frazier

1994
The news is broadcast for the first time on the Internet by America's ABC network.

What's news?

Any information or event that is current and important is news. For something to make the news headlines, it must have an impact, good or bad, on many people. Newsworthy items are often events that are out of the ordinary, from celebrity scandals to natural disasters.

In breaking news...
Seven of the world's best-selling newspapers are Japanese.

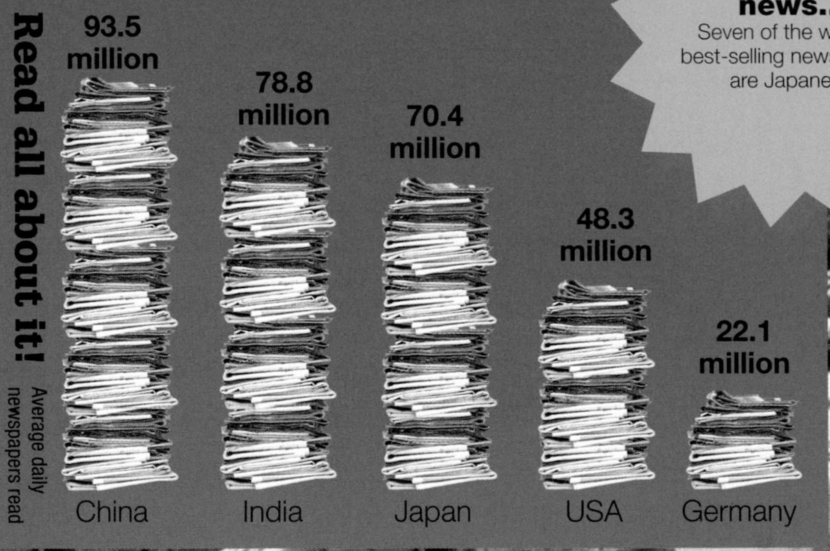

Five old ways of **spreading the news**

- Send a messenger
- Smoke and light signals
- Town crier
- Carrier pigeon
- Morse code and the electric telegraph

Four quicker ways of **getting the story**

- Radio
- Television
- Online/on the Internet
- Delivered to your phone

Media **censorship** is when published material is carefully monitored and controlled for moral, political, or religious reasons. Material that is highly offensive, hateful, or dangerous is removed. Censorship laws differ around the world.

What about me?

Freedom of speech is a human right under article 19 of the Universal Declaration of Human Rights.

Which stories make the news

Eyewitness
Bystanders provide first-hand accounts of news at the scene. In an accident or disaster, the report may come from an emergency services representative.

Exposé
Investigative journalism is when a reporter reveals a truth that has been hidden, avoided, or kept quiet. The truth exposed could be a crime, scandal, or political corruption.

Human interest
Ahuman interest story discusses a person or group of people in an emotional way that connects with the viewer and engage their compassion or sympathy.

Entertainment
This is usually light-hearted news and involves things that entertain people, such as movies, TV, fashion, or pop and rock music. Famous celebrities often appear in an entertainment story.

Odd spot
Humorous or quirky stories are usually reported at the end of a news bulletin. Who wouldn't want to know about record-breaking cheese!

Tell me more: **reading the news**

Eyes: Read the script from on the autocue beside the camera
Earpiece: This can transmit instructions from the program editors and producers
Make-up: You will need this to keep you looking polished on-air
Microphone: Necessary to amplify your voice for the broadcast
Script: Very useful just in case the autocue fails

In numbers

Bloggers can report news online immediately to readers worldwide.

133,000,000
Number of blogs indexed by Technorati since 2002

346,000,000
Number of people globally who read blogs

900,000
Number of blog posts ina 24-hour period

81
Number of languages in the blogosphere

WEIRD OR WHAT?

In the 1990s,people used the term "**Information Superhighway**" to describe the future of communication using the Internet.

Eight news agencies

Throughout the world there are organizations of journalists, called news agencies, that supply news stories to the news trade.

Agence France-Presse (AFP)
The first news agency, founded in Paris, France, in 1835.

Al-Jazeera
An independent news network in the Middle East, based in Qatar.

British Broadcasting Corporation (BBC)
The largest broadcasting news gatherer in the world, based in London, UK.

Cable News Network (CNN)
A cable news network based in Atlanta, USA, and the first to provide 24-hour TV news coverage.

Reuters
A Canadian controlled, UK-based news agency, that started out providing information for the financial markets.

RIA Novosti
A Russian information agency based in Moscow.

Xinhua
The official press agency of the Peoples Republic of China is state controlled.

Zuma Press
The world's largest independent press agency is based in California, USA.

Why is **pop music so popular?**

Pop music is the popular music of any time. Since the 1950s, pop music has become a softer style of rock and roll. It is easy to dance to, and usually has a catchy chorus designed to stick in your head.

Ten greatest singers

Aretha Franklin
The Queen of Soul and the winner of 18 Grammy Awards.

Ray Charles
Blinded at the age of seven, he pioneered soul music by mixing gospel, R&B, and jazz.

Elvis Presley
Also known as the "King of Rock and Roll", or quite simply the "King".

WHAT'S IN A NAME?

DJ is the shortened term for **disc jockey**. This was originally used when radio announcers played vinyl records on a turntable.

Tell me more: **Drums**

Ride cymbal: Maintains a steady, rhythmic pattern
Toms: Cylindrical pair of drums with no snare. It is mounted above the bass drum
Crash cymbal: Makes a loud, sharp "crash" sound
High hat cymbals: Two cymbals that clash using a pedal
Floor tom: Can be used as a small bass drum (usually in jazz)
Bass drum: Used to mark time in a song
Snare drum: Strands of wire stretched across the "skin" brighten the sound

How to: **play air guitar**

01. Put on your favourite heavy metal or hard rock album, and play it very, very loud!

02. Pretend that you are playing an electric guitar (your air guitar) to thousands of adoring fans.

03. Make wild windmill motions with your "free" arm as you rock some air. Do the splits!

04. When the song is done, thank your audience. Smash your air guitar on stage to seem more "rock".

WEIRD OR WHAT?

The first **World Air Guitar Championships** were held in Finland in 1996. Since then, 20 countries have joined the quest to find the world's most rocking air guitarist.

of all time

Recognize any of these golden oldies? This group of performers was voted the ten best singers of all time by Rolling Stone magazine. Apart from John Lennon, all are from the United States of America.

Sam Cooke
This soul singer owned his own record label and music publishing company.

John Lennon
The singer-songwriter and guitarist for the Beatles began his solo career in 1970.

Marvin Gaye
The singer-songwriter and instrumentalist was known as the "Prince of Motown".

Bod Dylan
A singer-songwriter, musician, painter, and poet who began as a folk artist.

Otis Redding
This powerful and emotional singer-songwriter was known as the "King of Soul".

Stevie Wonder
Born blind, the singer-songwriter is also an instrumentalist and record producer.

James Brown
A singer, songwriter, instrumentalist, dancer, and bandleader; he was the "Godfather of Soul".

I don't believe it!

Here's a mouthful: MP3 is a much quicker way of saying Moving Picture Experts Group-1 Audio Layer 3.

WEIRD OR WHAT?

Jazz pianist Yosuke Yamashita has been filmed playing a **burning grand piano** twice. The first fiery performance was in 1973, and the flaming encore was in 2008.

Virtual Band

- **Gorillaz** is the most successful "virtual band"– where people create the music, but it is performed by animated (cartoon) characters.
- The band has **four cartoon characters**: 2D, Murdoc Niccals, Noodle, and Russell Hobbs.

Anatomy of a five-part rock band

- The **lead singer** is considered the band's front person, and may also play harmonica, maracas, or tambourine.
- The **lead guitarist** plays melody lines, instrumental fills, and guitar solos within a song. He or she may also provide backing vocals.
- The **rhythm guitarist** provides chord progression, rhythm, and beat.
- The **bass guitarist** uses a four-stringed guitar (instead of six), and is part of the rhythm section.
- The **drummer** is the percussionist who drives the song's beat. He or she works with the bassist to create the rhythm section.

RECORD BREAKER

The 1995 music video for the duet "Scream" by Michael Jackson and his sister Janet is the **most expensive music video** ever made. It cost $7 million dollars.

Blasts from the past

1931 Adolph Rickenbacker invents the electric guitar

1946 Frank Sinatra releases his first studio album, *The Voice of Frank Sinatra* – it stays at the top spot on the US Billboard charts for seven weeks

1955 *Rock Around the Clock* by Bill Hayley is the first rock song used in a movie

1964 Sudden popularity of British pop and rock acts in the US dubbed the British Invasion

1977 Punk rock music bursts into mainstream popularity

1985 More than 400 million people watch televised Live Aid concerts broadcast from London, UK, and Philadelphia, USA

1999 The first portable MP3 players are sold

Why do we **dance?**

People have a natural urge to move in time to music. Some dances are spontaneous and some are structured. For many cultural and religious groups, dance is a strong unifying factor.

FAIRYTALE DANCERS

Many **ballets** re-tell classic fairytales and stories through dance. The dancers' movements and expressions create a narrative, along with the music, costumes, and sets.

Happy feet

Tap dancers are also percussionists as they tap out the beat with their shoes. Tap shoes have metal plates fixed to the ball and heel of the sole. The soun of the tap can be changed by tightening and looseni the screws on the metal plates.

China
Up to 50 people move the dragon on poles to a beating drum.

Mali
Dogon tribes dance in masks to honour their ancestors in *dama* ceremonies.

Poland
Spritely folk dance, the mazurka, became popular in ballrooms in the 19th century.

England
In this dance from the Middle Ages, Morris dancers wave handkerchiefs, sticks, or swords.

Spain
The flamenco is an intense dance, with rhythmic stomping and swift arm moves.

New Zealand
The Maori people perform the haka in welcoming ceremonies and, historically, before a battle.

India
Kathak is a classical Indian dance used to express myths, religious stories, and romance.

Dreamtime dance

At a **corroboree**, spiritual stories from Aboriginal Dreamtime are often retold through dance. Dancers may use their bodies to imitate Australian animals such as kangaroos and emus.

Breakdancing

Breakdancing is an athletic dancing style that began on the streets of New York City, USA, in the 1970s.

Toprock
These moves are made while standing up, and showcase the breaker's rhythm. Toprock may borrow from other dance styles, like hip-hop.

Downrock
Keeping low, these moves are made on the floor. When a breaker moves her legs in a circle supported by her arms, she is doing a 6-step.

Powermoves
The breaker's lower body spins above the head in moves such as the headspin – this one's only for the professionals!

Freezes
A freeze is when a breaker suspends a move as though frozen in mid air and usually signals the end of a routine.

Eight ballroom dances

01. Waltz Sliding German peasant dance from the 1600s.
02. Foxtrot Swift American dance from 1914.
03. Cha Cha Cha The name of this lively Cuban dance from 1953 describes the foot rhythm.
04. Tango Argentinian 19th-century dance.
05. Jive This 1940s American swing-dance is similar to the jitterbug.
06. Viennese An 18th-century Austrian type of waltz.
07. Quickstep Lightfooted English dance from 1927.
08. Samba Brazilian dance popular in the 1930s.

The **Limbo** – where dancers in a line try to dance under a lowering pole – was originally a ritual dance performed at Trinidadian funerals.

WEIRD OR WHAT?

In the 1970s, British **punks** invented a dance called the **pogo**. To pogo, you hold your torso stiff, keep your arms by your sides, and jump up and down on the spot.

In numbers

10,036
Number of people who broke the world record for the most people Irish dancing, set in Dublin, Ohio, USA, on 4 August 2007

2,028
Number of people holding hands in the world's longest contra dance line in Latvia on 25 October 2008

535
Number of people who broke the world record for the most people belly dancing in Malvern, UK, on 8 November 2008

I don't believe it!

In 2009, scientists found that some parrots dance to a musical beat. Their main study was Snowball, a cockatoo who became famous on YouTube, receiving more than 2 million hits.

13 dance crazes from the 1960s

- The twist
- The hitchhike
- The watusi
- The mashed potato
- The frug
- The stroll
- The bunny hop
- The chicken
- The monster mash
- The pony
- The dog
- The swim
- The locomotion

How to: **moonwalk**

01. Point your right toes down to the floor, behind your left foot. The weight is on your left leg, as the right toes balance.

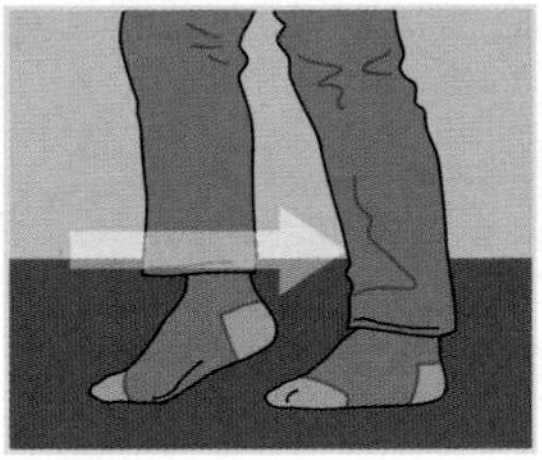

02. As smoothly as you can, slide your left foot behind your right foot. Your right foot will begin to fall flat on the floor.

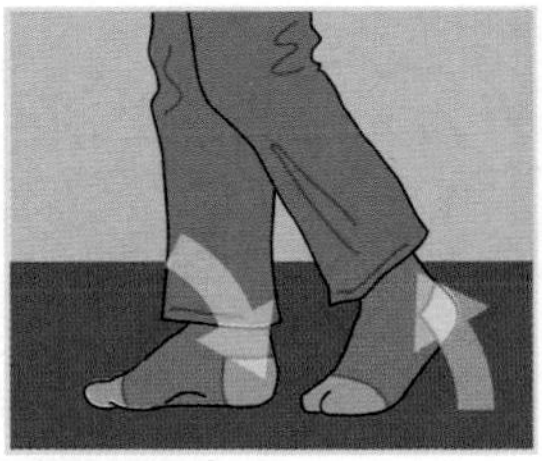

03. In one action, snap your right foot down to the floor as you snap your left heel up and point your left toes to the floor.

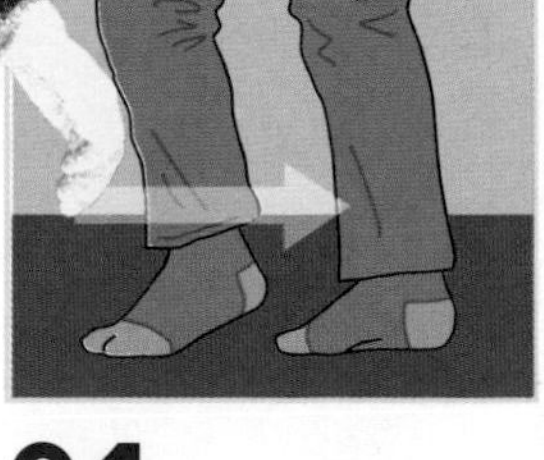

04. Repeat steps one to three, but this time start by sliding your right foot behind your left foot.

05. Now you must keep on practising until your moves are as smooth as Michael Jackson's.

Who decides what's fashion?

Fashion begins with designers presenting their collections to the media in catwalk parades. Fashion editors then promote their favourite catwalk styles in glossy magazines. Some celebrities help to influence fashion trends by the clothes they choose to wear. Finally, customers in shops decide what's fashionable.

Elle is the biggest-circulating fashion magazine in the world. Since launching in Paris in 1945, it has 42 international editions, and 28 websites around the globe.

Top five fashion capitals

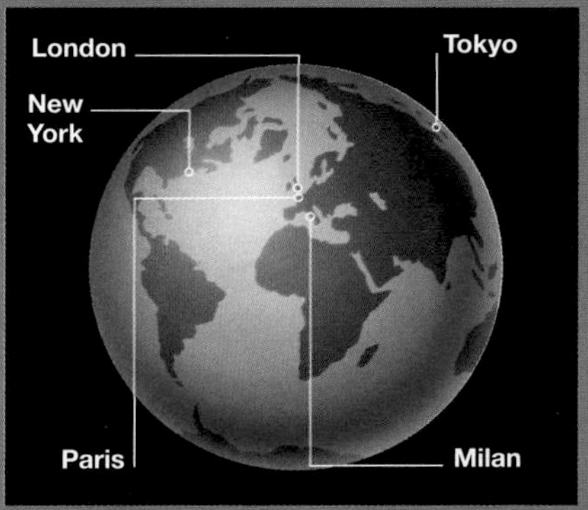

Haute Couture

Haute couture is high fashion that is fitted exclusively for a private client. In France, fashion houses are listed each year as haute couture designers. In order to belong to this exclusive club, designers must:

- Design custom clothing for private clients with one or more fittings.
- Have a Paris atelier (workshop) that employs at least 15 full-time staff.
- Present a collection twice a year to the Paris press. Each collection must have 35 "runs" for day and evening wear.

How to... be big in fashion

01. Design your fabulous collection and have it ready for Fashion Week in Paris, London, Milan, Tokyo, or New York.

02. Invite the right people to your show, such as fashion buyers, celebrities, and fashion editors.

03. Calling all photographers! You want your clothes seen around the world, so make sure the photographers get great snaps.

HAIRSTYLE GALLERY

Blasts from the past

1873
Levi Strauss creates the first pair of copper-riveted waist overalls, also known as blue jeans

1913
Paul Poiret is one of the first designers to create trousers for women – he called his loose-legged design "harem pants"

1917
Bastketball player Chuck Taylor adopts Converse All-Star as his preferrred shoe, leading to a long-lasting fashion craze

1947
Christian Dior's New Look makes skirts full and the female form curvy

1954
French shoe designer Roger Vivier creates the first stiletto heel

1960
The classic 1460 Dr Martens boot is created

1964
Andre Courreges brings the mini skirt into high fashion

models to show off your designs. If you have loads of money, hire a supermodel and you'll be taken seriously.

Big bucks

In 1990, Canadian supermodel Linda Evangelista famously said: "We don't wake up for less than $10,000 a day". She was talking about the huge amounts of money that top models were paid.

JEANS

01: The name jeans comes from the French *bleu de Genes* which means "blue of Genoa".

02: True jeans must be made of denim – a cotton fabric – and dyed indigo blue.

03: In the 1850s, merchant Levi Strauss began selling blue jeans to miners in California looking for gold.

04: In 1873, on the suggestion of one of his customers, Jacob Davis, Strauss began using copper rivets to reinforce weak points, like the corners of pockets and the base of the button fly.

05: In 1886, Strauss branded his jeans with a label showing a pair of horses trying to rip apart a pair of jeans, to show how tough the jeans were.

WEIRD OR WHAT!

The modern **bikini** was invented in 1946 by French engineer Louis Reard. He named the two-piece swimwear after the nuclear weapons test-site, Bikini Atoll, in the South Pacific Ocean.

I don't believe it!

During World War II, women were known to stain their legs with tea to get the appearance of wearing silk stockings.

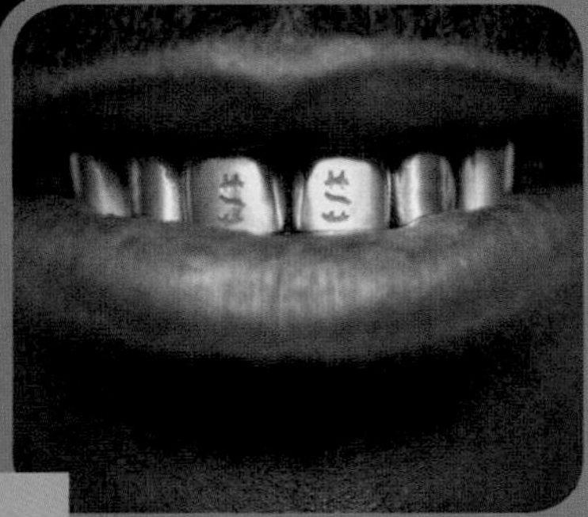

Bizarre dental fashion

Until the end of Japan's Meiji era in 1912, married Japanese women would dye their teeth black with iron that had been soaked in tea or rice wine.

Gold teeth are worn as a symbol of wealth in parts of the Caucasus and Central Asia. Sometimes real teeth are removed and replaced with gold ones.

Rap and hip-hop artists made "grills" popular in the 2000s. Grills are a removable layer of false teeth made of silver, gold, or diamonds.

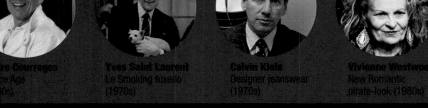

Famous fashion creations

Coco Chanel Little black dress (1920s)

Christian Dior New Look (1947)

Andre Courreges Space Age (1960s)

Yves Saint Laurent Le Smoking tuxedo (1970s)

Calvin Klein Designer jeanswear (1970s)

Vivienne Westwood New Romantic pirate-look (1980s)

Which country produces the most **films?**

RECORD BREAKER

The world's most expensive movie stunt was in the 1993 film, **Cliffhanger**. Stunt man Simon Crane was paid $1 million to cross between two planes at 4,572 m (15,000 ft).

India is in first place, producing about 1,000 films annually in various languages. Internationally, India's best-known films are the Hindi-language Bollywood blockbusters from Mumbai. Next in line is Nigeria, followed by the United States.

Top eight highest-earning films

01: ***Avatar*** (2010)
more than $2,462,821,000

02: ***Titanic*** (1997)
$1,843,201,268

03: ***The Lord of the Rings: The Return of the King*** (2003)
$1,119,110,941

04: ***Pirates of the Caribbean: Dead Man's Chest*** (2006)
$1,091,345,358

05: ***Batman: The Dark Knight*** (2008)
$1,022,345,358

06: ***Harry Potter and the Philosopher's Stone*** (2001)
$974,733,550

07: ***Pirates of the Caribbean: At World's End*** (2007)
$960,996,492

08: ***Harry Potter and the Order of the Phoenix*** (2007)
$958,212,738

Unusual places to **watch a movie**

Drive-in Watching films from cars was especially popular in the United States and Australia until many drive-ins closed in the 1980s.

Open air cinema FilmAid show films to people in need using giant inflatable screens. In 2009, 15,000 children from a Sudanese refugee camp in Tanzania attended a screening of *George of the Jungle*.

Inside a truck A travelling truck offers people in remote communities in the UK a chance to watch the latest films.

Genres of film

Action
Adventure
Animation
Biography
Children's
Comedy
Crime
Disaster
Documentary
Drama
Foreign
Espionage
Family
Fantasy
Horror
Musical
Mystery
Period piece
Romance
Science-fiction
Short
Sport
Suspense
Teen
Thriller
War
Western

Corny films

The American inventor Charles Cretor unveiled his **popcorn-making** machine at the Chicago World Fair in 1893. The cheap snack food became especially popular for film-goers during the Great Depression of the 1930s.

Blasts from the past

1824 The optical illusion machine, the thaumatrope, is one of the first of many magic lanterns to create the appearance of moving images

1839 Commercial photography is born with the daguerrotype, a method of capturing still images on silvered copper plates

1869 Celluloid, which is used in photographic film, is patented by John Wesley Hyatt

1879 Thomas Alva Edison demonstrates the incandescent light bulb, which is later used in movie projectors

1893 America's first movie production studio is built, the Black Maria at West Orange, New Jersey, USA

How to: **make a moving image**

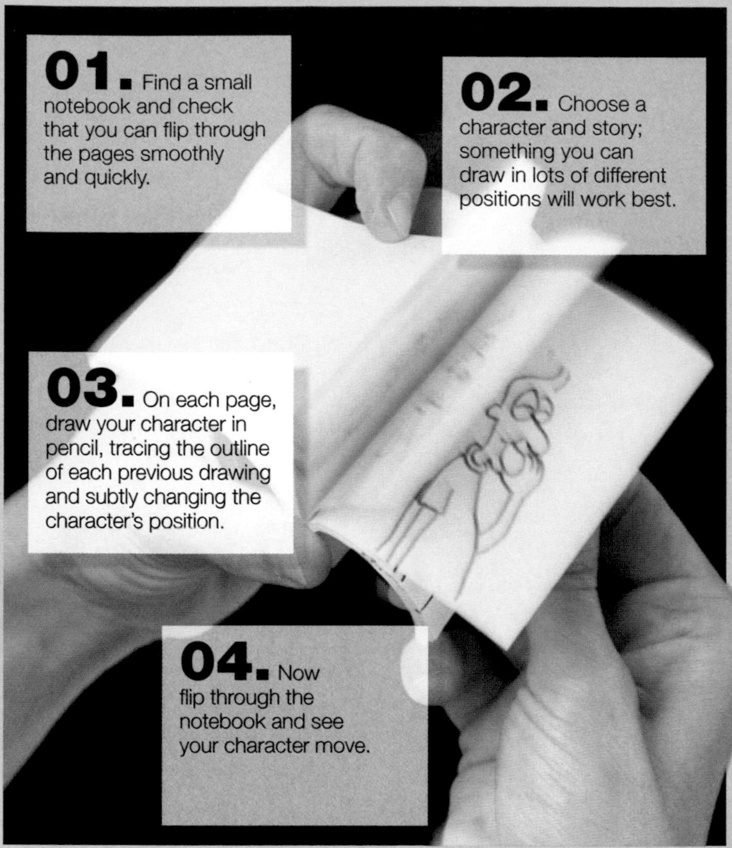

01. Find a small notebook and check that you can flip through the pages smoothly and quickly.

02. Choose a character and story; something you can draw in lots of different positions will work best.

03. On each page, draw your character in pencil, tracing the outline of each previous drawing and subtly changing the character's position.

04. Now flip through the notebook and see your character move.

Weird movie **crew names**

Gaffer
Often credited as Chief Lighting Technician, this position involves preparing, and sometimes designing, the lighting plan.

Grip
Responsible for maintaining and positioning equipment in a scene.

Dolly grip
This person positions the dolly, which is a small truck that runs on tracks carrying a camera, camera operator, and sometimes the director.

Best boy
The assistant to a gaffer or grip, and ensures the efficient daily running on set.

Body double
Some of the responsibilities of a body double include replacing actors in scenes involving nudity, or physically demanding stunts.

Clapper loader
Loads raw film stock into a camera magazine and operates the clapperboard.

Ten movie **sound effects**

Punching someone: Thump watermelons or punch a telephone book.

Bones breaking: Twist a head of celery or lettuce in two, with crackers glued on.

Bird flapping wings: Flap a pair of gloves.

Spaceship sliding door: Pull a piece of paper from an envelope.

Being sick: Take a bottle of salad cream and a bottle of water. First shake out a splodge of salad cream into a bowl and then pour a splash of water.

Fire crackling: Slowly press down on a packet of crisps with your hand.

Squelching of alien innards: Place a microphone close to your mouth. Open your mouth slowly, and let your tongue slackly "drip" from the roof of your mouth to create a gross noise.

In numbers

400,000
The number of extras used in the funeral scene of the 1982 film *Gandhi*

US$16.5 million
US dollars spent on the most expensive Bollywood film, *Love Story 2050* (2008)

999
The number of feature films that screened at the 2009 Cannes Film Festival, France

161
The number of Dracula movies

683
Number of running minutes in *The Lord of the Rings* movie trilogy

6
The age of Shirley Temple when she was the youngest person to ever receive an honorary Oscar in 1934

WHAT'S IN A NAME?

The person who creates the sound effects on a movie is called a **Foley Artist**, named after Jack Foley, one of the first great Hollywood masters of sound effects from the days of talking films.

Three types of **animation**

Animation is an optical illusion in which you see a rapid sequence of images as movement. There are three main animation techniques used for making movies.

Traditional animation
A series of drawn images, called cels, are photographed one by one and then put together in the same way as a flick book. Films such as *Pinocchio*, *Jungle Book*, and *The Simpsons* use this process.

Stop-motion
Clay models or puppets are manipulated and photographed frame by frame. This technique was used to make films such as *Chicken Run*, *Wallace and Gromit* (above), and to bring the dinosaurs to life in the *Jurassic Park* films.

Computer animation
A variety of digital techniques using a computer can create a film's scene and characters. Films such as *Up*, *Ice Age* (above), and *Toy Story* were created in this way, also known as computer-generated imagery (CGI).

Why do people **love to paint?**

Painting is a way for people to express feelings, relax, or capture their view of the world. By applying paint to a canvas, body part, or even a house, the painted object is immediately transformed. Painting can also be a lot of fun!

Six types of paint

Distemper
This is a traditional wall paint comprising water, pigment, and glue.

Oil paint
It is made by mixing pigment with an oil binder.

Acrylic
A paint made from plastics, such as latex.

Gouache
This is a type of watercolour, mixed with chalk to make it opaque.

Watercolour
These are paints that can be manipulated by water.

Primer/sealer
This is a surface for the finish coats of paint.

Bronzed tower

The Eiffel Tower has been painted 19 times since it was built to prevent it from oxidizing. It takes **25 painters** more than one year to paint it from the peak to the base. The current bronze colour is shaded towards the top so that it appears the same colour against the Paris skyline.

Aboriginal dot painting

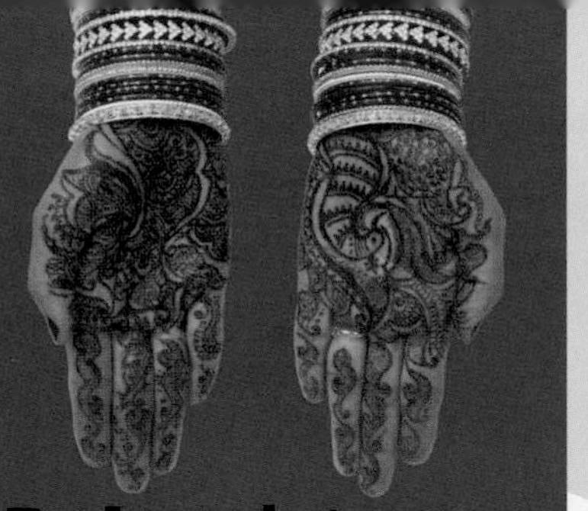

Body paint

- In the Middle East, India, Pakistan, and northern Africa, **henna paste** is used for bridal body art.
- Ancient Scottish Celts used **blue woad** (flower extract) for war paint.
- Aboriginal Australians use **clay and ochre** for paint on face and bodies.
- Ancient Egyptians used **green malachite** (copper oxide) to paint around eyes.
- In Elizabethan England the upper classes used a lead and white vinegar mix was used for painting faces white.

I don't believe it!

In the future, solar cells may be applied in paint form on the roofs of houses, factories, and public buildings to generate electricity.

Painted **cities**

These cities have brightened up their neighbourhoods by painting houses and flats in cheerful colours.

Jodphur, India

Bo-Kaap, Cape Town, South Africa

Venice, Italy

Manarola, Italy

Salvador, Brazil

Art movements and techniques

Impressionism
Paris-based movement of the 1870s and 1880s, aimed to paint what artists actually saw.

Cubism
Avant-garde art movement in early 20th century using abstract cube-like forms.

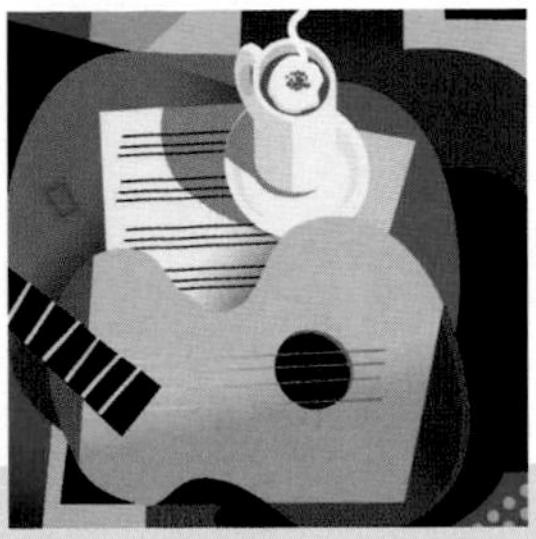

Art Deco
Art Design movement uses geometric shapes – a popular form in the 1920s to early 1940s.

Surrealism
Cultural movement that spread in the 1930s, known for "liquid" images and distorted distances.

Pop Art
Bright Pop Art images mimic advertising and popular culture in the 1950s and 1960s.

How to: **paint like Jackson Pollock**

01. Drip runny paint from a brush onto a canvas. Jackson Pollock preferred gloss enamel paint.

02. Pierce a hole in a paint can. Swirl the dripping can over the canvas a few times.

03. Experiment with other paint-dripping techniques until your artwork is complete.

It's all abstract
Jackson Pollock (1912–1956) was an American "abstract expressionist" artist. Abstract artists don't paint the "real world", but use colour and shape to show emotion. Pollock used liquid paint, which he poured and dripped over the canvas with brushes, sticks, or whatever took his imagination.

Van Gogh

01: Vincent van Gogh was a Dutch painter who lived from 1853–1890.

02: His best-known works are paintings of sunflowers.

03: The masterpieces were painted in Paris and Arles, France.

04: Van Gogh died poor, but today his paintings are worth millions.

Tell me more: **murals**

Mural artists think big. They paint on large surfaces, especially blank walls.

One of the most famous mural artists is Diego Rivera, who founded an art movement in the 1930s called Mexican Muralism.

Ancient Egyptians and Greeks, 2nd century Indian Buddhists, and Medieval and Renaissance artists all painted art on walls.

Four **painted faces**

Geisha
Japanese entertainers

Blue Man Group
American entertainers

Mime artists
Marcel Marceau

Sports fans
Swedish supporters

WEIRD OR WHAT!
British **clowns** can register their face paint at a society called Clowns International. Their face is painted onto an egg and kept in a gallery to prevent other clowns from using the same style.

What is **architecture?**

Architecture is the planning, designing, and construction of a building or structure. Over time, many architectural styles have developed. These styles reflect different cultures and civilizations, environments, and the building materials that are available.

Five groundbreaking architects

Christopher Wren, St Paul's Cathedral, UK
This Anglican cathedral was completed in London in 1710. The famous dome rises to about 111 m (365 ft).

Frank Lloyd Wright Falling Water, USA
This private modernist residence was completed in 1937. The floors are supported by one beam that hangs over a waterfall.

Antoni Gaudi Casa Mila, Spain
This lava-like apartment building was built in Barcelona in 1910. The stone front resembles a Catalan volcano.

Frank Gehry, Guggenheim Bilbao, Spain
Described as an "archisculpture", this titanium, limestone, and glass art museum was completed in 1997.

Jorn Utzon, Sydney Opera House, Australia
This performing arts venue was built in 1973. Ten white shells appear like boat sails overlooking Sydney Harbour.

Buildings fit for a king
(queen, emperor, or empress)

Winter Palace, Russia
This was the St Petersburg residence of Russian tsars from 1732 to 1917.

Alhambra, Spain
The Moorish palace was built to house the Muslim kings of the Nasrid dynasty in 1338.

Grand Palace, Thailand
This palace was built in Bangkok as the official residence of the King of Siam (Thailand) in 1783.

Neuschwanstein, Germany
Containing its very own concert hall, this fairytale palace was built by King Ludwig II in 1869.

Windsor Castle, UK
Dating back to 1086, the world's largest lived-in castle is home to Queen Elizabeth II.

Imperial Palace, China
Known as the Forbidden City, the Imperial Palace was built in 1420 and contains 9,000 rooms.

Top ten largest buildings (by floorspace)

01: Dubai International Airport Terminal 3
Dubai, UAE
1,500,000 sq m
(16.1 million sq ft)

02: Aaalsmeer Flower Auction
Aalsmeer, The Netherlands
990,000 sq m (10.6 million sq ft)

03: Beijing Capital International Airport Terminal 3
Beijing, China
986,000 sq m (10.6 million sq ft)

04: The Venetian Hotel and Casino
Macau, China
980,000 sq m (10.5 million sq ft)

05: Berjaya Times Square
Kuala Lumpur, Malaysia
700,000 sq m (7.5 million sq ft)

06: The Palazzo
Las Vegas, USA
645,581 sq m (6.9 million sq ft)

07: The Pentagon
Washington DC, USA
610,000 sq m (6.6 million sq ft)

08: K-25 power plant
Tennessee, USA
609,000 sq m (6.6 million sq ft)

09: Hong Kong International Airport
Hong Kong, China
570,000 sq m (6.3 million sq ft)

10: Suvarnabhumi Airport
Bangkok, Thailand
563,000 sq m (6.06 million sq ft)

The rise of Rome

In large, overpopulated cities, the Ancient Romans built timber or mudbrick apartment buildings called **insula**, which were about five storeys tall. Taverns and shops usually operated at the bottom, with living space above.

Housing through the ages

Mammoth bone hut
Found in parts of Russia and the Ukraine, these dwellings were built from bones between 27,000 and 12,000 years ago.

Hakka houses
These round, defensive structures – with houses inside – were built between the 12th and 20th centuries in Fujian province, China.

Earthen towers
High-rise apartments were built 400 years ago in the old town of Sanala, Yemen. They are made of earth and stucco (a type of plaster).

Sheep-skin yurt
The portable, wood-latticed homes of nomad shepherds in South Asia were insulated in felt, and made from the fleece of sheep.

How to: build a skyscraper

01. Create a building design. Find stable ground and dig until you hit solid rock. Then build concrete and steel foundations.

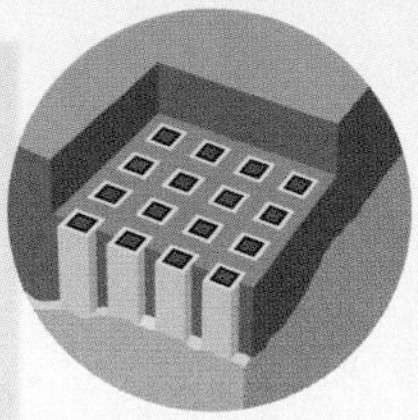

02. Place the vertical columns (steel beams cut to exact lengths and drilled with bolt holes) on to the foundation.

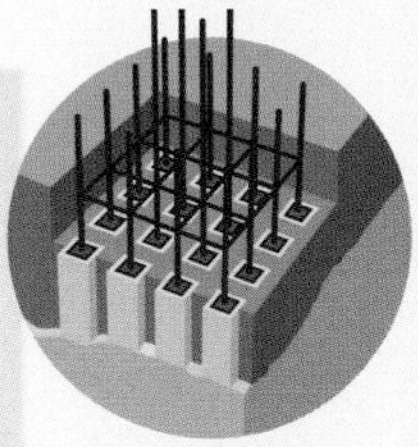

03. Fit the horizontal steel beams in place – the internal skeleton is now in place. Now it is time to begin work on the individual floors and walls. Ask the contractors to fit the electrical, plumbing, and air-conditioning equipment.

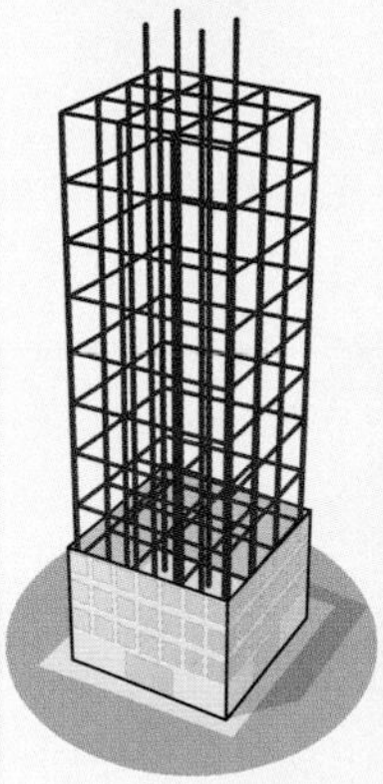

04. Finish the central core of the building, which includes lifts, piping, and staircases. Decorate the inside with beautiful marble floors and modern art. You are ready to move in!

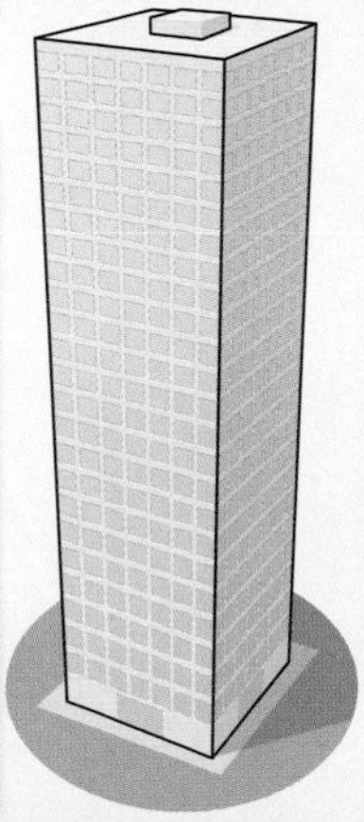

Round the world

If you haven't got time for an architecture tour of the world, just visit the casinos of Las Vegas, USA.

Ancient Egypt See the huge pyramid and the Great Sphinx of Gaza at the Luxor Casino.

Venice Tour a shopping mall with canals and singing gondoliers at the Venetian Casino.

Paris A hotel and casino with a giant-sized Eiffel Tower makes you feel like you are in France.

Manhattan The New York Hotel recreates the Manhattan skyline, and a model of the Empire State Building.

Ancient Rome With the Colosseum performing venue and Forum shops, Caesar's Palace recalls the time when Julius Caesar ruled Rome.

WHAT'S IN A NAME?

Modern houses that are quickly built, extremely large, and mix-and-match architectural styles are known as "**McMansions**". The name comes from a popular fast food chain.

The world's tallest man-made structure is the **Burj Khalifa**, formerly known as the Burj Dubai, in Dubai, UAE. It stands at 828 m (2,717 ft). It contains 900 private apartment residences, and an observation deck.

Amazing architecture

Allianz Arena Munich, Germany
A football stadium that can change colour.

Kunsthaus Graz, Austria
A landmark exhibition space for modern art.

Spaceport New Mexico, USA
Space tourists will be able to launch from here.

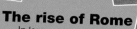

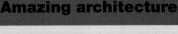

Pompidou Centre Paris, France
This "inside-out" building houses great modern art.

What can you play with a ball?

Ping-pong and table tennis are two different names for the same game. Ping-pong just sounds more fun.

Balls can be thrown, hit, kicked, bounced, dribbled, putted, hurled, bowled, pitched, head-butted, caught, and juggled. With a ball, you can play cricket, basketball, squash, polo, ping-pong, golf, snooker, pool, hockey, football, tennis, volleyball, and any other game you can think of that ends in "ball".

How to: **slam dunk**

01. First get fit and practise jumping. Take running leaps until you can touch the net ten times in a row. Then move on to touching the backboard. Never hang from the rim as it might snap.

02. Now you are ready to try the full shot. Get a good run up and dribble the ball towards the net, then take two steps and jump as high as you can.

03. As you jump, palm the ball into your dunking hand, stretching it out so it touches the rim of the net.

WHAT'S IN A NAME?

In **cricket**, a batsman who makes no runs is said to be "out for a duck". The duck's egg is the big, round zero recorded on the scoreboard.

Greatest **hits**

Baseball bat
In American Major League Baseball, the bat must be one solid piece of wood, not more than 106 cm (42 in) long, and 7 cm (2.75 in) in diameter.

Cricket bat
Traditionally, the cricket bat is made from willow wood, specifically from the Cricket-bat Willow tree (*Salix alba var. caerulea*). It is then treated with linseed oil.

Tennis racquet
Modern racquets are made from graphite and carbon metals. The head size is usually 68.5 cm (27 in) wide for professional players.

Hockey stick
The size and shape of field hockey sticks vary depending on a player's position. Defenders use "J hook" sticks with a thick head for stopping the ball.

Polo mallett
This has a hardwood head 25 cm (10 in) long is called the cigar. A sling wraps around the hand to prevent the player dropping it.

Get fit!
In Ancient Greece the physician Hippocrates used a type of ball, called a "**medicine ball**", to help his patients build strength. They were sewn from animal skins and filled with sand.

The modern game of golf originated around St Andrews, Scotland, with **12th century shepherds** knocking stones into rabbit holes.

Blasts from the past

1600 BCE Mesoamericans play a ball game that involves hitting a ball around a court surrounded by walls

364 BCE Roman soldiers play an early type of bowls between battles in the Punic wars

1300s Considered an early form of cricket, medieval milkmaids play a game called "stoolball" with their milking stools

1869 The first game of American football (or gridiron) is played between Rutgers and Princeton universities

1936 Gottfried Schmidt invents the mechanical pinsetter for ten-pin bowling; until then, teenage boys would usually do the job

1992 Beach volleyball is introduced at the summer Olympic Games in Barcelona, Spain

04. As you lift off, angle your wrist over the ball and when you reach the rim of the net, slam it down through the hoop. Dunk!

One of the **world's tallest basketball players** is Sun Ming Ming. The Chinese basketballer is 2.36 m (7 ft 9 in) tall, and wears a size 20 shoe!

Six ways to play polo

Polo began as a sport played on horseback, but there are lots of different variations:

- **Water polo** On horseback in water
- **Canoe polo** In canoes in water
- **Cycle polo** On bicycles
- **Segway polo** On Segways (two-wheeled, electronic vehicles)
- **Yak polo** On the backs of yaks
- **Elephant polo** On the backs of elephants

Three unusual **ball games to try**

Sepak Takraw
A bit like "kick volleyball", a team of three knock a hard ball over a net using any part of their body apart from the hands – usually the foot, knee, shoulder, or head.

Bossaball
A Belgian sport that combines volleyball, football, gymnastics, and the Brazilian martial art, capoeira. It is played on an inflatable court with built-in trampolines.

Hurling
A 15-player team has to get a ball into the opposition goal with an axe-shaped stick. The goal is H-shaped like a rugby goal, but also has a net. It is popular in Ireland.

In numbers

32
The number of panels stitched together to make a football, made up of 12 regular pentagons and 20 regular hexagons

52,200
The number of balls supplied to the Wimbledon tennis tournament each year

7.26 kg
(16 lb) The weight of a shot in men's shotput

20
The number of minutes in a single game of canoe polo

300
The perfect score in ten-pin bowling, which is achieved by getting 12 strikes in a row

31–0
The highest score in international football – Australia defeated American Samoa in the qualifying match for the 2002 FIFA World Cup

106.5 million
The number of American football fans that watched the 2010 Superbowl between New Orleans Saints and Indianapolis Colts

Six ball-sports greats

Roger Federer
The Swiss tennis player has won 16 single Grand Slam titles and is considered the greatest male tennis player of all time.

Claire Taylor
The UK cricketer Claire Taylor holds the record for the highest score in any one-day international at Lord's cricket ground.

Karch Kiraly
The world's best beach volleyball player, with a record-breaking 138 career wins. He is a three-time Olympic gold medalist.

Annika Sorenstam
This Swedish golfer (retired in 2008) won 90 international tournaments as a professional, giving her more wins than any other female player.

Stephen Hendry
In 1990, the Scotsman became the youngest snooker world champion at age 21. He holds 36 world titles, more than any other player.

Eri Yoshida
In 2009, the 16-year-old student was the first female to be drafted by a Japanese baseball team alongside male teammates.

Six team sports you can play on ice

Ice Hockey
Two teams use sticks to hit a puck into the opposite team's goal.

Curling
Two teams take turns sliding heavy stones along the ice towards a target.

Bandy
Two teams use sticks to hit a ball into the opposite team's goal. Similar rules to football.

Ringette
Two teams use cane-like sticks to guide a rubber ring into the opposite team's net.

Ice Stock Sport
Similar to curling, "ice stocks" with a 30 cm (11.8 in) handle are slid towards a target.

Sledge Hockey
A type of ice hockey where people with physical disabilities use a sledge.

Which sports are **hot in winter?**

Snow, ice, and frozen mountains provide exciting conditions for all types of winter sports, such as speed skating, ice climbing, skiing, and snowboarding. With modern indoor facilities, many winter sports can be played all year round.

How to: **ski jump**

01. Put on your skis at the top of the jumping ramp. Wait for the "go" signal, and then push off.

02. Crouch to help you accelerate down the snow-packed ramp towards the take-off point at the bottom.

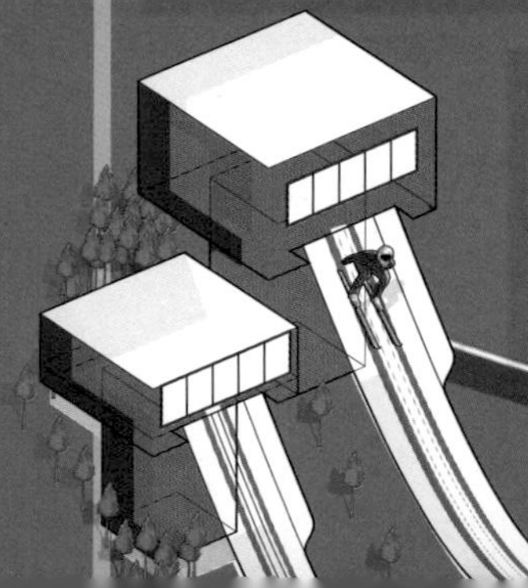

Snowball fight!
On 10 February 2006, the world's biggest snowball fight took place in Michigan, USA, between 3,745 university students and staff. They also rolled the world's **biggest snowball**, measuring 6.47 m (21.2 ft) all the way round.

Blasts from the past

6300 BCE
World's oldest known ski buried near Lake Sindor, Russia

4000 BCE
Rock carvings near Bola, Norway, depict humans on skis

1199 CE
The Battle of Finnmarkers and Danes is fought on skis

1767
In Norway, military skiing competitions are held

1812
Napoleon's retreating forces battle with Russian soldiers on skis

1850
Norwegian Sondre Norheim invents the heel strap by plaiting birch tree roots

1882
First US ski club opens – The Norske Ski Club in New Hampshire

1936
The world's first ski lifts operate at Sun Valley resort in Idaho, USA

1988
The Jamaican bobsled team make their debut in the 1988 Winter Olympic Games in Calgary, Canada; their story is the inspiration for the Hollywood film, *Cool Runnings*

The record for the world's **longest ski jump** is 239 m (784 ft). It was set in 2005 by the Norwegian ski jumper Bjorn Einar Romoren in Planica, Slovenia.

03. As you take off, stretch out, straighten up, and lean forwards. Spread the tips of your skis into a "V" shape, as you will travel further.

K POINT

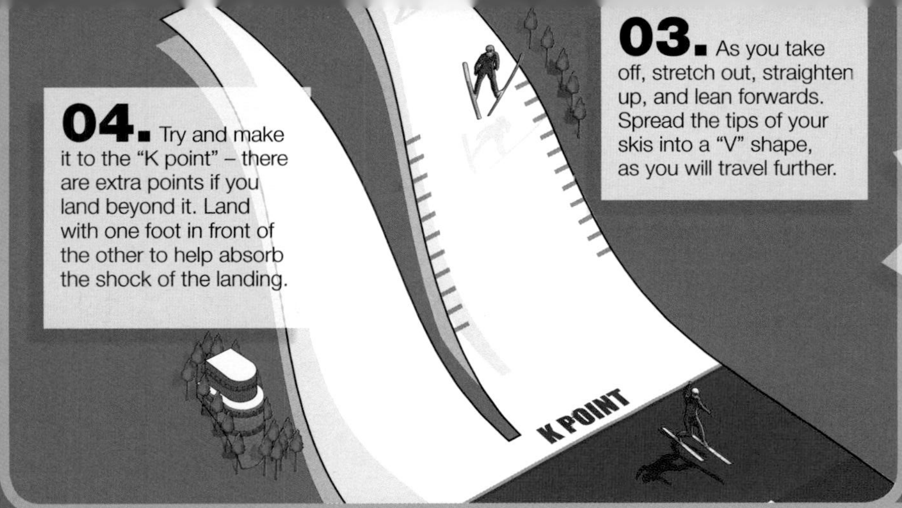

04. Try and make it to the "K point" — there are extra points if you land beyond it. Land with one foot in front of the other to help absorb the shock of the landing.

Multi-sport winter games

❄ **Winter Olympics** Held every four years since 1924.

❄ **Winter Paralympic Games** Held every four years since 1976.

❄ **Asian Winter Games** Held every four years since 1986.

❄ **Winter Universiade (World University Games)** Held every two years since 1960.

❄ **Arctic Winter Games** Held every two years since 1970.

❄ **World Eskimo-Indian Olympics** Held every year. Displays traditional skills of native American and Inuit peoples since 1961.

Ice fishing

✳ Ice fishing is a popular sport in frozen parts of Northern America, Europe, and Russia.

✳ Fishing takes place over a frozen body of still water (usually a lake). Anglers drill holes through the ice with an ice saw, auger, or chisel.

✳ Ice needs to be at least 10 cm (4 in) thick to support the weight of anglers.

✳ Some anglers use a stool to fish, while others build fancy cabins to live in for the season.

Tell me more: ice climbing

Boots: The boots have a stiff double-plastic to support the climber's ankles and bodyweight

Helmet: This protects a climber's head from falling clumps of ice

Ice tool: A double-sided pick and adze (chisel) to dig in to the ice

Gloves: Keep hands warm and protected in freezing conditions

Crampons: The spiky metal boot attachments are used to get a foot hold on ice

Ropes: This anchors the climber to the ice in case of a fall

Six cool **champs**

Lindsey Van
In 2009, American Lindsey Van became the first-ever female world ski-jumping champion at the Nordic World Ski championship in the Czech Republic. She soared to 97.5 m (319.8 ft).

Cindy Klassen
Speedskater Cindy Klassen is Canada's most successful female Olympian, winning five medals in the 2006 Winter Games in Turin, Italy. She featured on a Canadian 25-cent coin in 2010.

Jayne Torvill and Christopher Dean
The British skating couple received 12 perfect scores in the 1984 Winter Games in Sarajevo, Bosnia and Herzigovina, and went on to tour the world.

Wayne Gretzky
The retired Canadian hockey player with the National Hockey League was nicknamed the "Great One". He is also the only player to total 200 points in one season.

Ingemar Stenmark
The Swedish skier specializes in slalom and giant slalom. He has won more alpine ski competitions than any other skier, a total of 86 races, and has won the World Cup title three times.

Georg Hackl
Known as the "Flying Sausage", the German luge champion was the fastest in all four luge events at the 1998 Winter Olympics in Nagano, Japan.

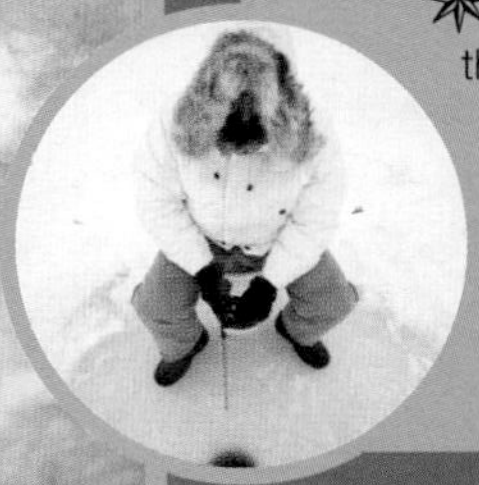

Rescue dogs
Some dogs are able to use their amazing sense of smell to track and locate missing people.

Herding dogs
These types of dog help farmers round up sheep or cattle, and move them to a new location.

Truffle dogs
These dogs can smell the rare underground truffle fungus, prized by chefs around the world as a delicacy.

Guide dogs
These clever dogs follow the commands of a visually impaired handler.

Guard dogs
Dogs with a fierce bark are used to guard private property and frighten intruders.

When does an **animal become a pet?**

When an animal has a name, it can be thought of as a pet. The first tamed beasts date back 14,000 years, with dogs trained to pull sleds or guard property. In this way, animals that could be relied upon to perform a particular task were eventually thought of as companions, or pets.

In numbers

61,080,000
The number of pet dogs in the USA

53,100,000
The number of pet cats in China

40
The number of babies that a female rabbit can produce each year

5,000
The number of British postal workers attacked by pet dogs each year

8 km
(4.9 miles) The distance that a caged hamster can run each day on its wheel

50 kph
(31 mph) The speed a domestic cat can run

Cat facts

- The first feline pet owners were the **Ancient Egyptians**. They tamed cats to hunt rodents, and protect their crops.
- In the Middle Ages, many cats were **considered to be witches**, and were killed on suspicion of witchcraft.
- When your cat drinks milk or water from a bowl, **tiny barbs on the cat's tongue** scoop it backwards into its mouth.
- Domestic cats can **purr when they inhale and exhale.** Purring can indicate contentment, fear, or pain.
- Cats use their **tail to balance.** About 10 per cent of the cat's bones are found in this part of the body.

Who's a bird brain?

Macaws
We can mimic a few words, but much prefer to screech! There are species of macaws living in Mexico, Central America, and South America.
African Greys
We are found in central Africa. I know about 1,000 words, so am undoubtedly the most intelligent parrot. Even so, I do enjoy mimicking household appliances.
Cockatoos
G'day mate! We sulphur-crested cockatoos are found in Australia, Indonesia, and New Guinea. With a bit of training, we can mimic human voices and pet sounds.
Crows
Many species of crows are found around the world. We are known to mimic humans talking, as well as the sounds of cats, dogs, hens, and roosters.

[redacted]

"Virtual" pets

- Computer pets are computer-generated and live on virtual pet websites (or software installed on your computer). You lose points if your pet gets hungry or dies.
- Electronic pets are sometimes attached to a keychain. You need to care for them by feeding them, or even taking them for "walks". They communicate with clicks and beeps.
- Stone age pets were the grooviest pets around in 1975. Pet rocks were sold with a training manual. According to the manual, pet rocks could be taught how to sit, roll over, and play dead. Did people have rocks in their heads?

ow to: **get a goldfish to eat from your hand**

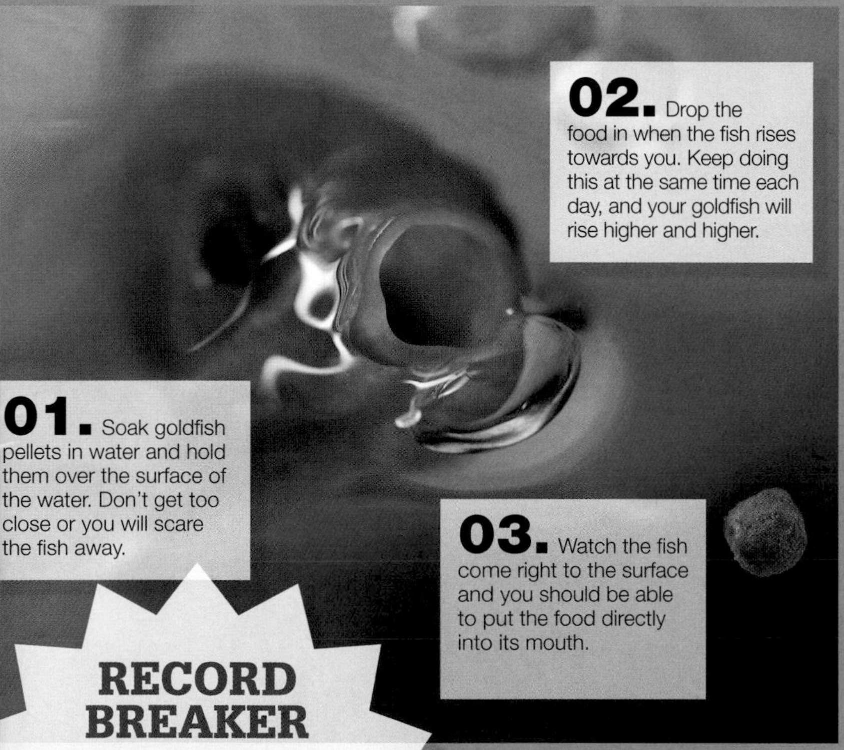

02. Drop the food in when the fish rises towards you. Keep doing this at the same time each day, and your goldfish will rise higher and higher.

01. Soak goldfish pellets in water and hold them over the surface of the water. Don't get too close or you will scare the fish away.

03. Watch the fish come right to the surface and you should be able to put the food directly into its mouth.

RECORD BREAKER

The world's **longest goldfish** was recorded in the Netherlands in 2003 measuring 47.4 cm (18.7 in).

Budgies
Budgerigars also hail from Australia. We are the most common pet parrot in the world. We can be trained to mimic human voices and whistle tunes.

Canine heroes

Bamse
This St Bernard dog that was known for his courage in the Norwegian navy during World War II, including saving a man who fell overboard in high seas.

Balto
A famous Siberian Husky that helped lead a dog sled team carrying a diptheria antitoxin to sick children in Nome, Alaska.

Hachiko
This loyal Japanese Akita dog waited every night for his owner at the railway station, 10 years after the owner's death.

Popular pets you can't cuddle

Salamander
This slippery amphibian species can grow back a missing arm, leg, or tail.

Scorpion
These arachnids have a sting in their tail. They need a good supply of beetles, spiders, or other creepy-crawlies for dinner.

Snake
This cold-blooded pet is known for its ability to escape from tanks. Make sure it isn't venomous or a constrictor.

Centipede
This mini-beast has between 20 and 300 legs. If you count them, you will always find an odd number of pairs.

Tarantulas
Be sure not to pat this hairy fellow. He may be one of the species of tarantulas that has hair that poisons and irritates when under attack.

Toads
Not the most attractive of pets, the "warts" on your toad are actually paratoid glands. These ooze a milky toxin to ward off predators.

[redacted]

[redacted]

[redacted]

[redacted]

[redacted]

[redacted]

[redacted]

WHAT'S IN A NAME?

In the 18th century, the **sandwich** was named after the 4th Earl of Sandwich, who liked eating beef served between slices of toast. This kept one hand free to play cards.

When was **ice cream invented?**

This deliciously frosty treat has royal beginnings. The Roman emperor Nero (37–68 CE) was said to enjoy ice shavings mixed with fruit. By the 6th century, China's Emperor Tang added milk to create a creamier confection. In 1672, England's King Charles II served ice cream at a royal banquet.

[redacted]

Pasta shapes

Everyone loves pasta, but if you don't speak Italian, you might not know exactly what you're eating. This list will help you make sense of all those names.

Campanelle – little bells
Canelloni – big pipes
Manicotti – sleeves
Tortellini – little turtles
Penne – quills (pens)
Conchiglie – shells
Farfalle – butterflies
Radiatori – radiators
Fusilli – rifles
Rotelle – wheels
Linguini – little tongues
Vermicelli – little worms
Orecchiette – little ears
Ditalini – little fingers
Gomito – elbow
Spaghetti – little twine
Capellini – fine hair
Fettucine – little ribbons

Creepy-crawly snacks

Tasty tarantulas
This spider is fried and served with spicy seasoning.

Roasted grasshoppers
A tasty treat seasoned with soy sauce and pepper.

Wriggly worms
Eat in salads or on toast for the full gastronomic experience.

Bamboo worms
Delicious to eat fried and served with Tom Yum powder.

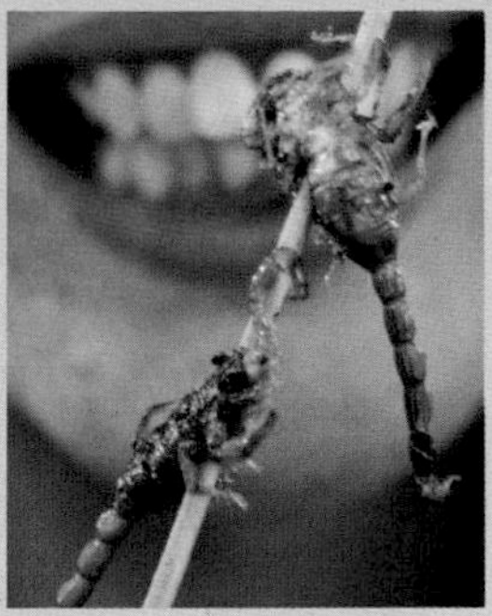

Snappy scorpions
Served dried and with dips, this snack has a bit of bite to it.

How to: **eat with chopsticks**

01. Hold one chopstick so it rests in the crook of your thumb and the top joint of your middle finger.

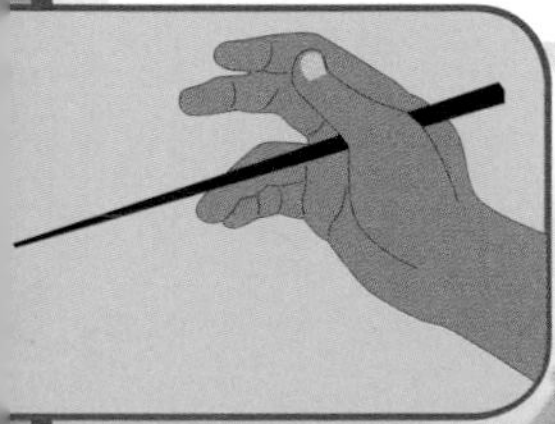

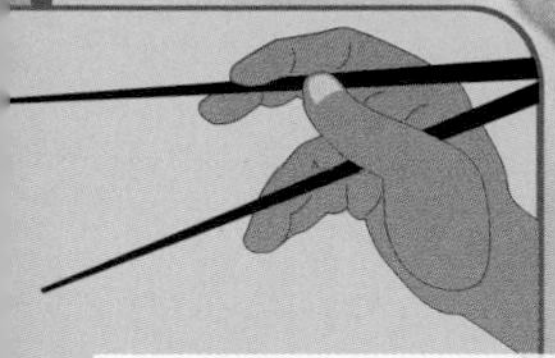

02. Hold the other chopstick above it between your thumb and forefinger.

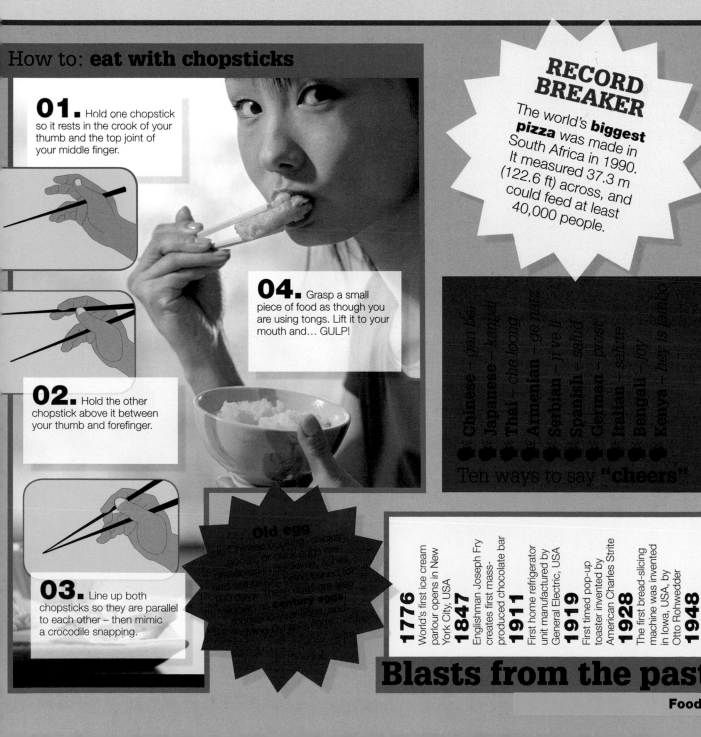

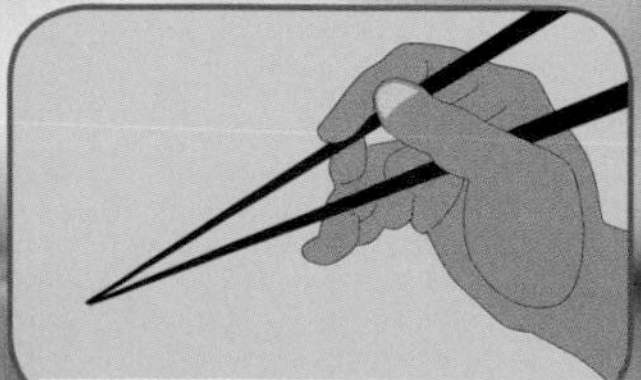

03. Line up both chopsticks so they are parallel to each other – then mimic a crocodile snapping.

04. Grasp a small piece of food as though you are using tongs. Lift it to your mouth and… GULP!

Old egg
In Chinese cooking, chicken, goose, or duck eggs are preserved in quicklime, ashes, and salt before being buried for 100 days. These eggs are also known as **century eggs**, thousand-year eggs, and Ming Dynasty eggs.

RECORD BREAKER
The world's **biggest pizza** was made in South Africa in 1990. It measured 37.3 m (122.6 ft) across, and could feed at least 40,000 people.

Ten ways to say **"cheers"**

- **Chinese** – *gan bei*
- **Japanese** – *kanpai*
- **Thai** – *che loong*
- **Armenian** – *ge naz*
- **Serbian** – *ji ve li*
- **Spanish** – *salud*
- **German** – *prost*
- **Italian** – *salute*
- **Bengali** – *joy*
- **Kenya** – *hey is jambo*

Blasts from the past

1776 World's first ice cream parlour opens in New York City, USA

1847 Englishman Joseph Fry creates first mass-produced chocolate bar

1911 First home refrigerator unit manufactured by General Electric, USA

1919 First timed pop-up toaster invented by American Charles Strite

1928 The first bread-slicing machine was invented in Iowa, USA, by Otto Rohwedder

1948 First drive-through burger restaurant with speaker system opened in USA

History

Who built **Stonehenge?**

Prehistoric farmers constructed the stone circle of Stonehenge in southern England about 5,000 years ago. It was an amazing feat of engineering, calling for careful planning, advanced construction skills, and the labour of vast numbers of people. This tells us that the site had great meaning and importance for the people who built it.

Lintel: Horizontal stone, lifted into place on wooden platforms
Trilithon: Stone arch made from two upright stones with a horizontal stone on top
Blocks: Cut to fit neatly into one another
Outer circle: Originally made up of a complete circle of linked stones

During the Stone Age, early humans used stone (as well as wood, shell, and bone) to make their weapons and tools. The **Stone Age** is divided into three periods: the Palaeolithic (Old Stone Age), Mesolithic (Middle Stone Age), and Neolithic (New Stone Age).

Five stone monuments **from around the world**

Great Pyramid
Built c. 2560 BCE as a tomb for the Egyptian pharaoh Khufu, this mountain of stone contains approximately 2,300,000 blocks.

Temple of the Sun
This huge pyramid was built c.300 CE in the ancient Mexican city of Teotihuacán, the largest city in Central America at that time.

Mayan pyramid
The Maya of Central America placed their ornately decorated temples at the top of steep-sided pyramids made of layers of stone.

Inca walls
The Incas of Peru slotted the blocks of their walls together so tightly, it is impossible to slip a knife blade between them.

Great Zimbabwe
Built about 700 years ago, the city of Great Zimbabwe was the centre of a rich gold-trading African kingdom.

Tell me more: **Stonehenge**

No one knows why Stonehenge was built, though there are many theories, ranging from an astronomical observatory to a place of human sacrifice. Sunlight pours into the centre at midwinter sunset and midsummer sunrise.

Blasts from the past

c. 2.6 million years ago
The start of the Palaeolithic Period; the first stone tools are used by early hominins (human ancestors) in Africa

40,000 years ago
Modern humans (*Homo sapiens*) have spread from Africa to Asia, Europe, and Australia

30,000 years ago
Hunters are using stone, bone, and antler tools, and the first cave art appears

c.10,000 years ago
The start of the Mesolithic Period; farming begins in the Middle East

8500 BCE
Wheat and barley are cultivated, and cattle, sheep, and pigs are domesticated in the Middle East

6500 BCE
Rice farming begins in China

c.4500 BCE
The start of the Neolithic Period in Europe; farming spreads throughout Europe

cle: Originally
sisted of
ween 60–80
/ stones
Bluestone: Brought from Preseli, Wales 386 km (240 miles) away
Sarsen: Upright stone, quarried 30 km (19 miles) away and probably brought to site on wooden rollers or sledges
Inner horseshoe: Made of five trilithons
Outer stones: Had been brought to the site by 2550 BCE – they replaced an earlier circle made of timber posts

WEIRD OR WHAT?

Contrary to popular belief, Celtic priests known as the **Druids** had nothing to do with Stonehenge. Druids were not around until more than 1,000 years after Stonehenge was completed.

I don't believe it!

Researchers in the USA recovered human DNA from a 14,300-year-old lump of fossilized human poo found in a cave in Oregon. The scientific name for fossilized poo is coprolite.

Mighty megaliths

- Prehistoric stone monuments are called "megaliths" (from the Greek word for "big stone").
- Megaliths are found in many parts of western Europe. They include menhirs (single standing stones), dolmens (two or more stone slabs capped by other slabs), passage graves, stone circles, and long stone avenues.
- At Newgrange in Ireland, a stone-lined passage grave was constructed so that a shaft of light would strike the back of the chamber at sunrise on the winter solstice (the shortest day of the year).
- Brittany, in western France, has impressive collections of megaliths. Most mysterious are those at Carnac, where more than 3,000 stones have been arranged in a series of straight lines.

Art class

- The earliest-known forms of body decoration are ostrich eggshell beads found at a burial site in Kenya. The beads are thought to be 46,000 years old.
- The Chauvet caves in southern France contain some of the earliest-known cave paintings, dating back 30,000 years.
- The Lascaux Caves, in southwestern France, have been closed to the public since 1963 as crowds were damaging the cave paintings. Exact replicas of the giant paintings of bulls, mammoth, wild oxen, and stags are on show at a visitor centre nearby.

Great leap forward

- During the Neolithic period (c. 4500 BCE – 2000 BCE in Britain), humans began to settle down in villages and grow their own food.
- This led to a rush of new inventions – pottery (to store grain), the wheeled cart (to carry heavy loads), and the plough.
- People started to make tools from copper and bronze. Iron-making spread between 1550 BCE and 700 BCE. Time to throw those stone tools away!

How to: make a hand axe

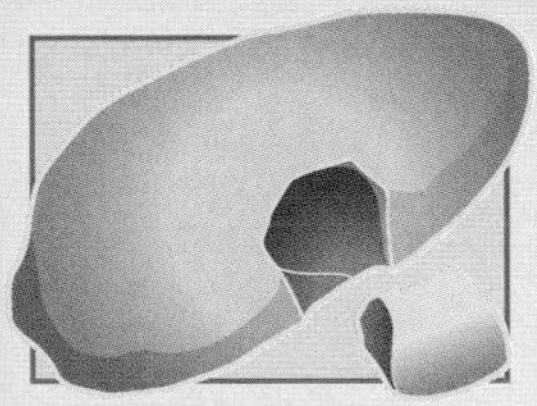

01. First, choose a hand-sized piece of flint for your axe. Then take a hard heavy stone (hammerstone) that will chip the flint.

02. Strike the hammerstone against the side of the flint and start to remove large broad flakes.

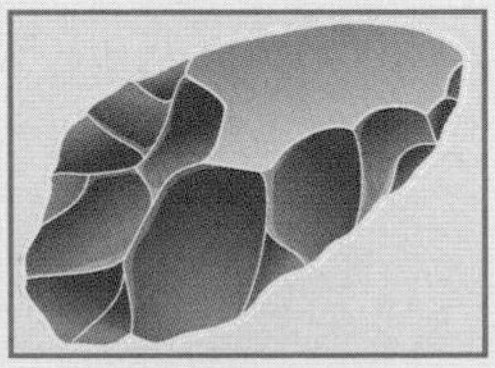

03. Carry on removing flakes from both sides of the flint until it is pear-shaped – rounded at one end and narrowing to a sharp tip at the other.

04. Now take a smaller hammerstone and work your way along the edges on both sides of the flint, polishing and smoothing away the sharp bits.

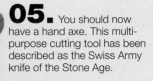

05. You should now have a hand axe. This multi-purpose cutting tool has been described as the Swiss Army knife of the Stone Age.

Early scripts

civilization	Sumerian (Iraq)	Egyptian	Chinese	Greek	Olmec (Mexico)
type of script	cuneiform	hieroglyphs	pictographs	alphabet	glyphs (symbols)
date	3200 BCE	3000 BCE	1400 BCE	800 BCE	500 BCE
writing method	blunt reed on wet clay	stone inscriptions; reed pen on papyrus (paper)	scratched on bones	carved on stone	carved on stone slabs

Record keepers
More than 5,000 years ago, farmers living in Sumeria in southern Mesopotamia (modern Iraq) began to draw pictures on **clay tablets** to keep track of how much grain they had in store, or how many sheep they owned.

When did people **start to write?**

There is no single date – writing emerged at different times in different parts of the world. The first writing began with people carving picture signs on wet clay, or on pieces of wood or stone (experts call these signs pictographs). Gradually, more signs were invented, giving rise to complex scripts.

Cunning cuneiform
Over time, Sumerian scribes found it was easier to make wedge-shaped stroke marks with a blunt reed pen than to draw pictures in wet clay. This form of writing is called **cuneiform** (from *cuneus*, the Latin word for "wedge").

Eight uses of early writing

01 Keeping track of goods, livestock, and business deals

02 Writing down laws for people to obey

03 Drawing up lists of goods for taxation

04 Sending messages over long distances

05 Writing letters to fellow rulers

06 Creating works of literature

07 Keeping records of rulers and events

08 Writing about the past, the gods, and the creation of the world

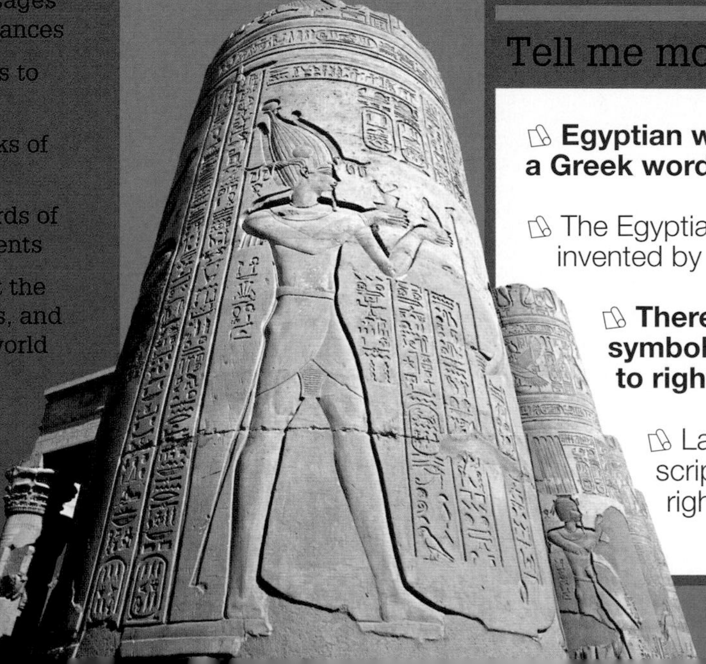

Tell me more: **Egyptian writing**

- **Egyptian writing is called hieroglyphs, from a Greek word meaning "sacred carvings".**
- The Egyptians believed that hieroglyphs were invented by Thoth, the god of learning.
- **There were more than 700 different symbols, which could be read from left to right, right to left, or top to bottom.**
- Later, the Egyptians developed a faster script called hieratic, which ran from right to left.

Language detective

When the Egyptian civilization ended, the use of hieroglyphs was forgotten – that is, until 1822, when a French scholar, Jean-François Champollion, studied the **Rosetta Stone**, a granite slab engraved with the same text written in three different scripts (hieroglyphs, a version of hieratic called demotic, and Greek). Champollion used the Greek script to crack the code.

Chinese writing

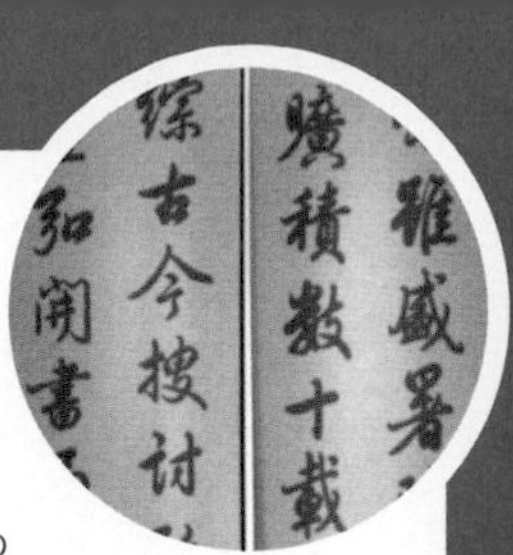

- The earliest Chinese writing was on oracle bones – pieces of ox bone or tortoise shell that were used to communicate with the gods.
- **By 500 BCE Chinese scribes were writing with ink and brushes on bamboo strips tied together to form a roll. They also wrote on silk cloth. Paper was invented in 104 CE.**
- Chinese is written with characters known as *hanzi*.
- **Twelve basic strokes are used to form the characters, and a character may consist of between 1 and 64 strokes.**

Indus
The people who lived in the Indus Valley (southern Asia) in about 2600 BCE wrote on tiny stone seals engraved with carvings of animals. No one has ever deciphered the script.

Etruscan
The Etruscans lived in Italy before the Romans. They used a form of the Greek alphabet and left thousands of stone inscriptions. Their language is unrelated to any known European language.

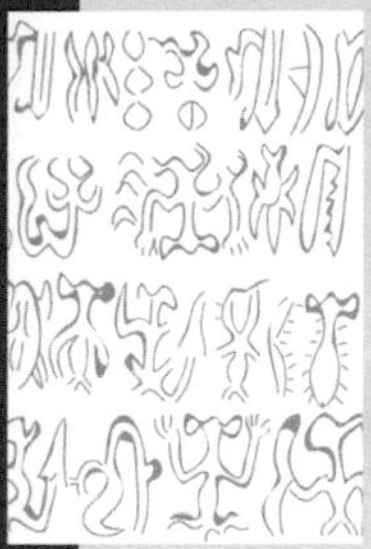

Rongorongo
This script was used by the people of Easter Island (Rapa Nui) in the Pacific Ocean. It has remained a mystery since its discovery in the 1860s.

How to: **make a sheet of papyrus**

01. Harvest the reeds with a sickle and trim off the bushy tops.

02. Cut the stems into lengths about 50 cm (20 in) long and peel away the outer skin. Slice the stems into strips.

03. Arrange the strips in a layer and then place another layer at right angles on top.

04. Cover with a piece of linen and put in a wooden press to release the sticky sap. This will bind the strips together. Hang out in the sun to dry.

05. When dry, write on one side of the papyrus sheet only.

WEIRD OR WHAT?

The Incas of Peru never learned to write, but they used **quipu** ("talking knots") to record and send information. Each quipu was made up of hundreds, sometimes thousands, of coloured strings made from llama or alpaca hair.

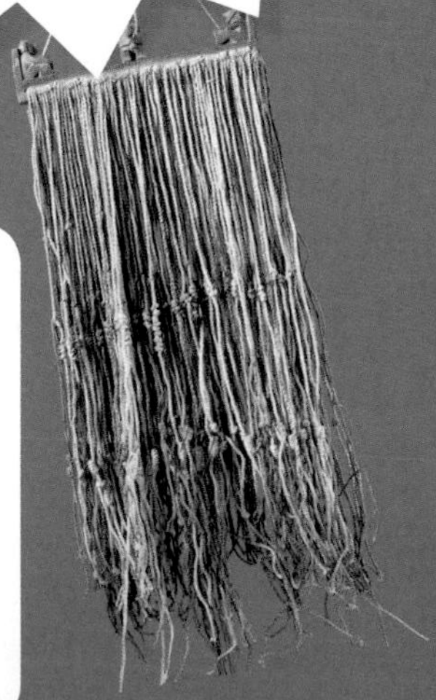

RECORD BREAKER

The oldest-known work of literature is ***The Epic of Gilgamesh***, a long poem from Sumeria that dates from about 2000 BCE.

Easy as ABC

01: The alphabet may have been invented by the Canaanites, who lived in the Gaza region 4,000 years ago.

02: They came up with the idea of using fewer than 30 letters or phonetic symbols (signs that represent speech sounds).

03: By 400 BCE, the alphabet had replaced cuneiform throughout the Middle East.

04: The Phoenicians, traders living in what is now Lebanon, passed the alphabet on to the Greeks, and it became the ancestor of all modern European alphabets.

FAST FACTS

Why would you want to be a mummy?

The word "mummy" was first used to describe the preserved bodies of Ancient Egyptians, but many other ancient cultures also mummified their dead, usually to prepare them for a life after death. Sometimes bodies are preserved naturally, in bogs or ice.

Taking care of mummy

The mummies of rich Egyptians were buried with lots of things they might need in the afterlife.

■ Models of slaves, called shabtis (below), were placed in the tomb to look after their masters in the afterlife.

■ Items of food, such as bread and figs, were left, and pictures of food were painted on the walls so the mummy did not go hungry.

■ For entertainment, toys and games were left in some tombs.

■ Glamorous mummies took combs, mirrors, wigs, and make-up to the grave.

WEIRD OR WHAT?

In east Asia, so-called **mermaid mummies** have been found. On closer inspection, these turned out to be made up of two different animals, such as the body of a monkey and the tail of a fish.

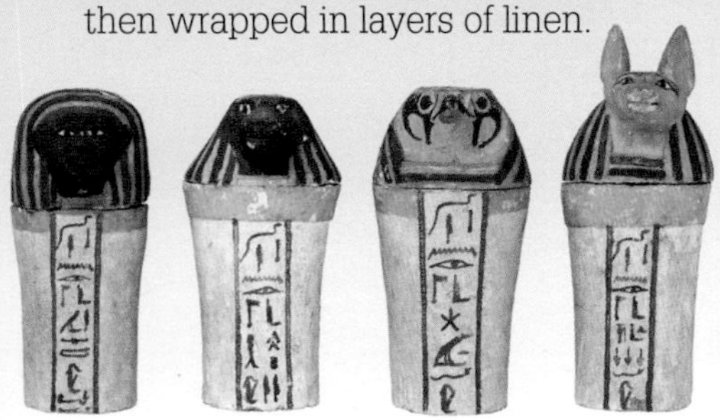

Tell me more: Egyptian mummy

After the mummy was wrapped in linen, a mask was fitted over the head, and amulets (magic charms) were put in place to protect the body from evil or to bring good luck.

Shroud: Final layer wrapping the body is called a shroud

Shabti figure: Model slave to help the dead person in the afterlife

Plaque of Anubis: Jackal-headed god of embalming and the guardian of cemeteries

Scarab beetle: Was a symbol of rebirth

Nut: Sky goddess, wraps her wings around the mummy

Rings: Personal jewellery was buried with the mummy

Gilded mask: Enabled a dead person's spirit to recognize its mummy

FAST FACTS

Stopping the rot

01: The Ancient Egyptians removed the liver, lungs, intestines, and stomach, and put them in canopic jars.

02: The brain was scooped out through the nose and thrown away as it was considered useless. The heart was left because it was thought to be the centre of intelligence.

03: The body was washed in wine and spices and covered with natron – a salt that dries out the body and kills bacteria – and left for 40 days.

04: When dry, the body was coated in oils to keep the skin lifelike.

05: The body was packed with linen, sand, or sawdust to give it shape then wrapped in layers of linen.

Liver Lungs Intestines Stomach

Canopic jars

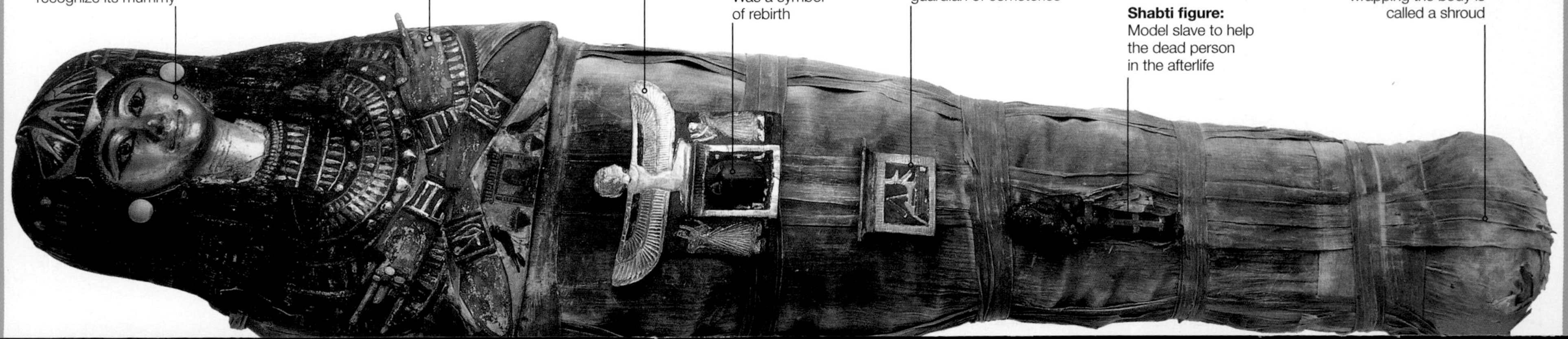

World of mummies

Many cultures have preserved their dead:

Greenland The Inuit preserved and prepared their dead for life in the "Land of the Dead"

China In the second century BCE, a Chinese princess was buried in a jade suit (right) in the mistaken belief that the gemstone would mummify her.

Crete Every year, the mummy of a Christian saint is carried through the streets of a Cretian town in a procession.

Andes The dead were preserved in ancient cultures across Columbia, Peru, Ecuador, and Chile. The Incas believed their dead king was a god and worshipped his mummy to keep him alive.

Sicily Around 400 years ago, on the Italian island of Sicily, mummification became fashionable. More than 6,000 mummies can be seen today in catacombs in Palermo.

Central Asia Scythian nomads, who roamed central Asia from 7th to the 3rd century BCE, were often mummified with their horses.

I don't believe it!

When experts in New York unwrapped an Egyptian mummy, the linen spanned an area of 895 sq m (9,634 sq ft) – enough to cover three tennis courts.

The curse of the mummy?

In 1923, Lord Carnarvon, one of the first to enter the tomb of **Tutankhamun**, died suddenly. It was said that he had been killed by the curse that protected the pharaoh, but no evidence of a curse has ever been found.

Top five ways to be naturally preserved

01: Covered in sand
A body dries out quickly in the desert, as the bacteria that cause a body to decay can't survive in the heat.

02: Bog bodies
Bodies have been preserved for thousands of years in peat bogs, where there is little oxygen.

03: Frozen solid
Decomposition is halted in extreme cold, such as at the polar regions.

04: Freeze-dried
Sometimes just very cold, dry conditions can preserve bodies.

05: Plaster casts
In 79 CE, the Roman residents of Pompeii in Italy were killed by ash from a volcano and became fossilized.

Gone but not forgotten

The bodies of these people have all been preserved.

Ötzi the Iceman
In 1991, walkers in the Alps discovered a body in the melting snow of a glacier. Ötzi, as the hunter was later named, turned out to be 5,300 years old.

Tutantkhamun
The tomb of this Egyptian pharaoh was intact when it was found in 1922. He was surrounded by all his treasures and wore this mask of solid gold.

Abraham Lincoln
When this great American president was assassinated in 1865, his body was embalmed so it could go on tour and people could pay their last respects.

Vladimir Lenin
When the revolutionary Russian leader Vladimir Lenin died in 1924, his body was preserved. His mummy can still be visited in Moscow's Red Square today.

Eva Perón
Known as Evita, the wife of the president of Argentina was much loved. When she died in 1952, her body was embalmed so the Argentinian people could still see her.

Ancient Egyptian animal mummies

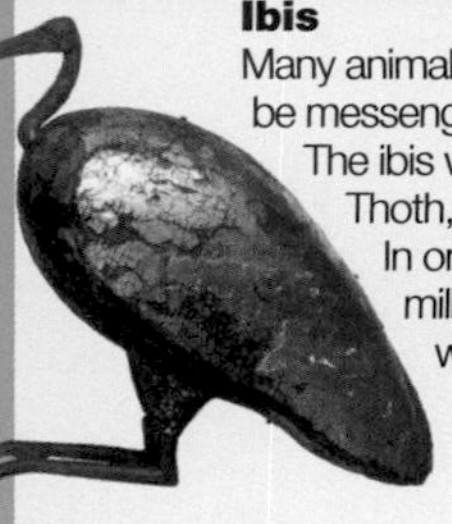

Ibis
Many animals were thought to be messengers of the gods. The ibis was sacred to Thoth, god of scribes. In one cemetery, four million ibis mummies were found.

Jackals
The jackal was sacred to Anubis, the jackal-headed god of embalming, and worshipped in life and death.

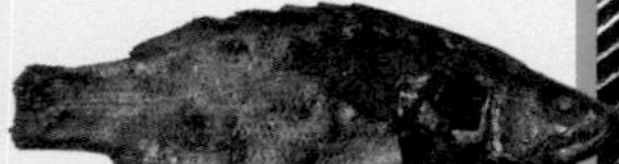

Fish
In some parts of Egypt, even fish were holy and were mummified and dedicated to the gods.

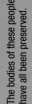

Crocodiles
Sacred to the river god, Sobek, many crocodile mummies have been discovered. The largest was 4.6 m (15 ft) long.

Cats
Cats were mummified to honour the cat goddess Bastet, and also because they were often favourite pets who could keep their owners company in the afterlife.

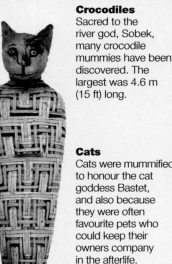

Who built the **first cities?**

The Sumerians – a people who lived in southern Mesopotamia (modern Iraq) more than 5,000 years ago. The Sumerians also invented wheeled carts and one of the earliest-known writing systems. These developments mark them out as the world's first true civilization.

Tell me more: **Teotihuacán**

In 300 CE, the ancient city of Teotihuacán covered an area of 31 sq km (12 sq miles), making it the largest city in Mesoamerica (Central America) at that time. All the buildings in the city were painted, many with mythological scenes.

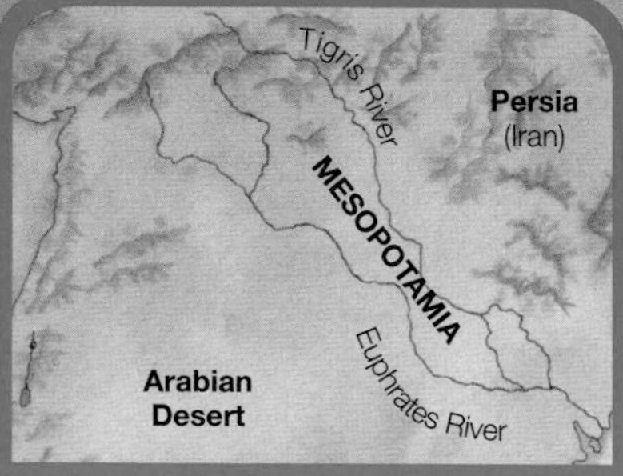

What's in a name?

Mesopotamia means "the land between two rivers" and refers to the fertile floodplain between the Tigris and Euphrates rivers.

The **Phoenicians** were a nation of seafarers and traders. They were famous for their purple dye extracted from the mucus of the murex sea snail. Snails were collected in large vats and left to rot, causing a foul stench – yuck!

RECORD BREAKER

The **Pyramid of the Sun** in the city of Teotihuacán was the largest pyramid in Mesoamerica, rising 63 m (207 ft) tall. A tunnel under the pyramid leads to caves that were once used for religious ceremonies.

Call yourself civilized?

You and your tribe have given up hunting and gathering to become settled farmers. Are you a civilization yet? Tick the boxes and check your score (bottom right) to find out.

- ❑ You build cities, and your farmers grow enough food to feed the urban population.
- ❑ You have a king and a powerful ruling elite.
- ❑ Your rulers build great tombs for themselves.
- ❑ You have priests to perform religious rituals to your gods.
- ❑ You have engineering skills and can organize huge teams to build temples and monuments.
- ❑ You are using bronze for weapons and decorative items.
- ❑ You have an army to fight against neighbouring states.
- ❑ You can write, keep records, and have a system of laws.

Blasts from the past

3400 BCE Cities develop in southern Mesopotamia

2600–1800 BCE Urban-based civilization settles in the Indus valley (southern Asia)

c.2530 BCE Great Pyramid of Khufu is built in Egypt

2000–1600 BCE Minoan civilization at its height in the Mediterranean

1766–1122 BCE The Shang dynasty rules in China

1400–800 BCE The Olmecs and Zapotecs establish the first states in Mexico

900–800 BCE City-states develop in Greece

559–530 BCE The Persians conquer Mesopotamia

509 BCE The Roman Republic is founded

490 BCE The Greeks defeat the Persians at the Battle of Marathon

334–330 BCE Alexander the Great conquers Egypt and Persia

221 BCE Shi Huangdi (the First Emperor) unites China

30 BCE The Romans take control of Egypt, ending 3,000 years of independent Egyptian civilization

Walled cities

The rulers of the **Shang Dynasty** of China (1766–1122 BCE) built large sprawling cities surrounded by strong walls of trampled earth. Within the walls were royal palaces, temples, workshops, and houses.

Coining it

Early civilizations did not have money, but traded by bartering (exchanging) goods of equal value. The first coins were issued in Lydia (in modern Turkey) in about 650 BCE.

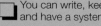

Quetzalcoatl
This carved stone head is of Quetzalcoatl, a Mesoamerican god of nature whose name means "feathered serpent".

Burial masks
The people of Teotihuacán covered the faces of their dead with burial masks, such as this one made of turquoise and coral.

Wall paintings
Frescoes and paintings discovered at Teotihuacán include images of people, gods, and animals such as coyotes and jaguars.

Mohenjo-Daro
From about 2600 BCE, the people of the Indus Valley in Asia started building the world's first planned cities. The city of Mohenjo-Daro is the best preserved **Indus city**. Built on a grid pattern, it had a population of up to 40,000 and contained mud-brick houses, temples, and workshops as well as a centrally heated public bath house.

Seven wonders **of the Ancient World**

01: Great Pyramid of Giza (above) Built in Egypt c.2530 BCE

02: Hanging Gardens of Babylon Thought to be the palace gardens of King Nebuchadnezzar II

03: Statue of Zeus at Olympia Carved by Greek sculptor Phidias c.435 BCE

04: Temple of Artemis at Ephesus Destroyed by Gothic tribes in 262 CE

05: Mausoleum at Halicarnassus Marble tomb of King Mausolus

06: Colossus of Rhodes Giant statue of the Sun god Helios

07: Lighthouse of Alexandria The second highest building after the pyramids, destroyed 1365 CE

FAST FACTS

Minoans and Mycenaeans

01: The Minoans, who lived on the island of Crete, were the first European civilization.

02: Their kings built great palaces decorated with wall paintings.

03: The Minoans were skilled sailors and traded throughout the Mediterranean.

04: Many Minoan palaces were damaged by a volcanic eruption that blew apart the neighbouring island of Thera in 1626 BCE.

05: In about 1450 BCE, the Mycenaeans invaded Crete, bringing Minoan civilization to an end.

06: The Mycenaeans were a warrior people from mainland Greece.

07: They lived in fortified palaces and loved gold, hunting, and warfare.

08: Their civilization collapsed c.1200 BCE when the eastern Mediterranean was attacked by invaders known as the Sea Peoples.

Mycenaean gold death mask

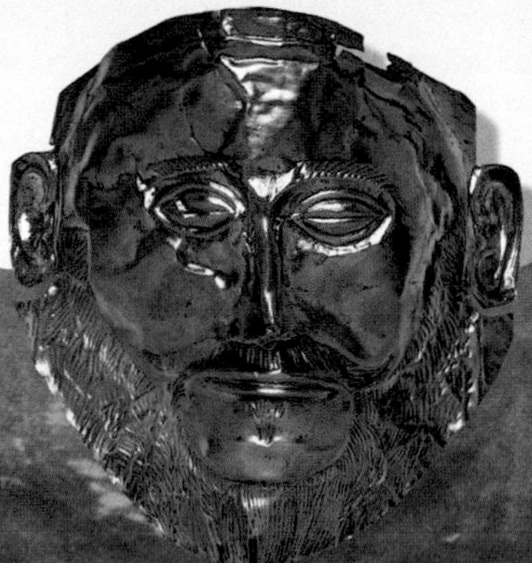

Ancient warfare

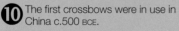

10 Wars, fought for control of water and trade, were frequent between the early city-states of Mesopotamia.

10 Light, highly mobile two-wheeled war chariots were in use by 1700 BCE.

10 The composite bow – a short bow that would bend without breaking – spread to the Middle East from Central Asia.

10 Iron swords came into use c.1000 BCE. They had a sharper edge than bronze swords, and were cheaper to produce.

10 The first crossbows were in use in China c.500 BCE.

10 The Greeks fought on foot with long spears. They charged the enemy in tight formations, called phalanxes, behind a wall of shields.

10 The Greeks also fought sea battles with warships called triremes.

10 The Romans had the first professional army in the world.

SCORES: 6 to 8: Well done, you're a class act
4 to 6: On the road to civilization, but not there yet **0 to 3:** Must try harder

Greeks versus Romans

Who had greater influence – the Greeks or the Romans? The Greeks were great thinkers and philosophers, while the Romans were skilled builders and engineers. Here are some of their great ideas to help you decide.

Ten Greek achievements

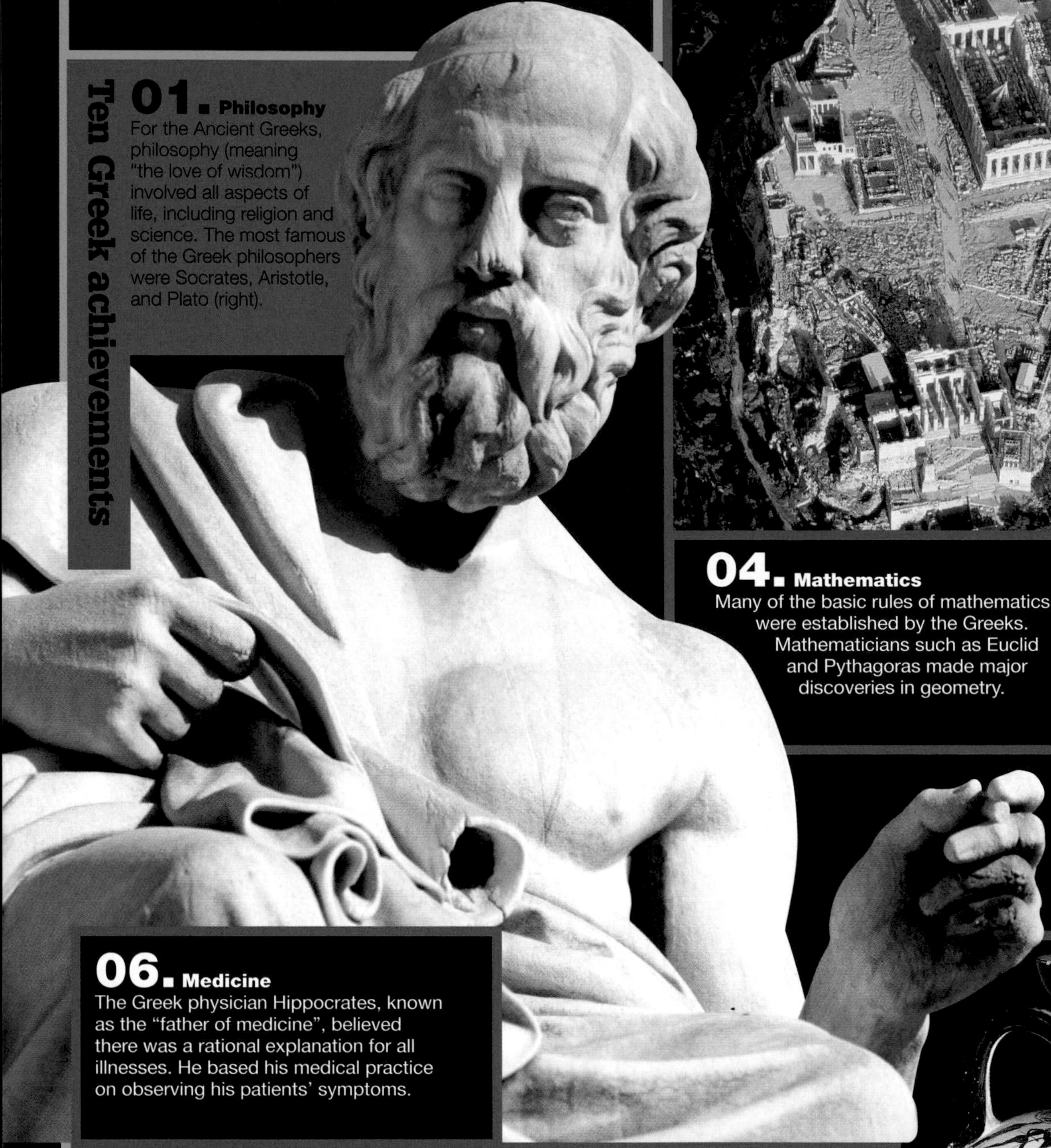

01. Philosophy
For the Ancient Greeks, philosophy (meaning "the love of wisdom") involved all aspects of life, including religion and science. The most famous of the Greek philosophers were Socrates, Aristotle, and Plato (right).

02. Architecture
The Greeks built large stone temples such as the Parthenon (left) in Athens. The proportions of classical Greek buildings were calculated to give an impression of balance and elegance.

03. Politics
Ancient Greece was made up of hundreds of separate city-states, each with its own laws, rulers, and system of government. Our word "politics" comes from the Greek word *polis*, meaning "city-state".

04. Mathematics
Many of the basic rules of mathematics were established by the Greeks. Mathematicians such as Euclid and Pythagoras made major discoveries in geometry.

05. Theatre
The Greeks built open-air theatres (such as the one above) where plays were performed as part of religious festivals. Many Greek plays can still be seen in theatres today.

06. Medicine
The Greek physician Hippocrates, known as the "father of medicine", believed there was a rational explanation for all illnesses. He based his medical practice on observing his patients' symptoms.

07. Archimedes' screw
This machine, shaped like a large screw, was designed to pump water. It is thought to have been invented by Archimedes, who is famous for shouting "*Eureka*" ("I've found it") after solving a mathematical problem in the bath.

08. Pottery
The Greeks were known for their highly decorated pottery, often showing scenes from everyday life. Artists painted black figures on red or orange backgrounds.

09. Olympic Games
The first Olympic Games were staged in Greece in 776 BCE. The most challenging event was the Pentathlon, which included jumping, running, wrestling, and throwing the discus and javelin.

10. History
The Greeks produced the first true historians, who wrote accurate accounts of the events of their day. Greek author Herodotus was the first historian to write about events in prose, rather than verse.

Ten Roman achievements

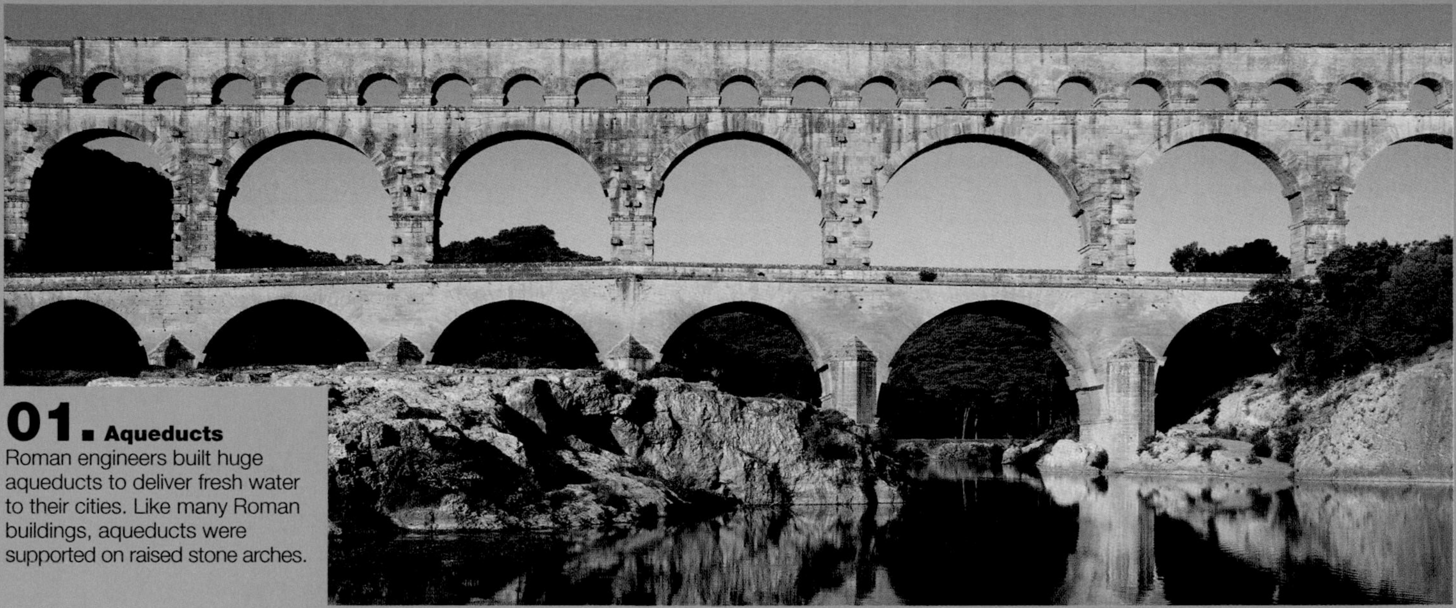

01. Aqueducts
Roman engineers built huge aqueducts to deliver fresh water to their cities. Like many Roman buildings, aqueducts were supported on raised stone arches.

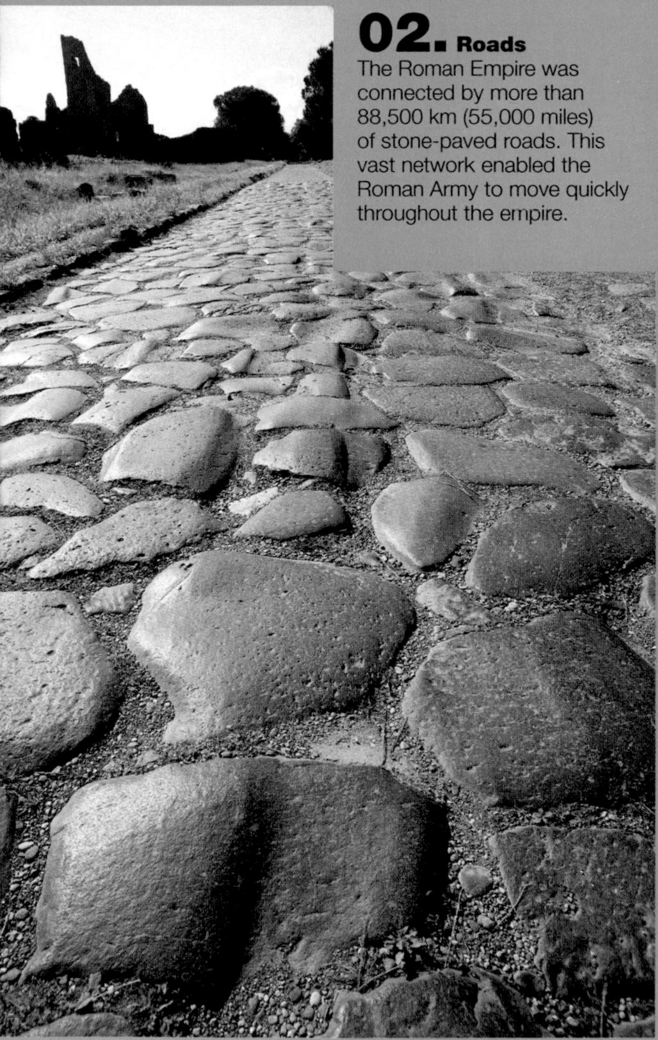

02. Roads
The Roman Empire was connected by more than 88,500 km (55,000 miles) of stone-paved roads. This vast network enabled the Roman Army to move quickly throughout the empire.

03. Concrete
The Romans made concrete from a mixture of burned chalk, volcanic sand, and crushed rocks. They also perfected a type of concrete that hardened in water, which was useful for building docks and harbours.

04. Central heating
Public baths, and villas belonging to wealthy Romans, were heated by underfloor heating systems called hypocausts. An underground furnace sent hot air through the floors and up through spaces between the walls.

05. Domes
The Romans were the first to create buildings with domed ceilings. The vast concrete dome of the Pantheon in Rome contains 140 hollow squares that help to reduce its weight.

06. Apartment blocks
Built to solve Rome's housing shortage, apartment blocks were often six or seven storeys high and lacked running water. Many were dangerously overcrowded.

07. Roman law
The Romans didn't invent laws, but the uniform system of law they imposed throughout their empire has been a major influence on all later Western legal systems.

08. Books
In the 2nd century CE, the Romans produced books with bound pages, called *codices*. These were much easier to read than long, rolled scrolls.

09. Calendar
The calendar we use today is based on the Roman calendar introduced by Julius Caesar in 45 BCE. Before Caesar, the Roman year was only 355 days long.

10. Glass
Though not the first to use glass, the Romans developed glassblowing techniques and invented window glass. One Roman glassmaker is even said to have come up with a formula for unbreakable glass!

Why did medieval people **build castles?**

Castles were fortified houses where kings and lords lived with their families, soldiers, and servants. They were built to provide shelter from enemy armies, and to show off the wealth and power of the people who lived in them – the bigger the castle, the more important you were.

Quick guide to castle building

01 The first medieval castles in Europe were built of wood, usually on top of a small mound.

02 Later, castles were built of stone with a central square tower (keep).

03 Stone castles then began to sprout towers and battlements.

04 European soldiers adapted Muslim castle-building techniques after the Crusades – wars between Christians and Muslims in the Middle East.

05 The most important castle in England was the Tower of London (above), built by William the Conqueror.

Tell me more: **inside a castle**

In medieval Europe, castles usually contained lavish private rooms for the lord and his guests, as well as a chapel, storerooms, and a Great Hall for entertaining.

Spicing it up
The crusaders brought back many new products from the **Middle East**, including spices, cosmetics (henna and rouge), perfumes, and tapestries (to hang on draughty castle walls).

Great Hall: The grandest room in the castle, used for banquets

Lord's rooms

Guard room: Where soldiers ate, slept, and relaxed

Murder hole: Designed for pouring boiling water or oil on the heads of attackers

Basement: Used for storage

Military parade

Agra Fort, India
Built for the Mughal emperors of India.

Carcassone, France
A medieval fortified city consisting of two ramparts and 53 towers.

Himeji Castle, Japan
Towering Japanese castle famous for its white walls.

Krak des Chevaliers, Syria
The largest and most formidable of the crusader castles.

I don't believe it!

Toilets in castles were small rooms where medieval people stored their clothes and other valuables. At one end was a hole with a wooden seat over it. This was the toilet, which emptied down a chute straight into the castle moat.

FAST FACTS

How the feudal system worked

01: Medieval kings granted land to their lords in return for military support.

02: Lords kept their own army of knights in their castles.

03: It became expensive having to feed a lot of knights, so the lord granted them estates of land, called manors.

04: Manors usually came with a house, church, village, fields, woods, and orchards.

05: Peasants did all the hard work on the manor. They had to farm the lord's fields, as well as their own, and pay him rent.

The lady of the castle **(châtelaine)** supervised spinning and weaving, organized the herb garden, and prepared **simples** (herbal remedies).

How to: rescue a damsel

01 Try knocking down the walls with a trebuchet – a contraption that hurls large stones.

02 Prop a tall ladder against the tower. Watch out for soldiers waiting to pour boiling oil on your head.

03 Pound the walls with a battering ram (a heavy log).

04 Dig tunnels under the tower and start brushwood fires to bring the foundations down.

05 If all else fails, bribe a servant to open the door and let you in.

Castle diner

- Meals were eaten in the castle hall at long wooden tables.
- The main meal was at midday and consisted of three or four courses.
- People used their own knives (forks were unknown).
- Food was served on wooden plates, or sometimes on slabs of dry bread (trenchers).
- Minstrels and jugglers provided live entertainment on special occasions.

Killer thriller

Knights honed their battle skills by fighting **tournaments** (mock battles). These could get out of hand. In 1241, 80 knights died in a single tournament at Neuss in Germany.

Malbork Castle, Poland
The largest medieval castle in Europe.

Neuschwanstein Castle, Germany
19th-century fantasy castle built by Bavarian king, Ludwig II.

Rumelian Castle, Turkey
Fortress guarding the narrowest part of the Bosporus Strait.

Windsor Castle, England
The world's largest inhabited castle and one of the official homes of the British monarch.

What was the Black Death?

It was deadly outbreak of bubonic plague that spread to Europe from Asia and killed an estimated 25 million people between 1348–1351. Victims developed painful lumps called buboes, which turned red and black. Most people died within three days of falling sick, many within 12 hours.

Beat that!
Medieval people had no idea that **fleas** were spreading the Black Death. They thought that God had sent the plague to punish them for their sins. To show remorse, groups of people called **flagellants** went from town to town whipping themselves with leather straps. It didn't help, and the Pope ordered them to stop.

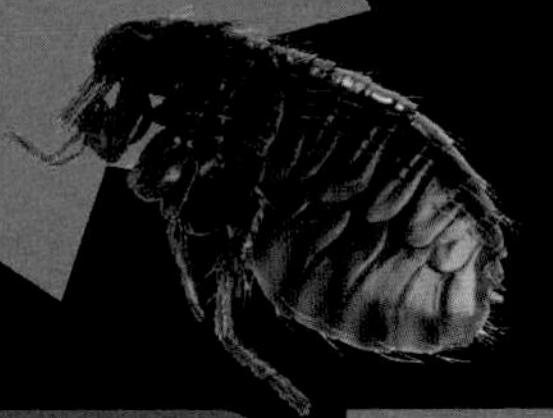

FAST FACTS

Bubonic plague

01: The first recorded outbreak of bubonic plague was in 542 CE, when it struck the city of Constantinople (now Istanbul, Turkey).

02: The Black Death killed 75 million people in Asia, three times more than in Europe.

03: Outbreaks of bubonic plague returned to Europe many times between 1400 and 1700.

04: In the 19th century, bubonic plague killed millions of people in China and India.

05: The cause of bubonic plague is a bacteria called *Yersinia pestis* (below).

06: Today, bubonic plague can be treated with antibiotics. Up to 3,000 cases are reported worldwide each year.

Tell me more: **how the Black Death spread**

- A series of bad harvests in Europe had caused widespread malnutrition, lowering the population's resistance to disease.
- Fleas, feeding on rats infected by the plague-causing bacteria, passed it on to humans.
- Rats were common on ships, and carried the disease along trade routes.
- Coughing and sneezing also helped to spread the disease.

Peasants revolt

- After the Black Death, many villages throughout England were deserted.
- Many peasants who did survive left their villages to work in towns.
- Wages fell, taxes rose, and the people began to feel very angry.
- In 1381, a peasant army, led by Wat Tyler, marched on London and rampaged through the city.
- King Richard II rode out to talk to the peasants. Tyler was killed, and the rest of the peasants slunk off home.

Three curious cures

01: Cut open the swelling with a sharp knife and cover with a warm layer of butter, onion, and figs to draw the poison out.

02: Take a live frog and rub its belly on the swelling (some people say a dried toad will do just as well).

03: Drink a glass of urine twice a day.

Plague symptoms

- Violent headache, chills, and vomiting
- Lumps the size of an orange under the arms
- Black boils and spots over the body
- Bloody flux (diarrhoea)
- Excruciating pain in every limb

Ten plagues of Egypt

According to the Bible, God unleashed ten plagues on Egypt when the pharaoh refused to let Moses lead the Jewish people out of captivity.

01: Nile turned to blood
02: Plague of frogs
03: Plague of gnats
04: Plague of flies
05: Death of livestock
06: Plague of boils
07: Hail
08: Plague of locusts
09: Darkness
10: Death of all firstborn sons

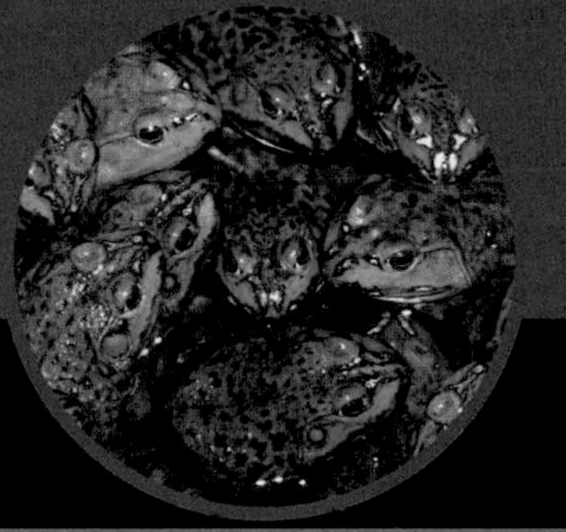

The **Arawaks**, the first people Christopher Columbus encountered in the New World, were virtually wiped out by disease within a few years of European contact. They had no immunity to common European diseases such as smallpox, measles, and influenza.

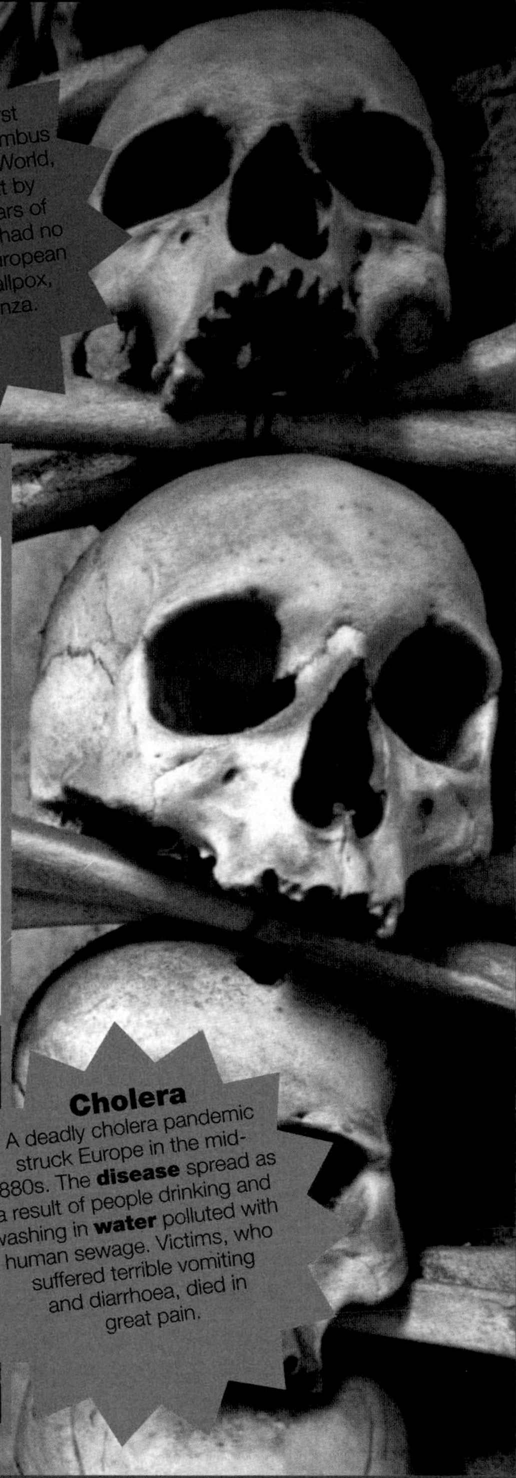

Tell me more: **pandemics**

- A pandemic is a disease that spreads around the world or throughout a whole country.
- A smallpox pandemic swept through the Roman Empire in the 2nd century CE.
- The deadliest pandemic in history was the outbreak of Spanish flu (1918–1919), which killed more than 50 million people worldwide.
- Spanish flu was caused by a strain of the influenza A (H1N1) virus, similar to the one responsible for the 2009 swine flu pandemic.

Workmen building London's Underground system dug into **plague pits** – communal graves for victims of the Great Plague of 1665. Luckily, they didn't come out in spots!

Cholera
A deadly cholera pandemic struck Europe in the mid-1880s. The **disease** spread as a result of people drinking and washing in **water** polluted with human sewage. Victims, who suffered terrible vomiting and diarrhoea, died in great pain.

Five pioneers in the fight against disease

Edward Jenner (1749–1823) Introduced vaccination to protect against smallpox.

Louis Pasteur (1822–1895) Developed the first vaccines and proved that most infectious diseases are caused by micro-organisms.

Joseph Lister (1827–1912) Championed the use of antiseptics during surgery.

Robert Koch (1843–1910) His research into bacteria led to life-saving changes in public health and sanitation.

Alexander Fleming (1881–1955) Discovered penicillin, the source of the first antibiotic drug.

What is **gunpowder** made of?

Gunpowder is an explosive mixture of sulphur, charcoal, and saltpetre (potassium nitrate). In the past, saltpetre was obtained from urine or animal manure. Gunpowder manufacturers collected urine in large vats and filtered it through straw to extract the nitrate salts.

Gunpowder was invented in the 9th century by the **Chinese**, who used it to make fireworks and weapons. It completely changed the face of warfare, both on land and at sea.

FAST FACTS

How gunpowder changed warfare

01: Firearms (guns) first appeared in Europe in the early 14th century.

02: Cannons could be used to knock down walls, so sieges became more common.

03: Bullets could penetrate armour and bring down horses from greater distances.

04: Gunpowder and weapons became so expensive that only kings could afford to go to war.

05: Unarmed nations were unable to resist armed invaders. As a result, European nations were able to colonize most of the world.

Crew members who kept the cannons supplied with gunpowder on warships were known as **powder monkeys**. They were often boys as young as 10 years old.

01. Open the small hatch at the side of the ship in front of the cannon, secure the hatch door with rope, then push the front of the cannon through.

02. Make sure the barrel of the cannon is clean – use a damp sponge to put out any sparks from the previous shot.

Sponge on a stick

03. Push a gunpowder charge down the barrel with a rammer. Then insert a rope wad and add the shot.

Rammer

Powder charge

Rope wad

Cannon ball
Heavy round ball usually made of iron. Used to put holes in enemy ships.

Chain shot
Two or more cannon balls linked by a chain. Used to tear down a ship's rigging.

Canister shot
Two or more pieces of shot joined by a bar.

Grape shot
Iron or lead balls bound in a canvas bag. Used to maim or kill the enemy.

Mons Meg (1449)
One of the world's oldest cannons, it was used in several battles against the English. It is now kept in Edinburgh Castle, Scotland.

Great Turkish Bombard (1464)
A Turkish cannon that could fire a stone ball weighing 300 kg (660 lb) more than 1.6 km (1 mile).

Tsar Cannon (1586)
Designed to fire grapeshot, the Tsar is the largest cannon ever made. It is now housed in the Kremlin, Moscow.

Big Bertha (1914)
Super-heavy gun built for the German Army in 1914 and named after Bertha, wife of the armaments manufacturer, Gustav Krupp.

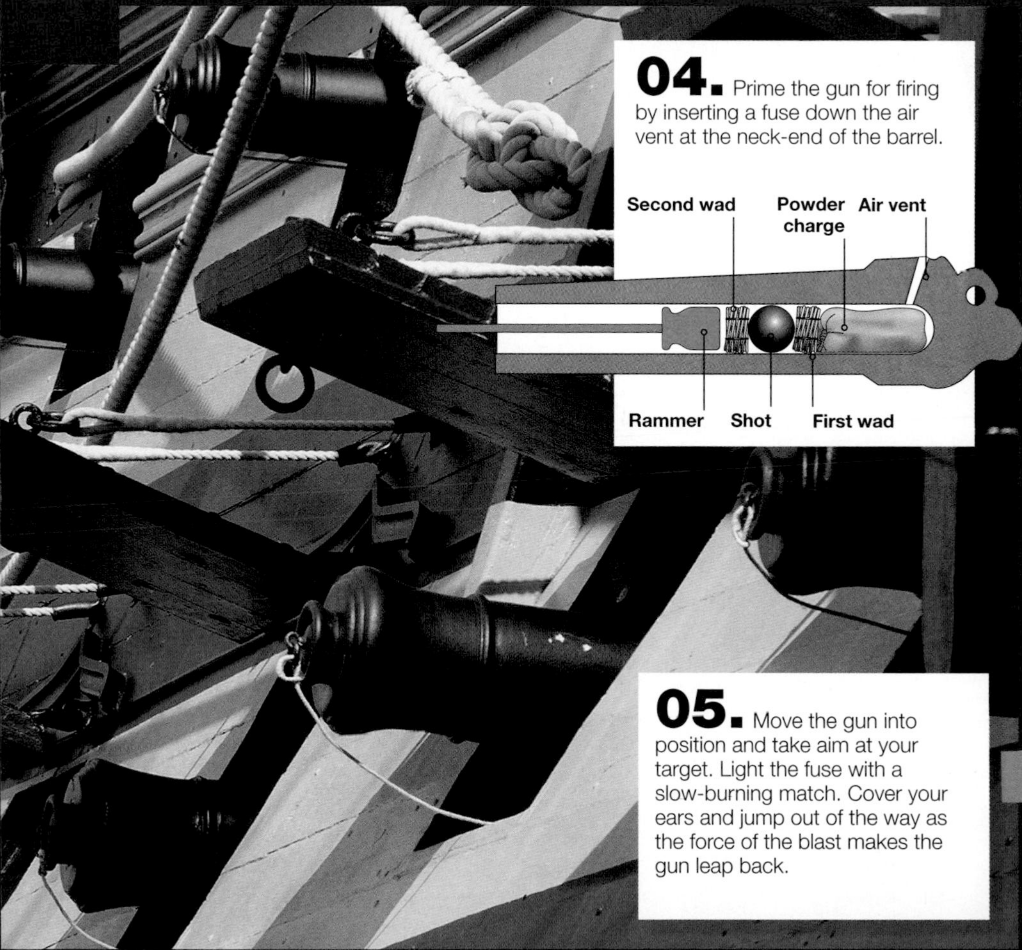

04. Prime the gun for firing by inserting a fuse down the air vent at the neck-end of the barrel.

05. Move the gun into position and take aim at your target. Light the fuse with a slow-burning match. Cover your ears and jump out of the way as the force of the blast makes the gun leap back.

A surgeon in Napoleon's army once used **gunpowder** to **season horsemeat** for the troops when supplies of salt ran low.

1126
The Chinese use bamboo tubes filled with gunpowder to launch flames; by the end of the 10th century, firebombs have begun to appear

1250
Knowledge of gunpowder has spread from China to Japan, central Asia, and the Middle East

1267
English scholar Roger Bacon describes how gunpowder is made

1326
The city of Florence in Italy orders the manufacture of cannons and cannon balls

1453
Ottoman sultan Mehmet II uses cannons to bring down the walls of Constantinople

1500
Hand cannons that can be fired by one man are in general use

Food notes

Gunpowder tea is a type of green tea produced in China. The leaves are steamed, rolled into small round pellets, and dried. The result is said to look like gunpowder.

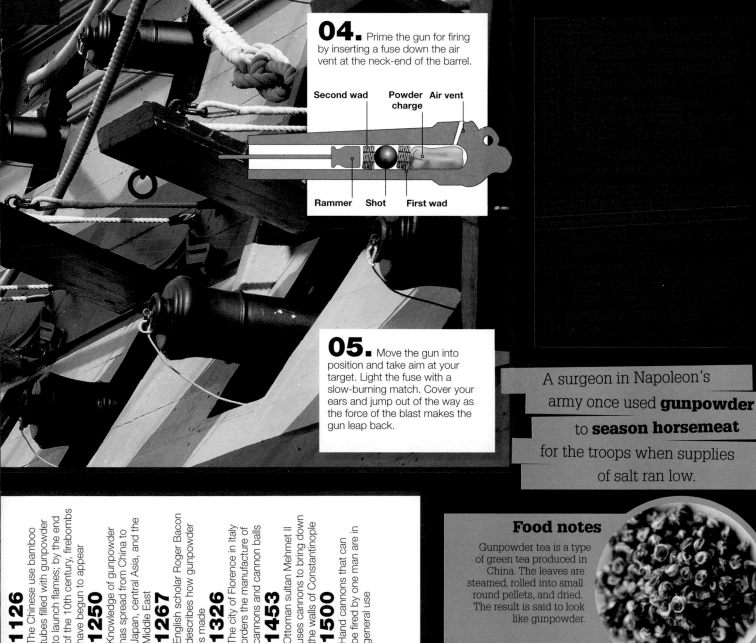

How did **trade** change the world?

In the 16th century, European sailors crossed the Atlantic to colonize the Americas and discovered new trade routes to the rich markets of Asia. As trade went global, European nations fought wars to defend their share of it, and transported people, food, plants, and livestock to their colonies around the world.

Tell me more: **the slave trade**

■ **British merchants sailed their ships, loaded with guns, cloth, and other goods, to trading forts in West Africa.**

■ There, they exchanged their cargoes for slaves who had been rounded up by African slave traders.

■ **Many slaves did not survive the terrible voyage to the Caribbean.**

■ On arrival, the slaves were sold to plantation owners and put to work.

■ **The ships were then loaded with cargoes of sugar, tobacco, or cotton and returned to their home ports.**

■ In 1807, the British Parliament voted to abolish the slave trade.

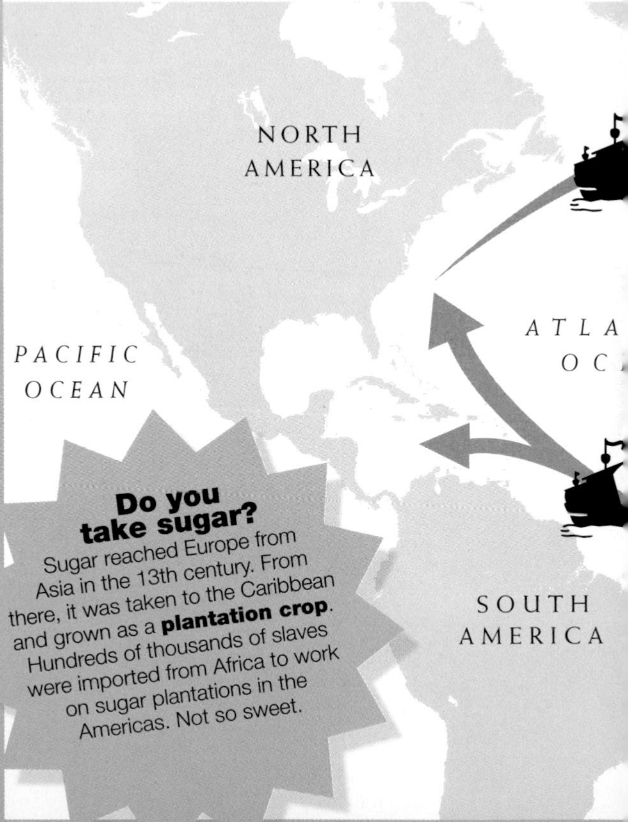

Do you take sugar?

Sugar reached Europe from Asia in the 13th century. From there, it was taken to the Caribbean and grown as a **plantation crop**. Hundreds of thousands of slaves were imported from Africa to work on sugar plantations in the Americas. Not so sweet.

Four things that enabled European sailors to conquer the oceans

01 Caravel: A small, fast ship, suitable for long ocean voyages.

02 Magnetic compass: Introduced in the 12th century, it contained a magnetic needle that pointed north.

03 Astrolabe: A navigational device adopted from the Arabs.

04 Ship-mounted cannon: Gave European sailors mastery of the seas and coastal waters and enabled them to set up colonies around the world.

Nutmeg wars

✸ Nutmegs are the seeds of an evergreen tree, the *Myristica fragrans*, which grew on only a few islands in Indonesia.

✸ The Portuguese were the first Europeans to find a sea route to the Spice Islands. They controlled the nutmeg trade for nearly 100 years.

✸ When Portuguese power came to an end, the Dutch and British fought a series of wars over the Spice Islands.

✸ Rather than give up the island of Run (the centre of the nutmeg trade) the Dutch gave New Amsterdam (New York) to the English in 1667.

Blasts from the past

1511 Portuguese sailors reach the Spice Islands in Indonesia

1545 The Spanish discover a huge silver mine at Potosí (Bolivia)

1557 The Portuguese found a trading port at Macau, China

1575 The Portuguese begin shipping slaves to Brazil from Angola

1606 The Dutch take control of the spice trade

1608 France founds Québec, Canada, to trade fur

1640 Sugar cane is grown on plantations in the Caribbean

1765 The British East India Company controls much of northern India

Supermarket sweep

⚙ Potatoes first arrived in Europe from South America in about 1565. For a long time, people thought they were poisonous and refused to eat them.

⚙ The Spanish caught the chocolate-drinking habit from the Mexican Aztecs. They liked it so much that they kept it a secret from the rest of Europe for almost 100 years.

⚙ Bananas, native to southeast Asia, were taken to Africa by Arab traders. In the 15th century, Portuguese sailors carried them to the Americas. The early bananas were green – the yellow variety

Tea trade

- Imported tea from China was a fashionable drink in 18th-century England.
- It was very expensive, and only the richest people could afford it.
- Tea began to be grown on plantations in British-owned India and Sri Lanka.
- It was shipped to Britain on fast sailing ships called tea clippers.

Plantation life

Slaves were forced to work long hours in the fields with no pay. Conditions were harsh and many died from disease and exhaustion.

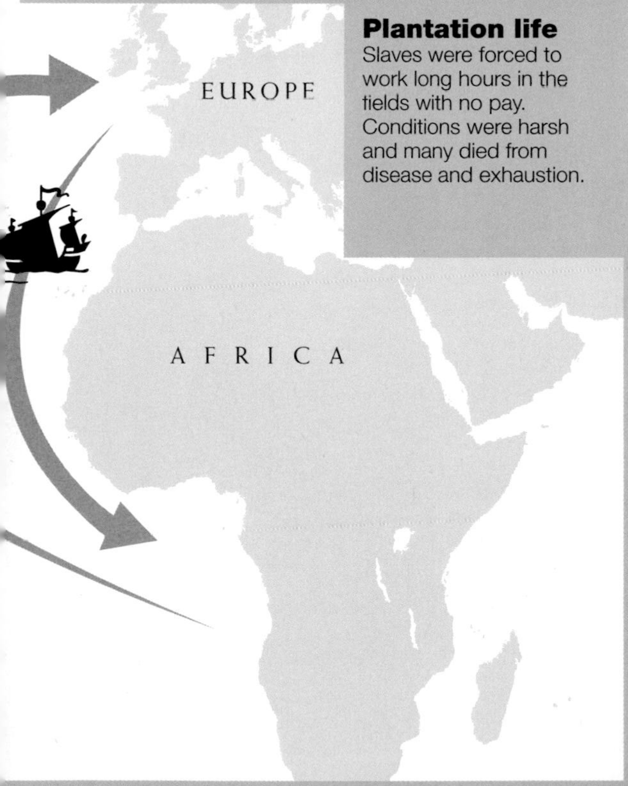

In numbers

13
The number of British colonies in North America that claimed independence in 1776

US$24
The value of goods Dutch merchant Peter Minuit paid for Manhattan, New York, in 1626

11,000
The number of tonnes of treasure shipped to Spain from South America

362,875 kg
(800,000 lb) The amount of tea imported annually to Britain in the early 1700s

What Europe gave to America

These are just some of the things that European traders introduced to America:

- **Christianity**
- **Guns**
- **Horses**
- **Influenza (flu)**
- **Measles**
- **Smallpox**

Pirates ahoy!

- In the 18th century, convoys of heavily guarded ships left Panama (Central America) for Spain, loaded with silver and gold.
- Pirates lurked in the Caribbean Islands, waiting for the chance to attack the ships, or raided Spanish settlements in Cuba, Panama, and Venezuela.
- Many pirates were privateers – owners of private ships who were licensed by their governments to attack other fleets.
- Pirates also preyed on European ships in the South China Sea and the Bay of Bengal.
- English pirate Edward Teach (Blackbeard) plundered ships in the Caribbean in the 18th century. He was one of the most feared pirates to sail the seas.

The Japanese considered they would be better off without foreign trade. In 1638, they **closed all their ports** to outside ships and did not allow them back for 200 years.

Hat trick

By the 17th century, **beavers** had been hunted to extinction in most of Europe to make hats for fashionable people in London and Paris. So business moved to North America, where French hunters began trading tools and guns for beaver pelts with Native American trappers, and demand for North American fur soared.

Changing tastes

Before 1600, Europeans would not have tasted any of the following foods, which are all native to South America:

Beans
Chillies
Chocolate
Potatoes
Sweetcorn (maize)
Tomatoes

What was the **Scientific Revolution?**

It was a period in European history when discoveries in astronomy, physics, and biology laid the foundations of modern science. These new ideas led people to challenge the teachings of the past and the way they thought about the world.

Printed word

The invention of the printing press (c.1450) helped to spread the ideas of the **Renaissance** (c.1400–1550) when scholars rediscovered Greek and Latin learning.

Printed books also played a key role in the **Reformation**, the religious controversy that divided the Church between Roman Catholics and Protestants in the 1500s.

The **Bible** was printed in most European languages. It was often the only book in people's homes, and helped to spread literacy.

Dutch scientist **Anton von Leeuwenhoek** built a powerful microscope that could magnify objects 270 times. When he placed a drop of water beneath the lens, he observed tiny life-forms swimming in it. He called them "animalcules". We know them as **bacteria**.

Star gazer

No one had thought of using a telescope for astronomical purposes until Italian astronomer and mathematician **Galileo Galilei** built one in 1608. He used it to observe the craters on the Moon, and later discovered the four major moons of Jupiter.

Astronomy row

In 1543, Polish astronomer and priest **Nicolaus Copernicus** published a book showing that the Sun is at the centre of the Solar System and is orbited by the Earth and other planets.

His argument directly opposed the teachings of the **Church**, which were taken from a verse in the Bible that says Earth is the fixed centre of the Universe.

Galileo, the leading astronomer and mathematician of his day, wrote a book supporting the views of Copernicus.

The Church authorities put Galileo on trial and he was forced to take back his words.

In 1992, 350 years after his death, the Roman Catholic Church publicly admitted that Galileo was right.

Blasts from the past

c.1450
German craftsman Johannes Gutenberg develops a printing press using moveable type

1517
Beginning of the Reformation

1543
Flemish anatomist Andreas Vesalius publishes the first modern study of human anatomy

1582
The Gregorian calendar (the one in use today) is introduced

1603
The Academy of the Lynx, in Rome, is the first scientific society

1609
German astronomer Johannes Kepler shows that the planets travel round the Sun in elliptical rather than circular orbits

1637
French mathematician and philosopher René Descartes publishes his findings on the links between geometry and algebra

1642
Frenchman Blaise Pascal invents a mechanical calculator

1660
The Royal Society for the study of science is founded in England

Ten useful inventions

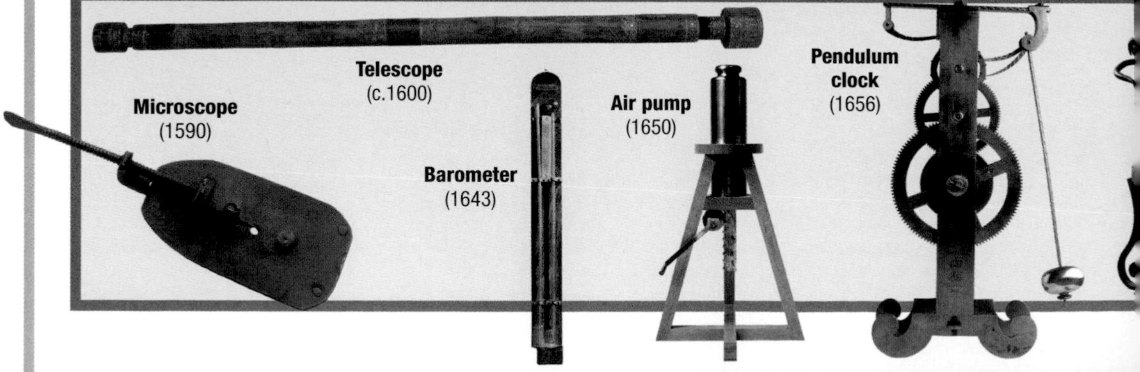

Tell me more: **Sir Isaac Newton (1642–1727)**

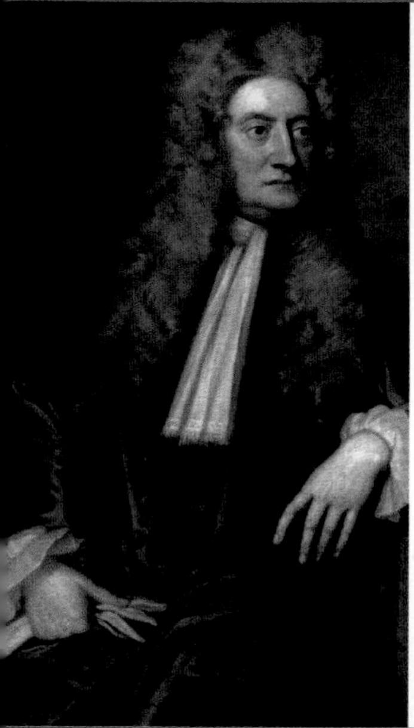

- He discovered the law of gravity and the three laws of motion (which explain how forces make objects move).
- **He showed that white light is a combination of all colours.**
- His most important work was the *Principia Mathematica*, published in 1687, in which he stated his laws of motion.
- **He dabbled in alchemy (the attempt to turn base metals into gold).**
- He was famous for his bad temper and quarrelled with many fellow scientists.
- **He was knighted for his work as Warden of the Mint, in charge of the English currency, not for his scientific achievements.**

I don't believe it!

One cold winter's day in 1626, English philosopher and scientist Sir Francis Bacon decided to see if he could preserve a chicken by stuffing it with snow. He caught a cold and died of pneumonia a week later.

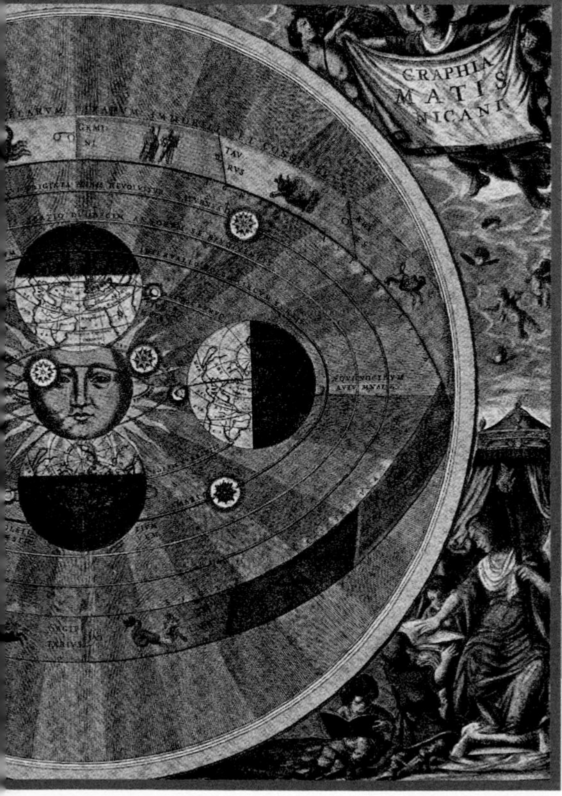

Live wire

American scientist **Benjamin Franklin** made important discoveries in electricity, invented the lightning conductor, mapped the Gulf Stream, was the first American ambassador in Paris – and still found time to help write the American Constitution!

Three 18th-century scientists

Carl Linnaeus
(1707–1778) Swedish botanist who invented a system for classifying living things.

Antoine Lavoisier
(1743–1794) French scientist who published the first modern account of chemistry.

Edward Jenner
(1749–1823) English doctor who discovered a vaccination against smallpox.

The Scientific Revolution saw a flood of new inventions and discoveries in the 17th and 18th centuries.

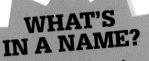

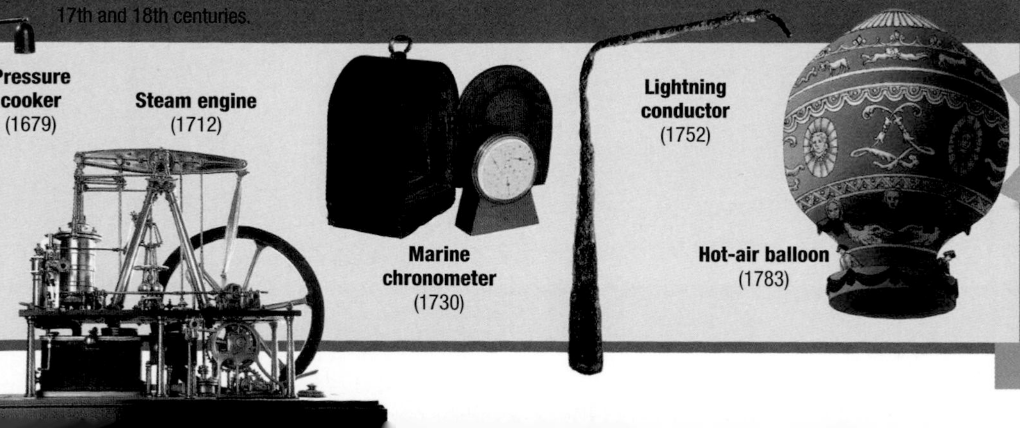

Pressure cooker (1679)

Steam engine (1712)

Marine chronometer (1730)

Lightning conductor (1752)

Hot-air balloon (1783)

WHAT'S IN A NAME?

The **Enlightenment** was a movement of important writers and thinkers in 18th-century Europe. They believed that individuals should think for themselves and not base their ideas on past traditions. Their ideas and discoveries helped to shape the modern world.

Leonardo da Vinci

About 100 years before the Scientific Revolution, one of the great geniuses of all time was living and working in Italy. Leonardo da Vinci is best known as an artist, yet he was also an inventor, scientist, architect, and mathematician, whose notebooks were filled with ingenious designs and observations.

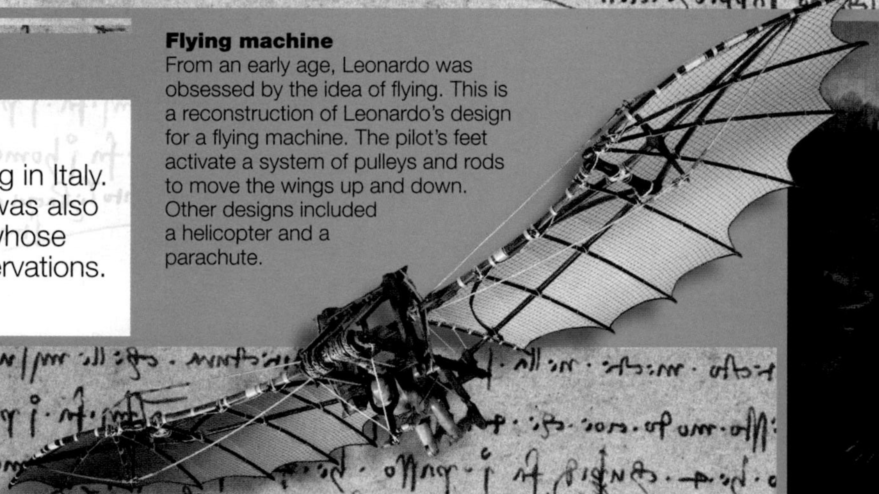

Flying machine
From an early age, Leonardo was obsessed by the idea of flying. This is a reconstruction of Leonardo's design for a flying machine. The pilot's feet activate a system of pulleys and rods to move the wings up and down. Other designs included a helicopter and a parachute.

Mona Lisa
It took Leonardo four years to paint the *Mona Lisa,* the world's most famous painting. Although he completed fewer than 30 paintings, Leonardo is regarded as one of the great masters of Renaissance art.

Leonardo the man
Born in 1452 in the small Italian town of Vinci, Leonardo was fascinated by how the world worked. Unusually for the times he was a vegetarian. This self-portrait shows him a few years before his death in France in 1519.

Nature studies
Leonardo's notebooks are filled with drawings of the natural world. He observed the wild flowers he saw around him in the Italian countryside, making detailed notes of their structure and the types of soils they grew in.

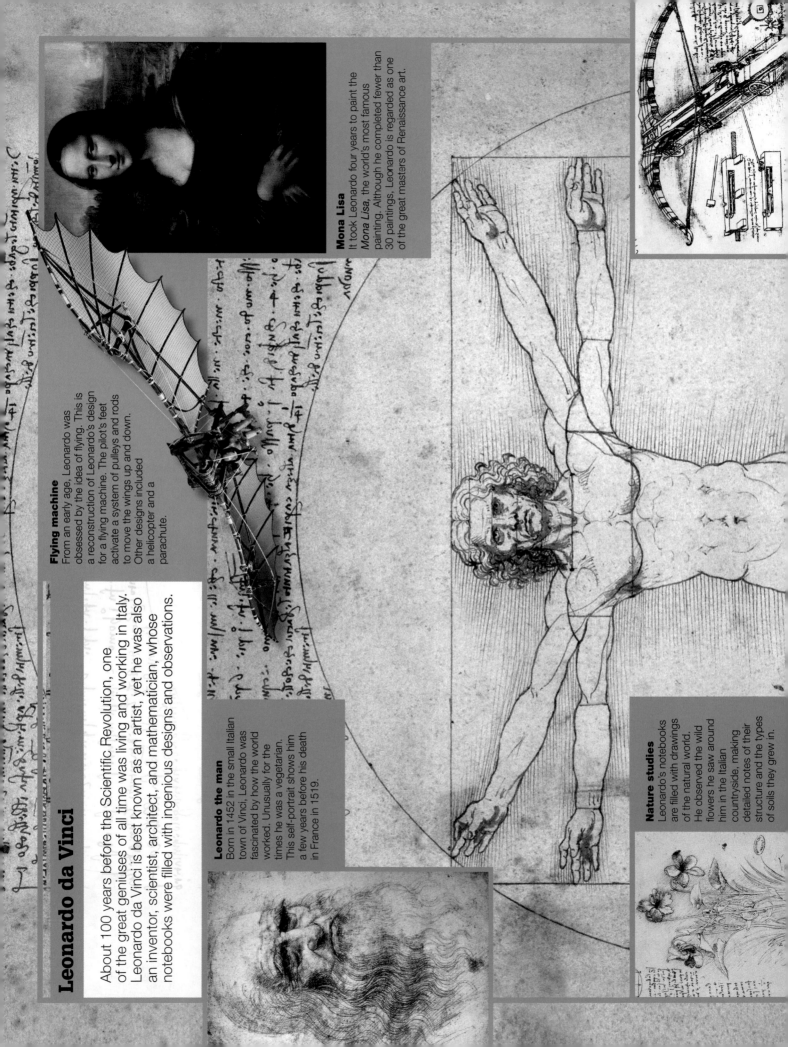

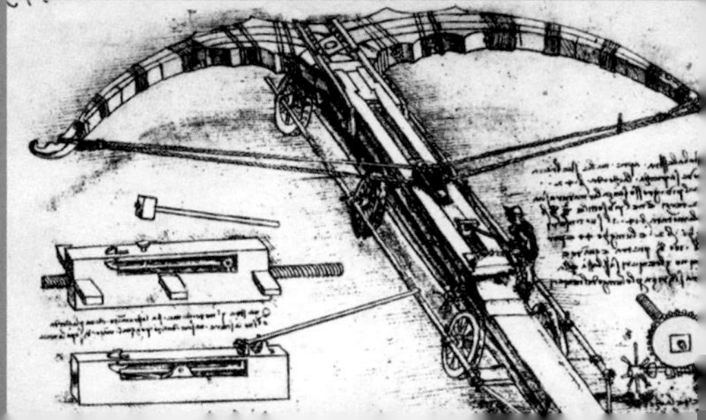

While in service to the Duke of Milan, Leonardo designed several war machines. His designs included a deadly crossbow (above), an armoured car, and a tank with guns around its rim – an idea that was 400 years ahead of its time!

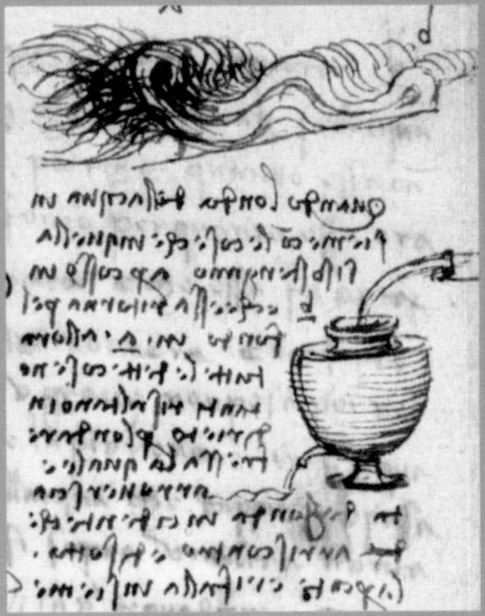

Movement of water
Leonardo was intrigued by water and the way it moves. He drew up plans for canals, locks, and dams, and designed pumps and other water devices. He even came up with an idea for an underwater diving suit!

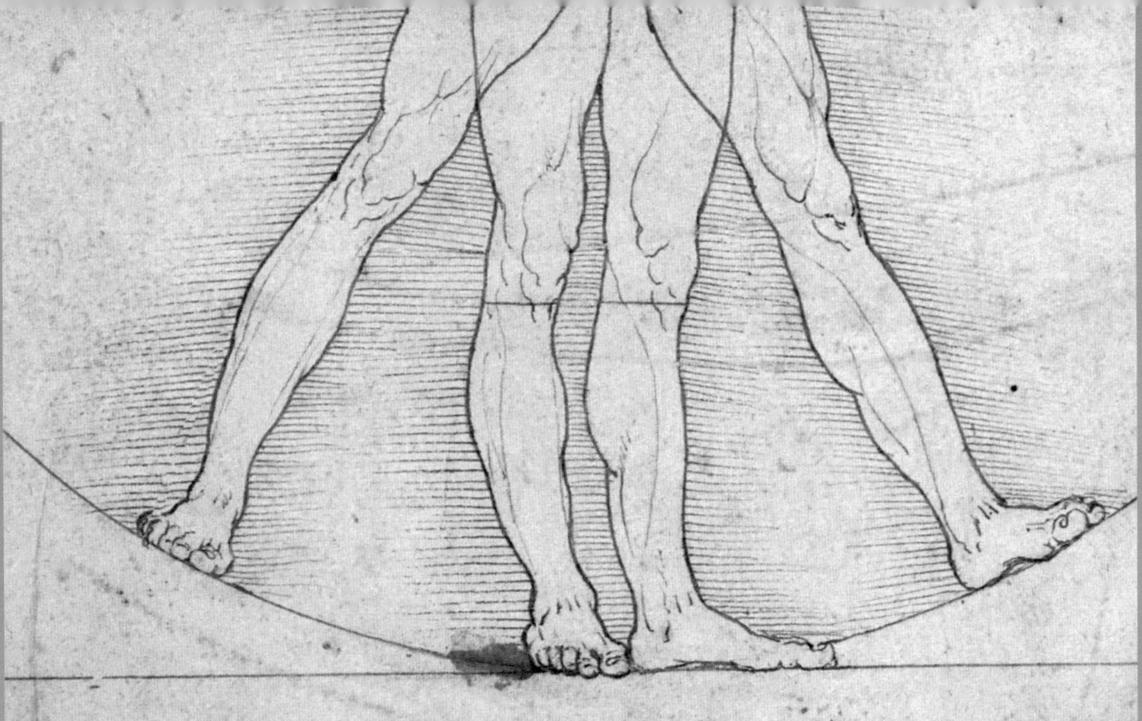

Vitruvian man
This drawing from Leonardo's notebooks represents the ideal proportions of the human body. It is basec on the ideas of the Roman architect Vitruvius.

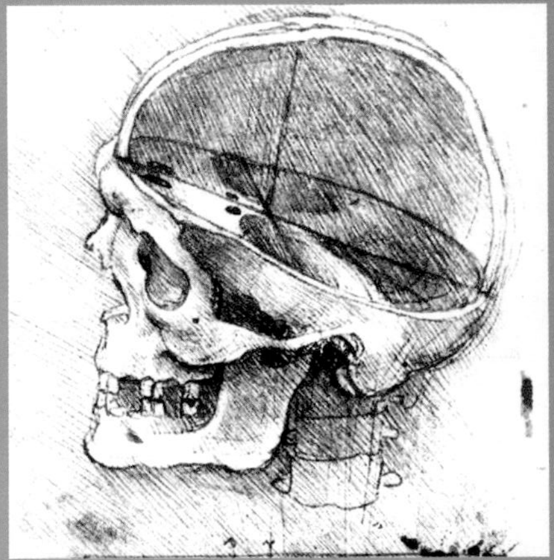

Anatomy
Leonardo was fascinated with the workings of the human body. He obtained dissected human corpses from hospitals to make more than 1,000 detailed anatomical drawings.

Maps
For Leonardo, drawing maps must have been the next best thing to flying. He was able to visualize a landscape as a bird passing overhead might see it.

Mirror writing
Leonardo used mirror writing in his notebooks, probably because he was left-handed. By moving his hand from right to left, he could get his ideas down quickly without smudging the ink.

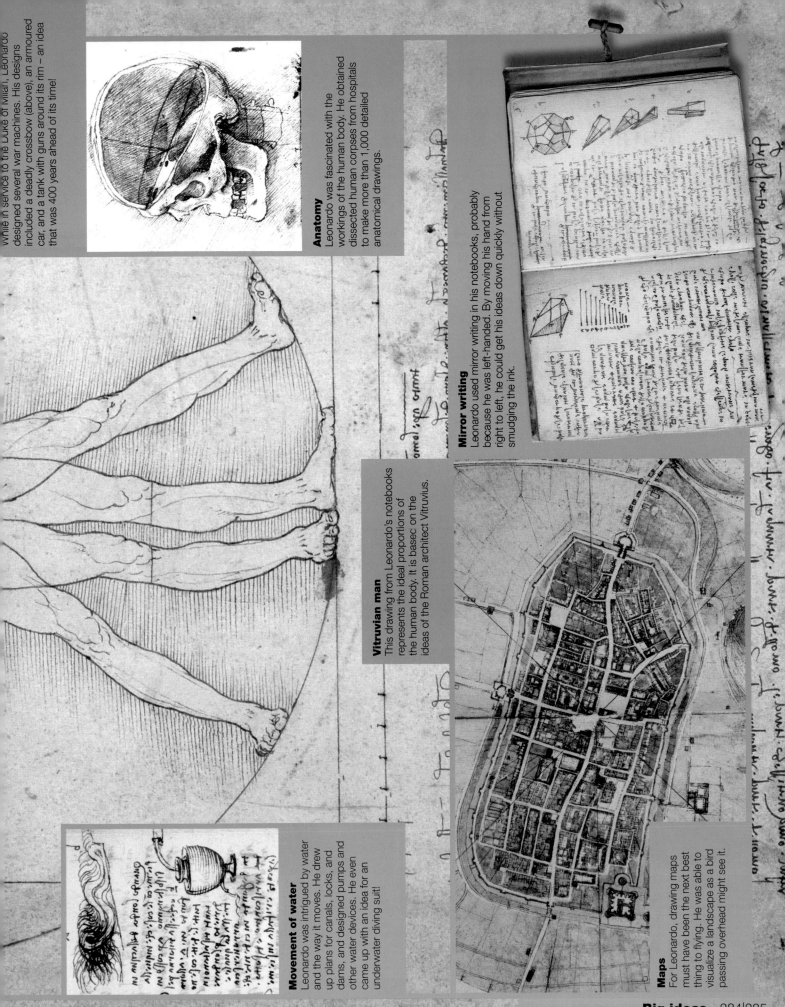

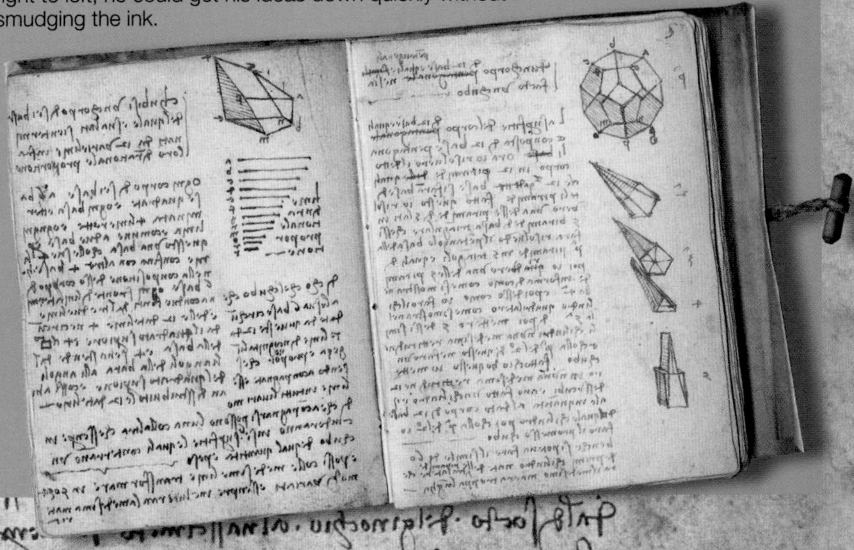

How did life change in the 19th century?

More and more people were moving to towns, working conditions were tough, and poverty was widespread. But advances in technology brought improved standards of living for many people. Travel became easier and people had more time for sport and leisure pursuits.

American inventor Thomas Edison (1847–1931) once famously said, **"Genius is one per cent inspiration, ninety-nine per cent perspiration."** The electric light bulb was one of Edison's many inventions.

Communications speed up

Steam locomotive
In 1804, British engineer Richard Trevithick built the first steam-powered locomotive.

Steamship
The steamship *Great Western* began the first regular transatlantic passenger service in 1838.

Telegraph
In 1866, the first transatlantic telegraph cable came into service.

Railway
The first transcontinental railway in the USA was completed in 1869.

Telephone
The first telephone call was made in 1876.

Petrol-powered car
The first petrol-powered car was built in Germany in 1885.

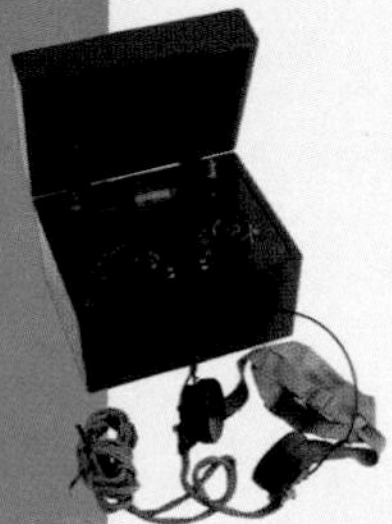

Radio
In 1901, the first transatlantic radio signal was sent.

Powered flight
The first powered aeroplane flight was made in 1903.

Children at work

- **Children as young as seven worked in mines and factories.**
- They tended machines and hauled heavy loads.
- **The work was dangerous and horrific accidents were frequent.**
- Hours were long – children sometimes worked up to 14 hours per day.
- **The estimated number of child labourers in the world today is 158 million.**

Tell me more: **urban poverty**

- Cities grew rapidly as people left the countryside to work in factories.
- **People were crowded together in dilapidated, unsanitary houses.**
- Deadly diseases such as typhus, cholera, and tuberculosis spread rapidly.
- **Workers were badly paid and had no rights or benefits.**
- Families without any means of support were split up and sent to the workhouse.

Five famous firsts

Photograph (1822)
The first photograph is taken by Joseph Niépce in France.

Postage stamp (1840)
The world's first postage stamp (Penny Black) is issued in Britain.

Female Dr (1849)
American Elizabeth Blackwell is the first female doctor.

Blast from the past

1811–1812
Luddite Riots – British craftsmen protest against job losses by breaking up industrial machines

1833
Factory Act bans employment of children under the age of nine in Britain

1836
Mill girls go on strike at Lowell, Massachusetts, USA

1845–1849
Potato famine in Ireland

1882
Labor Day holiday held in New York, USA for the first time

1889
Old age pensions in Germany are the first in the world

Urban life
In 1851, half the population of Britain was living in towns. This was the first time this had happened anywhere in the world.

Match strike!

- In 1888, female workers at a London match-making factory went on strike.
- They worked 14 hours per day for little pay.
- Many of them had "phossy jaw" (crumbling of the jaw bone) caused by exposure to white phosphorus, a highly toxic chemical used in match-making.
- Phosphorus had already been banned in many European countries.
- The "Matchgirls' Strike" won wide publicity and support. The factory girls succeeded in getting better working conditions for women, and white phosphorus was banned.

How to: ride a penny farthing bicycle

01. Stand behind the bike, and take hold of the handlebars.

02. Find the mounting step on the left-hand side of the bike and put your left foot on it.

03. Now use your right foot to push the bike forward. Keep looking ahead all the time.

04. When the bike is moving, heave yourself on to the saddle, throw your right foot forward to step on the right pedal. Start pedalling.

05. To stop, back-pedal and apply the brake via a lever on the handlebars. Good luck!

Skyscraper (1884)
The first skyscraper, the Home Insurance Office, built in Chicago, USA.

Movie (1895)
The Lumière brothers show the first public film screening in France.

Ten handy inventions

01 Canned meat (1810)
02 Waterproof raincoat (1823)
03 Sewing machine (1851)
04 Toilet paper (1857)
05 Heinz tomato ketchup (1867)
06 Vacuum cleaner (1876)
07 Domestic refrigerator (1879)
08 Light bulb (1879)
09 Aspirin (1898)
10 Washing machine (1907)

Brunel's suspension bridge, Bristol, UK

Transport links

Developments in building techniques led to more efficient transport systems. The engineering genius of the day was British architect Isambard Kingdom Brunel. His bridges, railways, viaducts, and steamships made long-distance travel faster and more affordable.

What is the American Constitution?

It is the framework of laws by which the USA is governed. Written in 1787, it declared that all men should have an equal voice in government. The American Constitution is one of the oldest written national constitutions in use today.

[redacted]

Tell me more: democracy

- A democracy is a political system in which citizens (members of a state or country) are given the opportunity to vote for their preferred candidate from a range of political parties.
- **Elections should be open and fair, and be held at regular intervals.**
- In almost all modern democracies, all adult citizens are able to vote.
- **All citizens should be free to express their political opinions without fear.**
- The law courts and judges (collectively called the judiciary) should be independent of the government.

[redacted]

FAST FACTS

Types of government

01: Monarchy: A country where the head of state is a monarch (king or queen). In a **constitutional monarchy**, the monarch usually has only limited powers. In an **absolute monarchy**, the monarch has ultimate control.

02: Republic: A country without a monarchy, where the head of state is usually an elected president.

03: Theocracy: A state governed by a religious leader, or leaders.

04: Dictatorship: A state ruled by a single person who may have seized power by force or been elected unopposed.

05: Single-party state: A state governed by a single political party where no other parties are allowed to put up candidates for election.

[redacted]

American Revolution
(1775–1783) Thirteen colonies break free from British rule and form the United States of America.

French Revolution
(1789–1799) The French monarchy is abolished and France sets itself up as a republic.

Chinese Revolution
(1911) The last imperial dynasty (the Qing Dynasty) is overthrown and China becomes a republic.

How to: hold a Boston Tea Party

01: Protest when the British government imposes a tax on tea on the American colonies in 1773.

02: Disguise yourself and about 50 of your friends as Native American Mohawks.

03: Sneak on board three British ships moored in Boston Harbour.

04: Break open the chests of tea stowed on deck and empty their contents into the sea.

05: Take up drinking coffee and prepare for revolutionary war.

Blasts from the past

1792 In France, the revolutionary government gives all adult males the vote (later withdrawn)

1867 All men over the age of 25 are able to vote for the German parliament

1869 African–American men are guaranteed the right to vote

1872 The secret ballot (the right to a confidential vote) is introduced in Britain

1884 All male householders can vote in Britain

1893 New Zealand is the first country to give women the vote

1906 Finland is the first European nation to give women the vote

1920 Women win the vote in the USA

1928 Universal suffrage (the right to vote for all adults) is introduced in the UK

1948 The United Nations declares universal suffrage to be a basic human right

Votes for women!

- The campaign for women to win the vote (suffrage) was fought on both sides of the Atlantic from the mid-1800s.
- Emmeline Pankhurst (1858–1928) was the founder of the women's suffrage movement in Britain.
- Her fellow campaigners, known as suffragettes, were frequently involved in violent clashes with the police.
- Their campaign was suspended during World War I. In 1918, women over the age of 30 won the vote in Britain.
- British women over the age of 21 voted for the first time in 1929.

RECORD BREAKER

Founded in 301 CE, the world's oldest surviving republic is the tiny European state of **San Marino**. Its constitution dates back to 1600.

When a group of people overthrow the government in power and set up a government of their own, it is a **volution**. When the army takes over the powers of the government, it is a **military coup**.

Communist states

- For much of the 20th century, Russia and the countries of Eastern Europe were **single-party states** ruled by the Communist Party.
- Since the collapse of communism in Eastern Europe in 1989, the only official communist states in the world today are China, Cuba, Laos, and Vietnam.

Five absolute monarchies

- Brunei
- Oman
- Qatar
- Saudi Arabia
- Swaziland

Russian Revolution (1917) The tsar is forced from power and the first communist state is created.

Iranian Revolution (1989) An Islamic republic is set up in Iran after the shah (king) is overthrown.

Of the 44 monarchies in the world today, 16 recognize the British queen, **Elizabeth II**, as their head of state.

The Sultan of Brunei

When did two million people leave Ireland?

During the Great Famine of 1845–1852, when more than one million people in Ireland died from starvation and disease, another two million were forced to migrate (move permanently to another country). The famine was caused by a disease that destroyed Ireland's entire potato crop.

WHAT'S IN A NAME?

An **emigrant** is someone who moves from one country to settle in another. An **immigrant** is someone who has moved into a new country.

Wrong side of the fence

- In 1947, two independent states – India and Pakistan – were born.
- Pakistan, in the northwest of the Indian Subcontinent, was created as a homeland for Muslims.
- This meant that Muslims whose families had lived for generations in India found themselves on the wrong side of the border, as did Hindus and Sikhs now living in Pakistan.
- Amid mounting violence, 14.5 million people left their homes to flee to the other side of the border.
- This was one of the biggest migrations that has ever taken place.

Tell me more: arriving in America

More than **12 million** immigrants checked through the US immigration station on **Ellis Island**, New York between 1892–1924. The first one to do so was a 15-year-old Irish girl, Annie Moore.

- From colonial times, America attracted large numbers of European immigrants.
- **Before 1850, most immigrants were from the UK, Ireland, or Germany.**
- Numbers increased after the 1880s when cheap steamship travel became available.
- **Most immigrants now came from southern or eastern Europe. Many were Jewish refugees, fleeing *pogroms* (organized massacres) in Russia.**
- Their first sight of America was the Statue of Liberty in New York Harbour.

Five reasons why people migrate

01 To start a new life with their families.

02 To find work so they can send money back to their families at home.

03 To escape famine or natural disasters.

04 To escape religious or political persecution.

05 To escape war or ethnic cleansing (the forcible removal of a people from their homeland).

Refugees fleeing civil war, Rwanda

In 1948, a small group of West Indians arrived in London, UK on board the ***Empire Windrush***. They had answered an appeal for workers to fill jobs in Britain. They were the first of thousands of migrants from the British Commonwealth to come to Great Britain after World War II.

More than 4.6 million Palestinians, Arab descendents of an area called Palestine, now in modern-day Israel, are today living in refugee camps and settlements throughout the Middle East.

Immigrants to the USA 1880–1930

from Italy	4.6 million
from Central Europe	4 million
from Russia	3.3 million
from Germany	2.8 million
from Britain	2.3 million

I don't believe it!

In 1900, only 13 per cent of the world's population lived in towns and cities. Today, more than 50 per cent of people live in urban areas.

An estimated **30 million people** worldwide were forced from their homes as refugees during the fighting and upheavals of **World War II** (1939–1945).

Home comforts

When people arrive in a new country, the language, food, and customs are often unfamiliar. Immigrants are drawn towards ethnic neighbourhoods – areas where people from their home country are already living.

San Francisco's historic Chinatown dates from the days of the American Gold Rush (1848–1855), when Chinese workers came to California in the hope of finding gold.

British railway workers in Argentina first introduced the game of football (or soccer) to the country in the 1880s. That's why many Argentine football clubs still have English names today.

World cities with one million or more foreign-born residents

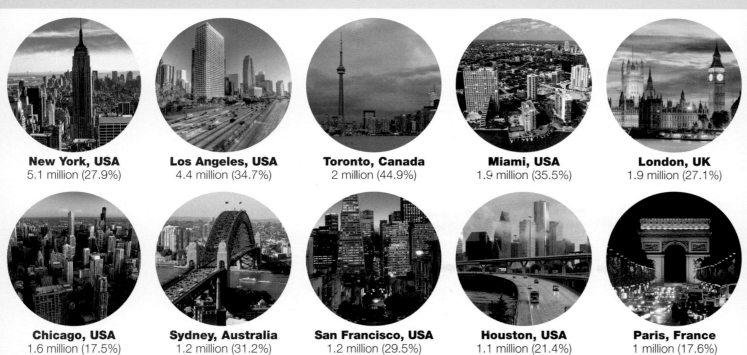

New York, USA
5.1 million (27.9%)

Los Angeles, USA
4.4 million (34.7%)

Toronto, Canada
2 million (44.9%)

Miami, USA
1.9 million (35.5%)

London, UK
1.9 million (27.1%)

Chicago, USA
1.6 million (17.5%)

Sydney, Australia
1.2 million (31.2%)

San Francisco, USA
1.2 million (29.5%)

Houston, USA
1.1 million (21.4%)

Paris, France
1 million (17.6%)

The estimated number of people living outside their birth country today is 200 million.

Tell me more: East and West Germany

■ **At the end of World War II, Germany was divided in two. The USSR controlled the eastern parts, while the USA, Britain, and France controlled the western parts.**

■ The city of Berlin was divided into western and eastern zones, although it lay entirely inside East Germany.

■ **In 1948, the USSR cut off all access to West Berlin. British and US aeroplanes had to fly in supplies to keep the people from starving.**

■ In 1961, the East German government erected a concrete wall across the city to prevent its citizens from fleeing to the west.

■ **The Berlin Wall stood for nearly 30 years, until the collapse of communism in Eastern Europe in 1989. A few months later, East and West Germany were reunited.**

Celebrating the fall of the Berlin Wall

USSR

01: It supported global communism.

02: After World War II, it stationed troops in Eastern Europe and took control of the "Eastern Bloc".

03: In 1955, it set up the Warsaw Pact – a military and political alliance of Eastern European communist states.

04: Its highest deployment of nuclear warheads was 45,000 (1986).

USSR

October 1957
Sputnik 1, the first artificial satellite in history, is launched

October 1959
Luna 3 sends back the first photos of the Moon's far side

April 1961
Yuri Gagarin completes the first manned space flight aboard Vostok 1

June 1963
Valentina Tereshkova is the first woman cosmonaut

March 1965
Alexei Leonov makes the first spacewalk

February 1966
Luna 9 makes the first successful landing of a craft on the Moon

What was the **Cold War?**

This was a period of tension between the USSR (the Soviet Union, now Russia) and the USA. The Cold War lasted for more than 40 years and brought the world close to conflict. During this time, the rival superpowers built up enough nuclear weapons to destroy the planet.

Former Eastern European communist countries

★ **Albania**
★ **Bulgaria**
★ **Czechoslovakia**
★ **East Germany**
★ **Hungary**
★ **Poland**
★ **Romania**
★ **Yugoslavia**

Superpowers

■ A superpower is an extremely powerful state that uses its military and economic might to dominate other nations and influence world politics.

■ Since the break up of the Soviet Union in 1991, the USA has been the world's only superpower.

■ There are signs that China's growing economic strength may give it superpower status in the future.

Blasts from the past

1949
The USSR tests its first atomic bomb

1950–1953
The US supports South Korea against invasion by communist North Korea

1956
Soviet tanks crush an anti-communist revolt in Hungary

1965
The US enters the war against communist North Vietnam

1968
Uprising in Czechoslovakia is put down by Soviet tanks

1969
The US and the USSR begin talks to reduce the number of nuclear weapons

USA

January 1958
Launch of the first US satellite, Explorer 1

May 1961
President Kennedy calls for a Moon landing before the end of the decade

February 1962
John Glenn makes the first US manned orbital flight

March 1966
Gemini 8 completes the first dual docking operation in space

December 1968
Apollo 8 completes the first manned mission around the Moon

July 1969
Apollo 11 astronauts are the first humans to walk on the surface of the Moon

FAST FACTS

USA

01: It supported democracy and free market economy (capitalism).

02: In 1949, it formed the North Atlantic Treaty Organization (NATO) with Canada, Britain, France, and other Western European countries.

03: In 1952, it developed the hydrogen bomb.

04: Its highest deployment of nuclear warheads was 32,000 (1965).

I don't believe it!

At the height of the Cold War, Soviet leader Nikita Khrushchev became so angry during a United Nations meeting in New York that he took off his shoe and banged it on the desk in front of him.

In August 1945, US planes dropped two **atomic bombs** on the Japanese cities of Hiroshima and Nagasaki killing 200,000 people. Six days later, Japan surrendered, ending World War II. But the age of nuclear weapons had begun.

Cuban Missile Crisis

In 1962, the Soviets built missile bases in communist Cuba. The **US**, only 145 km (90 miles) from Cuba, blockaded the island, causing a crisis between the two superpowers. The **USSR** finally withdrew its missiles, and the world narrowly avoided nuclear war.

Four superpowers in history

01: Roman Empire
For 700 years, its military power extended throughout Europe, around the Mediterranean, and into the Middle East.

02: Chinese Empire
Asian superpower that dominated its neighbours in central Asia, Korea, and Vietnam from 221 BCE – 1912 CE.

03: Ottoman Empire
At its height in the 16th century, this Islamic superpower controlled the eastern Mediterranean, Iraq, North Africa, and southeast Europe.

04: British Empire
The largest empire in history. In the late 19th century, it covered nearly a quarter of Earth's surface.

Animals in space

- The first animals in space were fruit flies, placed aboard a US V-2 rocket in 1947.
- Laika, a stray mongrel dog, was the first mammal to orbit Earth on board Russian satellite Sputnik 2 in 1957. She died after a few hours.
- [illegible]

Mutually Assured Destruction (MAD) was the idea that if both sides stockpiled enough nuclear weapons to wipe out the other, neither would strike first, thus avoiding nuclear war.

What was the **March on Washington?**

In August 1963, more than 200,000 people marched through Washington DC, USA, to demand full civil rights for African Americans. At that time, black people in the southern states of America did not enjoy the same rights as white people. They were unable to vote, had to attend separate schools, and could not eat in the same bars and cafés.

Bus boycott

African Americans using the municipal bus service in Montgomery, Alabama, were obliged to give up their seats to white people if the bus was full.

In 1955, Rosa Parks, a black woman from Montgomery, refused to give up her seat to a white man and was arrested.

In protest, African Americans refused to use the buses. In 1956, the Supreme Court outlawed segregation on buses, and the boycott came to an end.

Sporting protest

After winning gold and bronze medals at the 1968 Mexico Olympics, African-American athletes Tommie Smith and John Carlos raised black-gloved hands on the podium as a silent protest against racial discrimination. They were dismissed from the national team and sent home in disgrace.

In 2008, forty years after the death of civil rights leader Martin Luther King Jr, **Barack Obama** became the first African American to be elected President of the United States.

FAST FACTS

Martin Luther King Jr

01: Born in 1929 in Atlanta, Georgia, USA.

02: Minister of a Baptist church in Montgomery, Alabama.

03: Led the Montgomery Bus Boycott in 1955.

04: Influenced by Mohandas Gandhi, he believed in non-violent protest.

05: Led the March on Washington in August 1963.

06: Was awarded the Nobel Peace Prize in 1964.

07: Was assassinated in Memphis, Tennessee, in 1968.

08: His birthday is a US national holiday, celebrated on the third Monday in January.

Blasts from the past

1954 US Supreme Court declares segregated (separate) schools illegal

1957 Riots break out as nine African-American students enrol at a formerly all-white high school in Little Rock, Alabama

1960 Four black students, refused service at a whites-only food counter, stage a "sit-in"; their action inspires a wave of sit-ins across the southern states of America

1962 Civil rights protesters, known as "Freedom Riders" are attacked as they test a court ruling to end segregation on interstate buses

1963 March on Washington DC

1964 Civil Rights Act prohibits discrimination on grounds of race, colour, religion, or national origin

Ten facts about Mohandas Gandhi

01: He was born in Gujarat, India, in 1869.

02: He married Kasturba Makhanji at the age of 13.

03: He studied law in London and later moved to work in South Africa.

04: He devoted himself to ending British rule in India by means of non-violent protest.

05: He was often imprisoned for civil disobedience (refusing to obey British laws).

06: He led a march to the sea to collect salt as a protest against the salt tax.

07: He spun cotton for his own clothes on a traditional Indian spinning wheel.

08: He spoke up for India's "untouchable" class, whom he called "the children of God".

09: He fasted to stop violence between Hindus and Muslims.

10: He was assassinated in 1948 by a Hindu extremist.

WHAT'S IN A NAME?

Gandhi was known to his followers as **Mahatma**, which means "great soul" in Hindu. The name denotes a person of great spirituality and wisdom.

"I have a dream that my four little children will one day live in a nation where they will not be judged by the colour of their skin, but by the content of their character."
Martin Luther King Jr, addressing the crowds in Washington on 28 August, 1963

Long walk to freedom

Born in 1918, Nelson Mandela spent 27 years in prison – 18 of which were in solitary confinement – for his opposition to South Africa's apartheid (segregation) laws.

Black South Africans had no civil rights, even though they vastly outnumbered white South Africans.

Mandela led the military wing of the ANC (African National Congress), the party fighting for the unity of all Africans. He was charged with planning to overthrow the government.

Four years after his release in 1990, he led the ANC to victory in South Africa's first multi-racial election.

New nations

After World War II, colonies in Asia, Africa, the Pacific, and the Caribbean demanded the right to govern themselves. European countries, however, were often reluctant to hand over power. The years of decolonization (1945–1980) saw bitter conflicts in many parts of the world as about 90 new countries won their independence.

years of conflict	country fighting for independence	defeated power
1945–1949	Indonesia	Netherlands
1946–1954	Indochina (Vietnam)	France
1952–1956	Tunisia	France
1952–1960	Kenya	UK
1954–1962	Algeria	France
1961–1975	Angola	Portugal
1962–1974	Guinea-Bissau	Portugal
1964–1974	Mozambique	Portugal

In numbers

4 The number of independent African nations before 1950

23 The number of African nations that gained independence between 1950–1960

25 The number of African nations that gained independence between 1961–1990

53 The number of independent African nations today (Eritrea broke away from Ethiopia to become independent in 1993)

What is globalization?

It is the way multi-national companies, ideas, and lifestyles spread more and more around the world. Cheap air travel, 24-hour TV channels, and the Internet all help to make the planet seem a smaller place. But the downside of globalization is environmental pollution and a widening gap between rich and developing nations.

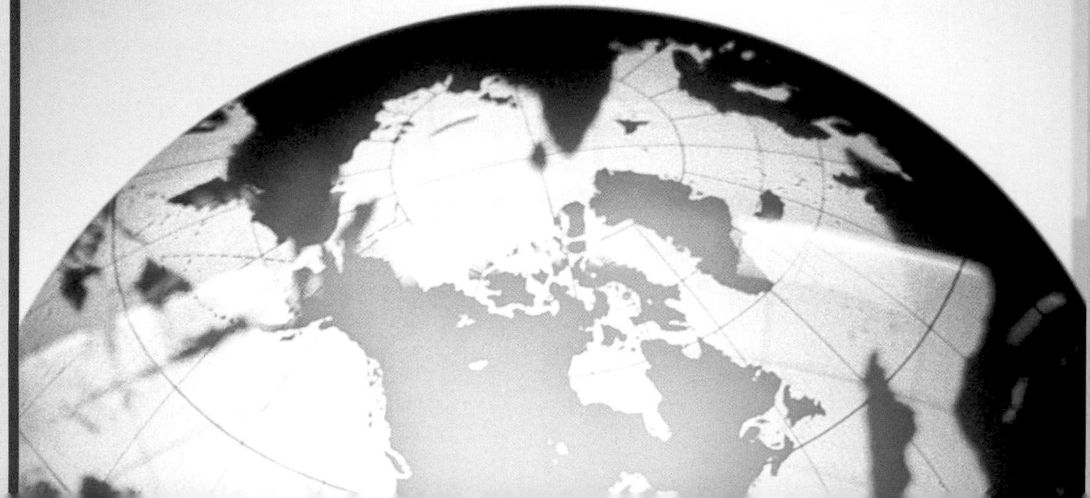

FAST FACTS

United Nations

01: The United Nations (UN) was founded in 1945.

02: It originally had 51 member states. Today, there are 192.

03: Its aims are world peace and cooperation between nations.

04: The UN's General Assembly, consisting of all member states, meets once a year.

05: The Security Council is responsible for international peace and security, and can meet at any time.

06: The Security Council is made up of 15 member states, five of them permanent (China, France, Russia, the UK, and the USA). The others are elected for two-year terms.

07: The UN is headed by the Secretary-General, who is elected every five years.

08: The UN Headquarters (below) are in New York, USA.

I don't believe it!

The government of the Maldives – islands in the Indian Ocean threatened by rising sea levels – held a cabinet meeting on the seabed in 2009 to highlight the danger of global warming.

Heated argument

In December 2009, 15,000 delegates from 192 countries and about 100 world leaders attended the UN Conference on **Climate Change**. After two weeks of talks, the conference failed to come to a legally binding agreement to limit temperature rise.

World financial markets

The globalization of the world's financial markets means that a crisis in one country is likely to have knock-on effects around the globe. In 2007–2009, the collapse of the US housing market caused a "credit crunch" (reduction of funds) that led banks to fail in many parts of the world and started a worldwide recession (decline in prosperity).

Global action

The UN heads up several agencies that work to promote human rights, fight disease and poverty, and protect the environment. In addition, there are thousands of voluntary international bodies known as NGOs (Non-governmental organizations). These include:

International Red Cross and **Red Crescent** Help victims of war and other violent catastrophes.

Save the Children Champions children's rights and helps disadvantaged and abused children.

Doctors without Borders (Médecins Sans Frontières) Organizes emergency medical help for victims of disaster.

Amnesty International Protects human rights and campaigns for political prisoners and victims of injustice

Fairtrade
Aims to secure better deals for farmers and producers in developing countries.

WWF
Campaigns for wildlife conservation and the protection of endangered species.

WHAT'S IN A NAME?

The name of **Google**, the world's most popular search engine, is a misspelling of the mathematical word **"googol"** (ten raised to the power of a hundred). "Google" is now a word in its own right, as in "I googled his name".

Global companies
A multi-national corporation is one that produces goods or services in several countries. Companies set up **factories** in parts of the globe where labour and materials are **cheap**, and sell their products **worldwide**. Brand names such as McDonalds, Coca Cola, Nike, and Disney have global recognition.

Ten busiest airports

Measured by passenger numbers

airport	no of passengers
Hartsfield-Jackson, Atlanta, USA	90,039,280
O'Hare International, Chicago, USA	69,353,876
London Heathrow, UK	67,056,379
Tokyo International, Japan	66,754,829
Paris Charles de Gaulle, France	60,874,829
Los Angeles International, USA	59,497,539
Dallas-Fort Worth International, USA	57,093,187
Beijing Capital International, China	55,937,289
Frankfurt, Germany	53,467,450
Denver International, USA	51,245,334

In North America, three out of four people have **access to the Internet**. In several African countries, less than 1% of the population has Internet access.

FAST FACTS

Plastic waste

01: 2.7 million tonnes of plastic are used to bottle water every year.

02: 80 per cent of all plastic bottles are simply thrown away.

03: Plastics take up to 500 years to break down.

04: That means that nearly all the plastic ever made still exists – somewhere.

05: Much of it ends up in the ocean, where it is a danger to marine life.

06: According to scientists, there is a "plastic soup" of waste floating in the Pacific Ocean twice the size of the United States.

The largest global TV audience for a single live event was 2.5 billion for the funeral of Diana, Princess of Wales, in 1997.

4.7 billion people – 70 per cent of the world's population – tuned in to watch the Olympic Games in Beijing in August 2008.

An estimated 1 billion people watched the singer Michael Jackson's memorial service in June 2009.

In numbers

1.7 billion
The number of Internet users

2.5 billion
The number of people without adequate sanitation

4.6 billion
The estimated number of mobile phones worldwide

4.8 billion
The number of air passengers in 2008

6.7 billion
The world population in 2010

884 million people in the world do not have access to safe drinking water.

Index

Credits

DK would like to thank: Peter Pawsey for creative technical support. Caitlin Doyle for proofreading. Jackie Brind for preparing the index.

The publisher would like to thank the following for their kind permission to reproduce their photographs:

Key: a–above; b–below/bottom; c–centre; f–far; l–left; r–right; t–top

3 Corbis: John Lamm/Transtock (bl/car); David Scharf/Science Faction (fcra/chigger). FLPA: Thomas Marent/Minden Pictures (tc/frog). **6** Corbis: (cb); Michael Benson/Kinetikon Pictures (bl). Getty Images: Purestock (br). **6-7** Corbis: Steve Nagy/Design Pics (c). Getty Images: Yoshinori Watabe (c/main image). **7** Corbis: NASA/Science Faction (bl) (br); Denis Scott (cb). Getty Images: Stocktrek Images (clb). **8** Corbis: Myron Jay Dorf (fbr); Mehau Kulyk/Science Photo Library (bl). NASA: Local Group Galaxies Survey Team, NOAO, AURA, NSF (br). Science Photo Library: Mark Garlick (cb). **8-9** Corbis: Tony Hallas/Science Faction (c/main image). **9** Corbis: Robert Gendler/Visuals Unlimited, Inc. (fbl); Stocktrek Images (bl); NASA (bl). **10** Galaxy Picture Library: NASA/JPL-Caltech/K.Gordon & S.Wilner (br); ROSAT (fbl); STScI (bc). NRAO / AUI / NSF: (fbr). Science Photo Library: NASA (tl). **11** Corbis: CNP (crb). Science Photo Library: European Space Agency (tr). **12** NASA: (cl) (cra/Chandra X-ray) (cra/Hubble near infrared); ESA/CXC/SSC/STScI (tl); ESA/The Hubble Heritage Team (STScI/AURA) (cb) (tr); STScI (bl); STScI/OPO/E.Karkoschka (University of Arizona) (br). **12-13** NASA: ESA/STScI (cb). **13** NASA: (br); CXC/MIT/Frederick Baganoff et al (tr); ESA/HEIC and the Hubble Heritage Team (STScI/AURA) (c); ESA/STScI/J. Hester and P. Scowen (Arizona State University) (tl), ESA/The Hubble SM4 ERO Team (bc); JPL-Caltech/University of Arizona (cr). **14** NASA: (cb). Science Photo Library: NASA/ H.E. Bond/E. Nelam/M. Barstow/J.B. Holberg/ESA/STScI (cra). **15** Corbis: Tony Hallas/Science Faction (tc). Science Photo Library: Johns Sanford (bl). **16** Corbis: (tr); NASA (cr). Getty Images: ESA/AFP (br). NASA: Lockheed-Martin (bl). Science Photo Library: (c). **17** NASA: (ftl) (ftr) (tc) (tl) (tr). Science Photo Library: NASA (cb); Friedrich Saurer (clb). **18** Corbis: (tl). **18-19** Corbis: NASA/Science Faction (c). **19** Corbis: Arianespace/Reuters (bl); Li Gang/Xinhua Press (bc). Getty Images: (tr) (fbl) (fbr); Stringer/AFP (br). **20** Corbis: (tr); Bettmann (tl). **20-21** Getty Images: Space Frontiers (c/main image). **21** Corbis: NASA/Reuters (br) (bc/Helmet) (bc/Underwear) (cr/Anousheh Ansari) (cra/Charles Simonyi). NASA: (crb/Mark Shuttleworth) (bl) (fbl) (fbr) (tr); Bill Ingalls (cr/Greg Olsen); KSC (crb/Dennis Tito); Victor Zelentsov (fcra/Richard Garriott). **22** NASA: (cl) (br) (fbr). **22-23** NASA: (c). **23** Corbis: Arthur Morris (tl). Getty Images: AFP (fbl); Bloomberg (fbr); Dibyangshu Sarkar/AFP (bc). NASA: (bl). Science Photo Library: NASA (br) (tr). **24** Corbis: (fbr); NASA and The Hubble Heritage Team (AURA/STScI) -Handout/Reuters (bc); NASA/JPL/Handout/Reuters (bl); NASA/STScI (br). **24-25** Corbis: NASA/STScI (c/main image). **25** Corbis: David Ljunggren (tc); NASA/JPL-Caltech (fbl); NASA/Science Faction (bl); Stocktrek (bc). European Southern Observatory (ESO) : (br). NASA: JPL-Caltech/D.Elmegreen (Vassar) (fbr). Science Photo Library: NASA (cr). **26** Corbis: Bettmann (cl/Venus); NASA (cl/earth). NASA: Johns Hopkins Universiity Applied Physics Lab (cla/Mercury). **26-27** Corbis: NASA/Roger Ressmeyer (c/main image). **27** Corbis: Atlantide Phototravel (tc); JPL/MSSS (cra). NASA: JPL/Caltech (tr). **28** Getty Images: Stocktrek Images (cl); Time & Life Pictures (bl); JPL/Cornell (bc). NASA: JPL-Caltech/Cornell/NMMNH (cra). **28-29** ESA: DLR/FU Berlin (G. Neukum) (c/Echus Chasma); NASA/JPL/CNP (cr); NASA/Roger Ressmeyer (tr). **29** Corbis: NASA/Science Faction (br). **30** Corbis: (fcra); NASA - Hubble Space Telescope-/Science Factiion (cra/Uranus). NASA: Robert Nemiroff (MTU) & Jerry Bonnell (USRA) (ca/Jupiter). **30-31** NASA: ESA and Erich Karkoschka (University of Arizona) (bc); NASA/CXC/STScI (tr). **31** Galaxy Picture Library: NASA/JPL/Space Science Institute (cr) (c) (fcr). NASA: JPL/Space Science Institute (cl). **32** Corbis: Tony Hallas/Science Faction (bl). Science Photo Library: Erik Viktor (c). **32-33** Corbis: Aaron Horowitz (c). **33** Alamy Images: Interfoto (cr/Donati); The Print Collector (cra). Corbis: Roger Ressmeyer (crb). Science Photo Library: Dr Fred Espenak (cr/Leonid meteors); Robert McNaught (tl); NASA (br) (cb). **34** Alamy Images: Jeff Smith (clb/Lunar meteorite); travelpixs (cla). Corbis: Visuals Unlimited (cl). Getty Images: Time Life Pictures/NASA (bl) (clb/Stony-irons). Science Photo Library: Detlev van Ravenswaay (cb). **34-35** Galaxy Picture Library: Nigel Evans (c). Getty Images: Cliff Leight/Aurora (bc). **35** Corbis: (bc). The Natural History Museum, London: (cr); NASA/Roger Ressmeyer (clb/Mars). **36** Corbis: NASA (clb). Getty Images: Dan Burn-Forti (cr); Time Life Pictures/JPL/NASA (bl). **36-37** Corbis: Stocktrek Images (c/background). **37** Corbis: NASA/epa (bc). NASA: G. Bacon/STScI (fbr). Science Photo Library: Lynette Cook (fbl); European Southern Observatory (bl); Mark Garlick (br/Gliese 581); Dr Seth Shostak (tr). **38** Corbis: Craig Lovel (br). **38-39** Corbis: Yann Arthus-Bertrand (c/main image). **39** Corbis: Tom Bean (cb); Fred Hirschmann/Science Faction (bl); Frans Lanting (cr); Macduff Everton (ca); George Steinmetz (clb); Visuals Unlimited (cl); Michele Westmorland/Science Faction (br). **40** Corbis: Image Source (cla). **40-41** Corbis: Brand X (c/background). **41** Getty Images: Teh Eng Koon/AFP (tc). Science Photo Library: W. K. Fletcher (br); David Parker (cr); Simon Terrey (tr). **42** Corbis: Peter Ginter/Science Faction (ca); Mark Schneider/Visuals Unlimited, Inc. (cr); Visuals Unlimited (bc). Dorling Kindersley: Harry Taylor/Courtesy of the Natural History Museum, London (tr). Getty Images: Ramzi Haidar/AFP (crb/bullets). Science Photo Library: Joel Arem (br); E.R. Degginger (bl); Arnold Fisher (fbr). **42-43** Getty Images: Dimitri Vervitsiotis (c). **43** Corbis: Tommy Flynn (cr/coins); Karen Hunt (crb); Helen King (cr/bicycles); Christian Liepe (tr); David Sailors (cra/copper); Phil Schermeister (ca); Gregor Schuster (br). Getty Images: Ken Lucas (fbl); National Geographic (cl); PhotoLink (cra/titanium). Science Photo Library: TH Foto-Werbung (bl). **44** Corbis: NASA (cl); Paul Seux/Hemis (c/background); Steve Terrill (bl). **45** Corbis: (br). NASA: GSFC/MITI/ERSDAC/JAROS (fbl); Johnson Space Centre (bl). Science Photo Library: Geoeye (fbr). **46** FLPA: Hiroya Minakuchi/Minden Pictures (br). Getty Images: Photolibrary/David B Fleetham (bl); Chris Jackson (fbl). **46-47** Ardea: D. Parer & E. Parer-Cook (c/main image). **47** FLPA: Imagebroker/FB-Fischer (fbr); Peter Oxford/Minden Pictures (br). Getty Images: The Bridgeman Art Library (bl); Andy Rouse (fbl). **48** Corbis: Image Plan (bc/K2); Imageshop (bl); Jane Sweeney/Jon Arnold Images (br); WildCountry (fbr). **48-49** Corbis: Desmond Boylan/Reuters (c/main image). **49** Corbis: Association Chantal Mauduit Nama (bc/Manaslu) (bl); Ed Darack/Science Faction (br); Didrik Johnck (crb); John Noble (fbl) (bc/Dhaulagiri); Galen Rowell (fbr). **50** Corbis: (bl); Shubroto Chattopadhyay (cl). **50-51** Corbis: Momatiuk-Eastcott (c/main image). **51** Alamy Images: JFox travel images (cr/helicopter). Corbis: Tom Bean (cra/walking); David Kadlubowski (tr); Craig Lovell (crb/rafting); Buddy Mays (br); David Samuel Robbins (cr/mule riding). **52** Alamy Images: Martin Harvey (tr). Corbis: Marcello Calandrini (ca). **52-53** Corbis: Gallo Images (c). **53** Corbis: Michael & Patricia Fogden (ftl); Blaine Harrington III (cl); Hoberman Collection (cb). FLPA: Imagebroker/Michael Krabs (tc/Gemsbok); Michael & Patricia Fogden/Minden Pictures (tc/Golden mole). NHPA / Photoshot: Anthony Bannister (tl); Martin Harvey (tr/Brown hyena); Ann & Steve Toon (ftr). **54** Alamy Images: Chris Howes/Wild Places Photography (fbl). Corbis: Atlantide Phototravel (bc); William James Warren (bl). Getty Images: National Geographic (br); David Silverman (br). **54-55** Corbis: Ashley Cooper (c/main image). **55** Alamy Images: Anthony Baker (cr). Corbis: Rainer Hackenberg (bc); Kevin Schafer (br). Getty Images: Rich Reid Photography (bl). **56** FLPA: Derek Middleton (bc). **56-57** Corbis: Michael Stuckey (c/background). **57** Corbis: Andrew Brown/Ecoscene (ftr); Creasource (ftl); Arvind Garg (bc); Roger Ressmeyer (cr); Mick Roessler (tl); Wolfgang Kaehler (tr). **58** Corbis: Bruno Burklin/Photex (ca). Science Photo Library: University of Dundee (bl). **58-59** Corbis: Jim Reed/Jim Reed Photography (c/main image). **59** Science Photo Library: John A Ey III (cra). **60** Corbis: Alejandro Ernesto/epa (tl). Science Photo Library: Wesley Bocxe (bl); Mike Theiss (cl). **60-61** Corbis: NOAA (c/main image). **61** Corbis: Bettmann (br); STR/Reuters (cr); Rhona Wise/epa (tr). **62** Corbis: NASA (tl); Kazuyoshi Nomachi (fbr). Getty Images: J P De Manne (br). **62-63** Corbis: Jose Fuste Raga. **63** Corbis: Bettmann (crb); Tibor Bognar (fbl); Lloyd Cluff (c); Michael Freeman (cl); The Gallery Collection (br); Blaine Harrington III (cra); Jon Arnold/AWL Images Ltd (cr); Reza/Webistan (bl). **64-65** Alamy Images: Neil McAllister (c). **65** Corbis: Walter Bibikow/Jon Arnold Images (fbr); Jose Fuste Raga (bc); Reuters (br); Supri/Reuters (cl); Nik Wheeler (c); Liu Yongqiu/Xinhua Press (bl). naturepl.com: Reinhard Dirscherl (tc/Manta ray). NHPA / Photoshot: Martin Harvey (tl); Burt Jones & Maurine Shimlock (tr); Oceans Image/Photoshot (ftl) (ftr); Woodfall Wild Images/Photoshot (tc/Komodo dragon). **66** Dorling Kindersley: Jonathan Hateley - modelmaker (fcl). **66-67** Corbis: Inspirestock (c/background). **68** Corbis: Kit Kittle (bc); Frans Lanting (fbr); Kevin Schafer (br); Michele Westmorland (fbl). **69** Corbis: Michael & Patricia Fogden (fbr); Image Source (bc/parrot); Mark A. Johnson (fcr/jellyfish); Naturfoto Honal (crb/dragonfly). Dorling Kindersley: Robert L. Braun (bc/lesothosaurus); Jon Hughes (bl); Jon Hughes / Bedrock Studios (br); Natural History Museum, London (cr); David Peart (fcrb/shark). **72-73** Getty Images: Siri Stafford (c/background). **75** Corbis: Frank Robichon/epa (cr). **76-77** Getty Images: Holger Spiering (c). **77** Dorling Kindersley: Jon Hughes (cr). **78** Dorling Kindersley: Jonathan Hateley - modelmaker (c). Getty Images: Wes Walker (c/background). **79** Dorling Kindersley: Natural History Museum, London (fbr); Luis Rey - modelmaker (bl). **81** Corbis: Mark A. Johnson (tr). Dorling Kindersley: Robert L. Braun (ca). **83** Dorling Kindersley: Jon Hughes (tr); Natural History Museum, London (clb). **84** Corbis: Sergei Cherkashin/Reuters (bl). **85** Ancient Art & Architecture Collection: (tl/woolly rhino). Corbis: Gianni Dagli Orti (tc/aurochs). Getty Images: Robert Frerck (ftl); Time & Life Pictures (tc/red deer stags). **86** Corbis: DLILLC (cla). Getty Images: Kenneth Garrett/National Geographic (bl). Science Photo Library: Javier Trueba/MSF (clb). **87** Dorling Kindersley: Pitt Rivers Museum, University of Oxford (cl). Science Photo Library: Sinclair Stammers (ca); Javier Trueba/MSF (clb/Homo heidelbergensis). **88** Dorling Kindersley: Jerry Young (clb). **89** Corbis: Steve Kaufman (cra/Arabian oryx); Hans Reinhard (cr); Paul Souders (br); Winifred Wisniewski (tr). Dorling Kindersley: The American Museum of Natural History (tl/museum); John Holmes - modelmaker (cla). FLPA: R & M Van Nostrand (crb); Jurgen & Christine Sohns (cr/Okapi). **90-91** Corbis: Louie Psihoyos (c). **92-93** Corbis: Gary W. Carter (c/main image). **93** Corbis: Hal Beral (ca); Bettmann (tr); DLILLC (cr); John Giustina (br); Image Source (c); Frans Lanting (cb). **94** FLPA: Maurice Nimmo (c); Rob Reijnen/Minden Pictures (fbr); Jurgen & Christine Sohns (br). **94-95** FLPA: Terry Whittaker (c). **95** FLPA: Michael Krabs/Imagebroker (bl); Frans Lanting (tr) (cra); Peter Oxford/Minden Pictures (fbl); Winifried Wisniewski (cr). naturepl.com: A.N.T Photolibrary (cb). Science Photo Library: P Rona/OAR/National Undersea Research Program/NOAA (br). **96** FLPA: David Hosking (clb/Medium tree finch) (ca) (cla) (cl/Woodpecker finch); Tui De Roy (bl) (clb). NHPA / Photoshot: Bill Coster (tl); Ken Griffiths (tc). **96-97** FLPA: Hiroya Minakuchi/Minden Pictures (bc). **97** FLPA: Mitsuhiko Imamori/Minden Pictures (cr); Donald M. Jones/Minden Pictures (tr/Bighorn sheep); Gerard Lacz (br); Phil McLean (c); Chris Newbert/Minden Pictures (cla). **98** Corbis: Frans Lanting (c) (bc/Orchid). NHPA / Photoshot: Rod Planck (fbl). **99** Corbis: Mark Bolton (bc); Jim Craigmyle (br); Daniel Hurst/AgStock (tc); Michael A. Keller (tc/apple); Radius Images (ftr); Isabelle Rozenbaum/PhotoAlto (tl); Johan Sorensson/JohnÉr Images (ftl). naturepl.com: De Cuveland/ARCO (cra/Lily of the valley); Hanne & Jens Eriksen (crb/Oleander); Juan Manuel Borrero (cra/Daphne); Rolf Nussbaumer (cra/Adonis); Reinhard/ARCO (cr/Deadly nightshade); Wild Wonders of Europe/Möllers (fbr). Photolibrary: Michael Habicht/Animal Animal (crb/Hemlock); Jose Oto/BSIP Medical (tr); ParollGalperti/Cuboimages (crb/Angels trumpet). **100** Getty Images: Jeri Gleiter (bc/Hedgehog cactus). **100-101** Corbis: Blaine Harrington III (c). **102** Corbis: Andrew Brown/Ecoscene (br); Brandon D. Cole (cl/Red algae); Jason Hosking (clb/Brown algae); Micha Pawlitzki (ca); Dr. Peter Siver/Visuals Unlimited, Inc. (clb/Golden algae); Visuals Unlimited (clb/Diatoms) (bl); Stuart Westmorland/Science Faction (c); Lawson Wood (cla/Green algae) (cb). Science Photo Library: Hamk Morgan (cr). **102-103** Corbis: Michael Macor/The Chronicle (c/lab flasks); George McCarthy (c/background). **103** Corbis: Alan Schein Photography (tr); Bernard Annebicque/Sygma (bc/Red algae); Tom Bean (fbr); Ashley Cooper (clb/fuel hose); Michael Macor/The Chronicle (ca/petri-dish); Jeffrey L. Rotman (br); Visuals Unlimited (bc/Diatom). **104** Corbis: Gallo Images (cl); Studios Sato/amanaimages (tl). Getty Images: Martin Dohrn/naturepl.com (cla); Flickr (clb); Visuals Unlimited (bl). **104-105** Getty Images: AFP (cb). **105** Ardea: Jean Paul Ferrero (tl). Corbis: Mark A.Johnson (cr); Marin Harvey (fcr); Steven Kaziowski/Science Faction (cb); Kevin Schafer (cl). FLPA: Mike Lane (c). **106** Corbis: Visuals Unlimited (bc). FLPA: ImageBroker (fbl). Getty Images: Gary Bell (br); Philippe Bourseiller (fbr); Jeff Rotman (bl). **107** Corbis: Ralph A. Clevenger (bc). FLPA: Panda Photo (tr). **108** Dorling Kindersley: Harry Taylor/Courtesy of the Natural History Museum, London (br). SeaPics.com: C & M Fallows (ca) (cr); Mark Conlin (bl); Tom Haight (fbl); Gwen Lowe (bc); Marty Snyderman (bc/sawshark). **108-109** SeaPics.com: C & M Fallows (c/main image). **109** Dorling Kindersley: Colin Keates/Courtesy of the Natural History Museum, London (br). FLPA: Colin Munro (tc). SeaPics.com: C & M Fallows (c); Jason Isley (ftl); Masa Ushioda (tl); James D. Watt (tr) (ftr). **110** Alamy Images: Nigel Cattlin (cla). Corbis: Richard T. Nowitz (bc). **110-111** Corbis: David Scharf/Science Faction (ca). **111** Alamy Images: David Kunkel Microscopy, Inc./Phototake (bc/whipworm); Wildlife GmbH (br/castor bean tick). Corbis: Ron Boardman/FLPA (cra/human flea); Dennis Kunkel Microscopy, Inc./Visuals Unlimited (cra/louse); Dennis Kunkel Microscopy,Inc/Visuals Unlimited (cra/tick); Micro Discovery (tr); David Scharf/Science Faction (bc/crab louse); Visuals Unlimited (crb/scabies mite). Getty Images: David Burder (fbl). Science Photo Library: David Scharf (bl/hookworm). **112** FLPA: Nigel Cattlin (bc/Cigarette beetle); Michael Krabs/Imagebroker (c); Mark Moffett/Minden Pictures (fbr). NHPA / Photoshot: Anthony Bannister (bl/Blister beetle) (br); Stephen Dalton (bl); Daniel Heuclin (bc/Large-headed beetle); Rod Planck (fbl). **113** Corbis: Andreas Lander/dpa (br); Elizabeth Sauer (cr/Diving beetle); Karl Switak/Gallo Images (cr/Dung beetle). FLPA: Ingo Arndt/Minden Pictures (tc); Richard Becker (crb) (fl); Nigel Cattlin (tl); Bert Pijs/Minden Pictures (tr); Cyril Ruoso/Minden Pictures (ftr). NHPA / Photoshot: David Slater (cra/Ground beetle). **114** Corbis: Wolfgang Kaehler (cb). FLPA: Nigel Cattlin (bc) (cla); Mark Moffett/Minden Pictures (clb) (tl). NHPA / Photoshot: Stephen Dalton (tr). **115** FLPA: Nigel Cattlin (tl); Gerry Ellis/Minden Pictures (br); G E Hyde (cr). NHPA / Photoshot: A.N.T. Photolibrary (tr); Stephen Dalton (crb); Daniel Heuclin (bl). **116** FLPA: Scott Linstead/Minden Pictures (c); Chris Mattisosn (br). NHPA / Photoshot: A.N.T. Photo Library (tr); Anthony Bannister (cla). **117** FLPA: Michael & Patricia Fogden (cra/Glass tree frog); Thomas Marent/Minden Pictures (tr); Mark Moffat/Minden Pictures (crb/Mossy frog); Larry West (bc). naturepl.com: John Downer Productions (cra/False-eyed frog); Pete Oxford (br/Giant Titicaca frog). NHPA / Photoshot: James Carmichael Jr (crb/Ornate Horned frog). **118** Alamy Images: Rob Walls (cla). Corbis: Martin Harvey/Gallo Images (br). FLPA: Theo Allofs/Minden Pictures (clb/Caiman). naturepl.com: Anup Shah (bl). Photolibrary: Philippe Henry (cl). **118-119** Getty Images: Ariadne Van Zandbergen (c/background). **119** Corbis: Jonathan Blair (clb). Getty Images: Shaen Adey/Gallo Images (fbr); Bob Elsdale/The Image Bank (bc). naturepl.com: Anup Shah (crb). **120** Corbis: Eric & David Hosking (bc/Falcon). FLPA: Harri Taavetti (c/Eagle). Getty Images: Thierry Grun (fbr); Dieter Schaefer (br). NHPA / Photoshot: Bill Coster (bl) (cl); Andy Rouse (c); R Sorensen & J Olsen (cr). **121** Corbis: John Hawkins/FLPA (bl); Chris Hellier (bc/Vulture); Andrew Parkinson (bc/Kite). Getty Images: Klaus Baier (fbr); John Giustina (br); Mark Hamblin/Photolibrary (tl). NHPA / Photoshot: Roger Tidman (fbl); David Tipling (cb/Condor). **122** FLPA: R. Dirscherl (ftl) (tc/Aye-aye); Frans Lanting (tc/Shrew). naturepl.com: Lynn M. Stone (ftr). NHPA / Photoshot: Daniel Heuclin (tr) (tl). **122-123** Corbis: Sanford Agliolo (c/background). **123** Alamy Images: Steve Bloom Images (tr). Ardea: Pat Morris (br). Corbis: Joe Mcdonald (tl). FLPA: Jurgen & Christine Sohns (bl). NHPA / Photoshot: Manfred Danegger (tc); Daniel Heuclin (ftl). **124** Corbis: Eric and David Hosking (ca). FLPA: Geoff Moon (bc). Getty Images: Bruce Dale/National Geographic (tr). naturepl.com: Dietmar Nill (bl). NHPA / Photoshot: Michael Leach & Meriel Lland (cla). **124-125** naturepl.com: Barry Mansell (c). **125** Corbis: Michael & Patricia Fogden (tr). Getty Images: Jupiterimages (br). naturepl.com: Tim Laman (bc). Photolibrary: Eyal Bartov/OSF (cr). **126** FLPA: Mammal Fund Earthviews (fbl); Flip Nicklin/Minden Pictures (bl). NHPA / Photoshot: A.N.T. Photo Library (br); Franco Banfi (cb); Douglas David Seifert (bc/Right whale) (cl). **126-1217** SeaPics.com: Duncan Murrel (cb). **126-127** NHPA / Photoshot: Saul Goner (c/main image). **127** FLPA: Foto Natura Stock (ftr); Flip Nicklin/Minden Pictures (tl); Terry Whittaker (tc/Indo-Pacific humpbacked). NHPA / Photoshot: Mike Hill (cr); Kevin Schafer (ftl). SeaPics.com: john K.B. Ford/Ursus (tc/narwhal); Michael S. Nolan (tr). **128** Corbis: Frans Lanting (tr). NHPA / Photoshot: Nigel J Dennis (br); Martin Harvey (bl) (fbr) (bc/jaguar) (bc/leopard); Andy Rouse (cl); James Warwick (fbl). **128-129** Getty Images: Daryl Balfour. **129** Corbis: Tom Brakefield (ftl) (tr). Getty Images: Araquem Alcantara (tc/jaguar); Joseph Van Os (bl) (tc/climbing leopard). NHPA / Photoshot: Jonathan & Angela Scott (ftr). **130** Getty Images: Rodger Jackman/Photolibrary (clb). iStockphoto.com: